AEROPOSTALE

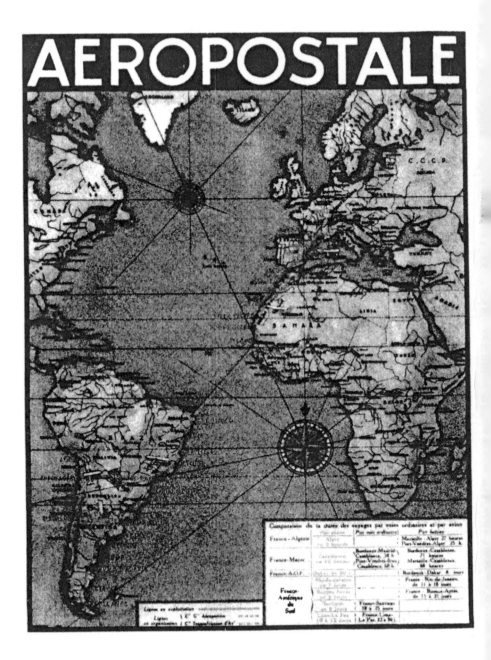

SAINT-EXUPÉRY

A Biography

STACY SCHIFF

A HOLT PAPERBACK
Henry Holt and Company
New York

Holt Paperbacks
Henry Holt and Company, LLC
Publishers since 1866
175 Fifth Avenue
New York, New York 10010
www.henryholt.com

A Holt Paperback® and 🅗🅟 ® are registered trademarks of
Henry Holt and Company, LLC.

Library of Congress Cataloging-in-Publication Data is available.
ISBN-13: 978-0-8050-7913-5

Henry Holt books are available for special promotions and
premiums. For details contact: Director, Special Markets.

Originally published in hardcover in 1994 by Alfred A. Knopf

First Holt Paperbacks Edition 2006

Printed in the United States of America

P1

This book was written for Marc de La Bruyère

Contents

~

Introduction

~

The predicament of his birth is summed up by one encyclopedia in two words, "impoverished aristocrat": Antoine de Saint-Exupéry began his professional life as a truck salesman. By 1929 he had distinguished himself as a pilot and published a first novel. Before another five years had passed he was unemployed, living hand-to-mouth. In 1939 he won both the American Bookseller Association's National Book Award and the Académie Française's Grand Prix du Roman for *Wind, Sand and Stars*; he seemed well on his way to a chair at the Académie Française. Five years later his politics—more accurately his lack thereof—made him so much a persona non grata that he lived in disgrace in Algiers, heartbroken and excommunicated, his books censored. That year he became the most famous French writer to go down as a casualty of World War II. He was forty-four years old.

Saint-Exupéry did not so much live fast as die early. Our fascination with him has grown as a result, as it does with all things that end before their time, from the *Titanic* to Marilyn Monroe. The mystery surrounding his death—so neatly presaged in *The Little Prince*, whose hero witnesses forty-four sunsets—has further enhanced the myth. To it have been added the eulogies: Saint-Exupéry's generation comes to an end only today, when he has been dead for over fifty years. Survived by a great number of eloquent friends he has been flattened under the collective weight of their decades of praise. That avalanche has naturally provoked a second one: those who have labored to remind us that Saint-Exupéry was a man, not a god, have delighted in doing so vitriolically. The detractors have done no more than the keepers of the cult to reveal Saint-Exupéry himself; they have tangled only with the legend, of which the writer is now twice the victim.

Under it all is buried one man, by no means ordinary, but not extraordinary either for the reasons we have come to believe. A pilot of indisputable audacity, Saint-Exupéry was anything but a disciplined flyer. He flew the mails only briefly, less than six years in all. He played a role in the pioneering age of aviation without having been one of its illustrious practitioners; he was more the Boswell of the early days. Relatedly, he was not much dedicated to routine. He displayed a stunning lack of personal ambition, and was a resolute nonjoiner. Disobedience was often to his mind the better part of valor. His friendships were solid but composed of equal parts loyalty and squabbling. His sentimental history is a thorny one. At the same time Saint-Exupéry was a man of tremendous, towering personality, of certain genius. Little of it crept into the tempest-tossed life, however; only a portion crept into the work. He was perhaps at the height of his powers recounting the tale of his near-death by thirst in the Libyan desert at the dinner table, over which his enchanted listeners plainly slumped with sympathetic dehydration. No one who met him ever forgot him.

How could an aviator write, or how could an aviator write as lyrically as did Saint-Exupéry? And how did an aristocrat come to fly as a mail pilot? There was nothing predetermined about either career, and the worlds of letters and aviation were further apart—especially in France in the 1920s—than a man with a foot in each realm might have liked. Generally speaking the two are not professions that go well together. The writer lives with some detachment from experience, which it is his task to recast; a pilot works his trade with a fierce immediacy, perfect presence. One may reshape events, the other must nimbly accommodate them. For Saint-Exupéry the two careers—and with them the life and the oeuvre— were inextricably bound. His biographer enjoys no greater advantage. Most of his work is journalism, romanticized, but still autobiographical; what is not journalism pure and simple is easily enough decoded. The pages hold little fiction, limited fantasy, a vast sea of fact. And while Saint-Exupéry could be absentminded—six years into his marriage he could not remember his wedding date—he neither reinvented nor muddied the past. He was not untruthful. He put a gloss on things, but he lived, too, for that gloss, for a quixotism that would be his undoing. The fashion in which he shaped the events he faithfully reported ultimately tells us as much about him as do the events themselves. It makes it possible to begin to imagine the truly critical hours of his life, those he spent alone at several thousand feet, moments no biographer can touch.

While the works are true to the life—the author's mind wanders on the page just as it did in the cockpit; a common literary construction for Saint-Exupéry is "over A I was thinking of B"—they do not entirely stand in for the man. They are simple; Saint-Exupéry was not. The anguished writer of petulant, indignant, downtrodden letters is nowhere to be found in the early books. Here, too, the myths have taken their toll: Saint-Exupéry's biographer commits to addressing the provenance of the Little Prince, that disarming visitor from Asteroid B612, and yet to date the chroniclers of his life have pretended that the man who wrote some of the most tender pages of our time had no private life, only a morass of a marriage. It is not easy to understand the Little Prince if one holds too much to the caped crusader of lore; it is at the same time too easy to write off Saint-Exupéry altogether if one takes him only at his written word. It is a richer life than he let on, poorer as it was in all the transcendent qualities that make the literature soar, so much more earthbound than it appears to have been.

A note on the name, which is pronounced Sant-Exoopairee, with all syllables accented equally: famous men famously change their names. Saint-Exupéry admitted he had "*un beau nom*" and enough attached to it that he forbade two women who shared it—an elder sister and his wife—from publishing under it. (Both ultimately defied him.) Friends and acquaintances were to take liberties even where he did not: after a childhood of nicknames, he was transformed by others into "Saint-Ex," who became the pilot of legend. He himself made only one concession on this front. When the writer settled in New York after the fall of France he authorized his American publisher to insert a hyphen into his name, so as to discourage those who insisted as addressing him as "Mr. Exupéry." I have retained the late-arriving hyphen here; to do otherwise in English leaves an odd impression. "Is he one of the saints of France?" a confused son of Charles Lindbergh asked his mother in 1940. Laughingly Anne Morrow Lindbergh—who had fallen under the Frenchman's spell the previous year—replied that he was indeed, if not in the usual sense of the word.

SAINT-EXUPÉRY

I

~

A King of Infinite Space
1927–1928

*The sky has stars—the desert only distance. The
sea has islands—the desert only more desert; build
a fort or a house upon it and you have achieved
nothing.*

BERYL MARKHAM, *West with the Night*

In 1928 Antoine de Saint-Exupéry was as settled as he would ever be.
He had no financial worries, no romantic entanglements, no concerns
regarding his employment. His home was the Western Sahara, his house
a wooden shack that had sailed from France to the desert five years before.
On one side it gave on the ocean, which at high tide lapped up against
his window; on the other it gave on to the desert. Dwarfed by an
impressive-looking Spanish fort with a crenellated wall, the shack was
meant to stand guard over an airplane hangar. Otherwise the perfectly flat
horizon was obstructed only, occasionally, by the tents of nomads. Saint-
Exupéry was twenty-eight years old, and since October of the previous
year had been chief of the airfield at Cape Juby. "I have never," he would
write fifteen years later, "loved my house more than when I lived in the
desert."

His furniture consisted of a plank lined with a thin straw mattress, on
which he slept, and a door balanced on two oil drums, on which he wrote.
The former was too short for the six-foot two-inch aviator; for the first
months at Cape Juby he extended the bed with a crate that served as his
pillow, until a friend suggested he might be more comfortable sleeping
in the opposite direction. To his mother, whom he wrote regularly, he sent
a list of the remainder of his worldly possessions: a water jug, a metal
basin, a typewriter, a shelf of books, a windup gramophone, a deck of

cards, and the Aéropostale records, the files of the airline for which he worked. Saint-Exupéry shared his home with four French mechanics and ten Moors, all fellow Aéropostale employees, a marmoset named Kiki, a dog, an outsized cat, and a hyena. For neighbors he counted the inhabitants of the Spanish fort, under the direction of an officious Castilian aristocrat named Colonel de la Peña. The northern coast of what was then the Spanish Río de Oro, an area roughly the size of Great Britain, today the Spanish Sahara, was further populated only by dissident Moors.

There was every reason to think of Cape Juby, today the Moroccan town of Tarfaya, as "the most desolate airstrip in the world." When its name was mentioned among Aéropostale pilots, a breed known for their sturdiness, the word "neurasthenic" sooner or later came up. The desert had its attractions—the aviator who had prospected the African line would swear to its incomparable beauty and claim the Sahara as his true mistress—but it was generally agreed that Cape Juby was a godforsaken place. A journalist who visited in 1929, just after Saint-Exupéry had left, commented on its "tragic solitude" before he had even landed on the strip of sand that served as the Juby runway. His observation was confirmed on entering the Spanish fort, where he was struck by the malaise of the men, by their "strange silhouettes of beggars or bandits. Their filth was so pronounced it seemed to be make-up. But even more than their slovenliness what was horrifying was their silence." He assumed this misery to be the work of an evil spell cast by Colonel de la Peña until a French mechanic enlightened him: "Did you really not know that Cape Juby serves as a Spanish military penitentiary?" Jean Mermoz, probably the most celebrated of French pilots and one renowned for his vigor, lived at Juby for a week in February 1927. He reported that he had never "had so much an impression of a state of siege, of suffocation. The guards were barely distinguishable from the prisoners, their uniforms were in tatters, their espadrilles shredded, they were filthy, idle, silent." Assisted by two Moors he had recruited as *sous-chefs*, Mermoz spent his week cooking for the French barrack, a revolver in his pocket. He slept fourteen-hour nights, practiced his Spanish, played a good deal of cards, and counted the days, which passed with an exasperating slowness.

The Juby shack stood 600 miles south of Casablanca and 1,700 miles north of Dakar; Saint-Exupéry barely exaggerated when he wrote to a friend that he was "1,000 kilometers from the nearest bistro." Water and provisions arrived by sailboat monthly from the Canary Islands; Juby offered no natural harbor, and its tides calmed enough to permit a landing only every four weeks. Its climate is not generally forgiving; temperatures rise to about 100 degrees during the day and the wind blows continuously, which meant that the Juby windsock remained stubbornly horizontal, usually filled by gusts from the northeast. With the wind blew sand, which

got into everything; it seasoned most meals, and proved especially pernicious in its invasion of airplane carburetors and fuel supplies. The Western Saharan coast is the world's most arid, but its air is exceptionally wet,
even in the hottest season. Humidity is no friend to an airplane and it was
even less so to the airplane of the 1920s: it soaked and inflated the cloth
wings, which then separated from their support, and corroded the metal.
Aviators can be forgiven for talking about the weather; for them it is a
subject of paramount importance. Today pilots consult satellite-generated
weather maps, but in the Spanish Sahara in the 1920s maps were cursory
at best and meteorology amounted less to science than to intuition. Years
after he had left Juby, Saint-Exupéry would remember having smelled a
sandstorm brewing; he was delighted to have learned to decipher the
"secret language" of the Sahara, to have "read the anger of the desert in
the beating wings of a dragonfly." Flying in such weather was not nearly
as poetic. From a practical aviation standpoint, Cape Juby was no paradise.

It is fair to say that had the mailplanes of the 1920s had a greater
range, the French would never have imposed on the relative calm of Cape
Juby. The Río de Oro was a misnomer on two counts: it is not a river, and
it has no gold.* The Spanish had set up house in an inhospitable place,
but that place happened to be strategically located for a mail line operating
between Toulouse, the seat of French aviation, and Dakar, the largest
French city in Africa, nearly 3,000 miles to the south. The mailplane of
the time, the Breguet 14, flew at a cruising speed of eighty miles per hour
and had an extreme range of well under 400 miles. These constraints had
led the budding air service to negotiate with the Spaniards for the use of
the only two refueling stops available in the Río de Oro, Cape Juby and
its southern neighbor, Villa Cisneros, settlements about as far apart as
Boston and Washington. When all went well the planes could make their
way from Toulouse to Dakar in about fifty-five hours, making stops every
250 to 350 miles and traveling only in daylight; word of their progress
traveled up and down the line by radio. The Breguet 14 was not an advanced aircraft: it was powered by a 300-horsepower engine, its propeller
was wood, its cockpit open; it had no radio, no suspension, no reliable
instruments, no brakes. One pilot observed that the gas gauge more accurately indicated the amount of sand in the conduits than of fuel in the
tank. Saint-Exupéry commented that the compass was a fine invention in
theory, but that in practice it resembled a weather vane.

On average, a Breguet 14 broke down every 15,500 miles, which
worked out to about one in every five Casablanca-Dakar round-trips. The
beauty of an unsophisticated airplane is that it is easy to repair: a hammer,

---

* In fact. the entire Western Sahara boasts not a single oasis or lake; the only mineral in
which the region is rich in phosphate.

nails, a saw, a block of wood, and glue were said to suffice in order to
jerry-rig a Breguet 14 back into service. As Mermoz boasted: "We had
created commercial aviation before there were any commercial planes."
If there were more casualties among planes than pilots, it may have been
due to a fact another great French pioneer, Louis Blériot, had pointed out
years before: "The ability to come crashing to the ground without hurting
oneself does not lie in any special cleverness on the part of the pilot. It
lies in what one might well term the elasticity of the aeroplane."

The African run had been inaugurated in May 1925, after which
Dakar, the administrative seat of a colonial empire nearly twenty times
the size of continental France, received its Casablanca mail in two days.
(By sea a letter had taken a week in summer and two weeks in winter.)
By the time Saint-Exupéry settled in Juby, the airline had begun to rely
on the outposts of the Río de Oro as stepping stones to South America as
well. Only when the Breguet 14's were replaced by Latécoère 26's, more
robust aircraft with more powerful and reliable engines, could the Río de
Oro be overflown. Until 1930, when that happened, the French were
largely at the mercy of the Spanish, who knew as much; the Río de Oro
is an oft-mentioned subject in the Madrid–Quai d'Orsay correspondence
of the 1920s. Geography is littered with places that sprang up for reasons
of utility and outlived their usefulness. The Breguet 14 and the African
mail put Cape Juby on the map; the Latécoère 26 and the South American
mail relegated it to oblivion.

The year before Saint-Exupéry was stationed at Juby, Charles Lindbergh, who had just flown the Atlantic, noted that fog and sleet were the
mail pilot's two greatest adversaries. He was not acquainted with dissident
Moors. The Río de Oro may have been a Spanish colony, but it was a
colony consisting entirely of two forts, secure only in that their proximity
to the sea facilitated speedy evacuation by boat. The Spanish did not
venture far beyond their garrison walls; in a humorous letter to his brother-
in-law, Saint-Exupéry wrote that if one strayed more than sixty feet beyond
the fort one was shot at. At 150 feet one was killed or sold into slavery,
depending on the season. Here again he exaggerated only slightly: months
before his arrival two Spaniards had disappeared from the fort walls themselves. It did not take the Moors long to discover the value of a French
aviator. The first pilots to be captured were held for ransom; in 1926, two
were murdered and a third died from wounds sustained during his captivity. The letters bound for Dakar were opened, and franc notes fell out,
and word got out quickly that the mail was a kind of airborne gold mine.
Shooting at the planes became commonplace; Saint-Exupéry reported that
the aviators were greeted like partridges. (He was also quick to note that
the Moors had blessedly bad aim when it came to shooting objects from

the sky, an art in which the Sahara offered little practice.) When an engine sputtered in midair it was a different story. There was ample reason for the French aviators to feel nervous about the Moors. They had been told that the head of the airline, Pierre-Georges Latécoère—known to be a very tough businessman—would not pay a ransom and that the Moors would cut them up slowly until the money was paid.

Pierre-Georges Latécoère owned the airline and built the planes, but the problem of the Río de Oro fell squarely to Didier Daurat, his operations director. Daurat is remembered, mostly thanks to the writings of Saint-Exupéry, for his military discipline and his taciturn rigor. He could as well be immortalized for his creativity. In the first years of the airline—well before the advent of radio—he had equipped Breguet 14's with carrier pigeons to be released in case of a crash; when the Río de Oro introduced greater dangers he armed the pilots. Then he sent them along the African route in twos, with explicit instructions that the pilot in distress was to facilitate the landing of the escort plane as close as possible to his own. He toyed briefly with the idea of equipping his planes with recordings for the Moors, which might better explain the French enterprise to them; he was convinced he could impress them with the grandeur of the Latécoère vision. Ultimately he arranged for native interpreters to accompany the pilots. Flying majestically along amid the mail sacks, their jewel-encrusted swords snug in their belts, the blue-robed Moors lent a new romance to the mails. They were unusual interpreters in that they were, with a few exceptions, unilingual; their mission was less to translate than to negotiate ransoms.

In 1927, after a number of grisly incidents and aware that the Spanish were lying in wait for one last disaster, Daurat realized he had still not solved the problem of Cape Juby. What he needed at this delicate outpost was an ambassador, someone who could convince the Spanish of the viability of the airline, who could make the French presence in the Río de Oro more palatable, who could manage the Moors. He turned quite naturally to Saint-Exupéry. An aristocratic name would impress the Spanish; it was already clear that the pilot had a certain charm; he was familiar with Juby, after nearly ten months flying the African mails. It has been suggested that Daurat may have been as eager to put Saint-Exupéry to work as an ambassador as he was to put him to work as an aviator. At the time Saint-Exupéry was on sick leave in France from the airline; a bout with dengue fever had left him crippled with joint pains. A hot, dry climate would alleviate his symptoms. He was recalled that fall to Toulouse and dispatched posthaste to Cape Juby, where he arrived on October 19, 1927. His mission was simple: to revive relations with the Spanish authorities, and "to set off to the rescue of any aviator in danger, at any hour, anywhere in the desert." He was to be a little bit the Saint Bernard of the Sahara. "The bearers of water in the desert," he wrote later, "are members of the greatest divinity there is."

~

As often happens in small places, the titles at Cape Juby were large. Colonel de la Peña was known as the inspector general of Cape Juby, though his rule barely extended beyond his fort. Saint-Exupéry was named chief of the airfield, and while he was aware of the modest size of his domain he was pleased with the responsibility the post entailed. It was partly a title that had brought him to Juby in the first place; "de Saint-Exupéry" is a fine aristocratic name, and Didier Daurat gambled correctly on the fact that Colonel de la Peña would be impressed with it. This was ironic, in light of the fact that earlier in the year Saint-Exupéry—never shy about telling anyone how or where to write him—had admonished his mother from Dakar: "Don't put 'Count' on my envelopes." His title kept him apart, as titles are meant to do, and one thing Saint-Exupéry had always felt, by nature as much as by birth, was painfully apart. He would turn his back on anyone who showed the poor taste to address him as "My dear Count." This behavior, of course, put him at a distance from another world, one for which his name and his relations if not his fortune—he had none—qualified him.

The beauty of Cape Juby was that, in its utter desolation, its remoteness, it minimized the chilling effect of the *de* which preceded his surname. Saint-Exupéry may himself have seldom noticed his *particule*, but those around him, especially at Aéropostale, could not help but do so: if a *grand nom* stood out anywhere in France in the 1920s it stood out on an airfield. At the same time Cape Juby was instrumental in making his name. From his colleagues he earned a good deal of respect for the amazing feats he would perform in the desert in 1928. While the pilots of *la Ligne* had always recognized Saint-Exupéry as a creature apart, they now cited his eccentricities instead of his name. For them he may never have been the Count de Saint-Exupéry but he had been *de* Saint-Exupéry; in the words of one Aéropostale mechanic, he was "a little bit our Queen of England." By the time he left the Sahara his name had shrunk to the more comfortable Saint-Ex. (The name would be abbreviated once again by the Americans during the war, for whom he became "Major X.") At the same time, the pilot grew into his family name.

When Saint-Exupéry arrived at Cape Juby, at the age of twenty-seven, he had published a story in a magazine, had been excruciatingly unlucky in love, and had flirted with a few careers, none successfully, before beginning to fly the mail the previous year. His letters to his mother, in whom he confided intimately in the correspondence of his twenties, resound with his fears that he would never amount to anything. He worried that he was lazy; he worried that he tired of himself so quickly; that he would not prove his worth; that he would never find a woman to love. It was as clear to him as to anyone that he did not fit in. "I have turned out so differently than I might have," he wrote plaintively in 1925. "Please try to appreciate me for what I am." It was clear, too, that he did not quite know yet what that was. He knew what he did not like: any happiness that rendered one immobile, satisfied, sedentary. Already he had a sense that he might take to a life of adventure, but adventure as he would describe it once he was flying over Africa—"a constant need to discover new places, to let my feet carry me along, to be unsure of the next day"—looked like something else altogether in the unemployed or half-committed. He was angry that the family thought him "a superficial, chattering layabout." He wanted very much to be taken seriously but could not seem to find the arena in which to prove himself. Before his first trip to Africa, early in 1927, he wrote his mother earnestly that he hoped he would come home "a marriageable man."

There were not a great number of professions open to a young aristocrat of Saint-Exupéry's time, particularly to one who did not like to play by the rules and was therefore excluded from a military or diplomatic future. These were and remain the two standard career tracks for the sons of noblemen; two-thirds of all French aristocratic families today include at least one active officer. In October 1926, the month he joined the airline, Saint-Exupéry wrote only half-humorously to Renée de Saussine, the sister of a close friend whom he was unsuccessfully attempting to court by letter, that he wished he could be *"un beau gigolo."* It was also one of the options, particularly if one were willing to marry his fortune, which could not have been less the case with Saint-Exupéry. "I wish I were a *'beau gigolo'* with a handsome tie and a magnificent record collection. I should have trained when I was younger; it's too late now. And I do regret it. Now that I'm balding it's not even worth trying," lamented the pilot.

Even before his hair had begun to thin Saint-Exupéry might have had trouble qualifying for the role. He was a good head taller than most Frenchmen, and awkward, and not handsome by the usual measure. He lumbered around like a bear. His "Mickey-Mouse nose, his black eyes jutting from the sockets, his luminous gaze" made him look almost otherworldly. He paid spectacular inattention to what he wore. What was more, once he had begun flying regularly he would show up at some of the best Parisian addresses with dirt under his nails. His hands were covered with oil; he complained to Renée that he alone found them beautiful. Once in the service of the airline he rather quickly began to turn his back on the world of the manicured, to crack jokes at its expense, a little, at first, out of spite. Within months he had written to another female friend that he was thrilled with his situation at Aéropostale: "I am delighted that it isn't a sport for gigolos, but a trade." To a former teacher he mailed a letter from Dakar: "When my engine coughs over the Río de Oro I consider myself very intelligent to see everything from a new angle, the memories, the hopes, and the circles of little literary gigolos." Ultimately the vocation to which he had faintly aspired became a code word for his worst nightmare: in his first novel, a pilot walks into a Dakar bar, "a heavy-footed explorer among all these gigolos." He had a taste for adventure, but had—as Anne Morrow Lindbergh astutely observed—to hurdle the "barriers of breeding, education, and delicatesse" in order to indulge it.

Still, there was the possibility he was making a mistake. He occasionally admitted to thinking himself idiotic for choosing the life he had. Why should he be sweating in the desert, in the land of eternal sand, "when in France there are good, green fields with streams and cows. And in Paris streets crowded with women. So sweet to touch. And the theater, music, pleasure?" Perhaps he was wrong to think that a life of risk counted for something more. After a time at Juby, these doubts plagued him less and less often, though on occasion he still needed to measure his world of high adventure against the potential of domestic bliss he had left behind. A little on the defensive, he responded to a Paris-based friend who had written to announce his impending marriage:

> You're engaged, you're happy. . . . All that is sweet, fresh and calm. I receive your news with an eight-day beard, bare feet, black hands. I receive your letter after returning from adventures from which I shouldn't have returned. . . . I've invited several Moorish chieftains over for tea. Here they are. They are greeting me hoarsely. Twenty kilometers from here I would hardly trust them. They are already regally settling on my chairs. I leave you; I return to my life. Your letter; what a breath of fresh air!

Within months of his arrival at Juby, Saint-Exupéry had reported to his mother that he had tamed a chameleon. "It is my role here to tame," he continued. "It suits me, it's a lovely word." He moved on to gazelles, had less luck with a kind of desert sand fox, known as a fennec, which he attempted to domesticate for his sister. He was done in only by the Spaniards' guard dog, who one night took a vicious interest in his shoulder. He had entirely grasped his mission vis-à-vis the Spanish, the Moors, and the desert; he had also found his calling. To tame (apprivoiser) would remain nearly a religious expression for Saint-Exupéry, who seemed to use the word in its larger sense for the first time on January 1, 1927, when he celebrated the New Year alone in an Alicante café. At 2:00 a.m. he sat down to write a letter, again to Renée de Saussine. He had been rejuvenated by a magical flight into the Spanish town and had caught its high spirits, though on paper his high spirits were often tempered with wistfulness. You have tamed me, he told her. "Frankly it's sweet to let oneself be tamed. Only you will also cost me sad days." It was a perfect vocation for a young nobleman: Saint-Exupéry described his work in the desert to his brother-in-law as one part aviator, one part ambassador, one part explorer. He had found a twentieth-century equivalent of the life of the troubador, the crusader, the knight-errant. He had, as he wrote his friend Charles Sallès, "tasted of the forbidden fruit . . . experienced the life of the *gentilhomme de fortune*." He was, in spirit and in deed, a *grand seigneur*, and this entirely by virtue of his personality, even if it had been his name that had landed him in the desert in the first place. Mostly, however, he was remembered by the French mechanics for his kindness, his reserve, and his late-night exuberance, all of which contributed to make Juby a newly popular spot on the African run.

Saint-Exupéry's technique in the desert was simple. He wasted no time in getting to know the nomads, something he had long wanted to do, though he had certainly never confessed as much to Didier Daurat. Within weeks of his arrival he was able to report that he was popular with the children of the desert, as he would be popular with children wherever he went; he was also taking Arabic lessons, though he was to be generally less successful with languages. He worked his diplomacy with a good deal of gracious mime and good humor. He offered teas to the chieftains, who reciprocated by inviting him a mile into the desert, to their tents, where no Spaniard had yet ventured. He was secure, he said, because the Moors were getting to know him, more accurately because they were impressed with his seeming fearlessness. He was earnestly fascinated with them, at least at first; they trusted him. In the words of Daurat, Saint-Exupéry's "goodness, his rectitude, his respect for form, custom, and tradition meant he was considered and respected as a sage." At the same time he was more than happy to invite the Spanish officers to the French barrack for dinner—even when, to the dismay of his colleagues, supplies were so low as to endanger the culinary reputation of the mother country—or to oblige them with a game of chess. He was accomplished at card tricks, which Juby allowed him time to perfect. He read a variety of technical manuals and took great pleasure in demonstrating his experiments, physical and metaphysical, for all concerned. He was, in short, a very capable ambassador. His success was immediate; within months of his arrival the Spanish flew the French flag along with their own at the passage of each airplane, and the Moors ran to greet the "great white dervish." Soon, too, he ac-

quired a title that fit. In early 1928 he proudly wrote his sister that the
Moors had dubbed him "Captain of the Birds."

~

The Aéropostale pilots did not often dress as glamorously as we imagine;
they were a motley crew who looked more like an assembly of Samuel
Beckett characters than the leather-suited archangels of legend. Saint-
Exupéry was no exception and shows up in photographs of Cape Juby in
an odd assortment of clothes, usually mismatched and never particularly
clean, sporting a wool scarf tied around his waist, a half-beard. He had
come as far as one can from the "*beau gigolo*" of his letters. Evidently he
took to wearing an old dressing gown that began to resemble a Moorish
robe. Tanned and unshaved, he was virtually indistinguishable from the
nomads. Henri Guillaumet, the pilot who would become Saint-Exupéry's
closest confidant on the airline, told of landing at Juby and being greeted
by Saint-Exupéry, "strangely dressed in a seroual and a gandourah."
"What are you doing here?" asked Guillaumet, who had evidently not
been informed of Saint-Exupéry's new posting. "This is my home," replied
the new chief of the airfield, "and tonight you are my guest."
     Saint-Exupéry was himself welcomed to his new home by Toto Lau-
berg, a Toulousian mechanic famous as much for his devotion to *la Ligne*
as that to red wine and Pernod, which he found in greater supply than
water in the desert. At his side was his pet monkey, who had obligingly
learned to share Toto's tastes. "Say hello to the boss, *ma cocotte*," Toto
advised Kiki. Toto, who doubled as the Cape Juby cook, repaired the
planes making stopovers at Juby; a second mechanic, Marchal, younger
and sturdier, made repairs farther from home. Toto reminded Saint-
Exupéry of a system the inhabitants of the barrack had ingeniously devised
to discourage nighttime visitors; the Spanish relied on fortress walls, so
well-guarded that Saint-Exupéry had once nearly met his death at the
hands of an overzealous sentry, baffled by the presence of a non-Spanish-
speaking caller during a late-night sandstorm. The French barrack
counted on a magneto that, powered by a small propeller, electrified the
door handle. Legend has it that Saint-Exupéry took note of the invention
but forgot about it come morning, when he brusquely opened the door.
The invention did fall out of use after his arrival; in Daurat's words, at
Juby "locks and bolts did not interest Saint-Exupéry much, as the magic
of his own personality was enough to protect him."
     Dinners at Juby, which took place around a long wooden table bor-
dered by a set of mismatched chairs, were nothing short of picturesque,
even with the pet hyena banished to the outdoors because of the smell.
Henry Delaunay, another Aéropostale pilot, left a priceless portrait of an

evening when Juby hosted a full house. To the regulars were added Henri Guillaumet and René Riguelle, who had flown the Dakar mail north that afternoon, and Mermoz and Delaunay, who would continue with it to Casablanca the next morning. The reigning atmosphere was that of a boys' dormitory: Mermoz, dressed only in pantaloons, sits handsomely in the corner, entirely engrossed in a crossword puzzle. Riguelle has tied the Juby dog to the slats of Mermoz's chair, and waits for the meal that is about to appear, guaranteed to activate the hungry animal. Marchal, eager to set the prank in motion, is negotiating with Toto about the order of the courses, a subject about which Toto's sense of propriety is not easily corrupted. Suddenly all attention is diverted by Kiki, who is noisily chomping on a razor blade. Every piece of fruit in sight is propelled in the monkey's direction before Marchal can explain that this is the third time in the course of a week that the animal has worked her cleverness. Meanwhile Toto lobbies for everyone to convey his dinner requests to the Moor who has been recruited as maître d'hôtel. Attila speaks not a word of French, and swaddled in his blue veils looks better suited to do battle with a sandstorm than with a group of boisterous Frenchmen. Guillaumet scribbles word games on the tablecloth, delighting in tripping up Saint-Exupéry, who plays along with grudging humor and induces general hilarity when he finally informs Guillaumet: "This is id-i-ot-ic." The evening draws to an end with Saint-Exupéry skillfully hypnotizing Toto while Delaunay tries not to think about what he will do the next morning if the fog rolls in as he follows Mermoz north, which it will.

Not every evening—or afternoon—was so entertaining. The mail passed through Juby only once every eight days, which left Saint-Exupéry seven days of silence in between. When the visiting pilots arrived they were grilled for news of the world, even before being offered a chance to wash up; they would unload their fabulous tales of *la Ligne*, each of which grew with its retelling, like those, Saint-Exupéry observed, of the Middle Ages. Aside from the regularity of these arrivals and departures—the high points of the week and the only rhythm by which time was measured— there was little routine. Saint-Exupéry occupied himself with his paper-work and flew the airfield's four planes every morning to rid them of condensation. The months at Juby would inform all of his writing, but it is particularly difficult to divorce the image of the Little Prince alone on his planet, carefully watering his rose every morning, from that of Saint-Exupéry in the Río de Oro, dutifully drying his planes. He played chess with the Spaniards; he wrote letters in which he lobbied for mail and for gramophone records; he visited the Moors. On occasion he flew the mail to Casablanca. He was acutely aware of his isolation. "Our nearest neighbors," he wrote in his first novel, *Southern Mail*, "were five to 600 miles away, also trapped by the Sahara, like flies in amber." "We are as much strangers," he wrote a friend in January 1928, "one from the other as planets in the solar system." In a fine mood he would report that he had read, or gone boating, or made a topographical study of the region. When the solitude weighed more heavily he reported: "Let me describe my life: It's morning, it's noon, it's evening. Every day repeats itself, without any events more interesting than these. I read a little; I smoke a lot; I take walks of about a quarter-mile." It was, he would write time and again, a monk's life.

Saint-Exupéry did not find this altogether disagreeable. He was, by his own admission, frightfully prone to abstraction, and few places favor meditation more than the desert. There was plenty of silence, of which he had for some time claimed a great need, and which he learned to classify:

> There is a silence of peace when the tribes are reconciled, when the cool evening falls. . . . There is a midday silence, when the sun suspends all thought and movement. There is a false silence, when the north wind has died and insects, torn like pollen from the interior oases, arrive to announce the sandstorms from the east. There is a silence of intrigue, when one learns that a faraway tribe is plotting something. There is a silence of mystery, when the Arabs discuss their incomprehensible differences among themselves. There is a tense silence when a messenger is late returning. A sharp silence when, at night, one holds one's breath to listen better. A melancholy silence, when one remembers those one loves.

He wrote repeatedly of his "monk's cell," of his "monkish" life and dispositions, but he did so always with fondness. His religion was the mail, and in his devotion to it he was bound inextricably to his comrades. It was said that for Mermoz "it was impossible to consider an immobile mail bag as anything less than a stalled heart." The zeal was contagious if curious, too. One day Saint-Exupéry cornered Delaunay to ask a question that had clearly been causing him tremendous anxiety: "By virtue of what emotion do we risk our lives, sometimes so casually, to move the mail?" Delaunay was of little help, but his floundering did not deter Saint-Exupéry, who went on, a believing soul who had not necessarily found God. "The mail is sacred," he wrote later, "what is inside has little importance." The isolation, the abnegation, the single-mindedness of Juby were a tonic to a young man undisciplined, a little frivolous, in great need of being needed. "Anyone who has known Saharan life, where everything appears to be solitude and nakedness, mourns those years as the most beautiful he has lived," he wrote two years before his death.

There was nonetheless a low point, and it began about two months after his arrival, at Christmas. The chief of the airfield spent Christmas Eve listening to the Moors prepare for a war, setting off flares, which illuminated the sky "like opera lights." It would end, he assured his mother cynically, "like all of the big Moorish spectacles, with the theft of four camels and three women." As the provisions were delayed from the Canary Islands, dinner amounted to a less-than-festive banquet of canned foods; the evening proved so melancholic that Saint-Exupéry turned in at ten o'clock. The good news: he had written six lines of a book. "That's a lot," he informed his mother. The New Year began on a similar note, less because of any new crises than because of a lack thereof. Relations with the Spanish were on as even a keel as they would ever be. The mail planes arrived and departed; Saint-Exupéry, feeling the mother hen, greeted and sent on his "chicks" weekly. If an airplane seemed to be late coming in he prepared to set off to the rescue: "I ready myself for great adventure with a certain vanity; but then a far-away hum announces that the plane will come in, announces that life is altogether more simple than I had thought, that romanticism has its limits, and that the lovely persona in which I have dressed myself is somewhat ridiculous." He was meant to be the king of desert repairmen, and yet from early December 1927 until the summer of 1928, when he was on duty, the Latécoère mail planes miraculously made their way to and from Juby, over 750 miles of dissident territory, without incident.

This rhythm altered a little late in February, when Saint-Exupéry reported to Casablanca with an inflammation of the eye. The condition may have resulted from his many hours of desert flying, impossible without dark glasses and dazzlingly bright under any circumstances; it may have been an infection that resulted from an earlier injury and that flared up with some regularity as he aged. It was clearly painful, though it does not appear to have impeded the pilot—who was not hospitalized in Casablanca—from enjoying himself during his convalescence. The condition would have cut into his desultory reading, of which he seems to have been doing a fair amount at Juby: he asked the pilots always for more technical manuals, for which he had a voracious appetite; by mid-1928 he had read a number of novels, of which he favored Margaret Kennedy's *The Constant Nymph* and Colette's *La naissance du jour* (*Break of Day*). For some time he had traveled with a volume of Baudelaire. It was later said of him that he was more likely to fondle than to read a book, and this habit seems to have been confirmed already at Juby. The wife of the chief of the Agadir airfield, four hours away by air and Saint-Exupéry's closest neighbor, remembered the pilot landing with a plane full of record albums that he would trade for books. He claimed not to be able to sleep at night without a pile by his bedside or on his bed: "He did not actually read them, but the thoughts which kept him company were there, locked in the books like precious medicines in their phials. It was indispensable for him to know they were within arm's reach, should the need for them arise." Saint-Exupéry returned to Juby from Casablanca, evidently cured, toward the end of March. He had missed the passage of the first France/South America mail, along with the dramatic search that ensued when the plane carrying it ran out of fuel fifty miles north of Villa Cisneros.

The first half of 1928 did not go entirely to waste. By the middle of January the six lines Saint-Exupéry had written before Christmas had grown to a hundred pages of a novel, the construction of which was proving difficult, as he was trying to tell his story from several points of view. By July he had completed a manuscript of 170 pages. He claimed not to know quite what to think of it, but hoped to show the manuscript on his return to Paris to André Gide or Ramon Fernandez, two of the literary popes of the decade, whom he had met through a cousin. The novel is *Southern Mail (Courrier Sud)*; it is the story of a failed love affair and of the France/South Africa mail, and is as neatly autobiographical as a novel can be. For one prominent reviewer it was remarkable for the contrast between the brutality of the world of action and the hero's "interior world of roses and fairies"; for an older Saint-Exupéry it was a work that would better have been left unpublished.

Southern Mail began a trend for its author, all of whose books were primarily written in exile, and all of which bear the stamp of Cape Juby. It was a novel written—as importantly in terms of his personal life—before any of his colleagues thought of him as a writer. Few at Juby were more than vaguely aware that he was working on a book, although his office was notoriously awash in paper and he was often observed scribbling and drawing in the cockpit. By the early months of 1928 he had begun to persuade his visitors to sit down for dramatic evening readings that— as imagined by Joseph Kessel, a journalist who knew him and who knew Juby—were delivered from the foot of his audience's bed, in Saint-Exupéry's muffled, flat voice, one which soon enough became incantatory. Outside, the far-off cry of "*Sentinella!*" passed from one Spanish guard post to the next, marking the quarter hour, and the wind rustled through the sands of the Río de Oro. Exhausted from their flights, Saint-Exupéry's early critics did not manage to stay awake long enough to appreciate many of their host's pages. In March 1928 he read the novel to Jean-Marie Conty in a Casablanca café at the end of a visit that began with a spirited game of chess and lasted thirteen hours. He told his wakeful colleague that he was the first to hear the work in its entirety.

Saint-Exupéry was a perfectionist, perhaps a more desirable trait in an aviator than in a writer. He corrected himself incessantly. Mermoz is reported to have interrupted Saint-Exupéry after a reading of his new pages of the novel with an impatient "But you've already read me that!" (On another occasion he evidently had to apologize for the transgressions of Lola, his pet monkey, who gulped down several pages of one draft of *Southern Mail* when no one was looking.) Mermoz may be forgiven his sins: it was he who found the title for Saint-Exupéry, pointing to a Dakar-bound mail sack on the barrack floor. The author found a more patient audience in Guillaumet, to whom he read often at Juby, as he would later in Paris and Buenos Aires. It was Guillaumet who encouraged him to keep on with *Southern Mail*. "Is it good?" Saint-Exupéry would ask, imploringly. "Yes," answered Guillaumet. "What a shame that I don't know how to write like you." He did not need to: Saint-Exupéry would immortalize Guillaumet in *Wind, Sand and Stars*, as he would the mysteries of the Spanish Sahara, as he would Bark, the venerable black slave.

It was most likely during this slow spring of 1928 that Saint-Exupéry actively took up the cause of Bark, whose fate he first lamented to his mother in his Christmas Eve letter. During these months the Juby chief took tea almost daily among the Moors. He had made various friends, especially among the Izarguin, the least hostile of the tribes of the northern Río de Oro. He was well used to seeing his tea prepared by black slaves; the Moors made no secret of the fact that they considered the French heathens ("You eat greens like the goat and pork like the pigs. . . . What good are your airplanes and wireless . . . if you do not possess the Truth?" Saint-Exupéry had been asked), but the blacks were lower still on the totem pole. For preparing the Moors' food and tending the camels they received a weekly salary; they were set free only when they were too old to work, at which point they were left to die in the desert. This, too, Saint-Exupéry had seen: "The children play in the vicinity of the dark wreck, running with each dawn to see if it is still stirring, yet without mocking the old servitor." What struck him was not the unfairness, or the pain, but the hoard of memories that went with a man: "It was then for the first time that it came on me that when a man dies, an unknown world passes away. . . . The hard bone of his skull was in a sense an old treasure chest; and I could not know what colored stuffs, what images of festivities, what vestiges, obsolete and vain in this desert, had here escaped the shipwreck."

Bark was the first slave whom Saint-Exupéry had met who spoke of this hoard of memories. He was called Bark, as were all slaves; his real name was Mohammed ben Lhaoussin. He had lived in Marrakech, where he had a wife and three children; he was a drover, and had not forgotten that he had once "held sway over a nation of ewes." A Senegalese, Bark had been kidnapped, then bought and sold over the course of three years before ending up the property of a Juby Moor. He had come to work part-time as a waiter in the Frenchmen's mess, for which he earned 300 francs monthly. Each month his owner appeared to claim his wages, greeted Bark's request for his salary with a beating, and disappeared from sight until the end of the following month. Insistently Bark pleaded with the

Aéropostale pilots to hide him in the Agadir plane; probably no one knew the schedule of the northern mail better than he. The Frenchmen hesitated to help him because they knew the Moors would avenge the theft of a slave; moreover such a reprisal would be directed at the Spanish, further upsetting delicate desert politics. After months of Bark's protests—and after soliciting funds from home, from a number of charitable organizations—Saint-Exupéry proposed a solution: he would buy the slave his freedom.

The color of his skin worked against him in attempting his purchase. It was not every day that the Moors met a European in quest of a slave, and they took advantage of this one by opening the negotiation at 20,000 francs, then about eight hundred dollars. Months went by before the nomads relented on their price, and then only after "a week of bargaining, which we spent, fifteen Moors and I, sitting in a circle of sand," did Bark become his for an undisclosed sum. The transaction was not made entirely in good faith: Saint-Exupéry had bribed two bandits who were friends of Bark's master to argue his case. One insisted that Bark was in ill health and advised the Moor to sell him while of some value. The second resorted to more convincing logic: "With the money you get from Bark," argued Raggi in exchange for fifty pesetas, "you will be able to buy camels and rifles and cartridges. Then you can go off on a *razzia* against these French." After an official ceremony of manumission, Saint-Exupéry locked Bark up in the French barrack. He knew the Moors well enough to know that anyone involved in the sale "would gladly have cut off Bark's head within fifty feet of the fort for the pleasure of doing me in the eye."

Bark lived in the French barrack for some time—in "comfortable captivity"—dreaming of his return, which he would ask to have described to him twenty times daily. The French mechanics, concerned about how he would reestablish himself in Marrakech, together presented him with 1,000 francs of their savings; it had not escaped their notice that he would be less wealthy as a free man than he had been in the service of the Moors. His departure from Juby was dramatic, not only in the eyes of Saint-Exupéry—now more than a tamer of gazelles or a mother hen—who felt he was sending his "fifty-year-old, newborn babe" out into the world. "Bark took his last look at the immense desolation of Cape Juby. Round the airplane 200 Moors were finding out what a slave looked like when he stood on the threshold of life. . . . 'Good-bye, Bark,' they called. 'No,' replied the free man. 'I am Mohammed ben Lhaoussin.'" In Agadir, Mohammed ben Lhaoussin evidently did what could be expected with his thousand francs. He had tea, poured for him by a waiter, and he visited the Berber prostitutes in the Kasbah. Then he spent every remaining franc on gifts, mostly golden *babouches*, for the children of the town. For Saint-Exupéry the former slave had made a brilliant transaction. He had landed in Agadir with too much freedom and plenty of money and had corrected the situation: "He felt the lack in him of that weight of human relations that trammels a man's progress; tears, farewells, joys." One thousand francs later "he felt the pull of his true weight. Bark dragged himself forward, pulling against the pull of a thousand children who had such great need of golden slippers." For the hermit of Cape Juby, bound to his fellow pilots by the urgency of a bag of letters, this was a working definition of happiness.

~

By the summer of 1928, the days of Saint-Exupéry's languid teas were over. Not so his protracted negotiations in the sand. On June 29 he was roused from his night's sleep by something that had never woken him before: the sound of an airplane. He quickly set up a number of runway flares that illuminated a Latécoère 25, almost certainly the first he had seen at Juby. It was less the sight of this impressive monoplane, which could fly 40 percent faster than a Breguet 14, that surprised him, however, than it was an unannounced nighttime arrival. (Regular night flights would debut the following year.) Out of the plane stepped Marcel Reine, the pilot; Edmond Serre, an engineer newly in charge of establishing radio communications over *la Ligne*; and a senior inspector. They had not been able to alert Juby to their arrival and the inspector now insisted that Reine and Serre continue on to Cisneros, although radio communication with Cisneros was equally impossible at this hour. Saint-Exupéry discouraged the idea on meteorological grounds; the coast had been socked in with fog for days and had only cleared that evening. He was a young pilot, however, and this was a senior inspector: at 2:30 on Saturday morning, June 30, Reine and Serre took off to the south, leaving the inspector at Juby. Seven hours later Saint-Exupéry radioed Cisneros and Port-Étienne, today the Mauritanian town of Nouadhibou, farther to the south. "We were sending out ship-like signals of distress," he wrote in *Southern Mail*. "*Request news mail-plane, request . . .*" No one along the line had heard from Reine and Serre.

Almost immediately, Saint-Exupéry was aloft in a Breguet 14, as he would be for much of the following months. He also sent word to the Moors, asking if they might help with his reconnaissance work. They knew only that Reine and Serre were in the desert or in the ocean; a heavy fog had indeed blanketed much of the coast south of Juby that evening, and a Latécoère 25 possessed only the most rudimentary instruments for flying without visibility. Neither fact augured well. On July 4, an expanded search party gathered at Port-Étienne. Saint-Exupéry flew the first plane, taking as passengers an interpreter and Albert Tête, the head of the airline in

Dakar. The second Breguet 14 was piloted by Riguelle, also accompanied
by an interpreter; the third by Henri Bourgat, who carried an additional
interpreter and Jean-René Lefèbvre, the airline's ace mechanic, then
posted to Villa Cisneros. Their mission was to cover as much of the Río
de Oro as possible. The trio took off from Port-Étienne but by Cape Barbas,
115 miles north, Riguelle's propeller had stopped and he was forced to
make an emergency landing. Expertly he guided Bourgat to a nearby spot
in the sand where he could land; Saint-Exupéry circled overhead while
waiting for a diagnosis, on the lookout for approaching caravans. Lefèbvre
ran to the ailing plane, whose connecting rods had ruptured and decom-
posed into what he sadly termed "a salad." There was no time for last
rites, though they may just as well have been performed. Riguelle was
quickly boarded onto Bourgat's airplane. The addition of an extra passenger meant that someone had to stay behind, and the Breguet took off
without its interpreter.

Minutes after takeoff Bourgat's Breguet developed an oil leak. He
turned to land next to Riguelle's plane, where the interpreter must have
been surprised to see that he was to have company after all. Lefèbvre's
report was this time less dire. The oil lines would have to be replaced, for
which he estimated a repair time of three to four hours. A sign was made
to Saint-Exupéry that he should land as well, which he did. The interpreters were dispatched as lookouts; as it was by now at least mid-
afternoon, Tête and Riguelle set about preparing a campsite for the
evening. The Breguet 14 was an unreliable aircraft, but a case where three
planes set off and none reached its destination was rare all the same.
Saint-Exupéry and Bourgat helped Lefèbvre to install the oil lines from
Riguelle's plane in Bourgat's, an operation that would have been hugely
facilitated by the presence of a stepladder. The operation finished, Saint-
Exupéry performed a run-up, running the engine at full power without
taking off. By now it was nearly dusk; all seemed in order for a dawn
departure. Happily the provisions were more reliable than the aircraft;
from the first-rate reserves Tête and Riguelle set out a modest dinner of
white ham, *pâté de foie*, sardines, and *pâté au fromage*. Lefèbvre noted
that the forlorn eight had no grounds on which to claim martyrdom as
they had been stranded as well with several excellent bottles of wine.

It was by no account—and Saint-Exupéry's and Lefèbvre's recollections vary mainly in their rhapsodics—a sad evening. The mechanic remembered that the group "did the reserves honor, no one having lost his
appetite" in all the drama, traded anecdotes, and played several games
of belote. Saint-Exupéry then entertained the group with his magnificent
card tricks, "happy as a child to demonstrate for us his talents as a con-
jurer." This night deep in dissident territory would indeed be remembered
as an emblematic one by Saint-Exupéry, who generally got a good deal

of literary mileage out of his misadventures. Here is his description of the evening in the passage that lent *Wind, Sand and Stars* its name:

> We unloaded five or six wooden cases of merchandise out of the hold, emptied them, and set them about in a circle. At the deep end of each case, as in a sentry-box, we set a lighted candle, its flame poorly sheltered from the wind. So in the heart of the desert, on the naked rind of the planet, in an isolation like that of the beginnings of the world, we built a village of men. Sitting in the flickering light of the candles on this kerchief of sand, on this village square, we waited in the night. We were waiting for the rescuing dawn—or for the Moors. Something, I know not what, lent this night a savor of Christmas. We told stories, we joked, we sang songs. In the air there was that slight fever that reigns over a gaily prepared feast. And yet we were infinitely poor. Wind, sand, and stars. The austerity of Trappists. But on this badly lighted cloth, a handful of men who possessed nothing in the world but their memories were sharing invisible riches. We had met at last. Men travel side by side for years, each locked up in his own silence or exchanging those words which carry no freight—till danger comes. Then they stand shoulder to shoulder.

Saint-Exupéry took a few artistic liberties with his account. When he first wrote up the evening for *Paris-Soir*, exactly ten years after it had happened, he mentioned that several aviators had been murdered by the Moors in the desert. By 1939, they had been murdered "exactly on the spot" on which the French now camped. He perhaps overstated the danger—Lefèbvre mentions only that the French were armed—but more indicative were the practical details he left out surrounding this transcendent evening. According to Lefèbvre, it was mostly Saint-Exupéry who talked and joked and sang, exercising a kind of magical fascination over his comrades. He carried on all night, possibly because he was happy, possibly to make the others forget the cold, probably both. First he spoke with great excitement of several Jules Verne-ish contraptions he had invented; he went on to suggest that Toulouse equip the Aéropostale planes with donkeys, convinced these animals would intimidate both the Moors and their camels. Ultimately he discoursed on the nature of existence itself. Clearly he could not have described the evening more accurately than he did, having been the magic at the center of it.

At a certain point even Saint-Exupéry's charms could not keep the group from sleep. It was decided that the mail trunks, suspended from the planes' wings, offered the best protection from the wind and the cold. They did for everyone but Saint-Exupéry who—despite numerous contortions—could not fold himself into a trunk and resolved instead to spend the night in an open cockpit. This arrangement did not last long, given the temperature, which could have fallen below thirty-five degrees and for which the Frenchmen were certainly unprepared. According to

Lefèbvre, who could not have been very comfortably installed in his trunk if he were able to report as much, Saint-Exupéry got out of the Breguet toward 3:00 or 4:00 a.m. "Covering himself with everything he could find in the baggage compartments, he walked in circles around the planes, like a ghost, attempting to keep warm. . . . In those moments when it would have been normal to give in to despair he seemed to experience extreme exaltation, intense happiness, before which our solitude in the immensity of the desert made him appreciate not only his craft as a pilot, but everything which among men elicited his love and admiration," Lefèbvre nearly prophetically observed. When the others woke, Saint-Exupéry went on at some length about the remarkable opportunity he had had to admire the North Star. His exuberance must have been infuriating, as Riguelle was quick to let him know: "The North Star," he informed the Juby chief, "has never been worth a few good hours of sleep." Two hours later the six Frenchmen arrived in Cisneros in two cramped planes; the interpreters were left for another night in the desert. A flurry of telegrams went out from Cisneros, assuring the airfields up and down the coast that the week had not, as feared, claimed any additional casualties.

That day the governor of Cisneros received a letter from Reine and Serre via a Moorish emissary. The fog had forced them to fly just above the ground on June 30, and a dune had knocked them out of the air about halfway between Juby and Villa Cisneros. Three hours later they had been taken prisoner by the R'Guibat, the most hostile of the tribes in the Río de Oro. An aerial search for their plane would have been futile; the R'Guibat had destroyed what they could of the 1,500-pound Latécoère. They had pulled apart Serre's luggage, evidently taking a special interest in his toiletries. Having elicited mimed explanations of each item they doused themselves in eau de cologne; it was a mild replay of a 1926 incident in which the Moors, fascinated by a first-aid kit, had downed a mixture of antigangrene and antitetanus serums, rubbing alcohol, and iodine salve, a potion that—fortunately for the French—claimed no casualties. Reine and Serre had fared better than their baggage and were intact. Naturally a ransom was proposed: the price of the two Frenchmen was one million camels, one million rifles, and the liberation of all R'Guibat prisoners— "a little nothing," Saint-Exupéry wrote his mother. The following morning he flew north to Juby and the others south to Port-Étienne. Lefèbvre, Riguelle, and Bourgat made a detour to pay their last respects to Riguelle's Breguet. Twenty-four hours after their departure, it had already been torn to pieces.

~

"At times like these," Saint-Exupéry wrote his mother that summer, "one risks one's life with a great deal of generosity." If anything, the Aéropostale management might have wished him to be less magnanimous in 1928. As summer wore on the mishaps multiplied, and as they did the man who would make a cult of adversity thrived. Reine and Serre were in their third week of captivity when, on July 18, a second team of aviators went down between Villa Cisneros and Juby. This time it was the escort plane that made an emergency landing south of Juby; it was piloted by Riguelle, who had as much bad luck as anyone could with the Breguet 14. Maurice Dumesnil flew on to Juby with the mail and the bad news, not having seen a suitable landing place next to Riguelle and not having wanted to risk damage to both aircraft in one of the most sensitive areas of the desert. On alerting Saint-Exupéry he took off again for Riguelle, who was only twenty miles from the fort. Either at this time or as the next set of aviators went down, as they did with stunning regularity over these months, Saint-Exupéry wrote home to tell of the magnificent feats being performed in the desert to rescue the mails. He had, he reported, covered 5,000 miles of the desert in five days. He had been fired at like a rabbit by *razzias* of 300 men; he had had some hair-raising adventures and—aside from his evening spent admiring the North Star—had landed four times in dissident territory. "I have never," he told his mother, "so often landed or slept in the Sahara, nor heard so many bullets fly."

Now he set about organizing the rescue of Riguelle's plane. It could not be transported back to the airfield over land, where no trail cut through the dunes, or by sea, because of the shoreline cliffs; Saint-Exupéry needed to fly the Breguet out of the desert as quickly as possible. Immediately he set out for the site with several Moors who had agreed to guard the machine; in the air, he passed Riguelle and Dumesnil, returning to the safety of Juby. His delight in seeing them must have been tempered with his distress at seeing the aircraft. It was only a twenty-minute flight from Juby but the Breguet required a good deal of repair. Regulations would have stipulated that it remain in the desert; Saint-Exupéry would consider no such thing. Happily he got on better with the Moors than with the rules, and on his return, evidently set off to consult with the chiefs camped in the vicinity. Sporting his famous bathrobe, he talked of the wind and the weather, downed the requisite three cups of tea, then politely asked for an escort, which—at a price and after some negotiation—was granted.

Over the course of the next two days he managed to organize a caravan of six armed Moors on horseback; nine workers on foot; two horses, one for the mechanic Marchal and one for himself; two mules, carrying supplies and water; one camel carrying tools; and two additional camels pulling a cart mounted on airplane wheels. This invention of Saint-Exupéry's

on which rode an airplane engine, a hoist, and a sawhorse, maneuvered
its way nicely over the dunes; it had evidently been the subject of some
derision at Juby, and Saint-Exupéry was particularly pleased by its performance. Later he could not restrain himself from adding an aside in his
official report to Toulouse: "This is the first time, at least in the Sahara,
that the camel has been used as a draft animal." This unusual caravan
set out to the south in the evening, reaching its destination on the morning
of July 21. The Juby chief could not have been pleased to find the aircraft
more damaged than when he had left it; the Moors he had stationed next
to the plane had either deserted or been scared away, and the Breguet
had been sabotaged. Its piston rod, he now noticed, had entirely sliced
the engine struts, which meant that new struts would be needed. Moreover,
it did not look as if it would be possible to drag the Breguet to a smoother
piece of ground, as he had intended. By camel he sent orders back to Juby
for a mechanic to disassemble several struts; Marchal set about removing
those of the wrecked plane. In the meantime, all hands were put to work
on an improvised runway, a project that took the better part of the next
two days. Saint-Exupéry reported that he put in a certain amount of time
with a pickax and shovel himself. Here his love of technical manuals served
him well. As the sand was soft he was not sure that he would actually be
able to take off from the runway without some sort of added lift. He had
a springboard of hard-packed sand built at the end of the strip, which he
could approach at high speed. The plane would either trampoline into the
air or sink if it could not attain sufficient air speed. In the event of the
latter, Saint-Exupéry constructed a sort of platform sixty feet farther on,
from which the plane would rebound or—in a worst-case scenario—crash,
but without any real danger to its pilot. These arrangements he did not
mention in his report to the company.

By nightfall the cameleer returned from Juby, engine mounts in tow.
He was preceded by the sound of gunshots in the distance, which had
sent the Moors racing for their guns. Toward midnight an Izarguin messenger galloped into the camp with the news that the bloodthirsty Aït-
Toussa would be upon them in minutes and that they would be killed; by
order of Colonel de la Peña, the men were to return to Juby. Instantly
they were off for the fort, the lucky ones three to a camel. Nine miles into
the retreat Saint-Exupéry learned that the alarm had not been sounded
by the colonel but by the kindhearted messenger himself. Furious, he
ordered a return to the half-built runway. This idea roundly displeased
the Moors. Ataf, his interpreter, informed him that he would be in great
trouble if he failed to prevent any further French deaths; what was more,
the Aït-Toussa could be counted on to kill everyone, which Ataf admitted
was to him cause for greater concern. Saint-Exupéry had his fair share
of coaxing to do; he appears to have successfully insulted the Moors along

with accusations of cowardice. His was by no means a euphoric evening under the stars. At 9:00 a.m., with order restored and work again under way, two Spanish planes flew overhead and delivered an official order from the colonel that Saint-Exupéry retreat. "I folded this paper carefully, as a souvenir, and decided to head back, but by plane, that evening," he reported later.

By noon the work was accompanied by a symphony of not-so-distant gunfire; the Moors had an understandable tendency to flatten to the ground every time a new series of shots rang out. Only late in the afternoon were the new engine mounted and the runway ready; Marchal had not had an easy time fitting the engine, and Saint-Exupéry admitted that "the name of God was compromised a certain number of times in the course of this adventure." At six he took off with Marchal for Juby. It was "a technically perfect takeoff from the spring-board, followed by an equally perfect landing at Juby," he reported privately. He allowed a touch of humor but no pride to creep into his official report, aside from the camels-as-draft-animals boast: the expenses, he explained, "come in a lump sum because (1) There were no bills and; (2) They are extremely muddled, having resulted from interminable discussions and complications." With fetching understatement he added, "I can't judge if the cost of this expedition is exaggerated, it being without precedent." When reporting back to Albert Tête he seemed well aware that the exploit would also remain without successor: "Don't reproach me this rescue, because it was reasonable to attempt it. If we stayed with the plane it was out of simple elegance. It's none of the company's business."

There was no question that Saint-Exupéry was, as one mechanic reported, particularly delighted by this rescue, which showed him to possess as much cleverness as courage. Legend soon had him stepping on the gas on his makeshift runway as blue turbans appeared on the horizon, performing aerobatics over Juby in Riguelle's plane until he remembered that Marchal had fit the engine to the plane with only four of its twenty-four bolts. It is easier to believe the legend that had him asleep at the Juby dinner table within minutes. Probably the most difficult part of the adventure was the drafting of the official report, which he filed on August 1, a week after his return. "Saint-Exupéry was never so unhappy, his forehead as wrinkled, than when he had to write an official report; he could not hold in his cutting, throwaway remarks, so lively was his intelligence," remembered Lefèbvre. The responsibility on which the Juby chief flourished was of the abstract and all-consuming variety. His bête noire would prove the administrative, the formulaic, that which obliged him to fold his odd, large frame into the confines of a box or a line or a category. The frustration that would lead him to exact his revenge—against small-minded inspectors, in *Night Flight*; against the sedentary, in *Wind, Sand and Stars*; against the politicians, in *Flight to Arras*; against bureaucrats, academics, businessmen in *The Little Prince* —was brewing already at his desk at Juby. He was turning out to be the living incarnation of two great French concepts: that of esprit de corps, which explained his new confidence in himself, and of which he would become one of the great literary spokesmen; and the spirit of noblesse oblige, which would separate him from it all, which would aggravate his impatience with the administrative demands of the company. The two made for a difficult balancing act.

This Saint-Exupéry amply demonstrated with a rogue attempt to rescue Reine and Serre, still held captive, on September 17. The aviators, who were being held separately, had talked in their letters of imminent assassination; all attempts to rescue them or to negotiate a rescue had proved futile. Through his contacts with the Moors Saint-Exupéry had on occasion learned their whereabouts (the prisoners were moved constantly) and he had several times managed to deliver food and clothing to them. This time, having assured himself that Tête would not be at Cisneros, he made an unauthorized trip south, stopping in a hollow among the interior cliffs where he dropped off a Moor with a few days' worth of rations and water. The Moor was to approach the R'Guibat, attempt to negotiate a reasonable ransom, then rendezvous with the pilot in the same place three days later. From his own pocket Saint-Exupéry furnished his accomplice the sum necessary for the purchase of two camels, with which he could make his expedition to the R'Guibat camp.

The trouble began not with Saint-Exupéry's takeoff—miraculous, given the fact that a strong wind prevented him from taking off in the direction he had hoped, which had meant he had had to jump over three dunes, stalling each time, before flying out of the hollow—but with his subsequent arrival at Cisneros. Colonel de la Peña had already radioed the airfield in consternation; he had seen an airplane head south although no mail was scheduled until the following day. Paul Nubalde, a Cisneros mechanic, received his call with some surprise. As no French flights were scheduled for that Monday he took the liberty of telling the colonel that he must have been watching one of his own planes depart without realizing it. He then set off, along with the rest of the Cisneros crew, to scour the skies; someone was wrong, and they must have been eager for it to have been the Spaniard. To make matters worse, Saint-Exupéry had been misinformed about the whereabouts of Tête. The director arrived at Cisneros shortly before Saint-Exupéry and was on the runway to greet him, which he did not do cordially. The Juby chief was ordered back to his airfield with the two mail planes scheduled for the following morning.

Had he followed Tête's orders, however, he would have missed his rendezvous in the desert two days off; it was perversely difficult to kill time, unnoticed, between Cisneros and Juby. Saint-Exupéry's ingenuity here joined with his persuasiveness. He immediately confessed his plan to the mechanic Nubalde. Both men knew there was no spare aircraft at Cisneros; the mechanic conspired to make sure that the engine of Saint-Exupéry's Breguet would not work in the morning. The northern mail came and went; the Juby pilot stayed, much to the fury of Tête. Nubalde pretended to work on the recalcitrant engine throughout the day, announcing success only in the evening. Saint-Exupéry took off—unescorted—the next morning at dawn.

Unfortunately, Nubalde's efforts on Saint-Exupéry's behalf were for nought. The Moor may or may not have made contact with the R'Guibat; he did see the mail planes heading north and set off all of his flares to attract their attention, evidently to no avail. By the time Saint-Exupéry came for him the Moor had no means of signaling his location; the pilot circled and circled without seeing a trace of his cohort. In his report Saint-Exupéry, of course, omitted the events following his arrival at Cisneros, contritely noting only that he had been informed by Tête that negotiations with the Moors were proceeding apace and in no way justified his "irregular conduct." The remorse went only so far, however. He had also learned from Tête that—relations with the Spanish having become delicate over the Reine and Serre issue—his rashness might have jeopardized the whole operation. With a twelve-year-old's logic Saint-Exupéry argued that Aéropostale had only to disclaim any responsibility for his flight. After all, he had acted without the company's authorization, for which, he added, he had not asked so that it could not be refused. On arrival at Juby, he sent a telegram to Nubalde assuring him of his safe arrival but notifying him of the failure of his mission. From Cisneros a note went out from Tête to Toulouse, informing the head office that the director was issuing a formal order that Saint-Exupéry—"who had been carried away by his generous nature"—henceforth be told to stay put at Juby.

~

Saint-Exupéry had been scheduled to leave Cape Juby in September 1928, and he continued to count on a return as soon as Reine and Serre were released. He dreamed, as he had all along, of the luxuries of France, of a place "where one politely greets people when one meets them instead of firing at them, where one doesn't get lost in the fog at 125 miles* an hour," but he was more than ever firmly entrenched in his life of adventure. He wrote his mother that he hoped to be home in September but that it

* If Saint-Exupéry managed to pilot a Breguet 14 at 125 miles an hour, he did so with a very stiff wind behind him. Cruising speeds were closer to 80 to 100 miles an hour.

was his *duty* to stay so long as the situation remained unresolved. It seems his first use of the word that would prove so crucial to his texts and his thinking: "It may be," he wrote, "that I'm actually good for something."

He was more than good for something, as he would continue, despite Tête's rebuke, to prove that fall. Another stellar rescue took place in October, when Saint-Exupéry came to the aid of a Spanish airplane shot down by the Moors 150 miles south of Juby. This time his bravado earned him accolades, not only because the venture had been successful. In the eyes of the company Saint-Exupéry had shown up the Spanish, who the French felt were proving the greatest obstacle to the liberation of the two hostages, now nearing the end of their 117 days in captivity. In his notes to Toulouse, which brim with frustration over the fate of Reine and Serre, Tête made a jubilant entry for October 18:

> Two Spanish planes leave Juby on a reconnaissance mission, one breaks down, the pilot lands, damages the plane; the Moorish interpreter is badly hurt, the pilot wounded as well. The escort plane doesn't dare land, returns to Juby. St Exupéry takes off to the rescue with a second Spanish plane. The second plane comes in to land. It crashes. St Exupéry executes an expert landing, brings back the two wounded men to Juby, takes off, and returns again with the second crew. What a lovely response to their authoritarian and petty attitude! I have instantly forgotten all the troubles that his adventure last month caused me. The lieutenant colonel had to write to the Company with his thanks!!!!

Saint-Exupéry had worked a certain amount of détente in the desert but it would have taken a miracle to eliminate the French-Spanish ill will of the 1920s. A game of chess between two aristocrats far from home was one thing, perfect trust between colonizing powers another, particularly since the Spanish could not help but be sorely aware of the French preeminence in northwest Africa. In a report on the Río de Oro filed after his return to France, Saint-Exupéry mentioned that he had been told point-blank by a Juby captain that the Spanish were disinclined to help the French, as every problem encountered by Aéropostale amounted to a boon to the projected Seville–Buenos Aires line. In the same report he vented some frustration with the Moors. His was perhaps a more anthropologically honest assessment of the nomads than the view shared by his colleagues, but it is not the romanticized picture later painted in *Wind, Sand and Stars*:

> One does not pacify the nomads any more than one pacifies the international underworld; the same tribe can be friend or foe depending on the time, the place, the circumstances. Above all else the Moors admire force, and a conversation will influence them only insofar as it is an expression of power, even if that power is not put to use. . . . The family of emotions

"gratitude, friendship, respect, etc." on which a stable society is based lose
their meaning when it comes to the nomads, whose social conditions have
created a different spirit. It is absurd to expect gratitude from the Moors,
as it would be absurd to condemn them for being ungrateful. The sentiment
of gratitude in its European sense follows from a set of social conditions
in which contacts and needs are permanent; a given nomadic tribe will
have a very different need tomorrow from the one it has today.

Neither of these persistent difficulties minimized the importance of the
Río de Oro for Saint-Exupéry, who had now spent over a year in the
desert. During that time he had been groomed by adversity. He had made
his first acquaintance with the ideas on which hang his books: the importance of responsibility, the fellowship it nurtures among men, the priority of an interior life. Thirteen years later, in New York, the celebrated
author would be described as walking "with a lifting motion from the
hips, as if he were on sand." When he returned to France at the end of
1928 a whiff of exoticism clung to him. He was no longer an awkward
loner with a name belied by his fingernails; he was Saint-Ex, whose legend
preceded him. The myth-making machine of the airline went to work on
him; by one of the more modest accounts, he had rescued fourteen aviators
during his thirteen months at Juby. His own writing testifies to these efforts:
in fourteen pages of *Wind, Sand and Stars*, he is forced down in the desert
three times, although not all of these incidents took place during his stay
at Cape Juby. And the derring-do went on until the last minute: His return
to France was delayed by the fact that his replacement crashed in the fog
en route for Juby. ("I am decidedly not lucky," the outgoing chief of the
airfield wrote his mother.) Louis Vidal had been flying toward Juby with
the payroll for the African mail; instead of delivering the 20,000 francs,
stolen by the Moors, he cost the company 22,600 francs in ransom and
rescue fees.

Like all exiles, Saint-Exupéry was capable of a fierce amount of nostalgia, and a rosy glow soon settled on Cape Juby. In his last months in
the Río de Oro he was apt to ridicule an outpost "where 200 men . . . live
in a fort which they never leave"; within a year he lamented his former
existence. For years he dined out on the accumulated tales of Juby as on
his later tales of the desert, always with an emphasis on the drama, the
foreignness, the tricks of nature, never on the heroics. He missed his
monk's life. The imagery of Cape Juby would color all of his work, though
the images of Juby are not all indigenous to the Sahara. *Southern Mail* is
a novel rich in flying gold and captive princesses and buried treasure and
velvet and amber and pearls, items with which the desert is frugal. This
"interior world of roses and fairies" was imported from another address;
it sustained Saint-Exupéry in the desolation of Juby, it was the reason he
understood the secret kingdom of the Moors, the treasure a man—any

man, even a Senegalese slave—carried inside him. When Saint-Exupéry thought of exile he thought not of Juby, but of a home richer still in legend and mystery. His wooden barrack remained the home he most loved, but the home he most missed was a less modest one. He claimed it was more real than the solitude, the sandstorms, the blazing moonlight of the desert. Its vestibule alone, he wrote his mother, "is more mysterious than the heart of Africa." It plays a role in *Southern Mail* and in *The Little Prince*; the first draft of *Night Flight* begins in it; it is described in some detail in *Wind, Sand and Stars*, when Saint-Exupéry has been forced down at night in the Río de Oro. Alone in the desert, he gives himself up to his memories:

> Somewhere there was a park dark with firs and linden trees and an old house that I loved. It mattered little that it was far away, that it could not warm me in my flesh, nor shelter me . . . It was enough that it existed to fill my night with its presence. I was no longer this body, flung up on a shore; I oriented myself; I was the child of this house.

II

~

The Mother Country
1900–1909

For the French, all children are barbarians who must be tamed and molded ruthlessly to adult standards.

JESSE R. PITTS, *In Search of France*

Antoine de Saint-Exupéry was born on the morning of June 29, 1900, at 8, rue du Peyrat, Lyons. He was baptized the following day as Antoine Jean-Baptiste Marie Roger de Saint-Exupéry; to his family he was Tonio. He would claim that it was entirely by accident that he was born in Lyons—neither of his parents was Lyonnais and the family spent little time there—and the city seems to have heard his protests. It is discreet about the birth of its famous son, commemorated only by a plaque over the entryway to the townhouse on what is now the rue Alphonse Fochier and in no imminent danger of being renamed. Saint-Exupéry would take little from France's second city, save for a Rabelaisian appetite for good food and a love-hate relationship with France's premier city. In a country in which Paris provides the measure of all things—in which distances are measured from a small stone sunk into the pavement in front of the portals of Notre Dame—Lyons remains proud of its provinciality. Ultimately it mattered less that Saint-Exupéry was from Lyons than that he was *not* from Paris.

His parents were both members of the provincial nobility, a class the Parisian nobility had dubbed *les hobereaux* in honor of a small falcon that hunts only small prey. The term was accurate in its suggestion that the respect accorded the provincial nobleman by his fellow townsmen was inversely proportional to the respect accorded him by the titled Parisian, who now tended his *cave* but who left the care of his vineyards to others.

The Saint-Exupéry family, one of France's oldest, dating back to the Crusades, came from the Limousin, in central France; Saint-Exupéry's paternal grandfather had married Alix Blouquier de Trélan, whose family was based in Tours. The Boyer de Fonscolombes, Saint-Exupéry's mother's family, hailed from Aix-en-Provence on the paternal side. Her mother's family, the Romanet de Lestranges, were also southerners, hailing from the Vivarais, now the Ardèche, in southeastern France. There were titles and châteaux and—less often—fortunes on both sides; Saint-Exupéry's paternal grandfather was a count and his maternal grandfather a baron. The genealogical details appeared to matter little to the aviator, who did not dwell on the glories of France's past except to explain the ills of the present, and then only in a most general way. (In one of the rare lines of his work in which he harks back to his ancestors he vaunts not the achievements of the family but the unaffected prose of his great-grandfather's cook.) He was, however, distinctly in possession of "*un joli nom.*" On his father's side he could count one member of the Académie Française and a host of distinguished military officers; his grandfather's grandfather had fought with Lafayette in America. Among his maternal ancestors he could claim an archbishop, a court chamberlain, several distinguished musicians, and a number of knights. Saint-Exupéry had his favorites in the family and relied heavily on the emotional and material support they came to offer him, but he did not view blood relation as a condition in itself sufficient to merit affection or even, much to his mother's dismay, civility. From his father's side he inherited a "marvelous gaiety" and much charm; from his mother's came an appreciation of things musical, artistic, and spiritual, along with the sensibility to match.

Jean de Saint-Exupéry, whom his son resembled physically and from whom he inherited his height, was born in 1863 in Florac, where Saint-Exupéry's grandfather, Fernand, was then *sous-préfet*. Later the family of nine settled in Le Mans, where Fernand de Saint-Exupéry joined an insurance company; it may not have been the obvious choice of profession for a count who had served as *sous-préfet* in four different *départements*, but it was a stable one, particularly in the post-1870, newly democratic world. Fernand de Saint-Exupéry appears to have recommended the profession to Jean, who began but did not finish his schooling as a military officer—a sin for which a younger brother later atoned—and who turned up in Lyons as an inspector for the Compagnie du Soleil in 1896. It says a good deal about the time in which he was born that on Antoine de Saint-Exupéry's birth certificate his father—then covering the company's affairs in two regions—described himself as being "*sans profession.*"

Jean de Saint-Exupéry probably met Marie Boyer de Fonscolombe, twelve years his junior, in Lyons the year of his arrival there. The two were distantly related and were introduced at the apartment of the Countess de Tricaud, Marie's great-aunt and godmother, who was to play a crucial role in the young family's life. By 1896 the countess, born Gabrielle de Lestrange, was sixty-three; she had long lost her husband and their only daughter, who had died before her fourth birthday in 1869. The Count de Tricaud had left his widow a fashionable apartment overlooking the central *place* of Lyons, where she installed herself during the winter months. Perhaps more dear to her was the château she had inherited forty-five miles northeast of the city, where on June 8, 1896, Jean de Saint-Exupéry and Marie de Fonscolombe were married. By January 1897 the couple had settled on the rue du Peyrat and produced their first daughter, Marie-Madeleine. A second daughter, Simone, the obvious candidate for the distinction of the Saint-Exupéry most likely to succeed, was born a year and a day later, on January 26, 1898. These two girls constituted the "elders" of the family. Antoine's birth in 1900 was followed by that of a second son, François, in 1902, and by that of a third daughter, Gabrielle, Saint-Exupéry's favorite sister, known as Didi, in May 1903.

The family was no sooner complete when, on the evening of March 14, 1904, Jean de Saint-Exupéry suffered a stroke in the waiting room of the train station near the home of his wife's family. He was forty-one years old. A doctor arrived minutes after his collapse but was unable to revive the young man; Jean de Saint-Exupéry received his last rites in the arms of his wife, in the La Foux station, as an eastbound train discharged its passengers. His children were not on hand at the time; it is unclear how the news was conveyed to them. Antoine was not yet four; his life was to be shaped to a remarkable extent by an event he may not have remembered. From this age on the preponderant influence on him would be a feminine one: the Countess de Tricaud, herself an expert at loss, rallied to the side of Marie de Saint-Exupéry, now a twenty-eight-year-old widow and mother of five with no fixed source of income. The apartment on the rue du Peyrat was abandoned and the family took to spending six months of the year at the countess's château at Saint-Maurice-de-Rémens, where they would almost certainly not have been installed had Jean de Saint-Exupéry lived on. The rest of the year they invaded the countess's Lyons apartment on the Place Bellecour or stayed with Marie de Saint-Exupéry's parents at the château de La Mole, a converted monastery with two medieval towers and its own tropical forest, near Saint-Tropez. The château had been in the family since 1770; it was here that Jean de Saint-Exupéry's funeral was held.

Marie de Saint-Exupéry acquitted herself of her familial responsibilities with grace and tenderness. She was a devoted mother who would remain unceasingly compassionate, attentive, giving, and pious, all qualities her elder son would put to the test. She was not always approving, which meant only that her blessing carried great weight. Her husband's

death made her presence doubly felt, which had on Antoine an effect that
defies the laws of physics: he could not get enough of her. Absent fathers
can be oddly present, too, and Jean de Saint-Exupéry's shadow was long.
His son never wrote about the loss of his father—although his oeuvre can
be read as a requiem to the male bonds of which he was deprived—and
seems not to have spoken of him. If he did not cave in to regret on this
subject he did, however, do battle with a very private anxiety. He thought
his father had died of syphilis, and he believed the disease to be hereditary.
His was not a far-fetched idea at a time when the illness—which Flaubert
had defined in his *Dictionary of Received Ideas* as something by which
more or less everybody was affected—accounted for some 15 percent of
all deaths. Still, this was not the kind of concern with which it is safe to
saddle a man with a prodigious imagination.

~

It was at the château of Saint-Maurice-de-Rémens that Saint-Exupéry
located his childhood. The house was dear enough to the family that when
Simone de Saint-Exupéry was prohibited by her more famous brother
from bringing out a collection of stories under the family name she published instead as Simone de Remens. Here was the "park dark with firs
and lindens," here was the "secret kingdom," the "interior world of roses
and fairies." Such enchantment might not have been obvious to the un-
initiated. The château, a handsome Louis XVI building, then a train and
carriage ride from Lyons, had been purchased for the Count and Countess
de Tricaud in the early 1850s and decorated by them in Second Empire
splendor, the style of the day. Its rooms were stately and dark, the long
front hallway paneled and cold and cavelike. To the right wing of the
house, which looks out over rolling foothills, the Tricauds had added a
chapel, in which were housed the remains of their daughter. Behind the
château lay a handsome, linden-lined park. The countess had entertained
both sides of her family—the Fonscolombes and the Lestranges—at Saint-
Maurice; Madame de Saint-Exupéry had long been made to feel at home
here. Now the house was opened to her "tribe" just before Easter and
served as the Saint-Exupérys' base of operations until October. Madame
de Saint-Exupéry and her elder daughters made their home on the ground
floor; the third was the province of the younger children and their governess, who for two very memorable years was an Austrian named Paula.
It was not long before the power of Antoine's personality made itself felt:
grills were placed over the third-floor windows to prevent nighttime
excursions on the roof. From that floor came the continual sound of
stampedes, especially at bathtime, when Paula or one of her successors,

sponge in hand, was obliged to do her best to outrun a screaming, naked Tonio.

The child whose full head of golden curls had earned him the nickname "the Sun King" was in fact happily attempting his first experiments with absolute power. He had a throne of his own, a miniature green chair very dear to him. He quickly distinguished himself with his *exigence*, making his mother the primary target of his tyranny: "He followed me throughout the house like a shadow, his little lacquered chair in hand, so that he might sit down at my side wherever I was." He was in quest of a story and would not release his mother until one was delivered. Madame de Saint-Exupéry encouraged her children to dramatize the many tales she told them with *tableaux vivants* or with charades; she saw to it that her sons, at least, were steeped in Jules Verne and Hans Christian Andersen. As a consequence the Saint-Exupéry children were committed litterateurs early on; Saint-Exupéry claimed to have written poetry from the age of six. Three would go on to publish, though none was quite so demanding of his first audiences as Antoine, who would beat François if his younger brother refused to listen to his work. At a cousin's home he and his sister Simone proved accomplished *metteurs en scène*; they composed short plays based on the tales they unearthed in their uncle's library, where they fell greedily upon all history books, memoirs, and adventure stories. These plays were performed with the assistance of numerous cousins, to the general delight of the assembled adults. Saint-Exupéry took this encouragement to its logical extreme. He wrote his poems mostly at night, when he prowled the house in search of an audience. Draped in a blanket or a tablecloth, he routinely woke his brother and sisters for dramatic readings of his newly minted verse. His protesting siblings in tow, he then led the way to Madame de Saint-Exupéry's room, where he would light a lamp and energetically repeat his performance, often prevailing until 1:00 a.m. His explanation for these intrusions was simple: "When you are awakened abruptly in such a way, you have a much greater clearness of mind," he informed his mother. Later in life, when he had to cross the city of Paris or dial an international number to deprive a friend of a night's sleep, he offered no such excuse.

His passions were not entirely literary, and his victims not exclusively members of the family. Anne-Marie Poncet, whose father directed the Lyons Opéra, made the trip to Saint-Maurice weekly to give the Saint-Exupéry children piano and singing lessons. One day she was asked repeatedly if she knew how a piston worked. She was finally obliged to banish the aspiring mechanic with a stern "Enough, Tonio, you're boring us." The opinion of Father Montessuy, the *curé* who visited Saint-Maurice every other day and returned the family's hospitality by consistently bettering them at the bridge table, carried great weight in the household; he in particular was not spared Tonio's enthusiasms. After having been assailed one evening by the twelve-year-old regarding his design for a motor for a flying bicycle, he slunk off to the card table with the reassuring news that "Antoine is extraordinarily talented in the sciences." His pronouncement gave the young inventor license; he was allowed to continue designing the contraption, for which he claimed he needed a small hot-oil motor. A search was made in the village and Tonio ultimately came to possess the coveted item, which he lovingly tuned and fondled for hours. "The bizarre object which vaguely resembled an octopus shorn of several tentacles" came to an untimely end, however: it exploded in François's face one afternoon and was confiscated.

Undaunted, the young engineer continued on with his design for a flying bicycle, a logical enough hybrid given that it had only been twenty years since the Prince de Sagan had begun a rage by pedaling through the Bois de Boulogne on a "little steel fairy" and nine since the Wright brothers had taken to the skies. Saint-Exupéry mounted a set of old sheets to a bicycle with wicker supports designed by the village carpenter but did not manage—even with the assistance of a steep ramp and, as one eyewitness remembered, with a good deal of frenzied pedaling—to take to the air. (His was not an entirely senseless exercise; nine years later a Frenchman in fact sailed forty feet through the air on a bicycle with wings and no propeller.) In his late twenties, when Saint-Exupéry flew aircraft not too much more complicated than the one he had designed, he would visit Saint-Maurice on leave and install himself at the side of Marguerite Chapeys, known as Moisie, in the sewing room. There he would harangue the devoted housekeeper, who had arrived in 1914 when the house's German staff was replaced, with tales of the labors from which he had just returned. In *Wind, Sand and Stars* he recorded her disappointing reaction: "You would say that I hadn't changed a whit. Already as a child I had torn my shirts—'How terrible!'—and skinned my knees, coming home as day fell to be bandaged. No, Mademoiselle, no! I have not come back from the other end of the park but from the other end of the world! . . . 'Of course!' you would say. 'Boys *will* run about, break their bones, and think themselves great fellows!' " (A village child remembered Tonio exactly as he described himself, always sporting at least one bandage.) His sister Simone remembered her brother's sessions with their housekeeper differently: the young aviator was enough his former self that he enjoyed tormenting the delicate Moisie with his tales of dissident landings. "Imaginative and willful, Antoine always got his way," she said, all evidence on her side.

Flying bicycles come naturally to twelve-year-old boys, but generally speaking Saint-Exupéry's childhood obsessions did correspond remarkably both to his time and to his adult fixations. In the year of his birth—when the only Frenchman to have flown had done so in what was known as a "mechanical bat"—Marconi's telegraph, X-rays, and intercity telephones were introduced at the Paris World's Fair, the first to display a wide selection of bicycles and automobiles. Before its disappearance, Antoine's cherished motor had been rigged up to power an irrigation system on which François half-willingly collaborated, the object of which was to plant vegetables to sell to Tante Tricaud at an inflated price. The enterprise ended when the motor exploded and was confiscated, though the failure of the venture did not prevent Saint-Exupéry from informing a cousin that they would all one day be gardeners, and though later in life he would repeatedly claim gardening as his true calling. Horticultural images proliferate in his writing; the highest compliment he could pay a woman was to compare her presence to a green field or a bed of flowers or a well-tended garden, something of an irony for a man who attempted to spend as little time as possible on the earth, and who by his twenties had developed a fierce allergy to lindens.

For animals the Saint-Exupéry children shared a collective passion, one that was not altogether reciprocated. The swallow fallen from its nest and coaxed to recovery on a diet of wine-soaked bread died of indigestion. The field mice of Saint-Maurice preferred their liberty to a generously stocked larder. The tamed crickets languished and died in their cardboard homes; they were diagnosed as suffering from thirst and carefully soaked in water. The snails of Saint-Maurice showed little interest in the dirt homes designed for them; those that had been trained for a race to commemorate Madame de Saint-Exupéry's birthday one year refused to budge from the starting line, probably because they had been dyed different colors for the tournament and been asphyxiated by the paint. Paula was one of the rare readers of *The Little Prince* who was not surprised by its author's atypical offering: the book greatly reminded her of Antoine's childhood ideas. "He often asked me to tell him what I had done when I had been a lion, an elephant, a monkey. He listened attentively to my tales of life as a wild beast." She remembered the walks she had taken with the Saint-Exupéry children at the château de La Mole, accompanied by their aunt Madeleine de Fonscolombe's cat, her dogs, and several turtles on leashes.

In his habits, too, Saint-Exupéry the child was a small and perfect advertisement for Saint-Exupéry the man. His celebrated ardor did not desert him at mealtime. One day after a walk in the mountains he sat down at the lunch table to admit contritely that he had just made a feast of four raw eggs at the home of the gardener. His appetite seemed to undermine the confession. Earlier the three youngest children had taken their meals in the kitchen with their governess, a measure that did not prevent the digestion of the adults next door from being troubled by piercing shrieks of "No carrots!" (Years later Saint-Exupéry informed one of his sisters that she did not love him anymore; in an act he considered treasonous she had served him green beans, which he detested.) His room was kept always in a perfect state of disorder, one with which only Gabrielle was authorized to tamper. Simone remembered this having been the case because the household staff refused the job. Her brother filed his papers away in a little velvet-lined trunk; only when it would no longer close would he begin to think of resigning himself to the necessary triage. He was happy when able to sit with these precious documents displayed all around him, more or less obliterating the floor of his room.

He was not much impressed by discipline. On the rare occasion when his mother lost her patience she would spank her son with a slipper or threaten him with a more austere *goûter* [afternoon snack] than he was used to. One method could be counted upon to keep the boisterous child tranquil: an aunt remembered having asked Antoine to feed a bottle of milk to an infant cousin, a task of which he acquitted himself with "an infinite gentleness." For one hour, not a sound was heard from either party. Outside of that, the aunt admitted, "He was a first-rate devil." According to his mother, however, he was as dreamy and sensitive as he was turbulent. The greatest hardship he could imagine—this before the world had yet heard of Combray—was to be put to bed without a good-night kiss, about which he would rhapsodize later: "Mother, you leaned over us, presiding over this flight of your angels; and so that our trip would be safe, so that nothing dared to disturb our dreams, you smoothed every wrinkle, every crease, every swell of the covers." He was as thin-skinned as he was dictatorial, domineering, in regular need of approbation and understanding. For this he looked to his mother. Arguably more than any other woman in his life, she provided it.

~

Marie de Saint-Exupéry was the incarnation of what we have come to think of as the archetypal mother: she was all solicitude and sympathy; her wisdoms were of the reason-transcending kind; hers was a cherishing, nourishing, sustaining goodness. Even when the fame of her elder son eclipsed the successes of her other children she refused to divide her loyalties: "Antoine was talented, of course, but all of my children were talented. I can't say that I noticed, when they were younger, that Antoine was more so than the others." The daughter and granddaughter of composers, she was herself an accomplished musician who played the harmonium in the village church every Sunday. It appears to have been she, with her trained contralto voice, who began to fill the château of Saint-

Maurice with music. André de Fonscolombe, a son of her brother who was nine years Antoine's junior, was struck by the "profound musical ambiance" of Saint-Maurice, where he also vacationed: "The house resonated with melodies of Reynaldo Hahn, Fauré, Schumann, Schubert or Massenet." Under Marie de Saint-Exupéry's direction the children formed a choir; they were taught a host of songs from the Middle Ages that formed the core of Saint-Exupéry's repertoire and were later performed in places his mother could not have imagined.

A talented pastelist, Marie de Saint-Exupéry painted all her life; in 1929, as *Southern Mail* was being reviewed, she sold three paintings to the city of Lyons, causing her son to remark proudly, "What a family we are!" In 1967, at the age of ninety-two, she published a book of poems, her second, mostly about her children and also about the years at Saint-Maurice. Her sensibility is uncannily similar to her son's. In one piece, entitled "Deception," she writes of her childhood disappointment when, in 1881, two "princes"—in fact the Duc de Chartres and the Comte de Paris—come to dinner. After days of anticipation she is forced to concede that there is nothing particularly remarkable about the visitors: "What? This man, a prince? This man who looks like a nobody! I'm very tempted to stick my tongue out at him!" Her wariness of convention was not her only legacy to her son. One of her nieces remembered her as utterly charming but often vague: "She sent delightful but sometimes imprecise letters. . . . Sending on news of a new baby of Gabrielle's she wrote: 'Didi has just had a little marvel,' without specifying whether it was a boy or a girl. She had no concept of exactitude." She was also hopelessly out of her element with financial affairs, not surprising in a woman who had married at twenty-one, was left alone with five children eight years later, appreciated well-made dresses, and had not been raised in a milieu in which women concerned themselves with the family accounts in the first place.

For the most part Marie de Saint-Exupéry was at the mercy, financially and geographically, of the family's kindnesses, even if—despite occasional sagging spirits—she never comported herself as such. She was not always in good health, although in the end she outlived all but two of her children. In March 1913 she took her two sons to the north of France for ten days to stay with a childhood friend who was herself widowed and the mother of four. The Countess du Mesnil du Buisson noted in her daybook that Madame de Saint-Exupéry was having trouble both with her eyes and her legs. The trip—which included a pilgrimage to Mont Saint-Michel—was deemed by Madame du Mesnil du Buisson to have done her friend much good, both physically and morally. The group spent a fair amount of time singing (Antoine's voice won unusual accolades) and attending masses with a visiting priest. Marie de Saint-Exupéry was unwavering in her

religious beliefs, a devotion that may have been fortified by her ill health
and by her frequent experiences with loss: in February 1907, just three
years after the death of her husband, she lost her father as well. Her life
and her household were held together, uncomplicatedly, by "a respect for
the real riches of Christianity." Her spirituality, if not entirely her faith,
would deeply mark her son.

Madame de Tricaud was, on the other hand, more lighthearted about
her faith and less so about discipline. It was incumbent on the members
of the household to join together in prayer at the Saint-Maurice chapel
after dinner every evening, but in the practice of this ritual Saint-Exupéry
found his aunt to be surprisingly casual: "As in truth this rite bored her
a little, she began the prayer loudly as she left the drawing room, carrying
along a whole procession behind her; then she kneeled and stood again,
without any attention whatever to the others." She reigned as something
of a local authority over the village of Saint-Maurice, though less so, after
the arrival of the Saint-Exupérys, over her own house. With all her heart
she had adopted Madame de Saint-Exupéry and her affection extended,
more fervently even, to her eldest daughter, Marie-Madeleine, who was
frail; on her death in 1920 Madame de Tricaud left Saint-Maurice and
its 250 hectares to the former and a large sum of money to the latter. She
thought differently of her great-great-nephews. They were in her opinion
"noisy, vulgar, messy, disobedient, demolishing everything they touched,
or at the very least dirtying it." Essentially she and they attempted to stay
out of each other's way. "My two brothers were," Simone de Saint-
Exupéry had to admit, "insufferable. But they were so like overly exuberant
children no longer reined in by a father who had disappeared too early.
They fought violently, accountable to no one."

It was the consensus of the extended family that the Saint-Exupéry
children were outrageously spoiled. Certainly they were altogether un-
versed in discipline, which meant they did not take well to those more
willing to dispense it than their mother. Saint-Exupéry's lifelong memory
of the dark, central hallway of Saint-Maurice was colored by his memory
of his mother's brother, Uncle Hubert, "the very image of severity," pacing
that corridor with another uncle while a five- or six-year-old Tonio cow-
ered in the shadows. "This man who never in his life had tweaked a child's
ear or pinched its cheek affectionately always threatened me when I had
been naughty with a terrifying frown and these words: 'The next time I
go to America I shall bring back a whipping machine. American machines
are the most modern in the world. That is why American children are the
best behaved in the world.' " A cousin remembered the eleven-year-old
Antoine as always having had a bone to pick with someone. The person
with whom he locked horns most often was his grandfather, Fernand de
Saint-Exupéry, with whom he spent several vacations. "My grandfather

and Antoine had this in common," recalled the cousin. "Both, being from the South, very much liked to talk, but my grandfather was deeply persuaded that only grown-ups were entitled to participate in conversation, while children were to listen sensibly without saying a word. Antoine was in no way convinced that silence suited youth. This difference of opinion was the cause of a great deal of recrimination and reproach." The ambiance of her husband's family, explained Marie de Saint-Exupéry smilingly to one of her son's intimates, "was like the reign of Marcus Aurelius." One uncle loudly prophesied that the Saint-Exupéry boys would amount to nothing. The forty-two-year-old Saint-Exupéry entrusted his response to the narrator of *The Little Prince*: "I have lived a great deal among grown-ups. I have seen them up close. That has not much improved my opinion."

~

When he came to face the adult world Saint-Exupéry often deferred to his youth. His are the best accounts we have of his childhood, and while his brief exercises in autobiography invite a host of questions about what memory may have consciously and unconsciously pushed aside, they also help to determine what mattered most to the man. His mother vouched for the accuracy of his many reports, even if she might have termed folly what he deemed adventure; she knew as well as anyone that for all his tale-spinning her son was no *affabulateur*. Simone de Saint-Exupéry's descriptions of the years at Saint-Maurice also bear out the images invoked by her younger brother:

> The life of Antoine, as a child, was one of total osmosis with his family and also with that more humble universe of plants and animals which was for us Saint-Maurice and its park. When the weather was good we built tree houses and cabins carpeted with moss in the lilac bushes. . . . When it rained we played charades, or we explored the attic. Oblivious to the clouds of dust and to the falling plaster, we probed the cracks in the walls and in the old beams, in search of *the* treasure, because, we thought, every old house contains its treasure.

This traffic in elusive riches was something Saint-Exupéry carried everywhere with him. Often it was the only baggage he had. It did not matter that the treasure went undiscovered, he reminds us in *The Little Prince*; it need only to exist to cast a spell over a house. He had no interest in a "house without secrets, without recesses, without mysteries . . . subterranean chambers, buried chests, treasures"; about his friends he felt similarly. The "quest for hidden gold" that will be transposed to the skies in *Night Flight* is still earthbound—and most literal—in *Southern Mail*:

When we were ten we found refuge in the attic's timber-work. Dead birds, old bursting trunks, extraordinary garments—the stage-wings of life. And this treasure we said was hidden, this secret treasure of old houses, so wondrously described in fairy-tales—sapphires, opals, diamonds. This treasure which shone softly. The raison d'être of each wall, each beam. Huge beams defending the house against we knew not what. But yes—against time. For time was the arch-enemy.

Restless as he may have been, Saint-Exupéry did not race to grow up, or make a lunge for his freedom. That—in the garden of Saint-Maurice, under the indulgent eye of his mother—he had in ample supply. Rather he returned to the park later, when his archenemy proved its ineluctability, when the world proved harsh. Over and over he wrote his mother that she was his refuge, his security, his "reservoir of peace," his "font of tenderness," his "all-powerful support." "It is you I think of when I am sick, when I am sad, when I am alone," he assured her in 1931, not long after his marriage. The previous year he had mailed her a particularly poignant letter: "What taught me the meaning of infinity was not the Milky Way, or aviation, or the sea, but the second bed in your room. It was a wonderful thing to be sick; each of us wanted to be so in his turn. That bed was an endless ocean to which the flu admitted us." At a more troubled time he would describe the very act of getting out of a warm bed to report to flying duty as "being torn from the maternal arms." He wore this fierce maternal love as a sort of cloak wherever he went, pulling it more closely around himself as he aged. "Once you are a man you are left to yourself. But who can avail against a little boy whose hand is firmly clasped in the hand of an all-powerful Paula?" he asked as he flew through German fire, phrasing his epitaph, in May 1940. In a similar way he conjured up images of Moisie and her stockpile of linens when stranded in the Sahara.

The "sovereign protection" provided Saint-Exupéry by the women of Saint-Maurice extended to the memories of the house itself: it was as if he advanced into the world cosseted by this retreat into the past. He claimed to learn the concept of eternity from Moisie, elsewhere to have inferred it from the pacing of his two uncles up and down the Saint-Maurice hallway, "like the tides," lamenting the future of France. He treasured the mysteries that filtered to his third-floor room from the bridge table at night. The image of clean, white, well-pressed sheets would comfort him in distress in Libya, in Guatemala, alone in the Sahara; it appears in his first story and in his last book, published posthumously more than twenty years later. The most rewarding, most reliable, most benevolent acquaintance he had ever made, the twenty-nine-year-old wrote his mother, was with "the little stove of the room upstairs at Saint-Maurice. Never has anything so much reassured me about existence. . . . I don't know why but it made me think of a faithful dog. That little stove protected us from everything; I've never had such a good friend." He would go so far as to recommend its unerring loyalty to his wife in a wartime letter: "You must be like the little stove of my childhood at Saint-Maurice, which puffed away peacefully in my room when the winter night frosted the windows. I would wake up and listen to the fat belly of the little stove purr away. I had the impression I was protected by this little household god—and I would go back to sleep, happy to be alive."

This magical childhood gurgles beneath the surface of every one of Saint-Exupéry's works. It turned him into a fine storyteller, but the lost world could also be distracting. To a man with a dizzyingly abstract mind it could seem more compelling than the tasks at hand. "This world of childhood memories," he cautioned his mother when he was thirty, "will always seem to me hopelessly more real than the other." Later in the same letter—written from Buenos Aires as he was battling homesickness and beginning *Night Flight*, the first draft of which opened at Saint-Maurice with an image of Madame de Saint-Exupéry—he added, "I am not sure I have lived since my childhood." It is as if the sandstorms and dissident tribes and mechanical failures of the desert had been a dream, Moisie's laundry closet a persistent reality. What Baudelaire described as genius—childhood recovered at will—could prove as much a curse as a blessing: for Saint-Exupéry it proved a constant occasion for regret. In his late thirties, on an occasion when his presence evoked a tribute of childish squeals, he remarked solemnly, "There is one thing that will always sadden me, which is to have grown up." Adulthood was for him an exile, by far a more painful one than the long, desolate months at Cape Juby. The narrator of *The Little Prince* is very lonely in the adult world—lonely, that is, until he meets the Little Prince, an emissary from another land, where children may conjure with weighty problems but remain, at no cost to themselves, children. The adult Saint-Exupéry would find that not everyone was as indulgent of his peccadillos and demands and independence of mind as had been the inhabitants of Saint-Maurice. A happy childhood, too, takes its hostages.

III

~

Things in Heaven and Earth
1909–1915

My desire for knowledge is intermittent, but my desire to bathe my head in atmospheres unknown to my feet is perennial and constant.

THOREAU, *Excursions*

At the end of the summer of 1909, Madame de Saint-Exupéry moved her family north to Le Mans, an industrial city of 70,000 people 140 miles southwest of Paris. Here her father-in-law had settled after his political career had come to an end, and here he—and two of his daughters—remained. A vestige of Le Mans or western France, not Lyons, remained always in Saint-Exupéry's speech, a considerate tribute to paternal tradition. The move appears to have been made with the boys' schooling in mind; Fernand de Saint-Exupéry had sent his two sons to the Collège Notre-Dame-de-Sainte-Croix, and it was with the Jesuits that his grandsons enrolled in October. Their cousin, Guy de Saint-Exupéry, was one year ahead of Antoine. Saint-Exupéry was placed in a class of *7ème,* or the equivalent of sixth grade, evidently having studied for a year or two at Mont-Saint-Barthélemy, a religious school in Lyons. He was a new student in a school of 250, which began with the first grade and at which half the students were boarders. Either to welcome him into the fold or to keep him in his place, his name was immediately corrupted by classmates to "Tatane."

The Saint-Exupéry homestead, a modest apartment with a small garden at number 21, rue du Clos-Margot, does not appear to have been one that placed a particular emphasis on order. This may have been due to Madame de Saint-Exupéry's occasional absences, when the boys were left to their aunts' care. It appears, for example, that the apartment's only clock did not work. Paul Gaultier, a neighbor on the northern side of the city and a fellow Sainte-Croix student, made the twenty-five-minute walk to school every morning with Antoine. The two were meant to start out at 7:30 so as to arrive in time for their 8:00 o'clock class. Bright and early each day Saint-Exupéry landed on the Gaultier doorstep and asked the time; invariably it was between 6:00 and 6:30. At least once he mentioned that the Saint-Exupérys did not have a clock on the rue Clos-Margot. It seems less likely that this explanation was believed than that he enjoyed a second breakfast before setting off to class.

Saint-Exupéry did not distinguish himself academically during his first years in Le Mans. Simone de Saint-Exupéry stated the case most succinctly when she declared that her younger brother was "in no way a child prodigy." The Sainte-Croix fathers, who taught a curriculum rich in Latin and Greek, remembered him as a child who was "incapable of sitting still, big-hearted, intelligent, but too often distracted." They had no shortage of reasons to detain him after class, given a succession of failed math tests, his fickle attention span, and the disorder of his desk and person, and they did. His grades fluctuated wildly, although overall he obtained better results than his disappointing marks for "general conduct" and "order, appearance, cleanliness" might have led one to expect.

Descriptions of Saint-Exupéry in Le Mans, between the ages of nine and fifteen, tally less with the rambunctious inventor of Saint-Maurice than with the introverted philosopher: his sister suggested that, removed from the warmth of his family, he became a secretive child. Jean-Marie Lelièvre, who had been a student at Sainte-Croix since 1905, remembered this new addition to the class as cheerless and slow to smile. His professors thought him "dreamy and meditative," qualities little understood by his classmates, who kidded him for being "off in space." He did not appreciate their gibes, although his anger was generally short-lived.

His literary efforts may not always have conformed to the program of study, but they in no way abated at Sainte-Croix. Here his correspondence with his mother, who was at times during the school year at Saint-Maurice or the château de La Mole, began. One of the first and longest of these letters was Saint-Exupéry's account of a field trip to the Benedictine monastery at Solesmes, a visit that would very nearly haunt him later in life. In *3ème*, at the age of thirteen, he approached Jean-Marie Lelièvre to ask if Lelièvre would like to collaborate on a magazine he was publishing. Saint-Exupéry had reserved the first page and the poetry column for himself but had already recruited a sportswriter, a caricaturist, and several other columnists. The publication did not survive its first issue, which won its editors private audiences with the *père préfet* and numerous hours of detention. The following year, however, he made off with the coveted prize for the year's best French composition. In *3ème*

Saint-Exupéry began for the first time to take an interest in the curriculum, under the tutelage of the Abbé Margotta, whom Lelièvre remembered as an uncommonly inspiring professor, a man who could have boasted—but did not—of having been the first for whom Saint-Exupéry wrote about aviation. By the time Antoine fell under the care of the *2ème* French professor, the dour Abbé Launay, he was recognized as a highly accomplished stylist, by his rhetoric professor's reckoning the best in the class. He cemented his reputation in the Abbé Launay's classroom with a 1914 composition titled "Odyssey of a Hat," one with which the priest was so impressed that "he made us read and discuss the piece for more than two hours," recalled Lelièvre, mollified in retrospect by its author's having made good on the essay's promise.

Saint-Exupéry's first claim to literary fame took the form of an autobiography of a top hat. The hat relates its birth in a factory, prior to its arrival in the window of the greatest hatter of Paris, where its elegance is the envy of all passersby and where the hat "lived in peace and quiet, awaiting the day when I would make my appearance in the world." One night it is sold to a gentleman so distinguished that the merchant doubles his asking price, "because his motto was never to miss an opportunity— or a bank note." The top hat's virtues are widely admired when it makes its debut at the gentleman's club; for several months it leads a pampered life, enjoying the special attentions of a valet who grooms it twice daily. Life changes dramatically, however, when the hat becomes a wedding present to the gentleman's coachman: "The first day I rolled three times in the mud and—oh, cruel fate—was not even wiped off." To avenge this neglect the hat shrinks; its cleverness backfires, however, and it is sold, for six francs, to a used-clothing merchant, "a dreadful Jew," as the fourteen-year-old Saint-Exupéry had it. On the next transaction his price drops to less than three francs, which wins him little respect from his new owner; happily, he is in his care only a short time when a furious gust of wind blows him to the birds on the Seine. After voyaging along with the fish he falls into the "avid hands" of a ragman, who entrusts him to the dim and dirty cottage that serves as the "store of the grand clothier of Their Majesties the Kings of Africa." Soon enough he overcomes his fright of his new master, the most powerful prince of his country, whose hands, he is reassured to observe, do not discolor what they touch. The top hat writes these lines during the last days of his life, in the hope that they will make their way to France, so that his compatriots "will know that I am in a country where the fashion of going hatless will never take root; and that when I have outlived my usefulness I may well be worshiped as a relic, for having once graced the head of my illustrious master, Bam-Boum II, King of Niger."

"Odyssey of a Hat" was returned to Saint-Exupéry with a grade roughly equivalent to an A —. Launay all the same returned it with the comment: "Far too many spelling errors, style occasionally clumsy." It is easy to forgive Saint-Exupéry the cultural stereotypes of his time in light of the political views he would have absorbed at home and in light of his schooling; it was entirely the privileged who sent their children to the Jesuits. At the age of fourteen he had probably met few people who were pro-Dreyfus and not yet anyone who was firmly pro-Republic. Literarily if not politically the document is almost too neatly anticipatory: Saint-Exupéry would stake his reputation on serving a master well; he would remain obsessed with the passage of time. The premium on fancy, and the whimsical indictment of adult mores, would prove the marks both of his life and his literature. He, too, would be swept off to Africa, blown in part by the winds, as, later, the Little Prince would "for his escape . . . take advantage of the migration of a flock of wild birds." In these travels Saint-Exupéry would shake off the cultural biases of his time. It is fair to say, however, that the political leanings of the average Sainte-Croix student—and a fourteen-year-old Frenchman is by no means too young to hold a political opinion—were decidedly Royalist, especially at a time when the separation of Church and State was being accomplished. This divorce took a painful toll on an institution like Sainte-Croix, forced by government decree and a failed countersuit to move to more modest quarters; there is no reason to think that the preadolescent Saint-Exupéry dissented from the school's prevailing monarchical leanings.

To his early literary habits he remained in Le Mans entirely true. Odette de Sinéty, the daughter of family friends who was two years his elder and whose brothers also attended Notre-Dame-de-Sainte-Croix, vividly remembered his visits to their château. His manner of expressing his admiration for her famous blond beauty took a familiar form: Antoine "wrote poems, tragedies, and repeatedly insisted on reading them to us. To tell the truth, at that age we preferred playing to listening. This did not deter him from frequently following me, declaiming as he went, his works in hand." Thanks to Odette de Sinéty a number of these early poems survive: the Abbé Launay would not have been impressed by the quantity of spelling errors, rivaled only by the depth of the young poet's romanticism, which visibly bore the traces of the nineteenth-century master Lamartine.

Together at the Sinéty home outside of Le Mans the Sinéty and the Saint-Exupéry children took dance lessons, instruction to which Antoine submitted only in the name of duty. He was particularly irked by the quadrille, which the group danced most often. "He put as much ill will into it as he possibly could, moving about more or less like a bear," reported Odette de Sinéty, who had the ill fortune of being his regular partner. At Le Mans as well he was better remembered for his clumsiness than for his academic brilliance. He enjoyed notoriously bad luck with his fountain pens, the rage of the moment, instruments that in his hands proved true to their name. Nor was he more talented for cycling. He made a number of excursions with Jean-Marie Lelièvre, but generally fell behind on these expeditions and when anything went wrong with his bicycle enlisted a friend's help to repair the machine. This did not prevent him, evidently, from having "hands as dirty, if not more so, as any one of us." A favored destination was the Lelièvre country home five miles south of Le Mans, in the pines of the Mulsanne forest, next to the racetrack in a tiny village called Hunaudières. This half-mile-long hippodrome carved out of a piney wasteland was hallowed ground, although Antoine had missed the consecration by just over a year.

~

On Saturday, August 8, 1908, two small boys had bicycled frantically into Le Mans, squeaking, "He flies! He flies!" For once their enthusiasm was not lost on the older generation; they had just witnessed the event that would usher in Europe's air age. Aloft for one minute forty-five seconds, Wilbur Wright had made two perfectly controlled circuits over the Hunaudières racetrack. It was not the longest flight yet witnessed in France (this was a year when endurance records were claimed monthly for flights of fifteen or sixteen-and-one-half or twenty minutes), nor was it Wright's longest flight to date. But what had been a routine demonstration for the American seemed nothing short of a miracle to the French, for whom flight had thus far been more a clumsy matter of lift than a scientific matter of control. Frenchmen had flown, but their aircraft had made lazy, shuddering takeoffs and uncertain landings; they would not have considered attempting a circuit in a field bordered on all sides by trees. No one at Hunaudières that day had ever seen a banked or tight turn, and hardly anyone expected as much from Wilbur Wright, who had been soundly written off by the French press as an "acrobat" and a "four-flusher."

Only a few hundred people were on hand for Wright's demonstration, which had been delayed for days because of rain and which had finally taken place at 6:30 in the evening, but among them was the indestructible French aviator Louis Blériot. Blériot had himself stayed aloft for eight and one-half minutes a month earlier; still, he knew the import of what he had just witnessed. "A new era in mechanical flight has commenced," he announced. "I am not sufficiently calm after the event to thoroughly express my opinion." Others did, however, and by Monday a crowd of 2,000 lined the racetrack. That day Wright flew twice, first executing a tight, 100-degree turn, later executing the first figure eight performed in Europe. "We are beaten," conceded *Le Matin* on Tuesday, when a crowd of 3,000 awaited the vindicated American, who flew three times around the track at an altitude of about seventy feet. "You never saw anything like the complete reversal of position that took place after two or three little flights of less than two minutes each," Wilbur wrote his brother on Friday, when it seemed abundantly clear that the Americans were not bluffing, and when their mastery of lateral control was not yet fully understood by the industry it was about to transform.

If France appeared to have taken the lead in aviation before Wright's demonstration at Le Mans, it was in large part due to a speech the French-born engineer Octave Chanute had made at the Aéro-Club de France five years earlier in which he reported on the Wrights' work, to which he had been a contributor at Kitty Hawk. Immediately French design had taken off. With Wright's demonstrations at Le Mans the gift of wing-warping —part of the Americans' solution to the control problem—was bestowed on the French, who lost no time in incorporating the advance into their machines.* Aviation took root quickly and conspicuously in France, where it was hardly favored by the weather, for many reasons. The countrymen of the ballooning Montgolfier brothers felt strongly that it was their birth-right to succeed in the field. The Aéro-Club de France, founded in 1898, was the first organization of its kind; a glimpse at its membership and its mores yields a number of clues as to the country's preeminence. A great quantity of Champagne was consumed at the club's meetings, which were held at Maxim's, a restaurant where the prices were intentionally kept high to guarantee an exclusive clientele. Most early members could boast a fortune, or a ranking position in the automobile industry, or, if nothing else, a *particule*. Flying began as a fantasy of the wealthy industrialist, or the well-placed engineer, or the society figure with a military background. It was to become the domain of the gentleman-pilot; later, aviation relied for its advancement on government subsidy. All of these commodities France had in great supply. It would have been difficult to locate such a confluence of wealth and gallantry and engineering acumen elsewhere in the world in the early part of the century; France was a country in which a perfectly respectable man might spend the afternoon in the Jardin d'Ac-climatation performing dirigible experiments instead of disappearing into the caverns of Wall Street or into the City of London. More a sport than a technology, aviation borrowed from the leisured classes of other coun-tries: it was the transplanted Brazilian Alberto Santos-Dumont who in 1906, in Paris, made the first powered flight in Europe. In this respect

---

* They would go far with this imported technology: France entered World War I with more aircraft than any nation save Germany and quickly became the premier producer of Allied planes. The United States would not recover its preeminence in the air until after Lindbergh's arrival in Paris in 1927.

the fledgling aviation business resembled the fashion industry: haute couture made its home in Paris, where a good number of its customers lived, even if its prime movers, like its founder, regularly hailed from elsewhere.

As it was to the fashion and automotive industries, in which France led the world, that country's dedication to high-quality, small-scale production was a blessing to the young aviation industry. So was the predominance in France of the family firm, where one man's vision could nimbly engage a specialized work force. Europeans, too, had reason to be acutely aware of their borders; the immediate applications of air travel were especially obvious to a modest-sized country hemmed in by former enemies. During the early years of the century the Germans lost ground in aviation because they were too much seduced by Count von Zeppelin's success with the rigid airship; the British had more reason than the French to feel secure. American apathy at the time may have had something to do with the greater distances to be covered, distances that the airplane initially appeared unqualified to traverse. France, too, benefited from a well-developed taste for public competition. Having just contributed the Eiffel Tower, the Suez Canal, and the Paris Métro to the wonders of the world, she was ripe for a new challenge.* In 1905, when it came time for the Wright brothers to sell their invention, they went first to their own government. After they were thrice rebuffed by a skeptical United States War Department and by the British authorities, they headed to France with the Flyer.

In March 1908, after months of negotiations, the Wrights signed a contract licensing the Flyer to a French syndicate. Their agreement called for two fifty-kilometer demonstration flights; it was in order to fulfill this obligation that Wilbur Wright set up shop in Le Mans. During the month of June he had considered a number of fields, ultimately settling on the race course at Hunaudières, his second choice, because it was far from the French limelight and because the president of the local flying club, Léon Bollée, had kindly offered the use of his auto factory and some assistance from his workers. Despite Bollée's generous hospitality and the attentions of a local canned foods manufacturer who saw to it that the American's shed was well-stocked with the finest sardines, anchovies, and asparagus available, Le Mans proved less than idyllic for Wilbur Wright, however. The customs officials had damaged his crated-up Flyer, which took seven weeks to reassemble; Bollée's workers spoke as little English as Wright spoke French; Wright had no assistant. To Octave Chanute he wrote that Le Mans was an old-fashioned town "almost as much out of this world in some respects as Kitty Hawk."

* Appropriately, Jacques de Lesseps, the son of the engineer of the Suez Canal, was the second man to fly across the English Channel.

Le Mans had no reason to complain of Wright. Between August 8, 1908, and January 2, 1909, he flew regularly in its immediate vicinity—nine times at Hunaudières and 120 at the artillery field of Auvours, his first-choice field, which the French army made available to him after the convincing miracles at Hunaudières. Daily two or three thousand people turned out to see him work his magic, half the time with a passenger beside him in the Flyer. He wrote Orville that nothing he had done had created as much astonishment as his having taken the 240-pound Bollée for a trip around the field. He spoke too soon: on December 31 he ended the year—one that had begun with a dramatic French circuit of 1½ minutes—with a flight of nearly 2½ hours, performed in subzero weather, for which he was awarded the Michelin Cup and, more or less simultaneously, the Légion d'Honneur.

If 1908 was the *annus mirabilis* of aviation, 1909 was the year aviation came of age, and it unquestionably did so on European soil. Wilbur Wright had only just sailed home when the French—most visibly in the form of Blériot—began to claim the lead in aviation. At 4:00 a.m. on Sunday, July 25, Blériot hobbled out of bed in Calais, on the northern coast of France, to his airplane. The monoplane was newly outfitted with warped wings, with which Blériot had been experimenting on and off—he had been the first to adapt ailerons, the form of lateral control preferred today—since before Wright's arrival in France. He walked on crutches, his foot having been badly burned in an earlier accident. Thirty-seven minutes after he had taken off from Calais he landed in a British meadow behind Dover Castle. His crutches strapped to the side of his airplane, he had crossed the English Channel with no navigational aid other than his own two eyes. The reaction to a Frenchman's having penetrated England's legendary isolation was not what it had been in 1066; Blériot was greeted like a demigod by the British. In London his airplane was displayed at Selfridge's department store, where 120,000 people came to admire it. In Paris later in the week the machine was drawn through the delirious city like an imperial chariot, armored Republican Guards flashing their sabers in salute as Blériot passed. (In photographs taken in both cities the triumphant hero appears steady on his feet and the crutches are nowhere in evidence.) A month later the Champagne manufacturers of Reims sponsored the world's first air meet, an event that proved a watershed event in the history of aviation. Thirty-eight airplanes entered the August competition; although the event was international all the pilots save an American and an Englishman were French. Well over 100,000 spectators flocked to Reims to see record after record fall. Of more enduring importance was the fact that six of the machines at Reims were on sale to the public. Along with two models offered later in the year these represented the first

complete generation of aircraft, from which every plane flying today is
descended.

It was in the wake of the excitement over Reims that Saint-Exupéry
moved to Le Mans. He was a year too late to witness the magic of Hunaudières, but Wright's spell hung palpably enough in the air.* French
aviation fever had set in; the persistent schoolboy was far from the only
one designing aircraft in these years. By the end of 1911 Frenchmen held
more flying licenses than the United States, England, and Germany combined; the world altitude, endurance, and speed records belonged to
France. That year the first long-distance competitions began, and French
pilots dominated them all. The same year it took an American seven weeks
and fifteen major crashes to coax a Wright biplane—almost entirely rebuilt
in the course of the ordeal—across the United States to claim a $50,000
Hearst prize. With the exception of Glenn Curtiss's seaplanes, European
machines were now measurably superior to American ones in design and
performance, and French aircraft were the most sophisticated of all.†
These were giddy, feverish days so far as aviation went, years when the
naysayers were proved foolish within minutes of their pronouncements.
There was no reason to think Saint-Exupéry any more sensitive to these
developments than any other preadolescent boy, but he could not have
escaped them. The years 1909 to 1914 saw a series of nonstop firsts, some
more happy than others—the first long-distance flight, the first airmail
delivery, the first intentional acrobatics, the first woman to be killed in an
airplane, the first midair collision, the first cat to cross the English
Channel—and the press had a field day. Saint-Exupéry's childhood was
steeped every bit as much in these events as it was in Hans Christian
Andersen or Jules Verne. The airplane had not existed in the year of his
birth; by the time he was fourteen a $50,000 prize had been offered for
the first nonstop transatlantic flight and $150,000 had been offered for
the fastest trip made around the world in fewer than ninety days. Events
would delay both of these competitions; Lindbergh would not land at
Le Bourget for another thirteen years, by which time the world already
felt smaller and the prize in question was worth half as much. Both for
aviation and for its future bard, these were the glorious—and the innocent—years.

~

---

* In central Le Mans it is now possible to walk from the rue Wilbur Wright, down the avenue
Bollée, to the rue Antoine de Saint-Exupéry.
† With one exception: in 1913 Igor Sikorsky built the first transport airplane in St. Petersburg.
In 1914 he flew in it, with four others, to Kiev, stopping only once.

Saint-Exupéry flew for the first time in late July 1912, while on vacation at Saint-Maurice. He and his sister Gabrielle bicycled regularly that summer to the recently opened airfield at Ambérieu, four miles from the château, where a number of Lyons industrialists experimented with the manufacture of aircraft. One in particular had met with success and lent his name—along with that of the two Polish brothers who had perfected the craft for him—to an early, all-metal plane. The Berthaud-Wroblewski resembled a bat as much as it did a modern airplane, but it held the air well despite its stem-operated controls, its considerable weight, and a seventy-horsepower motor. Three Berthaud-W planes were built, the second with a powerful engine in the hope of attracting an army contract. It says something about the science of early aviation that in March 1914, several days before the military contract was to be signed, the souped-up Berthaud-Wroblewski crashed at Ambérieu, killing both of the Wroblewski brothers.

It was in the third of these three planes, piloted by Gabriel Wroblewski, that Saint-Exupéry received his *"baptême de l'air."* He had become a familiar face at the hangars, where he brought his prodigious curiosity to bear on the work of the mechanics, whom he terrorized with a stream of questions. He was particularly eager to fly, something his mother—who had herself visited the field several times, possibly only to ensure that her son's wishes went unheeded—had strictly prohibited. One afternoon late in July Antoine arrived at the field triumphant, however. Alfred Thénoz, then a twenty-year-old mechanic, vividly remembered the twelve-year-old's exchange with Gabriel Wroblewski:

—Sir, *Maman* has now authorized me to receive my baptism.
—Is that true?
—Yes, sir, I promise you!

There is ample reason to think that this conversation has been reported verbatim, none that Madame de Saint-Exupéry had suddenly experienced a change of heart. The gambit worked, however, and on a perfectly clear, windless summer afternoon Antoine de Saint-Exupéry sailed twice around the field of Ambérieu in a Berthaud-Wroblewski. While history was hardly made—more than ten years would elapse before the passenger would earn his pilot's license—an obsession was. The young enthusiast was almost certainly unable to keep the exploit secret from his mother: Georges Thibaut, the village boy who had introduced Saint-Exupéry to the Ambérieu flyers, reported afterward that "he jumped for joy." Antoine also invited Thibaut back to the château to discuss aviation over a snack in the kitchen. Back in Le Mans he courted Odette de Sinéty with tales of aeronautical adventure; he put an airplane on the cover of his ill-fated magazine at Sainte-Croix; he penned a poem, beginning with the lines "The wings quivered in the evening breeze/The engine's song lulled the sleeping soul," for the Abbé Margotta, a work which does not suggest that this man and this machine would be linked forever on the page. When it came time to offer condolences to Madame Wroblewski on the death of her two sons, Madame de Saint-Exupéry wrote that Pierre and Gabriel had been extraordinarily indulgent toward "*mon petit Antoine*." Saint-Exupéry, too, sent a note from Le Mans, clearly dictated by his mother.

For Saint-Exupéry those few minutes at Ambérieu may have been the central event of these years. The rest of the world turned on what happened two summers later, in Sarajevo. On August 2, 1914, all Frenchmen over the age of twenty-one were mobilized; more than a million men—15 percent of the adult male population—made their way to the front lines. By the end of the summer, one month after the formal declaration of World War I, Antoine's godfather, Guy de Saint-Exupéry's father, was dead at the age of forty-nine. Madame de Saint-Exupéry was appointed head nurse at the hospital set up at the Ambérieu train station. So as to be nearer her, Antoine—and presumably François as well, although the record is unclear—were recalled from Le Mans and enrolled at a Jesuit school in Villefranche-sur-Saône, forty-five miles from Saint-Maurice. We do not know how the schoolboys felt about the outbreak of hostilities, but we do know that Notre-Dame-de-Mongré and the Saint-Exupéry boys did not take well to each other. Things began poorly for the timid, chubby-cheeked Antoine, whose turned-up nose and dreamy demeanor immediately earned him the nickname "*Pique-la-Lune,*" or "space cadet." The impression was again borne out by the testimony of his classmates. Louis Barjon, who went on to become a priest, found Saint-Exupéry most memorable for his otherworldliness: "He was above all a dreamer. I remember him, his chin resting on his hand, staring out the window at the cherry tree. . . . I recall an unassuming boy, an original, who was not bookish, and yet who was prone from time to time to certain explosions of joy, of exuberance." The portrait was to remain entirely accurate.

Academically Saint-Exupéry continued his affair with mediocrity. After consulting the school's records, the head of Mongré wrote in 1951: "Our man was an average student except in French, where his grades were still lower than they should have been, due to his appalling spelling." Antoine's fortes continued to be poetry and drawing. Both of these interests he pursued, with fervor, on his own; he penned a number of epic poems on the war and about Kaiser Wilhelm, which he illustrated with witty caricatures. Later he would disassociate himself from these early literary efforts, which he could not have thought anyone would have bothered to save. "Of course I was convinced I was a poet, and for two years composed verses madly, like all youngsters," he admitted regarding his juvenilia, which not unjustly has been called "bad Racine, massacred Hugo." He was as ever less methodical with his assignments, and with his neighbor in study hall heartily amused himself disturbing the peace and keeping his classmates from their work. He taught himself to write perfectly legible sentences in reverse: "At school I wrote interminable epic poems and learned to write them this way so the masters and fellow pupils could not read over my shoulder," he explained to a dazzled reporter in 1941. The Mongré administration could not have been entirely disappointed when, at the end of this first trimester, Madame de Saint-Exupéry, evidently acceding to her two sons' wishes, removed them from the school. The boys completed the 1914–15 academic year back in Le Mans, and the following fall were sent off for two happier years to a school run by the Marianist order in Switzerland. For the first time they were boarders, and for the first time they were far from their mother for months at a stretch.

For some reason the Saint-Exupéry brothers arrived in Fribourg at the Villa Saint-Jean several weeks into the term in November 1915. Antoine entered as a twelfth-grader, for what is in France the penultimate year of secondary school education. Charles Sallès made the acquaintance of the newcomer almost immediately, when Saint-Exupéry sat down next to him in the refectory. The two were summertime neighbors—Sallès's grandparents lived across the river from Ambérieu—and appear to have vaguely recognized each other. The introductions over, Saint-Exupéry exploded: "Guess what? I've been up in a plane. It's incredible!" He talked of nothing else for the course of the meal, his new friend rapt at his side. He had found a subject that engaged him entirely, one which brought him back, more or less, to earth. And he had met his destiny, even if it would spend the next eleven years eluding him.

IV

~

Lost Horizons
1915–1920

*In France being a barefooted boy is usually prep-
aration for becoming not President but a barefooted man.*

JANET FLANNER, *Paris Was Yesterday*

This first of Saint-Exupéry's exiles proved a tonic. Removed both from
the indulgences of Saint-Maurice and from the rigors of the Jesuits, the
fifteen-year-old seems to have begun to come into his own. The Villa
Saint-Jean was the only school to which we know he made a pilgrimage
as an adult; it was as well the only school he would visit in his writing,
facts that suggest a certain degree of attachment. "With melancholy" the
narrator of *Southern Mail* recalled his home, "a white-gabled house among
the pines, one window lighting up and then another." This was recognizably the Villa Saint-Jean, although Saint-Exupéry's description made
the handsome school sound more modest than it was; its campus was by
far the most luxurious he had yet known. A tidy red-roofed village unto
itself, the school overlooked the sleepy town of Fribourg; beyond its extensive playing fields lay a thick wood. It was a trilingual institution, of
which half the 1,000 students were Swiss and better than half the foreigners French. No wall separated its well-kept grounds from the outside
world; the prevailing sentiment was one of trust.

The Marianist school had been founded in 1903 in part as a tribute
to the British public school system. It was again an institution for the
privileged but it was also a liberal one, at which contact between teachers
and students was frequent and warm, news of the outside world welcome
(though in these years not generally happy; its alumni pool shrank con-
siderably in World War I), and excellence rewarded with independence.

The accomplished student could, for example, aspire to a private upper-story room near the professors, a distinction to which Saint-Exupéry never laid claim on academic grounds. The school's prospectus advised its staff "not to be less attentive to the boys' 'education' than to their instruction," a lesson imported directly from Britain. Its teachers were to "relax, to humanize, the regimen of boarding school life, in order to divorce it from its worst drawbacks." The administration very much took the attitude that discipline was better instilled in its students than imposed from above, an idea that may not have met with much visible success with the young Saint-Exupéry but which would get more than its due years later in his work. "I like it here," the Saint-Jean student informed his mother in a statement that could serve as an epigraph to his glory days. "It's a little severe, but everyone is imbued with a great sense of justice."

The Villa Saint-Jean was assuredly a better match than the Jesuits had been for the quixotic poet of Saint-Maurice, but it was still too early for this future champion of subordination to commit entirely to the demands of academic life. Regularly he was reprimanded for failing to speak German, as was required, at the dinner table; he responded to these accusations in French. While the German language—and in fact all foreign languages—would remain his undoing, he honed his Swiss accent to perfection and for years would regale friends with a singsong, Fribourgeois rendition of Hugo, Mallarmé, or Verlaine. In the classroom he continued on his erratic way, making off with an occasional high grade in French or Latin and as commonly functioning as the *lanterne rouge*—idiomatically, "taillight," said of that student who literally brought up the rear—in regular classroom work. His grades in geography were during both years the lowest in the class, a distinction he did not seem to forget and in which there was irony of several kinds. The narrator of *The Little Prince* regrets having given up a promising career as a painter for such prosaic matters as geography at the age of six. He comments dryly that, having flown all over the world, he now has reason to proclaim that subject useful. At a glance he can tell China from Arizona: "It's a helpful subject, if one loses one's way at night."

Childhood humiliations are perhaps more often revisited than childhood triumphs, even when outnumbered. It is, however, interesting to note that the memories Saint-Exupéry chose to record of his school days are Fribourg examples of distraction, failure, or punishment. At the outset of *Flight to Arras* he is a fifteen-year-old dedicated to a geometry problem, working away "dutifully with compass and rule and protractor." A few lines later a tree branch swaying in the breeze has caught his attention: "From an industrious pupil I have become an idle one." Under examination by his commanding officer after a 1940 reconnaissance flight he is reminded of his discomfort when asked how to integrate Bernoulli's equation, a paralysis with which he seemed well-acquainted: "You stiffened under the teacher's gaze, motionless, fixed in place like an insect on a pin." He will, he fears, "flunk like a schoolboy standing before all the class at a blackboard." The boarding school teachers whom the narrator of *Southern Mail* visits after he has begun his career as a mail pilot demonstrate a great indulgence for their protégé's "erstwhile sloth." For his part he is happy to reveal the limits of the masters' knowledge. They who had terrorized him with geography tests had never themselves visited Africa and now they quizzed him for the truth, for the secrets they had taught but only he had learned. It would hardly have been appropriate if the author of the line "Is being a man knowing the sum of the angles of a triangle and the longitude of Rangoon?" had turned out to have been a diligent student.

As usual Saint-Exupéry brought his talents to bear on everything outside of the assigned course of study. He continued to read widely—it was at this time that he discovered and feasted on Dostoyevsky ("I felt at once that I had entered into communication with something vast")—and was again famed for his poetry. "I worshiped Baudelaire," he wrote of his sixteen-year-old self in 1941, "and must admit shamefacedly that I learned all of Leconte de Lisle and Heredia by heart, and Mallarmé as well." Traces of Baudelaire, who would by no means have figured in the 1915 or 1916 Saint-Jean curriculum, turn up in Saint-Exupéry's Fribourg poems, all of them passionate but amateurish efforts, several of which indicate that Odette de Sinéty had been replaced in his affections. Valuable scraps of scribbled-upon paper littered his pockets, as later they would the cockpits in which he flew. Generally he had two or three poems in progress; he was inspired enough to produce, in his second year, two philosophy compositions for each one assigned, the second for a classmate in need. ("Already a great concern for bailing out his friends!" boasted an ex-professor in 1951, when he was presumably more good-natured about the practice than he had been at the time.)

One report from Fribourg has Saint-Exupéry excelling on the soccer field, on which he served as goalie and center forward, and at fencing, but if Saint-Jean's excellent facilities brought out this athleticism it was short-lived. He would remain a confirmed *non-sportif*. Whatever talent he did possess proved again a matter of will: his history professor described a clumsy child who "tipped over the table and, repeatedly, the pitcher of milk and the coffee pot, but whose big, long-fingered hands, when the time came to build a paper model, or take apart a complex mechanical object, took on all the nimbleness of a lacemaker." Years later he was asked, after the near-demise of a teacup he had let slip in a drawing room, if he was terribly clumsy or very agile. "Very agile," he responded, pointing out that in the end he had broken nothing.

On the literary front he proved more consistent. His memory for verse was excellent and his enthusiasm for theater as avid as it had been at Saint-Maurice. He played Molière beautifully, and proved as brilliant and witty an extracurricular debater as he was unremarkable in the classroom. Dressed as the doctor in *Le Malade imaginaire*, Saint-Exupéry looks much as he does in all photographs of the time: long-suffering, awkward, self-contained, ill at ease. By now he was a good head taller than his classmates; his height relegates him to the last row in every extant group photograph. He appears no more unhappy in a photo taken of him in detention at Saint-Jean than in any other shot. His blond curls had long flattened and darkened, so that his hair was less his most striking feature than the upturned nose, which would have been any schoolboy's undoing. Entirely like his father's, his flat, brown eyes floated up a little in their sockets, where they were dramatically anchored by dark, low brows. This lent the sixteen-year-old a sort of owlish appearance. Later Saint-Exupéry could look either very odd or very handsome, a cross between the actor Wallace Shawn and a young Orson Welles; as a schoolboy he appeared mostly gangly and sullen. With a single smile, however, he became mischief incarnate. The transformation was remarkable enough for a friend to comment in the 1930s that Saint-Exupéry "left permanent wounds in the hearts of those who saw him smile, even once." At Fribourg the child's smile was only just beginning to rival the childish timidity; it was more his distraction than his boisterousness that interfered with his studies. Saint-Exupéry did move enough out of himself at this time to make his first close friends, all three of them from the Lyons area. To Charles Sallès he added as his intimates Louis de Bonnevie and—possibly over the summer of 1916—Marc Sabran. Bonnevie's mother was evidently more able than Madame de Saint-Exupéry to make the trip to Switzerland and stood in for her on occasion when a maternal presence was called for; her handsome, sandy-haired son was twice as introverted as Saint-Exupéry and somewhat prone to depression. Witty and charming, a few years Saint-Exupéry's elder, Sabran, too, was a particularly sensitive boy, one who shared Saint-Exupéry's appreciation for music and poetry. Along with François, who was distinguishing himself in music and art at Saint-Jean, these were Antoine's first confidants.

Saint-Exupéry took these friends from the Fribourg years but left something as well. Despite his mother's piety and his years with the Jesuits he did not turn into much of a Catholic. He by no means turned his back on spirituality, with which his fascination only grew as he aged; he well understood the importance of religion, and often claimed to regret having lost his connection to the Church. Nor has his lapsed faith discouraged religious readings of his work, which are legion. Saint-Exupéry repeatedly declared, however, that he "lost his faith when he was *chez* the Marianists,"

who, it was true, were a liberal, egalitarian order more devoted to education
than to the Church. Religious instruction was not overly emphasized in
Saint-Exupéry's first year (its study was accorded two hours weekly, less
than were French, Latin, Greek, or German), and the subject was taught
alongside philosophy the second year.

Numerous reasons have been put forth to explain this loss of faith, or
to rediscover it tucked away in odd places. The alienation from the Church
assuredly had more to do with the man than with the Marianists, however;
his quirky, highly individualistic approach to things tallied as poorly with
organized religion as it did with organized education. In 1917 Saint-
Exupéry wrote his mother to say he was confessing weekly, although he
was then enrolled in a lay school and this was not required of him. After
this date no evidence exists of his ever having set foot in a church again
for religious reasons. The hero of his first novel does, "offering himself
up to faith as to any mental discipline," but finds in Notre-Dame-de-Paris
more cries of desperation than acts of faith and leaves the cathedral disappointed. Saint-Exupéry's Fribourg physics professor was impressed by
his student's scientific acumen when he demonstrated the power of metal
to block X-rays by placing a crucifix on a photographic plate exposed to
radiation. More than a show of scientific genius, the experiment represented a neat metaphor for the brilliant gaze the aviator would later cast
on the ideas with which he had first been educated.

In the fall of 1916 Saint-Exupéry bought himself a collapsible Kodak
camera, with which he hoped to experiment. He wrote his mother that
he was playing the violin a good deal and asked her to send on records.
He reported that he was working hard, although he was discouraged by
his thorough lack of aptitude for German. Otherwise he sounded happy.
A September letter offers a glimpse of his brand of whimsical ingenuity,
as of his ability to make light of his own folly. Returning to Fribourg
for the new semester, he had been smitten, at the Swiss border, by the
idea of traveling light: "*Maman*, you cannot know how pleasant it is
to be as light as air, as free as the wind." Accordingly he had stored
all of his belongings in his trunk, which he left, with his Saint-Jean
address, for its customs inspection; he knew he could send a porter to
the Swiss station to pick it up for him. On his arrival in Fribourg he ran
into one of his professors, who immediately remarked on the returning
student's lack of a suitcase. Saint-Exupéry explained his clever arrangements with pride. "And I was congratulating myself all over again on
my genius when the porter returned with the awful news: The trunk was
not there!" Thenceforth he had met every train at the Fribourg station,
waiting with the same hungry attention as a magpie in La Fontaine fixes
on the glittering attire of a nobleman. "And each time I went back to
school with a longer face, looking stranded; I must have resembled the

cast-offs of the Medusa. . . . I had nothing! Not even a shirt collar, not even a toothbrush." Several days later the trunk arrived safely. It was not difficult to see why its owner's professors so often termed their student "*un original.*"

Neither this letter nor any others surviving from the Fribourg years bear a trace of the war that had already claimed over a million French lives, save for that in which Saint-Exupéry took it upon himself to inform his mother that French nurses were entitled to three weeks' holiday in Switzerland at the government's expense. Why did she not take advantage of this leave to visit her sons at Fribourg? The war makes more of an appearance in Saint-Exupéry's poetry, in which he laments both its destruction and his distance from the front. At Saint-Jean he was as insulated from the war as one could have been on the Continent between 1915 and 1917; the school was rabidly pro-French, and daily communiqués from the front were posted for the boys, but the only contact with the reality of the conflict came in the unmenacing form of Swiss troops, who occasionally camped on the Saint-Jean lawns during maneuvers.

Two other trials claimed Saint-Exupéry's more immediate attention in Fribourg. All of his schooling to this time constituted preparation for the *baccalauréat* exam, the Frenchman's passport to higher learning. While not nearly as inevitable as it is today, the exam was compulsory for the son of a good family. Saint-Exupéry passed the first part of his *bac*, in literature, in June 1916 at the Sorbonne. He stayed with his great-aunt, the Baronne Fernand de Fonscolombe, with whom he made what was almost certainly his first visit to the Comédie-Française. If his letters to his mother regarding the practical details of this trip are any indication, he was as nervous as are today's candidates before the exam. He must have worked very hard in the weeks preceding the two-day ordeal; statistically, only one in two students passed the *bac* at the time. He certainly worked diligently in the examination hall. "I this minute left the Sorbonne," he reported to his mother, "where I've just finished my Latin essay as well as that of my neighbor, a very nice but entirely dim-witted boy. Tomorrow I shall do his Greek translation." To his second *baccalauréat*, in philosophy, he submitted successfully the following summer in Lyons. These were the first important exams in his life, and the last ones, officially speaking, he would pass.

Early in 1917 François de Saint-Exupéry fell ill and withdrew from school. By May he had still not returned to Fribourg, and Madame de Bonnevie broke the news to Antoine that his brother was suffering from rheumatic fever. On July 10, at the age of fifteen, François died of a heart attack in his bed at Saint-Maurice. He was buried in the small family cemetery on the estate.

Saint-Exupéry wrote directly about the event only once. By the time he did so twenty-five years had elapsed, and he was inaccurate on at least two counts. He claimed to have been fifteen at the time, when in fact it was François who had been fifteen. (Not too much should be made of this slip, as Saint-Exupéry was habitually inexact with dates.) And he claimed he had only recently learned of the body's relative lack of importance, a lesson he felt he should have gleaned—and clearly had—at the time of his brother's death. (As he phrased it in 1943, "The body is an old crock that nobody will miss.") Saint-Exupéry had lived the better portion of the intervening years in perfect defiance of this. Otherwise the account, the only one we have, is peculiar but could well be true: Twenty minutes before he was to die François had asked his nurse to call his brother to his bedside. It was 4:00 a.m. He was evidently in great pain, but this he waved away with his hand: " 'Don't worry,' " he assured Antoine, 'I'm all right. I can't help it. It's my body.' " With pride and embarrassment he settled his worldly possessions on his elder brother: "Had he been a builder of towers he would have bequeathed to me the finishing of his tower. Had he been a father, I should have inherited the education of his children. A reconnaissance pilot, he would have passed on to me the intelligence he had gleaned. But he was a child, and what he confided to my care was a toy steam engine, a bicycle, and a rifle." If the demise of another blond-haired boy in Saint-Exupéry's work has any connection with this event, François then "remained motionless for an instant. He did not cry out. He fell as gently as a tree falls." Shortly thereafter, Antoine photographed his brother on his deathbed.

To only one friend did he seem to speak at any length about François in the next few years. (He was in general circumspect with his emotions, and his silence is best read as an indication of an event's import.) Clearly he had lost his closest confidant: "He reckoned that he had lost a friend whose company would have been valuable to him at all times." Especially distraught by the loss was Gabrielle, who had been inseparable from François, to whom she was closest in age. Her surviving brother folded her in his arms after the death. Quietly he promised, "I will do my best to replace all the brothers in the world for you." He was now the only man in the family.

~

During the summer of 1917 Madame de Saint-Exupéry did all she could to distract her son from his sorrow. A change of locale seemed the most effective remedy, and late in July Antoine was shipped off for a series of visits, some more successful than others. (His sisters appear to have stayed with their mother.) He alighted first on his grandparents in Le Mans, where Fernand de Saint-Exupéry, who had been at work on a history of the family, attempted to interest him in his genealogical investigations. With his cousins he went to the family villa in Carnac, on the coast of Brittany, to which he had been a visitor during his Le Mans years. This time he was less than perfectly amused, on account of his cousin Guy, to whom he had developed a strong aversion. He journeyed next and more happily to the Bonnevie château in the Creuse, arriving for a monthlong visit in late August, during which he fell in love once again. He spent four hours a day on horseback and somewhat less time on math, which he seemed to enjoy; he wondered when he might hope to see his mother again.

Sometime during the summer it was decided—if it had not been already, in which case it was odd that Antoine had until now concentrated his studies on arts and letters—that he would aim for admission to the École Navale, the French equivalent of Annapolis. It was a natural choice for a Saint-Exupéry in 1917, if not for a future aviator. He was without the example of a father, which in the great majority of cases determines one's profession in a tradition-bound country (and in any event Jean de Saint-Exupéry had not blazed a particularly illustrious path for his son), but three and four generations back there were naval officers in the family. Moreover, there was a war on. Traditionally, too, in France the navy—the monarchist stronghold among the armed services—suffered fewer casualties than the other branches of the military. The first step toward the entrance exam for the naval academy was a preparatory school in Paris, where Saint-Exupéry—along with the candidates for some of the other *grandes écoles*, institutions that existed apart from the university system, to which no competitive exam was required—was to be steeped in higher mathematics. An assembly of the country's best and brightest, the Lycée Saint-Louis boys were divided into groups named for their destinations: the *flottards* for the naval academy, the *cyrards* for the military academy at St. Cyr, the *taupins* (or moles) for the École Polytechnique, the *pistons* for the school of engineering. A healthy rivalry kept them in their places; the *pistons* were the *flottards'* mortal enemies; the *flottards* were, in Saint-Exupéry's opinion, the most vivacious, the *cyrards* the least so. Together one day the graduates of these schools would, along with the alumni of the other *grandes écoles*, the great majority of them engineers by training, make up the mandarinate which ran, and still runs, France.*

Henry de Ségogne arrived at the École Bossuet, in Paris, in the fall of 1917 and was almost immediately assaulted by a hulking *cyrard*. He was saved by "a big guy, very strong, broad-shouldered, a bit ill at ease in his

---

* Today, one-half the chairmen of the 200 largest companies in France are graduates of either the École Polytechnique or the supreme École Nationale d'Administration.

body. He was hardly an Adonis, but his slanted eyes and turned-up nose hinted at a strong and unique personality." Immediately the two became friends—it was in Ségogne whom Saint-Exupéry confided his regret about François—and with three others formed an inseparable group that would make its way daily from the École Bossuet, where the boys boarded and studied, to the Lycée Saint-Louis, on the other side of the Luxembourg Gardens, where their courses were held. With Ségogne, Bertrand de Saussine, Albert de Dompierre, and Élie de Vassoigne (whose father was at the time an aide-de-camp of the French president), "Saint-Exu," as he now became, had a tight circle of friends. He seems to have thrived because of it, but he was not always available to the group either. He remained somewhat aloof: "A cloud would pass—and Saint-Exu would retreat into himself. . . . It was easy to think he was pouting, but that was not the case. He had momentarily withdrawn into his fortress." The *bande* concocted pranks of all kinds, but Saint-Exupéry's engagement with another world kept him from associating entirely with his friends; the man whose philosophy would be founded on the camaraderie of men was, during these years, more often described as shy, secretive, and unsociable. It was also true that the first social circle of this democratic champion of the work ethic was a thoroughly aristocratic one.

Saint-Exupéry worked, wrote Ségogne, the way he played: when he felt like it. He was capable of fierce concentration bordering on obsession; the tragedy, according to Ségogne, was that his gifted classmate could not seem to muster any interest in the assigned course work. In the highly directed, competitive atmosphere of Saint-Louis this was a huge liability. Had advanced mathematics not been part of the program it seemed sure that Saint-Exupéry would have devoted himself to its study, as he indeed did later, when it was too late to prepare for the École Navale. His unorthodox approach was not lost on his professors, although it may have been less apparent to his mother, who knew of her son's academic limitations but to whom he wrote always of how hard he was working. "I am well physically, morally, and mathematically speaking," he signed one letter; he reported that in his professor's opinion there was every hope that he would pass the Navale exam; he was moving up in the class, despite the fact that he had a good deal of catching up to do after three years in which he had prepared only letters; he had received the equivalent of a C−, which for him was not bad. No one seems to have wondered what this irrepressible litterateur was doing at Navale, least of all Saint-Exupéry himself; such questions were not asked in France, in wartime, in the 1910s, especially of young aristocrats.

Impressed by their student's obvious if undirected talents, Saint-Exupéry's professors mercifully did their best to play to his strengths. On occasion this proved impossible. In the Bossuet study hall Ségogne and

Saint-Exupéry enjoyed the rare privilege of working at individual desks at either end of the room, while the rest of the class of forty occupied wooden benches along a long communal table. The desks were luxurious in several respects: the chairs were markedly more comfortable than the bench, which had no back and which could not be rocked backward; those who worked at the communal table were forced to store their books neatly in a set of open cubbies, while the desks offered more privacy. Saint-Exupéry abused this privilege, to the extent that his desk was described as "an appalling mess." His disorder did not escape the attention of Abbé Genevois, who repeatedly asked his student to clean out the desk if he did not want to risk losing it. Saint-Exupéry ignored this advice, with the result that one day the Abbé—"like Jupiter unleashing his thunder"—announced that he was to spend his break changing places with a class-mate, to whom he was to relinquish his post. Always sensitive to criticism, Antoine was visibly shaken by this outburst. He did not, however, choose the obvious course of atonement.

First he vented his spleen, dissecting the Abbé's irreproachable char-acter before Ségogne, who had remained at his side. Then he calmly fished a clean sheet of paper from his desk and composed a ballad, one of the few to have been passed on to posterity from the Lycée Saint-Louis:

I sat in the back, to the side,	*J'étais dans le fond de l'étude*
a desk hardly worth a dollar.	*un petit bureau sans valeur.*
Yet I was like a badge of pride	*Je faisais la béatitude*
to my illustrious owner.	*de mon illustre possesseur*
Black as a native of the tropics,	*Noir comme un citoyen d'Afrique,*
worn down by years of bleakest tasks,	*usé par d'austères travaux,*
I was, prudent and pacific,	*j'étais, discret et pacifique,*
by far the most serene of desks.	*le plus paisible des bureaux.*
Well positioned by the window,	*Bien au frais sous une fenêtre,*
sunning myself like a lizard,	*gonflant mon dos comme un lézard,*
I was endowed by my master	*j'étais gratifié par mon maître*
with disorder, approaching art.	*d'un beau désordre, effet de l'art.*
Our serenity was profound.	*La paix, là-bas, était profonde.*
Nothing troubled our staid repose.	*Rien ne troublait notre repos.*
We were more sheltered from the world	*Nous étions retirés du monde*
than the happy dead in their tombs.	*mieux que les morts dans leur tombeau.*
Any wish I might have expressed	*Les souhaits que je pouvais faire*
was confined to the status quo.	*se bornaient tous au status quo.*
But my peace was evanescent.	*La paix ne fut que passagère.*
And I, old hunk of rococo,	*Et moi, vieux meuble rococo,*
was banished from this perfect calm.	*banni de cette quiétude,*

Like a king, I was driven out,	*je fus exilé, comme un roi.*
to moulder in another room,	*Je moisis dans une autre étude,*
o my dear master, far from thou.	*o mon vieux maître, loin de toi.*
ENVOI	*ENVOI*
You, who in a single motion,	*Prince, qui par un geste inique,*
denied all our good protests,	*êtes devenu son bourreau,*
please, touched by its petition,	*daignez, touché par sa supplique,*
do return to me my little desk.	*me rendre mon petit bureau.*

Once he had completed his petition he copied it on to the blackboard, from which the Abbé, on his return, asked that it be erased immediately. Ségogne saved the day, copying down the ballad and sharing it with the instructor in his office that evening. The Abbé, a man not known for the kind of outburst Saint-Exupéry had provoked from him, could not resist this elegant entreaty. Saint-Exupéry was told he could keep his desk, but advised to keep it in order. Charming though it may be, the incident could not have done much to disabuse him of the notion that a different set of rules applied to the rich in spirit.

Otherwise his high spirits were held much in check during his first year at Bossuet, partly by the financial constraints he experienced while a boarder in Paris. Ségogne theorized that his friend restrained himself from some of the boys' more outrageous episodes out of deference to his mother, who had made certain sacrifices for her son, and whom he did not want to disappoint. If this was indeed the case, Antoine almost certainly drove her to hand-wringing on other counts.

Demanding: This was the word that Saint-Exupéry's letters to his mother from Saint-Louis most often bring to mind. The first of these set the tone for the rest. In it the student requested a letter every day; his photo album ("the album, not the binder"); chocolate truffles, in quantity: He was particularly specific on this last count: "I don't like rissoles. . . . I like real *pâtisserie*, macaroons, chocolate truffles (not praline-flavored!!!) and candies." He reminded his mother that she was well-informed and, in jest, coined a formula that would seem less and less droll as it appeared over the next years more and more true: "*Antoine propose, et la famille dispose.*" Within a month or so he had asked for a bowler hat (or that the money with which he might buy one be sent to a friend of Madame de Saint-Exupéry's in Paris), toothpaste, shoelaces (purchased in Lyons and not in Ambérieu, because the Ambérieu laces were decidedly inferior), stamps, a sailor's hat, his atlas, photographs of his sister, more letters from home. His letters so habitually closed with requests that after a while he abbreviated them only to shopping lists: "shoes—rubbers—spending money."

As exacting as these letters were—and would remain, although soon enough the student would confine his demands to mail, money, and his mother's opinion—Saint-Exupéry showed himself to be "hugely tender-hearted." Ségogne was quick to recognize his acute sensitivity: "He had a fierce need for friendship, warmth, and trust, let us say for a good deal of affection, without which his personality did not flourish." He keenly felt the distance from his mother and his sisters, from the tenderness of Saint-Maurice. In his letters he was as adoring as demanding. He complained of his ten-hour workday but told his mother he was happy; if only she were nearer he would be in seventh heaven. Repeatedly he mentioned that when he was made an officer he would want her to come to live with him: "I will rent a little house where we will live the two of us together; I will have three days in port and four days at sea, and during the three days on land you and I will be together. It will be the first time I will be alone in life, and I will certainly need my mother to protect me a bit in the beginning! You will see, we will be happy." He made every attempt to divert her when he knew her to be ill, even when he claimed there was nothing "remotely amusing" to his days. He must have succeeded; the letters are charming, even when they consist mostly of gibberish and caricatures. And, too, he knew the way to Madame de Saint-Exupéry's heart. He issued a report on the morality of the Bossuet dormitories, in which he assured his mother that while there were obviously fewer religious souls than at a religious school, there was, "oddly enough, much more human respect." His classmates were more serious than the ones he had known in the past, regardless of their convictions. As for any fears Madame de Saint-Exupéry might have had about her adolescent son in the City of Light at a time when its morals were more than usually lax, he assured her that "I believe I will always remain your same Tonio who loves you so."

～

In fact Saint-Exupéry was, under the wings of various cousins and family friends, quickly discovering the glories of Paris. He had the best of guides. From his accounts of his social life it is difficult to believe that he was working ten-hour days and six-day weeks, much less that France was at war during his Saint-Louis period. He sought out a number of people, perhaps of his own initiative because he was a little lonely, perhaps at his mother's insistence. The Sinétys were in Paris from time to time, as were, more frequently, the Bonnevies; the Bonnevies allowed him the occasion to see Jeanne de Menthon again, with whom he had fallen in love during the summer of 1917 and who continued to charm him. Both Ségogne and Bertrand de Saussine invited him home regularly. He saw his aunts Alix and Anaïs de Saint-Exupéry, as well as his mother's younger brother,

Jacques de Fonscolombe, and the family of his great-aunt de Fonscolombe, as well as his mother's second cousin Yvonne de Lestrange. Among
the friends of his mother's on whom he called was Madame Jordan, whom
he visited weekly, occasionally spending Saturday night with her family.
Madame Jordan charged herself with the young man's moral supervision
and bestowed on him a series of brochures to forewarn him of the kinds
of dangers that he might encounter. He reported to his mother that he
had dutifully shared these with his classmates; their reaction can too easily
be imagined.

First among the relatives he ranked Yvonne de Lestrange, whom he
designated the most charming, creative, refined, intelligent, kind, superior
person he knew. "Yvonne is a marvel, she is exquisite, it is impossible to
be bored for a second with her, she explains all the wonders of Paris—
what a pleasure. She has ideas, she is interested in everything, in math
as well as the rest—in short, she is perfection." At the time the Duchess
de Trévise, Yvonne de Lestrange occupied a lavish *hôtel particulier* on the
quai Malaquais, steps from the Gallimard offices and very nearly the publisher's unofficial boardroom; most of the staff of the *La Nouvelle Revue
Française*, the prestigious, Gallimard-owned literary monthly known as
the *NRF*, went home at night via her salon. She not only took her young
cousin for walks through Paris but played the piano for him, invited him
to the opera, and read his verse, which she pronounced mediocre and
overly sentimental. If Saint-Exupéry was discouraged by this opinion we
have no record of it; in any event, Yvonne de Lestrange would later provide
Saint-the key to her cousin's literary future. Every bit as cultivated as
Antoine reported her to be, she proved to be a revelation to her sensitive
cousin, who for all of his fine education and privilege was still far from
being a Parisian.

As a measure of how impressionable the seventeen-year-old student
was we have his account of his lunch with the Duchess de Vendôme, sister
of the king of Belgium. His Aunt Anaïs, his father's sister, was the Duchess's lady-in-waiting and had wrangled an invitation for her nephew.
Saint-Exupéry proved far more taken with his brush with royalty than had
his mother in her youth. His fascination with the titled—and in the end
with many of Paris's indulgences—would prove short-lived, but in the fall
of 1917 he was still a wide-eyed provincial who burst with pride at having
made his way through a stately luncheon without a single gaffe or muddled
phrase. His savoir-faire was rewarded: the Duchess promised to invite him
one Sunday to the Comédie-Française, an offer on which she made good
several weeks later. He was as struck by the honor as by the location of
the Duchess's seats, each of which cost almost as much as his treasured
Kodak. To his Aunt Alix de Saint-Exupéry he grew closer as well at this
time; he attributed her kindnesses toward him as the direct result of his

"irreproachable" new wardrobe, the end result of the demands he had made on his mother. He painted a clear schoolboy's picture of an outing with his father's sister: "It was with her, Aunt Anaïs, Madame-I-don't-know-who (she went to Morocco and has the Légion d'Honneur and Aunt Anaïs is very fond of her, do you know who I mean?) and also another ardent and enthusiastic Royalist lady that we went to have tea in a well-stocked restaurant to which my stomach did justice."

The way to an adolescent's heart is not difficult to divine, especially in wartime. Parisian *pâtisseries* were by now open only four days a week and were less and less able, given shortages of sugar, butter, and flour, to turn out Saint-Exupéry's much-loved macaroons and truffles. They were instead creative with meringues, which, like all *pâtisserie*, were not by law to be consumed on the spot. Looking back, André Malraux wrote that, embarrassingly, his chief memory of the final days of the war was of margarine. He was less lucky than Saint-Exupéry, who in 1918 described another Lestrange aunt: "Aunt Rose is as ever a delight, and what is most delightful about her, aside from her sterling morals, are her *goûters*. She has me over for *goûter* on Sunday, and I swear to you that I leave with enough butter in my stomach for the whole week—fresh, melting, exquisite."

In Paris, despite the round of *goûters*, the theater-going, and the leisurely promenades, Saint-Exupéry had the war on his doorstep. Had he and his friends looked closely they would have seen patches of beans and carrots growing among the handsome chestnut paths of the Luxembourg. As of early 1918 the deepest subway stations were marked not "MÉTRO" but "REFUGE"; the city's concierges had happily taken charge of a series of neighborhood shelters, marked by black-and-white signs. Word had got around that a window to which paper was stuck would not shatter in a bombing, and soon every pane of Parisian glass, every mirror in the city, was taped, often decoratively, some to the point of mummification. The city was a virtual military parade ground as thousands of soldiers passed through in every conceivable kind of uniform, habitually mixing at the Café de la Paix with a host of admirers. All this proved an enchantment to an adolescent, even during the longest and coldest winter of the war. Saint-Exupéry's first account of an anxious Paris, late in 1917, in which nine out of ten streetlights had been extinguished, verged on the poetic: "All of Paris is painted blue. The trams have their blue lights; at the Lycée Saint-Louis the corridor lights are blue. Now when one looks out over Paris from a high window the city looks like a giant inkstain—not a single reflection, not a halo, a striking degree of nonluminosity!"

The blue-out interfered less with life as the city had known it than did the events of early 1918, at which point the nighttime streets of Paris were

empty save for *les hirondelles*, caped policemen on bicycles. In March Big
Bertha began to shell Paris from a forest seventy-five miles away; at about
this time the schoolboy excitement overran any artistic sensibility. To Louis
de Bonnevie Saint-Exupéry wrote with tremendous excitement that he
had finally "witnessed a bit of war":

> It was just after midnight; I was sleeping soundly and having the most
> exciting dream (I was dreaming that I was a railroad engineer and that my
> locomotive couldn't stop) when I was awakened by an odd noise. I opened
> my eyes to see a proctor in front of me, a candle in his hand, waking up
> the dormitory. I thought , "He's crazy! Why doesn't he turn on the lights?"
> I was certain it was time to get up. Equally perplexed, my neighbor checked
> his watch and suddenly jumped up:—But it's quarter to twelve. Ah, *zut,
> alors*! But it's the Zeppelins!—Great, that makes up for being awoken. . . .
> And in fact, I heard: *pan . . . panpan . . . panpan, panpanpan, panpan* . . .
> The cannon got louder and louder and all of a sudden rockets flew up on
> all sides; some headed out once launched, others blossomed into crowns
> and burst into a thousand stars. It's magical! . . . It's the first time I've seen
> the war and it's really incredible when it takes place in the air.

He acted out the drama in vivid detail for Bonnevie and Simone in March
1918, when the three took the train together to the south of France for
Easter vacation.

The result of this attack—which Saint-Exupéry assured his friend they
would find in no newspaper—was a significant casualty list. The Magasins
Réunis had been reduced to rubble; three bombs had fallen across from
the École des Mines on the Boulevard Saint-Michel; a six-story apartment
building had disappeared along with its forty inhabitants. Papers floated
down from the sky on which the Germans had scrawled "*À demain soir*"
and "*À bientôt*." (In all, the Gothas bombed Paris seventy-seven times,
and Big Bertha was responsible for forty-four attacks.) Saint-Exupéry
promised that if the enemy returned that evening he would race up to the
roof to observe the activity better. In the meantime, would Bonnevie mind
terribly sharing his letter with Simone, as it would be a bore to have to
write the same account twice? He hoped that Simone would understand
what a trial he had undergone and suggested she calm his shattered nerves
with chocolate truffles.

Saint-Exupéry's ebullience was general, and the next time the bombs
fell most of the Lycée Saint-Louis indeed clamored to the roof to watch.
The schoolboys' imprudence was shared by the population at large, which
demonstrated a marked preference for going up instead of down during
the bombings. The number of casualties—some five hundred people were
killed in all and more than twice as many wounded—was greatly inflated
by this curiosity, which kept Parisians glued to upper-story windows or
chatting in the streets when they should have been safely underground.

(On the rue de Fleurus Gertrude Stein and Alice B. Toklas never descended farther than the concierge's loge.) Saint-Exupéry missed not a second of this impressive display, for which he was "very well-seated." To his mother he regretted that he could not give a full accounting of the damages, on account of the censors, a consideration which seemed to hinder him only sporadically. He was happy to observe that the effect of the destruction was to turn the most committed pacifist into an ardent patriot, however: "That will put an end to the apathy about the war which is slowly infecting the population."

Watching Paris burn could not have had less of an effect on the Saint-Louis students, a great majority of whom would have their love of country put to the test twenty years later. Saint-Exupéry approved less and less of the administration's vow to pack the boys off to the basement during the next bombing: "What a bunch of chickens!" With the good-natured enthusiasm of a sportscaster he narrated the Germans' progress: "The Gothas are back. What a country! It's impossible to sleep! Today they made an unbelievable mess, ten times worse than the day before yesterday." The victims were this time innumerable and a huge number of buildings had been destroyed, many near the Lycée itself. Three bombs intended for the neighboring Ministry of War had fallen next to the Baronne de Fonscolombe's apartment on the rue Saint-Dominique. None of this was the kind of news a mother might wish to receive. "N.B.," Madame de Saint-Exupéry's son signed off after a detailed account of the destruction, "I am alive."

He may have prized his ringside seat but the *lycée* administration viewed it as a great danger: to cure the incorrigible habit of rooftop viewings, the older Saint-Louis students were, in the spring of 1918—probably just after a horrific Good Friday attack by Big Bertha that spurred the first real exodus from Paris—packed off to the Lycée Lakanal, twenty miles south of the city. Neither the students' fascination nor their viewing habits were cured by this displacement. "It's a beautiful evening, which means I can safely predict: Gothas, wake-up, cellar," wrote Saint-Exupéry to his mother. "I wish you were here to experience the artillery barrage just once. You would think yourself in the middle of a terrible storm, of a hurricane. It's magnificent." It was far from the last time that her son's enthusiasms must have cost Madame de Saint-Exupéry a night's sleep. He assured her, however, that were the Germans to enter Paris he would escape on foot. "Useless," he reasoned lucidly, "to take the train."

The Armistice was only months away but the bombs fell more and more frequently; by mid-June one could count on the Gothas at night and Big Bertha's shells by day. The city emptied—by the summer nearly one million Parisians had left—but also resiliently continued on her way, taking the new dangers, the higher prices, the stiffer rations in admirable stride. The Bois de Boulogne was jammed on Sundays. The theater, the cinema, the post, the banks, the markets did business more or less as usual. Restaurants and cafés remained open and crowded, although they did so with severely restricted menus and curtailed hours. *Pâtisseries* resorted to stocking their shelves with fresh fruit. At the Lycée Lakanal the severity of the situation impressed itself in gastronomic terms: Saint-Exupéry complained that his stomach was as empty as a cistern and that he was on the verge of dying of hunger. He was no longer in the market for chocolate truffles: he entreated his mother to send hard-boiled eggs, *pâté en croûte*, and bread, posthaste.

~

Events did not favor the naval candidate any more than he favored his studies. He spent part of the summer of 1918 in Besançon, in the east of France, as a guest of General Vidal and his wife, family friends who appear to have offered to supervise his studies. He wrote Simone that he was making a heroic effort with his work, getting up at 5:30 and putting in five hours of physics and five hours of German a day. He toyed with the idea of volunteering for the front in the event that he failed his entrance exam, for which he was now preparing furiously; the general had advised him that if he were to engage with the infantry he would have the option of choosing his battalion. Once on the front he would ask to be incorporated into aviation, his first reference to such an aspiration. Around the time that the Armistice was signed he presented himself for the naval exam and indeed failed, but by then there was no longer any war for which he could volunteer. Welcome though the news was, it cast an odd shadow over the Lycée Saint-Louis, to which Saint-Exupéry returned in the fall to prepare for a second try at his entrance exams.

The Armistice set off a massive series of hijinks in a school already racked by indiscipline; the boys proved so disruptive that Ségogne—who had held elected office as chief instigator—was ultimately expelled. (He was allowed to choose his own successor and passed the mantle to Saint-Exupéry, who wrote joyously of the honor to his mother.) In the pandemonium following the Armistice the students traipsed loudly through the brothels of Paris, with which at least some of them were familiar, opening doors and disrupting business as much as possible. These escapades may have seemed an odd way to celebrate peace, but the return of order was not necessarily welcome news to adolescents who had for four years profited from the distraction of their elders. To Ségogne the chaos represented a natural way to dissemble a grave concern: what were these eighteen- and nineteen-year-olds to do now that they were not in their turn to become the war heroes their older brothers had been? The few years that

stood between these boys and their older siblings made a world of difference: not a single member of the Saint-Cyr graduating class of 1914
survived the war. It made a difference, too, so far as one's literary education
went. Saint-Exupéry was locked up in the Lycée Saint-Louis as Hemingway watched pieces of the Madeleine's façade fall to the ground before
him; Dos Passos marveled over fishermen racing to the Seine to scoop up
the fish stunned by exploding shells; Joseph Kessel, the French author
with whom Saint-Exupéry initially seemed to have the most in common,
volunteered in 1916 and flew reconnaissance missions although he was
only two years Saint-Exupéry's elder. These writers would be able to claim
the war as their subject. Whether Saint-Exupéry shared Ségogne's
concern—which may in the end have made the risky business of aviation
that much more attractive—we do not know. The irony of his having
turned nineteen—the conscription age at last—the day after the Treaty
of Versailles was signed was not, however, lost on him.

He continued on at Bossuet that year and into the next, submitting to
his exams again the third week of June 1920. He passed his written test
—although one of the few autobiographical tall tales he fostered was to
pretend that he had received the lowest possible grade on his French
composition—but did indeed meet his demise in the oral examination,
administered in July in Brest at the naval academy. He was unpredictable
enough that timidity or defiance could equally well have cost him the test.
Lack of preparation may have had something to do with it as well, despite
the long hours he put in at Bossuet and the weeks he had spent in a study
of his design on the third floor of Saint-Maurice that summer. Doubtless
he felt, before and after the exam, like his golden-haired alter ego:
"Grown-ups never question you about the essential." He was now, after
three years of study, too old to submit to the examination a third time.

There is no record of any particular interest on Saint-Exupéry's part
in a naval career, although as an adolescent he was in general long on
pipe dreams and short on professional ambition. "When I'm an engineer,
when I earn a lot of money, when I have three cars, we'll drive together
to Constantinople," was the closest he came, in a 1919 letter to Simone.
With his literary ambition he was more explicit. He continued his versifying at Saint-Louis and reported proudly to his mother that his work had
met with kudos when he had read it aloud at the Vidals. He felt that he
would surely want to write for the theater, having been inspired by the
plays of Henry Bataille and Henry Bernstein, and having realized how
much raw emotion could be condensed in the form. There are diplomas
in France for many things—today there are four for laundry workers—
and there are diplomas appropriate to writers, but a young, fatherless man
named de Saint-Exupéry, even one who saw the arabesques of an art
edition in the formulae of his math workbook, would not have been an

obvious candidate for such a degree in 1920. He had set out to do what was expected of him and had foiled these plans, which he carried out as chaotically as possible. In the end he distinguished himself at Saint-Louis by winning a citation for drawing, an honor akin to winning the poetry prize at Cal Tech. He had missed the boat, in more ways than one. France's educational system is not a forgiving one; a perfect meritocracy, it has no need to offer third and fourth chances. The ex-naval candidate was now without prospects. On some level Saint-Exupéry must have known this. He was so aggravated by his failure that he succumbed to a *crise de foie*, from which he spent three weeks of the summer recuperating at Vichy.

The fall of 1920 found him back in Paris. His only source of funds was his mother, who was as accommodating as she could afford to be. Her son enrolled as an auditor at the École des Beaux-Arts, in architecture. He was more regularly to be found, however, down the rue Bonaparte a few steps, at the corner of the Quai Malaquais, not at a drafting but at a café table.

V

~

Silver Linings
1920–1922

I am like the king of a rainy country,
rich but powerless, young, yet already old.

BAUDELAIRE, *Les Fleurs du Mal*

Paris enjoyed a new lease on life in 1920, but it was an expensive one. The social whirl picked up where it had left off six years before—some circles had only been temporarily displaced to the provinces—and giggling and screaming *les années folles* were ushered in. That summer Ezra Pound and James Joyce both moved to Paris; they prowled the same Saint-Germain streets as did the Beaux-Arts student, streets that fairly buzzed with literary activity, expatriate and native. The lightness of relief filled the air, but in some ways life was more difficult than it had been in 1914. France had lost more than 10 percent of her work force in the war; her people complained of what they felt to be an unsatisfactory peace; as she would for the next years, the country began to shudder from political, fiscal, and industrial unrest. Prices had quadrupled since the beginning of the war and continued to rise; the *baguette* that had cost fifty centimes in December 1919 cost ninety centimes a month later. Madame de Saint-Exupéry did what she could to help her son, now living on his own for the first time. She may have been better positioned to do so since the death of Aunt Tricaud in April, but she could not have been substantially better off: Saint-Maurice was both an expensive property to maintain and an unprofitable one to farm. Her son's resources would by any count have been modest.

His ambitions, at least so far as architecture was concerned, were equally modest. Bernard Lamotte, the ebullient painter who spent the war years in New York and whose murals once hung over the White House pool, was among the first to welcome Saint-Exupéry to the École des

Beaux-Arts. He did not mince words when describing the new student, whom he thought to be about as much an architect as he was a dentist: "He himself must have occasionally wondered what he was doing at Beaux-Arts, because his love of architecture was not exactly overwhelming." When Lamotte and company left their ateliers for lunch at the neighborhood bistro they found Saint-Exupéry already well-installed at Chez Jarras, busily scribbling away, not in pictures but in words. This behavior made him the butt of a fair number of jokes. When he could not be ridiculed for his ardent devotion to the written word he was teased for other reasons: when it rains you had best bow your head, he was advised, else, given the shape of your nose ("*ton nez-en-trompette*"), you risk drowning. By now Saint-Exupéry must have been immune to gibes on both of these counts; still, the elfish Lamotte, well-positioned to take inventory of Saint-Exupéry's life of contrasts, noticed something curious about his friend. "A strange thing: this big man, this gentleman of such impressive size, next to whom I looked like a little boy, had in fact the sensibility of a little girl. It was bizarre; the two didn't go together. He was very sensitive, kind, and always a bit awkward."

This description would not have sat well with Saint-Exupéry, who with no certain future was at the same time experiencing some difficulty liberating himself from the past. His accomplishments were as yet few and his dependence great, no matter how well he may have disguised these matters for his friends, which he probably did not, given his propensity toward truth. It left him, however, in a never-never land in terms of maturity. In the fall he had dinner with the Saint-Pouloffs, distant relatives whom he had not previously met but to whom his mother had introduced her son by letter. Afterward he wrote her indignantly: "But . . . what the devil did you write them? When Tante saw me she seemed extremely surprised and asked me if it hadn't upset you too much to see me traveling alone. I looked stunned! Then she asked me, 'But how old are you?' 'Twenty.' 'Twenty years old! From your mother's letters I thought you were a little boy of fifteen!' They imagined that I had never left your side and Tante had not been looking forward to having to deal with someone who knew nothing of life! When I told them that I had been a student in Paris for three years they stood aghast for fifteen minutes and had a good laugh. What the devil did you write them?"

He did not, however, make any heroic attempts to get on with things. He was in a holding pattern, and coupled with his financial dependence, this put a strain on the relationship with his mother. He must have been frustrated, and Madame de Saint-Exupéry must have felt frustrated not to have been able to bail him out. He was certainly not the first Frenchman to be handicapped by a lack of a diploma. Notable failures include André Malraux, who held no degree; Louis Renault, who met his demise with

the Centrale exams; and Léon Blum, who left the École Normale Supérieure after having been done in by his first-year exams. It has even been
suggested that the high failure rate at French examinations has resulted
in a generally agitated and nervous population; France is a country where
one can be reminded daily of one's failure or success as a *lycéen,* where
a reputation as a brilliant nineteen-year-old test-taker can pave one's way
for life. Saint-Exupéry began to complain of depression at the end of his
Bossuet career, when he was probably exhausted as much as anything
else. His visits to Saint-Maurice were often followed, however, by apologies
for his brusqueness, or his irascibility, or his seeming ingratitude. He
promised always to make amends, as he knew his mother had a good deal
to contend with as things were, but he was forced all the same to ask for
money. His helplessness with financial matters dates from this period,
although in 1920 it seemed more a symptom of his directionlessness than
a character trait. We do not know how much his mother lent him over
the next years—in 1921 this allowance never amounted to less than a
generous five hundred francs, or thirty-five dollars monthly—but we do
know that Madame de Saint-Exupéry lent her son enough for the family
to have credited him later with her financial ruin.

It was probably during this period that he began to visit the Louvre
twice weekly to "feed my nascent artistic culture," and to call on a favorite
Bossuet professor, Abbé Sudour, who kindly—but severely—helped him
to shape his prose. He continued to see as much theater as he could, often
at the invitation of friends. Following Ségogne's lead he got himself hired
as an extra in a second-rate opera at the Théâtre des Champs-Élysées, in
which he appeared as a Praetorian guard. This occupation did not outlast
the ruckus Saint-Exupéry created when he dropped his lance on stage
and had no choice but to bend over in a skimpy tunic to retrieve it. His
violin and the volume of Baudelaire which his mother had given him were
constant companions; the melancholy of both must have suited him. He
seemed the perfect aesthete: ". . . everywhere I come across little things
which enchant me as never before. A note of Chopin, a verse of Samain,
a Flammarion binding, a diamond on the rue de la Paix," he had reported
the previous year.

His was not, however, the bohemian Saint-Germain life of a Joyce or
a Hemingway. As lost as Saint-Exupéry was, some of the best drawing
rooms of Paris were open to him. His existence became a chaotic one of
lavish dinners and low rents, skimpy meals and sumptuous lodgings, a
habit to which he ultimately became accustomed. We have no record of
how he dressed during these times, but he was neither the world's first
nor last impoverished aristocrat, and was eccentric enough to have been
allowed some latitude. At the Saussines he cut a familiar figure, declaiming
verse while wrapped in a sheet. He may at this time have perfected the

look that later became his style, as much out of insouciance as out of economy: a casualness verging on the shoddy.

Saint-Exupéry met with varied receptions at these fine addresses. With the Saussines the opinion divided between Monsieur de Saussine ("What a magnificent boy!") and Madame de Saussine and one of her five daughters, confounded by his unpredictable muteness. He uttered not a single word in the course of a weekend with Yvonne de Lestrange's parents, with whom the conversation ranged from politics to horses to finance to bridge; a report of his unacceptable behavior was conveyed to his mother. This "rampart of silence" posed less of an obstacle to the youngest of Saussine's elder sisters, Renée, who felt any child could make short work of Saint-Exupéry's inaccessibility and who either enjoyed this qualification or simply had a golden touch. The same could be said of the ravishing Louise de Vilmorin, whom Saint-Exupéry probably first met at this time. These were both of them households in which cleverness was not expected to conform to drawing room convention, and in which the eccentricities of this provincial count who had gone to all the right schools and was related to the Lestranges only added to the appeal. He must have seemed like a breath of fresh air.

For at least some of this period Saint-Exupéry lodged at the very affordable Hôtel La Louisiane, a few steps from the École des Beaux-Arts, and survived on a meager diet at the *prix fixe* restaurants of the neighborhood, where a good meal could be had for five francs, a decent bottle of wine for sixty centimes, and a bowl of stewed fruits could—with the right degree of charm, no obstacle to a persuasive and hungry young man—be parlayed into a side order of potatoes or Camembert. He did not want for friends. Charles Sallès was studying in Paris at HEC (Hautes Études Commerciales), France's premier undergraduate business school, and Ségogne and Bertrand de Saussine were quick to invite their versifying friend home with them. These two were particularly responsible for his life of contrasts. Saussine introduced Saint-Exupéry to his parents and to his sisters in a sumptuous *hôtel particulier* on the rue Saint-Guillaume, a building whose walls had been impregnated with the verse, melodies, and prose of Lamartine, Ernest Renan, Proust, Reynaldo Hahn, and Ravel. Saint-Exupéry hardly needed the encouragement of this tradition and was known to borrow Renée's violin for a little improvisation. Through a cousin, or possibly through Saussine, found his way as well to another of Paris's best addresses, that of the Vilmorins on the rue de la Chaise, where ministers and politicians congregated. These were the "well-liked friends who like me back" of whom he had written home the previous year. With the Saussine children he discussed his lack of future options; Renée proved particularly sympathetic to his plight.

His dual existence was no more apparent than in his lodgings. His address was not always the Hôtel La Louisiane; for some portion of his Beaux-Arts career Saint-Exupéry lodged with Yvonne de Lestrange, in an apartment whose proximity to the school was hardly its most attractive feature. Lamotte remembered a visit to his impoverished friend, who had suggested he paint the stunning view from his windows and asked that Lamotte call early some morning, by which he meant toward eleven. Lamotte was met at the door of 9, quai Malaquais by a valet who looked disdainfully at his easel and left him on the sidewalk; he was rescued from this ignominy by his friend, enveloped in a luxurious bathrobe. Up a spiral staircase the two went to Saint-Exupéry's quarters, where his breakfast had only just been touched. The room, a redux of the Bossuet desk, was an abominable mess: sheets of paper, bits of paper, balls of paper covered everything. (Yvonne de Lestrange later admitted that she dreaded the disorder her cousin created in the apartment. She was neither pleased nor surprised when, during one of his later stays, she was awakened by "the sound of Niagara Falls" in the apartment. Saint-Exupéry had run a bath in his room above hers and promptly fallen asleep, turning the staircase into a torrent of hot water. With some difficulty she awoke him for a little assistance. As he opened an eye his first words were, "Why are you being so nasty with me this morning?") The view, however, was indeed extraordinary. Two windows gave on to the Louvre, a third looked out over the school and the terrace of Chez Jarras. Lamotte sketched the scene many times during the winter of 1920 while Saint-Exupéry, seated on his bed in his bathrobe, wrote "*à la Balzac.*" As Balzac shut the noise of the Revolution of 1848 out and himself and his writing in with the words "And now, back to the real world," Saint-Exupéry may have been able to defer thoughts of his future with these bohemian dabblings.

Doubtless he was dragging his feet intentionally. The previous year his military service had been deferred in light of his expected naval career, and he would have known he would eventually be called up. But the theme song of these six Parisian months seemed one he would articulate later, during an equally stagnant period for which the winter of 1920–21 was but a dress rehearsal: "What I shall be in ten years is the last of my worries." He was all ability and little ambition.

~

He was called up to begin his two years of military service in April 1921. He had requested a posting in aviation, and on the ninth arrived in Strasbourg to join the Second Fighter Group, based in Neuhof, just south of the city. The Neuhof field was a large one, originally outfitted by the Germans; it became France's with the recovery of Alsace in 1918 and served both as a military and as a commercial airstrip. Saint-Exupéry joined the Group as a private second-class; he was assigned to the ground crew. He was one of the low men on the totem pole: in French such personnel are known as *rampants*, as are creeping plants or crawling animals or those who grovel. Moreover, as a conscript with no previous training, he did not qualify for flight instruction. He was inducted as any young man without a *bac*, or a *particule*, or three years of training in higher mathematics would have been, and he spent the next few weeks putting these advantages to work.

He could not have made himself less conspicuous by renting a small apartment in town, to which he retired when his schedule allowed. (He was free between 11:00 and 1:30, again between 5:00 and 9:00, after which he returned to Neuhof and spent the night at the barracks.) His Strasbourg letters home were by and large composed on the rue du 22 Novembre, a saner place from which to write than the barracks, as the young soldier relaxed with a cup of tea and a cigarette. The address was the best in Strasbourg; the landlord's telephone was at his disposal; he enjoyed the luxuries of central heating, electric lamps, and a bathtub. This clean, well-lighted room was not free, of course; for it Madame de Saint-Exupéry paid 120 francs a month. It was her son's first furnished apartment and he was for a while enchanted by it, as by Strasbourg, "an exquisite city, much bigger than Lyons."[*]

Despite a day that began punctually at six, the bohemian life came less to a screeching halt than he might have expected. Saint-Exupéry's first impression of the *métier militaire* was that "there is categorically nothing to do." He lobbied his mother for a motorcycle, with which he could make the commute from the airfield to the rue du 22 Novembre and with which he could, in his free time, tour Alsace. He claimed his life consisted of learning to salute, playing soccer, and keeping boredom at bay for hours, hands in his pockets and an unlighted cigarette in his mouth. More than anything the realm of military aviation—still entirely in its infancy, to be fair, to the extent that Saint-Exupéry arrived in Strasbourg before the uniforms did—seemed to him like a big soccer camp. It was hardly different from—and certainly no more boring than—the *lycée*. "Nothing to do between now and two o'clock. At two o'clock there will be nothing to do either, other than to move whoever was at place A to place B and whoever was at place B to place A, and then to do the opposite, which will allow us to start again from our original positions," he wrote his mother soon after his arrival. In May this was charming; by early June the drill had begun to depress him. But by then his efforts to bend the rules had begun to pay off.

---

[*] In fact the population of Lyons was at the time more than three times larger than that of Strasbourg.

The man who would never pull rank lost no time in Strasbourg pulling strings. He had requested a posting in aviation so that he might fly, not train as a ground crewman and gunner, and his proximity to a field of Hanriots and SPAD-Herbemonts in no way thwarted that ambition. The rules did; new military pilots were trained at many bases throughout France but not at Strasbourg. Furthermore, only those men who arrived in Strasbourg classified as student pilots were allowed to fly. Civilian training was easier to come by—in the 1920s some 2,000 licenses were issued in France—but it was expensive. Full-blast, Saint-Exupéry turned the pertinacity to which he had subjected the residents of Saint-Maurice to his cause. In his assault on the regulations he was assisted, if not encouraged, by two of his officers. With Captain de Billy and Major de Féligonde he had something in common, and the two looked out for this unusual recruit as one of their own. Major de Féligonde promised to look into Saint-Exupéry's request to become a student pilot, though he said it could take him at least two months to make the necessary arrangements. In the meantime he struck a deal with the well-educated private: as of May 26 Saint-Exupéry was to teach a course in aerodynamics and the physics of combustion. "I will have a classroom, a blackboard, and a handful of students. . . . What a blast! Can you see me as a professor?" he wrote his mother, profiting from the assignment to ask for money for his texts. (There is no evidence that Saint-Exupéry ever taught his course, although the funds and the texts did arrive.) He wondered if his mother knew Captain de Billy, who evidently had family in Lyons, and prevailed upon both his mother and his sister Gabrielle—now eighteen—to put in a good word for him with these supposed relatives.

Meanwhile Saint-Exupéry had paid a visit to the Compagnie Transaérienne de l'Est, one of the commercial firms that shared the Neuhof field with the military. Robert Aéby was the company's only staff pilot; the group had hoped to win the Strasbourg-Brussels-Antwerp line, but had been beaten out by the Compagnie Franco-Roumaine, their next-door neighbor on the airfield. With five aircraft the Compagnie Transaérienne de l'Est (CTE) had reinvented itself as a concern specializing in chartered flights, joyrides, and aerial photos. On a clear Sunday morning in early April, probably the tenth, a shoddily dressed young man inquired after the price of a flight. It was fifty francs, a fairly large sum at the time (ten francs more than the Duchess de Vendôme's box seats at the Comédie-Française), and Aéby doubted that his customer actually had the funds in hand. The young man agreed to the price, however, and Aéby took him up for his standard tour of the airfield, landing the Farman F-40 after about ten minutes. Aéby had taxied to the hangar and leapt out of the plane when his passenger asked if they might not try a second circuit. No one had made such a request before and Aéby was at first taken aback;

soon enough he decided, however, that it was "rather a pleasant thing to do business with a fanatic." Having made it clear that the second flight would cost an additional fifty francs, Aéby took off to inspect, at Saint-Exupéry's request, the south and north of the city, the Vosges, and the Rhine, a flight that would have taken well over ten minutes.

On at least a few other occasions Saint-Exupéry took to the air, although his obligatory training as a gunner had not yet begun. It was not unusual for the military pilots, many of whom were young aces covered with decorations, to indulge the *rampants* who wanted to go up; generally these flights were without successors, as the pilots liked to treat their passengers to "memorable acrobatics sessions." Saint-Exupéry only pleaded for more. His giddy report to his mother of his first experience of a SPAD-Herbemont, the premier fighter plane of the time, is also his first prose account of flight:

> My senses of space, of distance, and of direction entirely vanished. When I looked for the ground I sometimes looked down, sometimes up, sometimes left, sometimes right. I thought I was very high up when I would suddenly be thrown to earth in a near vertical spin. I thought I was very low to the ground and I was pulled up to 3,000 feet in two minutes by the 500-horsepower motor. It danced, it pitched, it tossed. . . . Ah! la la!

He looked forward to a second round the next day, when he anticipated with delight "the spins, the loops, the barrel rolls [which] will empty my stomach of a year's worth of lunches." How did he manage these flights in a SPAD? A corporal of the Group who was aware of the flights remained mystified by them. Saint-Exupéry told his mother only that he went up thanks to some acquaintances he had made. He hoped passionately to pilot a SPAD—"It holds the air like a shark holds the water, and even looks like a shark"—and lived for the moment when the regulations might allow him to do so. He was impetuous enough to consider volunteering for Morocco, where new French pilots were being trained in exchange for three years of service. (He was further tempted in this direction by the presence of his Rabat-stationed friend, Marc Sabran, with whom he kept up a healthy correspondence.) His letters brim with impatience. It was as if his awareness of lost time had caught up with him all at once.

Only one option would have allowed Saint-Exupéry to have qualified for military training as a pilot without having to prolong his commitment to the army. If he could obtain a civil license he would automatically qualify as a student pilot, and he would owe the army no more than the compulsory two years. This was the expensive (and highly unorthodox) alternative—if he had volunteered for an additional year the training would have been free—but it was also the one Saint-Exupéry chose. In the end, it was less his officers he needed to finesse than his mother. She must have had other ideas for her son, whom she had been pressuring to study during his service (he reported that this was next to impossible, given his exhaustion after all the physical exercise), and of whose schemes she must by now have grown wary. He could not make himself more clear in his letters, in which he writes directly to her now-lost objections: "*Maman,* if you only knew the irresistible thirst I have to fly." "It seems to me that you would like to discourage me. Tell me that you would never do that?" "I've *thought, questioned, discussed.*" "I swear to you that there is no cause for concern." "You told me in your letter only to make a well-thought-out decision; I promise you that this is one. I don't have a second to lose, hence my haste," wrote the young man in need of a significant sum of money. We have no way of knowing which of these arguments ultimately sent Madame de Saint-Exupéry to her banker for a loan; she must have been particularly susceptible, however, to her son's single-mindedness, as to his plea: "I need an occupation which suits me, otherwise I'll amount to nothing." He did not sound as if he had altogether enjoyed his six expensive, unproductive Parisian months. Early in June Madame de Saint-Exupéry sent the money.

At the other end the negotiations had been easier. Saint-Exupéry called again on Robert Aéby, this time in uniform, and asked if there were any way he might learn to fly. ("Do you remember me?" he asked, although ill-dressed aristocrats passionate about flying and serving as ground crewmen were generally in poor supply in Strasbourg.) Aéby told him he would need the authorization of his commanding officer, as well as the permission of the CTE. Not only was there no formal flight instruction at the Neuhof field at the time; Aéby had never taught anyone to fly. Moreover, it was unthinkable for a military man to pilot a civilian aircraft.

Not long afterward Commander Garde, acting with the complicity of Captain de Billy, convened a meeting in his office. Present were the head of the CTE, Saint-Exupéry, and Aéby, who was amazed at what transpired. Contrary to all regulations, Commander Garde authorized the private to submit to training. This exception had been made on no other field. Garde attached several conditions to his permission: Saint-Exupéry's lessons were to take place outside of his required hours; each man was to give his word of honor to keep the enterprise secret; no photographs were to be taken of the student with a CTE plane or in Aéby's company. Saint-Exupéry and the CTE director agreed on the sum of 2,000 francs for the instruction. The men swore, shook hands, and the matter—"a veritable conspiracy," in Aéby's words—was settled. "I beg you, Mother, not to speak of this with *anyone*," wrote Saint-Exupéry, requesting the funds, of the events that were to transform his life.

Lessons began in the Farman F-40 equipped with dual controls on June 18. On that day Saint-Exupéry made three circuits of the field and landed three times for a total of fifteen flying minutes. After the first landing Aéby advised his student that he could be less "brutal" with the controls, standard advice to the novice pilot. He flew regularly in the next weeks, before 8:00 a.m., at midday, or after 6:00 p.m.; he needed to complete twenty-five hours of training to obtain his license, and knew he was scheduled to be transferred imminently to Morocco. He set about realizing his dream with a vengeance, flying both the gunner flights required of a *rampant* and his CTE circuits daily. Aéby observed happily that his student's reactions were sure and his judgment quick. The Farman's motor was mounted at the tail, which allowed the two men to converse easily without being bothered by the noise of the propeller. Aéby found that conversations with his student were short, however; a certain gulf persisted between them. It could not have helped that in Aéby's logbook his student was "the Count de Saint-Exupéry," to be addressed as "Monsieur le Comte"; Saint-Exupéry probably thought Aéby unable to understand his passion. He would not have known that his instructor had an impressive history of his own in the fine art of circumventing regulation. A soldier in the German army, Aéby had learned to fly while recovering from a serious wound; in 1918 he injured himself with a propeller so as to avoid being sent back to the front. After the Armistice, when Alsace was returned to France, Aéby had joined the French army as an aviator but was assigned to the navy, a transfer that led him to resign from the military. In the three weeks the two men spent together the veteran was all the same unable to screw up the courage to tell his student that his landlady had twice come to see him in the hope that he might advise "Monsieur le Comte" that it was unwise to leave large bank bills crumpled up on the floor of his apartment, where she found them when she cleaned. (When, just before Saint-Exupéry's departure for Morocco, Aéby did mention these conversations, his student took offense, directing at Aéby the scorn that had accumulated for all those who ever asked him to tidy his room.)

At the end of two weeks, the two men had made twenty-one circuits in eleven lessons on the Farman: "conservative flying. . . . Careful and gradual turns. Slow, lazy landings—no spins or loops," as Saint-Exupéry described it to his mother. The Farman had seen better days, however, and Aéby—aware that his student did not have the patience to await its repair—introduced him to the Sopwith, a more rapid and delicate plane. In his letters Saint-Exupéry complained that the cantankerous Farman had already cost him several precious lessons; he doubtless shared his frustration with Aéby as well. The pair made two circuits in the British craft on July 8, both executed to Aéby's satisfaction. On the morning of the ninth they made a third, after which Aéby climbed out of the airplane.

"Take off!" he ordered Saint-Exupéry, who despite the fact that he had asked Aéby every day when he might solo now responded with a flabbergasted, "What?" A few minutes later, at 11:10, he was off, alone and aloft for the first time. He had only two and a half hours' flying time under his belt.

Saint-Exupéry's takeoff and circuit were without reproach; Aéby fired off a green flare to signal that he should land. His approach to the field was too high; five meters from the ground he realized his mistake and accelerated, a little too brusquely. The motor sputtered, but caught again after a second. Saint-Exupéry landed safely and took off on a second circuit, this one without incident. Aéby noticed afterward that as a result of the first landing Saint-Exupéry's puttees had been singed; his student reported that the airplane's engine had caught fire. Patiently Aéby informed him that it had not, but that in accelerating as quickly as he had he had caused it to backfire. He was generally pleased with his student and in the afternoon crossed the field to report on his progress to Commander Garde, whom he informed that the private had now soloed. The commander consulted his file and directed Aéby to stop the lessons there. Seventeen years later Saint-Exupéry and Aéby met again, when the student recognized his instructor on a café terrace in Vichy, where the Aébys and Saint-Exupéry were taking the cure. (Ironically, Saint-Exupéry was recovering from a serious crash in Guatemala.) The former pupil, now a celebrity, bought the Aébys an apéritif and conjured up his solo flight of that morning for Madame Aéby: "If you only knew, Madame, how happy I was up there, all alone for the first time. I never wanted to see a landing flare. And I do believe that if I had had enough gas I'd still be up there!"

From Aéby's point of view the events of the summer of 1921 were no less extraordinary. The *rampant* had not officially earned a license but he had learned to fly on a military field on which all instruction was prohibited, in uniform, aboard a civilian plane belonging to a company authorized only to offer joyrides, under the supervision of an ex-pilot of the German army who had never before trained a student. His protégé had indeed found friends in the right places. As if further proof of this fact were needed, a remarkable display of selective ignorance had been made by the Ministry of War on Saint-Exupéry's behalf late in June, probably after his mother's intercession: the Ministry delayed his transfer to Morocco by two weeks so that Saint-Exupéry might complete the training of which they had ostensibly known nothing.

~

It got hot in Strasbourg in mid-June, and Saint-Exupéry began to wilt. He did not record the effect the weather would have had on his flying—heat makes an airplane sluggish, notably at takeoff, and haze interferes with a pilot's vision—but complained bitterly of the toll it was taking on his chess partner, who was too sunstruck to prove a worthy opponent. He was so uncomfortable that he claimed to be judging art—of which he could not have been seeing a good deal at the time—solely on its calorific value. He told his mother he had lost all appreciation for the roseate, luscious eighteenth century and found his taste now ran to lithographs of the Mont-Blanc glacier and of the Russian campaign. How he was going to survive in Morocco remained to be seen, but he was eager to be off. "To go *as a pilot* to Rabat, I'm so happy. The desert seen from an airplane must be sublime," he sighed at the end of his three months in Strasbourg.

His pretransfer leave was abbreviated because of his training with Aéby, but he met his mother in Paris early in July before sailing from Marseilles to Tangier. Late in the month he joined the 37th Fighter Group, then stationed six miles outside of Casablanca, to find his Strasbourg hopes for a sublime desert dashed. "Where are the banana, the date, the coconut trees of my dreams?" he groused. He yearned for the verdant lawns of Saint-Maurice, for the gardens of France. "When I come across a bush, I pull off several leaves and stuff them in my pocket. Then back in my room I study them with love, I turn them gently. It does me good," wrote the man whose best-known hero would travel through interplanetary space on account of a rose. He did not yet know that the desert was to be his most fertile ground, his secret garden, the place where he grew more than anywhere else. "You cannot commune with the desert if you continue to carry with you the noise of the city," Saint-Exupéry concluded years later, and in the summer of 1921 Paris and Strasbourg rang still in his ears.

His love affair was not much assisted by the company he kept. It was noteworthy that from Strasbourg and Casablanca Saint-Exupéry took no new friends; he must have kept himself as much apart as his living arrangements in Alsace and his grumblings from Morocco suggested. He complained often of his unremarkable pilot friends, who could hardly have seemed otherwise to a military man who waxed poetic on the subject of the group's sleeping arrangements:

> The open-air barrack is filled with the kinds of complaints you hear on the seas; as the rain has surrounded it with lakes you can't help but be reminded of Noah's Ark. Inside, each of us has silently buried himself under his white mosquito netting, which gives the impression of a girls' boarding school. Just as you are getting used to this idea, as you feel yourself beginning to grow shy and charming, you are awakened by fierce swearing. To this you respond with equally fervent curses; around you the little white mosquito nettings seem to tremble with fright.

He wrote damningly of the routine, which was at first slow and unexacting;
he railed against a life of chess, raids on the natives' fig trees, and crab
fishing at low tide. Though he could be happily distracted by a Moroccan
sunrise or a visit to the souks, he made himself miserable with the thought
that he had bungled his life. His despair came to a head toward the end
of his exile, when, despite the fact that he was proceeding apace in his
training, he wrote home: "Still this anguish of not knowing which road
to take. Architecture school is so long [it was a three-year program], so
long, and I have so little faith in myself." Earlier the soldier had informed
his mother that he had discovered the vocation for which he was born and
which had escaped his notice at the Beaux-Arts: charcoal drawing. Now
that seemed as worthless as the correspondence courses in aeronautical
engineering he had considered. "Verse, drawing, all that comes naturally
to me. But what is it worth? Very little. I have no faith in myself."

Nonetheless he continued to write sonnets, which he submitted to his
mother for approval, and to request books (the works of Anna de Noailles,
the poetry of Charles Péguy) and periodicals. (He hoped his mother would
treat him to subscriptions to the *NRF* and *Arts Décoratifs* for Christmas.)
His descriptions, which still gleam with the magic of Hans Christian Andersen, begin as well to sound like someone else. In the souks of Casablanca, where he claimed his solitude was more easily forgotten because
the passageways can only be navigated single file, golden *babouches*—
destined to become Bark's *babouches*—talk to him. And in recounting for
his mother how he learned to fly with a compass he laid the groundwork
for one of the most indelible scenes in *Wind, Sand and Stars*. From Casablanca he reported:

> Tonight, by the peaceful light of a lamp, I learned to orient myself by
> compass. Maps are laid out over the table, and Sergeant Boileau explains:
> "Arrive here (and we lean intently over the diagrams) and you head 45
> degrees west." . . . I dream. . . . The sergeant wakes me: "Pay closer
> attention . . . now 180 degrees west, unless you prefer this shortcut." . . .
> Sergeant Boileau offers me a cup of tea. I drink it in slow sips. I dream
> that I am lost, in dissident territory. I yearn to join long missions through
> the desert.

Later, in Toulouse, he would sit down for a similar session with the
legendary Henri Guillaumet: "I spread out my maps and asked him hes-
itantly if he would mind going over the hop with me. And there, bent over
in the lamplight, shoulder to shoulder with the veteran, I felt a sort of
schoolboy peace." The tendency to dream while being instructed was
something he would never outgrow. Had he known about that second
lesson in navigation, however, only a little more than five years down the
road, he might have succumbed less to despair in Casablanca.

What ailed the student pilot commonly went by the name of home-sickness. All the music he most loved made him sad: it was too happy, too tender, too moving. He told his mother her letters were the only bright spots in his life. His missives to her were infinitely sweet—save when she did not write. The repeated refrain went something like this: "You've done everything for us and I've been so ungrateful. I've been selfish and clumsy. I haven't at all been the support which you've needed. It seems to me that every day I learn a bit better to know you and to love you more. It's true as ever; the Maman is the only real refuge for a man in need. But why don't you write me anymore? It's unfair to wait impatiently for the boat and not get any mail." At times he proved so needy he even forsook specificity: "Send me photos, send me letters, send me whatever you like, but send me something."

Two things, aside from the cooler weather, saved Saint-Exupéry from his melancholy. More and more often he was flying. Initially he made an average of six early-morning landings in a Breguet 14; soon he was con-fident enough of these to deem them masterpieces—and to push the en-velope of the official itinerary. By November, when he sat for his reserve officer exams in Rabat, he was flying 150-mile triangles from Berrechid to Rabat to Casablanca in the mornings and caving in to exhaustion in the afternoons. By the end of the year he was flying to the southern frontier and back, about a five-hour trip. (When he saw Casablanca, some fifty miles in the distance on his return, he reported that he felt the pride "of the Crusaders arriving in Jerusalem.") He offered his mother two portraits of himself, one of them in words. In the drawing he looks like a deep-sea diver of the 1920s.

> If you could see me in the morning, muffled up like an Eskimo and stout as an elephant, you would laugh. I have a balaclava which—like a mask —covers my entire face save for my eyes, and over the aforementioned eyes I wear goggles. A big scarf around the neck, your white sweater, and over it all a fur-lined flying suit. Enormous gloves and two pairs of socks in my huge shoes.

Still the morning cold at 7,000 feet was severe. But it was with an admixture of pride and fascination that the student pilot reported on having spent twenty minutes trying to fit his chilled hand into his pocket to withdraw a map.

Marc Sabran, too, came to the rescue. No one made Morocco more livable than the talented Lyons friend who had remained the standard by which all friendships were measured. Sabran was evidently now himself an officer posted in Rabat; if the two had not found each other sooner, they did at the end of the year when Saint-Exupéry spent eight days in Rabat for his exams. Sabran's presence clearly dulled the pain of the ordeal, for which the young pilot claimed to be unprepared and about which he remained nonchalant. He claimed not to be tempted by the few years in "an appalling school of military theory" to which the exams would admit him, and exerted himself very little. If he did pass he warned his mother that he planned to resign from the military. Faced with the prospect of "mechanical and insipid" military schooling, he decided that a degree in architecture again looked attractive. He was, however, entirely enchanted by squadron life, and Sabran now introduced him to another kind of squadron.

In Rabat Sabran took his friend to meet Captain Pierre Priou, the high commissioner of native affairs in Morocco. An artist and musician, Priou avidly welcomed the lettered and well-bred of the young French officers-in-training to his home. He lived high up among the labyrinth of Rabat's gleaming, white-washed homes: "One feels as if one is walking in the polar snow, this part of the Arab town is so bathed in moonlight," wrote Saint-Exupéry. The captain's house abutted a mosque set on slightly lower ground. Not only was the muezzin's cry closer and clearer than in the streets below, but his guests could look down into the mosque from above, as into a well. Otherwise the captain's visitors were doubtless unaware of the passage of time. Soon after Saint-Exupéry's exams Sabran was posted to Casablanca; he made a regular habit of taking his friend back to Priou's with him for forty-eight-hour leaves beginning on Saturday evenings. Typically, Sabran, Saint-Exupéry, and four other young men descended upon the captain. Their dinners were high-spirited; the conversation scintillating; the music exquisite; the poker consuming, at least until three or four in the morning. (Madame de Saint-Exupéry was presumably not overjoyed to learn that although her son sounded happy this new vocation was costing her up to sixteen francs a night.) She could not worry that she had been forgotten, however; here was a scene that moved her son to borrow a sheet of his host's stationery: "I write you from an adorable mauve drawing room, buried in big pillows, a cup of tea in front of me and a cigarette on my lips. Sabran is at the piano—Debussy or Ravel—and a group of other friends are playing bridge." The glow cast by the evenings in this oasis was warm enough to color the entire country, which Saint-Exupéry now saw sparkling under a carpet of red and yellow flowers. For the first time he had discovered a society that suited him perfectly. The hours were loose and the regulations lax, the friendships firm and the conversation invigorating. Insofar as it was possible he had transposed the aesthetic trappings of the family hearth onto military or dormitory life. It was the kind of situation in which he shone, and under the North African sun he now began to blossom, if not to put down roots. With the flying, and with the drawing room of Captain Priou, he was not a long way off from seeing that "greatness comes first—and always—from a goal outside of oneself. As soon as one locks a man within himself, he becomes poor."

By the time Saint-Exupéry boarded the boat back to France, in February 1922, nostalgia had begun to mist the air. "I can't complain about Morocco, it was good to me," he wrote from the boat. "I spent days of terrible depression in a rotten barrack"—earlier he had written his sister that mushrooms were sprouting both on his body and his brain—"but I remember it now as a life full of poetry." He was turning cartwheels in his mind as he crossed the Mediterranean from Tangier to Marseilles, commanding his mother to kill the fatted calf and heat his room well, challenging the *curé* to chess, sending hugs on to his governess, entreating Simone not to mention his return to the Bonnevies, so that he might surprise Louis. All's well that ends well: the ex–naval candidate discovered at this time that he was prone to seasickness.

~

The return to Saint-Maurice was to wait a little longer—probably, Saint-Exupéry thought, until late in the month. From Marseilles he made the short trip north to Istres, having passed his reserve officer training exam. This he did despite himself; he told a friend that he had gone to great pains to fail the exam, but had been held back by a certain sense of propriety from pushing this scheme too far. Probably he was held back as well by memories of his aborted naval career. He could at least congratulate himself on not having passed with flying colors: while only one in twelve applicants passed the exam, Saint-Exupéry distinguished himself by ranking sixty-eighth out of the victorious sixty-nine. (He was also the only qualifying student officer *à la particule*.) On the last day of January he received his pilot's license and on February 5 he was promoted to corporal. Two months later he was assigned to the airfield at Avord, outside Bourges, in central France, the field that had served as the primary training ground for World War I pilots. He did not resign at this time as he had warned he might; it is tempting to think he had begun to enjoy himself a little.

Jean Escot, a Lyons native who had remembered Saint-Exupéry's extraordinary triumph over the rules at Strasbourg and who would remain a fixture in his life over the next twenty years, recalled the comic figure the pilot cut on his arrival in Avord: "Pants too large, coat sleeves too short, indescribable leggings, regulation hat sprouting giant wings." The fault was not entirely that of Saint-Exupéry, who had in fact got his choice at the commissary; the air force was still so new that its uniforms were somewhat improvisational. When Saint-Exupéry earned his second-lieutenant's kepi that fall, there was still no regulation-issue headgear and he was given his choice of colors. (Only that year did the Ministry of War recognize the air force as a military branch on a par with the cavalry or infantry; it would not have its own ministry for another six years or its independence for eleven.) In October as in April Saint-Exupéry wore khaki; only the officers who had trained in metropolitan France had a right to regulation light blue. This, too, set him apart. He actively cultivated his reputation as an eccentric. When asked about his prior schooling he replied that he had come from Beaux-Arts, which was roughly akin to arriving at divinity school and claiming to have come by way of ROTC. When word got around that he had failed his oral exams for the naval academy he offered this explanation: "I didn't like the looks of the examiner. So I answered whatever I felt like!" His ability to attain, as one friend later termed it, "a surprising density of occupation of a room" did not go unnoticed any more than did his sartorial disarray. He reveled in his untidiness, writing his mother that summer:

> I am writing from my little room. An intimate and comforting disorder reigns. My books, my stove, my chessboard, my inkpot, and my toothbrush crowd around me on the table. I survey my kingdom in a long glance; my subjects do not run to cower in the drawers. Would you like a chocolate bar? Wait, here is one, between my compass and my bottle of methyl alcohol. Would you like a pen? Look over there in the basin.

He was in his element, although it was hardly a soldierly one. Even while he did astonishingly well on his exams, he did not conform to a military profile. As he had at Strasbourg he continued to write and to draw. He remained an incorrigible caricaturist. He performed technical experiments with his camera. One classmate remembered Saint-Exupéry drilling him—over the course of four hours—about the functioning of a metallurgical plant, with which he was familiar. As he illustrated the process, Saint-Exupéry, avidly following the explanation, embellished his diagrams with drawings of mischievous devils and nervous angels. He proved equally enchanted by the experiments an unusual classmate named Larrouy performed with hypnosis and made Escot one of his first victims, although his attempts to put him under were largely unsuccessful. Not so the card tricks he had been taught in the Strasbourg barracks: In the 1930s and early 1940s he met a great number of people who would remember nothing about Saint-Exupéry except that he was very tall, very famous, Saint-and could do sensational things with a pack of cards. In general he proved a far more outgoing colleague at Avord than he had earlier, although his taste for human contact could also be wearing. Escot remembered interminable discussions the two had as they traveled together to Lyons on leave. These were in fact soliloquies: Escot's compartment mate was inexhaustible on the subjects of Dostoyevsky, Baudelaire, Cocteau, and Giraudoux.

Escot and Saint-Exupéry were more effectively drawn together by a common problem. The Avord training was for an observer's license, which all aspiring officers needed to obtain. The curriculum consisted mainly of classroom work, with some flying as an observer; there was no scheduled piloting, and in fact only seven members of the class had earned pilot's licenses. The schedule was a full one—after their courses in navigation, meteorology, and bombardment the young men went up in Salmsons or Breguet 14's as passengers—but the Avord officers-in-training were allowed to rack up hours on the Sopwiths before the day's classes began, usually between 6:00 and 8:00 a.m. Escot swore he had never met anyone who was so much a fanatic about flying as Saint-Exupéry, whose sleeping habits seemed to corroborate the claim. He was notoriously difficult to rouse, but when it came to flying he was up and about and tugging at Escot's sleeve at dawn.

He was less eager—and less talented—as a student observer. His mishaps were legendary, and began with his colleagues having to shame him from his bed, then rearrange his uniform for roll call. Quickly he developed a reputation for being incorrigibly absentminded, a description that now began to trail him wherever he went.

In his letters he vacillated between a dawning independence and a clinging immaturity. He was angry with his mother when she did not write and could be severe with her, chastising her for shutting herself up in her "feudal Saint-Maurice." There is plenty of evidence that this treatment was reciprocal. At the same time Saint-Exupéry had not gained any appreciation for military discipline, or classes in tactics, or the humorlessness of his officers, and wrote that he fended off the dryness of military life by imagining his mother arranging flowers in the drawing room of Saint-Maurice. He felt her to be the antidote to the harshness of his superiors as she had been to the harshness of the *pères préfets* of his schooldays. Over and over again he wrote that he felt like a little boy, in need of a little boy's comforts. With joy he announced, happy for once with his fate, that he would soon begin training as a second lieutenant and would thenceforth receive a monthly 1,000-franc stipend. "Then I will marry, I will have a little apartment, a cook, and a delightful wife," he predicted. Without missing a beat he went on to tell his mother that the Avord tailor was a "hard and bitter man" who was, by damning insinuation, pestering him to pay his overdue bill. Could she send him 200 francs immediately?

Among his classmates these wire orders were as well-known as was Saint-Exupéry's seigneurial ignorance about money. He often made the trip to Paris on Sunday; if his mother's telegram did not arrive on time to fund the outing he had no qualms about soliciting contributions from his classmates. (He was obliged because he scrupulously repaid all debts. Later his literary agent in America, a frequent and generous lender of money, reported that Saint-Exupéry was the only author who ever reimbursed him.) In June the group spent two weeks at a special training camp at Mailly, from which Saint-Exupéry absented himself for a weekend when his cousin Guy was married in Paris. He clearly did so at his mother's request, and either suddenly realized how bedraggled he looked or thought the event a good excuse for another solicitation. He went to lengths to make Madame de Saint-Exupéry understand that she could not, under the circumstances, begrudge him his requests for funds; he could not be expected to make a threadbare appearance at a wedding. The month before his 1,000-franc stipend was to begin he lobbied for a 300-franc wire, although his mother had clearly been angry with him about these requests, which had been directed at his Paris relatives as well. Brusquely he repeated his demands, begging her not to be angry with him, and assuring her that he was more serious than nine out of ten of his comrades. He omitted to say that he had more expensive habits as well.

In August the student officers moved to Versailles for two months, to be trained in the various components of land war. The usual question presented itself to Escot and Saint-Exupéry: how to fly? Courses were held only in the mornings; the fanatics were advised that they were welcome to pilot so long as they made their own arrangements and were in their seats for the 9:00 a.m. lecture. Villacoublay, one of the early centers of French aviation, was only four miles away, and the two quickly arranged for Escot's brother to send the Escot brothers' jointly owned motorcycle from London. A small fortune—some of it doubtless originating in Saint-Maurice—made its way into the hands of the Saint-Lazare customs inspectors, but with the cycle in their possession the two were able to set out every morning at their leisure. At Villacoublay they presented themselves at the first hangar, in which gleamed a series of brand-new Caudron C59's. Escot's logbook was more impressive than that of Saint-Exupéry, who was warned that this fighter plane was faster than the Sopwiths to which he was accustomed. Both pilots performed two control circuits and then flew for a half hour, by Escot's report laughing to themselves the whole time. They were told they were welcome to come back every morning, weather permitting. Escot turned toward the motorcycle but Saint-Exupéry did not: another hangar, filled with Breguet 14's, had caught his eye. Soon enough the officers-in-training had completed a second set of introductions and control circuits, and were aloft for a second half hour. Thus, greedily, over the course of the next months, they built up flying hours. To his mother Saint-Exupéry wrote only that he was flying daily and was happy as a clam.

From Versailles he began to slip into Paris every evening, occasionally with Escot. He finished his training early in October 1922 and on the tenth was named a second lieutenant. As he was in the top half of the class*—it is important to all that came later that in the eyes of his air force superiors, who made no official mention of his distraction, Saint-Exupéry was a technically proficient and a promising pilot—he was allowed to choose his next posting. Probably he did not hesitate before requesting Paris. (Escot opted for Lyons, and would lose sight of his friend for two years, until a chance encounter on a Paris street reunited them. Both men's second choice was Morocco, a testament to the power of nostalgia on Saint-Exupéry's part.) He was assigned to the 34th Air Regiment, based at Paris's principal airport, Le Bourget, where Lindbergh would land five years later. Saint-Exupéry's responsibilities as a reserve officer were not taxing: he was to show up early each day at the airfield, and to fly a few times weekly.

To the site of his Beaux-Arts dabblings and his Bossuet disappointments he returned a happier soul. After his eighteen months with the army he was no more disciplined—these were years when one could be an iconoclast in the air force, when most of the French military still had trouble taking a so-called officer who had not survived the ordeals of Saint-Cyr or Saumur seriously—and disobedience remained for him the better part of valor. Nor was he, at twenty-two, any more responsible than he had been a year and a half earlier. But his idle years had allowed him a chance to cement a few important friendships, and he had emerged from under the cloud of his earlier failures. He had "delicious" friends and an enduring passion. While the Armistice had put a damper on one kind of future, the war had also offered up a new profession; Saint-Exupéry had turned his military service to his advantage. If he was still living in the present, he was at least no longer a precocious nostalgic, stuck in the past. His ambition loping along, he even began to think a little about the future. Or at least to dream about it: sometime late in the summer of 1922 he fell head over heels in love.

---

* He ranked twenty-seventh of sixty-two.

VI

~

Walking on Air
1922–1926

*The purpose of the aristocrat is most emphatically
not to work for money.*
NANCY MITFORD, *Noblesse Oblige*

The object of Saint-Exupéry's affection came as no surprise to his
friends, most of whom lived under the same thrall. The surprise more
likely came in the fact that the young officer's affections were reciprocated.
He was by no measure the most attractive of Louise de Vilmorin's suitors,
into which category fell nearly every man who mounted the three flights
to her room at the top of an imposing *hôtel particulier* on the rue de la
Chaise. It was a crowded staircase. In the salons below, Madame de Vilmorin, a lively, dark-haired beauty, entertained a wide circle of politicians
and ministers of the Republic: Édouard Herriot, Paul Painlevé, and Léon
Bérard were frequent callers. Her husband—a geneticist under whom the
family agricultural business had thrived—had died in Louise's youth; he
had been a great friend of the dramatists Sacha Guitry and Paul Claudel.
Madame de Vilmorin was absorbed enough in her conversations and indulgent enough as a parent to pay little attention to the army of visitors
that descended upon her four sons and two daughters; the house itself
was rambling and baroque, easily accommodating a great number of com-
ings and goings, more or less discreetly. The flow of traffic—and secrets
and telephone calls and *billets-doux*—was further assisted by the com-
plicitous concierge, Léon Hubert, who took special care of the Vilmorin
children. It was a festive and feted household and a hugely popular one,
perfumed as it was with a whiff of decadence. So much of the École Bossuet
found its way to 1, rue de la Chaise during the late-afternoon break that
the *abbé* who ran the school was forced to inquire: "I wonder what there

is *chez* Madame de Vilmorin which causes all these boys to rush over there all the time?"

Henry de Ségogne could have answered the question admirably:

> At the very top of the Vilmorins' townhouse, in a room which was a roost, an exquisite room, admirably appointed, there was, in a bed, the most exquisite creature imaginable, the quintessential young lady, in a light pink nightshirt, smoking Craven A's; she was poetry itself, poetry incarnate, charm incarnate; the small face of this creature was something from a dream, a waking dream, it was a marvelous vision, further enhanced by an entirely irresistible chirping. She was highly intelligent, entirely precious, she was absolutely stunning.

At no point in her life was Louise de Vilmorin a woman who evoked modest tributes. The youngest of the Vilmorins, known to her intimates as Loulou, suffered from a hip ailment that confined her to a cast and to her bed for nearly three years in the early 1920s. This allowed her to receive visitors in a somewhat unorthodox fashion, often said to be daringly unorthodox. It partially explained her four older brothers' tendency to dote on her; it encouraged the dreaminess to which all convalescents to some degree succumb; and it left her with a slight limp, which she turned into a supplementary charm later in life. In Saint-Exupéry's eyes the handicap transformed a perfect auburn-haired, pale-skinned, turquoise-eyed beauty into what he would most have liked to find ensconced at the top of a tower: a fairy princess.

Saint-Exupéry had probably made his way to the rue de la Chaise for the first time in 1918 or 1919, at the side of Bertrand de Saussine, whose family was closely linked to the Vilmorins. It is possible, too, that Honoré d'Estienne d'Orves, a fellow Saint-Louis student and a cousin to both families, made the introductions. (France is a small country with a big past: the Vilmorins also claimed a cousin of Joan of Arc as part of their family tree.) Louise would have been sixteen or seventeen at the time; her newfound cousin was two years her elder. Saint-Exupéry became a fairly frequent visitor to the house, which makes it difficult to say when exactly the *tête-à-têtes* and the poetry-making on the third floor gave way to love. It could not have been before the summer of 1922, when Saint-Exupéry, back from Strasbourg, Casablanca, and Avord, was based in Versailles. That summer his thoughts had certainly turned to love. Partly in jest he wrote his mother to help him find a girl like the three Americans he had just met, who enjoyed dancing because it was amusing, and music because it was pretty, and who claimed that the Eiffel Tower was ugly until told otherwise, when in unison they agreed that it was beautiful. "I don't need her to entertain me with literary theory," he wrote, regarding his prospective flame.

That June, under the auspices of Louise, a *"société humoristique"* called the GB Club—evidently for "Groupe Bossuet"—was founded. Its mission was "to foster among its members the growth of healthy ribaldry." The names of the founding committee members are familiar enough: Saussine was appointed archivist, Olivier de Vilmorin treasurer, Vassoigne the "frugal bursar." Saint-Exupéry's name appears at the end of the list of officers; the Count was given the title "Grand Poète Sentimental et Comique." The twenty-six bylaws of the club encouraged bawdiness, principally at table, and distinguished the tasteless humor appropriate to a cheese course from the banter appropriate to dessert. All discussion of politics and religion was banned, doubtless for reasons of aesthetics rather than of etiquette. Duels were authorized, scuffles encouraged, boxing and karate rewarded. In some ways the GB Club resembled all such juvenile associations, down to the official colors and the mascot. In other ways it belonged to a unique time and place: among its official suppliers figured not only a brand of cigarettes but of port, apéritif, *digestif*, and Champagne. (For the last, only certain Roederer and Moët et Chandon labels would do.)

The by-laws guaranteed a warm reception at the rue de la Chaise for all members, and by the end of the fall the Grand Poète Sentimental et Comique—who was evidently not present on June 20, when the club's charter was signed—had begun to take this invitation literally. He put his appointment to work on a familiar and arduous brand of courtship, the same kind he had used on his childhood interests, Odette de Sinéty, the mysterious beauty of Fribourg, and Jeanne de Menthon. This time he had a more appreciative victim. Few young women could have been as inspiring to a poet as was Louise de Vilmorin, and few would have so appreciated that poet's efforts than one who herself effortlessly constructed verse and recited whole libraries by heart. Louise charmed Saint-Exupéry with her fantastic stories; he courted her with sonnets.

They were both of them creatures of whimsy. Louise de Vilmorin was the issue of the same brand of enchanted-garden childhood as was Saint-Exupéry: in her sixties she was said by an admirer to remain still entirely attached to the magic of her childhood. Hers had in part taken place twelve miles southwest of Paris, at Verrières-le-Buisson, in a house with a romantic past of its own. It had been built by Louis XIV in 1680 for another Louise: Mademoiselle de La Vallière lost the King (to Madame de Maintenon) but got the house. What was more, Louise de Vilmorin's education had been blessedly free of such burdens as math, science, Latin, or Greek. She had been raised on a steady diet of letters. Two years before Saint-Exupéry arrived on the scene, her mother had chastised her for her dreaminess, which she thought made her daughter less attractive to men, a subject on which Madame de Vilmorin's expertise was unquestionable.

"You spend your days writing trivial things and looking out the window at what happens in the street. . . . Men don't like that." Louise's "trivialities" were poems or stories. She was known to begin: "The queen of Italy had a cat which was unusual in that it was a ghost-cat," or "There was once a man who married a huge bureau, in each drawer of which was a child." She played the cello, she painted, she doodled. It would have been difficult to imagine a more appropriate Countess de Saint-Exupéry.

Louise's room, like Captain Priou's or the Saussines' salons, was the kind of place in which Saint-Exupéry shone. His radiance was not lost on Louise, for whom he composed a great flurry—some say a formal volume—of poems, the bulk of which she seemed to lose. Twenty-two years later, in a statement as revealing of her voice as her suitor's charms, she described him: "The magician of our adolescence. A minstrel, a knight, a noble magus, a child of mystery, full of grace. Merry and serious, he distributed throughout our quarters—which were entirely those of the time—the customs, the accent, the virtues, the speech, of a province which might have been a neighboring one, but which appeared nowhere on our maps of the world." For a girl who claimed, with reason, that she was not of this world, who struck a friend later as "a tamed sprite who led you, almost illicitly, into a surreal world," it was a perfect match.

It was also an advantageous one. Louise de Vilmorin would have seemed an attractive catch for any man, not least of all an impoverished aristocrat. Her fortune could not have been of less importance to Saint-Exupéry; his lack of fortune was of great concern to the Vilmorins. Perversely, he could not have bothered with a marriage of convenience, although he knew he was expected to (as he put it in a 1928 letter to Louise, "They wanted to marry me off, they wanted me to marry some heiress and lead a peaceful, comfortable life"), and Louise de Vilmorin turned out to be hugely inconvenient. In the fall of 1922, when he had made his intentions known, he was living in an inexpensive hotel in the 12th arrondissement. He was flying at Villacoublay and at Le Bourget, piloting a Nieuport 29 with great delight, offering aerial baptisms to his friends, who obliged him by turning all shades of green. That was the extent of his professional life. His social rounds continued unabated: he saw the Bonnevies, the Vidals, Ségogne, his aunt Anaïs, the Jourdans, and Abbé Sudour. If he wrote of the early days of the relationship with Louise to his mother, whose opinion on all else carried such weight, the letters in which he did so have not been preserved; the first mention of his fiancée dates from 1923. It is almost certain, however, that in late 1922 his mother sent or carried to Paris an heirloom string of pearls intended as an engagement present for Louise. It did not measure up to Vilmorin standards—Louise sent the pearls out to be restrung, at her own expense, although a misunderstanding on the jeweler's part resulted in

Saint-Exupéry's being sent the bill—and constituted an additional strike against a suitor whom Madame de Vilmorin already found less than satisfactory. "If Louise loved him," wrote her brother André, "the same was not true of our mother, who barely understood his conversation, found him boring, and expected a more brilliant match for her daughter." The doting Vilmorin brothers might not have shared all of these concerns— they must have been more susceptible to Saint-Exupéry's magic—but it was difficult under any circumstances to endorse the choice of an aviator husband. Marrying a pilot was tantamount to putting in a claim on early widowhood, reasoned the Vilmorins, who were not alone in thinking the brash young man *"le condamné à mort."* Saint-Exupéry surely knew of these objections, but any arguments he may have made on his own behalf would have been seriously undermined on May 1, 1923, when the laws of nature betrayed him.

According to air force files, Saint-Exupéry took up a fellow second-lieutenant in a Hanriot HD14 that Tuesday morning at Le Bourget, presumably for a holiday joyride. The Hanriot was not an aircraft he was qualified to fly—he was authorized to pilot Caudron 59's—and the plane crashed to earth in a spin from a height of about three hundred feet within a minute of leaving the runway. Saint-Exupéry's passenger, Lieutenant Richaux, suffered a fractured skull; Saint-Exupéry was badly bruised all over, enough so that he would be bothered later by complications of his injuries. He had been entirely at fault; the mangled remains of the aircraft indicated that he had made some crucial mistakes at the controls. At the Hospital Villemin in Paris he found that, though badly shaken up and a little numb, he was alive. "I beg your forgiveness for having complained so much, but take my word for it without attempting the exercise: falling from 270 feet on your head makes you extraordinarily touchy and irritable," he wrote his mother. His sense of humor had not deserted him: he asked that she forward to him any tearful letters she might receive from the family.

He had plenty of visitors, first among them Henry de Ségogne, who was listed as the person to be contacted in case of accident and who appears to have spent most of the next ten days at the side of his friend's hospital bed. Saint-Exupéry reported that he had given the little lecture on his fall so many times that he had memorized the speech and forgotten the crash; it was a narrative technique with which he was to have a good deal of practice. Charles Sallès read in the papers that a "lieutenant Saint-Escupéry" had had a bad accident at Le Bourget, realized instantly that it was his airplane-obsessed Fribourg friend, and met him on his release from the hospital. Only the pilot's sisters remained oddly out of touch; as demanding post-fracture as he had been earlier, Saint-Exupéry wrote his mother that he did not forgive them their silence.

The official reaction to his close call was not exactly a damning one, despite the fact that the pilot was temporarily grounded for "his too-lively interest in trying all types of planes." There are smart and less smart ways to crash-land; today, learning the difference between the two makes up a significant part of a student pilot's education. "Made to be a fighter pilot. Excellent flyer. Inspired," applauded the official report. He was assigned fifteen days of the lightest possible punishment. The reaction to the mishap turned out to be less forgiving than the reaction to the misdemeanor: Louise de Vilmorin sent her sister, Marie-Pierre, to Saint-Exupéry's bedside to announce that Louise could not possibly tolerate a life of such close calls. On her sister's behalf, she demanded that he give up flying. The man who had fallen to earth was head over heels in love. After he had left the hospital but before he was entirely recovered he had agreed to do so.

~

The accident took no toll on Saint-Exupéry's spirits. He installed himself with cousins on the rue de Verneuil and continued on his social rounds, where he could not have wanted for attention. We do not know if he flew again that spring but he ultimately made good on his promise to Louise. On June 5, he was officially released from the military, having served his two years. As a reserve officer his only peacetime obligation to the armed services was to report to Villacoublay or Orly for annual two-week training sessions over the next years, a commitment to which he doubtless looked forward. A letter sent shortly after the accident allows a glimpse of his priorities: he reported on the one hand that his writing had continued apace and that he might have a story published by the NRF, on the other that "There is nothing new in my life because I am spending my days, quietly and sweetly, with Loulou."

All was not entirely well in paradise, however, beginning with Saint-Exupéry's health. Sometime in the summer of 1923 he checked into a clinic at Vichy as a result of the accident. In addition to the usual hydrotherapy, his treatment at the Villa des Acarins consisted, at least at the outset, of a certain amount of movie- and theater-going, story-writing, and chocolate-tasting. (The last could not have been of much help to his liver, which was evidently swollen.) He and Louise had by now settled on a late October or early November wedding, and this resolution seemed to have triggered a volley of objections from the Vilmorin front. The holdout was Louise's mother, although the Vilmorin boys—later referred to as Louise's "general staff of brothers"—did not help. They noticed Saint-Exupéry's appealing sturdiness—a build the French call "*style armoire à glace"* (politely, "a hulking brute")—less than his awkwardness, and took to calling him the "vague pachyderm." Behind the scenes an uncle of Louise's agreed that if the hand-wringing continued he would personally accompany the bride to the altar. He assured the young couple that arrangements could be made for the two to marry without Madame de Vilmorin's consent, if necessary. A Vilmorin family friend, Charles Daniel-Vincent, a former and future Minister of Labor and a decorated World War I aviator, promised to help find Saint-Exupéry a job, but the promise remained an abstract one for some time. Madame de Saint-Exupéry was still funding her son's life; the groom-to-be suddenly began to sound contrite on this subject. He suffered from his separation from Louise, more so after his doctor unexpectedly extended his treatment, concerned about the state of his liver. He had other worries as well: in light of his upcoming nuptials and what he believed to have been true of his father he arranged to be tested for syphilis, the first of many times he would do so. His fear proved entirely unfounded.

It began to get hot in Vichy, which did nothing either for Saint-Exupéry's spirits or his intellect. He felt his wits lagging and claimed he was incapable of so much as a simple pun; he no longer had the energy even to go to the theater. He had no interest in the races at Vichy. He drank and napped and dreamed, poor occupations under his circumstances; he thought only of Louise. "I've been trying to write a story," he wrote his mother. "So far it consists only of one line. And that's just the title. And it isn't even original; it's called 'Story.' "

Late in August the lovers were reunited far from all the concerns their engagement had provoked. Louise had gone to Switzerland with her governess, Mademoiselle Petermann, to recover from a bad cold. In Reconvilier, in the Jura Mountains, Saint-Exupéry joined her. He sold his Kodak in order to make the trip, which was partially financed by his mother as well. Louise wrote of her gratitude for this largesse to Madame de Saint-Exupéry; the two began to dispatch joint letters to Saint-Maurice, often finishing each other's sentences. The cooing and giggling fairly bounce off the page; at the end of one letter Louise complained, veering toward illegibility, that Saint-Exupéry was kissing her so much she could no longer hold the pen. They were happy—Louise assured Madame de Saint-Exupéry that she owed her the happiest days of her life—and in a dreamworld of their own, or at least dreamworlds of their own. As Louise described it, her fiancé the ex-pilot often thought only of aviation: "He describes for me terrifying or sublime moments spent between the sky and the earth, and I, who can think only of furnishing our future home, interrupt him to ask if he likes well-padded chairs."

Other moments of the Swiss idyll were more auspicious. At one point the two escaped from Mademoiselle Petermann, who must have found chaperoning the couple exhausting. Louise re-created the scene years later:

> Secretly, we manage an escape. For a few pennies, we take a little train; in sitting down I am careful not to wrinkle my skirt, I take off my white cotton gloves, and while he watches the birds, the clouds, the celestial currents, I survey the chalets, their starched curtains, the little gardens, and the plants on the embankment. Then, lost in each other's eyes, we trade observations until our arrival in Bienne. The sky is gray, the lake is dulled by black reflections, the day is ominous, and we are cold under the trees. "To warm ourselves, let's buy some chocolates, and smoke a cigarette or two; let's go sit in the train station where the posters are so pretty," he suggests. Couples who are about to separate do not hesitate to kiss in train stations. The whistle of the trains gives the signal to embrace and the lovers, about to leave each other, huddle in each other's arms. Well aware that we are cheating, we do the same.

The two returned to France at the end of the month via Geneva, where the state of their amorous (or natural) distraction was well-displayed. At the sound of military music that afternoon in the Swiss city Saint-Exupéry leaped from the lakeside lunch table, pulling Louise along with him. "Like all the youth born before the war of 1914, we were patriotic," explained Louise, who followed her fiancé through the streets in a daze, dreaming of the French flag, the indignities of the war, the tribulations of Alsace-Lorraine, finally bursting into tears as the music swept over her. Through her sobs she shouted, "*Vive la France!*" only to discover a Swiss flag waving before her. A Geneva regiment was returning from maneuvers in the field.

Back in Paris, at Louise's suggestion, Saint-Exupéry set about reminding Daniel-Vincent about the position he had promised. It was not the kind of persistence at which he excelled; if he undertook this self-promotion now at the insistence of his fiancée he would later entrust these kinds of entreaties as much as possible to women. It is said often enough that there is a woman behind every moment in French history; Saint-Exupéry's very masculine career was, both by default and concentrated effort, often directed by the women in his life. ("My wife's opinion is an invaluable thing," he wrote this fall, his only bald statement on the subject, to his mother.) Daniel-Vincent's devotion to the Vilmorin family paid off—after a number of what Saint-Exupéry politely referred to as "diplomatic calls"—in a position as a production supervisor at the Tuileries Boiron, at 56, rue du Faubourg-Saint-Honoré. He was to occupy himself with bookkeeping tasks, for which effort he earned 800 francs a month, not enough, unfortunately, to make his maternal petitions a thing of the past.

"The practical side of my life is not yet organized," he wrote his mother in a great display of understatement, probably in late September. His office was not far from the place de la Concorde, and the hotels in the heart of Paris were unaffordable on his budget; he stayed in one for a few weeks as an aunt tried to help him arrange an alternative. He was eager for the marriage and found the Vilmorins less disapproving; they had even led him to hope that they might put him up on their return to Paris the following month. Yet the financial problem remained a nagging one. He had borrowed money from family friends, who now balked a little at his requests. He signed a letter to his mother, "Your impoverished son, who has only 3F20 to his name," assuring her that he was living as economically as possible. This was a little untrue. While he was no longer flying he was eating well at the time, and probably displaying his congenital inability to let anyone else pick up the check. He still owed Le Bourget 190 francs from his accident and because of this did not dare see any of his pilot friends. He was lonely, too, as a good number of his other friends, and his fiancée, were still out of town for the summer.

Things began to go seriously awry the following month. Louise returned to Paris, as scheduled, but with second thoughts about the marriage. These were presented to Saint-Exupéry—who did not at first see them for what they were—as medical concerns. Her doctors were worried about the effect childbearing might have on her hip, and the marriage, which had been set for November 1, was postponed for six to eight months. Perhaps Louise's family's objections had begun to wear her down; perhaps Saint-Exupéry's indigence did. She was neither the first nor the last woman to remark that he was impossible to please: "Nothing satisfies Antoine; nothing is perfect; his demands are not limited by reason. He searches out gray areas and misunderstandings." At the beginning of October Saint-Exupéry made the trip to Saint-Maurice for Gabrielle's wedding to Pierre Giraud d'Agay, a Fonscolombe neighbor in the Midi with whom the Saint-Exupérys had been friendly since childhood. Louise was meant to have accompanied him but did not do so, and the young fiancé—who was watching his own nuptials crumble before him—put in a very solemn performance as brother-of-the-bride. His sullenness was much remarked upon and is borne out by photographs of the festivities of the tenth, in which he broods darkly. He was aware of having behaved badly and sent his mother an eloquent explanation—the letter stops just short of constituting an apology—on his return to Paris. She really could not hold his bitterness against him, he wrote; he had had such a difficult time of late. He had now taken the upper hand, however, and promised to be the sweetest son imaginable if she were to visit him in Paris. (He was in a rented apartment on the rue Vivienne.)

Louise went to Biarritz for the winter—the reason given was that some dispute with her paternal grandmother precluded a winter spent closer to

Paris at Verrières—leaving Saint-Exupéry to report that his greatest joy was in his work. From Biarritz he must have had disturbing news about the marriage because he made the trip to the resort town toward Christmastime to "clear things up." Louise was kind with him and asked for a month or two to sort out her thoughts, which were not sorted out in Saint-Exupéry's favor. In his next letter to his mother he begged that she not speak to him at all about the affair, about which he claimed he never again wanted to think, although he did for at least the next ten years. He relied a good deal on Louise's sister, Marie-Pierre—who presumably understood his fiancée better than any of his other confidants—to help him through this period, but was so heartbroken that he went so far as to make a pilgrimage to the Villemin hospital, where he had so much looked forward to his future happiness. He saw Louise again for the first time several years later, when he stumbled upon her getting out of a taxi. She did not see him, but Saint-Exupéry swore that if she had he would have turned away. She was pregnant, but it was he who nearly fainted.

~

Saint-Exupéry had fallen for one of the great seductresses of his time, a woman who energetically lived a line for which she was famous: "*Je t'aimerai, d'amour, toujours ce soir.*" ("I shall love you, forever, tonight.") He was her second fiancé; probably he should have given more thought to the naval lieutenant who preceded him. The same frivolity that endeared Louise to Saint-Exupéry made her perfectly unreliable, as no one knew better than she. "I have no faith in my fidelity," she announced years later. It would be some time before he could bear to see her again, and he was surprised by the persistence of his attachment. In 1925 he felt still that she was the only woman he had met whom he could have married. From Cape Juby two years after that he wrote her frequently, still analyzing her heart and their relationship. "Oh, Loulou, you do weigh heavily!" he remarked at the time. In early 1929 he asked if they might not correspond; he was ready to forgive her even if she were to hurt him from time to time. He promised not to speak to her of love—as he repeatedly had in a series of letters in the intervening five years—although this was not to say he had forgotten what had come before. That, he had to admit, was impossible: "What I need is a happy love affair, but I don't give a damn about any romance save one. That is my illness . . ." he confessed. It was courtship of a kind. He had not stopped sending Louise his literary efforts, and with this letter enclosed a draft of *Southern Mail*, which he hoped she might allow him to dedicate to her. Along with a finished copy of the book he sent a long, explicit love letter. In Louise he confided what he

called the secret of his novel about the airmails: The work amounted to
a conversation with the fairy of an enchanted kingdom, the kind of fairy
she had been for him, who reigned over the kind of kingdom he so wanted
to inhabit. "Do not forget me too much," he closed.

At the time he wrote this letter his ex-fiancée was married and a
mother. Almost inadvertently Louise de Vilmorin had wound up the wife
of an American sixteen years her elder. Henry Leigh Hunt, the son of
Leigh S. J. Hunt, a roving entrepreneur who had made a fortune in mining
in Korea and had gone on to invest heavily in the development of Las
Vegas, had fought for France in the war and became a Vilmorin family
friend. He serenaded Louise with tales of the South American tropics, of
parakeets and monkeys and orchids and birds of paradise. "I should so
much like to see all that," sighed Louise, to which Hunt responded that
she need only marry him to do so. If it seemed she should pay the price
for having broken the heart of a peripatetic aviator she did, albeit briefly:
she was installed in arid Las Vegas in her father-in-law's home while her
husband returned to his business—and the orchids and monkeys and birds
of paradise—in Brazil. This was Las Vegas in the 1920s, a dusty frontier
town of 5,000 people. When Louise strolled down Carson Street to post
her letters at the end of the day the cowboys and miners got off their
horses to whistle as the Frenchwoman passed. She lasted four years, the
better part of two of them in a Santa Fe sanitorium.

Exile had the same effect on Louise de Vilmorin as it had on her ex-
fiancé: she became a writer. Her first novel appeared—with Gallimard,
thanks to Saint-Exupéry, who introduced her to the Lestrange pipeline—
in 1934; she would publish fourteen novels and three volumes of poetry
before her death in 1969. The dedications say a good deal about their
author: Among others, her works are offered as tributes to Orson Welles,
René Clair, and Jean Cocteau. A great number of men, many with celebrated names, waited at the bottom of a great number of staircases for
Louise de Vilmorin, who left no heads unturned. "She knew the sesame
for smiles, the sole password to the heart," wrote Saint-Exupéry of the
heroine of his first novel, *Southern Mail*. Or as another admirer put it,
"She was a woman who well understood the profession of women: to put
men through the paces."

Years later, in one of the odd coincidences that would forever link
together the names of two men who had little to say to each other in their
lifetimes, Louise de Vilmorin became the companion of André Malraux,
with whom she had had a brief liaison in the 1930s. With sly accuracy
she referred to herself as "Marilyn Malraux." The writer and statesman
was a domineering man and Louise's was not an easy role: "Her union
with Malraux," commented the same admirer, "was like the marriage of

a bird and an elephant." At the end of her life, still living with Malraux, she volunteered the names of the five men she had truly loved. Neither of her two husbands, nor Malraux, nor Saint-Exupéry made the list.*

~

The role Louise de Vilmorin played in Saint-Exupéry's sentimental life has been disputed—though never by the men who knew him intimately —but the role she played in his literature is unassailable. Much of the heartbreak over Louise is to be found embedded in *Southern Mail*, a novel that grew like sedimentary rock, the first layer of which probably dates from 1924. Saint-Exupéry had always believed in fairy princesses and now he had known one. The women in his books—aside from Fabian's wife in *Night Flight*, herself described as a little girl—would generally amount to frail, childlike wood sprites, more part of the animal kingdom than of the world of man. Although the published novel is not, the manuscript of *Southern Mail* is indeed dedicated to Louise, for whom Saint-Exupéry confessed he had in part written the book. (The typescript of the story of Bark from *Wind, Sand and Stars* was also dedicated to Louise. Saint-Exupéry was never to dedicate a published book to a woman, however.) *Southern Mail* was in fact a twin tribute, one part written to Louise, one part to aviation, with results as mixed as had been those of the Swiss marriage of padded upholsteries and wind currents. The novel's two primary layers—the love story and the tracking of the ill-fated Paris–Dakar mail—are not, as the critics observed, well-integrated. It is hardly a great novel, but it is a healthy exorcism.

Jacques Bernis, who first appears in "L'Aviateur," and the narrator, mail pilots both, are best friends. The two have lived under the spell of Geneviève since their childhoods. She was their princess of the lindens, the oaks, the flocks; she was the "frail child," the "little girl," the "underwater fairy." She is a thinly disguised Louise, although Saint-Exupéry may also have been thinking of his golden-haired sister Gabrielle. Geneviève was the wellspring of the two men's childhoods, and as the novel opens she appears older, at least chronologically, unhappily married to the pompous Herlin, an insensitive bourgeois who neither appreciates nor understands his prize. After the sudden death of their child—clearly modeled on Gabrielle d'Agay's loss of her son in 1925—she allows the mighty Bernis, "the heavy-footed explorer," to spirit her, "light-footed as the moon," away, an effort that the novel's narrator knows to be futile. Geneviève's existence is founded on "a habit of fortune, of which she's un-

* The winners: Alexandre de Millo, Sacha de Manziarly, Jean Hugo, Gaston Gallimard, and Duff Cooper.

aware," and despite his best intentions Bernis is going to empty her life of "the 1,000 objects one no longer noticed but of which it was composed." Love is one thing, living quite another; Bernis is taking Geneviève away from her Verrières. The narrator's thoughts here are one of the few tributes to pragmatism in the work of Saint-Exupéry, who had clearly learned a lesson from Louise.

The practical world indeed conspires against Jacques Bernis, as it would often enough against his creator. As Bernis carries his prize off into the night, away from Paris and Herlin, the car headlights work badly, the heavens open, a sparkplug dies. He finds he has forgotten a flashlight. The hotels in Sens are shut, or have no vacancies. Freedom proves elusive for Geneviève. She is inextricable from the world of Persian rugs, the bric-a-brac, the well-pressed linens, to which Bernis returns her after a night in a third-rate hotel. "It was as if I had been trying to drag her down beneath the sea," he tells the narrator; their "underwater fairy" turns out to be no mermaid. For Bernis, the sweet enchanted world of which Geneviève was meant to be guardian proves irretrievable as well. Even later, Saint-Exupéry seemed unable to forgive women their growing up. "The day dawns when the woman wakes in the young girl . . . and then an imbecile comes along. . . . And the imbecile drags off the princess into slavery," he would write in *Wind, Sand and Stars*. It is clear from *Southern Mail* that Saint-Exupéry saw in Louise not the great enchantress, not "the smile of superiority, the face which reminded me of all the paintings of French history depicting aristocracy and pride," described by Anaïs Nin, but a kind of child-goddess, a force of nature.

Southern Mail is the only one of Saint-Exupéry's works in which a female character plays a substantial role, unless one counts the rose in *The Little Prince*, the offshoot of another love. Even then the story of the Little Prince and his vain, capricious flower speaks to the debacle that was the Louise affair: It is the misunderstanding with the rose that sends the prince off on his voyage to the planet Earth. Unwittingly Louise in effect supplied the rose's lines in a poem appearing in a volume called *L'Écho des Fantaisies*: "Love me, I am pretty and wise / And will renounce all vanity / If you will take me at your side / To the land of realities." Her work is less easy to parse for signs of the grounded aviator—her sentimental life having been declared one of the most tumultuous of the century—but it should be noted that in the 1958 *Lettre dans un taxi*, a passionless and appropriate marriage also survives the assault of true love.

This was ironic in light of Louise's famous inconstancy. Saint-Exupéry accused her of having an urgent need for a world "in which no action leaves a trace; you feel a near-animal anguish in leaving your footprint on the sand. You are made to live at the bottom of the seas, where no movement disturbs the surface," a judgment with which her brother André concurred. In the end, however, it is Bernis, as he disappears for good over the Sahara, who becomes lighter than air, who leaves no impression on sands so forgiving that they scarcely "retain the light imprint of a child." The light-footed Geneviève leaves an unmistakable trace on the life of Bernis, as the sprightly Louise leaves footprints all over the work of the aviator whom she brings down to earth. It turned out to be she who was bound to the stable world of objects and he who thrived on the ethereal.

~

Louise de Vilmorin's legacy was an ironic one. The effect of the affair was to plunge her ex-fiancé more deeply into the bourgeois world that was anathema to him. From the fall of 1923 to the fall of 1924 he reported every morning to a fifth-floor cubicle at the offices of the Tuileries Boiron. It did not take him long to conclude that "I wasn't made for a twenty-square-foot office"; he referred to this office as his cage. He occupied himself with the bookkeeping and with the filing, a task that seemed to him particularly onerous given the fact that the papers he so carefully filed away were never again consulted.

His primary occupation consisted of the futile effort of urging on the hands of his watch. He waxed supremely eloquent on the subject of boredom: "I've tried every trick to make time fly; I am now a master of the subject," he bragged to Sallès. Staring out the window at the brick wall on the other side of the courtyard proved an ineffective method; the best was to leave an urgent task until the last minute when, with a supervisor breathing down his neck, the clock hands flew like those of a windmill. "It is precisely 11:10. It is precisely 11:11. It is precisely 11:12. I feel as if I am climbing an interminable staircase. It is precisely 11:13 and several seconds. . . . When I think that a little while ago it was four minutes to eleven it gives me hope; I will probably make it to noon." He had no colleagues to whom he could complain; his best friend was the second hand on his watch, the only one that consistently offered the sense that time was indeed passing. He was free for two hours at midday, during which he could, he wrote Sallès, lunch, visit anarchist clubs, make love. Only he had three francs fifty to his name; he would be virtuous and pretend he was being so on principle.

He readily confessed that the job suited him "like an evening gown." His employers were not oblivious to this fact. Saint-Exupéry was forced to abandon his habit of sleeping at his desk—a foolproof method of passing the time—when his boss and a group of executives paid the slumbering employee a visit one day. Some very curious looks must have been exchanged when Saint-Exupéry, startled back to consciousness, awoke with a shriek of "*Maman!*" The management may have thought him crazy but kept him on, and even indulged him a little. In the summer of 1924 he was dispatched to the company's booth at the Paris Fair, where he presented their wares with great dignity. "You would laugh to see me there," he wrote his mother. He himself must have laughed when the company asked him to take some aerial photographs of their factory that June.

The letters sparkle, but the life did not. The young bureaucrat was virtually homeless, bunking in for a few months with Captain Priou, now returned from Morocco, in his apartment on the rue Petit near the Buttes-Chaumont, later making his way from one modest hotel to another. More than anything else he yearned for a place he could call his own, where he could cultivate some of the "*douce intimité*" Louise had provided and on which he thrived. He played the lottery, although the lucky star that was to shine with uncanny constancy on Saint-Exupéry the aviator in distress made no appearance now. The hope that it might, at least, kept him afloat. "Like a broken heart, it keeps you busy," he wrote.

He realized he was stuck—the full impact of his failed exams must have hit him now, as his friends were collecting their advanced degrees —and cast about for a way out of his quandary. One of the few remaining prospects seemed to be journalism, but he had no time to do the reporting (nor for that matter any aptitude for this kind of detail), and the columns open to stringers were hardly enticing. Early in 1924 he heard that China was recruiting flight instructors and thought this might be the answer to his pecuniary difficulties. Doubtless he picked up this bit of news, which came to nothing, at Orly, where he had begun flying again on the occasional Sunday. Twelve hundred feet above the ground, communing with his motor, he was able to forget the miseries of a life that had kept him so much off balance. It was the only subject on which he seemed still inclined to ambitious reverie. "When I am rich," he resolved in a letter to Gabrielle, "I will have a little airplane of my own and will come to visit you at Saint-Raphaël."

He remained, however, as threadbare as ever. His spirits could not have been improved by the news that his mother needed to sell Saint-Maurice—the house had quickly become a financial burden—although he promised to help her do so and thought he might be able to take advantage of the expected arrival of 300,000 Americans in Paris for the 1924 summer Olympics. It was perhaps this news that was responsible for the acute regret he now evinced at the bills he piled up. He began to sound as tired of asking for money as his mother must have been tired of fielding his requests. He made several trips to Saint-Maurice—including one that summer with friends and a second in the fall—but kept all travel to a minimum in light of his limited resources. On one occasion he painfully explained to his mother that were he to journey to the south he would only be forced to ask her again for money the day of his return to Paris. He was equally apologetic with Didi, who had a baby in August and who wrote him asking for a visit. A ticket to the Midi would claim half his monthly salary; to Gabrielle he explained the constraints on his life and replied wistfully that in the course of fifteen months he had seen her only for three days. (The following year the count was equally dispiriting: eight days in two years. "I will probably get to be 100 without having seen the inside of your house or met my nephew again," he wrote.) He accepted an invitation to visit his cousins in Le Mans primarily because it would spare him his living expenses for four days. "I am the most discouraged man in the world," he wrote that summer, probably just before his sister Marie-Madeleine was diagnosed as suffering from epilepsy.

His situation improved a little in the fall. On October 24 he moved to the Hôtel Titania on the boulevard Ornano, one of Paris's less chic addresses. The 18th arrondissement is about as far from the rue de la Chaise or the quai Malaquais as one can get, but it was affordable, and for the next eleven months the Titania provided Saint-Exupéry with a Paris address. He started out with a room on the sixth floor, the tiny balcony of which offered a view of Montmartre and Sacré-Coeur. He was disgusted with these lodgings—as much as he always maintained a distance from the material world his appreciation for comfort never lapsed—although his discontent did not prevent him from prevailing upon Jean Escot to move to the same address when the two ran into each other on the street this winter. Escot was at the time comfortably installed in a furnished room near the École Militaire; he proved as incapable as ever of resisting Saint-Exupéry's will. (This was, after all, the friend who, given a shortage of aircraft, argued, "Let me go first, you know it certainly matters more to me than to you!" and who, before a serving of caviar, bargained, "Leave me the bigger portion, you know I like it more than you do!") Shortly after Escot's arrival Saint-Exupéry managed to flood his room—he may have been perfecting the technique he would use later at Yvonne de Lestrange's—and was resettled in more luxurious quarters on the fourth floor. These soon disappeared under the detritus of his life. He wrote his mother that she would have to come and live with him when he was rich; as things stood he hadn't the courage to separate his shirt collars from his socks.

He also wrote her in the fall with the happy news that he was very close to getting a new job, this one in the automotive industry. "It will be my first joy in a year," wrote the man who had astutely pointed out elsewhere that no two joys resemble each other. This was a different kind of pleasure from the one he had anticipated the previous autumn, but it was consolation of a kind. He was rescued from his bookkeeping by the Saurer truck company, which hired him in October as a traveling salesman at what seemed to Saint-Exupéry the munificent salary of 12,000 francs yearly, an annual commission of about 25,000 francs, and a company car. The position began with a three-month training period (Saint-Exupéry mistakenly thought it two months long) at a salary more in keeping with his Boiron wage. Decked out in a pair of blue workman's overalls, he learned, piece by greasy piece, the secrets of a truck engine. Proudly he reported to Sallès that he felt capable of disassembling his friend's Citroën single-handedly. This was the kind of engineering school at which Saint-Exupéry excelled, although it was not the kind of engineering school the privileged generally attended. French news magazines can today eke out cover stories on the number of aristocrats working for the Parisian transit authority, a still-fascinating subject, but in the 1920s a count in overalls was an unusual sight. Of all the ill-fitting uniforms Saint-Exupéry wore in his life, none was more inappropriate than the workman's blues with which he now claimed to be enchanted. The language of the mechanics charmed him too with its earthiness; he found the fast wit of the garage irresistible. "*Je me porte*," he wrote home, "*comme le Pont-Neuf*" ("I'm a new man").

He was no longer bored, but exhausted. The Saurer plant was located in Suresnes, now a western suburb of Paris, at the time a good hour and a half from the Titania doorstep. When the hotel porter and Escot succeeded in their herculean efforts, Saint-Exupéry awoke between 5:30 and 6:00 so as to travel across the Bois de Boulogne to Suresnes as the winter sun began to rise. Between the work and the commute thirteen hours of his day were spoken for, which left him the time to have dinner and the time to delay Escot's night's sleep but not the energy to write. It was not exactly a life of letters—he complained he no longer read or wrote—but he was, oddly, in his element. It was his first taste of working with his hands, on a team, in an unacademic setting, and he relished it. The joys of vocational school did not change him entirely: He continued to rent an airplane at Orly on Sundays when he could afford to and doubtless as well when he could not. He often enough defied all efforts to rouse him and had to race to Suresnes in a taxi, a trip that could put a dent in any budget. He lobbied for a significant sum to "*refaire son trousseau*," a somewhat literal plea as he had not had a new suit since his discharge from the army.

Early in the winter of 1925 he traded his overalls for a suit and made a two-week tour of northern France with a colleague who was to teach him the art of the traveling salesman. Afterward he was dispatched to Montluçon, the headquarters from which he was to cover three departments of central France: the Creuse, the Cher, and the Allier. These first few weeks as a traveling salesman were for Saint-Exupéry giddy ones. Although he did not yet have a car and was at first forced to travel by

train he was solvent, employed, independent, mobile. For the next months
he rarely spent two consecutive nights in the same place, moving from
hotel to hotel, café to café, racing back to Paris whenever his schedule
permitted. In such a way he made the close acquaintance of the third-
rate hotels to which Jacques Bernis applied with Geneviève, the kind with
"special rates for traveling salesmen." On the road, save for a visit by
Henry de Ségogne and a number of excursions he made with Charles
Sallès in Sallès's 5CV—excursions that generally kept the duo out until
dawn—he was alone. It was an existence he described, with jubilation and
frustration, as an exile, "*une cure de silence*," that of a pilgrim, the wandering Jew. It was, down to the *poste restante* Montluçon address, all of
it a rehearsal for another life.

Saint-Exupéry was a man who needed an audience, and it was his
friends and family who kept him afloat, as much when he was in Paris
as on the road. The letters he dispatched during the Saurer year have few
rivals and constitute early proof that—as he was to argue as loudly as any
writer of our century—a writer is well off employed. Their letterheads
provide a stylish map of the itinerant year: he wrote on elaborate Beaux-
Arts stationery from the Hotel Aucouturier in Boussac, from the Grand
Hôtel du Boeuf in Vierzon, from the office of a mechanic in Monteil-au-
Vicomte, from a café-restaurant in Bourges. He prepared his friends and
family well for the flurry of letters they would ultimately receive from Port-
Étienne, Dakar, Buenos Aires, Punta Arenas; through his eyes the Saurer
rounds became themselves a kind of *tour du monde*. These letters begin
to reveal that he lived to a different rhythm. He occasionally overcame his
lifelong aversion to dating his correspondence—something of a statement
in a culture in which it is as customary to date a letter as to sign one—
during this year on the road, when time did not exactly fly. "The I-haven't-
the-foggiest-idea," he began one later. "Midnight sharp, is it tomorrow
or yesterday?" he dated another. "The twentieth century," he marked a
note to Escot in which he sketched portions of the three legs of his journey
from Paris to Vierzon, the last leg of which is illustrated by a fat black
square, "because it was nighttime."

In a letter dated "the day after yesterday," he reported on a meeting
with a potential client who had put him off with the promise of buying a
truck at a future date. "I don't give a damn about later; I will already have
died of hunger," grumbled Saint-Exupéry, who included in this lavishly
illustrated letter a prototype of the Little Prince's tippler, meant to illustrate
the commercial traveler at rest. Escot's missives in particular very nearly
resemble comic strips: Saint-Exupéry illustrated his toothache, and the
main street of Bourges; he provided a sketch of himself in bed (in an
uncharacteristic lapse of imagination he indicated the position of his
guardian angel but claimed he could not draw her). He provided a little

bar graph of how the traveling salesman spent his time, the bulk of which was devoted to putting people back in their places, the smallest fraction of which to interesting reading.

Life in the provinces left something to be desired in the eyes of this ex-provincial, who turned to it both a caricaturist's eye and an anthropologist's ear. For Escot he drew the symbols of provincial life (a calendar draped in spider webs) and of Parisian life (a speedometer powered by a 300-horsepower engine, held in place by a naked woman). An illustration of a Bourges café shows an empty room and is marked "The annual client has just left." He had a little irreverence meter that went off whenever he encountered the self-important or the self-satisfied, and it rang a good deal this year. He confided to Sallès his terror of defacing the ornate stationery of the Café Riche: "What a responsibility to write on this paper! It comes from the most important café in Montluçon, what presumption on my part!" He was taken with the accents, the mores, the foibles of *la France profonde* and described to Sallès a Montluçon "full of little shopkeepers who travel twenty yards in their lives. The grocer, the fruit vendor, the undertaker all fit in a tiny space. Existence can amount to such a short trip." This was his first close encounter with the life of the *petite bourgeoisie*—what some might call the real world—and it was an eye-opener.

He could be charmed, too, by the quaintness of provincial France, as he was by a dance he and Sallès attended. They had thought a Montluçon gathering would be great fun but arrived to find no bar, no cocktails, no jazz. At the "*sous-préfet's* ball" one *waltzed*, under the protective eyes of the girls' mothers, who lined the four walls of the room, surveying the proceedings like a jury. This "old guard" chatted pleasantly among itself while their daughters twirled away on the dance floor. Their escorts, a group of cyclists, sported stiff dinner jackets reeking of mothballs; they pulled at their sleeves, checked their reflections in the mirrors, tried to make peace with their scratchy, starched collars. On the subject of Argenton-sur-Creuse, a hamlet disturbed only every four hours by the noise of its tiny steam train, Saint-Exupéry was equally rhapsodic. One afternoon he settled on the parapet of the town's old stone bridge after a walk. "I set my hat down beside me and felt a great sense of freedom. As did my hat—it is at present sailing toward America. I watched it slowly head off, intelligently take a curve, then disappear," he wrote after watching his Sainte-Croix essay come to life, bewitched as always by objects carried off by the wind. As much as anything else these letters were desperate attempts to amuse himself. Within months of his arrival in Montluçon he admitted to being bored silly: "My life is empty. I get up, I drive, I have my lunch. I have dinner, I think of nothing. It's sad."

He was not made to be a traveling salesman any more than he was to be a bureaucrat; there was more genius in the letters than in the sales-

manship. It has been postulated that the aristocrat was ill-adapted for
survival in a consumer society because doing business defied the laws of
the Old World: an aristocrat-salesman opened himself up to rejection by
a member of the *bourgeoisie*, empowering the customer—in this case the
general public—at the expense of the vendor, the traditional leader. Probably as much on account of his thin skin as on account of his name Saint-
Exupéry found his rounds difficult. "Customers are selfish," he concluded,
sketching a bug-eyed manager seated in an office decorated with a gun
display and a salesman-skin rug. The company safe sported a sign that
read: "Don't even bother. The keys are lost." It was a life of rebuffs and
dead ends, and he was as hilarious on the subject of his lack of aptitude
for it as on any subject. He asked Escot to pray to Saint Fiacre for him.
He closed a letter with a tombstone marked "Here lies the last Saurer
customer. RIP."

He did not report on his triumphs because there were none. In his
year or so on the road Saint-Exupéry sold, depending on the account,
somewhere between one truck and no trucks at all. (The average Saurer
salesman took a commission on three to four trucks monthly.) If his position was ever in jeopardy he was saved by the very traits that proved so
undesirable in a salesman. He had a reputation as an artist, an eccentric,
a practical joker, but the head of the company happened to have the soul
of a poet and a weakness for eccentrics. He could not discuss Baudelaire
with most of his employees; he had reason not to discuss sales figures with
Saint-Exupéry. This was not the last time Saint-Exupéry would benefit
from the place of honor in which France places literature. Despite all the
country's rigorous categorizing, her politicians are commonly published
authors, her generals are members of the Académie Française, and the
intelligentsia sits close to the seat of power. To take as examples only
some of those whose paths Saint-Exupéry crossed, at the Vilmorins' or
later: Poincaré was elected to the Académie Française; Herriot had been
a professor of literature and in any capacity sounded the part; de Gaulle
was an intellectual who had fallen out with Pétain when he got too noisy
about the volumes he had ghostwritten for his mentor; Vilmorin was said
to be able to recite *Ubu roi* by heart; Pierre-Georges Latécoère collected
rare books.

In the end, late in the winter of 1926, Saint-Exupéry left Saurer of his
own volition. He appears to have done so without any visible prospects,
although he had an idea at the time that his literary efforts were soon to
pay off. Otherwise the future remained uncertain. He returned to Paris,
where he had never entirely fit in and where he now fit in less than ever.
As often as he had been able to during the Saurer exile he had rejoined
his Parisian friends. He did so in the manner that would become Jacques

Bernis's, slowly finding that "After so long an absence one loses one's place, one is no longer at home." He learned that a stranger who comes to town provokes curiosity and that a stranger who comes to the city has to earn this attention. To his mother he wistfully described his homecomings, almost exactly in the words with which he would paint Bernis's in *Southern Mail*. He returned to the metropolis—still before he was to become one—"like an explorer from Africa." He called around, only to find that life had gone on without him, that his friends were busy or out of town. In *Southern Mail*, Bernis goes off to a dance hall; in 1926, Saint-Exupéry fell back on the ever-accommodating Jean Escot, whom he dragged off to the cinema—and out of the cinema in mid-film if the feature did not meet with his expectations—or kept up late. (The films that most seemed to delight were Chaplin's *The Pilgrim* and Murnau's *The Last Laugh*.) One evening early in the year he sat Escot down in the Café Napolitain and watched as he read his story "L'Aviateur." He then drilled him on his reactions. He saw a certain amount of his sister Simone, who was studying in Paris to be an archivist and was as engrossed in her work as her brother was indifferent to his. He discovered that there is nothing longer than a rainy Paris Sunday spent alone.

The *beau monde* slowly welcomed him back, but the truth of the matter was that Saint-Exupéry had lost his taste for their life. Probably the lingering memory of the broken engagement soured him in part. He began to complain of the posturings and chatterings of various factions of the idle upper class, which he now referred to as "*cette fausse culture*." His disdain for the life of a gigolo found its origins here. He savaged this world in a letter to his mother: "I don't like people who feel chivalrous when they dress up as musketeers for a costume ball." She thought he was being difficult. He insisted, however, on the virulence of this new allergy, and began to talk a good deal about the supremacy of the interior life, which he opposed to the flamboyant, rigged-up emotions of the drawing room. This world seemed the only one of any integrity, although he knew this was not a socially convenient address. "You must forgive me for not being accessible and for remaining so much inside myself," he wrote his mother. Idle conversation bored him; facile reasoning angered him; pretention and posturing silenced him; public revelations of intimate details made him roar. He could be garrulous but remained entirely mute—on paper and in conversation—on the subject of his personal life. He was so in late 1925, when Gabrielle lost her infant son, as well as in the summer of 1926, when Marie-Madeleine died and he watched his mother bury a second child. "The more intimate the feeling, the more I am unable and the more I find it repugnant to show it," he wrote her later by way of explanation, although he would not always be so apologetic about his silences. He did not hesitate to condemn those who violated his code, or failed to appreciate it, or who lived grandly and publicly. To his mother's extreme displeasure, he was particularly vitriolic on the subject of certain family members, whom he found hypocritical. He complained that she could not expect him to like this kind of person.

Saint-Exupéry's impatience with all that glittered extended to his views of literature. He had begun to offer literary counsel to Bertrand de Saussine's lovely sister Renée in the fall of 1923, when his engagement was unraveling. "One needs to learn not to write but to see," the unpublished poet had advised, with feeling, that fall. Three and a half years later he was proclaiming, "One needs to live in order to write." The relationship narrowly escaped a premature end when Renée's elder sister dared to compare Pirandello to Ibsen in a *salon de thé* one afternoon. "*Métaphysique de concierge*," muttered Saint-Exupéry, upsetting a café table as he stormed out of La Dame Blanche, leaving a silenced restaurant in his wake. He could not forgive Pirandello for allowing the theatergoer the illusion of thought; he felt the playwright misled his audience by allowing them to toy with metaphysics with the same ease with which they might manipulate a deck of cards. Nothing was more unforgivable in his mind than this kind of facility. He worried that glibness too easily obscured meaning, that we learned how to write well and to speak well but not to reason well. He detested people who wrote to amuse themselves, who "concerned themselves overly with style," and fell out with Marc Sabran on this subject. Only one thing mattered to a writer: "One needs," insisted the twenty-four-year-old, "to have something to say."

His Saurer year distanced him, too, from his past in that it made him something of a populist. Already in 1924 he had begun to romanticize squadron life: "I have never loved anything so much as that life of a draftee, that affectionate camaraderie with the mechanics and the clerks. I even loved that prison in which we sang all those lugubrious songs." This seemed a curious statement coming from the soldier who would daily escape the Strasbourg barracks for his apartment in town. It was his first paean to the community of men, the kind of statement on which his reputation was later staked. Not unimportantly, it was written—to his mother—while he was still in his Boiron cage. He had been blissfully happy among the Saurer mechanics, who probably had not known what to make of him. He had not been slumming; he needed a job. But he had not needed to be seduced by this one. He was reacting to a heartbreak, to the frivolous society that had caused it, to a world in which he had no place and now knew that he desperately wanted one. There was no pretense at Saurer, no gratuitousness. "Café society never taught me anything," he wrote Renée de Saussine in the same letter in which he reduced

Pirandello's art to metaphysical froth. "I like people who have been tied more closely to life by the need to eat, to feed their children, and to survive until the end of the month. They are wiser." Jean Escot was not the only friend to note that Saint-Exupéry preferred to talk to an honest street sweeper than to a cultured man-about-town. He would always be an elitist—it was in his bones—but he had now sounded his democratic version of the seigneurial battle cry.

None of the months following the broken engagement favored literary effort and yet they were months that introduced Saint-Exupéry to his themes. He learned an enormous amount from his two insular years marked by purposelessness, loneliness, homelessness. He grew more and more impatient with the comfortable life out of which he had, sometimes unintentionally, so many times now opted. The unpaid bills, the uncertain future, the unhappy heart, the vanishing youth were godsends; they were the first labors to teach him what cyclones and sandstorms and a fledgling mail service would, in years to come, appear to have taught him. They turned him around, though not in the direction in which he was born to have headed. Originally of necessity, he developed a respect for that which made a man labor. The French edition of *Wind, Sand and Stars* opens with a tribute to "the obstacle." Just as only an ex-loner could convincingly sing the praises of camaraderie, only a man who had very nearly fallen through the cracks of the system could write with passion of the tragedy of wasted potential, a situation Saint-Exupéry immortalized as "*Mozart assassiné.*"

For years Saint-Exupéry had lobbied for financial support with the plea that he could not live at odds with the world. In French this is phrased more poetically: "*Je ne peux pas vivre comme un ours*" ("I cannot live like a bear"). It was precisely the opposite advice Flaubert had offered the aspiring nineteenth-century writer: "Break with the world. *Il faut vivre comme un ours,*" and Saint-Exupéry, the idler who came to appreciate the preeminence of action, the indulged, profligate son who would make a near-religious appeal for the stoic, responsible life, began after two miserable years to see the wisdom in it. An aristocrat in a republic that no longer had a use for one, he was from the start at odds with his world. He may have been born privileged, but not to the world to which he now aspired. If family connections made him a writer sooner than he might otherwise have been there was nothing preordained about a Saint-Exupéry piloting an airplane. On this count his name and his station conspired against him. It took all of Saint-Exupéry's tenacity to overcome the advantages of his birth; doing so was one of his greatest achievements. His education, the expectations of his family, the demands of a socially prominent fiancée took him far out of his way. When Gallimard first considered bringing out a collection of his work during the winter of 1925 Saint-Exupéry was a traveling salesman. In April 1926, when *Le Navire d'Argent* published him for the first time, the author of "L'Aviateur" was an ex-pilot. Evidently it was his nostalgia for the air that captured the attention of the magazine editor who signed him on.

VII

~

Friends in High Places
1926

*There is nothing I dread more in life than being
bound by the opinions of other people and being
tied to a permanent routine.*
                    CHARLES LINDBERGH,
     The Wartime Journals of Charles A. Lindbergh

Jean Prévost, the literary editor of *Le Navire d'Argent*, met Saint-Exupéry
for the first time at Yvonne de Lestrange's during the second half of 1925.
In a drawing room frequented by Gaston Gallimard, André Gide, and
Jean Schlumberger the two men were very much the youngsters; side by
side, especially in a salon full of lovely, fragile objects, they would also
have looked like visiting *footballeurs*. Prévost was another *armoire à glace*,
thick-necked, large-faced, and broad-shouldered; aware that his parents
lived in the Champagne, Gide nicknamed him "the wild boar of the
Ardennes." Both physically and intellectually, he resembled a charging
bull. Prévost prided himself on his athletic ability and was the only Frenchman who enjoyed a regular boxing match with Hemingway, whose robust
prose he championed early on. In the first of these encounters Hemingway
broke his thumb on Prévost's skull; later he admitted to F. Scott Fitzgerald
that he had made special arrangements with the timekeeper to cut the
rounds short were Prévost to pummel him without mercy. (On at least one
occasion their referee put an end to a two-minute round after forty-five
seconds.) Years later, when Saint-Exupéry took Prévost up in his Simoun,
the two men's combined weights posed a problem. Before one takeoff
Saint-Exupéry hastily scribbled on the cover of a book Prévost had brought
aboard, "Go sit in the back."

    If Prévost was the first Frenchman to begin a literary career in the
realm of athletics—his first book, *Plaisirs des sports: Essais sur le corps*

humain came out this year—he was, unlike the Saurer salesman, no misfit in the world of letters. A graduate of the École Normale Supérieure, as close to a breeding ground for an intelligentsia as exists, Prévost had a prodigious memory, especially for verse, which he was said to be able to recite for forty-eight hours straight. This brand of genius was not always a winning one: Marcelle Auclair, who also met Saint-Exupéry at this time and would become Prévost's wife the following year, once informed her husband that he could easily be replaced by a sports coach and the *Encyclopaedia Britannica*. Prévost had every reason to be proud and easily found reason to be temperamental, if not downright disrespectful. He had a famous intolerance, for example, for Gide, another of Saint-Exupéry's early advocates. The relationship with Saint-Exupéry, whose lack of presumptuousness and refinement would in themselves have won him over, seems to have been cemented in song: both commanded a vast repertoire of old French songs and delighted each other—as well, presumably, as Yvonne de Lestrange's other guests—by pulling one after another of these forgotten tunes out of their oversized hats.

Prévost's affection for Saint-Exupéry took the form of that of an older brother for a younger, which says something about how the truck salesman, taller and a year older than the editor, must have come across in his cousin's living room. To Prévost as to other intimates later in life, Saint-Exupéry was known by his childhood name; Yvonne de Lestrange would almost certainly have introduced him as "Tonio." Early on Prévost learned of Saint-Exupéry's writing—this was no secret at Yvonne de Lestrange's, where Gallimard had talked with him about a collection of stories earlier in the year—and expressed an interest in his work on behalf of *Le Navire d'Argent*, the literary magazine he had edited for Adrienne Monnier since the previous June. In the note that follows "L'Aviateur" Prévost gives a sense of the haphazard way Saint-Exupéry found his way into print: "I met him through friends, and had long admired the force and the finesse with which he described his impressions when I learned that he had written them down. I had a great interest in reading them; I think that he lost his manuscript, then reconstituted it from memory. (He composes everything in his head before setting it down.)" Clearly, Prévost, as well equipped as anyone could have been to appreciate Saint-Exupéry and his tales of adventure—traditionally there is as little nature as sport in French literature—had not had to lay siege to the famous ramparts. He had had his ear talked off.

In the late winter Saint-Exupéry put the finishing touches on his story, part of a larger tale called "L'Évasion de Jacques Bernis" on which he had been working for some time. Some part of it had been offered, unsuccessfully, to the *Nouvelle Revue Française* in 1924; subsequently it had turned into a loosely constructed novel. In a vastly reworked version,

Jacques Bernis's story, simmering all of these years as if in wait for a plot, would become *Southern Mail*. Generous as ever, Saint-Exupéry had shared the manuscript of his work-in-progress with his friends in 1925. Bonnevie and Sabran professed great admiration for it. Escot, who had read "L'Aviateur" with Saint-Exupéry hovering over him just before its author was scheduled to share it with Prévost, pronounced it fine. Saint-Exupéry agreed to deliver his pages to Prévost at the Deux-Magots, one of the literary watering holes of the 1920s and '30s. Prévost appeared at the appointed time at the Place Saint-Germain-des-Prés but the aspiring writer did not, and the editor ultimately left the café empty-handed. When he stopped by several hours later a sheaf of papers awaited him; so it was that the honor of submitting Saint-Exupéry's first published story to its editor fell to the Deux-Magots cashier. Unconsciously this time, Saint-Exupéry had managed to leave his affairs in the hands of a woman. This arrangement may have been for the best as the accompanying submission letter ranks among the least enticing ever written:

> Dear Sir: I regret to have missed you and leave you herewith my aviation story. I've corrected a few typing errors, but many have doubtless escaped me. If you find anything idiotic, blame it on me. There are a few errors in detail, especially in punctuation—I know nothing of these things—and if something strikes you as off please do tell me. If you want to be truly wonderful read this quickly; I am so eager to know what you think. I leave both you and the inviting bistro from which I write. I shall hope to see you soon. Saint-Exupéry

Prévost must have read the story quickly; the nonmeeting would have taken place in January or February and "L'Aviateur" appeared in *Le Navire*'s April 1926 issue. Prévost introduced its author as "an aviation and mechanical expert," as good a description as any of the reserve air force lieutenant (he had been promoted in January) and former truck salesman. France is not a country in which aviators or truck salesmen publish—especially in a literary review alongside Rilke, Blaise Cendrars, and Martin Luther—and Saint-Exupéry was in any event unemployed in the spring. "L'Aviateur" reads as a pastiche of several tales, the first of which finds Jacques Bernis, after a splendid flight, making his familiar, poignant return to the city in which he feels so much an alien. Nearly word for word this passage finds its way into *Southern Mail*. The second capitalizes on the inherent drama of flight: An airplane one of Bernis's students has taken up has not yet come down when a thick fog rolls in. Mortier—"who flies like a pig"—botches his landing as Bernis, on the ground, hisses, "Shut down, shut down, shut down" through clenched teeth. Mortier crashes; a group of soldiers gathers awkwardly around the wounded pilot. Bernis, who exhibits the discipline and reserve Saint-

Exupéry would lend *Night Flight*'s steely Rivière, dismisses them all with a gruff professionalism that the author clearly already admired. When a second student, proud to have witnessed this brush with death, assures his instructor that he will in no way be deterred from flying the next day, Bernis refuses to applaud his courage. He shrugs off the tragedy as a common, work-related incident. In the last section of the story Bernis is himself sacrificed to the sport when—contrivedly—the left wing of his plane snaps off after a spontaneous display of acrobatics. The story proves equally brittle; the pieces do not add up to a whole, and the metaphors creak loudly. But already the twenty-six-year-old author had begun to articulate his favorite theme. Bernis, lunching in the pub near the military airstrip, listens in on the pilots' conversations. He delights in the contrast between the brutal heroism of their exploits and the modesty of their language. Among them it is possible, he thinks, to be simple: *"Ils font un métier. J'aime ces hommes."* ("They have a métier. I like these men.")

Toward those who made literature their métier Saint-Exupéry was less drawn. All of the critical, early encounters of his literary career took place on the quai Malaquais—it was here that he met Prévost, Gallimard, Gide, and Ramon Fernandez—but the center of literary Paris was a ten-minute walk away, up the rue Bonaparte, past the Deux-Magots, east a few blocks along the boulevard Saint-Germain to the celebrated rue de l'Odéon. Resonating between Sylvia Beach's Shakespeare and Company at number 12 and Adrienne Monnier's Maison des Amis des Livres, the seat of *Le Navire d'Argent*, at number 7 was the epicenter of Parisian literary activity. On April 20, en route to the opening reception of a Walt Whitman exhibit at Shakespeare and Company, James Joyce termed this vibrant corner of the world Stratford-on-Odéon, an epithet that stuck. Beach's guests that evening included Paul Valéry, Schlumberger, Valery Larbaud, Prévost and Auclair, T. S. Eliot, Monnier, Harry and Caresse Crosby, Hemingway, and Ezra Pound. In short it was a fine cross-section of the international literary community that had invaded postwar Paris. Had Saint-Exupéry attended the reception (he had not been invited) he might have met Lewis Galantière, who was to become his English-language translator, a stalwart support during his American years. Like Hemingway, he was, however, just on the brink of success. (The all-American March issue of *Le Navire* had been the first to introduce Hemingway to the French, with a short story; *The Sun Also Rises* was published in America in 1926.) Saint-Exupéry did not speak English, and by his mid-twenties had largely lost his taste for fiction. His impatience with clever conversation probably did not exempt the shop talk of writers. We have no evidence that he read any of the authors whom Beach and Monnier and *Le Navire* championed—he makes no bows to Whitman, Eliot, Hemingway, or Joyce—and certainly he did not socialize with the latter three. Singing old

French songs with his boxing partner was as close as Saint-Exupéry seems to have got to Hemingway, although the two writers' paths would cross again and their works would inevitably be classed together after their deaths. While it is easy to imagine Saint-Exupéry at Monnier's table, feasting on her famous roast chicken in the dining room above the shop, we have no reason to think that he did so. At her address he may briefly have met Léon-Paul Fargue, for whom a place was always set at Monnier's table and with whom he would while away a good deal of time in the 1930s, or André Maurois, a closer friend in American exile than on French soil, or Léon Werth, to whom *The Little Prince* was dedicated. If so, he left no lasting impression on these men of letters now.

As much as his inclusion in *Le Navire* allowed Saint-Exupéry some entrée to Stratford-on-Odéon, it was very much a closed world. The Republic of Letters, wrote the influential essayist Jean Guéhenno later, "is wholly contained in a few Parisian houses, some cramped magazine or publishing offices, some drawing rooms, some cafés, some artists' studios, some attic rooms. It is not easy to penetrate this world. The real dialogue takes place between a few dozen writers who acknowledge each other, and that is all." There was a bias against those writers who lived on the wrong bank (or as Gaston Gallimard's biographer has put it, one could not pretend to have "*l'esprit NRF*" and live on the Right Bank), who published with the wrong houses, who frequented the wrong cafés. If Saint-Exupéry was not entirely of the literary village of Saint-Germain— one that would, by 1935, turn into the world's artistic crossroads and one that, with his connections, he could more easily have entered than could many others—this, too, was by choice. A man with a great thirst for fraternity, he disliked clubbiness, and Saint-Germain of the 1920s was a particularly inbred community, as all-consuming as it was small. When Jean Prévost wrote to Marcelle Auclair's parents to ask for their daughter's hand in marriage he did so on *Navire d'Argent* letterhead. When the two married in April 1926, one week after Beach's Whitman exhibit, François Mauriac and Ramon Fernandez stood up for them. Both the bride and the groom published with Gallimard; their first marital home was a closet in Monnier's shop. Yvonne de Lestrange was the godmother of their daughter, Françoise; she also happened to be a particularly close friend of Fernandez's. This was literature as occupation as well as social obligation; to some the insularity of Saint-Germain represented its charm. The appeal of the close quarters of the *super-gratin littéraire* was lost, however, on a writer who craved action and who would on all occasions refuse the opportunity to play the intellectual. If there was one thing Saint-Exupéry hated it was a small world.

After Prévost took "L'Aviateur," Renée de Saussine—who, along with Saint-Exupéry's other friends, had very much suffered from his Saurer position along with him—breathed a sigh of relief. So the great versifier was to be a writer at last! Nothing doing, countered Saint-Exupéry; writing came as a consequence of experience. Once again, he began a search for gainful employment.

~

In the summer General Édouard Barès, who not only oversaw the Centre d'Études d'Aéronautiques at Versailles but also commanded military aviation in the Paris region, lent a hand, arranging for Saint-Exupéry to join the Compagnie Aérienne Française (CAF), a commercial airline specializing in tourist flights at Le Bourget. (General Barès had long been, by way of both his mother and sister, a Saint-Exupéry family friend; his word with the CAF—staffed primarily with army-trained pilots—was golden.) The position marked a turning point for Saint-Exupéry: for the first time he was to fly for a living. On June 23 he received his airline transport rating, still a relatively rare license that permitted its bearer to carry passengers. In retrospect he acknowledged the General's intervention as the godsend it was: without him, Saint-Exupéry wrote in Barès's copy of *Wind, Sand and Stars*, he would not have entered commercial aviation, would not have known the métier, would never have flown with Aéropostale, or written this book.

On July 10 Saint-Exupéry began a series of training flights on a Dorand AM-1, a biplane that had been produced in quantity for wartime reconnaissance missions. Two weeks later he took up his first passenger for a scenic circuit over Paris, a flight that would have cost about 150 francs. It lasted twenty-two minutes. Aerial baptisms lasted for six, and he generally did not fly more than twice daily; his logbook began, like a dance card, to fill up with these short excursions, but his was not a hugely demanding life. He rarely spent more than an hour in the air a day and did not work regularly, which left him plenty of time to visit with his friends. Probably he flew as often as any other CAF pilot; he brought the same fierce logic with which he had so often bullied Escot to bear on Madame Fontaine, the CAF manager in charge of flight assignments. "Madame, let me fly! I will give you cigarettes!" proposed the new recruit. "Monsieur, I don't smoke, but you may do the next baptism!" promised the incorruptible Madame Fontaine.

The CAF position provided some consolation during a difficult summer. Marie-Madeleine had died during the first week of June, in the end of tuberculosis, and Madame de Saint-Exupéry did not bear the loss of her firstborn easily. From the lack of correspondence between Saint-Exupéry and his mother it seems fair to speculate that he spent some portion of the early summer in Saint-Maurice. There is no record of where he lodged in Paris at the end of his Saurer tenure; although he gave the Titania as his address on at least one occasion the hotel's ledgers show him as having ended his stay there in late 1925. He may have camped out again on the quai Malaquais. He was no more flush, on the CAF's meager wage, than he had been before. While he had a published story to his credit these were years when it took a good deal to set the literary world on end; he had hardly done so, and did in any event not dwell on this success. His family alone allowed itself to be impressed by his publication: Saint-Exupéry complained to Escot that the relatives who had so long despaired of him had suddenly begun to search him out. (It should be said that these were the same relatives who had generously offered him funds and lodging in the past.) Moreover, *Le Navire* had, with its May issue, ceased publication. Its year of life had so bankrupted Adrienne Monnier that in mid-May she was forced to sell her private library—"with sadness and humiliation"—to meet the expenses. Again and again the world seemed to disappear out from behind Saint-Exupéry; as much as the theme of his work was progress the theme of his life was often nostalgia. There was something sadly appropriate about the fact that he should make his literary debut in *Le Navire*'s penultimate issue.

Famously, Paris played host to a batch of young expatriates who, in music and letters and café life, reenergized the city. The Surrealists drank loudly at the Dôme; George Antheil, Paul Robeson, and Josephine Baker sent the musical and theatrical worlds spinning; the book-making on the rue de l'Odéon further kept the neighborhood humming. American jazz was, however, the wrong soundtrack in 1926 for Saint-Exupéry, who was beginning to feel his age. This was partly in contrast to his friends, who had now begun to settle down; partly because he was losing his hair, a fact that had troubled him for several years, although if anything he now seemed to have grown into his awkward body and was better-looking than he had been. He wrote his mother that nothing made him happier than an exclamation over his youth; he needed terribly to feel young. There was no disguising his loneliness. More and more often he expressed a desire to marry. He was sick of "this perpetually temporary life"; he wanted children, "*beaucoup de petits Antoines.*" However, he lamented, he had only met one woman to whom he had been tempted to make this commitment.

On the subject of domestic bliss Saint-Exupéry was of two minds. He wavered between thinking of being ill at ease as an artistic advantage and as a disease. He told his mother that what he hoped for in a woman was above all someone who could calm his anxiety. "That's what one needs most. You cannot imagine how life weighs heavily, how useless one's youth can feel. You cannot imagine what a woman can offer, what she would be able to offer," he wrote to one woman who surely did know. In the same letter he admitted he feared the stultifying comforts of marriage. He had noticed that the settled, satisfied man failed to develop further, a criticism he leveled against one friend in particular. Already he held in disdain the kind of person he—and the Little Prince—termed "mushrooms"; many years later he defined this type as he who, clinging to a tree of which he is wholly unaware, naïvely pursues his "unreal little existence." Later, too, he would complain that when his friends settled down they were entirely lost to him: "All my friends get married, after which things are different: they build their little barriers. Then I always have the feeling of being left out." He despaired of ever finding a woman who would be right for him and was disappointed over and over again. (The qualifications as he outlined them for his sister Gabrielle were stringent: his *"petite jeune fille"* had to be beautiful, intelligent, charming, serene, calming, and loyal.) His mother found him far too critical; he replied that he was demanding of himself and that it was therefore within his rights to be demanding of others. He was now in the market for an intelligent woman who only liked intelligent people, a woman who could comfort but not dull him. Surely this was not too much to ask?

His high standards did not preclude romance. Saint-Exupéry flirted and dated in Paris as he had during his year as a traveling salesman, characteristically reporting only on the failed conquests. These included the hat seller in Dompierre-sur-Besbre and a Czech manicurist so pretty he had been forced to profess his love. ("You are not the first," came the pert reply.) He had had his eye on a small but voluptuous Saurer secretary who would not give him the time of day. He spent some time with the sister of a friend's fiancée, Lucie-Marie Decour, blond, stunning, conservatory-trained, and at least for a time enchanted by his storytelling; she would prove a loyal correspondent later. In 1925 a Russian fortuneteller had read his cards and predicted an imminent marriage with a young widow he would meet within eight days. He was intrigued, but his young widow was to keep him waiting for seven more years.

His friends were again his consolation, although they were increasingly, to his frustration, officers, professionals, husbands. (Ségogne was married this year; Bonnevie had not only completed Centrale but been an army lieutenant since the previous year; Saussine had gone on to Navale and was made an officer in 1924.) He began to grow more attached to Renée de Saussine, who, oblivious to his growing affection, saw him regularly over the summer. She was an accomplished musician and shared as well a lively interest in literature, serving as an early reader for her friend's work. Only later did Saint-Exupéry realize that he had been in love with her—this was a very different love from what he had felt and continued to feel for Louise de Vilmorin, much more of an *amitié amoureuse*. Ségogne was far quicker to see the affair develop; because of the

Louise fiasco, Saint-Exupéry refused to admit to any tenderness. Throughout the second half of 1926 he nonetheless wrote Renée routinely to say he was exasperated by her uncommunicativeness and would never write her another letter, only to sit down before the week was out to do so again. In 1927 he was ready to concede that he had indeed felt love for her and that he had been sadly disappointed, having unwittingly *"trop aventuré mon coeur."* (Renée de Saussine—who that year began to win acclaim in Europe and South America as a concert violinist and who went on to publish several volumes of her own, including a biography of Paganini— never married.) In Paris, on a meager salary and with no home of his own, Saint-Exupéry muddled by, more lonely than alone. "Drearily I court these Colettes and Paulettes and Lucys and Daisys and Gabys, all of whom resemble each other, all of whom bore me at the end of two hours," he wrote Gabrielle. He termed these women his "waiting rooms." He was in a stall, like Jacques Bernis, in search of a plot. And then in September, suddenly, superbly, the wait was over.

~

The aerial baptism business was not brisk, and Saint-Exupéry's CAF salary offered scant relief from his financial worries. A pilot seeking to earn a living in 1926 would have been well-advised to turn to the mail lines, which had begun to function just after the war and were now generating some excitement, in France especially, where they were among the most advanced. Passenger transport no longer amounted to airline-supplied hot-water bottles, gloves, goggles, and greatcoats, but it remained an expensive, deafening, irritating, chilling—in both senses of the word—experience, far more stylish than comfortable. It had only just established its operational viability; the main call for commercial pilots was in the burgeoning mail industry. In the summer of 1926 Saint-Exupéry prevailed upon Abbé Sudour, the Bossuet mentor who had so often encouraged his literary efforts and with whom he had remained in touch, to put in a word for him with Sudour's old friend Beppo de Massimi, the general manager of the Compagnie Latécoère, France's most ambitious mail line. In doing so he was unwittingly following the counsel of a postwar text evaluating the best professions in which to make a fortune. The publication touted commerce and industry as the careers of the future but warned that all desirable jobs were obtained through influence, patronage, and luck, as was to be Saint-Exupéry's case. By September, Sudour—whom Saint-Exupéry had evidently pestered repeatedly—had arranged an interview for him with the Latécoère manager. That same month Charles Lindbergh, carrying the New York mail from St. Louis to Chicago in a decrepit World War I de Havilland biplane—exactly like the one he had crashed a week earlier in an Illinois field—began to think about what he could do in a more reliable plane, given fuel enough and time.

Both highly cultivated men, Sudour and Massimi had known each other in the trenches of the Somme, where the soldier-priest and the Italian count (Massimi had flown as a volunteer) had talked literature. After the war the two men remained close; Massimi had entrusted his son to Sudour's care at Bossuet. The Abbé could not and did not vouch for his former student's skill as a pilot but sang his praises as a writer to the manager of the company, adding that Saint-Exupéry's only ambition, despite the promise he had already displayed in the field of letters, was to become an airline pilot. This intrigued Massimi, himself a playwright and translator. In his seven years with Latécoère he had hired mostly wartime aces for the company.

Massimi met with his friend's protégé in Paris, probably during the first days of October, and never forgot the impression made on him by "this tall young man who seemed terribly conscious of his size and annoyed at taking up so much room in his chair." He seemed to suffer from amnesia; he was incapable of discussing anything that might have reflected well on him. Only on the subject of the airline and its day-to-day operations did he spring to life. Under other circumstances it might well have been an interview without sequel. Massimi told Saint-Exupéry that he would have to submit to a series of tests in Toulouse, where the firm was based. Were he to fly well he would be allowed to pilot for a certain period on one of the Latécoère lines then being prospected. "And then?" asked the candidate, sounding worried. "And then . . . well!" temporized the Italian, taken aback by the question. "Our operations director needs a lieutenant." He was interrupted by Saint-Exupéry, red-faced and sputtering. "Monsieur, I especially want to fly . . . only to fly." He made it clear that he would be willing to leave for Toulouse that evening. Massimi, for whom this was in all ways an exceptional interview, was moved by his ardor. He could not make the candidate any promises but agreed to put in a call to Toulouse to see what could be arranged. He expected then to talk to Saint-Exupéry about his writing, but the author of "L'Aviateur" was already halfway out the door.

Either in this meeting or during a subsequent conversation Saint-Exupéry was told he would be summoned by letter to Toulouse; it was agreed that the offer of employment would be sent to him at his sister's home in Agay, and that week, having submitted to the obligatory medical exam at Le Bourget, he packed his bags. His spirits did not soar as he said his Parisian good-byes. He felt defeated by a city that held out so many promises and kept none; from this point on Paris would represent a gilded cage for him. He took full responsibility for his failures, which made him feel worse: "I'm not a very nice guy. I'm good only to be packed off alone to some far-off line, the farthest off," he wrote Renée de Saussine in a note accompanying a manuscript of what was probably an unpublished short story called "Manon Danseuse." This story—a Jean Rhys–like tale of the unhappy affair of a Pigalle dancer and a man twice her age, images from which were presumably layered into *Southern Mail*—he also shared with an ex-professor before his departure.

The move from Paris exhausted him. He was unable to detach himself from a host of odd objects for which he had no use but suddenly experienced an irresistible need; he had a long series of errands to run; the storage of his heavy trunks was a complicated affair. As if in revenge, he never put down roots again. In the end, all arrangements made, he was left with fifteen empty minutes before he needed to leave for the station. He spent them alone on the quai Malaquais. It was late afternoon; his friends had all deserted him for films and concerts and the countryside. His head ached, he could feel a cold coming on; he had Renée de Saussine and their not-altogether-satisfying friendship on his mind. In his hat and coat he sank uncomfortably into an armchair, where his melancholy got the better of him. He did not look like a man finally about to embark on his future.

On October 11 the letter from the airline's owner, Pierre-Georges Latécoère, arrived in Agay, summoning Saint-Exupéry to the Montaudran airfield outside of Toulouse. As was standard procedure, he was to bring with him his licenses, his logbook, and a passport valid for travel to Spain. He was requested to report to Didier Daurat—Monsieur Daurat to all who knew him—the company's operations director. Saint-Exupéry borrowed the train fare from his family and made his way immediately to Toulouse. On the fourteenth he stood before Daurat, the man he would render immortal in a portrait so powerful that the airline director would spend the rest of his life attempting to detach himself from his fictional alter ego. Daurat can only be said to have returned the favor.

Didier Daurat, a hero of Verdun, from which battle he emerged with the Croix de Guerre, five citations, and a collection of shrapnel; a man who convalesced by earning his pilot's license and wound up as a fighter squadron leader in 1917; the only surviving pilot of sixty-four after the second battle of the Marne in 1918; the flyer who located Big Bertha from the air, and the man who devoted twelve years to building what was to become the most extensive airmail operation in the world by 1930; Daurat—who died at seventy-nine in 1969, having created an ill-fated airline of his own and having spent five years as chief of Air France's operations at Orly—was quizzed about no moment of his distinguished life more often than about his first meeting with Saint-Exupéry. True to his reputation for perfect precision, he offered up the story with little variation. And true to his reputation for conciseness—it was said that no conversation with him lasted for more than three minutes—he left a certain amount unsaid. Daurat, who had signed on with Latécoère in August of 1919 and had himself flown the first Toulouse/Rabat mail that September, was, at all times, a man with a mission. For him it was said the war had not ended, it had only changed fields. He was to turn an industrialist's quixotic dream into a reality. "People write every day," Pierre-Georges Latécoère had observed. "The mail service doesn't make sense unless it, too, is daily." If the trick of most of life is to make some event of the day-to-day, to fan some spark of the unusual in the quotidian, the challenge of the early airmails was to make the quotidian as eventless, as *usual* as possible. This was the methodical Daurat's accomplishment; it was the mission he instilled in the bedraggled group of war veterans and young Turks who had assembled, *Lord of the Rings*-style, in Toulouse, and who were to become France's first set of post–World War I heroes. These included the young man who now stood before Daurat, to whom such a philosophy was so foreign that he arrived an hour late for his interview.

The thickset Daurat, a cigarette glued to his lips, received Saint-Exupéry in his austere office at the airfield just before lunch. His desk had long since disappeared under a sea of paper; behind him hung a huge map of Spain across which were flung a series of colored lines. His trademark attire, indoors and out, included a wilting felt hat, a rumpled raincoat, and a five-o'clock shadow. Daurat's welcome to other pilots has been described as glacial; it is doubtful that Saint-Exupéry's greeting was any warmer, given what the director admitted were some misgivings about the newcomer with the lily-white hands. His logbook was thin, not much more impressive, Daurat noted in his memoirs, than that of a hobby pilot. Two years earlier Daurat had refused to be impressed with Jean Mermoz's 600 flying hours, as much as twice as many as Saint-Exupéry had amassed at this time. (By comparison, Charles Lindbergh, who had also been flying since 1922, had by this autumn logged close to 2,000 hours in the air.) Saint-Exupéry's logbook would also have included his accident at Le Bourget, which the director presumably asked him to explain. More worrisome, Daurat noticed that this young man "possessed a clear moral and intellectual distinction; he seemed more inclined to dreaming than made for flying." He spoke with the soft voice of a poet. In a field that invited hubris he was anything but self-assertive. He carried himself awkwardly; Daurat noticed the same lack of grace that had so much concerned the mothers of eligible young women. What Daurat looked for in a pilot was evidence of *débrouillardise*, or resourcefulness. He was one of the first arbiters of "the right stuff."

The pilot of the 1920s was less a scientist or an engineer than an adventurer. Flyers were still widely considered marginal characters by the public; not too much earlier Louis Breguet had been told that it was preferable he abandon himself to drink than continue to build aircraft. No one yet believed entirely in air transport, and no one had less reason to, observed Daurat, than the pilots themselves. They knew better than anyone the limits of their fragile machines; they could not imagine how these unreliable contraptions were one day going to be asked to cross oceans. In the first years of the mails Daurat had been obliged to fire an excellent pilot when, returning to Toulouse from Casablanca, the pilot had been forced down on a Spanish beach by bad weather and had had the poor judgment to advise his passenger: "You should take the boat! It's so much safer." Daurat had no reason to be convinced of Saint-Exupéry's professional aptitude; there was even less proof that Saint-Exupéry would bring the required brand of confident, even-tempered tenacity to the job.

The director had further reason to be wary. Sudour, whom Daurat had known as well at the front, had indeed said kind things about his ex-pupil, but the point of a recommendation, observed the matter-of-fact Daurat later, is after all to say kind things. While the priest's word was good, it carried less weight on an airstrip than in the intellectual village of the 6th arrondissement, where Saint-Exupéry looked very much to belong. What was more, Daurat could not entirely overlook the fact that Saint-Exupéry came to him via his aristocratic colleague. On this he commented tersely: "Massimi referred him to me; they shared *la particule*." Massimi had dropped his, but Daurat noticed that Sudour's protégé signed always "de Saint-Exupéry." He was the only one of Daurat's approximately seventy pilots who could do so.

Why, then, did he take Saint-Exupéry on, at least provisionally, sending him on to the workshops where all pilots began? Perhaps he was intrigued; perhaps he felt a certain amount of sympathy, although this was hardly the virtue for which Daurat was best known. He may simply have needed a pilot (of the 126 flyers recruited between 1923 and 1926, fifty-five had left the company and seven had died in the line of duty). He knew as well as anyone that good pilots come in all brands, and he had little to lose. He claimed to have felt acutely Saint-Exupéry's need for a success during their short interview. In Daurat's view the only realm in which the young man had made any headway was in society; he could not have known that this had been a very qualified success. He suspected that what had first struck him as affectation in the young man was in fact shyness, pure and simple. This was not what he expected to find in a man like Saint-Exupéry, but modesty was a more promising quality than pretension or overconfidence, which he abhorred. (When Mermoz went up for his first flight test in a Breguet 14, he took it upon himself to perform acrobatics for Daurat. He was very nearly fired before being hired.) The exacting chief, known for being a stickler about schedules, the devotion to which after all constituted his life's work, chose to forgive the applicant who had arrived at noon for an eleven o'clock interview, a crime of which Saint-Exupéry must quickly have realized the gravity. Under Daurat's care, that same man, only partially reformed, would write of his first day with the mail line: "I learned that any delay is a dishonor, regardless of why it occurs."

~

Saint-Exupéry began his Latécoère career as a mechanic. Daurat had designed this apprenticeship with an eye to the war veterans who filled the bulk of the airline's original ranks. Most of them lived off their remembered glories; Daurat felt he needed to strip them of their bulky "armor of pride" and teach them to appreciate routine, monotony, teamwork. Many of the veterans found this training beneath them; the ex-Saurer mechanic did not. During his first weeks with Latécoère, decked out once again in workman's blues, Saint-Exupéry learned to wield a wrench, to dismantle a motor, to check for oil and water leaks, to anticipate a ruptured connecting rod, to weld and clean cylinders. Daurat was pleasantly surprised by the quick transformation of the new recruit's manicured hands, which came for him to represent the transfiguration of the man himself, whom Daurat saw as propelled by his earlier ordeals to turn a passion into a profession. What was more, even Saint-Exupéry's much-noted clumsiness could not mask a remarkable aptitude for mechanics.

He was on familiar turf. The Breguet 14—the warplane that was the staple of the Latécoère fleet in 1926 and 1927 and in which Saint-Exupéry would perform his feats at Juby—was hardly more complicated a machine than was a Saurer truck. A total of 5,500 biplanes had been built during the war, equipped as either light bombers or reconnaissance planes; nearly 150 were purchased by the United States, to whose de Havilland D.H.4B the Breguet probably best compared. It was not an aircraft that rivaled other fighter craft in its appearance or its prestige; it was neither rapid (its cruising speed was eighty miles per hour, half that of a French high-speed train today) nor particularly manageable. But a Breguet 14 A2 was the most reliable aircraft of the time, which was to say that it broke down only every 15,500 miles traveled or, by another gauge, that it flew well even with an incomplete wing or with only half its pistons firing. It was an aircraft with which Saint-Exupéry had some experience, in part thanks to his enterprising outings with Escot at Villacoublay. Several weeks after his arrival in Toulouse he submitted to his first flight test, which he passed, though Daurat deemed the performance to have been "without brio." There was ample room for improvement, and over the course of the next training flights Saint-Exupéry made steady progress. Daurat followed this progress especially closely, not because he meant to cosset the man who would become the bard of the airline, but, conversely, because he had more reason to worry about Saint-Exupéry than about most of his new recruits.

Daurat was not the only one at Montaudran watching Saint-Exupéry carefully. All young pilots were looked upon with suspicion by the war veterans, who accepted them only grudgingly. But among his fellow greenhorns Saint-Exupéry stood out as well, initially because of his name and his decidedly bohemian airs, soon enough because of his famous capriciousness. He was not taken altogether seriously. Léon Antoine, a young pilot who had arrived at Latécoère earlier in the year, remembered a morning when Saint-Exupéry did not appear to board the tram that carried the pilots from their Toulouse hotel to the airstrip, a capital offense. Someone ran up to his room to see what was keeping him; the truant was discovered asleep in his bath, a book floating in the water before him. Such tales circulated quickly. Later, at a Spanish airfield, the man who was to write odes to the punctuality of the early airmails announced just before he was meant to take off that he could not do so. "Are you sick?" asked the chief of the airfield. "No, but I forgot my gloves at the hotel," explained Saint-Exupéry. "You will leave without gloves, my friend!" he was advised tartly. One of the historians of the line noted that men with no sense of time in their personal lives adopted a rigorous exactitude when it came to the mail. Those who resisted were forced to adapt to the discipline by their colleagues, "like skeptics lost in a religious community." Saint-Exupéry submitted with near relief to the metaphor, if not always to the practice. "When I joined the Aéropostale Service," he wrote six years later, "I felt that I was entering a monastery."

The Latécoère cloister was to be found just off Toulouse's main square, eight miles from the airstrip, at the corner of the rue Romiguières and the rue des Lois. The Grand Balcon, a five-story hotel built of the pink brick that makes France's southwestern capital glow with rosy light early in the morning and at the end of an afternoon, offered respectable rooms with board at seven francs a night. (For a special client, like the ferociously handsome Mermoz, the rate could go as low as five francs nightly.) Along with two additional restaurants, Le Site and Les Pyrénées, which also housed aviators, the hotel came to serve as the Latécoère priory, probably for the simple reason that Toulouse boasted few hotels at the time and this affordable one was on the Montaudran tramline. (Toto, the Juby mechanic, as partial to liquids in France as in the desert, would stumble to the airfield after an all-night bender by tapping his way blindly along the rail with a cane.) Three unmarried women, two of them sisters, ran the benevolent *pension*, which by the time Saint-Exupéry arrived was entirely overrun by the vagabondish Latécoère family. Just as important to the newcomer, the hotel was a stone's throw from Toulouse's best cafés, all on or near the place du Capitole or the place Wilson. From here he kept up a busy correspondence during his first six months on *la Ligne*; a great number of these envelopes were addressed to Renée de Saussine. At the Grand Balcon the fortunate Saint-Exupéry was assigned a spacious fourth-floor room with a fireplace and two windows, overlooking the square.

Daurat, who lived in town with his wife, arrived at the Montaudran field in the company car at 4:00 a.m. The mail arrived, by overnight train from Paris's Gare d'Orsay and by truck, at 8:00. The Latécoère crew waited in front of the Grand Balcon for the number 10 tram; by the time it rattled to the door of the hotel a group of men had assembled on the pavement in the dark, their hands stuffed in the pockets of their leather jackets, cigarettes dangling from their mouths. Off they rode to Montaudran, where their holy orders were sealed in oil, in boring but critical meteorology lessons held in a freezing hangar, in fear of the labors to be accomplished and in awe at those who had already accomplished them. (In all, 120 employees died in the service of the mail line, an average of about ten men a year.) The streetcar dropped the pilots a quarter-mile from the field; this final stretch was covered on foot. Saint-Exupéry made a practice of stopping in at Le Site, at the end of the line. Marius Fabre, an eagle-eyed Latécoère mechanic, noticed that a ritual evolved around the pilot's two-croissant-and-café-au-lait breakfast: When Saint-Exupéry was broke he discreetly sat down at Le Site with the mechanics, who understood they were to treat him to his one-franc meal. "But, on the other hand, when he was flush, he conducted himself royally and bought breakfast not only for our table but for all the others," remembered Fabre.

Saint-Exupéry rose to the challenge of this new life with gusto, although the work was not always transcendent or even remotely glamorous. He moved on from his mechanic's *stage* to flying the Breguets as they were delivered, which was irregularly. One Friday he took a new airplane up for an hour's test flight at 300 feet in heavy rain, a flight during which he observed that aviation resembled nothing more than taking a bath. That Sunday he woke at six to take up another plane but was forced down (as he put it, the aircraft "manifested the imperious desire to return to the stable") after ten minutes, because of which he spent the rest of the day bored and half-asleep. He bought matches, cigarettes, and stamps so as to have something to do; he reported that he already had thirty boxes of matches and enough stamps for the next forty years in his room. His salary was probably close to 1,000 francs a month—his first letter home from Toulouse was the last in which he lobbied for money—but once he began flying he would have found that no distinction existed among weekdays, weekends, and holidays. The previous year Mermoz had reported flying 600-mile, seven-hour days, with one day off for every two he worked. Still, Saint-Exupéry was far from disconsolate. The departure of the mail at dawn, under a light drizzle, was a beautiful sight, and he was quick to appreciate a brand of aviation that seemed less a sport than a kind of war. The danger, the pioneering aspect of the venture, the sacrifice for the greater, abstract good, and the transient lifestyle brought a man out of himself, something Saint-Exupéry had complained he had trouble doing on his own. "One is who one is, but this is sometimes limited," he had written his mother. Under the weight of greater responsibility, yoked into a team, he began to rise above his melancholy. It is not easy to resist the triple lure of a demanding family that with its own creed wages a very personal war, and Saint-Exupéry—who may have needed these structures more than most of the Latécoère personnel—bought in hook, line, and sinker. Though the religious trappings were there for all to see, he began to distill and romanticize the spiritual dimensions of his new life. This time the nonjoiner—having found a cause worthy of his ideals, or simply having run out of options—became a zealot.

After several weeks of flying new aircraft and after a number of flights to Perpignan, just under two hours from Toulouse, Saint-Exupéry was sent off as a passenger on the Toulouse-Barcelona-Alicante line, halfway to Casablanca along the Latécoère route. His pilot was Henri Guillaumet, whom Mermoz had brought to the company—the two had met during their military service—during the winter of 1925. Guillaumet was the recipient of two of the hardest-won accolades in Latécoère history. Daurat thought him the best pilot he had known. And the stern chief, who held that a pilot lost three-quarters of his value when he married, allowed that Guillaumet was the sole exception to his rule. (This was perhaps more of a tribute to Madame Guillaumet.) Two years younger than Saint-Exupéry, Guillaumet was a man of no visible ego. He was frank and humble and taciturn. Mermoz, too, was a quiet man and a hero—among his innumerable breathtaking feats he had once risked his life for a corpse—but he had a certain vanity. Arguably this was through no fault of his own: Mermoz was a man of such godlike good looks that when he first arrived in Toulouse even Daurat felt compelled to comment on his extraordinary head of wavy hair. He was revered for his person and his exploits; he was the kind of man for whom a woman would—and did, at his side, while he slept, after being told their affair would end in the morning—kill herself. Mermoz was the more visible of the two, more the front man: as the Latécoère adage went, "*Mermoz défriche, Guillaumet laboure*" ("Mermoz clears, Guillaumet plows"). If Guillaumet has a place today in the crowded pantheon of French aviators it is in part thanks to Saint-Exupéry, who told his tales for him. Mermoz is remembered—and forgotten—on his own merits and demerits.* It happened, not accidentally since Daurat was involved, that most of Saint-Exupéry's initiations in 1926 took place under the supervision of the masterful Guillaumet.

After Guillaumet had twice carried Saint-Exupéry as a passenger on the Toulouse/Alicante run, Daurat entrusted the newcomer with his first mail. He delivered this news to him in his office one evening late in November or early in December, in a conversation that could not have much differed from the way Saint-Exupéry reported it in *Wind, Sand and Stars*:

> He said: "You leave tomorrow." I stood motionless, waiting for him to dismiss me. After a moment of silence he added: "I take it you know the regulations?" In those days the motor was not what it is today. It would drop out, for example, without warning and with a great rattle like the crash of crockery. And one would simply throw in one's hand: there was no hope of refuge on the rocky crust of Spain. . . . Still, the important thing was to avoid a collision with the range; and blind flying through a sea of clouds in the mountain zones was subject to the severest penalties. A pilot in trouble who buried himself in the white cotton-wool of the clouds might all unseeing run straight into a peak. This was why, that night, the deliberate voice repeated insistently its warning: "Navigating by the compass in a sea of clouds over Spain is all very well, it is very dashing, but—" And I was struck by the graphic image: "But you want to remember that below the sea of clouds lies eternity."

Saint-Exupéry wrote that he left Daurat that evening with a sense of childish pride. He was by no means oblivious to the dangers that awaited him the next morning, however. Turbulence, fog, and snowstorms amid the Pyrenees represented significant obstacles to the pilot of an open-cockpit Breguet 14, which had an operational ceiling of 13,500 feet; in the mountains it is easier, and more dangerous, to get lost, and more difficult to manage an emergency landing. The Pyrenees, moreover, are no ordinary mountain range; from the point of view of the pilot of a small craft they are more formidable than the much taller Alps, harboring sudden, magnetic storms, extreme turbulence, and high cloud cover in all seasons. The previous year, Willy Coppens, the Belgian ace, had been advised by his pilot to brace himself as they overflew the Pyrenees; the

---

* It is said that when the Banque de France, anticipating a series of banknotes that would celebrate French technology, polled French schoolchildren for the name of the country's foremost aviator, the answer came back resoundingly, "Mermoz." A man can endear himself to history and offend her, too: in the 1930s, Mermoz joined the avowedly fascist Croix-de-Feu organization, an affiliation that did not make him banknote material in the eyes of a Socialist administration. Saint-Exupéry profited from his colleague's disfavor and in 1993 appeared in Mermoz's place on the fifty-franc bill.

pilot had lost his previous passenger. The same fate had befallen Pierre Jaladieu, who preceded Saint-Exupéry at Juby. In the hope that Guillaumet might go over the route with him Saint-Exupéry sought him out that night at the Grand Balcon, where the news that he was to make his maiden flight had preceded him. Guillaumet asked how the debutant felt, and produced two glasses and a bottle of port. "It's easier than you think," promised the veteran, who in his shirtsleeves spread out Saint-Exupéry's maps on the table before them.

Saint-Exupéry was that night to receive the most unorthodox geography lesson of his life and the first he would enjoy. "Guillaumet did not teach Spain to me, he made the country my friend. He did not talk to me about provinces or people or livestock," he remembered. Nor did the veteran pilot talk of wind sheer or radio navigation. The Latécoère maps were rudimentary Michelin or general survey maps; Saint-Exupéry reported that he had had to reprimand the countryside for its impertinent refusal to conform to the indications on his papers. At Daurat's insistence, the pilots flew always below the clouds, following the natural landmarks across the border, even if this meant treehopping. Guillaumet introduced Saint-Exupéry to a different way to survey the earth. He talked about a row of tall orange trees, about a farmer and his wife who lived alone on a remote mountain slope and were like lighthouse keepers to the pilots, about a brook that meandered quietly through an emergency landing field and could turn up where it was least expected, about a herd of thirty sheep that could appear out of nowhere to tangle with a plane's wheels. He taught Saint-Exupéry about the color of a river, from which a pilot could tell whether it was safe to land nearby or whether he would be putting down in swampland. This was Saint-Exupéry's kind of geography, Guillaumet his kind of Virgil. "Little by little, under the lamp, the Spain of my map became a sort of fairyland," he wrote later. The *Aeneid*, he would claim in a scene in *Southern Mail* based on this tutorial with Guillaumet, had failed to yield up a single secret capable of saving him from death. Guillaumet's orange orchards, streams, and shepherdesses did. These wisdoms belonged to the secret language the Saint-Jean instructors had been unable to impart, a secret language not unlike that of the attics of Saint-Maurice. Saint-Exupéry liked his dose of the natural world flavored with a hint of mysticism, which this flying by vision and instinct—or "*à l'oeil et à la fesse*" ("by the seat of the pants"), as one mechanic more colorfully put it—surely provided. Like all French aristocrats he had an abiding attachment to the earth; like all early aviators he enjoyed as close a relationship with the ground as with the air.

As it turned out, that evening at the Grand Balcon was a pivotal one not only for Saint-Exupéry and for his friendship with Guillaumet, to whom the French edition of *Wind, Sand and Stars* would later be dedicated. At Montaudran Daurat was said to be everywhere and to hear and see everything; he did not miss this *tête-à-tête*, which astonished him. His account may be more telling than Saint-Exupéry's:

> Late in the night, I saw Saint-Exupéry seated at Guillaumet's side; they were concentrating on a map laid out in front of them. The silent Guillaumet was speaking, with increasing warmth; he was speaking of his kingdom, rich in scope, rich because of his unique discoveries. . . . the conversation intensified, bringing out in Guillaumet the soul of the poet-guide. He was discovering himself through his contact with Saint-Exupéry, and I knew instantly that a rare friendship had just been born.

In an interview in which he himself proved more forthcoming than usual, Daurat admitted that it was only at this moment, in the dim light of the Grand Balcon sitting room as he watched Guillaumet warm to Saint-Exupéry's questions and the newcomer carefully mark up his map, that he felt certain he had not made a mistake in hiring Sudour's ex-student.

~

When Saint-Exupéry left Guillaumet that winter evening he headed out for a brisk walk. The twelve hours that followed, beginning with this late-night promenade through a chilly city, became, at least in retrospect, emblematic, the keystone of his philosophy. In 1926 he was still more concerned with his own evolution than with that of man in general, but this changed as he came into his own, as he quite literally broadened his horizons. As he saw it—and Saint-Exupéry often enough telescoped events but rarely misrepresented them—those hours came to illustrate the power of work, of craft, of a mission, to lift man above himself. (He had indeed been reading Nietzsche—"I am immensely fond of this writer," he admitted that fall—but this was something else altogether.) He strolled through the Toulousian streets, his collar turned up against the cold, drunk with that sweet mixture of pride and nervous fervor that any new lover knows. The people he passed in the street had no idea they were about to confide their most cherished hopes, their precious business interests to his care so that he might convey them across mountain ranges and boundaries; he was a shepherd, a warrior, a magician. "I alone was in the confidence of the stars," he thought, savoring his newfound responsibility, the religious flavor of his appointment. Walking past lighted shop windows, he found himself in "a paradise of sweet things" and yet tasted only "the proud intoxication of renunciation." He had no need for these earthly trinkets, he who was luxuriously "wrapped in the aura of friendship, dazed a little like a child on Christmas Eve, expectant of surprise and palpitatingly prepared for happiness."

He awoke, at three, to rain. Thirty minutes later he was dressed and seated on his little suitcase, waiting on the wet pavement in front of the Grand Balcon for the tram,* which this morning was also enchanted. It carried in it his previous life; suddenly Saint-Exupéry came face-to-face with his near death by bureaucracy. He did not handle this encounter with a surfeit of charity. The streetcar was redolent of stale tobacco and of wet clothes; to Saint-Exupéry it "smelled of the dust of government offices into which the life of a man sinks as into a quicksand." Every 500 yards or so it stopped to pick up a notary, a guard, a customs inspector, each of whom fell asleep immediately or quietly swapped tales of domestic woes with his neighbor as the tram groaned along. Saint-Exupéry reveled in his disguise: he was indistinguishable from these bureaucrats, yet hours later they would be locked in offices, victims of "their dreary diurnal tasks, their red tape, their monotonous lives" and he would be battling dragons in the sky. The streetcar became a sort of chrysalis—a favorite image for Saint-Exupéry the nature writer—from which a man might emerge transformed. And on this particular morning he felt "the birth within him of the sovereign":

> Old bureaucrat . . . you, like a termite, built your peace by blocking up with cement every chink and cranny through which the light might pierce. You rolled yourself up into a ball in your genteel security, in routine, in the stifling conventions of provincial life, raising a modest rampart against the winds and the tides and the stars. You have chosen not to be perturbed by great problems, having trouble enough to forget your own fate as man. You are not the dweller upon an errant planet and do not ask yourself questions to which there are no answers. You are a petty bourgeois of Toulouse. Nobody grasped you by the shoulder while there was still time.

He pitied but did not blame the "old bureaucrat," who had never been allowed to escape. No one had been on hand to awaken the hidden musician, the poet, the astronomer, in his soul. There was, as Saint-Exupéry was always eager to point out, no gardener for men, no doctor of souls, no one willing, like the Little Prince, to protect, shelter, and cultivate his rose, no matter how uncooperative or undeserving that rose might be. He may not have spoken or written of having been orphaned at four—as was the authority-lover who had preceded him, Nietzsche, at five—but this loss had clearly left its mark.

If Saint-Exupéry's analysis of his fellow commuters rings like an indictment it should be heard more as a loud sigh of relief. Any man could succumb to this fate, as the pilot well knew. If he seemed to recoil from

---

* Saint-Exupéry's *"omnibus,"* or tram, mistakenly turned into a bus in the English-language version of *Terre des hommes.*

these men it was with the terror of recognition; he flinched as a Henry V might from a Falstaff. He would not end either as a sedentary or as a gigolo, a broken man in a sedate line of work. Latécoère had grasped him by the shoulder while there was still time; Didier Daurat was his gardener. In a roundabout way he had stumbled upon one of the few true crusades the twentieth century had to offer. His natural modesty did not blind him to this parallel. Daurat's copy of *Wind, Sand and Stars* came inscribed to a man who had alone built "a sort of separate civilization in which men felt more noble than elsewhere." He was grateful, not immodest. He saw that he could put to use the name which, in the words of another pilot, sounded so much like that of "a knight of the Holy Grail." Responsibility may well be another name for aristocracy; Saint-Exupéry had discovered a last bastion of *noblesse oblige*. The irony was that Daurat never tired of reminding his pilots, for the sake of their work, that they were mere day laborers: "Don't forget that imagination, heroism do not belong here. You are workmen."

As much as he was a man of the people, despite his condemnation of the Parisian drawing rooms, despite his thoroughgoing respect for Guillaumet and his dedication to the Latécoère team, there was, in fact, a decidedly undemocratic ring to Saint-Exupéry's humanitarian vision. On the one hand he claimed to admire above all else the steady-working gardener, the devoted mother of five. On the other he loathed all that reeked of the subjugation of the individual to his task. His very belief in a cosmic gardener on earth was elitist. It was an idea he would probe most deeply in his last book, a quasi-religious text in which he makes a quiet case for oligarchy. He knew it was the universal that bound men together but he never stopped despairing of the baseness of that standard, could not understand why it was Pirandello instead of Ibsen, jazz instead of Mozart, a cheap print instead of a van Gogh or a Cézanne that won out. He loved the life of the barracks but generally lived apart; in Toulouse he decamped soon enough from the Grand Balcon to a nearby apartment on the rue d'Alsace-Lorraine, although this was not as uncommon among the Latécoère staff as it had been in Strasbourg. He relished his separateness the way another man might have relished his *particule*.

To a friend he wrote from a Toulouse café not long after his first flight. Seated at a table to which he had for several evenings laid claim, he surveyed a room of mute card players. They silently downed their *apéritifs*; he ruminated in his corner. He compared their incomparable silences. These men were considering their next hand; he was dreaming of Moors and planes. "The proprietor and the waiter already take me for their prisoner; they pull out my chair for me, smile benevolently over the three sugars I dissolve in my coffee, beam radiantly as I order a beer afterward, fail to contain their joy when at 10:00 o'clock sharp I send for cigarettes, reminding me, 'It's time for Monsieur's cigarettes.' They think me theirs for the next twenty years. How I am going to disappoint them!" To Renée de Saussine he described the "little provincial path" he traced daily. He would play perfectly at his routine until—overwhelmed by the desire to escape and explore new territory—he would emigrate to a new chair in a new café and a new newspaper vendor, for whom he would coin a new, formulaic greeting. Elsewhere he admitted to a terrific fear of habit, a diet of which gave rise to "mushrooms." If he threw himself humbly, whole-heartedly into the métier, he did not bow to consistency. He had always seemed congenitally, unapologetically incapable of it; now he began to write it off as little-mindedness. There were plenty of reasons why some Latécoère personnel should think Daurat kept Saint-Exupéry on purely because of his name, which he did not.

Saint-Exupéry's affair with the transcendent got off to a soggy start. At the airfield on the morning of his first Alicante run the rain continued to fall. The wind whipped up waves in the puddles. "Would you call this bad weather?" he asked Daurat, who looked out the window as if doing so for the first time and mumbled: "It doesn't mean anything." Saint-Exupéry was left to wonder what might constitute bad weather. He felt emptied, suddenly, of all of the confidence Guillaumet had instilled in him. One line returned to haunt him: Guillaumet had said that he pitied the man who did not know the whole line, pebble by pebble, especially if that man were to run into a snowstorm.

He took off in the rain. Five hours later, after a stopover in Barcelona, he landed in Alicante, the warmest town in Europe, the only one, he wrote giddily later, "where dates ripen." He saw no snow, save for that safely blanketing the Pyrenees. His return flight the next day was slightly more eventful. He again cleared the mountains without difficulty but met with a heavy fog—and an early evening—between Carcassonne and Toulouse. Several miles short of Montaudran he was forced down in a field. A search committee set out immediately by car and after a number of hours finally located him. Raymond Vanier, Daurat's second-in-command, found the pilot seated under a wing of his plane in the wet grass. "Monsieur," said Saint-Exupéry, "the plane is intact. I apologize for not having fully completed my first mail flight; I did my best." It was a far cry from the Bossuet ballad of the lost desk.

VIII

~

The Swift Completion of Their
Appointed Rounds
1927–1929

Orders are orders.

SAINT-EXUPÉRY, *The Little Prince*

Saint-Exupéry's mishap was an insignificant one in the early annals of Latécoère, as rich in bravura as in misadventure. The two were often one and the same; at other times the early days resembled nothing more than a pilot's version of a Keystone comedy. At the end of the war France was left not only with one of the most productive aeronautics industries in the world, but also with 12,000 aviators and very nearly as many planes. These facts did not escape the notice of Pierre-Georges Latécoère, an ambitious young industrialist who, upon completing engineering school, had returned to the family timber business, and was perennially on the lookout for a venture he could call his own. Initially he had turned to the construction of railway cars, with which he had much success. But by 1917 it was clear to the thirty-four-year-old, whose poor eyesight had kept him from the front, that the railroad was a creature of the nineteenth century. That October, at a time when it was estimated that no fewer than three months were needed to produce the first aircraft in a new series in an efficient, existing factory (of which he had none), he entered into a government contract to manufacture 1,000 Salmson reconnaissance planes within the year. He was late with his first delivery of 600 planes, but only slightly so, and he made a fortune, having by the terms of his agreement profited as much from the Armistice as from the war. Even before the peace Latécoère began to think about the airplane's potential in the postwar world; he needed a new challenge, and he did not by nature think small.

In May 1918 Latécoère shared his vision with Beppo de Massimi, a childhood friend whose wartime flying experience Latécoère—who would never himself pilot an airplane—prized. He did not consider a simple Paris/London or Paris/Amsterdam line; these were cities that were already well-connected by train. Nor did he begin to dream of passenger aviation, a business for which open-cockpit Breguets and Salmsons seemed ill-suited. Instead he turned toward what lay south of France and toward the Americas, and thought in terms of the far-flung business interests of the early-twentieth-century empires. At this time France was, after Britain, the second largest colonial power in the world; her holdings in Africa alone totaled nearly 4 million square miles, well over fifteen times the size of continental France herself. French trade with Morocco, one of the jewels in her colonial crown, had tripled in the four prewar years. The war had driven home—as the next one would even more forcefully—the strategic and economic importance of these possessions. Latécoère imagined a network that would link Rabat and Casablanca to France via stops along the Spanish coast, a line which would later extend to the south through the Rio de Oro and along the Mauritanian coast to Saint-Louis-du-Sénégal and Dakar, the administrative seat of the French West African empire. Dakar was a bustling, inclement city of 40,000 people; its French population was small, but it was France's third largest port. With the advent of air travel it suddenly became one of the world's best-located cities as well; the 1,620 nautical miles that separated it from the New World shrank overnight. When the technology caught up with his vision—Latécoère had conceived of this network with 400-mile-hopping converted warplanes in mind—Latécoère thought that Dakar's Cape Verde peninsula, the westernmost point in Africa, could serve as a jumping-off point for the Americas. The airline might then continue toward Buenos Aires, Rio de Janeiro, and Montevideo, ultimately on toward North America.

The windmill-tilting for which Pierre-Georges Latécoère would be best remembered began when he presented his fantastic scheme to Massimi that May. The underlying argument, according to the Italian, seemed to be: "I've reworked all the numbers. They confirm the opinion of the specialists: It cannot be done. We have only one option: To go ahead and do it." Before the Armistice had been signed Latécoère had presented his bold proposal for a commercial airline to the government; he felt he could reduce the distance between Toulouse and Casablanca to two days at most (by rail and boat from Paris a letter to Casablanca at this time took seven to eleven days, depending on the season), between Toulouse and Dakar to five days in lieu of twelve to fourteen. Before the government's position was made clear, Massimi—who reveled in the art of diplomacy and was to practice more of it than he might have counted on for Latécoère—had been dispatched to Spain to negotiate an authorization for overflying Spanish territory and building and equipping coastline airstrips.

Latécoère celebrated Christmas 1918 in a Salmson over the Pyrenees. He and his pilot executed the maiden Toulouse/Barcelona flight, a trip of 200 miles. Two months later Massimi was flown from Toulouse to Alicante, 250 miles south of Barcelona, where he had arranged for a 600-meter landing strip to be cleared. Unfortunately his request had been understood to mean 600 square meters; some time before or after the plane crashed and Massimi's nose began to gush blood the Italian accurately noted, "It's a handkerchief, not a landing strip!" He and his pilot immediately set out to clear a suitable runway, as Latécoère was himself en route. Happily for the grooming committee, Latécoère's arrival was delayed. His pilot had lost his glasses to turbulence in the Pyrenees and had gone on to overfly Barcelona, where he should have stopped to refuel, without seeing the city. With an empty tank he landed on a strip of sand about one-third of the way between Barcelona and Alicante. Here he and Latécoère managed to refuel, and the two continued on their way. With his passenger's help the pilot was able to make out the airstrip at Alicante but not the windsock, which indicated that he was landing with a tremendous tailwind. The airplane raced down the length of the newly extended runway to crash against the rocks at its end. After being helped from the wreckage, the incorrigible Latécoère concluded, "That didn't go so badly. We'll have to repair these planes. In a month we'll go all the way to Morocco." All the same, he chose to return to France that evening by train.

Less than a month later, at a time when Saint-Exupéry's sights were still fixed on his naval exams, Latécoère indeed stepped out of a Salmson to a triumphant welcome in Rabat. Maréchal Lyautey—not yet named a *maréchal*, but as *résident général* acknowledged to be the uncrowned king of Morocco—was on hand to congratulate the industrialist. Latécoère presented Lyautey with a copy of the previous day's Paris newspaper; he bestowed on his wife a bouquet of violets that had traveled from Toulouse in a hatbox. He had made the trip from France in fewer than twenty-four hours, or in a quarter of the time it took a boat traveling under the most favorable conditions. It was the fastest Lyautey had ever received his newspaper; its delivery won Latécoère an important ally. Lyautey had his own budget, from which he immediately offered the industrialist an important subsidy. Effectively guaranteed a monopoly on the France-bound mail, Latécoère had a contract in hand for the southern mail by the end of the summer. Several pilots were recruited; Massimi called on his squadron leader, Daurat, who arrived in Toulouse in August. *La Ligne* was off and running, if a little erratically.

On September 1, 1919, Daurat inaugurated service between Toulouse and Casablanca. The equipment remained so unreliable—and Latécoère's determination so strong—that seven planes were lined up for the trip although only three were to make the flight. The enterprise suffered its first casualty that December, when a pilot went down near the Pyrenees. A host of accidents followed. There were all kinds of problems—of morale, diplomacy, matériel, security, finances. The headaches seemed disproportionate to the task at hand, which was simply to take off and land on schedule. The Spanish proved as unpredictable and adversarial as the winds over the Pyrenees: that autumn both Daurat and another pilot, making separate emergency landings on Spanish soil, were taken prisoner by the Spanish, who claimed not to have been informed that the French had been authorized to land on their territory. Anti-French sentiment ran high in Spain, where neither the Court nor the military smiled upon her neighbor; the Germans had generously lent a hand in the supply and development of the country's infant airlines and continued to lobby effectively in Madrid. Overflying Spain could be legal for Latécoère one day and illegal the next. As late as 1928, the French ambassador to Spain was writing the Quai d'Orsay of the passive resistance the Spanish were demonstrating toward the airline: "We have a fair amount of proof that the standing orders have been not to favor, and even to hinder, the operations of the France-Morocco line; we often find that promises extracted from recently installed ministers are suddenly withdrawn." In 1937 the London *Times* reported that Saint-Exupéry had flown to Timbuktu to investigate an alternate France–South America route because the French and Spanish continued to squabble.

Still, through a series of mishaps and miracles, the Latécoère enterprise forged ahead. In 1920, one year after Daurat's flight to Casablanca, the company consisted of thirteen pilots, thirty mechanics, and sixty airplanes, or one-third of the entire French commercial fleet and one-fifth of its active commercial pilots. And Latécoère continued to expand: in 1923 the Casablanca–Dakar route was prospected, although not without difficulties of its own. Two years later, when that route—an empty boulevard of desert—was officially opened, it was as true as ever that *la Ligne* amounted to "a series of forays based on luck and the grit of the men who fly them." This did not prevent Latécoère from boarding a boat to Rio—almost exactly one month to the day after Saint-Exupéry first appeared before Daurat—to see if he might tilt at some windmills in South America. Less than two years later, a letter posted from Paris arrived in eight days in Buenos Aires, in a quarter of the time the same envelope would have taken when Latécoère made his 1926 trip.

In 1920 Latécoère transported 200,000 letters. Ten years later—when service had been extended to Africa and South America—the airline would carry 32 million. The quality of its service and that of its equipment remained hugely divergent. In 1927 the pilots complained that they spent half their time bailing out their broken-down colleagues, that they could count on a malfunction every third trip, that the planes stumbled along at low altitudes without the power to climb, that they took off only on whim. And yet of the 1,462 bags of mail carried that year only one—at least according to the company's annual report—failed to reach its destination. In the short term at any rate the Latécoère story was one of stunning success. By 1930 it had grown into the longest line in the world and represented the largest of Europe's commercial fleets. Latécoère's personal sense of invincibility had penetrated the ranks; the airline boasted an esprit de corps that no other could rival and that it could claim as its greatest asset.

With its mail lines, France capitalized on the breadth of its empire, its prewar achievements in aviation, and its wartime industry. It was also true that French soil proved naturally hospitable to the Latécoère vision in the first place. While his countrymen may not have entirely understood the premium Latécoère placed on speed, they appreciated as well as anyone his devotion to the written word, sacred in France. The French love their mail, so much so that they long resisted the telephone, which is invasive, and which overrides the laws of social intercourse, and for which even today one has to make excuses in good company. (Saint-Exupéry had few such reservations about the telephone, which he abused. The written word never traveled fast enough for his tastes, and even when his own missives did he felt compelled to call to explicate or correct his texts. He chastised Renée de Saussine for having sent a letter by boat in 1930: "It's hardly worth our knocking ourselves out to move the mail if our letters come to us by boat.") Today Parisians enjoy three mail deliveries a day, and a letter sent from any point in France to any other reliably arrives overnight.

The reasons why Latécoère thrived in the 1920s were not primarily cultural or colonial, however. No government did more to encourage the aviation industry after the war than the French. The British and the Americans were by comparison apathetic; the Germans were hamstrung by the terms of the peace. The French set up a National Weather Bureau. The Comité Francais de Propagande Aéronautique—a sort of educational public relations committee—was established by the industrialist André Michelin in 1921; its mission was to instill "*l'esprit aviateur*" in every Frenchman. The state helped to train pilots, to develop aircraft. Flying clubs were established all over the country. Subsidies were available—

Saint-Exupéry may have benefited from one in 1935—for those interested in purchasing an airplane for personal use; at least 40 percent of the price was underwritten by the state. The French were further motivated by their anti-German spirit, which piqued their well-developed appetite for public competition, of which this one was among the more glorious. The Quai d'Orsay had its own interest in tying the French empire closely together: the more speedily the colonies could communicate with the Ministère des Affaires Étrangères, the more the colonial governors were forced to defer to Parisian-based decision-making. Aviation in fact helped to put an end to the age of the diplomat-adventurer, the *gentilhomme de fortune*. By the mid-1930s—when pilots had begun to complain as well that the age of "*la belle aventure*" had skidded to an end—colonialization had become the domain of the civil servant. The government was generous with Latécoère, who routinely performed a sort of Columbus-before-Queen-Isabella dance before its ministers, and their investment paid off handsomely in prestige and historical firsts.

By the early 1930s, when that government began to prove a fickle benefactor, when the Latécoère-founded enterprise had begun to creak on its uneasy economic foundations, most countries flew their mail from city to city. Germany and Holland were, and had been, well in advance of the rest of the world in building transport machines. The U.S. mail had made its way from New York to San Francisco in forty-eight hours as early as mid-1927. Lindbergh's flight of that year transformed America's laggard attitude toward aviation. France herself had four other mail lines, and Latécoère had a new name, having been sold to Marcel Bouilloux-Lafont, a South American–based Frenchman, after whose entrance on the scene in 1927 the company was known colloquially as Aéropostale. (Its official name was the Compagnie Générale Aéropostale.) Pierre-Georges Latécoère's brainstorm was an impressive but short chapter in the frenetic and crowded history of early aviation; it was not the longest-lived airline but it was arguably the most ambitious. In some ways it was simply a compelling commercial for the insignificance of distance, for the potential of technology. If it was remembered for far more even after the noisy scandals that brought it down were forgotten, that was largely thanks to a misfit of a pilot who wrote indelibly of its heroic age although he was not himself one of its heroes and never claimed that he was. He never figured in the company's annual report, but was to do for *la Ligne* what *Life* would do for the Mercury 7 astronauts. History belongs to the eloquent.

~

No one described flying over fogged-in mountain peaks, battling down-drafts, navigating in snowstorms better than Saint-Exupéry. He flew through the Pyrenees regularly in December 1926 and January 1927, during which time he grew more and more accustomed to the discipline of the métier and the indiscipline of the machines. He wrote Renée de Saussine of the mountain gods that guarded the French-Spanish border:

> You apply for the right to pass. At 9,000 feet, you feel very proud. But the hostile gods drag you down and the altimeter plummets "9,000 . . . 7,000 . . . 5,000 . . . 4,500 . . . 3,000" as do you along with it; you're forced to turn around because the mountain is now higher than you are and the gods are laughing. And you try to escape through a valley, with the confidence of an omelette in a frying pan, because the hostile gods are playing tennis, and you are the ball.

After another trip he reported that he piloted with one hand and held on for his life with the other; on occasion he held on for his life with both, while his airplane "took the opportunity to dance a little Charleston." At 100 miles per hour he made his way in a snowstorm through two walls of mountain he could not see. He had only his compass to guide him; it got him out of the snowstorm but took him entirely off course. This was the flight that caused him to remark on the unfortunate similarity between a compass and a weathervane. On another occasion he reported that it had taken him nine hours to make the trip from Toulouse to Alicante, normally a five- or six-hour flight. He was exhausted after these excursions, which in early 1927 began to extend to Casablanca and occasionally on to Tangier. He might fly as much as 2,500 miles in four days. If he stood after such a trip he claimed he looked drunk; if he talked he stuttered; he was never quite sure where he was. The only time the word "heroic" entered his mind was when, after such an ordeal, he made the superhuman effort to sit down and write a letter before keeling over with fatigue.

By mid-January he was considered a seasoned enough pilot to graduate to the Casablanca–Dakar line, now a little over eighteen months old. Understandably, he was a little uneasy, particularly on account of the Moors, who only a month after his arrival at Latécoère had murdered two of his colleagues. Probably it did not help much that he was told to be ready to leave for Dakar several weeks before he was actually sent on his way; fear, he was to say later, was a result of having nothing to do. He packed his bags and lived, unhappily, in what may well have been the tidiest room he ever occupied, until early February. Since moving to the apartment on the rue d'Alsace-Lorraine he had waged war against his landlady's porcelain figurines, which he routinely hid in the closet only to find miraculously resurrected on the mantelpiece on his return. Now he allowed these two statuettes, a hunchbacked Zouave and a shepherdess, trappings of a life he so much resisted, to win; he let them reign over his desolate room full of boxes. Claiming the order enforced by these kitsch gods to be painful, he spent as little time as possible in his quarters. He felt like a fifteen-year-old about to head off to boarding school, with all of his memories neatly tucked away for the trip. Sometime in January, probably before the bags were packed, Madame de Saint-Exupéry paid her son a visit in Toulouse, as she had been hoping to do for some time. He was moody and sullen. He claimed this was because he had felt unable to cheer his mother, who was not feeling up to par. Just before he left he wrote contritely that he would return to France solvent, a marriageable man, the son of her dreams.

On February 6 Saint-Exupéry flew an empty aircraft to Agadir, midway between Casablanca and Cape Juby. From here he was to continue on to Dakar as a passenger. On the seventh Guillaumet and an interpreter took off from Agadir in one Breguet with the mail; René Riguelle took off with Saint-Exupéry in another. There was a moment of drama when the two planes lost each other after Villa Cisneros, but they landed in tandem at Port-Étienne, refueled, and quickly headed off on the next and longest lap, the penultimate one. Despite his excitement Saint-Exupéry succumbed to the heat and drifted off to sleep, waking momentarily to note that Riguelle had moved the Breguet a mile or so out to sea in an effort to find cooler air. He was not particularly happy about this decision—were anything to go wrong they would surely drown, he thought—but dozed off again nonetheless.

> I was startled out of my sleep by a crash, a sudden silence, and then the voice of Riguelle saying, "Damn! There goes a connecting rod!" As I half rose out of my seat to send a regretful look at that white coastline, now more precious than ever, he shouted to me angrily to stay as I was. I knew Riguelle had been wrong to go out to sea; I had been on the point of mentioning it; and now I felt a complete and savage satisfaction in our predicament. "This," I said to myself, "will teach him a lesson."
>
> But this gratifying sense of superiority could obviously not last very long. Riguelle sent the plane earthward in a long diagonal line that brought us within sixty feet of the sand—an altitude at which there was no question of picking out a landing place. We lost both wheels against one sand dune, a wing against another, and crashed with a sudden jerk into a third.
>
> "You hurt?" Riguelle called out.
>
> "Not a bit," I said.
>
> "That's what I call piloting a ship!" he boasted cheerfully.

The airplane had ploughed into the dunes at seventy miles per hour; it was, Saint-Exupéry reported to Ségogne, one of the many people he wrote of his memorable Saharan initiation, "a handsome crash." Saint-Exupéry crawled on all fours from the wreckage; he was indeed unhurt, but ached all over. He reckoned the two were hundreds of miles from help of any kind, with two revolvers, three tins of food, and no water save that in the Breguet's radiator. (Mermoz had discovered the pernicious effects of this beverage the previous year when, stranded near Juby, he had on his third day been reduced to drinking his radiator water. He suffered less from having been captured by the Moors on this exploit than from the damage the acidic fluid had done to his intestines.) Riguelle assured Saint-Exupéry that Guillaumet would be along to rescue them; sure enough Guillaumet touched down shortly, on the flat stretch of nearby sand to which Riguelle had been headed. There was not room in his Breguet for all of them, however, and it was decided that Saint-Exupéry would stay behind while Guillaumet and Riguelle flew the mail on to safety, after which they would return for him.

On his first day in the Sahara Saint-Exupéry was left in the middle of a vast sea of rolling dunes, armed, with the instructions to shoot at anything he saw. Riguelle and Guillaumet handed over to him their extra ammunition, which led him to expect the worst, but what he remembered having felt was something else altogether. He was alone—in his first account of the afternoon he referred to it as his "*baptême de solitude*"— and he could sense the mystery of the desert, the hum of its silence. It had the rich appeal of an old house. He was very far from Paris, or even Toulouse. "Sitting on the dune, I laid out beside me my gun and my five cartridge clips. For the first time since I was born it seemed to me that my life was my own and that I was responsible for it." He climbed a dune and surveyed the horizon like a captain from his ship, enchanted by the empty sea around him. A gazelle turned up, as did, toward the end of the golden-tinted afternoon, Guillaumet. "You weren't frightened?" asked the veteran, who had neglected to mention that he had abandoned his colleague in one of the safest stretches of the Sahara, well within the boundaries of Mauritania. "I said no, and thought, Gazelles are not frightening," remembered Saint-Exupéry. To his mother he wrote nonchalantly of the initiation: "The trip went well, aside from a breakdown and the plane crashing in the desert."

He was not so matter-of-fact concerning his accommodations that evening. Only his description of the evening of February 8 has survived, but it has in so many versions that it is fairly easy to gauge its accuracy. Together, too, these variations on a theme reveal a good deal about the narrative and spiritual drama Saint-Exupéry could extract from a single image-heavy event. Riguelle had been lucky to crash not far from the French fort at Nouakchott, on the Mauritanian coast, the site today of that country's capital. A single French sergeant had manned the outpost for several years with his fifteen Senegalese soldiers; nothing was more

welcome to this misplaced bit of France than the arrival of three compatriots, who were to him like gifts from heaven. He had not seen a
Frenchman in six months; the original victim of poor communications,
the sergeant received his mail twice a year, at which point the responses
to his letters no longer made much sense. His luxury in life consisted of
a supply of candles, by which he kept up his off-kilter correspondence
from his spartan bedroom. In one account Saint-Exupéry has the sergeant
weeping at the sight of his visitors. By all accounts he began to pour out
his heart—and his provisions—for these emissaries from the homeland.
Proudly he treated the aviators to the best of his cellar, after which the
group filed up to the parapet of the fort and discussed the stars. (They
were, Saint-Exupéry noted, "all present, all accounted for.") The four
men smoked, they surveyed the heavens, they traded intimate confidences in the moonlight. Guillaumet and Riguelle reminisced about
women they knew in France, whose charms they celebrated; so as not to
be outdone Saint-Exupéry invented a girlfriend for the occasion. The
sergeant talked about his lieutenant and his captain, whom he had not
seen in months and who were, twice a year, his only visitors. Saint-Exupéry
realized that for a man marooned in the desert these were no less memories
of love.

To Ségogne he wrote a rhapsodic letter the following week from
Dakar:

> We went to sleep on the sand, but toward three in the morning our wool
> blankets became thin, transparent; the moon had cast an evil spell. At three
> in the morning we were freezing and had to get up. We went back up to
> the terrace where we sat on the wall; we were three to watch over the desert
> while the sergeant slept. And I could tell you how many jackals, how many
> hyenas made love that night. I could tell you the number of shooting stars,
> those that took advantage of the sergeant's sleep: they were three. On the
> first, I made a wish: that this night last a thousand years. On the second,
> which fell to the north, that everyone would write me. On the third, that
> all women in the world might be tender. Then it was so calm, so quiet, it
> was such a marvelous night that I did not dare further disturb the stars.

Ségogne saved this letter, which struck him as particularly polished;
he guessed at the time it was to become a draft of something. He was
right: the incident found its way into two newspaper pieces, *Southern Mail*,
and *Wind, Sand and Stars*. Although Ségogne surely got the most
personal—and the most poetic—account of the evening, all five were trial
runs for the sixth, more abstract version, that of *The Little Prince*. In
Southern Mail Saint-Exupéry reduced the cast to two men, one of whom
has dropped in on the other from interplanetary space; alone in the desert,

the two trade confidences about their respective planets. Bernis follows the sergeant up to the parapet for a cigarette. "Are you the Sergeant of the Stars?" he asks, but gets no answer. In the moonlight the two men break into a rousing chorus of the children's song "Il Pleut, Il Pleut Bergère." By the time they finish it is daylight, and the sergeant helps Bernis to repair his plane, sending off the "young god" with a heavy heart. "From what paradise, beyond the sands, do such handsome messengers so noiselessly descend?" he asks himself. It is the riddle that, sixteen years later, will plague the narrator of *The Little Prince*, whose fable is prefigured in many ways at Nouakchott, where a different course in astronomy takes place. In an early version of the manuscript Saint-Exupéry goes so far as to give the captain-governor of Port-Étienne, who otherwise resembles the Nouakchott sergeant, a wife. Toward the end of the evening, in mid-desert,

> Our hostess shows us her garden. Three cases of real earth had been shipped to her from Montluçon; they had therefore traveled 2,500 miles. She sprays them every night with water, which arrives once a month from Bordeaux. From this earth grow three green plants. We caress their leaves gently, as if they are jewels. The captain says: "It's my park. And when the wind whips up the sand, drying everything, we take it down to the cellar."

Like the shipwrecked evening that lent *Wind, Sand and Stars* its name, this was an incident that stayed with Saint-Exupéry. He recycled it several times, turning and turning it like a prism for the purpose of his narratives. Guillaumet and Riguelle were probably no less moved by the jewels in the desert sky, by the glint of moonlight on the Breguet's wings; it does not take a poet to recognize the poetry of the Sahara at night. Saint-Exupéry, who could be off-handed but who in none of these accounts felt the need to exaggerate (save that he gives the sergeant twenty Senegalese guards in *Southern Mail*), was taken by the more human elements of the fantastic evening, by the twin powers of distance and isolation, by the ready intimacy they created, by the uncommon importance of home and of homeland and all that represents the two, by the mythmaking that goes on in the mind of a man, especially a solitary man, especially a solitary man in God's country, the desert. His profession had the effect of making man larger than life but Saint-Exupéry, as he practiced it, began to see man as smaller and smaller, everywhere as isolated as the sergeant at Nouakchott, until urgency or a heartfelt cause drew him to his fellows. He was hundreds of miles from, but had not forgotten, Saint-Germain-des-Prés. "It is a little lonely in the desert," observes the Little Prince. "It is also lonely among men," replies the snake.

~

A day or two later the pilot found himself in Dakar, a city that might have been on another planet from Nouakchott and to which he took an immediate dislike. There was nothing transcendent about flat, gray, modern Dakar, then about half the size of Le Mans. At all times of the year Dakar is humid, even when it is not hot; in February Saint-Exupéry complained that he sweated profusely from the minute he got up in the morning. He compared Senegal's premier city to Asnières, a rather glum suburb of Paris; he wrote his mother, with scorn, that he had traveled three thousand miles to find himself in a suburb of Lyons. Dakar was more bourgeois than bourgeois France, more provincial than the provinces, he wrote, railing against the uselessness of the small, inbred community that—with its petty politics and heightened sense of self-importance—was an inevitable fixture of the colonial world. He felt stifled, and was stuck in Dakar until the twenty-fourth of the month, when he was to begin flying up and down the coast to Casablanca.

At first Saint-Exupéry joined his colleagues in various nightclubs in town, in one of which he met Guillaumet's future wife for the first time. (He would be a witness at the couple's wedding in 1929.) Noëlle Guillaumet never forgot her first impression of Saint-Exupéry, flailing about on the dance floor of a Dakar club with a girl who barely came up to his shoulder, a sock garter trailing behind him. He was not much for the nightlife Dakar had to offer, the colonial decadence of which he found repugnant; another account has him off in a corner of a Dakar nightclub reading Plato's *Dialogues*. In all the wrong ways the city reminded him of the prisons of habit in which the provincial bureaucrat lived out his days; it brought to mind "those little village bistros along the roadside where one sometimes winds up to gulp down a quick lemonade, and in which one rediscovers, like the walls of a prison, like an impossible escape, the player piano, the calendar, the pool table, and above all the smell and the greasy tables and the waitress shuffling around in her slippers." It was worse still. Everything in the city seemed to Saint-Exupéry either unfinished or dilapidated. No water ran in the sinks; doors refused to close; the municipal clocks had been broken for ten years. "Everything is here, but none of it works," he lamented.

Even on a monthly salary of about 6,000 francs, or about two hundred and thirty-five 1927 dollars, Dakar was expensive for Saint-Exupéry. His room alone, at the Hôtel de l'Europe, cost five hundred francs a month. He made himself feel a little at home by displaying one of his mother's pastels on his night table, along with a crumbling branch of a hazelnut tree she had given him; he tucked away three years of her letters in his drawer. The month before he had bought himself a little Moroccan carpet in the Casablanca souk, which presumably decorated his Dakar room as well. He reported that he had felt a different man since making this purchase, almost too neatly appropriate for a footloose aviator living an Arabian tale: "I have a little parcel of land, I have a homeland, I have a little rolled-up carpet." Sometime this winter he went lion hunting, an obligatory sport in Dakar; he wounded but did not kill his prey, and admitted that he would have felt equally challenged hunting rabbit. He toyed with the beginnings of *Southern Mail* and he complained, at least in his letters. But he also knew that it was from Dakar that he would head off in search of the kind of magic he had known at Nouakchott. He could only hope that his crankshaft would give way, so that he might realize the kind of adventures of which he dreamed. This wish, unlike those made from the parapet at Nouakchott, was regularly granted.

From the end of February until early in the summer Saint-Exupéry flew the mail up and down the coast. His letters—which went to all the usual correspondents save for Renée de Saussine, on whom he now began to give up—are postmarked Port-Étienne, Cape Juby, Villa Cisernos, Dakar; often enough he carried them himself the 1,700 miles up the desert coast, a trip that would have taught anyone the meaning of infinity. A Breguet 14 moving at eighty miles per hour over rolling sand gave an impression mostly of immobility, like a rowboat on the high sea. He was happy, and reported to his mother—in the same letter in which he asked that she leave the word "Count" off his envelopes—that he had finally found his calling. He managed only on his fourth or fifth attempt to make some sense of his new life in a letter to Sallès; he was still feeling out its virtues, the appeal of which surprised him a little. In particular Saint-Exupéry marveled over the distance, which was at once liberating and poignant; his past seemed as far-off and immaterial as the headlines in a provincial newspaper sound to a nonnative. "I know that I am terribly independent," he finally concluded. "I have a great need for solitude. I suffocate if I live for fifteen days among the same twenty people."

With the women in his life he allowed himself to be less than perfectly affirming. The same mail that took an envelope to Sallès extolling the virtues of isolation included one to his friend Lucie-Marie Decour in which he wrangled with some last reservations. The next morning at six he would be aloft over dissident territory, between Cisneros and Juby, fired at like a partridge. "Sometimes I think I must be an idiot," he confessed. "I wonder what I'm looking for in all this, if the more intelligent choice is not simply to be happy. . . . I have chosen the most difficult life—and the most uncertain—because I think that otherwise one amounts to nothing, and because people like the ———— disgust me. But what if I'm wrong? What if it's all a matter of pride? What if it only serves to wear me out?" His female friends and his mother represented a world he saw as incompatible with the realm of action but which a part of him nonetheless still craved. Half in jest he wrote his brother-in-law, Pierre d'Agay, to find him a ravishing girl with whom he might have a family. He dreamed of elevators and bathrooms and eau-de-cologne and of that eminent symbol of civilization: of well-pressed sheets. He got down from his Breguet covered in oil; he asked Sallès to send him some industrial-strength soap, for which he would be reimbursed, saying that it took him hours to clean up after a flight without it.

His doubts extended beyond the luxuries he knew he was missing. From Casablanca in January he wrote Renée de Saussine openly of his fears. He was not happy when he was told to expect fog on his flights. He did not want to die. ("The world would not lose much but I'd lose everything," he wrote.) He may have been made more aware of his own mortality by the apparent death eighteen months earlier of Sabran in Tangier; in May a second Fribourg friend, Louis de Bonnevie, would pass away as well. He trembled a little at the idea of heading off to Dakar, of overflying dissident zones. He was fixated on the Moors. He had a decided taste for risk but only during the day; at night his anxieties got the better of him. Then his world, and the ties that bound him to it, seemed hugely fragile. At night, too, courage struck him as nothing short of ridiculous: "It's hogwash," he wrote Lucie-Marie Decour. (He may have said more about himself than he meant to when he wrote his mother that he only ever lived after nine at night. At that time he could see through the virtues that made other men proud, and at that time his anxieties ran wild.) Courage seemed to him more a matter of contempt than anything else. It was not in his eyes a particularly admirable trait: "I don't even know whether I'm courageous or not. The only things I worry about are the tachometer, the pressure gauges, the altimeter. Those are the only things that count." The quality of bravery seemed to him increasingly flimsy the more he crashed, the more he came to know the dangers of the desert. To Yvonne de Lestrange he wrote memorably the next year that he had come to understand why courage came last on Plato's list of virtues. It amounted to "a touch of anger, a spice of vanity, a lot of obstinacy, and a tawdry 'sporting' thrill." There are, of course, many definitions of courage: the man who regularly piloted an unreliable plane over hostile territory for the sake of the mail and who succeeded most of the time, often enough by the skin of his teeth, could not help but see the quality differently from the man who meticulously prepared himself and his airplane for several months for a thirty-three-and-one-half-hour solo flight across the Atlantic in quest of a $25,000 prize.

Saint-Exupéry succumbed neither to any sense of self-importance nor to his misgivings. After these first few months on the African route, after a first crash in Senegal, he began to rise well above his misgivings. He got used to the danger, the heat (which could keep a Breguet from climbing above 600 feet), the glaring sun, the traveling interpreters, the long days, the layovers. What may once have been fear soon turned into fascination; in a very short time he went from being green to being wise beyond his years. And the distraction that had on occasion concerned his colleagues began to evidence itself as abstraction.

In May 1927, with Lefèbvre, then chief mechanic at Villa Cisneros, as his passenger, Saint-Exupéry flew from Cisneros south to Port-Étienne. He had arrived in Cisneros with the mail, which was slow in being unloaded; the escort plane meanwhile turned circles overhead. The discharging of the mail took a long time, however, which did not make the Breguet's air-cooled engine, slowed during this period, very happy. Several minutes after Saint-Exupéry and Lefèbvre took off, somewhere just over—and barely over, as Lefèbvre remembered it—the Bay of the Río de Oro, the engine began to cough and clang and sputter. It had overheated, a condition that would have been further aggravated should Saint-Exupéry have tried to gain any altitude. He had little choice but to skim the waves, which he now did, serenely, the escort plane at his side. Lefèbvre, as well acquainted with the humors of an engine as anyone, thought it prudent to prepare for the inevitable swim: he removed his shoes and set about disrobing. What was Saint-Exupéry doing during this time? He was making sketches that he passed backward with broad smiles to his passenger. In them the two men appeared as deep-sea swimmers, as Robinson Crusoe look-alikes on a tiny island, as prisoners of the desert.

Ultimately, Saint-Exupéry flew back toward land and—despite a long mechanical series of coughs and hiccoughs—on to Port-Étienne without incident. At the Port-Étienne airfield, to Lefèbvre's great surprise, he noted in the Breguet's journey log: "Good aircraft. All okay." That evening at dinner the mechanic could not help but question the pilot's judgment. Saint-Exupéry replied, a little slyly: "Look here, Lefèbvre, it can't be a bad airplane if it carried us all the way here."

This conversation did not prevent the pilot from assuring Lefèbvre on another occasion: "Flying an airplane is different from driving a car; you don't have to watch the road. An airplane is made to fly straight, on its own." His claim sounded curiously like that made some years later by William T. Piper, the president of the Piper Aircaft Corporation: "Once you have learned to fly your plane, it is far less fatiguing to fly than it is to drive a car. You don't have to watch every second for cats, dogs, children, lights, road signs, ladies with baby carriages and citizens who drive out into the middle of the block against the lights. . . . Nobody who has not been up in the sky on a glorious morning can possibly imagine the way a pilot feels in free heaven." For the very reason that he manifested this nonchalance under conditions where it amounted, in the late 1920s, to either courage or idiocy, Saint-Exupéry was no Latécoère mechanic's first-choice pilot. (One went so far as to say that he was much esteemed by his colleagues except on those occasions when they were required to fly with him.) What he demonstrated amounted less to grace than insouciance under pressure. But posterity had much to gain from his imperturbability, at least as much as it did from Lindbergh's determination, which this month set the world on end. It seems entirely likely that Saint-Exupéry did some of his clearest thinking during his flights up and down the African coast in 1927, when he was flying the most primitive plane he would ever fly. "How is it possible," Anne Morrow Lindbergh wondered of him several years later, "that he kept his mind on the gas consumption while pondering the mysteries of the universe? How can he navigate by stars when they are to him 'the frozen glitter of diamonds'?"

Saint-Exupéry's first logbook has been lost, but like all of the Latécoère pilots he made plenty of unscheduled landings between 1927 and 1929, certainly more than found their way into *Wind, Sand and Stars*. It was not an accident that won him a leave in the summer of 1927, however, but a serious attack of dengue fever, an infectious disease that causes serious muscle and joint pains. It landed him in a Dakar hospital for a few weeks, a nightmarish stay he liked to describe for his friends afterward, dwelling on the condition of the roommate whose body played host to a tenacious army of fat, red worms. Saint-Exupéry's illness won him a reprieve from the brutal Dakar summer, so hot and windy that the French women and children were routinely sent back to Paris. He returned to Gabrielle and her husband's home at Agay, on the Riviera—the house that would henceforth take the place of Saint-Maurice as his refuge—to recover his strength. It was from this leave that he was recalled posthaste by Daurat to Toulouse and packed off, with a few hours' warning, early in October, for what turned into his thirteen-month stay as chief of the airfield at Juby.

~

By the time Saint-Exupéry returned to France at the end of 1928, he was legendary along *la Ligne*, now as much for his resourcefulness as for his distraction. He had discovered the luxury of urgency, which he wore well. It transformed his childish persistence into an impressive sangfroid in the face of danger, his love of performance into a welcome ingenuity when it came to diverting the tired, the despondent, the shipwrecked. His childish tyranny—still an element in his friendships—looked, on the mail line, more like leadership, confidence. (In all guises it could cause friction, however: the mail pilots thought it their right to test-fly any newly repaired aircraft at Juby before heading off over the desert, but the chief of the airfield firmly insisted on taking these machines up himself.) He had grown close to Mermoz and to Guillaumet and was now within the bosom of the Aéropostale family as within his own. He discovered that "there is no fraternity more welcoming than a professional one . . . [that] the winds, the storms, and the long, nocturnal anguishes make for a common homeland."

Tales of his bravado circulated quickly. One night in a Casablanca restaurant in January 1929 Joseph Kessel heard about Saint-Exupéry's magnificent desert rescue missions, of the détente he had orchestrated at Juby. He wrote that these exploits were narrated by a sort of fevered chorus and included the tales in his own passenger's-eye view of the mail line. (Kessel's *Vent de sable* followed the publication of *Southern Mail* by a matter of months. Saint-Exupéry's first novel did not merit a review in *Le Figaro Littéraire*, but the excerpt from *Vent de sable* that appeared in that publication in November happened to be one describing his camelback rescue of the Breguet.) Blaise Cendrars, returning to France from Brazil by boat the following year, was treated to a long catalogue of the herculean tasks accomplished by this ace, this soldier, this paladin, this adventurer, this knight-errant, this broad-shouldered *tendre*, the most taciturn man in the company but also its *enfant terrible*. He was most struck by the account of an episode that had taken place in early December 1927, when Saint-Exupéry and Maurice Dumesnil waded for three hours through a hip-high Senegalese swamp to rescue a downed Guillaumet. Most of these tales swelled in the retelling: Cendrars heard that Guillaumet, Saint-Exupéry, and Dumesnil spent the next three days entirely absorbed by a furious game of chess while they waited to be rescued, an account that added two full days to the misadventure. (Cendrars admitted to having been most impressed by Saint-Exupéry's purported insouciance in the midst of this wait; he found this a sure mark of heroism.) It was, however, clear to the men with whom Saint-Exupéry worked—and to no one more so than Didier Daurat, who was most responsible for having nurtured the transformation—that a different creature had emerged from the desert. Now there was Saint-Exupéry and also Saint-Ex: Kessel wrote that an infinite margin separated these two distinct individuals.

Early in 1929, Saint-Exupéry the man of letters submitted his manuscript of *Southern Mail* to Gallimard. It was accepted—a contract was signed on February 20—and the publisher made its traditional commitment to the author's next seven volumes. This gave Saint-Exupéry something a little different to celebrate from his colleagues, who had been, during his time at Juby, concentrating on opening up South America to airmail service. In May 1928 Mermoz linked Rio de Janiero and Buenos Aires by thirteen hours in a Latécoère 28, a staggering feat in the eyes of the South Americans, who had never dreamed that the 1,250 miles separating the two cities could be forded in the course of a day. On Bastille Day 1929, Mermoz officially inaugurated Buenos Aires–Santiago service with Guillaumet, to whom it was entrusted. The glory of Aéropostale had now begun to be celebrated widely: these advances figured prominently in the newspapers. In large part they were due to a number of new planes that Latécoère—sorely aware of the limitations of the Breguet 14—had been developing in 1927 and 1928.

By early 1929, the Latécoère 25 and 26, the latter capable of 425-mile hops, had by and large replaced the Breguet 14. These two airplanes— the first Latécoère machines designed specifically to carry the mail—were not only more powerful than the Breguet; they carried passengers and were equipped with radiotelegraph. They did not routinely break down; they could be flown at night, and began, as of mid-1928, to speed service all along the airline. But the Paris–Buenos Aires mail, as Mermoz complained that year, spent eight to ten of its fourteen days in motion on a slow-moving French boat, an insult to the men who knocked themselves out to move the envelopes from Paris to Dakar, then on from Natal, on the Brazilian coast, to Buenos Aires, in a total of two days at either end. It remained still to cross the 1,600 miles of ocean between Dakar and Natal by air. The technology with which to do so was clearly in the offing; what was needed was a skilled pilot for the grueling Senegal–Brazil leg, one who could navigate by the stars and also fly a hydroplane.

Proof that, at least by now, he had come to respect the writer as a pilot, Daurat thought of Saint-Exupéry for the task. He was rare among the Latécoère staff in that he had had training in higher mathematics, the stuff of which navigation is made. Early in 1929, he was enrolled in an elite course in celestial navigation offered at the naval academy to promising young lieutenants and to a few pilots from the private sector. So it was that in April, after a brief stay in Paris during which he did some preparatory work at Saint-Cyr, Saint-Exupéry found himself in Brest after all. He was only ten years late.

General Lionel-Max Chassin, then a brilliant naval lieutenant, headed up the specialized course. He was eager to get off to an informal start with his eleven students, not much younger than himself, and arranged for a first meeting of his class to take place on the terrace of the Café Continental, Brest's best café, at 6:00 p.m. Ten young men and a second instructor assembled at the appointed hour. Some time later an apologetic Saint-Exupéry appeared; he had lost his way in the winding streets of

Brest's old city, where he had rented a room. He made an unforgettable entrance. If Saint-Exupéry had stood out on an airfield Saint-Ex now stood out among precisely the kind of men whose background and schooling resembled his own. Chassin remembered the effect produced by his massive student, "this big, rough-hewn devil with the shock of dark, unruly hair, his powerful forehead, and his luminous expression of intelligence and ·kindness." Saint-Exupéry and the course's sole engineer were the only two men not in uniform; the pilot was five or six years older than his classmates (and two years older than his instructor) and balding. If his fame had not preceded him his classmates at Brest were well aware all the same that the Aéropostale pilots were not exactly paper-pushers. He was immediately baptized "Juby."

Chassin's course got off to a lively start. The genial professor ordered a round of vermouth and cassis, after which the senior officer among the students did the same, as was proper. Chassin's colleague offered up the next round; Saint-Exupéry then broke with tradition, proposing a round of vermouth and cassis on behalf of the civilian students. Thirteen Noilly cassis and a few drunken choruses later the group was on familiar terms. Saint-Exupéry clearly felt comfortable within this circle, in which company he elaborated on the terrors he had caused at Bossuet. He must have taken particular pleasure in relating the story of the failed entrance exams to the naval academy, which he now attributed—as any writer whose first book was on the presses that April would have been tempted to—to a failing grade in French. The group's camaraderie was cemented in the evenings, not only in the brasseries of the city, but on the roof of the old château where the courses were held. Here Chassin and his students assembled, sextants in hand, to map the evening sky. When the clouds rolled in, as they do often in Brest, the astronomers chatted happily for hours, in the chill, as they waited for the skies to clear.

If Saint-Exupéry was famous in Brest it was neither for his tales of the desert nor for his schoolboy antics, however. He distinguished himself immediately with his "clumsiness and his lively intelligence," proving as brilliant on the theoretical plane as he was hopelessly maladroit on the practical one. Chassin noted that his student had an innate feel for mathematics: though he had been lost in the educational system he had not forgotten any of his earlier training, and had as good a grasp of calculus as any of the young lieutenants. He displayed a remarkable ability to locate subtle relationships between two seemingly unrelated phenomena; as Daurat had also observed, he could disassemble a complex question into its simple components with alacrity. Invention came naturally to him. He was a genius as an engineer, more successful now than he had been with his flying bicycle or his irrigation system. There was only one difficulty with the navigational apparatuses Saint-Exupéry devised at Brest and shared in confidence with Chassin: by and large, they existed already.

He did not win high marks on the practical level; his missteps were still being catalogued years later. He smashed an expensive quadrant, broke a magnetic compass, misplaced a hydrographic circle. He miserably failed a pop quiz on magnetic derivation, spending an entire afternoon in a panic-stricken sweat only to arrive at a series of outlandish answers. He ignored Chassin's repeated reminders that the pilot of a hydroplane pulled back on his stick to take off rather than forward, as in a conventional tail-dragger; Saint-Exupéry dutifully pushed the stick forward, thrusting the floats downward into the water. The plane, its pilot, and his instructor ploughed into a ferocious whirlpool. On another occasion he very nearly drowned himself. Chassin had been teaching his students to fly a two-motor Latham hydroplane, one peculiarity of which was that its drift-ometer hatch was exceedingly difficult to close. He had issued specific instructions that the driftometer was as a consequence not to be touched for any reason, instructions that Saint-Exupéry alone ignored, consulting the mechanism and then neglecting to close the hatch before landing. After much frantic hand-waving, he and the Latham, both of them wa-terlogged, were lifted from the bay by a dockside crane. Saved from the waters he began to make excuses for his awkwardness; Chassin confined himself to treating Saint-Exupéry coldly, a punishment from which his student suffered more than he might have from any other.

In his letters from Brest he does not sound as if he is thriving, probably because of the workload. He wrote his mother that Brest was "not much fun" and that he would love her to visit but (inexplicably) had only debts at the moment. He missed Saint-Maurice terribly and reported that he needed a vacation. In a melancholic mood he wrote Ségogne in May, after the birth of his friend's daughter. He reported that he was tired of his life, which seemed to consist of either sand or sea, both of which were noto-riously poor in greenery and women. He was sure Ségogne, as a new father, would be proud and insufferable, which he conceded was only natural under the circumstances. He could be a solitary creature, as one friend with whom he watched a leisurely Brest sunset—seated thirty feet from each other without exchanging a word—was quick to note.

At Brest as at Bossuet, he was distracted by literature, this time more legitimately. He was greatly preoccupied—too much so, in Chassin's opinion—by the correction of the proofs of *Southern Mail*, which he must have received early in May, the same month that an excerpt from the book appeared in the *NRF*. As soon as the novel's proofs arrived Saint-Exupéry shared them with his instructor, whose opinion he valued greatly. (Chassin was favorably impressed.) In the end the novel became so much a part of life in Brest that spring that the entire class was able to recite the first page of the book by heart. Nor did Saint-Exupéry's obsession confine itself to his classmates. His Parisian cousin, Honoré d'Estienne d'Orves, himself a naval officer, remembered having been deprived of a night's sleep by a dramatic reading of *Southern Mail* just after Saint-Exupéry had received the proofs.

The young author was not always so emboldened. Also in April, at Gallimard's suggestion, he paid a call on André Beucler, a writer of about his age who already had a number of publications to his credit and who was something of a permanent fixture at the publishing firm. Beucler remembered feeling an immediate sympathy for the shy, robust individual who darkened his doorway and awkwardly pulled a set of proofs from his pocket with the words: "My publisher, who is also yours, has sent me to ask you for a short introduction to the book I have here. I apologize for disturbing you." (Beucler would have been forewarned of the intrusion: evidently Saint-Exupéry had called the previous day and left word with Beucler's family. Moreover, Beucler, who had a few years earlier been Gaston Gallimard's roommate and who now very much played the role of his emissary-at-large, had recently complained that his ambassadorial duties left him little time to write. Gallimard countered that Beucler was living a privileged life in his employ but all the same threw him the Saint-Exupéry preface—which he requested for the next day at noon—to placate him.) The introduction, largely a meditation on the heroism of the Aéro-postale crew, indeed appeared on Gallimard's desk the day after Saint-Exupéry's visit. In it Beucler presented the first novelist as one of the company's star pilots. "Saint-Exupéry is not a writer," he explained, making an impressive case instead for his being a hero. Months later, when Beucler and Saint-Exupéry had become friends, Beucler regretted not having been more effusive in his praise for the work. He found its author astonishing, radiant, the kind of man for whom heads turned in the street. He was interested in everything, always eager to divulge a subtle observation on which he had clearly meditated for some time. Said Beucler, recalling a series of walks and dinners, bookstore visits and afternoons in cafés: "He seemed to hold a degree in all subjects."

This was ironic in light of his fate in Brest. In July Saint-Exupéry passed his final examination, as did all of his classmates. At the end of the term, however, the air force colonel in charge of the program paid a visit to the academy, partly to remind Chassin of the prestige of his course. Its reputation had only been enhanced by its association with Joseph Le Brix, an early instructor and a hero since 1927 for having made the first nonstop crossing of the South Atlantic. For the course to retain its cachet, the colonel explained, it was necessary that Chassin flunk two students. The young lieutenant protested but so did his superior; ultimately Chassin relented and handed over the names of the last two of his eleven students. One of them, the next-to-last, happened to be a very promising officer whose career the Ministry wanted in no way jeopardized. "Give me the name of the ninth," ordered the Colonel, forcing the professor to deliver up Saint-Exupéry, who had fallen to ninth place only because of the points his mishaps had cost him. (Such interventions were not unheard of. Five years earlier Philippe Pétain had stepped in on Charles de Gaulle's behalf at the École Supérieure de Guerre, when a costly "*assez bien*," the lowest grade accorded, was raised to a "*bien*," without which de Gaulle's entire career would have been compromised.) Saint-Exupéry was failed; it was as if the system could only conspire against him. Mercifully, this was to be his last academic experience.

~

Southern Mail, meanwhile, was published in July. Suzanne Verneilh and her husband, who had been the chief of the Agadir airfield when Saint-Exupéry had been posted to Juby, ran into their ex-neighbor that month in Paris and made a dinner date with him at a favorite restaurant in the 17th arrondissement, near their apartment. Saint-Exupéry arrived at the Maisonette Basque a little late and greatly distracted, a copy of *Southern Mail* under his arm. The book had come off the press that day. He put the volume down on the table next to him without saying a word, but Madame Verneilh noticed a look of secret delight cross his face as he did so. Uncharacteristically, he paid no attention to what he was eating; he let Verneilh make all the conversation. He was oblivious even to the "superb blonde" who stared at him from across the restaurant all evening and to whom Verneilh had to direct his attention. Occasionally he reached out furtively, dreamily, to caress the cover of the book. Madame Verneilh doubted that the first novelist even remembered having eaten that evening, much less where and with whom. She and her husband left him at the corner of the avenue Carnot and watched as he headed off toward the Arc de Triomphe, the slim volume pressed tightly to his broad chest.

Southern Mail's first major reviewer was the eminent Edmond Jaloux, writing in *Les Nouvelles Littéraires*. Responding to Beucler's preface he observed that heroes generally wrote poorly, but was quick to note that this author was an exception to the rule. He was much taken with the novel—though understandably more so with its impressions of aviation than with the love story of Geneviève and Bernis, which struck him as superficially treated—and Saint-Exupéry was much pleased by the notice. Literary circles are small everywhere but especially so in France: Jean Prévost did not feel disqualified from writing about *Southern Mail* although he had been the first to put Saint-Exupéry into print and had helped to steer him to the Gallimard stable. He reviewed the book glowingly in the September edition of the *NRF*. He too had high praise for

Saint-Exupéry's ability to render action on the page; he found the discontinuity of the story consistent with the reality of experienced adventure. An indulgent friend and reviewer, he was all the same forced to admit that the sentimental part of the novel was awkwardly handled. (Except for *The Little Prince*, this observation would prove as true of the work as of the man. Stung by these comments and reined in by his natural discretion, Saint-Exupéry henceforth steered wide of matters of the heart on the page.) Prévost was struck in particular by a line of Saint-Exupéry's quoted in Beucler's preface: "I have loved this life that I have never really understood, a life that is not at all regular. I don't even know how I got here; it was all a lark."

In August Saint-Exupéry was back at that life. Didier Daurat seemed in no way put off by his pilot's failure at Brest, although he must have concluded from Chassin's reports that Saint-Exupéry was not meant to be the first man to pilot a hydroplane across the South Atlantic. (The honor fell to Mermoz the following year.) He put Saint-Exupéry to work on the Toulouse–Casablanca route, now piloting Latécoère 25's and 26's, the aircraft that would change the geography of the African coast. That month, in the middle of a heat wave, Saint-Exupéry and Henry Delaunay, who had joined the company at about the same time, flew through the night with two mechanics from Alicante to the beach of Valencia to rescue a downed Latécoère. The mechanics set to work immediately on their arrival, at 10:00 a.m. Delaunay voted to nap on the beach under an airplane wing as they worked, but Saint-Exupéry vetoed the idea and insisted on visiting the ancient city, one with a rich history, having passed through the hands of nearly every conquering people since Greek times. For the next few hours he dragged a sulking Delaunay through hot, dusty streets, from sad church to crumbling fortification. It seemed to Delaunay that the deserted, sun-struck city consisted mainly of beggars and flies; his ill humor—which he made no attempt to conceal—was not improved by the fact that the two found nothing to drink except warm beer.

Only that night, at dinner in Alicante with Saint-Exupéry and two pilots bound for Oran, did Delaunay discover Valencia. His colleague's description of the city was rigorously accurate, save that when Saint-Exupéry talked "the old city practically became a daughter of the sun; suddenly she was less dulled by the heat than richly carved out of light." That night Delaunay claimed to discover the pleasure of "the music-lover listening to the virtuoso, following along on a one-dimensional score." This was Saint-Exupéry in his element, Saint-Ex Scheherazade, the twenty-nine-year-old version of the late-night versifier of Saint-Maurice. He was more a natural litterateur than a born pilot; it seemed to Delaunay, that he lived entirely "*pour avoir à exprimer*" ("in order to have something to say"). In the commitment to the mails he certainly did not see what the others saw: it was for him a romance and a culture as much as a religion. Aéropostale gave him his subject, as well as a mantle of responsibility that brought him into his own. After all of his run-ins with discipline, the highly regulated life won him over. Ironically, it was in the sacrifice to the regularity of the mails that the erratic Saint-Exupéry felt himself to be in the service of a higher good. His was far more than an honest job to a man for whom an honest job would never have sufficed. In this respect he found himself among equals: nearly all the Aéropostale pilots were, in the words of Noëlle Guillaumet, "bad businessmen . . . [who] did not want to hear about money. In the end they attached only the faintest importance to those things that men traditionally care most about." The grandeur of *la Ligne* freed Saint-Exupéry not only from a dreaded routine but also from the tyranny of petty things. Unfortunately, within two years the grandeur of *la Ligne* was to be found more in his writing than anywhere else.

I X

~

Toward the Country
Where the Stones Fly
1929–1931

*If we except those miraculous and isolated mo-
ments fate can bestow on a man, loving your work
(unfortunately the privilege of a few) represents
the best, most concrete approximation of happiness on earth. But this is a truth not many know.
This boundless region, the region of* le boulot, *the*
job, il rusco—*of daily work, in other words, is less
known than the Antarctic . . .*

PRIMO LEVI, *The Monkey's Wrench*

Early in September 1929, on landing in Toulouse with the Spanish
mail, Saint-Exupéry learned that he was to be transferred to South America, possibly for as long as two years. He was told nothing more and given
six days to put his affairs in order. He spent them charging about chaotically, saying his good-byes in Agay and Saint-Maurice, running errands
in Lyons, making a last stop in Paris. In the capital he felt much as he
had before his departure for Toulouse three years earlier. He had few
friends he truly cared about and they—Lucie-Marie Decour, Henry de
Ségogne, Yvonne de Lestrange among them—were all out of town. As he
had been a poor correspondent he had no one to blame for this but himself,
which he did poignantly: "No one was around for this reunion, which I
had arranged rather too silently." He concluded that his friendships were
in a state of great disorder, a condition he began to remedy as the distance
from France increased.

Yvonne de Lestrange was on the dock in Bordeaux to see him off the third week of the month. He was delighted to learn from her that the literary world was talking about *Southern Mail*; he probably told her that he had also received encouraging words from Gallimard, who wanted another book from him as soon as he could produce one. Either Yvonne de Lestrange or another friend delivered to him a letter from Decour before he set sail. His ship took a leisurely eighteen days to make its way from Bordeaux to Buenos Aires: Saint-Exupéry discharged a letter from Bilbao to his mother, from Lisbon to Renée de Saussine, from Dakar— where word from home awaited him—to Decour. He reported that he was spending his time at sea entertaining a group of young girls, under the careful supervision of their thick-waisted mothers. They dressed up in costume; they played charades; they admired the sharks and the schools of flying fish. In such company Saint-Exupéry felt at times fifteen again, at times inexpressibly old. Decour's letter did nothing to alleviate his despair on that count: she had written to say she was engaged. From the Dakar harbor, alone in the ship's bar after midnight, he acknowledged this happy news with mixed feelings. He had not himself been a candidate for Decour's hand and did not begrudge her the marriage, especially as he had met and approved of the fiancé, a charismatic young lawyer who had been blinded in the war. He did, however, reproach her her timing. His whole world was in flux, he was off again for the unknown, and she had chosen this moment to deprive him of one of his few anchors. He repeated to her his observation that married friends were soon lost to him—this probably because they were less easy to coax from bed for a 3:00 a.m. literary discussion—and predicted that the same fate would befall her. Several months later he tried sheepishly, but without apologizing, to explain away this ornery letter. The best he could do was to say that his sadness could not be held against him as he did not himself know the cause of it. He suggested that he simply did not know how to write a letter of congratulations, itself a coy admission of wrongdoing. A little as a peace offering, he asked if Decour would allow him to have Gallimard send on to her the author's proofs of *Southern Mail*.

If Saint-Exupéry had been disappointed by his Parisian sendoff, he had no reason to be with his arrival. On the dock to greet him in Buenos Aires on October 12 were Mermoz, Guillaumet, and Reine, who welcomed him like the prodigal son. The hardy Reine raced forward to announce exuberantly that he had found him a luxurious apartment. "You'll be more comfortable than in your Juby shack!" he promised. Saint-Exupéry responded with a firm and solemn handshake, one generally described as bone-crushing. He spent his first few weeks at the Majestic Hotel on the Avenida de Mayo, not far from the Aéropostale offices. At the end of the month he decamped to his new quarters, off the Calle Florida, the city's most animated shopping street, though as it turned out the well-

intentioned Reine had been wrong: he would have much preferred the
Juby barracks. In his furnished apartment on the eighth floor of a fifteen-
story building, one of the capital's concrete marvels, he claimed to enjoy
the same agreeable sensation of lightness he might were he to have been
entombed in the Great Pyramid. He was to spend slightly longer in Buenos
Aires than he had at Cape Juby, but he resisted the city with all his might.
This time he truly felt exiled to the desert.

After three massive waves of immigration, Buenos Aires in 1929 was
a vast, flat, bustling metropolis of more than two million people. Its population was nearly as great as that of Paris, with the difference that Paris
was 2,000 years old and for most of that time had been a pedestrian city;
Buenos Aires was less than 400 years old and had been designed—most
of it in the previous forty years—around the trolley car. Sixty years earlier
the population of the Argentine capital had been one-tenth that of Paris;
compared to the French city—and the citizens of Buenos Aires unabashedly made the comparison—Buenos Aires had been built in a day,
and that without the benefit of a Baron Haussmann. To Saint-Exupéry
the city resembled "a giant slab of badly cooked dough." It had more in
common with Chicago or Melbourne, spanking new, laid out in a hurry
for maximum profit, rich in all things but history, a more successful human
than architectural melting pot, true to its reputation as "the world's most
prodigious mushroom." Every well-bred Argentine thought himself spiritually and culturally a Frenchman, but all her love of France could not
make Buenos Aires look like Paris. A house dating from 1890 was considered old; the city's architecture was a jumble of steel-and-concrete,
New York–style skyscrapers, French-inspired *hôtels particuliers*, and small
colonial homes, all piled atop one another. Saint-Exupéry noted, as did
other early visitors, that the architects of Buenos Aires had been ingenious
in their ability to suppress all perspective, even on their better work.

The central part of town, where Saint-Exupéry lived and spent most
of his time, was confined to a few narrow streets, poorly paved and generally mobbed, streaming with traffic, although one drove into town more
for ostentation's sake than for expediency's. The Calle Florida, roughly
equivalent to London's Bond Street but more the width of Wall Street,
may well have been one of the prides of Buenos Aires—it boasted a Har-
rods and the city's most exclusive club—but it was not a primary attraction
to a man in love with the open sky. Most remarkable and most unnerving
for Saint-Exupéry was the thoroughgoing absence of nature within the
Argentine capital. Buenos Aires was almost entirely lacking in parks; built
upon an estuary—"Río de la Plata" was as much a misnomer as "Río de
Oro"—it is a city in which one can live for a year without once seeing
water. Justifiably, Saint-Exupéry felt a prisoner of a concrete kingdom.
So disenchanted was Le Corbusier by "the speculative chaos" of Buenos

Aires when he visited that same year that he proposed the city establish an outer limit, around which it create a green belt, and beyond which it could continue to expand.*

A man of the Old World, Saint-Exupéry did not take to the flamboyance of Buenos Aires's *nouveau riche* society any more than to the city itself. In all fairness he had touched down amid a particularly closed society, one in which even the best-credentialed visitor found that doors opened slowly. He took his consolation in his frequent absences; he almost certainly flew more in his fifteen months in Argentina than at any other time in his life. Two days after his arrival in Buenos Aires he traveled 400 miles south to Bahía Blanca, the first stop on a proposed Patagonian line, as the passenger of Paul Vachet, then operations manager of the Argentine company. The two men continued on, over 600 miles of desolate coastline, to Comodoro Rivadavia, a frontier town that looked to Saint-Exupéry like a set for Chaplin's *Gold Rush*. The crust of the earth around the low-lying settlement was as dented, he wrote later, as that of an old boiler; the community was itself hardly more picturesque. Comodoro Rivadavia owed its existence to oil, which had been discovered beneath it in 1907; blackened derricks presided over a town that otherwise consisted entirely of corrugated iron. On October 17 the two men returned to Buenos Aires with the second Comodoro Rivadavia mail, delivering it to the capital in twelve hours instead of the four to five days it had previously taken by boat. Since February Vachet had been busy organizing the route, which was nearly ready to be opened to regular service.

If Saint-Exupéry was wondering what exactly he was doing in South America he was at last enlightened on the twenty-fifth, when he was told he would be replacing Vachet as operations manager. (Evidently without rancor for having to abandon to a colleague a route he had spent months prospecting, Vachet went off to set up a Venezuelan operation.) In his new position Saint-Exupéry, aside from opening up the Patagonian route, was to supervise the entire Argentine operation from an administrative point of view, to hire and manage its personnel and outfit and oversee its airfields. His annual salary was set at a princely 225,000 francs. He was a little proud, although he cloaked his satisfaction in melancholy, pining for the simpler life of the African coast. He wrote his mother that he hoped she would find in his success a "gratifying revenge" for all the reproaches she had had to endure from the family concerning his education. She had clearly "succeeded not so badly," he wrote another family member, deflecting the credit a little. In a new twist on an old theme, he began immediately to send money home. A banquet for the changing of the

---

* The city benefited from no zoning at all until 1934, by which time it was far too late to consider Le Corbusier's suggestion.

guard was held for the Aéropostale personnel in Buenos Aires on October 29, 1929; in a photograph of the evening, Saint-Exupéry, a cigarette in hand, looks serious and settled, and, true to his word, suddenly a little old. Probably the next morning, he set off again for Comodoro Rivadavia.

Ever since Marcel Bouilloux-Lafont, the Brazilian-based French magnate, had bought out Latécoère in 1927, arrangements had been under way to span South America with mail routes. Argentina and Uruguay exchanged volumes of mail with Europe every year; the larger country alone received 3.5 million letters from the Continent. In February of that year Bouilloux-Lafont came to agreements with the Argentine, Uruguayan, and Chilean governments, much to the dismay of the Americans and the Germans. Mermoz, Vachet, and their colleagues forged ahead in establishing the new routes, inaugurating service with Paraguay on January 1, 1929; night service between Rio de Janeiro and Buenos Aires in April; and service to Santiago, Chile, in July. Single-handedly, with matériel imported from France and with a staff composed mostly of South Americans, Bouilloux-Lafont built up a vast network. By the time he was done nearly twenty airfields were in service, many of them carved out of virgin forest. The operation was hugely expensive but also a potential gold mine, especially once Peru had been yoked into the empire late in 1930, unlocking the shortest route from Europe to the Pacific.

A sister company of Aéropostale, the South American enterprise went by the name of Aeroposta Argentina. Its best-known representative was Jean Mermoz: in two years he had quite literally opened up the sky of South America, landing in Brazil, in Patagonia, in Chile, in Paraguay, in Bolivia, and in Peru, never once failing in a mission—despite a harrowing crash in the Andes and an equally hair-raising experience in the the forests of the Paraguayan Chaco, where he lived like a character out of James Fenimore Cooper for a week. He was a most welcome conqueror, and his legend grew enormous. In a country well-attuned to commercial opportunities his portrait soon decorated cigarette packs, ashtrays, matchboxes, perfume bottles. Certainly Mermoz's repute went a long way toward paving the way for Saint-Exupéry and the rest of his colleagues, welcomed with open arms as bearers of the future in most of the continent's outposts, save those where pro-German sympathy continued to flourish. Mermoz returned to France four months after Saint-Exupéry's arrival; when he did so it was said that he distributed the keys of his kingdom to his friends. To Étienne went Brazil, to Reine Paraguay, to Guillaumet the Santiago–Buenos Aires route over the Andes, to Saint-Exupéry Patagonia.

At the end of October, when Saint-Exupéry returned in his new capacity to Comodoro Rivadavia, he carried an Argentine pilot named Rufino Luro Cambaceres along with him in his Latécoère 25. Cambaceres left him in the oil town and continued south by car to prospect airfields that would allow the mail line to continue to Tierra del Fuego. En route the two men had stopped in San Antonio Oeste, a third of the way between Bahía Blanca and Comodoro Rivadavia, where no Laté 25 had yet landed. The coastal community's airstrip was too short for the aircraft, and Saint-Exupéry was forced to land in a dry lagoon a few miles from town. On the thirty-first he returned alone to Pacheco, the aerodrome thirty miles outside of Buenos Aires that was rented to the Aéropostale operation and where he now laid claim to an office. The next day Mermoz, in a newly arrived Latécoère 28, officially inaugurated mail service to Comodoro Rivadavia. It would fall to Saint-Exupéry to open the full 1,500-mile coast Cambaceres was then prospecting to Río Gallegos, fifty miles north of the Strait of Magellan, the following year. He spent the intermediate months, or the Argentine summer, familiarizing himself with his new territory, organizing the existing but primitive airfields at Bahía Blanca, San Antonio Oeste, and Trelew, creating those south of Comodoro Rivadavia. He flew west to Santiago for a few days, north to Asunción to survey the new Paraguayan route. He no longer had to battle Moors and sandstorms but had exchanged them for wind and night, for airfields that were dusty in fine weather and swampy most of the time, overrun, as was that of Bahía Blanca, by snakes or scorpions, illuminated only by storm lamps and faint triangles of gasoline flares, on which a nocturnal windsock could consist of a handkerchief held at arm's length by a radio operator helpfully waving an electric lamp in his other hand. These hardships, rather than the man-made ones of Buenos Aires, were those with which Saint-Exupéry liked to contend. Among them, none was as formidable as the Patagonian wind.

~

The speed limit for Patagonian motorists in the early 1930s was set at twenty miles per hour and reinforced by bumps built into the pavement of the region's few roads. To drive any faster was to risk a potentially fatal encounter with the stones that flew along the ground, carried by ferocious gusts that rushed down from the Andes. The wind picked up in San Antonio Oeste, grew fiercer as one continued south, and was unceasing beyond Comodoro Rivadavia, where—among the strongest in the world—it could reach velocities of 125 miles per hour. It regularly flattened crops, knocked down herds, carried away roofs, bowled over trucks. Saint-Exupéry liked to laugh later about an order he had purportedly signed at Comodoro Rivadavia, prohibiting pilots from landing in that town when the wind speed exceeded ninety miles per hour. Given that the average speed of a Laté 25 or 26 was nearly the same, the effect, in one direction anyway, was that of revving the engine of a car mounted on blocks, if rather more dangerous.

The visibility in South America could be exceedingly good: When a pilot can see 125 miles ahead of him and is opposed by a strong wind, he is more than anything prone to believe that he will never arrive at his destination. Often enough in Patagonia in the 1930s the struggle ended in the wind's favor; a Latécoère 25 could be forced to retreat. Daurat recalled a day when the gales so overpowered Saint-Exupéry that he could not make it to the coast 600 feet away. On another occasion he could still see the airport at Río Gallegos an hour after he had left it. He put five hours into the 150 miles that separated Río Gallegos from Punta Arenas, the town of 25,000 people perched on the Strait of Magellan, finally running out of fuel a third of the way from his destination. The return trip was accomplished in under sixty minutes. It could take over an hour to climb 900 feet in such weather; landing was another ordeal altogether. The Argentine government arranged for soldiers to assist the aviators; twelve to fourteen of them were on hand for a Comodoro Rivadavia landing under the most favorable of conditions. They divided into two groups, forming a 150-foot-long, ninety-foot-wide corridor between them, into which the pilot would fly at nearly full throttle. Tail high, the pilot kept his throttle up so that the air speed of the machine remained equal to that of the wind. Several members of the ground crew then rolled a cart under the tail skid of the immobile machine; the aircraft thus remained horizontal, presenting a streamlined profile to the wind. At the same time, the soldiers rushed forward with long bamboo poles, which they hooked through metal eyes installed on the underside of the wings. In this way the aircraft was secured to the ground despite the winds. Slowly, on signal, the pilot then advanced full throttle into the hangar, guided by his Lilliputian captors on either side, cutting the engine only once he was partially sheltered. It was a dangerous and time-consuming exercise; jauntily Saint-Exupéry told friends that it combined elements of harpoon-fishing and rappeling. On one occasion a violent gust poured down from the mountains just as the soldiers had caught onto the plane, lifting one column of men six feet off the ground, shaking them loose in midair, and forcing the plane down on its opposite wing, crushing to death two of the men on its leeward side.

Saint-Exupéry's best-known encounter with the elements took place around the new year, when he regularly traveled the Patagonian route in a Laté 25. He was to remember the adventure as his most brutal, but while he held dinner tables spellbound with the tale for years he did not write it up until 1938, at the urging of his American publisher.* He

---

* The account of Saint-Exupéry and the cyclone, which belongs to the English- but not the French-language edition of *Wind, Sand and Stars*, appeared in France as a newspaper piece in 1939.

had been flying south to Comodoro Rivadavia, long enough into his South American tenure to be on the lookout for the gray-blue tint in the sky that—past the marshes of Trelew—indicated he should brace himself for trouble. Generally this battle lasted about an hour; it was, claimed the pilot, an ordeal but not a drama. On this day, however, the sky south of Trelew was a disconcertingly pure blue. This was the sign of an invisible enemy; he would have preferred a good, black, ominous-looking storm, which he would have known how to circumvent. Moreover, to his right, on a level with the Andes, floated "a sort of ash-colored streamer in the sky." Saint-Exupéry felt a tremor; minutes later the sky blew up around him. The Latécoère came to a dead stop in midair, then began to plunge to earth in an abrupt series of spins and shivers and slides. One image came to his mind: "I was a man who, carrying a pile of plates, had slipped on a waxed floor and let his scaffolding of porcelain crash." One escape came to mind: he had to reach the sea, which was flat, and over which the wind would not be bottled up with the intensity it was in the valley.

Suddenly the aircraft—at this time only about 200 feet off the ground—was swept 1,500 feet into the air. Saint-Exupéry was indeed sent out to sea, but he was not himself at the controls: "I had been spat out to sea by a monstrous cough, vomited out of my valley as from the mouth of a howitzer." Five miles from the coast he was again powerless to move; he felt as if he were single-handedly battling the whole sky. He worried that his wings would hold, that his hands, frozen to the wheel for forty minutes, would continue to obey him, that his gas pumps would continue firing; already his engine had begun to sputter from all the turbulence. Later he was to find that his storage batteries had been pried by the storm up out of the roof of the plane, that his wings had come unglued (only the forward part of the aircraft was reinforced with metal; the rear portion remained fabric-covered), that some of the Latécoère's steel cables had been whittled down to single strands. (Later, too, he was to say that he was carrying a passenger with him on this occasion, an Argentine journalist who was so shaken he had tried to jump.) He attempted desperately but unsuccessfully to climb; each time he was thrown off balance by a new gust. He let himself be blown south, and in one hour managed finally to cover the five miles to shore. Using the coast as shelter he was able to continue toward Comodoro Rivadavia. He had seen the worst of the storm, and was able, at an altitude of about 900 feet, to reach the town's airfield. A platoon of soldiers had been called out to meet him and to tame the Laté into its hangar, an operation that took an hour. Saint-Exupéry's shoulders ached; his hands were cramped; he was exhausted; internally he felt as if he had been crushed; he must have looked a sight for having been lashed about by the wind in an open cockpit. In all of this he claimed there was no obvious drama of which to speak. He had been far too busy for emotion. "I climbed out of the cockpit and walked off," reported Saint-Exupéry. "There was nothing to say."

On the exoticism of the Argentine south he was far more loquacious. Patagonia proved a rich consolation for Buenos Aires and Saint-Exupéry succumbed to it immediately, finding in this wilderness an ample supply of the enchantment he so prized. In Buenos Aires culture was in its infancy; in Patagonia, civilization felt only weeks old. Over desolate towns fitted between glaciers and volcanoes he was able to reflect anew on the things that bring men together, on the "fragile gildings" of civilization. The sheer dimensions of the territory must have awed him—the five regions that make up Patagonia are alone one and a half times the size of France— and the virgin expanses of the place must have been a feast for the eyes, especially to a pilot who claimed to be familiar with every rock and dune that lay between Toulouse and Dakar. He was far from the first to appreciate the majesty of this uniformly gray region, a desolate, stony plain populated mostly by sheep, where all is somber and windswept and fantastically seductive. Charles Darwin had perfectly enunciated the riddle of the place a century earlier: "Yet, in passing over these scenes, without one bright object near, an ill-defined but strong sense of pleasure is vividly excited." Bustling Comodoro Rivadavia did not excite Saint-Exupéry; the center of the Argentine petrol industry, around which more than 350 wells operated, was not to his mind a town in which one could live. Entirely devoid of trees, women, homes, it was a town "in which one traded ten years of one's life for gold. . . . It was a settlement lost amid the winds and rejected by the earth." Twelve miles away was a beach thick with seals, however (naturally he flew one back to Buenos Aires in the fall of 1929); farther on was one overrun by penguins. And in the towns huddled against the wind farther south he thought the miraculous nature of man, very much by contrast, abundantly clear.

If indeed there are different kinds of silence, one of the densest in the world hung over these outposts of Patagonia, the southernmost settlements on the globe. The dwellers of this region had not seen their families in years; until the arrival of Aéropostale, they had been connected to the capital only by an unreliable ten-day boat service and Morse code. When the aviators appeared they did so, then, as heaven-sent emissaries. Five minutes after a landing in South America, observed Saint-Exupéry, hands were held out; in Patagonia, whole towns opened their doors. "Imagine," he wrote, "that just as you were to step out of the Dijon train station, a stranger were to accost you and say, 'I welcome you, partly on behalf of the city of Dijon. Man cannot live without friendships; he can create nothing without assistance. You have a right to do both. Do not thank me.' " On one occasion—not in Patagonia but 500 miles north of Buenos Aires—the welcoming committee turned out, to Saint-Exupéry's astonishment, to be French. These were not, however, the French of Dijon; this couple had been recast in the mores of their new land. Descending from a beat-up Ford, Monsieur and Madame Fuchs announced to a man on whom they had never before set eyes, whom they found in a meadow tinkering with a recalcitrant airplane, "We will come to fetch you for dinner."

In Puerto Deseado, a coastal town of 200 low-lying houses situated at the mouth of a river, he got a hero's welcome and a tour from the mayor. He was entirely seduced. "Nowhere have I encountered a more noble race of men than that of the Argentines of the south," he wrote the following year in a passage that should have but did not become part of *Wind, Sand and Stars*:

> Arrived to build cities on these deserted lands, they built them. A city in their hands became a living thing, to be shaped, to be protected, to be cherished like a child. These men did not dream of exploiting the land to return, enriched, to their paradises. They had come to establish themselves here for good, to found a race of men. It would be difficult to find elsewhere so developed a sense of society, of cooperation, so much serenity. Theirs was the serenity of men who address only the great problems. Once again I had here the opposite impression of that of Comodoro, a sense of brushing up against another era, one in which man settled himself on earth, chose his campsite, and lay the first stone of his new town's fortifications.

These were towns so new they had built schools for a generation of children not yet conceived. Their cemeteries were empty; they were only just surviving their first brush with adultery. In Puerto Deseado Saint-Exupéry visited the spacious compound the town had designed for a leper; having had none of their own, they had gone to great lengths to import one from Buenos Aires. He made a lasting impression on the pilot, who watched over a barbed-wire fence as the sick man emerged from his house. Leaning heavily on his cane, he made a slow tour of his yard. After a quick glance at the ocean and without acknowledging his visitors, he disappeared again into his cheerful, red-tiled home. Saint-Exupéry felt that after his long separation from the affairs of men the leper oriented himself with the natural world, turned to the sound of the ocean and not toward that of the town. He had lost a good deal along with his fingers and yet he had lost nothing at all: "Ambition, jealousy, honor—all of the emotions to which society entitles a man—none of these could stir him any longer. He had attained an inhuman peace."

The night flying—of which he would do more this year than ever again—inspired Saint-Exupéry to rise to descriptive heights in his next novel, written in South America in 1930. He would expound at dinners on the oddities of Patagonia for the rest of his life: on Punta Arenas, "a

town born of the chance presence of a little mud between the timeless
lava and the austral ice"; on the Indians who wore only guanaco skins,
which they turned fur- or hide-side out depending on the direction of the
wind; on the sheep of Tierra del Fuego who, when asleep, disappeared
in the snow, but whose frozen breath looked from the air like hundreds
of tiny chimneys. What he mostly treasured and what he preserved for
himself from his arduous exploration of the Patagonian route were the
odd encounters in the primitive landscape, however; the balls held in the
aviators' honor in corrugated iron shacks, probably the only official ban-
quets of his life at which he shone; the glow that humanity emitted in a
cold climate. To his mother he wrote rhapsodically of the towns along the
Strait of Magellan, towns farther south even than Río Gallegos, the offical
terminus of the mail route. Here all suddenly became green. Saint-
Exupéry was enchanted by "these men who, accustomed to being cold,
to huddling around fires, had become so warm-hearted." This new attempt
to settle an ancient corner of the world was for him an advertisement for
the fragility of all that glitters, for the essentials too quickly forgotten in
Buenos Aires or Saint-Germain. Here earthly law still prevailed; Saint-
Exupéry could feel the tug of nature. It was this corner of the world that
led him, in a 1933 *NRF* article, to use for the first time the expression "*la
terre des hommes.*" In the Patagonian context he did so ironically. Nowhere
could it have seemed clearer that this was not "man's own earth"; nowhere
did man look punier. Yet Saint-Exupéry stood in awe of the modest race
of men who settled here, a race to which he did not belong. They were
the carpenters, the gardeners, the smiths, the creative and custodial men
whose quiet heroism he lauded in all of his later writings. For him these
frontiersmen were the true noblemen, tiny but seigneurial in a barren
landscape punctuated by volcanoes, from the occasional crater of which
rose—"as if from a cracked pot"—a green tree. Visions of the Little Prince
danced in his head.

~

Garlanded in bulbs, dazzling, especially to a European eye, in its profligate
nighttime display of electricity, boasting entertainments that did rival those
of Paris, Buenos Aires moved to a different rhythm. So did Saint-Exupéry
when he was at home. He saw as much as he could of the newly married
Guillaumet, also based in Buenos Aires, although given both men's travels
these visits occurred less frequently than Saint-Exupéry might have hoped.
He lit up visibly when reunited with his friend; he was clearly loath to
leave him in the evenings, as Madame Guillaumet's tales of Saint-Exupéry
falling asleep in their elevator, or in the taxi on his way home, attest. In
a piece he wrote later about Mermoz, Saint-Exupéry paid tribute to the

traveling hearth of his professional family at which—in Casablanca, in Buenos Aires, in Dakar—he stopped to warm his hands and to finish a sentence begun long before, often on another continent, likely to be continued on a third. In Buenos Aires the exchange of tales of snowstorms and cyclones and hair-raising landings with Mermoz, Guillaumet, Reine, Étienne, Antoine, and Delaunay continued in congenial restaurants, over immense steaks, chased down by an abundant supply of Mendozan wine, until early morning.

Impossible as it was to take a leisurely stroll through Buenos Aires, it was agreeable to go swimming or boating at the city's resort at El Tigre, the lush delta formed at the intersection of the Paraná and Uruguay rivers just north of the city, an area described approvingly by another Frenchman as "the delta of the Nile made to resemble the lakes of the Bois de Boulogne." Probably Saint-Exupéry joined his colleagues here during the last months of 1929 and the first few of 1930. The Argentine summer is the only time of year when the Buenos Aires climate can be called disagreeable; toward February and March the humidity can be oppressive enough that a billiard cue will seem as if it has been retrieved from the bath. He reported regularly to the Aéropostale offices, not far from his apartment, on Buenos Aires's international banking street; the bistro at the corner was a popular gathering place for all of the airline's employees. A table was at all times reserved for the Aéropostale personnel at a small hotel called the Père Bach, much frequented by the French colony; for *apéritifs* the aviators favored the Richmond Bar, not far from Saint-Exupéry's front door; the nightclub of choice was the Tabaris, where the rituals concerning the sexes were a little less elaborate than elsewhere and the floor show of fairly good quality. If he had not learned to enjoy this kind of nightlife, Saint-Exupéry had since Dakar at least come to appreciate some of its better-known attractions. His taste ran to the blonde and French-speaking.

Mostly, however, and to the point of exhaustion, he flew. He took his role as an inspector seriously and put a good deal of time into prospecting, outfitting, and supervising the mail lines to Patagonia and Paraguay. He reported having covered the 1,500 miles from Patagonia to Buenos Aires in one day. He might fly for eighteen or twenty hours straight, stopping only to refuel; he reported he could now pilot half-asleep; he had time to write mostly when back in Buenos Aires or, as he was renowned for doing when the weather was fine and the plane flying more or less of its own accord, in midair. His cockpits were littered with papers; passages of *Night Flight* were composed as well in the lobbies of some not very prepossessing backwater hotels a few hours before dawn. Although Saint-Exupéry had ascended to the administrative echelon he was still part of that well-coordinated, herculean race against the clock that would animate this next novel, and he flew the occasional mail as well. While there were fewer misadventures than there had been at Juby the life continued to be one of permanent adventure. The mail flights offered a full catalogue of hazards and their pilots demonstrated all kinds of bravado: Saint-Exupéry was forced down on narrow beaches bordered by impenetrable forests. He sailed neatly under electrical wires in order to avoid what some pilots might have deemed the lesser risk of landing long on a runway. He expertly treated a mechanic stung by a scorpion, making an incision around the bite with a penknife and sucking the venom from the mechanic's shoulder. He enlisted the aid—after having landed hard in a field, with a heavily loaded plane—of a village blacksmith so as to get the mail through on time. Two of the rivets holding the cabin to the fuselage had given way, and one of the aircraft's four longerons had cracked. The blacksmith had no trouble rebolting the cabin but was a little mystified by the longeron problem. He settled on a length of fence wire for the repair, attaching it to the two ends of the tubing and knotting it tightly, thereby forcing the two long metal supports back together. In flight the repair began progressively to give way, so that the radio operator—new to the South American line—was left to survey expanses of Argentine dandelions through the fuselage. By the time Saint-Exupéry reached Buenos Aires the crack was clearly visible from the ground; it sent Raoul Roubes, the chief Pacheco mechanic, running out to the airstrip to meet the Latécoère as it landed. Before Roubes could say a word, Saint-Exupéry had him up on the running board admiring the blacksmith's handiwork. "But you're sick," Roubes informed the pilot, "the fuselage was on the verge of breaking in half!" "We would have got out our parachutes!" responded Saint-Exupéry airily, without a glimpse at his pale-faced radio operator.

In May 1930 he prepared to make a Buenos Aires–Asunción run in a newly arrived Latécoère 28, one which had not yet been entirely broken in. A troupe of actors from one of France's national theaters was in town, and like most visiting dignitaries paid a visit to the terrain at Pacheco. Saint-Exupéry invited the nine men and women to join him on the trip to Asunción, an invitation that was readily accepted. Presumably because he had already filled the plane to capacity, he did not take a radio operator along on the flight. The trip north went off without a hitch but the next day, long after Asunción had announced Saint-Exupéry's departure, the Latécoère had yet to return to Buenos Aires. The head of the Pacheco field began to pace nervously. When there was no sign of Saint-Exupéry the following day he sent out a search party; it turned up no trace of plane or pilot. Late that second afternoon Raoul Roubes looked up to see the Laté 28 come in for a landing. He ran to greet the pilot, who emerged from the cockpit unshaven, his shoes barely holding to his feet, covered up to his knees in mud, and entirely radiant. He had been caught in a violent storm and been forced down in the countryside, where he and his passengers had opted, after a long, muddy trek, to spend the evening in a rustic hotel. In the gift shop of this establishment they had each purchased a change of clothes. As they filed off the plane the actors looked more like the company of a traveling circus, outfitted in pajamas and bathrobes of every imaginable color. Monkeys and parrots rode on the women's shoulders, to which hung their disheveled hair; a collection of bras and panties had been left to dry from the windows of the airplane. The travelers were in far better humor than the Pacheco chief, who had been worried sick for two days. He informed the exuberant pilot that if he had come to Buenos Aires "to play the fool" he could count on a speedy return to France.

Saint-Exupéry complained to Renée de Saussine in January, when the Argentine heat is at its peak, that the network of 2,400 miles over which he presided was sucking from him "second by second, all that remains of my beloved youth and liberty." This was ironic, in light of the fact that those same 2,400 miles offered him some of his best subjects. He was worn out, too, by the money he felt obligated to spend each month. Buenos Aires had been called "one of the most remarkably easy places in the world for getting rid of money quickly," and Saint-Exupéry bowed to the local mores. Here was a city in which the trades had not yet matured and repair was unheard of; one bought a new foreign-made watch—at the city's greatly inflated prices—rather than attempting a vain search for someone who might be able to fix an old one. Saint-Exupéry sent about 3,000 francs to his mother monthly, which left him a purse of more than 15,000. Like most of the money he earned in his life this sum disappeared quickly, sometimes in short shopping sprees, sometimes in spontaneous, lordly displays of philanthropy. Daurat once commented that Saint-Exupéry's scorn for lucre was equaled only by his need for it, and it was true that he seemed as bewildered by its presence, of which this was his first experience, as by its absence. (In a city obsessed with style, he remained all the same as eccentrically dressed as ever.) To Renée Saint-Exupéry complained that he was drained by all of his shopping. His acquisitions had begun to crowd him out of his apartment, and while he did not have the remotest need for any of them he could not seem to stop collecting. What was worse, longing made the world a magnificent place. Now that he had bought himself the supple leather carrying case, the fine felt hat, and the sophisticated chronometer of which he dreamed, what had he left to hope for?

This lifestyle, of course, did little to staunch a steady flow of nostalgia. Later Saint-Exupéry was to write that he had always before him the image of his first night flight in Argentina, but in Argentina, at least when at rest, he had eyes only for a corner of France. Exhausted though he was he slept little, and the book he now began, at night, about the night,

originally opened in the front vestibule of Saint-Maurice. The perils of an
Argentine flight among the stars made him dream of the sanctuary of his
mother's room, of the bliss of being tucked into bed at night, the sheets
smoothed around him. (The image, a little abbreviated, wound up in *Night
Flight*, as in nearly every work of Saint-Exupéry's.) He wrote to thank his
mother for the rich store of childhood memories she had bestowed upon
him, which he now realized to be his prized possession. He read and raved
about Rosamond Lehmann's *Dusty Answer* (*Poussière*), a melancholic
novel about the tenacity of adolescent impressions, one which reminded
him of the importance of what he called "tribe."

Repeatedly in South America he sought out the kinds of enchantments
for which he had developed a taste in childhood. Nowhere was this more
true than in Concordia, to which the hospitable couple in the old Ford
had brought him for dinner. In an evening that he wrote up in 1932 and
that later became a part of *Wind, Sand and Stars*, he made the acquaintance of an old house very much in the league of Saint-Maurice. A crumbling, once-luxurious 1886 citadel, this run-down mansion with its
caved-in floors, its decaying lintels, had more charm for Saint-Exupéry
than all of the steel girders of Buenos Aires. In his eyes it was not dilapidated but "a friend of time." He took great aristocratic satisfaction in its
decay—even more in the Fuchses' refusal to apologize for its condition
—and began at once to muse about its underground chambers, its buried
chests, its treasures. The girls of the house, said by their father to be wholly
untamed, were of a breed he knew and cherished. The Fuchses' two
adolescent daughters looked on visitors with well-placed suspicion; they
tamed iguanas, mongeese, foxes, monkeys, bees; they did their best to
make Saint-Exupéry squirm at the dinner table with tales of the snakes
that nested under his chair. Their crumbling wild garden became for him
a perfect symbol of the endurance of mystery, the girls another incarnation
of the kind of fairy princesses he had always known existed. Even the
leper of Puerto Deseado took Saint-Exupéry back to his early years, reminding him of the time he had spent recovering from bronchitis in the
boarding school infirmary. He remembered how the noises of the school
had reached him but had meant nothing to him, sounding—in his land
of temperature charts and medications—like the murmurs of a dream
world. This sensation of living outside of time must, he mused, be precisely
that of the leper.

Mail from his Paris-based friends could send Saint-Exupéry off on a
long riff in praise of the Brasserie Lipp or the chestnut trees of the boulevard Saint-Germain, even while he readily admitted that he did not feel
at home in Paris. "I would be so incapable of living in France," he wrote
his mother in July. Exile was a complicated business: "You vaguely hold
to the idea of returning and finding everything as you left it. You know

The Saint-Exupéry
children, toward 1906.
From left to right:
Marie-Madeleine,
Gabrielle, François,
Antoine, Simone

The château of Saint-
Maurice-de-Rémens, as it
appears today from the edge
of its "park dark with firs
and linden trees"

(LEFT)
Jean de Saint-Exupéry,
the writer's father

(BELOW)
Marie de Saint-Exupéry,
the writer's mother

Antoine, the "first-rate devil"

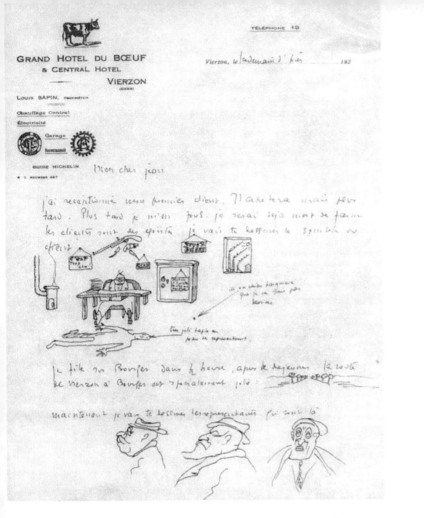

(ABOVE) Page one of a two-page letter to Jean Escot, written in 1925 but dated by Saint-Exupéry, the truck salesman, "the day after yesterday." Saint-Exupéry's rendering of his hard-hearted customer—the safe is marked "Don't even bother; the keys are lost" and the office is decorated with a salesman-skin rug—bears a striking resemblance to an early drawing (RIGHT) of the Little Prince's businessman, made seventeen years later.

Saint-Exupéry, chief of the Cape Juby airfield, with his colleagues

(ABOVE) Cape Juby, circa 1928

(RIGHT) Three ages of aviation: (*top*) a Breguet 14, the World War I biplane in which Saint-Exupéry began his career; (*center*) a Caudron-Simoun, which, he discovered, was not nearly so elastic; (*bottom*) a Lockheed P-38, one of the fastest planes in the sky in 1943 and the aircraft in which Saint-Exupéry disappeared

Marcel Bouilloux-Lafont (*center*) and Saint-Exupéry (*a few steps to his right*) at the ceremony for the opening of the Buenos Aires–Río Gallegos line, the only route which Saint-Exupéry actually in part prospected. The two men continued to keep their distance: the day after this photograph was taken the pilot incurred the public wrath of Bouilloux-Lafont when he landed a brand-new Latécoère 28 in a ditch, with the airline owner aboard.

Saint-Exupéry with an arm around Henri Guillaumet in Mendoza, Argentina, just after Guillaumet's superhuman trek through the Andes, immortalized by Saint-Exupéry in *Wind, Sand and Stars*: "I stared at your face: it was splotched and swollen, like an overripe fruit that has been repeatedly dropped on the ground. You were dreadful to see . . ." Jean-René Lefèbvre stands at Guillaumet's right, in the fedora.

Consuelo de Saint-Exupéry

The couple together in the early 1930s

"He left permanent wounds in the hearts of those who saw him smile, even once," wrote Saint-Exupéry's cohort of the 1930s, Léon-Paul Fargue.

Saint-Exupéry and his mechanic, André Prévot, before an intact Simoun. Prévot's loyalty to the pilot was largely to be rewarded in medical bills.

The same Simoun as it looked after its encounter with the Libyan desert, at a speed of 170 miles per hour. "Our situation was hardly ideal," wrote Saint-Exupéry later in his official report. He inscribed a photo of the remains of the aircraft to his sister with the words, "In memory of an evening of despair."

Consuelo seeing her husband off, before a flight of 1935

The two Madames de Saint-Exupéry in Paris on January 5, 1936, reading the telegrams of congratulation which flooded in when their son and husband was reported alive and well after he had disappeared into thin air for four days, which he spent walking through the Libyan desert.

(LEFT) Saint-Exupéry conferring with airline officials in Brownsville, Texas, hours before the crash that was to be the end of his second Simoun and—very nearly—of its pilot

(BELOW) The second Simoun in Guatemala City, hours later. Its pilot was only moderately more intact. The demolished cockpit—from which Saint-Exupéry was extracted—can be seen in the foreground.

Saint-Exupéry at the luncheon held in his honor at the Dog Team Tavern in Middlebury, Vermont, August 12, 1939. Dorothy Thompson turns to face the camera. Pierre de Lanux—whose conversation was as brilliant as the card tricks Saint-Exupéry performed at this table that afternoon—sits between her and the other visiting dignitary.

Renée de Saussine (*standing at left*) and
Louise de Vilmorin (*to her right*) with friends
on the beach in Rio de Janeiro, 1930

Louise de Vilmorin

Natalie Paley

Silvia Reinhardt

Saint-Exupéry writing *The Little Prince* in Silvia Reinhardt's Park Avenue apartment, 1942. Silvia had propped the yellow-haired doll, purchased in a New York candy shop, on the arm of the sofa.

The "chaser of butterflies" with his own version of a hothouse flower, on what was to become the Little Prince's planet.

An unused sketch of the Little Prince, which bears the marks of having been crumpled into a ball by the author

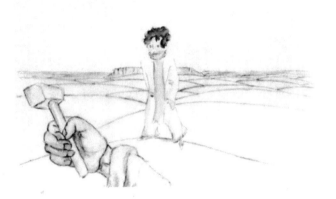

One of several early sketches for *The Little Prince* in which the aviator appears, although he is not pictured in the published book

"He is the best friend I have in the world," wrote Saint-Exupéry of Léon Werth (*right*), to whom he dedicated *The Little Prince* and for whom he wrote *Lettre à un otage*.

The author's inscription in Dorothy Barclay's copy of *The Little Prince*. Barclay had earned Saint-Exupéry's gratitude for having researched a question crucial to him in the writing of the book: How many stars were in the sky? "You would have to be crazy to choose this planet. It is agreeable only at night, when its inhabitants are asleep," laments the Prince on her half-title page. Underneath, the author begs to differ with his hero, on account, he argues, of such generous souls as Dorothy Barclay.

The artist Jean Pagès's sketch of Saint-Exupéry performing his *oranges sur le piano*, which he did a great deal over his grounded ten months in Algiers, 1943–44. To most ears the result—which could be obtained as well with hard-boiled eggs or lemons—sounded like Debussy.

John Phillips and Saint-Exupéry in the midst of a furious round of the "game of the six-letter words," Sardinia, 1944. Phillips was not meant to prevail over the esteemed *homme de lettres* and found the room automatically emptied whenever he seemed on the verge of doing so.

French and American members of the 23rd Photo Reconnaissance Squadron having polished off the better part of a 230-liter belly tank of wine, May 28, 1944. A particularly radiant Saint-Exupéry stands with his arm around his commanding officer, René Gavoille.

René Gavoille dressing the pilot for a high-altitude mission. A year earlier Saint-Exupéry had written his wife that he could not so much as get out of bed, carry a five-pound package, or bend to the ground without pain. "When he was getting dressed," remembered an American reconnaissance expert, "he was an old grouch."

this is impossible, but you so much hate the fact that life hurries so." He saw it, a little sadly, very much as Breyten Breytenbach would in our day, as "an engagement with an elsewhere that cannot be reached." There was nothing charming about living as an expatriate, an idea Saint-Exupéry tried to impress upon his mother when at this time his sister Simone began to talk about leaving for Indochina to work as an archivist. He was firmly opposed to the idea: Indochina was expensive, it was hot, it was thick with opium, and Simone could not be counted on to choose her friends wisely, he argued. (It was clear that generally speaking Saint-Exupéry did not think a woman, let alone one of his sisters, to be suited to such an adventure.)

In his greater objections it is difficult not to read his doubts about his own life. Exile is never temporary, he warned. One gets ambushed by it, taken prisoner forever, one becomes someone else: "And it gets no better over the course of a vacation, one day, in France. The vacation over, you always leave again. It's the worst of diseases." The subtext of the letter was that Saint-Exupéry knew of what he spoke, having traveled more than the rest of the family put together. The distance from France could only have been increased by the fact that he could not seem to impose his will on his far-off kin: Simone left, against his counsel, for Indochina, where she spent more than twenty happy years. He was as insistent now that the funds he sent be acknowledged speedily as he had once been that the money he requested be sent immediately. It rarely was. Worse, his mother could not be relied upon to use these funds as he directed her to, which was essentially on a life at Saint-Maurice. This threw him into a rage.

The closest Saint-Exupéry came to revisiting the pleasures of Saint-Germain in Argentina was probably in the company of Paul Dony, chief financial officer of Aéropostale in Buenos Aires, and his wife. With Dony Saint-Exupéry reprised some of his early literary habits, uprooting the executive from his Pacheco desk or his bed with a good deal of charm and a sheaf of freshly minted prose. (Cementing his reputation as the world's worst roommate, Saint-Exupéry once pried Dony from sleep at 2:00 a.m. in Concordia with an authoritative, "Listen to this, and tell me if it's good.") But it was at the Donys' Buenos Aires apartment, late at night, often after a movie, that Saint-Exupéry proved his most winning. Profiting from the couple's French library, he entertained them with word games, most of his own invention. He would seize their *dictionnaire analogique*, a sort of loose-limbed thesaurus arranged by clusters of meaning, and torture the couple by asking for the relationship between two seemingly unrelated, or two obviously related, words. What rapport was there, he would inquire, between *une caisse* and *un roulement*? When the answer came back "finances" (the first term most commonly indicated a cash register, and the second applied to the use of money), he was triumphant; the correct response was "percussion" (less often *une caisse* meant a drum, and *un roulement* a drumroll). He solicited subjects from the couple on which he spontaneously composed sonnets. At other times he chose a volume of verse from the shelf, settled on a second-rate sonnet, and in fifteen minutes tossed off a new version of the poem that not only respected its themes but adhered to the same end rhymes. "*Je recommence la littérature française,*" he announced as he set about transforming these stanzas. He was clearly much amused by these exercises, which showed him in his best light, at his favorite time of day. His gaiety was not of the boisterous kind, Dony noted, but seemed to bubble, when all circumstances were favorable, from a kind of interior well. Unfortunately, if one believes Saint-Exupéry the letter writer, circumstances all too rarely smiled upon him in Buenos Aires, and the Donys' salon was a rare refuge.

Despite all the complaints—Buenos Aires was odious, he felt old, he regretted the administration-free life of Juby, he hoped to marry—Saint-Exupéry was unquestionably good at what he did. Later one of his Argentine pilots sat long into a stormy, Río Gallegos night with Joseph Kessel explaining why he continued to fly eleven months of the year against an absurd wind when he had no need of the money: "I began out of a love for the sport, but Saint-Ex put the métier in my blood." As an administrator Saint-Exupéry was a stickler for discipline if not for the rules: the same pilot told Kessel how his boss had once flown the mail for a colleague he had had to penalize, recording his hours in the pilot's logbook so as not to cost him any of his salary. In midyear Guillaumet sang their friend's praises to Mermoz:

> The Argentines are crazy about him. . . . The mail goes through despite the winds, and—despite his absentminded demeanor—our friend manages the Aeroposta Argentina with a firm hand. He flies all day, delivers the mails, lands suddenly 600 miles from Buenos Aires on an airfield whose chief—thinking himself far outside anyone's purview—is tending to his bridge game and not to his field. Saint-Exupéry rights the situation, takes off again, returns to Pacheco as night falls, picks up his car, races home at full speed, and spends the rest of the night writing. I wonder when he sleeps, this phenomenon!

At about the same time accolades arrived from another quarter. For his service at Juby Saint-Exupéry was nominated for the Légion d'Honneur in March. The honor was accorded him a year later, in acknowledgment of his having "demonstrated a remarkable sangfroid and a rare sense of self-sacrifice" in the desert. His sponsor had been Abbé Sudour, to whom he already owed so much.

~

Nineteen-thirty proved something of a banner year for Aéropostale in South America. The Patagonia route was soon to be, under Saint-Exupéry's supervision, up and running; the mail went regularly from Buenos Aires east to Rio de Janeiro and north to Asunción; day and night the planes flew up and down the coast, from Natal south. On the Pacific side of the continent, Bolivia and Chile were linked; Vachet set up an operation in Venezuela. The Latécoère 28, a luxuriously robust machine with a 600-horsepower motor, an outside range of 700 miles, and a cruising speed of 150 miles per hour, had begun to arrive in numbers. Once a pilot flew in the closed cabin of the Laté 28—a feature necessary at this speed—he was likely to turn his nose up at the Laté 25 and 26, which were slowly retired. (This may have come as particularly welcome news to Saint-Exupéry. The Latécoère 25 had been designed to the measure of its test pilot, Elisée Negrin, who was very short. The long-legged Saint-Exupéry evidently had to engage in a series of acrobatics to get into the machine.) There had been a miraculous shortage of serious accidents, even while fatalities continued to plague the Toulouse–Dakar route. The fame of Mermoz, who had been seen off to France on January 20 by Saint-Exupéry, Guillaumet, Reine, and a crowd of thousands, had grown to the point where all of his colleagues basked in it. On the street, in theaters, in restaurants, people jostled for better views of "*los aviadores franceses,*" about whom they whispered breathlessly.

Late in March 1930 the Buenos Aires–Río Gallegos route was at last ready to be opened in both directions to regular service. Two aircraft made the inaugural voyage, a Laté 25 flown by Luro Cambaceres, who had prospected the route's southernmost points, and a Laté 28, piloted by Negrin, then inspector general of the South American network. Marcel Bouilloux-Lafont made the trip in Negrin's plane, as did Captain Vicente Almandos Almonacid, now the company's technical director; Julien Pranville, Daurat's highest-placed representative in South America; Alexandre Collenot, Mermoz's ace mechanic; Saint-Exupéry; and an Argentine journalist. Saint-Exupéry flew the Laté 28 on the return trip, during the course of which he landed badly, wedging one of the airplane's wheels in a ditch at Comodoro Rivadavia in such a way that the machine—which was brand new, having arrived from Paris the week before—nosed over on hitting the ground and was badly damaged. His sloppiness won him a stern and public rebuke from the company's owner, which he did not forget; he never managed to warm up to Bouilloux-Lafont afterward. Paul Dony remembered Saint-Exupéry as having been so ashamed after the incident that he refused to show his face in Buenos Aires for ten days. He spent as much time as he could in the air, flying the mail, and slept in the Pacheco canteen.

A little over a month later, Mermoz flew into the Natal harbor from Saint-Louis, Senegal, in a specially equipped Laté 28, the first air arrival from Europe. Carrying 280 pounds of mail, he made the trip in a little more than nineteen hours, a feat that the French felt confirmed their supremacy in the air. (This despite the fact that a regular commercial link between the two continents was still some years off and despite the difficulty Mermoz had with the 1930 return: he took off on his fifty-third attempt and then watched the seaplane sink some 450 miles shy of the African coast.) The delirium created by Mermoz's return to South America was tempered only by an accident that had occurred two days earlier. A Laté 28 bound for Natal to greet Mermoz had met with fog and crashed off the coast of Montevideo, leaving Negrin, Pranville, and three others to drown in the chilly waters. Only an Argentine journalist had managed to make it to shore; he had been thrown an inflatable cushion because he was the only man aboard who could not swim. The mail was retrieved off the Uruguayan coast and matter-of-factly marked: AIRCRAFT ACCIDENT MAIL RECOVERED IN OCEAN NO POSTAGE REQUIRED (Saint-Exupéry received the news badly in the small Argentine town in which he had stopped for repairs but did not attend the funeral). The day after his arrival Mermoz flew down to Buenos Aires for a five-day stay, partly to dispel the cloud cast by the Negrin incident. If he had not already met up with Saint-Exupéry in Natal he surely did so now.

France's eminence in the air was further confirmed in September 1930 when Dieudonné Costes and Maurice Bellonte triumphed over the North Atlantic in a Breguet 19,* completing the first Paris–New York flight in just over thirty-seven hours, earning a tickertape parade down Broadway, a week's worth of headlines, and a visit with President Hoover, and setting off the first transatlantic broadcast of the "Marseillaise." The hero's welcome Saint-Exupéry had described receiving in Patagonia was extended to Costes and Bellonte all over America, where the two pilots made an extended goodwill tour. Their success had some happy side effects in some unexpected places. The French ambassadorial staff, overwhelmed by the Francophilia occasioned by the pilots' arrival in America, wired the Quai d'Orsay for permission to contribute publicly to the Franco-American lovefest. In October, Charles Lindbergh was named a commander of the Légion d'Honneur.

For Saint-Exupéry, nothing better typified this golden age of heroics

---

* An exquisite, sterling-silver replica of the airplane, crafted by Tiffany's and offered to La Maison Française at Rockefeller Center by the French government, sits today in the lobby of 610 Fifth Avenue.

than a misadventure. In the middle of the winter, a month after Mermoz's crossing of the South Atlantic, Guillaumet took off from Santiago for Buenos Aires in a Potez 25. He had been flying the east-west route for a year; this was to be his ninety-second crossing of the Andes, no small feat given that the summits of the mountains—which look from the air like a prolongation of the Rockies—reach heights of more than 18,000 feet and the ceiling of a Potez was significantly lower. A pilot threaded his way through the passes on his wits and a clever manipulation of updrafts. The date was Friday, June 13. The weather was not good—in forty-eight hours fifteen feet of snow had fallen in the Andes—but undaunted, having already delayed the flight by a day, Guillaumet set out, convinced that he could avert the storm by making a detour to the south. At 17,000 feet he was caught in a fierce gale that dropped him 10,000 feet in what felt like an instant: he held not to the controls but to his seat. Underneath him as he pitched and rolled he caught sight of a dark spot that he recognized to be a lake. Descending toward Laguna Diamante seemed his only escape from the winds; the lake was surrounded by mountains, and he had been told its shores were flat and firm. Guillaumet descended to about 150 feet and flew round and round the lake until he ran out of fuel, at about 11:30, three and a half hours after having set out from Santiago. The plane was immediately swept over on landing, its propeller and its ailerons mangled; Guillaumet was knocked over—again and again—on standing. The ground was frozen and he was cold, but shoveling with a piece of the capsized plane's fuselage he managed to dig a hole in the snow under the wings, in which, the wind howling over him, he stuffed himself and sat out the next forty-eight hours. "I leave to my readers the task of imagining what those first few days were like," the laconic Guillaumet wrote later in his preface to the report to the company. In fact, he left the tale of his ordeal to Saint-Exupéry, who made of it probably the best-known passage of *Wind, Sand and Stars*.

During the course of the second night Guillaumet opened his eyes and saw a star in the sky. The winds had calmed; on the third day he emerged from his shelter. He had already unloaded the mail bags from the Potez and placed them on a parachute, weighing the baggage down with rocks. On the two sides of the fuselage he scrawled in flint: "My last thought to my wife, with a kiss. I was forced to land here because of the storm. Not having been spotted from the air, I am heading east. Farewell to all." In his suitcase he placed his reserves: a half bottle of rum, a tin of pâté, one of corned beef, two of sardines, two boxes of condensed milk, a few crackers. He was at an altitude of 10,500 feet, forty miles from Argentina as a bird flies and not counting the chain of frozen mountains that stood in the way. He knew that from the air he was invisible, having already been overflown several times, and that, not knowing what route he had taken, no one would have known where in the Andes to search for him. At ten o'clock on Sunday morning he set out, on foot. For the next five days and four nights he walked, his hands and feet frozen, swelling, and bleeding, exhausted beyond reason, covered in ice, aware that at these temperatures to sleep was to die. He saw puma tracks, and a number of guanacos; he stumbled and slid and crawled and walked on. The most difficult thing, he told Saint-Exupéry later, was to keep his mind off the snow. The easiest thing was to contemplate a silent, cold defeat. What saved him was less strength or ingenuity than love and pride: "My wife, if she believes I am alive, believes I am walking. My friends believe I am walking. They all have confidence in me. So I am a *salaud* if I don't walk," Saint-Exupéry quoted him as having reasoned. Facedown on a snow-covered slope he was roused to his feet by the demonic tug of bureaucracy. A line of fine print appeared before his eyes: without a corpse, the insurance company was not obligated to pay his wife any benefits for four years. He was indeed *un salaud* if he failed to go on; if he did not his wife would be penniless. At the top of the peak Guillaumet saw a slab of stone on which he could die and be sure the evidence would be found. With great pain, he climbed to the rock. And once there, he thought, why not continue? "What saves a man is to take a step. Then another step. It is always the same step, but you have to take it," was the way Saint-Exupéry remembered Guillaumet having explained his superhuman endurance.

Jean-René Lefèbvre, then chief of the airfield in Mendoza, the temperate Argentine town in the eastern foothills of the Andes, had been waiting for Guillaumet to land since the morning of the thirteenth. That afternoon he alerted Saint-Exupéry in Buenos Aires and Pierre Deley, the Santiago chief, to Guillaumet's disappearance. Both men flew to Mendoza and spent the next five days overflying the Andes in search of the Potez, a tiny, white needle in a vast, white haystack. Later Guillaumet told Saint-Exupéry he had seen him; he had known it was Saint-Exupéry because no reasonable pilot would have ventured so low among the mountains. On Friday, the twentieth, as Lefèbvre steeled himself to tell Madame Guillaumet she had been widowed, a call came from the police in San Carlos, seventy-five miles to the south, to say that Guillaumet had been found. Once again the documentary details fall to the Mendoza chief, who in his years with the company seemed always to be on hand in moments of high drama. Evidently he raced from the airfield to the Plaza Hotel, where Saint-Exupéry was lunching, to share the news. As Lefèbvre remembered it, the jubilant Saint-Exupéry rose from his table to shout, throughout the hotel, in French, "Guillaumet is saved!" Saint-Exupéry reported only that everyone in the dining room embraced. (In any event, word traveled around town in minutes, recalled Lefèbvre, like powder in the wind.) Instantly Saint-Exupéry was aloft in a Potez 29 with Lefèbvre and a second Mendoza mechanic, headed south toward San Carlos. As he had taken off without having had time to locate a map of the region, he was obliged to follow the southbound trail, flying at an altitude of about fifty feet. A good hour into the trip, the three saw a procession of horses and autos that could only have been that of Guillaumet's saviors. The gauchos signaled to the aircraft, waving their ponchos wildly. Saint-Exupéry's enthusiasm could not be contained. Lefèbvre reported that the pilot barely cleared a row of poplars to land in a meadow, coming to a stop inches from a ditch that had been invisible from the air. The mechanic, who knew of what he spoke, deemed it "without a doubt one of the most spectacular of Saint-Exupéry's landings."

All three men fell upon Guillaumet, who crawled into his friend's arms. The Argentines, like the French, dissolved in tears. Saint-Exupéry must have been as thrilled by the sight of Guillaumet as concerned by what he saw: his friend was a shriveled, frostbitten, sun-baked shadow of his former self. His face, reported the writer, "was splotched and swollen, like an overripe fruit that has been repeatedly dropped on the ground." Guillaumet dismissed the tears that ran down his face in a quiet voice: "They're from joy. Up there, I was not so weak." In his report, Guillaumet stated simply that this first reunion with friends "had been exceedingly moving." Lefèbvre and Saint-Exupéry remembered a few additional details and one line in particular, although each man felt it had been addressed to him. Guillaumet asked if his plane had been recovered. When hearing that it had not, he realized that, torturous though the week had been, he had been right to walk. Probably in response to this he added: "I swear that what I went through, no animal would have gone through." For Saint-Exupéry it was the noblest line any man had uttered, one that splendidly defined his place in the universe. On no other count did Lefèbvre quibble with Saint-Exupéry's version of events as recorded in *Wind, Sand and Stars*, save to say that the reunion had been, if anything, more overwhelming in reality.

Guillaumet had, on his seventh day in the mountains, stumbled upon a farmwoman, the wife of a grizzled smuggler, who had had trouble believing her eyes when she saw a man stumble out of the Andes. "*Yo soy l'aviador perdido, muchos pesos,*" Guillaumet shouted, with whatever strength was left to him. Introductions could be difficult under such circumstances; this was one of those casual lines created by the urgent shorthand of aviation. It was in a league with Beryl Markham, crashed off the coast of Newfoundland after having been the first to fly the Atlantic solo nonstop from east to west, introducing herself to two fishermen, blood dripping from her forehead, with "I'm Mrs. Markham. I've just flown from England," or Charles Lindbergh's "Which way is Ireland?" to the trawler below him while en route to Paris in 1927. The family had taken Guil-

laumet in, installing him in their only bed, and delivering him the following day by mule to the San Carlos authorities. In Mendoza, Guillaumet
was met at the airfield by festive crowds, which he ultimately escaped to
slip into a borrowed suit and call his wife, a beaming Saint-Exupéry at
his side. Saint-Exupéry tucked him into a warm bed in Mendoza and
nursed him with herbal teas over the next day and a half, returning him
on Sunday afternoon, the twenty-second, to Buenos Aires. At the airfield
crowds turned out to meet Guillaumet, whose ordeal had made the front
page of every newspaper in South America, and whose fate was immediately written into a Chilean folk song. In Buenos Aires, Saint-Exupéry
installed himself on the Guillaumets' couch, from which he began an
exuberant performance of the bawdiest songs in his repertoire, interrupting
himself only to remind Guillaumet how hopeless the search had seemed
from the air or to pry from his friend another detail of the ordeal. Evidently
he wore out the convalescent a little. This revel went on all night with
Saint-Exupéry tirelessly serenading and interrogating and serenading
again, oblivious to the excited accompaniment provided by the Guillaumets' dog, Looping, until Guillaumet somewhere found the strength to
say, "It's obscenely late, go to sleep."

Guillaumet, who went on to fly more than an additional 100 trips over
the Andes in a single-engined plane, was asked for his official report on
the crash the day after his return to Buenos Aires. He delivered it immediately. It took Saint-Exupéry, who stuck to the facts but extracted from
them something close to parable, seven years to set the by then oft-told
tale to paper. He grafted his view of man to the adventure, finding in
Guillaumet's stamina the acceptance of responsibility that was to his mind
what made man great; it was the theme of the novel on which he was at
work the year of the crash, as that of all of his subsequent writing. If
Guillaumet had moved mountains it was a moral quality—and not an
adventurer's disdain for death—that had saved him. He had walked out
of the Andes because he had turned his body into a tool, because he had
remained steadfast to his fellow men and their common enterprise. (He
made no mention of Madame Guillaumet.) In honoring these modest
bonds Guillaumet had proved himself a man of courage. Saint-Exupéry
wrote no more of the slayers of dragons who had peopled his first story
and novel. It was to the nobility of a gardener—a man bound by love to
his cultivable land—that he compared the triumphant Guillaumet, in an
image that recalled that of the newborn Bark, or of the Patagonian settler.
Here was another man who, dwarfed by his environment, had proved
anything but puny.

This account of Guillaumet's ordeal, which began to take shape in a
preface Saint-Exupéry contributed to a 1932 biography, which was first
published integrally in a newspaper in 1937, and which found its home

in *Wind, Sand and Stars* two years later, typified the way Saint-Exupéry inadvertently wrote himself into the history books. He did not mean to appropriate Guillaumet's best lines, but over time they detached themselves from Guillaumet and got themselves attributed to Saint-Exupéry. People who heard Guillaumet's story over dinner—and many did between 1931 and 1939, although not from Guillaumet—remembered its narrator; many would testify later that Saint-Exupéry had been the one to utter the line about man and the animal. Originally the story of Guillaumet's story became Saint-Exupéry's; later Guillaumet's story became Saint-Exupéry's. Today Hollywood would be a contender for the rights to dramatize the ordeal, and even in 1939 Saint-Exupéry was not alone in doing so. That year Jean-Gérard Fleury, a young lawyer and journalist who knew both men well, brought out his fine book on Aéropostale, which includes a version of the same events. His account is richer than Saint-Exupéry's in the practical details and he, too, reprises the famous line, but it was left to Saint-Exupéry to supply Guillaumet's interior dialogue, to add the rhetorical flourishes. Others too would have liked to have attached themselves to Guillaumet's heroism. When Saint-Exupéry told Gide the story in France the following spring and mentioned that he hoped to make it a part of his next book, Gide asked if he could go over his text for him. "I shall never," the veteran of French letters confided to his journal, "forgive him for spoiling it." There was little cause for concern. Saint-Exupéry knew how to tell a tale, and it was in his words that Guillaumet's feat was burnished into legend. It became a kind of fable, which he recounted over and over again, with remarkable consistency.

~

Consuelo de Saint-Exupéry, on the other hand, never told the story of having met her husband the same way twice. It seems safe to say that the twenty-eight-year-old widow—who claimed she had been nineteen at the time—first laid eyes on the pilot early in the fall of 1930.* The introductions were almost certainly made by Benjamin Crémieux, then the head of French PEN and an acquaintance of Saint-Exupéry's from *NRF* and Monnier circles. Probably best remembered for having translated and brought to French attention the works of Luigi Pirandello, Alberto Moravia, and Italo Svevo, the inexhaustible diplomat–author–cultural em-

---

* There is a five-year discrepancy between the birthdate on Consuelo's marriage license—1902—and the birthdate officially reported at the time of her death—1907. Neither figure is verifiable. I have assumed the former to be true as we more commonly err in the opposite direction when misstating such facts, and as Saint-Exupéry would—insofar as he was interested in such things—have believed his wife was born in 1902.

issary traveled that August to Buenos Aires to deliver a series of lectures. It would have been altogether appropriate for this energetic internationalist to have been the one to introduce Saint-Exupéry to Señora Gómez Carrillo, a native of El Salvador, the widow of a well-established journalist, and a longtime resident of France. Crémieux was forty-three at the time; he may only have met Señora Carrillo on the boat en route to Buenos Aires, but he would have known of her already. He almost certainly spoke of Saint-Exupéry, whose writing he admired and whose lifestyle was as ever a subject of fascination, before introducing the two. There is no reason to think he did so other than off-handedly, even if he himself admired the young woman's liveliness, the ivory skin, the dancing eyes, the jet-black hair.

The presentations were made at a reception, either during the last week of August or the first of September, when demonstrations against the ruling radical party filled the streets, or just after September 6, when, with a brief show of force, a conservative government came to power in the first of Argentina's modern army-led coups. These were not welcome events to Señora Gómez Carrillo, whose husband had enjoyed close ties with the ousted regime, or for Saint-Exupéry, who had the mail to worry about. Sometime after this first encounter, when Consuelo's tiny hand—she was half Saint-Exupéry's weight and her head came just to his shoulder—slipped into the aviator's bearlike paw, the pilot introduced the widow to his great love, taking her up for her first flight in a Laté 28. On all other counts the record of the early days of their courtship was irrevocably if imaginatively obscured by Consuelo's forty-eight years of variations on the theme.

A vivacious, fine-boned beauty, Consuelo Gómez Carrillo already had in 1930 some experience as the wife of a man of letters. A native of Guatemala City, Enrique Gómez Carrillo had arrived in Paris in 1892 as the correspondent for a Madrid newspaper. There he cut a dashing and reckless figure, rubbing shoulders with Joyce, Wilde, Verlaine, Zola, dueling at the slightest provocation, traveling widely, trailing behind him a hefty reputation as a syphilitic, traveling incessantly, publishing prolifically. Maurice Maeterlinck said of him that he had been a true Renaissance man, cramming three or four existences into one life and living them all more completely than most do one. He died, probably a suicide, in 1927. Gómez Carrillo's second wife had been a popular music-hall singer named Raquel Meller, whom he had divorced six years before marrying Consuelo Suncin in 1926. He had been fifty-three at the time; she was probably in her early twenties. It was his third marriage, Consuelo's second. Evidently he fell instantly for the Central American beauty, who either innately appreciated or quickly assimilated his flamboyance. We do not know how or when Consuelo Suncin arrived in Paris, and for certain only that she was born in Armenia, El Salvador. She was fond of saying that her father owned a vast coffee plantation but generally passed over all other references to her family, saying of her early years only that she had been born prematurely in an earthquake, which had turned the Suncin house around on its foundation and swallowed up her mother. (On hearing this story one reasonable friend asked how she could be sure that the earthquake had precipitated her early birth and not that her birth had precipitated the earthquake. The friend could have been wiser still: there was no earthquake in Armenia in either 1902 or 1907.) At the time she met Saint-Exupéry, she made her home in Paris, in a ground-floor apartment on the rue de Castellane, behind the Madeleine, and in a villa at Cimiez, above Nice, both of them homes left to her by Gómez Carrillo. Her friends were artists and writers, some of them left to her as well by her husband, her hobbies painting and sculpture, her lifestyle wholly bohemian. Didier Daurat described Consuelo de Saint-Exupéry as having much in common with her volcanic country: she was vehement, rash, bubbly, volatile, bursting with energy. Certainly she was more Latin than European, a fact that would have been clear in Buenos Aires, the most European of South American cities, where she may not have looked but certainly—to Saint-Exupéry—would have sounded exotic. Her voice was raspy, her French always colorful and approximate, buzzing with thickly rolled r's. She was rarely described by anyone without recourse to the word "capricious," an adjective that trailed her as inevitably as the word "distracted" did her husband.

All of Consuelo's versions of her courtship with Saint-Exupéry have in common one element: that short trip in a Laté 28 during the first week of September. Assuming that the couple's destiny was indeed sealed 2,000 feet above the Río de la Plata one evening early in the month, the events were said by Consuelo to have proceeded as follows: Not long after meeting him, possibly the very evening of Crémieux's introduction, Consuelo found herself aloft with Saint-Exupéry. In order to coax her out on this excursion, the pilot had had to invite along eight or ten of her friends as well; he may have promised them a view of the revolution from the air. The friends filled the Latécoère's cabin; Consuelo found herself alone in the cockpit with the pilot. Suddenly, over the noise of the motor, Saint-Exupéry asked for a kiss. She virtuously responded either a) that she was a widow, b) that in her country one only kissed people one loved, c) that there were places in the world where certain flowers, when brusquely approached, closed up, or d) that she never kissed anyone under duress. The response, which rings true and on which Consuelo permitted herself no variation, came back: "I know why you don't want to kiss me. I'm too ugly." To this the young widow made no answer. A few seconds later the dejected pilot threatened, "Oh well, since you don't want to kiss me I'm going to dive

into the Río de la Plata and we are all going to drown!" With this, tears
evidently welled up in his eyes. Terror-stricken and a little moved, Consuelo deposited a meek kiss on Saint-Exupéry's cheek. Under her breath
she added, "You're not ugly". The aircraft returned safely to the field at
Pacheco some minutes later, but not soon enough to return Consuelo's
musician friends to a concert engagement in Buenos Aires. A small scandal
reportedly ensued. This version of events may have been tacked on to the
story, inspired by the June episode with the visiting French actors who
had been held over in Paraguay.

Consuelo returned to France before the next few months were out,
having made some claim on the pilot's heart, enough for him to have
shown her an early draft of *Night Flight*, possibly to have asked as well
for her hand in marriage. Her version of these events is irresistible, if
undocumentable: Late one night, in a restaurant that she felt Saint-
Exupéry had kept open expressly for his purposes, he offered her a letter
of eighty pages. It was in fact an early draft of *Night Flight*, signed with
the line "Your husband, if you consent." If such a document ever existed
it has never turned up. Saint-Exupéry himself left no record of the courtship: we do not even know if the marriage proposal was made on Argentine
or French soil, in 1930 or 1931. He did not write home regarding his
intentions this fall, something he might have been a little reluctant to do
in any event, having already set off one false alarm. His silence may all
the same have been telling. In mid-December he received a ceremoniously
worded reprimand from Daurat. The company, while it recognized that
such matters were of a private nature and did not like to meddle in them,
wished to inform Monsieur de Saint-Exupéry that its Toulouse office had
received a visit from one of his relatives. Saint-Exupéry had not written
his mother since early October. It was hoped that he would demonstrate
a little less negligence in the future.

Even allowing for Saint-Exupéry's reticence on the subject of the courtship, we do know a certain amount about the background to it. For eight
years now the pilot claimed to have been looking for a wife. He felt his
age acutely. From July to September Renée de Saussine had been in Brazil,
where she played a number of enthusiastically reviewed concerts; although
she had warned Saint-Exupéry of the trip, she had not gone out of her
way to contact him on her arrival. He found out by accident that she was
in Rio and then had trouble getting her to fix a date when they might
meet. He was pained by these slights. (Ironically, Renée was traveling with
Louise de Vilmorin, for whom his affection had by no means diminished.)
Insofar as the courtship itself can be reconstructed we know this: Saint-
Exupéry was a lousy if successful flirt. He tended to sidle up to a woman
who caught his eye a little bashfully, with a mathematical formula or a
work-in-progress; it makes sense that he approached Consuelo in this

way. He was not promiscuous, and was clearly in 1930 more interested in the tenderness and shelter a woman could provide than in her social standing. He had little reason to think he would ever again live—or wish to live—in France, and may have felt he could play a little looser and faster with her social rules because of this. For five years now he had had no fixed address. Despite his protests, he clearly preferred some degree of nomadism to the numbing effects of bourgeois life that he feared marriage entailed. Consuelo could be relied upon to keep any man off the ground, off balance, on a perpetual adventure; here was an antidote to the numbing effect of conventional marriage, or at least marriage to a conventional party. Presumably this mattered more to him now than it had in 1923; he could not have been unaware that Consuelo seemed an odd choice for him in the milieu in which he was raised, which may have explained his silence of October and November.

Consuelo did not on any count seem the type to settle down. She was a woman who appeared to be lighter than air, free as the wind, who could move at a moment's notice. She was arguably better at doing so than at making plans in advance. Hers was decidedly not the motto of Isabel Burton, the explorer's wife, who had learned to "Pay, pack, and follow"; Consuelo had trouble with at least two of those directives. When she attempted them—as she did once in the early days of the marriage, when she was to meet her husband at Charles Sallès's home in the south of France—her baggage arrived but she, and the mink coat with which she was traveling, did not, although they, too, parted ways. In Paris she was known to wave her lovely pale arms but not her pocketbook in the air as she waltzed out of taxis and past the guardians of the city's finest eating establishments with the vague—and generally untrue—assurance, "The Count de Saint-Exupéry will be arriving shortly."

If Consuelo did not correspond to Saint-Exupéry's physical taste in women she did fill his need for what his American translator described as "frail, young, gentle persons with whom he could feel perfectly secure." She was the perfect match for a man who would be said to violate all sense of time and space, "who scorned both the customary sequence of the hours and their usage." Far more so than even Louise de Vilmorin— to whom he had recently written that he wanted for a woman to spirit him away to a private "little eternity," where he could feel at home— Consuelo Gómez Carrillo hailed from another planet. To her Saint- Exupéry was a tree, a camel, a dragon, a lumbering bear; initially she was his "little tropical bird." In his letters, she was more often than not "*Ma petite fille*," or "*Petite fille poète*." He had years before confided in Renée de Saussine his very un-French conviction that a fault of grammar was pardonable but that a fault of rhythm was not: Consuelo's command of grammar was original at best, but she had abundant rhythm. Her strong suit was the spinning of tales. Some call this mythomania. To Saint-Exupéry, a man who worried that the Fuchs daughters of Concordia would one day be swept off by a suitor who claimed to admire their wild gardens but in fact intended to turn them into the manicured grounds of Versailles, it was charm incarnate. He had, in short, met a woman who would see in a drawing of a hat a boa constrictor digesting an elephant.

In January 1931, if his long-range plans were, as Consuelo claimed in her various accounts, already clear to him, Saint-Exupéry had a chance to reveal them to his mother. She arrived in Buenos Aires for a month-long visit at the beginning of the year. The Countess and the future Countess de Saint-Exupéry did not have a chance to meet in South America, as Consuelo had already returned to France, where her suitor was soon to follow. Assuming that Consuelo left Buenos Aires at the last possible moment—it has been suggested that the two women's ships crossed in the harbor, although the truth is certainly less tidy—this allowed, at most, for a four-month courtship.

Madame de Saint-Exupéry arrived in Buenos Aires for the hottest weeks of the year. Her son had seemed to want to forestall the visit, possibly because of his sentimental life, possibly because, as he claimed, he was flying a great deal, and had an enormous amount of work, and could not be certain that he would be on hand to welcome his mother to the capital. Early in the month, in what was almost certainly the first flight she made with her son, she joined him on a trip to Asunción. He introduced her to the Donys, with whom the Saint-Exupérys dined on January 31, 1931, the night before they were to sail together for France, Saint-Exupéry having been accorded a leave. The pilot insisted on ending the evening at the Buenos Aires amusement park, where he hauled Paul Dony on every ride. (Or on nearly every ride: Noëlle Guillaumet remembered having been unable during her time in Buenos Aires to convince either Saint-Exupéry or her husband to join her on the park's loop-the-loop, which the two pilots found too violent.) Madame Dony and Madame de Saint-Exupéry watched from below as husband and son whirled and tilted and tumbled; Saint-Exupéry had the time of his life. Three weeks earlier, he had carried the mail from Buenos Aires to Asunción in what he knew was to be his last South American flight, inviting Dony to join him. At Posadas, 200 miles southeast of Asunción, they dropped off a passenger. From this point on the pilot hedge-hopped his way to the Paraguayan capital, barely clearing the fences around fields, sending the livestock off in all directions, heading directly down roads even as they led through woods. Turning up the Río Paraná toward Asunción, he forced a fisherman to dive into his boat for cover so as not to be hit by the landing gear. The Paraguayan ventured up only to wave a fist in the air. In the cockpit Saint-Exupéry was exultant.

On the morning of February 1, the pilot and his mother boarded the *Alsina*, along with the pet puma Saint-Exupéry insisted on bringing back to France for Gabrielle. (The animal never made it to Agay. After it attacked an officer of the ship, it was sold on the high seas to another passenger.*) Presumably Saint-Exupéry left for France with as little idea of his next posting as he had had in setting sail for Buenos Aires in September 1929; in any case, he was never again to set eyes upon the coast of South America. Exactly ten years later Eve Curie would overfly it while making a war correspondent's tour of all anti-Axis territories, from North America to China. The abandoned French hangars that dotted the South American coast made, she wrote, for a miserable sight. They revealed nothing of the greatness of Mermoz and Guillaumet; they were rotten and moldy.

---

* Saint-Exupéry was not the only one to give in to the temptation of exporting South American fauna, with which he had often enough flown. Blaise Cendrars sailed from Brazil to France at about this time in the company of 250 tropical birds and sixty-seven marmosets, few of which ever saw the Continent either.

X

~

Brightness Falls
1931–1933

Mistily I realized that the harsh days of my solitary battling had passed.

T. E. LAWRENCE,
The Seven Pillars of Wisdom

Not since the summer of 1926 had Saint-Exupéry been footloose in France for any extended period of time. Never before had he been at liberty and solvent. He was now a published writer, carrying his new manuscript— along with a screenplay penned in Argentina—around with him in his bag; he was gainfully employed; he was in love, and this spring officially engaged. Early in April he was awarded his Légion d'Honneur. He was thirty years old. He appears to have made the rounds, in high spirits. There was much to celebrate. Unsurprisingly, not a single piece of personal correspondence survives from this period.

On the return to France in mid-February Madame de Saint-Exupéry had gone to Agay and her son had immediately sought out Consuelo, who claimed she had spent the intermittent weeks in mourning out of fear that her new suitor would not come for her. Evidently she thought it preferable to observe his death than to risk being stood up. Reunited, the lovers spent the better part of March in the south of France, mostly at Consuelo's home in Nice, where Saint-Exupéry set about energetically cutting and revising the 400-page manuscript of *Night Flight*, which he was to trim by more than half. Consuelo most likely introduced her fiancé at this time to the Maeterlincks, who lived in a palatial home nearby; Saint-Exupéry intro- duced Consuelo to Yvonne de Lestrange in Agay, where his fiancée had already met the family, at the end of the month. Vacationing with Yvonne de Lestrange at the Hôtel de la Baumette was André Gide, to whom Saint-Exupéry now recounted Guillaumet's tale. At the same time he shared with him the manuscript of *Night Flight*, with which Gide was much impressed, and which he offered to preface. This proposal must have surprised as much as delighted author and publisher. It was true that Gide admired and had translated Conrad, but he was better known as a champion of personal freedom than as an endorser of duty. In his journal on March 31 the senior statesman of French letters noted: "Greatly enjoyed seeing Saint-Exupéry again at Agay . . . he has brought back from Argentina a new book and a fiancée. Read one, seen the other. Congratulated him heartily, but more for the book; I hope the fiancée is as satisfactory."

In the end it was Madame de Saint-Exupéry more than anyone who hastened the marriage. She was uncomfortable with the fact that the couple had set up house forty miles away, not very discreetly, without having taken any vows. Consuelo reported that her future mother-in-law made frequent trips to the villa at Cimiez, inquiring at each visit, "When will you finally marry?" The wedding was held in the chapel of Agay on April 12; Abbé Sudour, who had probably not yet had a chance to congratulate Saint-Exupéry on the Légion d'Honneur he had been instrumental in securing for him, officiated. Twice-widowed, the bride wore black lace, in which she looked stunning; Pierre and Gabrielle d'Agay's three children, the two daughters in long, organdy skirts and their son, François, in a crisp white sailor suit, served as attendants, accompanied by Consuelo's Pekingese, Youti. In photographs, taken in the château garden, in full bloom and sweetly scented by purple and white stock, the bride and groom look solemn but not unhappy. A small crowd assembled in the afternoon to celebrate at Agay's finest restaurant, Les Roches Rouges, with an elaborate meal. The union was made official only on the twenty-second of the month, when the couple paid a visit to the town hall in Nice to obtain their civil license, a formality that traditionally precedes the religious ceremony and is in France the binding one. Saint-Exupéry gave his address as the Château d'Agay, Consuelo as an apartment on the avenue David in Nice. As his profession, Saint-Exupéry listed "*pilote-aviateur.*" At four that afternoon the couple were pronounced legally wed. The honeymoon, insofar as it had not been taken already, was spent on the Riviera, between Agay and Cimiez.

It is to be hoped that Saint-Exupéry was distracted by the preparations for these festivities, by his version of domestic bliss, by the manuscript of *Night Flight*. If not his heart may well have been breaking during these months. Practically since his return to France, Aéropostale had been in the news, rarely in a favorable light. As a result of the October 1930 revolution in Brazil and the fallout from Wall Street in 1929, three of Marcel Bouilloux-Lafont's banks had filed for bankruptcy. The owner's

financial situation consequently came under close scrutiny. He may have
been the head of the world's longest airline, one that trumpeted the glory
of France around the globe, but he was also the beneficiary of generous
government subsidies. To some it now looked as if these funds had been
misappropriated. The first of these facts may have proved more offensive
than the second, government subsidies being something of a common
denominator in France but resounding success a subject of some resentment. Early in March, the Chamber of Deputies voted against according
the airline a new subsidy; late in the month—less than a year after Mermoz's triumph over the South Atlantic and just as Bouilloux-Lafont had
begun planning an assault on North America—Aéropostale was forced
into liquidation.

Shortly after Saint-Exupéry's wedding, Mermoz was heard on the radio, expounding upon the injustice of the company having been "done in
by political and financial scheming." On May 5 the *Journal de l'aviation
française* commented harshly on the irresponsibility of the ministries of
air and finance, which had allowed "banking rivalries, envious foreigners,
jealous Frenchmen, and socialist intrigues" to eat away at one of France's
finer institutions. There was no end to the finger-pointing involved in a
particularly messy affair, played out as publicly as it was negotiated covertly, in the end reflecting poorly on all concerned. In the spring of 1931
the battle had only just begun, but already the airline to which Saint-
Exupéry was to return in May was a different operation from the flour-
ishing company of 1930. It had had trouble meeting its February payroll;
in South America, the mail went on even in the absence of paychecks,
which after three months were finally supplied by the French embassy.
The company began cutting back on personnel and by June suspended
service to five countries. By the end of the year, additional routes would
be shut down, and the airplane that might have claimed the North Atlantic
for the French, the Latécoère 38, retreated to its hangar, where it would
corrode to death. Already Aéropostale—provisionally operating under a
state-assigned board of directors—had become a subject of hand-wringing
and embarrassment and outrage instead of one of national pride. In disgust
one pilot concluded that the age of "*belle aventure*" had come skidding
to an end and that "*l'ère de l'administration aérienne*" had dawned. Saint-
Exupéry, perhaps because his mind was elsewhere, perhaps because he
was so gifted at the sustaining of nostalgia, certainly because he had little
patience for political intrigue, was all the same able to put off that dawn
a little longer.

By summer, having delivered his manuscript to Gallimard and having
made a mid-June trip to Paris with Consuelo, he was back at work on the
African run. Cutbacks in the Aéropostale budget evidently prevented him
from returning to South America (they likely played a role in securing

him the January leave), a decision he could not have minded. Now in a
Laté 26 he began to fly the mail from Casablanca south to Port-Étienne,
leaving Morocco late on a Sunday afternoon and adhering to a tight
schedule down the coast, one that provided the rites by which he lived for
a good part of the next two years. At Agadir he and the mail changed
aircraft; the relay plane was up and running on their arrival. In his ten
minutes of ground time Saint-Exupéry chatted with the mechanics as he
gulped down an hors d'oeuvre of chocolate followed by a plate of fried
eggs, a banana, and a glass of wine. Alexandre Baïle, the chief of the
airfield, provided a word on the weather and—the mail having been
transferred—saw to it that the pilot made a prompt departure. As the sun
set over the desert Saint-Exupéry forged on to Juby, three and a half hours
to the south. Here another plate of fried eggs awaited him; in his ten
minutes on the ground he traded memories with the Spanish officers who
still occupied his former home. Jean-Gérard Fleury, who met Saint-
Exupéry this September when the pilot was asked to take him along to
Port-Étienne as a passenger (Fleury was at the time preparing a report
on the convoluted Aéropostale scandal for a popular newspaper), never
forgot the reception that greeted the aviator at Juby. He had traveled to
the outpost—against the wishes of the pilot, whom Fleury had heard
protesting to the chief of the Casablanca airfield that a passenger of
Fleury's size was going to cost him thirty gallons of fuel—in a wicker
chair, which bounced around amid the mailbags in an open compartment
behind the radio operator of the Laté. The plane had barely arrived at
Juby when a troop of blue-veiled Moors threw themselves upon Saint-
Exupéry, kissing his hand. They assembled around him, all speaking at
once until orchestrated by the pilot, from whom they clearly wanted an
opinion. A little embarrassed to be playing the role of desert chieftain,
Saint-Exupéry held court quickly, over a glass of water and a plate of
eggs, settling the pressing issue with the little Arabic he possessed. Now
in the hands of a well-connected journalist, the account of his diplomacy
traveled back to France, where it did much to enhance his Parisian reputation as a tamer of the desert.

The glory days were not entirely over: the Río de Oro remained dissident territory, and at Juby the interpreter was replaced with another,
friendly with the R'Guibats of the south. Through the night the Latécoère
continued on toward Port-Étienne, overflying Villa Cisneros to drop, quite
literally, the mail, whereupon the chief of the airfield waved the plane on
from the ground. With the dawn, Saint-Exupéry arrived at Port-Étienne,
having flown for nearly twelve hours, a period of duty and under conditions
that would be abhorrent to any member of the pilots' union today. His
stay in Port-Étienne lasted until the end of the week, when—the Buenos
Aires mail having been sent up from Dakar—the trip would be repeated

in reverse, landing Saint-Exupéry in Casablanca on Sunday morning, in time for an early breakfast of warm croissants and cafés au lait. The bulk of the newlywed's week was thus spent in a Saharan outpost consisting entirely of a fort, an airfield, a barracks, and a fishery; Consuelo was in France, occasionally in the company of her new mother-in-law, or later in Casablanca for most of this time.

Though larger, Port-Étienne boasted the same number of attractions as had Juby in 1927. The fishing was better, but swimming in the shark-infested waters was out of the question. Sandstorms and sandflies were so prevalent that the pilots had little choice but to live as shut-ins. Saint-Exupéry slept a good deal, generally during the day, writing at night. So much did he hold to his nocturnal schedule that he was said to be utterly confounded by the full moon, which can brilliantly illuminate a desert sky. At these times he generally slept for a full twenty-four-hour stretch. When awake he was in his element and, as always, quick to supply the much-needed entertainment. He traveled with a record of Ravel's *Boléro*, to which he forced the inhabitants of Port-Étienne to listen ad nauseam. He recited Baudelaire for them (at the time *"La Mort des Amants"* was at the top of his list); he spun tales of a fictional childhood; he hypnotized the ground crew; he played an improvised version of battleship.

For most of this period he was teamed up with a Corsican radio operator named Jacques Néri, as brilliant a match as could have been made. A 1929 recruit, Néri was a hugely talented radio-navigator; his preferred means of communication with his pilot was drawing, however. Not only was this easier to understand, he felt, but it was aesthetically more interesting. Once, having been advised by radio of less turbulence at a higher altitude, he chose to communicate this information to his pilot with a sketch of Saint-Exupéry laboring up a steep staircase with his aircraft on his shoulders, Néri trailing along behind at the end of the radio antenna. The staircase was marked 1,000 meters; a chubby-cheeked angel presided over it, blowing gently. Few could have appreciated Néri's extra-aerial talent more than Saint-Exupéry, who may have been back in his element but knew as well as anyone how monotonous flying over the desert could be and who appreciated a quick wit under any circumstances. He needed no encouragement to respond to Néri's creations in kind; the resulting correspondence turned into a sort of artistic competition. Saint-Exupéry went on to pay tribute to Néri in one of the more amusing episodes of *Wind, Sand and Stars*, but Néri did him one better: he saved a great quantity of the little scraps of paper passed between pilot and navigator during the second half of 1931. Taken together, these relics make for an alternate version of *Night Flight*. The preserved Néri–Saint-Exupéry correspondence, as published in the French review *Icare*, consists less of the ideograms that Saint-Exupéry later claimed he found so reassuring in the middle of a dark night than of the text of the terse, tragicomic drama that played itself out in the open cockpit of an airplane plying a night sky. Often the notes betray an eerily modern sense of two men, trapped alone in the dark in a tiny space, unable to communicate: "I told you to write instead of gesturing," Saint-Exupéry instructed Néri, who replied: "I was saying I'd seen a flare." More often they serve as fitting reminders of the still-unscientific nature of night flying: "Sure looks like land to me," scribbled Saint-Exupéry, with a big question mark. "I'd love to know where we are (at this speed we could run out of gas), but I can't afford to waste time detouring west." Occasionally all went well: "Doesn't look too bad," reported Saint-Exupéry, "give me a cigarette." Sophisticated though a Latécoère 26 was by comparison with a Breguet 14, instrument flying was still a thing of the future. "The compass is completely inaccurate, it's shameful, it's turning halfway around for five degrees," grumbled the pilot who, perhaps on the same trip, informed Néri, "In my opinion we can't be more than thirty miles from the sea. At daybreak we'll head west and we'll see, but for the moment I'm staying away because the fog will give me trouble with this idiotic compass. It turns like a top if we so much as angle west."

In *Wind, Sand and Stars*, it is with Néri that Saint-Exupéry has been drawn off course in the middle of a foggy night, en route for Cisneros. No airport can tell the two men their bearings, which makes them feel as if they have "slipped beyond the confines of this world." The two set their cap on star after star, each time in the vain hope that they are actually headed toward an airport beacon. The first time the skies yield up a light, Néri, singing, begins to pound the fuselage with his fists. Lost in interplanetary space, hungry and thirsty, Saint-Exupéry dreams of the breakfast with which the two will celebrate if ever they return to earth; all the joy of being alive will be his in that first rich, burning mouthful of coffee. But the two remain hopelessly lost. When Néri asks that Cisneros blink its beacon three times, the light ahead "would not, incorruptible star, so much as wink." ("The old flirt doesn't want to wink at us! It's a star," wrote Néri during the actual flight.) Finally Néri hands his pilot a scrap of paper. "All's well. Great news." He has received a transmission from Casablanca, which he expects will save them. In fact the message has been delayed somewhere in the 1,250 miles of night sky and dates from the previous evening, when a government representative had sent out word that Saint-Exupéry was to be disciplined on his return for having flown too close to the Casablanca hangars. He had indeed done so but was never happy to be reprimanded, least of all when he was lost on the company's behalf, in the night sky, in a dense fog, hoping for some more pertinent information. It was as if he had jumped overboard to save a shipmate and—upon asking from the open sea for a buoy—had been told that his socks were mismatched.

Later, in a perfect illustration of his accelerated capacity for nostalgia, Saint-Exupéry was to bemoan the passage of the Breguet 14, the days when every trip constituted an adventure, when a pilot necessarily entered into an intimate relationship with the land below him. "I find," he sighed not long after these flights with Néri,

> and in this I am not alone, that the Aéropostale has lost much of its charm since the advent of reliable motors and radiotelegraph. We no longer experience those little palpitations which were so pleasant: Will I make it? Will I not break down? Where am I? Those are the questions which we asked ourselves on each of our trips, in the olden days. Now our engines are foolproof; there is no reason to know our route because the direction-finder indicates it for us. Frankly, flying under these conditions is a bureaucrat's affair. It's a life without surprises. We like it as well, but the other . . .

Even with Néri he worried that the desert—*his* desert, *his* dissidents, *his* R'Guibats, as Néri heard him express it—held little adventure anymore. He asked his radio operator countless times to tell him the stories of the olden days, which Néri did, with gusto. Yet he clearly still delighted in the work, making new sport of the radio navigators. An operator who flew with him during this period* told of a harrowing experience he had had one night, between Agadir and Cisernos, when the hole through which his trailing antenna was meant to fit turned out to be blocked. Over the radio both Cisneros and Agadir were calling for the aircraft's position, but he was unable to respond without the 350-foot antenna in place. Finally, trying not to think what Daurat would say were he to see him in action, he hammered a hole in the plane with a screwdriver and a pair of plyers. Through this he inserted the weight at the end of the antenna, then the length of cord itself, insulating it from the metal of the fuselage with his socks. He turned the power on; sparks flew out in all directions. Saint-Exupéry knocked on the divider and passed back a note: "You're going to set us on fire, what the hell are you doing?" Already exasperated, the radio operator scribbled back, "It's not as bad as that. We have parachutes, don't we?" Saint-Exupéry smiled as he turned around; if there was room for insubordination clearly there was no cause for concern. The navigator added his scarf to the improvised insulation job and tried his radio again; it worked, although the antenna continued to fly free in the air, knocking

---

* This radio navigator may have been Néri, but he chose to relate the incident anonymously (which was not like Néri). in *Présence des Retraités d'Air France* (April 1973).

against the side of the fuselage, producing a sea of violet sparks toward the tail. At this the interpreter woke up, not very reassured to be surrounded by a display of fireworks. The navigator ignored him and set about re-contacting the ground with a system that may well have been jerry-rigged but which, for all its pyrotechnics, functioned.

He was happily broadcasting away when a bright flame suddenly burst out on the port side of the ship where the antenna surfaced. Without a moment's hesitation he sent out an SOS. Agadir emerged from the night to ask him to repeat the message, which had been garbled by static. Saint-Exupéry, half out of his seat, turned and gestured frantically: "Parachute, buckle up quickly, we're going to jump!" The agitated navigator fumbled with his gear; the straps were stuck, he could not find the buckle. Mean-while, from the radio came a worried, regular "Acknowledge, what's going on?" At this point, leaning over to examine the port-side fire, he discovered that Saint-Exupéry had set off a flare, intended for emergency landings. The pilot's shoulders heaved as he exploded with laughter at the controls; when the beleaguered navigator turned around, he found that the inter-preter was also doubled over with laughter. Hugely pleased with himself, Saint-Exupéry spent his ground time retelling the story, all the way down the coast.

Néri knew that information on two subjects was to be communicated to his pilot with special urgency: news regarding the whereabouts of Guil-laumet, of whom Saint-Exupéry felt, after the Andes incident, more pos-sessive than ever (he could be more nervous about his safe passage than Noëlle Guillaumet, whom he one night repeatedly abandoned in a Ca-sablanca cinema to call the airfield while Madame Guillaumet, surely no less aware of the weather, calmly watched the movie), and news regarding mail from Consuelo, for the routing of which everyone on the African run had explicit instructions. Evidently Saint-Exupéry spent a good deal of time in the cockpit calculating where, exactly, he would intercept his next letter. As much in the first days as at the end, theirs was an unusual twist on domestic life. Consuelo was not particularly happy about her husband's long absences, although she had certainly developed no habit of stability in her year's marriage to the restless Gómez Carrillo. In Casablanca she told Néri that she wished Saint-Exupéry was not a pilot but a minister, a word which was pronounced "*ministrou*" in her Spanish-laced French. She came finally to live in Casablanca late in 1931—she would join her husband here again during the second half of 1932—at which time the two moved into the apartment that was to be their first marital home. "Come live with me," Saint-Exupéry had written in a letter in which he promised she would be entirely happy in Morocco, "and fill my house with your marvelous chaos. Write on all the tables. They are yours. And put lots of disorder in my heart."

On this he could rely, as Consuelo's domestic habits rivaled her husband's. Fleury, invited to look up Saint-Exupéry in Casablanca after the memorable flight to Port-Étienne, did so at the first available opportunity. One afternoon he and the pilot were long in savoring their noontime apéritif and returned to the Saint-Exupérys' apartment later than expected for lunch. Consuelo welcomed them graciously but appeared crestfallen: they were late, and her soufflé was ruined. They would have to make the best of a tin of sardines. Fleury thought nothing of this incident until it was replayed under similar circumstances, down to the last detail. Léon Antoine, who had so clearly remembered Saint-Exupéry's grand entrance in Toulouse, was invited with his wife for a before-dinner drink at the Saint-Exupérys' one evening in Casablanca. On their arrival their host opened a bottle. It was empty, as were all those that followed. He called in his domestic to ask where the Cinzano might have gone, a question that was answered with a shrug. Saint-Exupéry asked the young man to go out and buy a new bottle, a request that was met with a second shrug; although he had been given fifty francs that morning, the domestic was out of money. When pressed he came up with a list of items, clearly invented on the spot, on which he had spent the sum. After his performance Saint-Exupéry reached into his pockets for the money with which to send the young man out for a new bottle. Turning them inside out, he produced not a cent. In the end it was Léon Antoine who purchased his host and hostess their next bottle of Cinzano.

Consuelo's arrival in Casablanca did not go unnoticed. Henri Comte, a worldly general surgeon based in Casablanca who came to know the Saint-Exupérys well, was told by a fellow colonial that he had lunched recently at the Hôtel Excelsior at the side of a ravishing, unaccompanied young woman. Unable to contain his curiosity, he had leaned over and asked where she was from. Replied the young woman with the utmost seriousness, "I have come down from the sky, the stars are my sisters." The day after hearing this story Comte was asked by a friend in Lyons to look up Saint-Exupéry; he was flabbergasted to discover that the celestial creature of whom he had just heard was the aviator's wife. Comte and his wife could not help but be fascinated by the couple, who were quickly adopted by all of their friends. Together they spent many evenings at a seaside bistro called Chez Zézé, a favorite of Casablanca taxi drivers. The Comtes would pick Saint-Exupéry up at the airfield and drive him to the twenty-four-hour restaurant, animated by two mechanical pianos and a colorful clientele, where they would listen for hours to his tales. The pilot, having been up all night, was generally the last to succumb to fatigue. The departure of the Saint-Exupérys late in 1932 was perceived by the French community as a disaster: the herculean poet and his fragile wife were the source of much fascination. Said a friend who was to know the

Saint-Exupérys a little later, on their return to Paris: "I have never forgotten the way Saint-Ex looked at her. So fragile and small, she charmed him . . . she surprised him, she fascinated him; in short, he adored her. That little bird never kept still. She perched according to her whim on her huge stuffed bear, that huge, flying stuffed bear that was Saint-Ex. They seemed to have walked out of an animated movie—a very animated movie—by Walt Disney."

~

From this decidedly colorful life Saint-Exupéry was abruptly removed several times: once in 1931, by good fortune; a second time by orders he might have preferred to have ignored; a third and final time, in late 1932, by tragedy. *Night Flight*, the novel he had written on scraps of mismatched paper all over South America the previous year and whittled down to 180 pages on the Riviera that spring, was published in Paris in October 1931. The reviews were glowing. Saint-Exupéry had given France something she had not seen since the days of Corneille and *La Princesse de Clèves*, when duty and honor reigned supreme; here was a tale of heroism, a slim, modern epic, one that might speak to the defeatism that had crept into the French novel since *Madame Bovary*. *Night Flight* "will relegate all novels of earthly chivalry to the nursery," opined the reviewer from *Le Matin*. "It is not a novel; better yet, it is a great book," announced *Les Nouvelles Littéraires*. The pilot at its center, wrote one admirer, was "the man of the century." Simpler and more tightly reined in than *Southern Mail*, possibly in response to the critiques of that novel, *Night Flight* hums with contained emotion. Saint-Exupéry could not entirely forgo a certain lyricism—ironically this now won him the accolade Maeterlinck had applied to Gómez Carrillo, and for a second time Consuelo found herself married to "a poet in prose"—but *Night Flight* is crisp and lean as well, classic in its proportions, a battle with the elements on a scale with *The Old Man and the Sea*. Three mail planes head through dark skies toward Buenos Aires, one north from Patagonia, the second east from Chile, the third south from Paraguay. In Buenos Aires the pilot of the European mail will await them, flying east at midnight. In the end, however, only two aircraft arrive; the European mail will take off as scheduled but without the Patagonian mail, lost with its pilot to a ferocious cyclone.

No one follows the mail's progress more attentively than the steely Rivière, operations manager of the enterprise, whom Saint-Exupéry lent his own title but who got tangled up in 1931—as he does still today—in the legend of Didier Daurat. He, and not Fabien, the ill-fated flyer who perishes with the Patagonian mail, is the hero of the novel. Rivière dresses like Daurat and shares his fiber and bearing, but he thinks like Saint-

Exupéry. His mission, as he sees it, is to temper his men like steel, to knead them into shape, to make them rise above themselves for the success of the gargantuan enterprise that is the mail. With few words and much severity he keeps his men in line, sending them out to do the impossible. It is because of Rivière that "the service of the mails was paramount over 20,000 miles of land and sea. 'The men are happy,' he would say, 'because they like their work, and they like it because I am hard.' " And hard he is, shaking his men up so that the elements will not, seeing to it that they are held responsible not only for their own peccadilloes but for the faults of the weather as well. Rivière's battle cry—which will echo throughout the work of Saint-Exupéry—is "Those are the orders." His secret, according to his second-in-command: "If only you punish men enough, the weather will improve." He himself wonders: "Am I just or unjust? I've no idea. All I know is that when I hit hard there are fewer accidents." In France, in 1931, Rivière won comparisons with Moses, with the heroes of Greek drama. Raving about the novel the following year to Anaïs Nin, Henry Miller billed Rivière as "a Jack London superman, with more sophisticated ruminations." (Miller rightly suspected that French literature is by no means crowded with such characters: there are plenty of heroes in French literature, but—outside of the seventeenth century—they are more prone to swashbuckling than to the exercise of ruthless discipline, and they rarely find their adversary in nature.) In Hollywood a measure of his strength could be taken from the fact that Rivière was seen as the greatest role that could have been written for John Barrymore. A few years later, when the stirrings of fascism had grown louder, the duty-obsessed head of the South American service would seem an advertisement for something far more dangerous. In 1931, however, Saint-Exupéry could do little wrong.

While Rivière may seem a perfectly Nietzschean figure, while he looked to his men to be "Rivière the Great, Rivière the Conqueror," the "old lion" reserved his highest admiration for a different brand of courage. He marveled most over the quiet satisfaction of a carpenter, the modest industry of a blacksmith before his anvil, the power of a gardener cultivating ground that forests would only be too happy to reclaim. If his interior dialogue is, as Miller noted, a step up from that which Jack London might have lent him, it is also familiar: Rivière asks himself the same questions with which Saint-Exupéry badgered Delaunay in Cape Juby. Is any amenity worth the crushed face of the worker injured during its construction, Rivière asks himself, thinking of a country bridge erected at a high cost in a far-off country. "Not one of the peasants using the road would ever have wished to mutilate this face so hideously just to save the extra walk to the next bridge," he reasons. What is this higher value for which we strive, which we seem to think more precious than human life? "By virtue of what emotion," Saint-Exupéry had interrogated Delaunay, "do we risk our lives, sometimes so casually, to move the mail?" Even if he cannot quite put his finger on what it is, Rivière knows that there is a greater good, which consists of whatever makes man eternal. "The mail," Saint-Exupéry had concluded at Juby, "is sacred. What is inside has little importance."

For his portrait of man and superman he certainly relied on the operations director, who was to spend the rest of his life vainly attempting to pry himself loose from his fictional counterpart. But well before Daurat existed for him Saint-Exupéry had invented him: Rivière amounts to a fully fleshed-out incarnation of the gruff, taciturn Bernis, the hero of Saint-Exupéry's first story, written and published before he had met Daurat. It was a figure for whom the fatherless son had a predisposition, as the indulged, iconoclastic aristocrat did for the stoicism, the steadfastness, the rigorous professionalism of the mail pilots. Military posturing meant little to him, but bowing to duty did. Arguably these were qualities he could fully admire because they were not naturally his own; Aéropostale transformed his life to a greater extent than it did most of its pilots. Saint-Exupéry always remained reverent before Daurat, whom he never addressed as anything but Monsieur Daurat, with whom he was not friendly until years later, and to whom he presented himself always like a small boy in search of a blessing. To him—ultimately probably to both men's regret—he dedicated this novel. If Daurat provided living proof of something that Saint-Exupéry had for a long time thought existed, for which he carried around the Platonic template, he also later justified Saint-Exupéry's abiding faith in that ideal. Saint-Exupéry's posthumous and most ambitious book amounts to a long meditation on the father-son, ruler-subject dynamic, a study that can be said to have begun, on the page, with *Night Flight*. In 1941, at a time when France was most at a loss for leaders, Rivière's creator wrote in a sort of Hegelian twist on the theme:

On what does our salvation depend? On leaders. But we must agree on what we mean by a leader. A leader is one who governs without doubt. The manager [*gérant*] also governs—he arbitrates and administers—but the manager is not a leader. . . . A leader is one who needs us, needs us ardently. He is one who cannot forgo our participation, who solicits not only our effort in the task at hand but our constant invention, that which transforms us into creators. Because he needs our creations. . . . The leader is one who shows us enough respect to need us. Because almost anyone can give orders, can impose himself upon us from the height of a throne. But in what way do these posturings of a corporal have anything to do with authority? Authority entails creation.

He had come a long way from the black-and-white reasoning of *Night Flight*, but the image of Daurat clearly still burned bright. Unlike most people in his life, his Aéropostale boss never disappointed him, nor could Saint-Exupéry, clinging to the ideal, ever let him.

Much more of the pilot made its way into *Night Flight* than simply the consciousness he breathed into the character of Rivière. The novel is rich in autobiographical touches; it is, after all, the story of a struggle Saint-Exupéry had often enough lived firsthand. Once again he cribbed from his letters, painting a picture of a flight over the Andes exactly as he had described it in 1930 to his mother. The harbor of his childhood bed became that of the pilot of the European mail, whose sheets are smoothed by his wife, "as a divine hand calms the sea." Rivière remembers a poignant conversation he had had with a young mother who had lost a child, a drama that had, by way of Gabrielle's experience in 1925 and Louise de Vilmorin's sister the previous year, already made its way as well into *Southern Mail*. Early on in the novel Rivière mercilessly fires a mechanic named Roblet who had worked in aviation since 1910 and who had outlived his usefulness; Saint-Exupéry had in fact himself been forced to terminate a veteran with the same name whom Mermoz had brought to South America and who had been the chief mechanic at San Antonio Oeste. Taxing work for any man, the position proved to be too much for a sixty-year-old. A thin layer of fairy dust still hangs over the story, which for all of its sobriety still sparkles with frozen jewels and buried treasure, even if it does not succumb to the overblown lyricism of *Southern Mail*.

Nearly every element in the novel testifies to Saint-Exupéry's love affair with the abstract. Its characters are not so much characters as they are walking moral entities. For Daurat, the inveterate leader, Saint-Exupéry invents the foil of Robineau, the small-minded inspector, the consummate "*gérant*" of his 1941 piece. (Robineau was modeled on an actual inspector, reputed to have borrowed and never returned a collection of rocks Saint-Exupéry assembled at Cape Juby, and on whom he now vented his rancor. Robineau is made to suffer from eczema and from a pathetic lack of intelligence; he wants nothing more than to save the company from some mortal danger but manages only to locate one rusting screw. He is isolated from the pilots once because it is his job to give orders, a second time because his orders do not earn him the respect accorded Rivière. Saint-Exupéry allows him all the same a little of their transcendence; he gives the fictional Robineau a rock collection, his "talismans to open doors of mystery." Robineau longs to share his pebbles with someone: "All his long life only the stones had not been hard on him," wrote Saint-Exupéry, confessing later to having been much amused by this unsubtle airing of his grievance.) Fabien and the pilot who is to carry the mail to Europe are portrayed as young archangels, both of whom remain faceless, one of whom never merits a name. Their wives, the only two women in the novel, represent a world apart, one that answers to different rules and that Saint-Exupéry pits squarely against that of Rivière. Again Saint-Exupéry explored what he saw as the divide between the heroic arena and the domestic front. While the scene in which the Europe-bound pilot's wife wakes and prepares her husband for his evening battle with the stars may be the tenderest Saint-Exupéry ever wrote for a man and a woman, the forbearing wife amounts still to nothing more substantive than a little girl. Her husband draws on his heavy armor; she is shunted aside by the call of duty. When Fabien's wife appears at the airfield for an explanation of her husband's tardiness, Rivière dreads the encounter; she does not so much represent a lost pilot's wife as "another theory of life."

One can dive deep into *Night Flight* for autobiographical traces but not for symbols, all of which are walking about on the novel's surface, posing as characters. It is a work in which the sky is described in detail but which is otherwise entirely devoid of place. There is nothing vaguely South American about it, and if the meteorological conditions could be reproduced the story could equally well take place in the sky over Mars. Saint-Exupéry clears the stage, the better to force us inside the hearts and minds of these men. His first novel had been a moody, autobiographical work. With *Night Flight*, he began to reach for the moralistic underpinnings that would anchor all his later work, more accurately categorized —with the possible exception of *The Little Prince*—as essay than as fiction, and that would ultimately evolve from essay to parable. His admirers like to say that Saint-Exupéry deserted the novelistic form because *Night Flight* was so widely misconstrued; in fact even in this work he is clearly headed toward the territory of the *moralistes*, an aviator in search of a higher world.

Saint-Exupéry managed to fuse the active and the contemplative as skillfully as he ever would in the pages of *Night Flight*, among the finest he would write. This he accomplished through a series of narrative devices of which he was himself no doubt unaware. They were not purely literary; he could not have written a *Lord Jim*. The story is told in telegrams, flashbacks, emotional close-ups, a sort of literary montage, all of which struck an occasional reviewer as a camera's-eye view of the world. More accurately it was a pilot's-eye view. Fabien and the narrator make poetry of the night sky; Rivière thinks and communicates in a telegraphic shorthand reminiscent of Daurat but belonging to early aviation in general, as witnessed by Saint-Exupéry and Néri's in-flight correspondence. The novel's dialogue is so pared down as to resemble that of a screenplay more than a novel, a virtue that in the end played better on the page than on the screen, partly because what seemed an elemental struggle between man and the universe was in its themes and in its language a far subtler

tale. One of the first to recognize Saint-Exupéry's crystalline prose as
deceptively simple was Stuart Gilbert, a translator of *Ulysses*, whom Caresse Crosby introduced to the aviator in the hope that he might render
Night Flight into English. As Gilbert told an earlier Saint-Exupéry biographer, the limpid text proved far more troublesome than it had seemed
at first glance. "And before I was through, I was taking passages to Joyce
and saying: 'Now how would you translate this?' And Joyce would take a
long squint and then say: 'Well, let's see . . .' And I'd get my pages back
later, revised by the Master." The Joyce-enhanced Gilbert translation
failed all the same to win over the English-language critics, a backhanded
tribute, given Gilbert's considerable gifts, to Saint-Exupéry and *le mot
juste*.

The writer thought of his book as an exploration of the dark; we know
he began it thinking of his childhood evenings at Saint-Maurice. Later
he cited as his literary influence a little-known work of Jules Verne, *Les
Indes noires*, which he claimed to have read when he was ten: "Usually
considered rather tedious, [it] seemed to me an infinitely majestic and
mysterious work." Its fantastic images persisted in his mind for years: in
1941 he recalled that "the action takes place in subterranean passages
dug thousands of feet below the earth's surface, where light never pen-
etrates." One critic counted sixty-three uses of the word "night" in the
novel, and it is true that the book amounts, as Gide stated in his short
preface, to a meditation on "the night's dark treachery." Only one kind
of imagery is more prevalent: *Night Flight* is bloated with ocean-going
references. The book overflows with seas, waves, anchors, submarines,
tides, ships, divers, harbors, with metaphors concerning all things nautical.
Saint-Exupéry had been overflying the South American coast for a good
year, but it is impossible not to think of him in 1929 at Brest, during that
short summer when he lived among and learned from sailors. It was
entirely appropriate that reviewers of *Night Flight* should start to give way
to the temptation to compare Saint-Exupéry with Conrad, and *Night Flight*
to *Typhoon*.

On both sides of the ocean Saint-Exupéry was hailed as a classicist,
which must have made the author of a book about aviation—even one
with a decidedly Old World name—smile. In 1932, when the novel was
published in America, it was greeted as "an enduring modern classic," as
a superb portrait of "modern courage," as the best description of flight in
print, a distinction it arguably holds still today. In a mixed notice in *The
New York Times Book Review*, Louis Kronenberger conceded, "For the
first time the airplane achieves at least a nodding acquaintance with art."
Some friends proved loyal: Benjamin Crémieux, a Gallimard reader to
begin with, managed to review *Night Flight* not once but twice, in *Les

Annales in September and again in the *NRF* in October. In the second
piece he found himself addressing the thorny question of what an airline
pilot was doing writing a book. From a publicity point of view this worked
to Saint-Exupéry's advantage in 1931—as did the Gide preface and the
fine reviews and the Gallimard imprimatur, often a necessary if not sufficient condition for the winning of awards in France—and it came as no
surprise that the book was rumored in November to be a serious contender
for the Prix Fémina, one of the country's most prestigious literary awards.
The other short-listed title was Jacques Chardonne's *Claire*; both men
were said to be in the running for the Prix Goncourt. Of the two Saint-
Exupéry was the lesser-known writer, and the only one who happened to
be flying the mail between Casablanca and Port-Étienne while the jury
deliberated.

On December 4 he received at least three cables. The Fémina jury
had, by a vote of twelve to three, awarded him the prize. A second cable,
from the company, granted him permission to return to Paris to accept
the honor, although he was expected to fly the South American mail with
him to Toulouse. And in what may have in the end amounted to the most
significant of the dispatches, Mermoz sent his heartfelt congratulations.
Saint-Exupéry arrived in Toulouse toward mid-month after a twenty-hour
flight, drenched in grease and further disguised by a three-day beard. The
1931 Fémina laureate wore a decaying pair of espadrilles, stained trousers,
and—over a bare chest—a blue cotton overcoat, belted at the waist with
a piece of string. Two hours later he was on the Paris-bound train, having
rustled up a wrinkled suit. He checked into the Hôtel Lutétia, a grand
old Left Bank establishment, where Consuelo and his mother joined him.
A bellboy was charged with the revitalization of his wardrobe, and a barber
was sent to his room to make the pilot look a little less like a latter-day
Robinson Crusoe. None of these efforts would have put him any more at
ease at the Fémina reception, where his vanity no doubt deserted him, as
it reliably did on such occasions, rendering him awkward, red-faced, and
mute. "If a friend approached him at such a time," wrote a woman who
would see him through many of these tortures in the next ten years, "he
glommed on to him as to a life vest, crushing his hand in silence."

Otherwise Saint-Exupéry seemed to have his dual existence firmly
under control. He appeared to be a man doubly blessed: He was an exotic
creature in two worlds, much valued in them both. While one newspaper
marveled that the Fémina laureate was not a professional writer, another
noted that he liked to draw his flying colleagues into discussions of Valéry,
Spinoza, and German Romanticism. Unfortunately, Saint-Exupéry would
soon enough find this a more difficult balancing act than navigating amid
the stars, one that would require more from the department of explanations

than that of stoic brevity. Still on leave, he spent Christmas with Consuelo at Saint-Maurice, the last time the family was to do so.

~

Sometime before the Fémina jury had cast its votes, Saint-Exupéry read several reviews of *Night Flight* that displeased him. From Port-Étienne he fired off a bitter letter to Crémieux, who, presumably with its author's permission, published it in excerpted form in the December 15 issue of *Les Annales.* No writer is immune to criticism, but it was typical of Saint-Exupéry to have focused on the dissenting voices in what was otherwise a torrent of praise. He was a thoroughgoing malcontent: he told Yvonne de Lestrange he was disappointed to have won the Fémina and not the Goncourt, a complaint for which she had little sympathy.* His letter, written in November, doubtless carried more weight for having appeared after he had been named as the Fémina winner. So began a period of his life that constituted a sort of apologia, in which the author of *Night Flight* was to do more talking than flying.

The charges against Saint-Exupéry were threefold and somewhat contradictory. He had been taken to task for a certain mysticism, an element he could not and did not deny in his work, although he did dismiss the suggestion that he was a disciple of Tagore, the Nobel Prize–winning Indian poet very much in vogue at the time. He was more aggrieved to read that his imagery was precious, in any way contrived. What could be more natural, he asked, than for an image to pop spontaneously into one's mind in a situation so dire that it precluded rational thought? To illustrate his point he referred back to the evening with Néri—which he first let congeal into prose in this letter—when the two men had been "lost in interplanetary space." Over and over he had set his cap on stars; they had had to head toward something. Having repeated this exercise a number of times, he had said to himself, "I'll never be able to find the one on which I live!" The image of "a single inhabitable star" had come to him naturally, as much he claimed, belaboring his point a little, an invention of his body as his mind. In moments of equal duress even the most primitive of men resorted to a rarified dream world well above language, he argued; the results represented near-subconscious attempts to make sense of a situation. On another occasion, bouncing along among the stars without the benefit either of a horizon or an artificial horizon, a single image had

---

* He was right about the weight of the Goncourt, an award so hotly contested that the publishers of runners-up have been known to print bellybands for their losing candidates that read "PRIX GONCOURT" and, in small print, "Four votes out of ten." Today writers maneuver their way around lesser awards so as to remain *Goncourable.*

come to mind: he had been performing a trapeze act on an apparatus suspended from the stars. The image might sound precious but it was not a matter of literary fakery, which he disdained as much as anyone. "Any farmer has equally poetic dreams every night," he assured his critics, who surely knew as little on that score as he did. He had answered Anne Morrow Lindbergh's question: he did indeed conjure with these images while flying an airplane; he was somehow able to navigate by what looked to him to be "the frozen glitter of diamonds." And he had amply illustrated what set him apart from most pilots, who might well have found their thoughts—especially at 2:00 a.m., in the hold of an endless, inky fog, low on fuel, and having lost their bearings—confined to technical matters instead of veering off to the oneiric.

At the same time he defended himself against the charge that he had no business writing about his métier. The division of labor is more strictly adhered to in France than elsewhere: French taxi drivers write but rarely publish their memoirs; aspiring litterateurs write but do not support themselves driving taxis, having come to their field early or never. "Must one then be a eunuch to speak of love? And not be a literary critic to speak of books?" asked Saint-Exupéry, sensibly enough. A village blacksmith who had written a bad book about his anvil was not likely to fare any better on the subject of château life, of which he knew nothing. Here Saint-Exupéry somewhat ducked the issue. He knew full well that he was pushing the envelope of the literary world with his other life, and he knew equally well that no village blacksmith was likely to come thundering into Saint-Germain to claim the 1932 Prix Fémina. He had benefited from loopholes in the regulations that governed membership in both worlds, and now began to find that having footholds in two camps amounted to having a place in none. For the next few years he would be a little like Voltaire, exhausting himself in attempts to pacify both Church and State.

After the holidays, for reasons that may have had to do with the continued unraveling of Aéropostale, Saint-Exupéry did not return to the African line. Instead, in mid-February, he reported to Marseilles, along with Mermoz, to begin work on the Marseilles–Algiers route. From here he would have read countless newspaper accounts of the political-industrial intrigue swirling around Bouilloux-Lafont, which was now uglier than ever. He was scheduled to make two round-trips as copilot, after which he would train for his seaplane airline transport rating. Thereafter he would be entrusted with the five-hour flight over the Mediterranean, one that amounted in good weather to what Saint-Exupéry called "an afternoon stroll" but that continued to claim one or two lives annually. Marseilles did not hold the same attractions as the Río de Oro or even Argentina, but it did have the virtue of being a short flight away from Agay and Nice, where Consuelo presumably resettled. Gabrielle d'Agay's younger daughter vividly remembered the morning when her uncle swooped down on the bay in what looked to her four-year-old eyes to be a "fat green mosquito," interrupting the children's work on a sandcastle and attracting a crowd on the beach. She was slow to recognize the figure who strode to shore in helmet and goggles and not terribly pleased when she did to learn that her uncle was about to carry her mother off for a short flight. The two departed laughing, Gabrielle wearing a jacket over her bathing suit so as not to catch cold. Her daughter clung to her father's leg as she watched the aircraft take off.

Probably this was one of Saint-Exupéry's happier moments that spring, when the grumblings of a second group who held that one does not write about one's profession began to be heard. Saint-Exupéry's sudden bout with literary fame did not sit well with many of his colleagues, who felt it had been won at their expense. If, as the adage went, Mermoz cleared and Guillaumet ploughed, it now looked as if Saint-Exupéry—single-handedly—reaped. The pilots resented as well his near-deification of the operations director, who was hardly the one who risked his life. As the Saint-Germain crowd felt a writer was not meant to have dirt under his nails, the Aéropostale pilots could not help but assume that a Fémina laureate was pretentious. Saint-Exupéry began to pay the price for having been—despite his years of service—always a little exceptional, a little distracted, a little unpredictable, a little too refined. It is less likely that the success of *Night Flight* put a swagger in his step than that he was plainly taken to task for having violated a cardinal law of the profession. Didier Daurat had impressed upon his men that they were manual laborers, public servants: "You should see your name in the newspaper exactly once, the day you have been careless enough to get yourself killed," he counseled. This advice Saint-Exupéry had ignored. He may in the end have been the one responsible for the immortality of their enterprise but he now paid dearly for having portrayed its glories. In the early 1930s he was as popular among some of his peers—the pilots more than the mechanics—as John Glenn initially made himself among the early astronauts. In their own ways, both men reached out toward the public, violating a fraternal code of silence.

None of Saint-Exupéry's colleagues confessed to turning a cold shoulder that spring, but Saint-Exupéry wrote several pained reports of having been frozen out by his peers. He appealed to Guillaumet's sympathies:

> For having written this ill-fated book I have been condemned to poverty and to the enmity of my colleagues. Mermoz will tell you what has been said about me by those whom I no longer see and of whom I was once so fond. They will tell you how pretentious I am. And there is not a soul, from Toulouse to Dakar, who doubts this. One of my most serious concerns has

been my debts; I haven't always been able to pay the gas bill, and am wearing clothes I bought three years ago. . . . My repeated disillusionment, this injustice, have kept me from writing you. Maybe you, too, thought I had changed. And I could not bear to justify myself to the one man whom I consider a brother. . . . So my whole life is ruined if my best friends turn their backs on me, if it has become a scandal that I fly on the line after the crime I have committed by writing *Vol de nuit*.

A year or two later, he claimed he no longer had the courage to set foot at Le Bourget. Brokenhearted, he wrote Guillaumet: "You don't know, you can't imagine, how much I have suffered these last two years. . . . Life is indeed merciless." His timing only made the matter worse: he had chosen the worst possible moment to write a book that appeared to sing the praises of Didier Daurat.

By summer the Aéropostale scandal had escalated to the point where the company was reduced to issuing a twenty-five-page brochure in its own defense, entitled *La Vérité sur l'Aéropostale*. In June, in a particularly ugly turn of events, Daurat was accused of having tampered with the mail. In an interview on the twenty-seventh with Abel Verdurand, who had replaced Beppo de Massimi on the Marquis's resignation a year earlier, Daurat was asked over and over why he had intercepted, opened, and ultimately burned envelopes bound for Buenos Aires. The record shows him capable mostly of sputtering "Infamies!" "Calumny!" Why, he asked, pointing out that his accusers were men who disliked him in the first place (one was Édouard Serre, who claimed that the letters he had sent to his wife while he was held prisoner in the desert in 1928 had been opened), would he stoop to such behavior after twelve years of arduous service? Why, countered Verdurand, don't you speak to the accusations? It was agreed that Daurat would resign at noon on Wednesday morning, the twenty-ninth, in Toulouse. Unflappable, he reported to his office that morning and left at his usual time for lunch. When he returned two hours later he found that the lock on his office door had been changed. Evidently he stood immobile for a minute before the door. Then, without displaying the least hint of emotion, he walked off without saying a word. His admirers did not share his restraint. Mermoz, for one, immediately and loudly began to argue for his return. Saint-Exupéry said he spoke as well for him and for Guillaumet when, on July 15, the three were asked by the company's interim management what improvements they would like to see, and Mermoz responded that if Daurat remained in place the improvements would take care of themselves. (Daurat was replaced by Serre. In early 1933 Daurat, the original operations director, won a suit for his back salary; he was rehired that summer in a lesser capacity.) Mermoz had his quibbles with Daurat—"he has obvious failings, but his virtues are solid and his integrity is beyond reproach," he wrote a friend—but he firmly believed that the enterprise belonged to those who had built it, and in his mind that was first and foremost its operations director. Even if he had hoped to avoid being caught up in the Daurat maelstrom, Saint-Exupéry found himself automatically involved in the affair. He had written what now seemed a hugely political book, in which he had taken a contentious, highly public stand on his ex-boss's behalf.

He was recalled from or left Marseilles the same month, for reasons that are unclear but which he attributed later to his literary sins. His presence on the run had not been welcomed by his peers: "The most insignificant of my actions served as the pretext for absurd dramas," he wrote of his short tenure in the port city. Most likely he was recalled and, in angry response, requested a leave of absence from the company. He had personal reasons to request a vacation at the time: this year his mother finally sold the Saint-Maurice château to the city of Lyons—it became a summer retreat for children—and the house needed to be emptied. In July Saint-Exupéry returned to help with the packing. This exercise in loss and order could not have improved his spirits. Earlier he had warned that without Saint-Maurice, the only family seat he recognized, he and his sisters would be "like lost chicks."

Whatever the terms of his departure from Marseilles, all was clearly not well between the pilot and the company this summer. According to a letter he received from Toulouse late in the month, he had asked for a two-week leave as of July 1, then requested an extension, which he had never bothered to confirm. Nor had he put in an appearance at the airfield. He was asked to notify Toulouse as to his return date and crisply informed that he was currently enjoying an unsalaried leave. If only to secure a paycheck, the letter sent him scurrying back to Montaudran. By August he was based again in Morocco, having taken an apartment with Consuelo on the rue Nolly in Casablanca. Consuelo had been troubled by a series of asthma attacks; Saint-Exupéry requested this two-month posting at least in part with her health in mind. He now picked up again where he had left off when news of the Fémina had reached him, but much of the pleasure was gone. He was demoralized, all the more so because he felt he was flying only for money, which failed to equal what he and Consuelo were spending.

From Port-Étienne he wrote despondent letters. He was short even with his mother, who did not entirely approve of the way her son was running his life, socially or spiritually, and who begrudged him a little his marriage. Firmly he assured her that her fears were misplaced, that she was in no danger of losing another son. If anything he needed her tenderness now more than ever: "*Maman*, the more I've seen of the world, of hard countries, hard lives, hard men, the more it seems to me the only great virtue," he wrote her this month. He was off-balance, no longer grounded by the exotic conventions of a country that had once entirely charmed him, probably too aware of the tenuousness of his position. His financial concerns were aggravated in the fall by a serious automobile accident Consuelo had in Nice, for which she was at fault. The repair bill for the couple's Bugatti came to 3,600 francs but a far costlier lawsuit followed, necessitating the rental and ultimately the sale of the villa at Cimiez. It was the second refuge Saint-Exupéry was to lose this winter.

~

October 1932 found the Saint-Exupérys back on the rue de Castellane in Paris, their bad luck in tow. Saint-Exupéry was once again on leave from the company, this time entirely of his own volition. Earlier in the year, he had promised Gaston Gallimard a series of articles on aviation for Gallimard's new journal, *Marianne*, founded as an answer to the highly successful, right-leaning *Candide*. These pieces—the first fragments of what would become *Wind, Sand and Stars*—appeared now, just as the Aéropostale affair was reaching its tawdriest. While in every newspaper the company's name was dragged through the mud, Saint-Exupéry could be read, in four of the first issues of the weekly, singing the praises of Bouilloux-Lafont's great enterprise.

By this time, Marcel Bouilloux-Lafont's bookkeeping practices were of interest to no one, having been supplanted by the confessions of one Lucien Collin, secret agent. Posing as a disinterested newspaper reporter, "Lucco" had supplied a number of documents to Bouilloux-Lafont's son, André, allegedly proving that a powerful French industrialist and the country's director of civil aviation—acting with the collusion of Pierre Latécoère and Beppo de Massimi—had conspired to gain control of Aéropostale. They had done so with the sole purpose of putting the company in the hands of Deutsche Lufthansa.* The documents had been taken by an outraged Bouilloux-Lafont to the head of the Ministry of War, who had confiscated them. One of the letters had evidently come to Bouilloux-Lafont from André Tardieu, the former French prime minister; by now the Aéropostale scandal had grown to include not only secret agents and international conspiracies but a number of top-level ministers. Lucco, in reality a police informer, grandly testified that he had falsified the doc-

---

* Lucco's was not a wholly far-fetched idea. A British air ministry report of 1931 reveals that there had been talk that year of combining French and German efforts in South America. These discussions would have taken place at a governmental level and out of the earshot of Bouilloux-Lafont, whose patriotism had led him to invest in the airline in the first place, and who would have been offended by such a suggestion. In 1934 Air France entered into a pooled agreement with Deutsche Lufthansa.

uments at the instruction of André Bouilloux-Lafont, who, he claimed, had dictated several of them. As a result of the trial young Bouilloux-Lafont, no one's favorite in the first place, was arrested and sentenced to four months in prison. By now it was eminently clear to all concerned not only that Aéropostale had ceased to exist, but that the Bouilloux-Lafonts were finished as well.

The October 26, 1932, issue of *Marianne*—the newspaper's premiere—was crowded with articles on the scandal, studded with references to Lucco. Page two was given over entirely to Saint-Exupéry. The first of four "Pilotes de Ligne" essays began:

> Although there is a scandal in the Aéropostale service, we must not forget that pilots still devote themselves to their difficult calling far from political and financial discussions. Airplanes are flying along the route from France to South America as well as along the route from Marseilles to Algiers. Every day there are judicial hearings, but every day some pilot is called before another tribunal, dramatic and important in quite a different way. He is entrusted with bags of mail and human lives that he may have to defend a few hours later with more courage than one needs in an ordinary court, for he confronts single-handed a vast tribunal of storms, mountains, and seas, the three most common perils the airline pilot has to face. I am not today attempting to describe our work but simply what is peculiar to our existence and why—if this network of elaborate air routes were to disappear—we should feel as if we were losing with it a special way of thinking, feeling, and passing judgment which is unique in the world. This network represents a little, closed civilization whose language one cannot learn overnight. When I think of my colleagues I realize that if they were to vanish we should lose with them a fine race of men, born of the conventions and customs of the air and subject to its special morality, never to be replaced.

Saint-Exupéry went on to celebrate his harrowing flight with Néri, Mermoz's trials in crossing the South Atlantic, one of his magical encounters with the virgin desert. Doubtless he paid more attention to his choice of adjectives than to his political angle, but once again his name appeared in the wrong place at the wrong time. Taken as a whole, the issue seems an odd combination of the sacred and the profane; it is not easy to reconcile the pettiness of the accusations that flew fast and furious with Saint-Exupéry's remembered grandeurs. The fallout was immediate.

On October 31, the pilot wrote a long and indignant letter to Raoul Dautry, the president of the bankrupt company's acting board of directors, a brilliant administrator who had made his reputation in railroads. Mermoz had told Saint-Exupéry what emotion his piece had stirred up; all sorts of political motives were being assigned to him when he was nothing more than a victim of coincidence. Six months earlier he had promised

Gallimard three articles (four would run in all) for *Marianne*; he was not a man to go back on his word, and he had delivered his texts. At the time he had had no reason to think that when *Marianne* was launched Aéropostale would be so much in the public eye. Nor could he have foreseen that his article would follow a highly explosive piece by Emmanuel Berl, the paper's editor, calling for the routing of Emmanuel Chaumié, the director of civil aviation implicated in the Lucco affair and an ally of Dautry's. He could not and did not intend to address Bouilloux-Lafont's financial practices, of which he was entirely ignorant, but he did intend to defend the noble enterprise itself. "This seemed to me," wrote Saint-Exupéry, in an attempt to rise above the pettiness, "the only thing that was important." The paper by no means represented his own political opinions: he could at the same time admire Daurat, Bouilloux-Lafont, and Chaumié and he did so, odd though that might seem in the present climate, when the three were waging an all-out war with one another, the first for his job and his reputation, the second for his company and his fortune, the third for the interests of the State.

Moreover, Saint-Exupéry continued, this was not the first time he had been unfairly accused of partisanship. He claimed he had been recalled from the Marseilles–Algiers line "in a brutal and painful manner" for his literary sins. *Night Flight* could hardly be termed a political tract as it had been written the year before the events on which it was now said to bear had happened. Had no one noticed that the little book that had cost him his job in fact constituted an advertisement for the company? Nothing could have been less his intention than polemic, nor had he any favor to gain from Daurat. (He did not in this letter express his conviction that Daurat was innocent, a point he argued elsewhere without acknowledging that it constituted a political opinion.) Doubtless again from Mermoz, he had heard that he was being reproached because he was no longer flying. "But it seems to me," he protested, "that I would still be flying if M. Verdurand had not recalled me to Paris with the sole objective of scoring a point against M. Daurat, as if I were a pawn, as if the company and not M. Daurat could not—out of gratitude for everything I had brought [to the airline], having asked for nothing in exchange, and which would have cost dearly coming from anyone else—let me simply work in peace, far from the critics, on one of the most difficult lines, one which I loved." He had no desire to return to work now, and did not intend to do so until "the petty grudges were put to rest." With the letter, as a courtesy, he enclosed his second piece for *Marianne*, which was to appear on November 2.

A week after it did—this time Saint-Exupéry wrote of his initiation in Toulouse, his first experience of the desert, the enchanting night in Nouakchott—Dautry responded to his letter. While the acting board of directors was not particularly delighted with Saint-Exupéry's eulogies to the company, they were happy to hear that the author intended to remain above the political fray. Artfully, Dautry suggested that it would be "infinitely regrettable" if a name like Saint-Exupéry's were muddied in the scandal. So far as his assignment to the Marseilles–Algiers route went, the company had only been acting on Daurat's instructions. The Marseilles–Algiers run had known a great number of accidents; while the company appreciated Saint-Exupéry's thirst for new adventure, no one wanted to risk assigning a pilot unfamiliar with seaplanes to the dangerous route. It is unlikely that Saint-Exupéry felt better for having been told he had been turned away not for his political beliefs, but because he was a second-rate pilot. In an elegantly disingenuous twist, Dautry appealed to Saint-Exupéry's own work: surely Saint-Exupéry must approve of such decisions, given the respect he had accorded discipline in his novel?

Night Flight had turned out to be a Pyrrhic victory. When the pilot wrote Dautry again—he mailed an impassioned defense of Daurat on February 20, 1933—he had plenty of time on his hands; he had been unemployed for four months. As if to add insult to injury, the novel—inspired by a work of Jules Verne's and by Saint-Exupéry's memories of the refuge that was his childhood bed—could not escape political interpretation. In January 1933, Hitler came to power; to many, *Night Flight* suddenly read like a paean to fascism. Reviewing the novel in the *Nation* in September 1932, Clifton Fadiman had raised a red flag to this effect, calling *Night Flight* "a dangerous book." Its reverence for Rivière sounded to Fadiman perilously like an endorsement of Mussolini; the novel was all the more dangerous because it was beautifully written, because it romanticized the triumph of the will. (It would not help that the novel was as successful in Germany as it had been elsewhere, nor, later, that Saint-Exupéry's works would be held up by the Germans as an example of what was best about French literature.) Everything about the book seemed cursed. Even Gide carped that his preface had been misquoted and misconstrued, although Gide filed this complaint with some regularity, often with relish. In the fall of 1933, Clarence Brown's film of *Night Flight* appeared in American theaters. John Barrymore claimed the role of Rivière and Lionel Barrymore somehow ended up as Robineau; Helen Hayes, Clark Gable, Robert Montgomery, and Myrna Loy filled out the cast. Not unreasonably, *Vanity Fair*'s reviewer termed the result "as terrible an exhibition of gas-light acting as I've ever seen in my life." For Clarence Brown the reviews of *Night Flight* were no more unpleasant than the filming had been: he had had to direct a hopelessly drunk John Barrymore.

By the time Aéropostale had, for better or worse, made its way to the screen, the company had ceased to exist. Along with France's four other airlines, it was folded on August 30, 1933, into a temporary company, of which one-quarter was state-owned, an entity that was soon to become Air France. If the comprehensiveness with which Aéropostale was swept under the new company's carpet was any indication, Bouilloux-Lafont was either a very guilty or a very innocent man. Modern histories glide easily from the vision of Pierre-Georges Latécoère to the sophistication of Air France without pausing to remember his capitalistic ambitions; both bask in the reflected glory of the unmentioned middle era, purged from the record with remarkable vigor. (Bouilloux-Lafont does not so much as appear in a *Larousse*.) Didier Daurat would be resurrected, but the ex-magnate would die in a run-down hotel room in Rio de Janeiro in 1944, mostly, it appears, of a broken heart. A farewell luncheon for Aéropostale was given by Dautry in Paris on July 31, 1933, to which Saint-Exupéry was not invited.

Divisiveness runs deep in France, a country distinguished by what has been called its "people's ineradicable love of political squabbles." (De Gaulle made the same quality sound nearly romantic, referring to it as "*notre vieille propension gauloise aux divisions*.") The characteristic was on full view in France between the wars, when the country exhausted forty-three governments in twenty-two years. To this day the Aéropostale scandal holds its mysteries, but few would argue with Jean-Gérard Fleury's description of it as a clear-cut illustration of "the France of the Right and the France of the Left, the France of parties and clans." Every step of it was political, from the early days, when Bouilloux-Lafont's alleged mis-management was seen by the leftists as a weapon to be used against Pierre Laval's government, to the nationalizing instinct that guided and ulti-mately resolved the affair, government connections having been recog-nized as the single greatest asset to an airline company in these years. (It should be said that the idea to nationalize—which Bouilloux-Lafont would have resisted with all his might had he been given a choice—had been secretly bandied about as early as December 1930.)

"Our country does not smile upon enthusiasm, demonstrations of faith, cooperative ventures," noted Mermoz. Bouilloux-Lafont was a man who had in his control the world's most ambitious airline, who had secured access to three continents and, in 1930, exclusive landing rights in the Azores, the key to the North Atlantic and thus to a fourth. His dazzling prosperity did not sit well with all concerned. The entrepreneurial spirit seems foreign in France, where the meaning of the word gets changed in the nontranslation: in French an *entrepreneur* is a contractor. For whatever political or financial reason, it seemed more important in 1932 that Bouilloux-Lafont—guilty or not of financial impropriety—be sacrificed than that a valuable state interest be left in his independent hands. A promising if not always profitable enterprise was scuttled in the process, and Aéropostale was thrown out with the Bouilloux-Lafont bathwater.

Those who most benefited from its demise were the Americans, the British, and the Germans, to whom fell the spoils—including the North Atlantic, the best spoil of all, which Mermoz could have been flying by mid-decade.*

The scandal went a long way to push the disillusioned Mermoz into the arms of the right-wing Croix-de-Feu. He had been sickened by the mess made of the airline and by 1936 was giving political speeches brightly tinted by his earlier anger:

> A ship's captain is second only to God. We are dying in France for want of captains, and when we have one we spend our time criticizing and judging him. Among us, on the airline, a leader, the ship's captain, isn't criticized, isn't judged. In any crew the copilot may be Front Populaire, the mechanic a Communist, the navigator a Socialist. None gives a damn about politics. We know we have 7,500 miles ahead of us, which represent sixty hours. . . . Of course I am accustomed, when I return to my earthbound life, to the usual betrayals and cowardice. This is the worst part of my life, but when one has a goal, an ideal, one surveys the obstacles along the road with contempt.

Saint-Exupéry, too, subscribed to the mystique of leadership, but in search of a substitute for it went off in his own direction; the Aéropostale debacle did much to wean him from politics altogether. It was afterward abundantly clear to him that the "fine race of men" celebrated in his first *Marianne* piece had indeed not managed to survive the enterprise that had called them into being. Once burned, twice shy, he had no desire to take part in the backstabbing and blackballing of 1932 all over again; when faced with the fall of France he would attempt to play a neutral hand. Doubtless this would not have seemed so urgent a priority in 1940 were it not for the dire repercussions he suffered now. "It is terribly difficult, at a time like this, to remain true to oneself, to be of no party," he wrote Dautry in 1932, during what must at the time have seemed the darkest autumn of his life.

---

* The exclusive landing rights Bouilloux-Lafont had secured for the French in the Azores were canceled by the Portuguese for nonperformance on October 7, 1933.

XI

~

Beyond the Call of Duty
1933–1935

What is true in a man's life is not what he does,
but the legend which grows up around him.

OSCAR WILDE

If there was a second act in Saint-Exupéry's life it began here, in early
1933. For the next three years the aviator·had more reason than opportunity to leave Paris, his new home. These were the last years in which
he found work as a commercial pilot. Despite himself, he gradually became
what so many aspire to be: a Parisian-based *homme de lettres*, a regular
at the Brasserie Lipp and the Deux-Magots, a card-carrying member of
the Republic of Letters, which—during the tumultuous 1930s, when governments came and went with dizzying regularity—staunchly, powerfully
held its own. These are the largely undocumented years of his life, and
he spent them documenting what had come before. They feel and must
have felt slack to Saint-Exupéry, who spent them on the defensive, animated more by need than desire. "Saint-Ex had not an ounce of personal
ambition," noted a cohort of the 1930s, when it showed. He stood as a
perfect incarnation of Kierkegaard's unhappiest man: his future lay behind
him, his past before him.

Early in 1933 Didier Daurat arranged for Saint-Exupéry to return to
Toulouse as a test pilot for Latécoère, then operating solely as an airplane
manufacturer. He met with varying degrees of success in this line of work.
As one colleague observed, test-flying did not exactly play to his strengths,
requiring as it does fierce attention to detail. It was, however, remunerative,
especially in a depressed economy. In four months Saint-Exupéry's salary
and bonuses totaled 33,000 francs, or the equivalent of $16,000 today.
That July he test-flew forty torpedo seaplanes destined for the navy; if the

Laté 290's passed muster at Montaudran they were sent south to the base at Saint-Laurent-de-la-Salanque, where they were equipped with floats and test-flown on the adjacent lake. Louis Marty, the chief mechanic at Montaudran in 1933, recalled that Saint-Exupéry experienced some initial difficulties putting down the aircraft but adapted quickly and soon piled up more than 200 hours as a seaplane pilot. The forty aircraft were checked out and delivered to the navy without incident; Marty and Saint-Exupéry—who regularly lunched together during this period—drank heartily to the occasion.

With other assignments Saint-Exupéry was, notoriously, less successful. He took off one day in a Latécoère 350 although one of the aircraft's engines was clanging loudly on the runway and the trimotor sputtered and smoked as it climbed. As he initiated his approach to the airfield a huge piece of sheet metal detached itself from the plane and spiraled to the ground. It was the Latécoère's door, which the pilot had forgotten to lock before takeoff. In another Laté 350 he flew to Paris, where the aircraft was to be examined by a group of air ministry officials. The trip ended with an emergency landing outside the city because of mechanical difficulties. (As if to add insult to injury, the Laté 350 never advanced beyond the prototype stage.) Equally memorable was the test flight Saint-Exupéry made in April in a Latécoère 28, one of a series bound for Venezuela. He was to take each aircraft to an altitude of 10,000 feet and fly it at full throttle over a three-mile course, noting any difficulties that arose. On his return from one such flight he reported that the aircraft had leaned so severely to one side that he had nearly lost control of it. He was entirely unable to say which way the Latécoère had listed, however. Asked for his flight pad, on which he was meant to record his observations, he displayed a lovely sketch of a woman. Jean Gonord, a fellow pilot who spent the first few weeks of May in Saint-Exupéry's company, took away from the experience an impression of a man "floating above the concerns of the world." He remembered that Saint-Exupéry and his pen were inseparable in the cockpit, although he hesitated to say if they were so in the name of official business.

Gonord lodged with the writer at the Hôtel de France in Perpignan, seven miles from the test center at Saint-Laurent. He met his doom nightly at the chess table. The two would begin a game after dinner, from which Saint-Exupéry excused himself at midnight to telephone Consuelo. One-half hour later he would return to checkmate Gonord in minutes. These small triumphs did nothing to endear the life of a test pilot to him. To a friend in Paris he described, ears abuzz, hands black with oil, the endlessness of a Perpignan evening. "I know no one here and want to even less," he wrote from his café table in a particularly misanthropic mood. "The laughter and snatches of conversation that make their way to my corner are a torture. These people seem to be simmering quietly away—like a stew pot—to the end of their days. What point is there to their lives?" Essentially this was a reprise of his 1926 letter to Renée de Saussine, from the Toulouse café where he was mistaken for a regular. From Perpignan, however, he was not to set out to do battle with the Pyrenees or the Moors; he must have worried that the prosaic was contagious. His spirits were not improved by a visit from two happily married friends (possibly Ségogne and his wife), whose domestic bliss he found suffocating. He admitted that there was a certain peace, a security that he hated. His environment only served to remind him of his dread of stagnation; the rotting seaweed that perfumed Saint-Laurent provided a neat correlative for his inner state. He wrote that he was most attracted to what was close but inaccessible, his recipe for adventure.

Saint-Exupéry's career as a test pilot came to a soggy and definite end a few days before Christmas in a Laté 293. The floats of a 293 had been designed to angle slightly downward to assist takeoff, making it imperative for the pilot to land with the aircraft's nose well up. Such an approach came as second nature to a naval aviator but less so to a pilot like Saint-Exupéry, accustomed to landing a tail-dragger on a runway, which is done tail high. On December 21, carrying with him a naval lieutenant, a staff engineer sent from Paris especially for the flight, and a mechanic, Saint-Exupéry landed the 293 in the bay of Saint-Raphaël as he might have landed a ground plane, ploughing the tip of the floats brutally into the water. The impact was so great that one of the floats cracked; the aircraft flipped over, catapulting the naval lieutenant—who had been seated next to Saint-Exupéry, had seen what was coming, and had opened his escape hatch—out over the ocean. The mechanic managed a miraculous escape through the machine-gun aperture and, with the assistance of the sailors on a patrol boat that rushed to the scene, forced a door open to rescue the engineer, who could not swim. Saint-Exupéry, who could see nothing in the moss-green water and who blindly groped for a door in what he thought was the ceiling of the Latécoère but what was in fact the floor, disorientedly made his way to the back of the aircraft, swallowing water as he did so. Serenely he resigned himself to death. In the tail of the plane he bobbed into an air pocket that allowed him momentarily to clear his lungs; he was surprised to find the convulsions of the return to life so brutal when death had been so gentle. "In truth, death isn't nearly as disagreeable as they say," he marveled later. He made a good deal of this observation, as of the fact that in his confusion he had not noticed how cold the water was. In the end—after what could not have been more than a few minutes but were surely among the longest few of his life—he was saved by his colleagues, who heaved him, half-drowned, onto the patrol boat. He coughed up seawater for some time.

Few men write elegies to 800-horsepower motors but Saint-Exupéry did, in *Wind, Sand and Stars*:

> Air and water, and not machinery, are the concern of the hydroplane pilot about to take off. The motors are running free and the plane is already ploughing the surface of the sea. Under the dizzying whirl of the scythelike propellers, clusters of silvery water bloom and drown the flotation gear. The element smacks the sides of the hull with a sound like a gong, and the pilot can sense this tumult in the quivering of his body. He feels the ship charging itself with power as from second to second it picks up speed. He feels the development, in these fifteen tons of matter, of a maturity that is about to make flight possible. He closes his hands over the controls, and little by little in his bare palms he receives the gift of this power. The metal organs of the controls, progressively as this gift is made him, become the messengers of the power in his hands. And when his power is ripe, then, in a gesture gentler than the culling of a flower, the pilot severs the ship from the water and establishes it in the air.

He referred to the close call at Saint-Raphaël in print only in passing, notably in *Flight to Arras*, imagining what a fellow reconnaissance pilot must have felt when his plane burst into flames around him. All his friends, however, heard the story and learned how agreeable Saint-Exupéry had found this near-surrender, for which he later claimed he had, underwater, run a comb through his hair. How much easier it had been, he told the Gallimards, to succumb to death than to contemplate a return to life, to the debts and trivialities.

Back in Paris after the holidays he continued the good fight. He lobbied Dautry on Daurat's behalf in February. Unemployed, he wrote a long and urgent letter to Monsieur Foa, Air France's new operations director. He was furious that in the airline's eyes he continued to pay the price of his celebrity and heatedly argued his case. *Night Flight* should have done the company some good, he reasoned, whether Rivière resembled Daurat or not; it had been written long before the Aéropostale scandal began; he had explained as much to Dautry; he had been denied a position in the new company; in the end he had taken a salaried position at Latécoère only in order to survive. His bitterness verges on the pathetic as he is forced—-uncharacteristically—to boast a little: "After all I've done for you, how can you object to my return? I've done everything—for Reine and Serre alone I landed more than ten times, without a radio, without an escort, in the most remote corners of dissident territory." He was humiliated to be reduced to begging, particularly since "*la Ligne* should be for me a bit like a family." The letter—like the conversations that preceded and followed it—fell on deaf ears. Foa continued to hold to the party line, insisting that the company was not in a position to hire supplementary personnel and that taking on Saint-Exupéry would constitute precisely that.

As his fortunes waned his celebrity increased. One year after its publication *Night Flight* found its way onto the reading lists of most of France's *lycées* and universities; the number of the country's student pilots promptly doubled. Nearly 150,000 copies of the book had been sold by early 1933. In March 1934, Clarence Brown's film of the novel opened in Paris, where it enjoyed a ten-week run. Often Saint-Exupéry was recognized on the street, by those who neither wrote nor published. French culture is preserved in the names of the finer things in life: in 1862, when Flaubert's *Salammbô* caused a sensation, a new kind of petit four was christened; Chateaubriand and Brillat-Savarin are guaranteed their immortality the gastronomic way. In 1933 Guerlain introduced a pert, spicy perfume in a bottle emblazoned with a constellation of propellers. It was dedicated to Saint-Exupéry and his colleagues and named "Vol de Nuit."

Saint-Exupéry's feelings about the fragrance have not been recorded; his nostalgia for night flying often enough was. In a preface to a history of aviation published by Maurice Bourdet the same year, Saint-Exupéry remembered how the early morning sky can cleanse a man's heart, especially that of the pilot flying the mail north from Dakar to Casablanca: "As you slowly descend the stairway of the stars toward the dawn, you feel purged. . . . When—engine throttled and idling—the pilot drifts down toward the landing field, surveying the city in which men dwell with all their afflictions, their financial concerns, their baseness, envy, spite, he feels pure and invulnerable." His four pages were an ode to another time and place as, appropriately enough, was Bourdet's text, in which mention was made of France's having fallen behind in military aviation while Lufthansa bounded ahead. Saint-Exupéry had as well another kind of past glory in mind. More and more, aviation had become a science, its pilots technicians. The airplane for him—a key perhaps to his lack of success as a test pilot—remained not a "collection of parameters, but an organism of which one takes the pulse." He was stalled in the days of flying by what the French call *pifomètre* and we call instinct, by meditation rather than calculation. These days were now over. "Before writing, one must live," he had counseled Renée de Saussine in the 1920s. It would often seem as if he stopped living when Aéropostale stopped flying; the creation of Air France made him a writer. In 1934 he applied for a passport and listed "aviator" as his profession. Six years later, a new passport was issued to Antoine de Saint-Exupéry, "man of letters."

~

Four days after Saint-Exupéry wrote his plea to Foa, Paris erupted in a
bloody riot. Protests against high taxes and an escalating cost of living
had begun the previous year, but on February 6, 1934, hundreds of thousands of Parisians took to the streets—converging on the Place de la
Concorde—to express with paving bricks their feelings about government
corruption and state-supported swindling; the Aéropostale imbroglio had
been far from an isolated event. The day turned into "bloody Tuesday"
when the Gardes Mobiles began to fire into the crowd. The official death
toll came to twenty, although over 2,000 machine-gun shots were fired at
the Place de la Concorde and as many people were wounded. The next
year was spent reading about Stavisky and the related tangle of political
developments, out of which ultimately arose Léon Blum's Front Populaire.

Saint-Exupéry—who now set up shop on the Left Bank, where he and
Consuelo moved to a modest rue de Chanaleilles apartment in July—was
not sheltered from these political winds. Neither was he, unlike a great
number of intellectuals, swept away by them. He read Marx, and he met
Victor Serge and Gaston Bergéry, the eloquent, independent Deputy; like
everyone else he spent long evenings at café tables discussing France's
shift to the Left and her neighbors' disconcerting lunges to the Right. The
day after the riots, on the terrace of the Café Weber, he drilled a new
acquaintance on the events of February 6 well into the morning. His
mentor André Gide committed briefly to Communism, which he glorified
in the daily press; André Malraux, whose *La Condition humaine* had won
him a Goncourt in December and who had been the toast of Paris ever
since, took his vows, traveling to Moscow several times, delivering ninety-
eight brilliant speeches for the Communist Party in 1934 and 1935. No
one was more bitten by the Communist bug than Paris's wealthy intellectuals, a society to which Saint-Exupéry maintained his connections.
For all of his fascination with theory he evinced little interest in party
membership of any kind, however. His name and his background would
have inclined him more naturally to the Right but he was too much of a
nonconformist to endorse their dogma; his cousin André de Fonscolombe
theorized that if Saint-Exupéry was more drawn to Marxism than to fascism it was simply because the former held, in his estimation, more intellectual interest. Still, it is not entirely easy to be a gentleman Marxist
with a name like "de Saint-Exupéry." Mermoz's formal association with
the neofascist Colonel de La Rocque began in 1935, and though this
sprouted largely from his disenchantment with the state of French aviation,
Saint-Exupéry, who shared his sentiments, made no attempt to follow in
his footsteps. "I have no taste for polemics," he had written to Foa in
February. For the next years, while everyone in France succumbed to
round-the-clock polemicizing, he stubbornly remained his own man.

Beginning in 1935 Saint-Exupéry traveled with a thin leather notebook in his breast pocket. His impatience with party lines rings loud and clear in these pages, published after his death as *Carnets*. In 1935 he confessed to "an immense difficulty in distinguishing the aims of the French Left from the aims of the Right." He felt the two carried on their debate without knowing anything of each other's stance and in complete ignorance of the facts: no fascist really knew what was happening in Germany; no advocate of the Front Populaire understood Spain's troubles. His mistrust of politics is writ large in *Carnets*; fundamentally he objected to labels, which limit a man's freedom. "To sell a man into slavery is one hundred times less unjust . . . than these divisions between the orthodox and the heretical. I could equally well choose as labels 'rice and prunes'; the outrageousness of the situation would be clearer." There is, of course, always a discrepancy between a man's life and his letters. Saint-Exupéry's *Carnets* read like a workbook of political economics; he lived above the fray. Gide dabbled in politics all his life and in the Communist fervor of the early 1930s appeared as one of the great believers, yet it was he who recorded that he was reading Goethe in German a month after the fall of France. During the war, he flatly penned lines like "Finished *Le Rouge et le Noir* in the night during a rather heavy bombardment."

Nothing better illustrated Saint-Exupéry's neutrality than the company he kept. The closest friend he made outside the Aéropostale family began to play a major role in his life now, although Saint-Exupéry and Léon Werth had met in 1931. An essayist and novelist probably best-known for his art criticism, Werth could not have had less in common with Saint-Exupéry. Twenty-two years his elder, he was an anarchist and a Jew; his writing—in all he was the author of twelve volumes and a great number of magazine pieces—verged on the surrealistic. As angular and lithe as Saint-Exupéry was round and portly, Werth had a track record as a nonconformist. His months in the trenches in World War I had made him a pacifist; a trip to French Indochina in 1924 had made him an anticolonialist. A man of the Left and a Bolshevik supporter, he won a reputation as a "fierce free-thinker" for having been quick to denounce Stalin. He was a man who took little for granted and great pleasure in the exchange of ideas, and it was no wonder that when the two men were introduced by the newspaperman René Delange it was a *coup de foudre*. The two were said not to have left each other's sides for days. Werth's shadow hangs over Saint-Exupéry's *Carnets*; Saint-Exupéry would go on to refer to Werth in three books and dedicate two others to him. In the lines that preface *The Little Prince*—one of the most charming dedications ever written and one that has earned Werth his place in the French edition of Trivial Pursuit—Saint-Exupéry describes him as "the best friend I have in the world." At the armistice, which Saint-Exupéry did not live to see, Werth turned to Jean Lucas, the former chief of the airfield at Port-Étienne: "Peace, without Tonio, isn't entirely peace."

More remarkable than the friendship with Werth, cemented during these idle, Left Bank years, was that Saint-Exupéry could at once consort with a confirmed anarchist and the right hand of Colonel de La Rocque. Jean-Gérard Fleury—whose sympathies, like most people's, lay somewhere between the two—remembered Saint-Exupéry's open-minded, eclectic approach to political discourse. He painted a picture of him at his prime in 1935, when political discussions were heated. In his tiny rue de Chanaleilles living room the ex-pilot one night received more guests than he could seat. Present, on chairs or on the floor, were an adherent of the right-wing Action Française, a Communist, a Croix-de-Feu, and one or two others, representing among them a complete spectrum of the era's political views. Naturally the discussion turned to politics. Saint-Exupéry patiently heard each of his guests out, questioning them in turn, coaxing them into cogent summaries of their philosophies. Finally, recapitulating each man's argument, he demonstrated in a flourish of intellectual sleight-of-hand that they were all of them in perfect agreement with one another. His guests were horrified.

His interests were universal and yet Saint-Exupéry remained—possibly because of his allergy to dogma—surprisingly naïve as well. Before he journeyed to Russia in May 1935 as a special correspondent for *Paris-Soir* he asked an acquaintance of Léon-Paul Fargue for a crash course in Soviet history. Prince Alexander Makinsky, a White Russian refugee, was shocked to find Saint-Exupéry ignorant even of the most recent and much publicized events. He saw different things in Russia than most French intellectuals, nearly all of whom made pilgrimages east in the 1930s and nearly all of whom wrote about their trips. Malraux investigated dogma and made the standard tour of the factories. If Saint-Exupéry set foot in a Soviet factory he did not write about the visit; he sent home tales of old French governesses, of Polish workers crammed into an eastbound train, of border guards and porters in stations. His focus strayed always from the sweep of history to the individual. Seduced though he had been with Marx on the page—and especially by Marxist economics—he came home from Russia as fearful of the tyranny of the majority as he was of dictatorship pure and simple. There were other nonjoiners—Louis-Ferdinand Céline was one—but Céline denounced Communism before declaring his independence. Almost irresponsibly in a country where nothing lies outside of political interpretation, Saint-Exupéry neither advocated nor denounced, leaving himself open to interpretation by anyone who wanted to claim him.

Revolution was everywhere in the air and current events all-consuming; Saint-Exupéry, casting about in the midst of the chaos for something to do, continued to dream of escape. While he saw more and more of his literary friends, he continued to damn the success that had obscured his greater love and exiled him from *la Ligne*. To an Argentine colleague who had evidently kept up a hefty, one-sided correspondence with him since his departure he wrote of his despair; he said he had given up hope of ever knowing the peace he had known in South America, the very memory of which now pained him. "When I read your letters I could so clearly see the vast open spaces of the South that my heart would break," wrote the man whose existence was increasingly confined to two Parisian arrondissements. He compared himself to a lovesick suitor, compelled to destroy the portraits of the woman at the root of his illness. In April he attempted to buy a used Farman 402 but for some reason the airplane never came through. Possibly because, as a result of the February uprising, new Air Ministry officials were appointed that spring, or possibly because, as a sort of walking icon, Saint-Exupéry was a dangerous man to leave on the streets at a dangerous time, he was at last approached by Air France about a job.

Jean Chitry, public relations director for the new company, was responsible for contacting the ex-pilot in March. Either he or his superiors had recognized the potential embarrassment of leaving Saint-Exupéry out in the cold while the venture with which he was so much associated in the public's mind fought to establish itself. Chitry and the pilot made each other's acquaintance at the Brasserie Lipp, where Chitry tackled the matter head-on. "You're not up to anything these days?" "No," replied Saint-Exupéry. "Wouldn't you like to join Air France's propaganda service?" he ventured, evidently unaware that he could just as well have been offering Cyrano de Bergerac an office job. Saint-Exupéry exploded: "You must be joking. Can you see me flying a desk? Clearly you don't understand. . . . Of course I'm broke, I'm in a hell of a jam right now, but all the same you must be kidding."

Chitry made the best of his unpleasant task, assuring Saint-Exupéry that he would not be installed behind a desk. He needed a technical adviser on films for the company (one on the soon-to-be-opened Marseilles–Algiers line was already under discussion), a writer who could spell things out accurately for the press, a lecturer who could speak intelligently about Air France's glories. Saint-Exupéry seemed mollified by this explanation, or, after a few moments' reflection, reminded of the attractions of a paycheck. He asked about salary; Chitry got back to him with a modest figure. "It's not much, but it will pay for my cigarettes," mumbled Saint-Exupéry, who late in April received a letter confirming that a place could not be found for him in the cockpit but offering him a position, in France and abroad, as a publicist. He was to receive 3,000 francs monthly as well as a minimum bonus of 1,000 francs each time his work took him up in a plane. (As a Latécoère test pilot his base monthly salary had been 5,000 francs.) The irony of Saint-Exupéry's having been assigned to do public relations for an enterprise from which he had been blackballed because of his fame seems to have been lost on all concerned.

As Saint-Exupéry must have expected, the job proved to be a sinecure, though not an especially profitable one. He did not complain about this, nor did he express any concern that the position was a sop. There was no work until June, when Saint-Exupéry flew to Algiers with Chitry, the director Félix Forestier, the head of Air France in Marseilles, and two journalists to make the documentary Chitry had alluded to in his initial conversation with Saint-Exupéry, released as *Week-end à Alger*. Saint-Exupéry immersed himself so deeply in the project and proved so helpful on all fronts that Chitry put him to work on a second film with Forestier. A celebration of the early days of Aéropostale, *Atlantique Sud* opened in July 1936 to commemorate the one-hundredth crossing of the South Atlantic. According to Chitry it was primarily Saint-Exupéry who directed the thirty-minute documentary, which went on to play in cinemas for nearly twelve years. The film brought in not a cent for the ex-pilot, who had not wanted his name attached to the project. Generally he kept his distance from his film projects, too much a purist for collaborations of the artistic variety.

He kept his distance, too, from the articles he contributed over the next few years to the *Revue Air France*, few of which were signed. Again these heralded back to the early days of Aéropostale. In a piece that ran in the magazine's spring 1935 issue—and that, like most of what Saint-Exupéry published during these years, was folded into *Wind, Sand and Stars*—he wrote of three Moorish chieftains with whom he spoke in 1931 after their visit to France. Unimpressed by the *Normandie* and the Eiffel Tower, they had succumbed to the majesty of a tree, the reality of a cow. They had been held spellbound by a waterfall that convinced them once and for all—along with, Saint-Exupéry admitted, the Folies-Bergère— that the god of the French was more generous than the god of the Moors. In the last lines of the article, which did not make their way into *Wind, Sand and Stars*, Saint-Exupéry wrote of the price the Moors had paid on their return home, the price every traveler pays for having his horizons broadened: "The Sahara seems to them emptier, the game of war more illusory. For the first time they realize the Sahara is a desert."

In mid-July, without great enthusiasm, he left for Indochina for a one-month research trip. Flying by way of Damascus, he arrived on the nine-teenth in Saigon. He was greeted at the airfield by Pierre Gaudillère, a floatplane pilot and radio-navigation specialist who had been a classmate at Brest. Presumably he saw his sister Simone in these first hours as well;

in any event, Saint-Exupéry did not stay long in Saigon. The afternoon after his arrival he and Gaudillère set out in a Lioré et Olivier 190, accompanied by three colleagues, to visit the Cambodian temples of Angkor. Twenty minutes into the flight the engine abruptly died; Saint-Exupéry made an expert landing on the Mekong River, and the Vietnamese mechanic ministered to the floatplane. Five minutes after a second takeoff they were forced down again, at the muddy confluence of the Vaico and Soirap rivers, with an engine that refused to turn over. Here, on the edge of the jungle, in an eerie wilderness of scruffy trees and yellow water sixty miles from Saigon, anchored to a mangrove tree, they were forced to spend the night. They knew they would be rescued by a launch bearing a towing cable and a solid breakfast in the morning; Gaudillère's only concern was for Saint-Exupéry's health, as he was the only one of the five men unaccustomed to the climate and at risk of catching malaria.

Such concerns were far from Saint-Exupéry's mind in what was for him clearly a reprise of the Río de Oro evening that lent *Wind, Sand and Stars* its title. He was jubilant, having in his misadventures never before encountered snake- and spider-infested tropical swamp. As the sun set he and Gaudillère made themselves comfortable on the upper wing of the Lioré, legs dangling over the silent motor; their colleagues bedded down in the hull. Accompanied by the occasional splash of a fish and the constant drone of mosquitoes, Saint-Exupéry unpacked his bag of tales for his friend. He spoke of the world of men, from which this delta seemed exempt; he sang old French folksongs, adapted slightly to accommodate Asian history. Presumably the night was worth any embarrassment the trip might otherwise have cost him: an empty gas tank had been the cause of the engine trouble, and Saint-Exupéry did fall ill afterward, flying back to France as a passenger. He arrived in Marseilles on August 12. He would continue to collect an Air France salary for at least three years but aside from a two-week lecture tour of the eastern Mediterranean in late 1935 and a few additional articles he did little more to earn it. It kept him on the bandwagon, however, even if his method for promoting Air France's new ventures consisted largely of appeals to the past. Professionally he now amounted to what Jean Prévost termed him posthumously: "*un artiste en souvenirs.*"

It was not a profitable line of work. Saint-Exupéry reported a gross income in 1934 of just over 48,000 francs—one fifth of what he had earned in Argentina. Slightly less than half represented monies Gallimard had advanced him for his writing; the remainder was his Air France salary. He spent more than every cent of it. Jean Mermoz estimated that until late 1935 Saint-Exupéry cost him about 350,000 francs, none of which he saw again. As a borrower Saint-Exupéry could not have been more winning, or more demanding: clearly he subscribed to Montaigne's belief

that a service asked a true friend amounts to an honor bestowed upon
him, as the principal aim of each friend is to find occasion to cater to the
other. Penniless, Saint-Exupéry comported himself as ever *en grand seigneur*. Fleury reported that the writer might equally well treat an intimate
to a sumptuous meal with an extraordinary selection of wines or relieve
him of half the money in his pocket. ("How much do you have on you?"
he asked Fleury on a day when the journalist confessed to be carrying
sixty francs. "Good. I'm leaving you half. Give me thirty francs," instructed
Saint-Exupéry.) If the Bugatti he drove during these years—which was
his on loan from Gaston Gallimard, a great lover of automobiles—was
not at his disposal, Saint-Exupéry might without warning requisition the
car of a friend. It is always practical to have a lawyer in the family, and
Fleury dedicated his services to the former Aéropostale pilot. On several
occasions he intervened when Saint-Exupéry's distraction combined with
his poverty to cause him serious embarrassments. In the most dramatic
of these episodes, Fleury was asked to rescue the writer from jail, where
he had spent the previous forty-eight hours, deprived of his tie and shoelaces. His crime: he had neglected to attend to a series of summonses sent
him for a speeding ticket. Two gendarmes had arrested him on his
doorstep.*

Consuelo de Saint-Exupéry's disregard for money was bohemian
where her husband's was aristocratic; it yielded the same results. Her
tastes were expensive, her grasp of numbers vague. Her asthma took its
toll both in medical and travel bills; she felt as if she were suffocating in
wintry Paris, and repeatedly during these years Saint-Exupéry was forced
to find accommodations for her in the south of France. On the rue de
Chanaleilles the couple carelessly stored their money in an entryway vase;
legend has it that their savings went up in smoke one day when a friend
extinguished a cigarette in the family bank. The franc was cheap in 1934,
when a cup of coffee and two croissants could be had for a few sous and
the rate of exchange was twenty francs to the dollar, but neither of the
Saint-Exupérys was able to make deflation—or any future windfalls—
work to his advantage. Few things mattered less to Saint-Exupéry than
money and yet—with a wife to support and time on his hands in a city
full of distractions—that was precisely what these years were about. He
was nonetheless never too hard up to disdain the stuff. In a 1935 *Marianne*
article written, like all the others, solely for financial gain, he extolled the
virtues of friendship, all that which was too priceless to be bought. "A
night flight, with its hundred thousand stars, its serenity, its few hours of

* His cellmate was a petty thief. confounded by the arrival of Saint-Exupéry. "What? They
also arrest les Légion d'Honneur!"

sovereignty," he wrote toward midyear, just before he and Consuelo had reached the breaking point, "money cannot buy."

Saint-Exupéry's predicaments met with varied reactions among his creditors. He could count on a backroom drink and a loan of 500 francs from Jarras, the café proprietor on the rue Bonaparte, to whom he had remembered to send the occasional postcard from South America. It seems that Gallimard was to some extent obliging. Crémieux was to say of him: "Gaston Gallimard is something like this. If you ask him for a raise, he moans that he can't afford it, that business is too bad. On the other hand, if you tell him you dropped 10,000 francs at the gaming table, he'll give you that amount right away." The landlord on the rue de Chanaleilles was not as broad-minded. Shortly after the *Marianne* piece had appeared—after the gas and electricity had been cut off for lack of payment, and after Consuelo had dramatically offered to find a job scrubbing floors—the Saint-Exupérys decamped for a series of hotel rooms, leaving Consuelo's Pekingese with their former concierge.

~

Saint-Exupéry's only permanent address in the 1930s was at the lively intersection of the rue de Rennes and the boulevard Saint-Germain. He set up shop in the afternoons at the Café des Deux-Magots, in the evenings at the Brasserie Lipp. He scheduled his meetings, he worked, he ate, he socialized here; together the two cafés constituted his office, his drawing room, his social club, his retreat, the Grand Balcon of his thirties. One friend was to say later that his ten years of friendship with Saint-Exupéry were spent almost to a meeting in a succession of public places; most of what was to become *Wind, Sand and Stars* was written at the Deux-Magots. These were the years when Saint-Exupéry sat still to a large extent, and the great majority of the portraits we have of him paint him here, in 1934 and the five years that follow, drinking, recounting, sulking, expounding, correcting his texts, shutting the two establishments down. There were many reasons for doing so, not least of all because the writer had at times in the thirties no other place to work. In attempting to make sense of his own ambivalence toward objects Jean-Paul Sartre explained that he preferred "to sit on chairs which belong to nobody (or, if you like, to everybody), in front of tables which belong to nobody: that's why I go to work in cafés—I achieve a kind of solitude and abstraction." Saint-Exupéry, who never owned more than a few sticks of furniture, was of the same school. Nor was he alone in making Lipp his headquarters. Léon-Paul Fargue, the silver-tongued bard of Saint-Germain, perhaps its most cultivated full-time *flâneur*, wrote of the brasserie: "One couldn't write thirty lines in a newspaper in Paris, paint a painting, or hold strong political opinions without devoting at least one evening a week to this café restaurant. . . . Lipp is certainly one of the places, the only one perhaps, where for the price of a draft beer one can have a faithful and complete summing-up of a political or intellectual day in France." He was himself a late-night fixture at the establishment, to which he had a special connection: his father, a glassware-factory owner on whose fortune Fargue still lived, had designed the restaurant's ceramic tiles.

It seems fair to say that a little of Léon-Paul Fargue wore off on Saint-Exupéry. Fargue had a long-standing reputation for arriving hours late at his destinations (and then with a superb *bon mot*), closing cafés, leaving taxis idling in streets while his brilliant conversation rushed on, habits for which Saint-Exupéry was soon also renowned. He needed no encouragement to lead the life of a Parisian night owl but got it from Fargue, who often turned up at the Boeuf sur le Toit when Lipp had closed its doors, sometimes with the author-aviator in tow. On one occasion he issued Saint-Exupéry a certificate: "I the undersigned, Léon-Paul Fargue, officer of the Académie Française [an untruth], certify that I have kept Antoine de Saint-Exupéry, commander of all things, out to an ungodly hour, because when I see him I cannot let him go." Often the two left each other only when harassed by a café waiter or a hotel porter. Together they made the gastronomic tour of Paris. Blaise Cendrars remembered his first glimpse of Saint-Exupéry, at the Brasserie Lipp. "Straddling a chair, among a circle of admirers listening to Léon-Paul Fargue telling his imaginary tales after midnight, he listened along with the others but laughed more loudly."

He was by no means uniquely the sorcerer's apprentice. When in form Saint-Exupéry could hold not only whole tables but whole restaurants under his spell. Beucler, with whom his friendship had blossomed after the *Southern Mail* preface, told of a long summer evening with Fargue, another friend, and a model who seems either to have been accompanying Saint-Exupéry or the friend. The five piled into a taxi and set out from the terrace of the Deux-Magots in search of a restaurant acceptable to everyone. They inspected neighborhood after neighborhood, winding their way from the east side of the city to the west and back again, clearly as pleased to be loose on the town in one another's company—practically in one another's laps—as they were eager to sit down to dinner. They wound up in Neuilly, when their glamorous escort could no longer stave off hunger. Fargue began the meal with a story and promised to read, over dessert, pages from a typescript he had in hand. In the meantime, something he said prompted Saint-Exupéry to begin to weave a colorful fairy tale. One by one the restaurant's tables fell silent as his cadences took over the room. When he finished his audience sat paralyzed, as one, recalled Beucler, watching the credits roll at the end of a powerful film. Fargue returned his typewritten pages to his coat pocket. "A shooting star has just fallen in my glass," he declared.

At a great number of café and dinner tables in the 1930s, Saint-Exupéry told and retold his tales. He had little choice, as he would add few new ones to his arsenal between his near-death in the bay of Saint-Raphaël in 1933 and his near-death in the Libyan desert in 1936. In effect he was trying out his drafts of *Wind, Sand and Stars*, although no one knew so at the time and few would have cared, privileged to be on hand when he chose to perform. He was not bombastic, and he did not play-act. He was neither a bore nor a rhetorician; he did not—like Fargue—have a brilliantly rich and varied flood of phrases at his disposal. He resorted instead to long trains of simple words, melted down by a flat, nearly faltering voice that brought his precise images to life. Henri Jeanson, a quick-witted satirical writer of whom Saint-Exupéry was particularly fond, submitted as everyone to his not-so-special effects: "If it was cold in his story you were cold, and if it was hot you wiped your brow. You died of thirst, and inevitably someone would venture, on tiptoe, to open a window." In the right company he could hold forth all night, moving from club to club across Paris until breakfast, or reading until dawn in the apartment on the rue de Chanaleilles from the pages he kept, badly sorted, in a hatbox. Jean Galtier-Boissière, the influential, radical left-wing editor who chronicled these years in detail, met Saint-Exupéry for the first time at an official banquet at the ministry of air, probably in 1936. Jeanson was there as well, as were a number of flying aces, including Maurice Bellonte. The two nonflyers took it upon themselves to lighten up a stuffy evening by provoking the solemn, overdressed maîtres d'hôtel into laughter; they felt everyone else was kowtowing to the minister, which made for a miserable dinner. Finally they got an assist from Saint-Exupéry, who had sat silently throughout the meal. Over petits fours he unexpectedly lit up and launched into a vigorous account of his days in the desert, of Guillaumet's triumph over the Andes. The party broke up at 4:00 a.m.

Jeanson had introduced Saint-Exupéry to Galtier-Boissière—he introduced him as well to Louis Jouvet and Gaston Bergéry—but for all of his new acquaintances his circles stayed small. He liked familiar faces. One day he and Jean Prévost sat down to lunch together on the rue Saint-Dominique, five minutes from the rue de Chanaleilles. They were hesitating between the poached and the fried fish when Beucler and Jean Giraudoux walked in; the four resolved to lunch together as often as possible, which amounted to three or four times a year, until the war. "The only problem," commented Prévost at one of these gatherings, in a Russian restaurant, "is that we all speak at once." Happily the four men agreed on most things, above all that the world was becoming a less and less hospitable place. "The essential," Saint-Exupéry would murmur, "is to be alive. We can't forget that. But nowadays the living are obliged to defend themselves as if they were threatened at all times." To his oldest friends he remained loyal; he continued to keep Escot from sleep. He dragged him to an all-night Montmartre bistro, where Escot struggled to stay awake as Saint-Exupéry covered page after page with algebraic equations. Escot better appreciated the caricatures Saint-Exupéry drew of the bistro's other patrons, not always an innocent art. One night he attracted the attention of a man at a neighboring table who felt the artist had stared a bit too long at his wife. Saint-Exupéry amiably started up from his chair to supply the reason for his attentions; rising to his full height proved to be explanation enough for his jealous neighbor.

Occasionally he could be persuaded to drink on the Right Bank by Néri, Guillaumet, and company, who frequented the cafés of the Champs-Élysées because of their proximity to the Air France offices at the corner of the avenue George V and the rue Marbeuf. He turned up one day in the company of Maryse Bastié, the aviatrix, to meet a group of dancers and gymnasts in a studio near the Place Clichy. Nadia Boulanger's studio, which he also visited on occasion, was nearby. He mixed his company, at least the best friends of his companies, some of whom—depending on their affiliation—called him Tonio (his wife and family), some Antoine (most of the other women in his life), some Saint-Ex (the Aéropostale staff and anyone who met him after he was famous, although he did not appreciate their familiarity). With pride he introduced Guillaumet to Werth with a simple, declarative "*Ça, c'est Guillaumet.*" He got as far as Versailles, when André Chamson, the writer and radical socialist politician, became the curator of the palace and entertained there on Sundays. He and Consuelo journeyed to Caresse Crosby's house on the edge of the forest of Chantilly, where Consuelo did all the talking. Her attention alone drifted when her husband spoke; an irrepressible raconteuse herself, she was jealous of his hold on the spotlight. As often as not, however, she had plans, and audiences, of her own. Saint-Exupéry might tempt a cohort into a jaunt to what he billed as a friend's house in the country; the house turned out to be the prepossessing château of Yvonne de Lestrange at Chitré. Gaston Gallimard joined him for a visit to Chitré one day when the two were out motoring together and the writer realized they were nearby. Both men were in casual clothes; Saint-Exupéry breezed in by the service entrance, borrowing a domestic's tie as he waited to be announced.

Mostly, however, he could be glimpsed on the Left Bank, in Montparnasse or Saint-Germain, where he was best-known. While he lived in the middle of this world, he fit into it only around the edges. He does not seem to have taken part, for example, in the June 1935 International Writers Congress for the Defense of Culture, an antifascist gathering and one of the most important literary events of the 1930s, but two weeks earlier did attend a Fernandez-moderated panel on Malraux. Afterward he continued on to the Deux-Magots and to dinner—at a long outdoor table animated by Malraux, Guéhenno, Fernandez, Gide, and a host of others—at the Saint-Benoît, one of his favorites. On the Left Bank the world was small: it was no more than a ten-minute walk from the rue de Chanaleilles to Gallimard's offices, to the Brasserie Lipp, to the Saint-Benoît, to Gide's apartment on the rue Vaneau, to Yvonne de Lestrange's, to Léon Werth's. This was fortunate for Saint-Exupéry, who had an aversion to exercise of all kinds. One day he called Werth on the rue d'Assas to say, "I'd very much like to see you, but my means of mobility are feeble." When he did have money in hand he was a taxi driver's dream, hailing a car for short distances, suspending meters with his late-night conversations. Georges Pélissier, a doctor friend who met Saint-Exupéry in 1931, spent the latter half of an evening parked before his hotel in a taxi—hours earlier the driver had been instructed to choose his destination—listening to Saint-Exupéry deliver a monologue on his search for God. In the front seat the driver slept. Behind the wheel of a car he was his passenger's nightmare, piloting at breakneck speed around Paris, which was how he endeared himself to his American publisher, Curtice Hitchcock, when the two met for the first time in 1932. Said Bernard Lamotte after an excursion that deposited him breathless in front of La Coupole: "That day, I understood what aviation was."

Everyone was happy to remark on Saint-Exupéry's tastes, if only because a list of his favorite things furnished an excuse for long-windedness. Above all, said Beucler, he loved to sing, to invent disguises, to perform his card tricks. Above all, wrote Beucler elsewhere, "he liked honesty, women, cheese, and practical jokes," an observation no less true for being perfectly alliterative in French. It was still easy to recognize the chief of the Cape Juby airfield: "He appreciated disguises; word games; strolls; simple, bawdy old French songs; concision; literary truth. He liked Bach, Nietzsche, Élie Faure, Puccini, André Gide, jazz, the cinema, humor, solitude, great gatherings of friends, with one well-mannered drunk in attendance, on the condition that he was in reality less drunk than he let on." He had, probably a function of his size, a great capacity to hold his liquor, and he had, particularly in his idle thirties, a fairly constant thirst. He smoked up a storm. He loved a good *aïoli*, available in a restaurant on the rue Gît-le-Coeur; a little bar on the Right Bank where the obliging *patronne* cut hefty slices of ham; the temple of cheeses that is Androuet. He would climb stairs for a superbly prepared plate of *pieds de cochon grillés*. For the most intimate evenings he preferred a little bistro on the corner of the rue Vaneau and the rue de Chanaleilles, where dessert was accompanied by cries of "Tonio, sing!" and where he would oblige. The list of subjects that interested him was exhaustive: He talked, with Fargue, of Balzac, the Middle Ages, Gérard de Nerval, Mallarmé, Roosevelt, boxing, comic books, Marxism, mythology, snobbism, Picasso, psychoanalysis, the Medicis; with Pélissier, about genetics, astronomy, sociology, mysticism, Bach, van Gogh; with Beucler, of Spinoza, Greek beauty, poetry, free love, algebra, word games, social structures; in his notebooks, of Christianity, the problems of capitalism, banking, taxation, chemistry, Einstein, Planck, Newton, liberty, justice, language. When someone told him of something new he listened with fanatical attention, opening his mouth a little, arching his long eyebrows, jotting down a few lines in his notebook, and never failing to double-check the information the next day, by telephone. When he spoke he often sketched, or—if more vested in his conversation—gesticulated madly, slapping his thighs. His discourse proceeded with a series of "Have you noticed?" and "That reminds me," openings that allowed him plenty of latitude.

While his meditations were, in the words of Léon Werth, "lighter than air," he performed the games he so adored with great seriousness. His card tricks were unforgettable. Against amazing odds and often without himself handling the deck, he could pick out a card on which he had asked someone to focus. For one particular demonstration he chose a willing assistant—a woman, for example. His powers worked most effectively if she were the most attractive one on hand. Saint-Exupéry would ask her to shuffle and reshuffle his deck and to focus on a card; if she then lay the cards out on a table, facedown, he could get her, as if guided by some mystical force, to point to the back of the card she had selected but never shown him. Although his victims made claims to the contrary— Saint-Exupéry was particularly pleased by the stupefaction of a *polytechnicien* who took him aside and whispered, "You're a sorcerer, aren't you?"—there was no trick in his repertoire that an intuitive card-handler with a good grasp of probabilities, a deft touch, and plenty of time could not master. There was reason why he preferred to work with a virgin deck and reason why he refused to perform in front of certain very skeptical friends, whom he accused of ruining his concentration.

A deck of cards provided a convenient way of ducking attention, a better tack than the insolence of which Saint-Exupéry was also capable. To the woman who asked him one day how many hours he had spent flying he responded, more out of abashedness than anything else, "Dunno. Do you count the hours you've spent in an elevator?" With a card trick he could charm and deflect; he could also cultivate the kind of childish wonder he felt to be in such short supply in the world. Best of all he did not need an Indochinese swamp or a Saharan dune to do so; in the right mood, he could create it anywhere. And he did: "He spent less time writing," lamented Jean Prévost, "than he did picking out the ten of spades." He invented word games and other conundrums: Beucler remembered a game with matches, one with anagrams, another involving a series of apéritif stains on the table. He devised psychological tests; one split the world into two kinds of people, those who needed to understand everything, and those who could believe in miracles. He liked to torment acquaintances with odd questions: Why wasn't the image reflected in a spoon reversed horizontally as well as vertically? Are you aware, he asked an Aéropostale colleague one day, that you are in the process of creating your past? He could be fascinated by the functioning of an eyedropper. His love of gadgets—which he would be able to indulge fully in America—continued. He fiddled with a variety of inventions, mostly on paper.* He envisioned an early kind of pay-per-view television; he described to Pélissier the workings of photoelectric cells; he laid out the idea of a genetic code. At the end of 1934 he filed the first of his ten patents, for a blind landing device operated by radio waves.

The lists of what Saint-Exupéry ate, drank, and enthused about are long. The list of friends to whom he wholly unburdened himself is short. The mainstays of these years were Guillaumet, Werth, and his old friend Ségogne; Beucler, Prévost, André Chamson, Jeanson, Jean Lucas, Fargue, and Ramon Fernandez were intimates. He opened up slowly; Saint-Exupéry and André Maurois knew each other for ten years before they became friends in America, during the war. His personal life remained always a closed book, at least to his male friends, even when he acknowledged it to be problematic. He asked about no one else's. He had a low tolerance for gossip and lost his temper when others did not. Several years earlier, after Madame de Saint-Exupéry had questioned Consuelo about Gide and Yvonne de Lestrange and after Consuelo's answers had elicited some disapproving remarks (with which she had then bludgeoned her husband), he wrote his mother: "Only with difficulty have I forgiven her for having trafficked in idle gossip, for having shared with you insignificant details concerning private lives, which are nobody's business at all, details which I reproach you for having solicited and which I ask you now to forget." Among friends he could be, as Jeanson put it, "slow to take off," waiting hours to join the conversation, even then wandering off on his own for some time. He did not suffer fools gladly, clamming up immediately in their presence. "He would leave us his body, out of politeness,

---

* One nearly made its way into the literature. In an early manuscript of *The Little Prince*, a merchant hawks a futuristic machine which can be programmed to assume most functions for its user, whom it could transport anywhere. Not only could it offer a lighted cigarette, it could smoke it, too.

for appearance's sake, and come back for it later, after the nuisances had left," wrote Jeanson of such occasions. He was more quirky than he was effortlessly, brilliantly spontaneous, as were the premier conversationalists of his generation, Cocteau and Malraux. When he felt he was attracting attention in a public place he buried himself in his newspaper or looked away, a delinquent schoolboy trying to make himself invisible. When asked for an autograph, which he was regularly as the 1930s wore on, he blushed and made polite conversation while nervously rubbing a finger behind his ear. Henri Jeanson knew a surefire way to get his goat. If he came across the writer strolling about Saint-Germain he would bellow from as great a distance as possible, in as distinct a voice as possible, "Saint-Exupéry! Saint-Exupéry!" In a panic his friend would race toward him, begging for mercy.

He was as ill-suited to deal with celebrity as he was ill-equipped to master politics. These were indeed the convivial years, yet at the end of the day Saint-Exupéry spent them alone at a series of small tables, a drink at his elbow, a cigarette in hand, doing silent battle with a sheet of paper. A caged bird, he did what a caged bird does: he sang. By 1938 he had produced—all of it in the guise of magazine articles, most of it, under duress, for the money on which to live—the bulk of *Wind, Sand and Stars*, a book that bears no sign of Paris and in general no clues to the prosaic details of its author's life. Once, from across a café, Blaise Cendrars furtively observed him at work on a set of page proofs. Like so many of the portraits drawn of Saint-Exupéry in his thirties Cendrars's is a still-life: "He gestured with his left hand, not as if he were reciting verse, but rather as if he needed to shoo away the pesky shadow of an airplane, which wandered like a fly across his pages."

~

In the spring of 1935, Hervé Mille and Pierre Lazareff, editors of *Paris-Soir*, proposed that Saint-Exupéry travel to Russia as a special correspondent for the four-year-old paper. The two newspapermen may have thought of Saint-Exupéry for the assignment because an impressive flyover had been planned in Moscow to mark May Day. Since his *Marianne* series three years earlier he had contributed only one piece to the *NRF*—the four-page description of Punta Arenas, published in April 1933, had been written on café stationery at the Royale and *chez* Lipp—and three short aviation pieces to *Marianne*. The *Paris-Soir* assignment represented a great stride forward for Saint-Exupéry, who was offered a handsome amount for the trip. A wildly successful combination of sensational reporting, serious journalism, and photographs, *Paris-Soir* was France's most popular paper, with a circulation more than ten times greater than that of *Marianne*. It was the property of Jean Prouvost (to whom Jean Prévost had introduced Saint-Exupéry), who was always happy to see a prestigious writer in its pages, even if he may not have been the obvious choice for the assignment at hand.

Characteristically, Saint-Exupéry did not jump at the opportunity. He had few others, however, and after his crash course on Russian history—doubtless he also picked the brains of his cousin André de Fonscolombe, who was half-Russian—he set off by train for Moscow, arriving on April 29. He would protest always that journalism was beneath him—reporting and screenwriting were, to his mind, the twin vampires of the literary life—but his dispatches from this short trip are among his more successful efforts. Saint-Exupéry did his best to defy deadlines and revised beyond the last possible minute. (He was not above distracting printers with a bottle while he re-edited his texts.) His Russian pieces, however, conveyed by telephone to Paris, are among his freshest; in them there was less poetry and more of the man, less gloss and more sparkle. In the first of them, telephoned to Paris three days after his arrival and acknowledged in the second as "an outright surrender on my part to headline pressures," he described a May Day he had nearly missed. He had found Soviet bureaucracy as uncongenial as any other, and had been unable to obtain a spectator's permit for the Red Square celebration.

He rose on the first to find the doors of the Hotel Savoy securely locked; it seemed for a minute as if he would be barred from doing what 4 million Muscovites were about to do. The noise of a thousand planes descending upon Moscow was all it took for him to slip his chains; he made his way into the street by way of a hotel window. As the airplanes roared overhead in formation the crowds advanced like an ice floe through the freezing streets toward Red Square. They were directed on their march by police barriers and gatekeepers; as Saint-Exupéry watched they were commanded to stop, presumably to allow for some other ice floe, easing its way down another street, to empty into Red Square. The wait was long, and the air was cold. The Frenchman then witnessed a miracle: the "unified solid mass suddenly melted into single human beings." On their way to Red Square thousands of men and women fell into ragged circles and began to sing and dance. For a moment Moscow appeared to Saint-Exupéry—who chose to forget the snow—"like any Paris suburb on a July 14th night." Then the musical instruments were put away and the banners were raised and the lines re-formed and the crowd continued on its sober way, to pay tribute to Stalin. Even in a sea of unfamiliar gray faces Saint-Exupéry had eyes only for the individual; he had tipped his only political hand early on in his reportage.

Eleven days went by before his next piece—because, according to legend, there were few good cigarettes to be had in Moscow and Saint-Exupéry could not write without them. Probably he could have come up with a better excuse himself; years later he was patiently to explain to his American publisher that he was late with a chapter of *Flight to Arras* because his guardian angel had appeared and demanded that he attend instead to a different project. The angel had stayed to talk; he could not very well have shown a guardian angel the door! Evidently having obtained a nicotine fix—possibly from the French embassy, possibly from Joseph Kessel's journalist brother, Georges, who had met him at the station on his arrival and who shepherded him around Moscow—he called Paris on the thirteenth with his best-known piece. Ostensibly an account of his trip across the continent to the Soviet Union, he reported that his train had "cut an unswerving path across a Europe torn by anxieties and hostility," then went on to ignore current events altogether. The third-class cars of the train had been crowded with Polish workmen, expelled from a depressed France in a fresh rash of xenophobia. For the second time public transportation offered Saint-Exupéry a great epiphany: he saw in the workers the same uncultivated, defeated men, the "lumps of clay" he had glimpsed in the Toulouse tram. In 1935, however, he thought not only like a hero of the sky but like an aristocrat. Taking a seat across from one couple, he was surprised to discover a cherubic blond child sleeping soundly between his parents. "Forth from this sluggish scum had sprung this miracle of delight and grace," he explained in a line one could get away with, barely, in a front-page article in France in 1935. (He neglected to point out that these very "lumps of clay" were the miners, the gardeners, the blacksmiths whose work he celebrated elsewhere.)

Hervé Mille impatiently awaited this second of Saint-Exupéry's dispatches in the *Paris-Soir* offices on the morning of May 13. He expected the piece for the next day's front page, for which press time was fast approaching. Finally, near noon, his correspondent called in; to save time, Mille put him on the line directly with Madame La Rosa, the paper's ablest secretary, who typed as Saint-Exupéry read. Mille sat down next to her in the cubicle, reading over her shoulder. All went well until Madame La Rosa reached the third page of the article and began to transcribe the story of the golden-haired child. "This is the child Mozart. This is a life full of beautiful promise. Little princes in legends are not different from this," she typed, transcribing the line which would provide Mille with the piece's title. "This little Mozart will love shoddy music in the stench of night dives. This little Mozart is condemned," continued Saint-Exupéry, but Madame La Rosa was at a standstill. "What's wrong?" demanded Mille. "I can't continue, I can't. It's too beautiful," she sobbed, tears streaming down her face.

On the nineteenth the writer became the first foreigner to fly in the *Maxim Gorki*, the world's largest aircraft and the pride of the Soviet Union. The next day he became the last, when the forty-two-ton plane collided in midair with one of its escort planes and crashed, killing forty-three people. Saint-Exupéry's description of the propaganda plane—equipped with a cinema, printing presses, a radio station, and conference rooms—turned then into what was increasingly becoming his specialty: a eulogy. For *Paris-Soir* he wrote up an account of his inspection of the 7,000-horsepower monster, of its communications system (the *Maxim Gorki* had loudspeakers enabling it to "speak above the roar of its motors to those listening on the ground"), its on-board pneumatic tube system, its electric-power plant, its telephone operators, its secretaries. Doubtless the gadget-lover in him was impressed, even if the Breguet 14 pilot was horrified. "My impression was of a complex, highly organized group activity such as I had never experienced in my own flying," he reported evenly. For the *Journal de Moscou* on the twenty-third he wrote an elegiac account of the camaraderie that had produced the *Maxim Gorki*. It sounded like an endorsement of Communism but was instead his usual expression of admiration for *"la camaraderie professionelle"*: "This dedication to the métier gave me—every bit as much as the roar of the eight motors—the impression of a force on the move." No one should too much mourn the *Maxim Gorki*, wrote Saint-Exupéry, surely more inclined than most people to admit that accidents happen; its memory would surely spawn new triumphs.

His last Russian piece, headlined "A Curious Evening with 'Mademoiselle Xavier' and Ten Tipsy Old Ladies Lamenting Their Youth," appeared on the twenty-second. He was always clever on the page but in the longest of his Russian articles he was downright droll; he had reached the end of his assignment and was this time entirely in his element as a foreign correspondent. He had learned that some 300 Frenchwomen in their sixties and seventies, governesses of the daughters of the old regime, were still scurrying around a transformed Soviet Union, "as invisible as virtue, duty, and good breeding." Unemployed and forgotten, they lived from hand to mouth. After an unpromising start—he asked directions in French and got them in Russian, English, and Danish before he finally found his way—he caught up with one "Mlle. Xavier." He landed on her doorstep much as he had arrived on that of the Nouakchott sergeant; he was the first Frenchman to cross Mlle. Xavier's threshold in thirty years, and she wept at the sight of him. So proud was she to share a bottle of Madeira and a plate of cakes with her visitor that she left the door to her room open. The seventy-two-year-old wanted the neighbors to be jealous of her gentleman caller. Saint-Exupéry quizzed her about current events—"What does a revolution mean to the gray mouse? How does the mouse survive when everything is tumbling down around its ears?" he wondered—and reveled on the page in her story of its having passed her by.

That evening Mlle. Xavier arranged for her visitor to meet ten of her friends. He provided the Port and the wine and the liqueurs, they provided the tearful memories of their far-off French years. Saint-Exupéry had a fine time, describing himself as a "Prince Charming, drunk on glory and vodka and surrounded by lots of little old ladies who kept kissing my cheeks." Before the drink and song had ended a rival appeared on the scene in the form of a sober Russian gentleman. He was made to reveal to Saint-Exupéry his claim to fame in the governesses' eyes: in 1906 he had played roulette in Monaco. It was 1:00 a.m. when Mlle. Xavier and a colleague ceremoniously escorted the correspondent to a taxi. His first friend leaned unsteadily on his arm, whispering that he must come back the following year. "You'll come to see me before the others? I'll be the first, won't I?" she entreated, leaning closer to his ear, staggering ever so slightly. Sent to investigate a brave new world, he had unearthed the relics of a vanished one.

Saint-Exupéry's account of the evening with Mlle. Xavier, like all of his *Paris-Soir* pieces, met with an enthusiastic reception. On his return to Paris he would have a more difficult time than ever staving off distractions: he was now in demand as a reporter and could easily have managed a substantial Parisian rent on the salary of one. What was more, at about the same time he proved to be a successful screenwriter; either just before or just after the Russian trip he sold a screenplay to the director Raymond Bernard, Tristan Bernard's son. Escot remembered that he had tossed it off quickly, in a matter of days; a final draft was typed up while Saint-Exupéry was in Moscow. A love story, *Anne-Marie* is by far the frothiest of his literary efforts. The title character is a stunning twenty-year-old engineer who is adopted and taught to fly by an inseparable group of pilots who—paternally and selfishly—do their best to shield her from love, who appears on the scene in the form of a happy-go-lucky inventor.

The screenplay's tone is frivolous but its themes are familiar. The Bach-playing inventor tends a rose garden on his terrace, which he tenderly removes to his apartment at night, when it is cold; in the screenplay (though not in the film) his father was a wealthy cultivator of roses. The pilots—who are relieved from any great need to identify themselves, as they are named the Farmer, the Detective, the Thinker, the Lover, and the Boxer—live entirely for their brand of masculine friendship. They can easily justify keeping Anne-Marie to themselves: "Theirs is a hard and bitter life. After the night, the storms, they are entitled to rediscover a calm garden and their childhood games. . . . They have no rosebushes, no stars, no music to console them their fatigue, their fear." They need their protégée; she may well be a pilot, but locked up in the tower of their devotion she remains, more importantly, a chaste and loyal little girl. They understand that she is sentimental and so as to occupy her heart nominate the Thinker to court her with an anonymous series of *billets-doux*. Love triumphs, contrivedly, in the end, after the Thinker is sacrificed to the plot, after that tragedy reveals the depths of Anne-Marie's feelings for the inventor, after the inventor ingeniously saves her life when she has lost her bearings in the night sky.

None of this worked much better on the screen than on the page, although Annabella—who would go on to become Mrs. Tyrone Power and a good friend to Saint-Exupéry in America—pranced her way through the title role with aplomb, and although the inventor's rescue of Anne-Marie—he leads the five aces to an electrical power plant where he signals in Morse code to the lost plane with the lights of the entire city of Angoulême—is stunning. Released in 1936, *Anne-Marie* set no box office records. Graham Greene, who reviewed the film that year, was not alone in finding it themeless and "quite amazingly silly." Others remarked on the production's similarities to *The Perils of Pauline*. Somehow the collision of the world of men and adventure and the world of roses and music worked less well when bullied into a happy ending.

Most likely *Anne-Marie* was not the screenplay with which Saint-Exupéry had been toying in South America during the summer of 1930. That project almost certainly turned into a thriller called *Igor*, of which he wrote several different versions. Never filmed, *Igor* traced the voyage of a political agitator from the dock in Rio de Janeiro to Europe, aboard a French vessel. The story delights in irony: in one version the celebrated criminal manages to impose his authority on several of the passengers on this ship of fools, all of whom should recognize him from police descriptions. In another, he appears to be apprehended at the end of his crossing. In the last scene we discover we have been trailing the wrong man; Igor is seen back at work, happily fomenting far-off revolution. Later Saint-Exupéry was to dispense with the Igor character altogether and write many of the same elements into a second screenplay for Raymond Bernard. *Sonia* took its name from one of the Spanish dancers who, with her generous embraces, helped spread disease throughout the ship. Essentially her story is that of Igor transformed into a rousing tale of heroism, courtesy of a group of aviators who fly serums from all over the continent to the Bordeaux harbor, arriving in the nick of time to save the 5,000 ailing passengers of the quarantined ship. (The speedy transport of medicines was to prove the fulcrum for the plot in the movie version of *Night Flight* as well; on the screen it spoke with an urgency the mail did not.) At some point in 1935 Saint-Exupéry began to think as well about a film adaptation of *Southern Mail*, to which he was to devote himself the following year.

He saw these projects as a means of paying the rent, not as a future; once again he was biding his time while his heart was elsewhere. In March his name had been added to the end of a list of clients for whom Renault expected to turn out airplanes, to be delivered after the twenty-ninth of April.

If the dream of every man is to fly, the dream of every pilot is to own an aircraft. This spring Daurat was busily organizing an ambitious—and short-lived—domestic airline with Beppo de Massimi; inaugurated in July, Air Bleu relied on night flights to promise next-day mail service anywhere along the six lines of its network for a three-franc stamp. It was not a popular idea politically—Air Bleu's interests did not always coincide with Air France's—although Saint-Exupéry did not hesitate to lend it his support; Daurat credited him with having written a number of unsigned newspaper pieces in Air Bleu's defense. Daurat had involved Renault as an investor in the new company, which had received the government's blessing on the condition that it receive no subsidy. Its services were to be performed in a Renault-manufactured Caudron-Simoun, a rapid new 180-horsepower airplane which sported the luscious curves of a 1940s automobile. The first French aircraft with a variable-pitch propeller, a standard feature on virtually all modern propeller-driven planes, the Simoun was a particularly light and efficient aircraft. Equipped with other contemporary amenities (like brakes on the wheels), it also boasted instruments which made flying without visibility possible. Quickly it went on to set most of the 1935 speed records.

Why Saint-Exupéry did not enter the Air Bleu ranks is unclear. A life of routine night flights over France may not have been of interest to him; he may not have been offered a job. He did turn up often at Le Bourget at Daurat's side, freely offering his advice, and in some capacity Daurat was almost certainly instrumental in helping him to secure an airplane. Daurat may have managed to acquire a Simoun for Saint-Exupéry at the Air Bleu discount. It seems more likely that Caudron's director, Henri Peyrecave, made the pilot a gift of the aircraft for publicity reasons, possibly at Daurat's suggestion. If—in a less likely scenario—Saint-Exupéry purchased the Simoun by himself with his *Paris-Soir* and *Anne-Marie* earnings, he took advantage of a government subsidy that reduced its price from 128,000 francs to about 96,000 francs. He almost certainly took possession of the airplane early in the summer, on his return from Moscow and fresh from a two-week training program required periodically of reserve air force officers. Borrowing the first two letters of "Antoine" and the last two of "Saint-Exupéry" he christened the Simoun F-ANRY. Immediately he set out to introduce his friends to the new acquisition, in which he took a childish pride. It was by far the nimblest aircraft he had yet flown, and he showed off a little. After one such hair-raising demonstration he half-apologized to his passenger, Léon Werth, "I wanted to dazzle you a little."

Saint-Exupéry did not venture out of France in his Simoun until his old Aéropostale colleague Jean-Marie Conty—holder of the *Southern Mail* audience endurance prize seven years before in Casablanca—devised a means for him to do so. A wiry, vibrant engineer with a fierce intellect and a pronounced taste for the mystical, Conty had a background similar to Saint-Exupéry's. His father had been a high-ranking diplomat; four years Saint-Exupéry's junior, Conty was also an alumnus of the École Bossuet. He had gone on to Polytechnique, and joined the airline in 1927. In his youth he had known Louise de Vilmorin, whom he had recognized in the *Southern Mail* portrait of Geneviève. It had been he who had tipped off Saint-Exupéry about the French governesses in Moscow, where he had observed them furtively stuffing their bags full of hors d'oeuvres at a Bastille Day celebration in 1934. Conty knew Saint-Exupéry was chomping at the bit, and one day, without realizing what he was doing, prevailed upon a friend visiting from Egypt for help. "Come and see me in Egypt," she told him as she boarded her train at the Gare de Lyon. "I will come by air, with Saint-Exupéry in his Simoun, if you can guarantee us a lecture there," replied Conty. Days after her return to Cairo the friend cabled that she had arranged for five speaking engagements. Conty then took his proposal to Air France, convincing them that a lecture tour would put Saint-Exupéry to good use and well justify its nominal cost. In November, having recruited André Prévot, an Air Bleu mechanic who was to have a colorful career with the pilot, they set out in the Simoun for a 7,000-mile tour around the eastern Mediterranean.

From Paris the three men flew south to Casablanca, then east, via Algiers and Tunis, to Tripoli, Benghazi, and Cairo. Saint-Exupéry did the flying; Conty served as navigator. This was not difficult work: Conty described the in-flight conversations as going something like this: Saint-Exupéry: "Do you see ground?" Conty: "Yes, I see the ground." Managing the budget proved more of an effort. The three spent every cent of what they earned on the road, consistently landing with empty pockets; although they played to full houses, the profits were nominal. In Cairo, where Conty and Saint-Exupéry visited a recently excavated tomb, Saint-Exupéry succumbed to the bronchitis which had plagued him since Tunis. Conty was obliged to treat him with the cure of the day: leeches. These he applied to his friend's broad back one night while the cooperative patient talked nonstop into his pillow. The narrator's voice was a little muffled, but it was in this way that Conty heard the epic tale of Saint-Exupéry and the Patagonian cyclone. The three continued on to Damascus and Beirut, where they gave their talks on the fourteenth. The High Commissioner of France in Syria and Lebanon reported on their Beirut talk. Conty— meant to discuss the Air France network, past and future—did not get high marks, having in the diplomat's mind delivered a vague, rambling talk. "As for Monsieur de Saint-Exupéry, in a speech devoid of all pretension, but in well-chosen words, the precision of which betrayed no particular effort, he very successfully revealed the psychology of the airline pilot." He had been much applauded by the audience who had seen him at his best, despite a troublesome cough and a scratchy voice; generally Saint-Exupéry seized up when forced to speak publicly. All the same, the diplomat did not feel that the agreeable hour justified its expense, as no one went away from the lecture particularly well-informed about Air France's operations. His reaction was representative. Despite Saint-Exupéry's lectures, despite the records Mermoz continued to set throughout these years, France had by now largely lost her interest in the air.

There was a bit of a problem at the Turkish border, where Saint-Exupéry was taken first, by a farmer, for a Bolshevik and then, by an unhelpful French consul, for a Turk, but the three pushed on to Istanbul and later to Athens, where they arrived on the twenty-second. With a Greek acquaintance, Saint-Exupéry and Conty set out for lunch in a little harborfront restaurant one afternoon. (Prévot, who was generally not greeted with the same pomp as the celebrity-lecturers, did not join them.) At the end of the meal there was a struggle over the check; the Greek insisted he must be the one to settle it, as he could guarantee it would be inaccurate. Sure enough, three dozen unconsumed oysters turned up among the hors d'oeuvres and a few more padded out the desserts. Summoned to the table, the restaurant manager acknowledged his mistake. "Yes, gentlemen, there were a few errors," he admitted. "But you must forgive us; the times are so hard." Saint-Exupéry adored this eminently humane explanation. Conty settled the bill, without paying for the oysters.

From Athens Conty flew separately back to Paris, where his desk called. Saint-Exupéry sent immediately for Consuelo, without whom, his friend recalled, he suddenly could not go on. She arrived after Conty's departure and flew home in the Simoun with her husband and Prévot on the twenty-fifth. It was a less than happy homecoming, partly because there was no longer a home to speak of.

~

Consuelo's address for part of the winter of 1935 was the Hôtel Pont-Royal on the rue Montalembert. Her husband did not join her there immediately; he continued to camp out on the rue de Chanaleilles, where he must have become expert at dodging the landlord. Increasingly the couple had begun to go their separate ways. The second-floor apartment on the rue de Chanaleilles was small—Werth described it as being so minuscule that the limbs from the trees in the courtyard garden took it over—and Consuelo had filled it with her friends, her sculpting materials, her disorder. Saint-Exupéry was by no measure in danger of being suffocated by bourgeois comfort, by the kind of wife Hemingway dismissed in "The Snows of Kilimanjaro" as the "kindly caretaker and destroyer of his talent." Years later Saint-Exupéry drafted a prayer for Consuelo, which she was to say each night. In part it read: "Dear Lord, save my husband, because he truly loves me and without him I would be an orphan. But make sure, dear Lord, that he is the first of us to die, because while he looks sturdy he suffers terribly when he does not hear me bustling about the house. Lord, spare him above all from this anguish. See to it that I always make noise in the house, even if I must, from time to time, break something."

These prayers were answered, but made for a more exhausting drill than Saint-Exupéry might have liked. His wife proved not so much capricious as unreliable: she could perform an amazing disappearing act when this was least desirable. Madeleine Goisot, an artist who met Consuelo in the Café Weber late in the evening of the February 1934 riot and exchanged addresses with her while the injured were wheeled in, saw a good deal of her in the years that followed. She served as Consuelo's unofficial *garde de coeur*: Saint-Exupéry knew that if his wife went out with Madeleine Goisot she would return, something she could not otherwise be relied upon to do. Consuelo made her husband look punctual; on one occasion when she was meant to accompany him to an official reception she sent a telegram in her stead. "Can you hear the bell of your little lost lamb in the Alps? Please come and rescue me," she wrote from Switzerland. Her husband was, by his own admission, ill at ease in love, which made it difficult for him to express himself. He claimed, however —in a letter to a lover of the 1940s—to be a fine shepherd. Consuelo gave him plenty of practice. She precipitated herself on various people in her inimitable manner, half simper, half assault, and told outrageous stories; she elaborated publicly on her husband's habits. Her mythomania was so accomplished as to be infectious. Even Gaston Gallimard caught it. He could speak inexhaustibly on the subject of Consuelo's eccentricities.

While it was clear to Consuelo that the Saint-Exupérys thought her husband crazy to have married her, Madame de Saint-Exupéry in no way hesitated to welcome her daughter-in-law into the family. If anything she proved a model of patience and generosity. Simone de Saint-Exupéry may have been less accommodating, if it is fair to marshal forth her 1943 short story as evidence. In "Pèlerinages" ("Pilgrimages"), a tale rich in enchanted houses and closets of snowy linens, a young man returns with his foreign-born wife from Saigon to France. His friends had warned him against the marriage: "She's a tough little number who will do you in, because unless she dances every night life will be a chore for her." Having ignored their advice he is eager to introduce Denyse to the French countryside, to the family's old housekeeper in whose ramshackle home they are to spend the night. (The family's home has been sold, dispersing its inhabitants to the four corners of France.) Nothing could bore Denyse more; dreaming of shopping sprees and nights on the town, she behaves wretchedly, barely disguising her condescension, throwing tantrums. When her husband leaves the two women alone for a minute, Mademoiselle confides in Denyse: "He has always been so improvident, so reckless. How he kept us on our toes! Fortunately you are here now; you will watch over him. You will stop him from embarking on his adventures. He needs a kind woman to keep his closets in order, because by nature he isn't neat; he has too much on his mind. You must run his house well." Denyse can only laugh, while Mademoiselle goes on to vaunt the glories of the four linen closets that were her charge in the husband's childhood home. By the end of the story the housekeeper has every reason to conclude the new wife a selfish vixen who will do her husband in.

The state of the Saint-Exupéry marriage was well-known. The two cut each other off in midsentence, clearly taunted each other, and discussed divorce "like two kids teasing each other." Unlike her husband, Consuelo had no objection to making herself talked about; she provided ample grist for the mill. Saint-Exupéry's letters to her from the 1940s read as one long plea to come home on time at night and not make herself the subject of conversation. While he spoke little of his affairs of the heart, others were always happy to do so for him. In 1935 Michel Georges-Michel published an offensive novel called *Le baiser à Consuelo* (*Consuelo's Kiss*), a thinly disguised portrait of a failed marriage. Consuelo de Hautebrive is a manipulative, hysterical seductress whose looks point directly to her namesake; her husband, a former Toulouse–Casablanca pilot posted to Africa for the first half of the novel, is portrayed as a barbarian, a clod, a naïf, a big, hulking, cuckolded fool. Faced with evidence of his wife's indiscretions during his absence he responds that a lover cannot be faulted for performing his "*métier d'homme.*" As for the wife: "From the moment you decide to risk your life, every day, to carry bills and shopkeeper's records between Buenos Aires and Caputzcoa, you prefer to know that your wife is enjoying herself on this earth. . . . Sexual jealousy is the most monstrous sort of selfishness. Would you think of forbidding your wife to eat or sleep while you were away?"

This kind of chatter was particularly unwelcome to a man who was so

easily hurt, who placed a premium on discretion.* By the end of the 1930s
Saint-Exupéry had had plenty of experience of *ad hominem* attacks but
suffered all the same from any kind of hostility. In responding to a newspaper survey on vivisection he had written that the sacrifice of hundreds
of dogs could be justified if their deaths could save the life of one child.
He received an avalanche of letters and confided his distress in Pélissier:
"The first three, four, five, fine. You shrug your shoulders. But when, every
day, you find vicious letters in your mail, the accumulated reproach makes
you miserable." His *Paris-Soir* description of the Polish workers won him
another 200 abusive letters, by which he was equally stung. He anguished
not only over his wife's behavior but over every one of Louise de Vilmorin's
liaisons, although—despite his best efforts—he continued to have no claim
whatever on her fidelity, and although this concern reduced him to a
pettiness he generally abhorred. "Put your mind on the strategy of the
fight and you will not feel the other man's punches," he wrote in *Flight
to Arras*, but in the 1930s he felt every one of the punches thrown him,
as if the battle were beneath him and not worthy of his pulling out his
armor.

A tumultuous home life was something to which Saint-Exupéry aspired
when the world around him had seemed unnervingly calm. What he
needed now—when the world was in flux and he was penniless and directionless and under fire, afflicted by what he referred to as his many
"*litiges*" (disputes)—was a refuge from the storm. He met Madame de B,
the woman who was to play this role in his life, for the first time in 1929,
falling back on his usual introduction: a sheaf of papers. On this occasion
it was the page proofs of *Southern Mail*, an ironic choice of texts given
the fact that the meeting took place at the home of Louise de Vilmorin.
Saint-Exupéry stood like a bashful schoolboy as his new acquaintance
read. Madame de B had been married two years earlier; Saint-Exupéry
was just back from Cape Juby. He was abashed a second time, when,
several years later, having heard of his financial woes from Yvonne de
Lestrange, his new friend sent him a check. It went uncashed, although
Saint-Exupéry was made to promise that he would signal should he ever
be entirely hard up. In 1934 he swallowed his pride: Consuelo had been
in another auto accident, and Saint-Exupéry needed to join her immediately in Dijon. Madame de B met him at the station with the train fare
and a picnic lunch; the two traveled south together late in the afternoon.
In Dijon he set out in search of his wife; his benefactress changed quais

---

* "Does a husband go from house to house crying out to his neighbors that his wife is a
strumpet? Is it thus that he can preserve his honor? No, for his wife is one with his home.
No, for he cannot establish his dignity against her. Let him go home to her, and there
unburden himself of his anger," he was to write in *Flight to Arras*.

and returned on the next train to Paris. She was to regret her marriage
—into a prominent, wealthy, titled Catholic family—from this point on.*

For the next ten years, to varying degrees, Madame de B—who in
a lifetime of attempts to erase herself from the Saint-Exupéry record
has managed to cast a longer and longer shadow, not least of all because
those efforts have included writing a biography of her friend, under the
pseudonym Pierre Chevrier—was to prove a formidable force in Saint-
Exupéry's life. She has been described over the years as "his sweet Egeria,"
as someone "who brought him both the 'space' and the 'grounding' so
crucial to him," as Saint-Exupéry's "guardian angel," as "a charming
and intelligent woman well-known in the literary and social life of the
capital," simply as "*la blonde*." Madame de B was all of these things,
stunning and golden-haired and long-legged and supremely aristocratic.
She was also deeply in love with Saint-Exupéry. To her detractors she
was a virago; to her admirers she was astute and quick-witted, able to
accomplish anything she set her mind to. She was a childhood friend of
Edmund Wilson's fourth wife, Elena; Wilson's daughter felt years later
there may have been "some girlish rivalry about who had the biggest man
of letters on her charm bracelet." In *Near the Magician*, Rosalind Baker
Wilson remembered that her father had a theory that "one's wife always
had a blond friend the husband didn't like." With Elena, "——— was
it." (Wilson's opinion may have had something to do with the fact that
the Frenchwoman informed her American friend that she had married
an inelegant man.) Madame de B had gone to Beaux-Arts; she painted,
and wrote fiction; she spoke flawless English; she was well-versed in literature and marvelously well-connected, as refined as Consuelo was wild,
as skilled in the rules of the world as Consuelo was stunningly naïve. She
was, unlike Consuelo, eminently presentable, which was important to a
man who knew that a wife did not always take well to dining with her
husband's mechanic. By marriage both women were countesses; one used
the title, the other played the part. Madame de B was, in short, that kind
of Frenchwoman of whom Gertrude Stein's sister was speaking when she
quipped that an American wife rises wonderfully to a crisis but that a
Frenchwoman sees to it that a crisis never arises.

Consuelo, of course, took poorly to the attachment and saw that crises
arose. For all her trouble her husband remained, however, devoted to her:
a frail and wayward woman is what every *chevalier-servant* needs. (A man
on whom Consuelo worked her charms years later reported that he was
made to feel like her Zorro.) There are many ways to love in France,
where it is sometimes necessary to specify that two people "*s'aiment
d'amour*," and Saint-Exupéry—who had ample opportunity to do so—

* Madame de B has requested that her real name not be disclosed.

could never truly imagine life without his wife. He could not live with her; he fretted, and wrote her what his American agent described as "sizzling letters," when away from her. He spoke repeatedly of his profound need to protect her; she gave him plenty of occasion to do so. He needed to exercise his sense of responsibility and somehow—in a wet cockpit on a cold night, perhaps—had learned that this should taste bitter. He was attracted—in women, at least—to the fragile and the damned, even while he at all times required a woman in his life to provide large doses of maternal solicitude. It fell to Madame de B to look after him, to counsel him, to sort out his affairs, a role for which she was supremely qualified. It fell to the rebellious Consuelo to play the part of what he called his "*sorcière*," to distract him with her tall tales and her half-truths.

And so he remained bound to both women in a kind of syzygy. "*L'une le déséquilibrait*," remarked a relative, "*l'autre lui rendait son équilibre.*" ("One threw him off balance, the other righted him.") Saint-Exupéry's was not an altogether unusual arrangement—one could argue that it is in France more common than not—but this *ménage* attracted its share of attention because of Consuelo's flamboyance and Madame de B's high profile. At the end of 1935 the situation was fairly new and not yet awkward; still, it made for drama on the domestic front, the kind Saint-Exupéry liked least. It was enough to make a man—especially a broke, harried man who was not particularly invested in the future in the first place—dream of escape.

XII

~

"Tayara Boum-Boum, Tayara Boum-Boum!"
1935–1937

Any fool can find his way, a poet alone knows how to lose it.

STUART GILBERT

"Aviation unites men as childbirth makes all women one," declared André Malraux, who never learned to pilot an airplane. Late in 1935, Saint-Exupéry's flying friends rallied—some, when they knew what was involved, against their better judgment—to bolster his sagging spirits. Mermoz took up the case of his distraught friend with General René Davet, then a high-ranking air force staff officer who had made the pilot's acquaintance years earlier. Under no circumstances should we lend him money, warned Mermoz, whom Saint-Exupéry had already cost a small fortune; surely, however, there was another way to bail out a destitute man? The two hit on the idea of a long-distance flight; at the time the French air ministry offered two prizes for record-setting flights completed before December 31: 150,000 francs (about 80,000 1994 dollars) for the fastest Paris–Saigon, and 500,000 francs for the fastest Paris–Tananarive (Madagascar). The aircraft of choice for such a flight, known in French as a *raid*, was a Simoun; Saint-Exupéry already knew the route to Saigon. It seemed an obvious arrangement, an easy way to hit the jackpot.

Saint-Exupéry's Simoun was not configured for such a flight, and he was not back in Paris until late November. Moreover, he had been quoted—when asked several years earlier if the life of a mail pilot was not terribly monotonous—as having said that nothing was more boring than a *raid*. It was a gratuitous mission, undertaken when convenient and propitious for the pilot; the mail had about it a practical urgency that lent it its flavor. All the same he embraced Mermoz's idea and began to talk excitedly about his Paris–Saigon flight. He had little to lose. By mid-December his mission was clear: he needed to beat the record set on the sixteenth by André Japy, who had made the flight—and front-page headlines—in ninety-eight hours and fifty-two minutes in a Simoun less powerful than Saint-Exupéry's. With a 180-horsepower engine Saint-Exupéry thought he could easily cut twenty hours off Japy's record.

Mermoz was to say that a *raid* required one to two years of preparation; Japy had made a series of preliminary flights—round-trips to Oslo, Oran, and Tunis—before his Paris–Saigon; Lindbergh spent weeks compiling the short list of emergency equipment he carried with him when he flew across the ocean in 1927. Saint-Exupéry had two weeks until the end of the year, and his preparations were casual. He spent crucial hours chasing Consuelo—who was not at all happy about his plans—around Paris. The three days at the Pont-Royal immediately preceding his departure have been described as "a combination tea party and comic opera." Daurat and the Air Bleu mechanics saw to it that the Simoun was overhauled for the trip. Andre Prévot, who in the years that followed must have come to feel like Saint-Exupéry's Sancho Panza, volunteered to join him. His Aéropostale colleague Jean Lucas prepared his compass readings and maps while, on the other side of the Pont-Royal room, the pilot spent as long arguing with his wife. He found the time to report to Davet's office for regular plenary sessions—meetings he generally left with a fresh packet of Lucky Strikes, the only commodity Davet dared lend him—but in general his was a *raid* proposed and prepared by friends, even those, like Mermoz, who in the end thought him far too distracted to succeed. Saint-Exupéry made two crucial decisions himself: to carry no radio, so as to take on extra fuel instead, and to finance the trip partially by selling the account of it, in advance, to René Delange, the editor-in-chief of *Paris-Soir*'s rival, *L'Intransigeant*.

On Saturday, December 28, 1935, Lucas accompanied his friend to the Le Bourget weather bureau, where Saint-Exupéry, who had already made up his mind to leave the following morning and who was in any event running out of time, heard a mixed forecast. That evening he and Consuelo dined with Raymond Bernard and his wife in a Montmartre bistro; afterward they strolled along the street fair that lined the boulevard de Clichy. The pilot abruptly excused himself after a few minutes and headed off to visit a fortune-teller. He returned a few minutes later visibly shaken; the woman had predicted disaster. Saint-Exupéry refused to elaborate on her prophecy but steered the group to an all-night drugstore. He wanted to buy something that could be counted on to keep him from sleep in the cockpit. He was by no means rested when Lucas woke him the next morning at 4:00 a.m., having spent the latter half of Saturday evening chasing around Montmartre clubs in search of his wife, who had disappeared again. Despite Davet's and Mermoz's advice that he be in top physical condition for the three-day trip, he had on the morning of his departure barely slept for forty-eight hours. Ségogne drove him to Le Bourget, where Daurat, Lucas, and the Werths were to see him off. Two detours were made en route to the airfield, one to another drugstore for a thermos, a second to a bistro just opening for the day, so that the thermos could be filled with the coffee Saint-Exupéry had forgotten. At 7:01 a.m. on Sunday, December 29, Saint-Exupéry and Prévot were aloft and en route. *Le Figaro* carried the news of the departure—and of the fact that Saint-Exupéry was trying his hand at *"l'aviation sportive"*—in their lead headline.

At 2:45 a.m. on the thirtieth, searching for the lights of Cairo in a sky thick with cumulus clouds, Saint-Exupéry ploughed into a sand dune in the Libyan desert at a speed of 170 miles per hour. He had been flying blind, under the impression that the winds were behind him. As he made his descent he assumed he had already overflown the Nile; in the end he really did not know if he was closer to Libya or the Sinai. In fact the winds had been against him, and he was still some 125 miles west of the Egyptian capital. It was a mistake from which only a radio could have saved him: his instruments were of little use as Saint-Exupéry did not know either his location or the barometric pressure, by which an altimeter is regulated. The Simoun's crash was cushioned by a field of round pebbles that acted like ball bearings under the airplane, allowing it to skate across the ground although shorn of its front landing gear. When it finally skidded to a smooth patch of sand, the Simoun stopped so abruptly that the aircraft's contents were thrown 150 feet from the window. Anticipating an explosion Saint-Exupéry and Prévot dove out immediately. They found themselves standing side by side in the dark, unexpectedly alive. "I was sure he was going to keel over any minute and split open from head to navel before my eyes," wrote the pilot of Prévot, who could complain only of having bruised his knee in the leap from the Simoun. It was not to matter much but—one-third of the way to Saigon—Saint-Exupéry had already shaved two hours off Japy's record.

"Our situation was hardly ideal," admitted the pilot later in his official report. Unsure of their whereabouts the two men spent what remained of the evening in the cockpit, doubtless privately taking inventory of their rations, which consisted of a thermos of very sweet coffee, some chocolate, and a few crackers.* In the morning they set out to the north, but after a walk of some thirty miles encountered nothing but sand. The second day they ventured west, where Saint-Exupéry was certain Cairo lay. A "vague

---

* Or so Saint-Exupéry told reporters following the crash. In hindsight these became the white wine, orange, and grapes of *Wind, Sand and Stars*.

foreboding" stopped him in his tracks, however. Reason dictated that Cairo lay to the west, but his feet would only take him east. Later he realized that he must on this count, as on many others, have been thinking of Guillaumet in the Andes, and that "in a confused way the east had become for me the direction of life." In fact a walk west would have been a walk toward nothingness; once again the pilot's instincts served him well. Years later Prévot was asked why he had so willingly followed Saint-Exupéry in the desert. "Oh, because of that," responded the mechanic, touching a finger to his nose. "Saint-Exupéry, he always knows the way!" The second day's walking proved futile, however, and the two spent a miserably dry New Year's Eve. Saint-Exupéry was haunted by the vision of Consuelo's eyes peering out at him from under the brim of her hat, "like a scream for help, like the flares of a sinking ship." (The sturdy Prévot suffered from similar concerns. On the second day he began to weep. "Do you think it's me I'm bawling about?" he asked Saint-Exupéry, when the pilot tried to console him.) As Guillaumet had been, Saint-Exupéry was shamed by the vision of his wife. He was far too impractical to think in terms of insurance payments, however. Just after his rescue he wrote his mother that he had fought tooth and nail to survive because he knew Consuelo needed him; he was prepared to move mountains in the name of duty.

On the third day, parched, discouraged, and ultimately delirious, having seen no sign of a rescue plane, the two set out toward the northeast, to walk until they could do so no longer. They took with them the Simoun's parachutes, with which they hoped they might collect the morning dew. Probably again with Guillaumet in mind, Saint-Exupéry scrawled his adieu on the side of the fuselage. He left the other side to Prévot, who was concise: "I ask my wife's forgiveness for whatever hurt I have caused her." In the sand the two men stamped out in thirty-foot-high letters: "WE HAVE HEADED NORTHEAST. SOS."

On January 1, when Parisian newspaper vendors' cries alerted the city to Saint-Exupéry's disappearance, a small group had already assembled around Consuelo at the Hôtel Pont-Royal. A sort of command center was set up here, much to the dismay of the hotel's telephone operator, who nearly went mad in the hours that followed. At all times eight to ten of Saint-Exupéry's friends and relatives could be found in the Pont-Royal lobby; Madame de Saint-Exupéry arrived to be at her daughter-in-law's side on the first; Madeleine Goisot was on hand, requested by the Ségognes to bunk in with the frazzled Consuelo; Yvonne de Lestrange, Werth, Gallimard, Daurat, Kessel, Fleury, Lucas, Fargue, Jeanson, and a host of other friends, many of whom now met for the first time, kept up the vigil. A number of journalists installed themselves at the hotel; café waiters, hotel porters, passersby stuck their heads in to make solemn inquiries.

Few of the acquaintances with whom Saint-Exupéry had shared a café table in the preceding years failed to put in an appearance. Among them his friends divided the tasks of the watch. Lucas served as official liaison with Air France; Ségogne took it upon himself to hound the Quai d'Orsay, which in his estimation was making neither a concerned nor a concerted effort to locate Saint-Exupéry. He paid a call on the minister of foreign affairs himself—who happened at the time to be Pierre Laval, also the prime minister—to ask that the rescue effort be given a little more attention. RAF planes from Iraq, French planes from Damascus, Italian and Egyptian aircraft were at one point or another dispatched to comb the desert but Saint-Exupéry, who customarily took up so much room and created such a stir around him, had disappeared into thin air. It did not help that two men walking in the desert are as good as invisible, or that no one knew exactly where to begin to search. Generally it was assumed that the Frenchmen had been carried north by the wind, to Palestine.

No one could have felt as frustrated by this turn of events than Daurat, who had doubted that Saint-Exupéry could succeed in his *raid* but had done so much to ensure that he would. He had more experience in the waiting game than anyone else, however, and hid his concern well. At one point a young woman sidled up to him in the Pont-Royal lobby and asked wide-eyed if Saint-Exupéry would be found. "Ah, Saint-Exupéry, he's gotten himself into a hell of a mess [*il s'est foutu dans un épouvantable merdier*] and, as usual, at the last minute he'll get out of it," replied Daurat. When Fleury telephoned him with the same question he was equally sanguine but more elegant: "Have no fear, he is a man of great battles. Of course he'll make it. I've seen him disarmed only by the little things, by pettiness, stupidity." Consuelo meanwhile discovered that she had never been better suited to being an aviator's wife than she was now, the near-widow of a celebrity flyer. There was ample reason for melodramatics, and she was, or appeared, at her wit's end. One of Saint-Exupéry's editors remembered her publicly refusing all food while privately tucking into a plate of sauerkraut hidden under a carpet. She offended some of his friends, dramatically offering to "carry the torch" ["*reprendre le flambeau*"] now that her husband was gone. When she sat down in a café the day after his departure, spread a map before her, and nervously began to talk to the person at the next table about the *raid*, she made sure that that person happened to be a *Figaro* reporter. She paid frequent visits to Notre-Dame-des-Victoires, a small church on the place des Petits-Pères, where she claimed to know from her prayers that her husband had been found. Her confidence was reinforced on Thursday, January 2, by Madame Luce Vidi, eminent clairvoyant. Saint-Exupéry's overcoat in hand, Madame Vidi swore that the pilot was alive and well, having been rescued by a caravan. Consuelo fainted at the news, leaving Madame Vidi's in such a state that she did so without the coat. The proprietor of Lipp described a particularly memorable entrance Consuelo made that week in the brasserie: "Held up by two friends, bathed in tears, she was grief personified. Then she sat down calmly to await condolences." In Agay, Gabrielle and her family kept up a different kind of vigil, praying ceaselessly, daring to hope for what they knew full well would be a miracle.

Saint-Exupéry's misadventure would sell books; now it sold newspapers. His departure had been front-page news in the popular press, as had all the *raids* of the time and aviation news in general. Paris–Saigon and Paris–Tananarive efforts regularly found their way to the front page; Christmas week *Paris-Soir* ran a series called "The Glorious and Dramatic Life of Charles Lindbergh." If a record-breaking flight boosted circulation a lost aviator was even better; between the first, when Saint-Exupéry was reported missing somewhere east of Benghazi, and January 3, much news was generated by a complete absence of news. About the most that could be said was that a search effort was under way. Finally on the second, late in the evening, Lucas was called to the telephone at the Pont-Royal. The air ministry was on the line. At the same time it was announced that Consuelo was wanted on the telephone—by Monsieur de Saint-Exupéry, calling from Cairo. The lobby exploded with joy. Consuelo may have fainted for the second time that evening; if she actually did so she first let out a piercing shriek that Saint-Exupéry was to say would ring forever in his ears. He asked his wife for what all record-setting aviators, successful or not, need on landing: a change of shirt. Off went the Pont-Royal group to celebrate *chez* Lipp, then at a Saint-Germain apartment, where the singing kept the neighbors up until about 5:00 a.m. Gide, who had been worried sick about his protégé, woke the rue Vaneau a little later with the good news. At a more respectable hour he reported to the Pont-Royal, where Consuelo was no longer receiving. Exhausted from the previous evening's revel, she had taken a sleeping pill and had allowed herself to be disturbed only once, by a second call from her husband. The other Madame de Saint-Exupéry was very much up and about. Dressed discreetly in a long black dress, she fended off a reporter's questions, preferring that he speak later with her daughter-in-law. She had spent the morning running errands for her son.

~

For a man who had often assured his mother that the world was small it must have seemed for three days supremely vast. Seventy hours after their departure from Paris Saint-Exupéry and Prévot should have been in Saigon; instead, they were tramping northeast through the rolling dunes of the Libyan desert. They had a compass, but it was of no use as they were

entirely disoriented. Their condition had not been improved by a freezing
night in the open air, followed by a dewless morning; their spirits were
not improved by the search planes that overflew them regularly without
seeing them. By the fourth day, like men "canoeing in mid-ocean," they
were so exhausted that they advanced only by steps of 600 yards. They
had no saliva, no strength, no emotion. Years later Saint-Exupéry was
asked if he had been afraid, lost in a desert three times bigger than France.
"After three days of walking under a hot sun, you no longer answer to
courage but to mirages. . . . You are no longer capable of emotion. Emotions require humidity!" he responded. His throat had contracted; his
tongue felt like plaster of paris; he did not dare part his lips for fear he
would be unable to retract his tongue; bright spots flickered before his
eyes; he was hallucinating. Around him the landscape began to change,
however, and scrubby vegetation began to appear. At last the two men
stumbled upon human footprints. Encouraged by "that caravan swaying
somewhere in the desert, heavy with its cargo of treasure," the pilot forged
on. Then suddenly he and Prévot had the same hallucination: a Bedouin
on camelback appeared from behind a dune, leading a caravan. Summoning all of his strength and all of his knowledge of Arabic, Saint-
Exupéry rushed at the men squawking, "*Tayara boum-boum! Tayara
boum-boum!*" ("Airplane fall! Airplane fall!") The Bedouins understood
the essential; before them were two men who could not take three steps
without falling on their faces. Immediately they produced a basin of fresh
water, into which Saint-Exupéry and Prévot—flat on their stomachs in
the sand—plunged their faces "like young calves" and with an ardor they
would later regret. Hoisting the Frenchmen onto a camel, the Bedouins
began to lead them back to civilization. The arrangement lasted only for
about nine miles, as the pilot and his mechanic proved too weak to hold
to their mounts.

Twelve miles away, Madame Raccaud was getting her children ready
for bed at Wadi Natroun when two Bedouins arrived at her door with an
urgent message for her husband, the Swiss director of the Egyptian Salt
& Soda Company, Ltd. "Could you pay my guide three guineas," it read,

> I have no local currency. After five [sic] days of walking in the desert with
> hardly a drop of water, my mechanic and I have just arrived at a small
> oasis. We are being brought to your home by camel but no longer have
> the strength to bear this form of transport. May we count on your great
> indulgence and ask you to come fetch us as soon as possible by car or boat.
> Our guide will explain to you where we are. Antoine de Saint-Exupéry.
> We thank you in advance.

Madame Raccaud, whose husband was in Alexandria, was confused.
She knew who Antoine de Saint-Exupéry was, and she knew he had been

in Cairo the previous month. It made no sense that he was back again; Wadi Natroun being somewhat off the beaten track, she had not yet heard of the attempted *raid*. (Had she turned over the paper in her hand she would have found a clue: a neatly typed list of descriptions of Middle Eastern landing strips.) And what in the world did the celebrated writer want with a boat, miles from water? She nonetheless sent the guide off with a company truck, which returned at 6:00 p.m. with the two Frenchmen. It was not much easier to understand their situation once Saint-Exupéry and Prévot began to explain it: in a state of nervous exhaustion, they got tangled up in their accounts, leaping around in time and interrupting each other. In the middle of this jumbled narration Monsieur Raccaud returned. He had in his hands the papers announcing that the aviators had been lost and was rather surprised to open the door of his home to find them seated in his living room, smoking cigarettes. As he walked in he heard Saint-Exupéry saying to his wife, "When you have nothing left to hope for, it is easy to die!" Raccaud proposed that the aviators' story be interrupted for tea and a bite to eat. "Yes, tea—and whiskey," suggested Saint-Exupéry. "We suffered such terrible thirst in the desert."

At 8:00 o'clock Raccaud set off with the two men in his car for Cairo, inviting along an armed Bedouin as an escort. In its way the trip must have seemed to Saint-Exupéry like a tribute to the olden days: four miles from the Pyramids, Raccaud ran out of gas. For this reason it was not until much later that the pilot was able, from a Giza hotel, fifteen miles outside of Cairo, to get to a telephone. His first call, to the French minister in Cairo, was met with some skepticism. Pierre de Witasse had been in bed for some time; when he appeared in his office to take the call an aide warned him, "Don't forget, sir, that it is past midnight, and the call has come from a bar." Witasse agreed to call the Air Ministry on the pilot's behalf; Saint-Exupéry appears to have waited until his arrival in Cairo to make the remainder of his calls. Raccaud deposited the aviators on the steps of the Hotel Continental and disappeared for a few minutes, presumably to park the car. In doing so he left the Frenchmen to one of the greatest labors of their odyssey: getting past the Continental's porter. He took one look at their tattered clothes, their unshaven faces, and announced that the hotel did not lodge beggars. Evidently at this moment a procession of spectacularly well-dressed conference-goers happened on the scene. An international surgical congress was under way in Cairo, and the representatives of twenty countries—in white tie and dripping with medals—were making their way from a banquet at the Faculté de Médecine to the city's red light district. The ruckus in front of the hotel on the Place de l'Opéra caught their attention; slumped on the steps, at the mercy of the porter, were what appeared to be two drunks. "Get lost, I want a room, I am Saint-Ex," the heavier one was saying, over and over.

Within minutes Saint-Exupéry had not only a room, a bath, and a whiskey, but a team of the world's most eminent surgeons leaning over his naked body, listening to his heartbeat, monitoring his pulse, examining his eyes. (The record yields no clue as to the attentions Prévot may or may not have received at the same time, apart from the glass of champagne served him in the hotel lobby. He appeared generally unwilling to speak to reporters, deferring to Saint-Exupéry, perhaps more wed to the advice Daurat had years before given the Aéropostale pilots about seeing their names in newspapers. For this he paid the price: one of the greatest casualties of the Libya crash would be Prévot's rather ordinary name, which would rarely be spelled the same way twice and never correctly.) Raccaud returned after a few minutes and was able to clear up the confusion over how Saint-Exupéry had crawled out of the desert and, incognito, onto the steps of the Hotel Continental, an explanation that others would later choose to ignore. Gabriel Dardaud, *L'Intransigeant's* reporter who observed these first moments at the hotel, swiftly called the news of the rescue in to the paper. He was surprised to hear that no one wanted his account of the misadventure, Saint-Exupéry being under exclusive contract to the newspaper himself. The flyer was by no means disposed to write a piece that evening, however, and Dardaud left him to sleep. Consequently *Paris-Soir* became the first paper to carry the news of the rescue and an interview with the pilot in a special edition published on January 3. That morning toward eleven Dardaud found Saint-Exupéry on the terrace of the hotel. As he was asked to do he bluntly reminded the aviator of his commitment to the paper, which had already advanced him the bulk of his payment for the *raid* pieces. "A large smile illuminated the face of my interlocutor. 'Tell them for me that the accident was not included in our agreement.' "

After eighty-seven hours in the desert Saint-Exupéry returned quickly to the world of men. An army of reporters called on him in the morning; they found him refreshed and lighthearted, emotional only when talking about how sick with worry his wife must have been. His wardrobe alone showed signs of distress. His clothes having been frayed in the trek, he began the interviews in a bathrobe and finished them in a shirt the concierge had bought for him, without tie or cuff links. Otherwise he was in fine form, eighteen pounds lighter than he had been, more garrulous than usual, no doubt feeling for once that earthly impositions were all of them, in the scheme of things, pleasures. He received a flurry of telegrams, including one from his family that touched him deeply: "ARE SO HAPPY." (He had sent one of his own: "SAFE AND SOUND SEND ALL MY LOVE.") He was inundated by notes, letters, calling cards. He had a shave and a haircut, talking with a reporter while he did so. He comported himself like a man reprieved. Evidently Witasse called on him in the morning and found three bottles lined up on the floor of his room, one of champagne, one of whiskey, one of Vichy water. Saint-Exupéry explained that they represented the three stages of a man's life, the last being, of course, the age of reason. "A few hours' sleep restored all of his lucidity," reported the *Figaro*'s correspondent. Dardaud, who watched as Saint-Exupéry tucked into a hearty breakfast, found this to be true. Breakfasts in the desert were exorbitantly priced, remarked the aviator gaily as he ate; to gather a tiny quantity of dew he had had to sacrifice a 6,200-franc parachute. There was about him no trace of embarrassment or failure, as there was in the press mainly wild praise for his heroism. (*Marseille-Matin* went so far as to contrast the purity of his feat with the elaborate machinations of France's elected officials.) He talked with reporters of his desire to make a second attempt at the trip. He responded to a letter from his mother: "I cried reading your brief note, so full of meaning, because I had called to you in the desert. I was in a rage against all men because of their absence, their silence, and I called for my mother. . . . It is a little for Consuelo that I came back, but it is by you, *Maman*, that I was brought back." The order Witasse had placed with a Cairo funeral parlor at the instruction of the Quai d'Orsay for two lead-lined coffins was canceled.

Saint-Exupéry drank a great number of toasts, doubtless remembering the words of Joseph Le Brix, who, rescued from the desert, swore that in his delirium he had seen parade before his eyes every frosted beer glass he had refused in his life. Late that morning he did so with seven or eight compatriots, one of whom was a young Cairo-based engineer who, as a reserve air force officer, followed French aviation news closely. Paul Barthe-Dejean arrived at the Continental on the third with his copy of *Vol de nuit*, which Saint-Exupéry giddily inscribed. He drew a little man, lounging on the book's title. Below the figure he began, then crossed out, what was clearly to be an earnest inscription. Over it he scrawled: "I started a sentence I can't get out of. Rather than exhausting myself on grandiose pronouncements I prefer to admit that I have had too much to drink. But I swear that I behaved perfectly in the desert." Barthe-Dejean invited his new friend and a few others to his parents' Cairo home, where the family's Nubian cook prepared a lavish lunch, washed down, to Saint-Exupéry's delight, with champagne. He was enough revived to finish off the meal with a flurry of card tricks.

On the seventh an expedition of three cars set out at 6:00 a.m. for Wadi Natroun, four hours west of Cairo, to visit the remains of the Simoun. Saint-Exupéry and the Renault insurance adjusters were followed by two cars of friends and journalists; Prévot, who had been at work on the airplane since the third, had preceded them to the site. Not having seen each other for several days, the pilot and his mechanic shook hands with obvious emotion. Barthe-Dejean was struck by the sight of the fuselage, stripped of its wings, its propeller, the engine cowling, the windows, and a door, lying flat on its belly in the sand. Saint-Exupéry asked the group to keep its distance and discreetly erased his premature farewell to the world. Over the wreckage he then delivered a miniature press conference, explaining his attempts to find Cairo, all of them based on the hypothesis that he had already overflown the Nile. The insurance experts thought the wreckage best deserted but the pilot insisted that an attempt be made to salvage the parts of the unfortunate airplane. Several morsels were handed out as souvenirs; over the next two weeks the Raccauds' home became the base of operations as Prévot set about disassembling the rest of the Simoun. In a handcart of Raccaud's design its remains were transported to Alexandria and shipped back to France, an effort Saint-Exupéry would describe later as a *"tour de force."* The debris was sold to a Valence businessman in 1938.

Only on the eighteenth, having written the better part of his six articles for *L'Intransigeant* in one of the most productive literary sprints of his life, did Saint-Exupéry himself set sail from Alexandria in an Egyptian boat, the *Kawsar.* He had for over a week entirely dominated the news: toward January 9 he had been eased off the front page by Lindbergh's arrival in Europe and by the Hauptmann trial, by a new record-setting flight by Japy, and, on the fifteenth, by word of Howard Hughes's trans-American flight in a Northrop Gamma, made in nine hours and twenty-seven minutes. Reporters hungered for every detail of the accident, searching out Prévot's family (a native of Picardy, he turned out to be the son of a mechanic), even managing a few minutes with the Bedouins to whom the Frenchmen owed their lives. It was no secret that Saint-Exupéry had taken off in haste; still, he was hailed as an authentic hero, a portrait of courage, a man with a claim on what La Bruyère termed *"la véritable grandeur."* There were of course occasional dissenters: the aviation journal *Les Ailes* wrote up the accident with some incredulity, implying that no pilot could be both so careless and so lucky to have survived such carelessness. Gallimard meanwhile profited from the headlines, running ads for *Vol de nuit* and *Courrier Sud,* along with their author's photo. All of this coverage would pale in comparison to Saint-Exupéry's own account of the desert, which began to run in *L'Intransigeant* under the title "Prison de Sable" on the thirtieth.

Leaving Prévot behind, Saint-Exupéry arrived in Marseilles, where he was greeted by his wife, his mother, his sister, and a horde of reporters, on January 21. As the *Kawsar* slowly steamed into port toward noon that day, the pilot waved to the crowd from the boat's promenade deck. In tears, Consuelo cried out, "Finally, you've come!" Everyone plied him with questions at once; Saint-Exupéry, by now more used to the attention, read from a prepared statement into a microphone, Consuelo at his side. Afterward, in a smoking room of the *Kawsar*, a reception was held in his honor; late in the afternoon he was feted by the Aéro-Club de Provence. Copies of *Vol de nuit* and *Courrier Sud* surfaced everywhere and were dutifully autographed.

In Paris the celebrations continued around Saint-Germain. The Lipp proprietor did not easily forget the welcome home thrown in his establishment. Word of Saint-Exupéry's return traveled quickly around the neighborhood, and his friends rushed to Lipp to drink to his health. The place was mobbed; it was understood that each of the revelers would pay his share on leaving. When the party broke up at 3:00 a.m. not a single one of the pilot's euphoric friends remembered to settle his bill. Saint-Exupéry himself ate like a man who had been marooned in the desert for three days, whipping up a storm of *boudin, steak tartare, aïoli*, and chocolate. He was unapologetic about his indulgences, explaining to Fargue: "I suffered such thirst that my mechanic and I swore that for the rest of our lives we would never turn down a drink." There were, all the same, certain constraints. The flier returned to a hero's welcome but with an empty purse; the trip that should have relined the coffers ended up costing him money. Several days after his return he called Jeanson to ask if his friend might meet him at the Deux-Magots. He had a great favor to ask him. Jeanson ran to the café, where Saint-Exupéry explained that he was afraid to go back to the rue de Chanaleilles alone. He owed several months' back rent, and thought if the concierge saw him with company she might refrain from comment. He had not yet dared to venture back to the apartment. Jeanson told him he was out of his mind; he had, after all, been in every newspaper for the last weeks. "She's going to throw her arms around you, kiss you, and offer you a drink, your concierge!" "Possible," replied Saint-Exupéry, "but come with me anyway, you never know." Jeanson's prediction proved correct, reinforcing Daurat's claim that the pilot was a man undone only by the little things. Later he asked Saint-Exupéry why he had chosen him for this delicate mission. Saint-Exupéry admitted that he could not have spoken of his embarrassment to many people. There was another reason, too: "If I had appealed to another friend he might have lent me money, while you—for all your goodwill—could not have," he told Jeanson.

~

The evening after the return to Paris, the Saint-Exupérys joined the Bernards for a late dinner in the same Montmartre bistro they had frequented the night before the attempted *raid*. The meal was barely over when the pilot pulled a writing pad from his inside coat pocket. He spent a moment shuffling pages, then began to read his story of the accident and his miraculous resurrection. Nothing about the desert ordeal could have prepared anyone for the lush poetry of his account of it, which these three were probably the first to hear. Consuelo burst instantly into tears. Bernard thought these the most beautiful of his friend's pages, a case it remains easy to argue. General Davet and Jean-Gérard Fleury were treated to an account at about the same time, in the deserted basement of a Champs-Élysées café. They proved equally impressed. When the six pieces appeared in *L'Intransigeant* between January 30 and February 4, they created a sensation: Never would Saint-Exupéry's celebrity stock rise so high in France save, perhaps, when these pages reappeared as the longest section of *Terre des hommes* in a somewhat condensed form. (They are barely reworked in the English edition, published as *Wind, Sand and Stars*.) He had set off for Saigon for the most prosaic of reasons; from his failure to reach Indochina he had emerged a hero, as odd a twist, surely, as was his having been cast from the bosom of the Aéropostale family for having publicly glorified the enterprise. His mail in the following months was heavy, enough so that he initially hired Madeleine Goisot as a secretary, then allowed a friend to fix him up with a professional. The sober Mademoiselle Zaclav saw to his constant and demanding correspondence of the next months: Could Saint-Exupéry attend the opening of *Anne-Marie* in Dijon? In Nancy? A viewing of *Vol de nuit* at the Fédération Aéronautique de France? A gala in Limoges? Could he lecture at any number of provincial aeroclubs?

Luminaries do not always make attractive tenants, and the Saint-Exupérys' landlord proved more interested in seeing his rent paid on time than in sheltering a hero of France and his eccentric wife. The rue de Chanaleilles lease was rescinded on February 9. The couple's few pieces of furniture—officially now government property in lieu of back taxes—stayed until later in the month, when they were removed to a storage depot. Saint-Exupéry moved temporarily to the Hôtel Lutétia, next door to the Pont-Royal; even before her frenzied January stay at the Pont-Royal, Consuelo had been settled in a modest apartment on the rue Froidevaux, across from the Montparnasse cemetery, where the air was cleaner than elsewhere in Paris. Her husband's move made sense in terms of the couple's nomadic lifestyle—he spent part of February in the south, where he did some writing, and continued to travel throughout the year —but did little to ease the strain on their finances. He was as ever forced to go to unhappy lengths to pay the rent, although in 1936 these efforts did not take him as far afield as Libya. (The lesson of that experience seems to have been that such concerns were truly immaterial: not all of the hotel bills of these years were paid.) He groused about his finances, but charmingly so. At the time it was said that 200 families controlled all of France's wealth. Pondering his frayed cuffs at the Lutétia one day, Saint-Exupéry told Françoise Giroud, then the young script girl on the screen adaptation of *Courrier Sud*, that one would be well advised to find a way to join one of these families for eight days, just long enough to "refresh one's wardrobe." A few years later Prévot alerted the pilot to the fact that he had found a used Simoun for sale for 300,000 francs. "I am going to write him that he would have been better advised to have found the 300,000 francs; I would have taken it upon myself to find the Simoun," Saint-Exupéry informed Pélissier.

Fundamentally he was too much a malcontent to enjoy any sustained euphoria at being alive and back in Paris, a city incapacitated in the spring of 1936 by labor strikes of all kinds. Artistically he found himself caught up in a vicious cycle. He was not in a position to turn down journalistic or screenwriting assignments that came his way and took these on with some bitterness. "I feel like a prisoner, spending his time weaving baskets, when I could be so much more useful, so much better off elsewhere," he wrote Madame de B late in the year. He found such work provided no satisfaction whatsoever; each opportunity to write a screenplay provided not only one less opportunity to write a book, but one more to write a screenplay. There was little consolation in this. Nor was any forthcoming from his wife, more invested in her husband's celebrity than in his career. Early in March Émile Raccaud wrote that a tiny red airplane had overflown Wadi Natroun and had made him think of Saint-Exupéry. He enclosed with his letter photos taken during the towing of the Simoun. Saint-Exupéry wrote back cordially on the twentieth, sending on a small compass as a sign of his continuing gratitude. He had not forgotten the warm welcome he had received. "Furthermore, I already miss Wadi Natroun and its peace," he wrote Raccaud. "Here the world seems to be less of a desert, but is much more of one."

Each time a new assignment came his way, Saint-Exupéry managed to spend the income straight away. "Money burned a hole in his pocket," said Consuelo openly of her husband; he made no public observations regarding her habits. Early in the year he was approached about a screen adaptation of his first novel; months later Jeanson directed another film project his way; when the Spanish Civil War broke out in July he was asked by *L'Intransigeant* for a series of articles. He said yes to all of these projects because he was in debt and felt he had to: by early summer he and Consuelo were decorating a lavish duplex in a new Art Déco building on the place Vauban—an apartment with a rent three times that of the rue de Chanaleilles—into which the couple moved in July. Saint-Exupéry laid claim to the lower floor and Consuelo to the upper, an arrangement that suited their increasingly parallel lives better than had any previous abode; a conciliatory Consuelo told her husband she was granting him "a spousal holiday." Each had a separate telephone. The apartment overlooked the Esplanade des Invalides and beyond it the Right Bank; on its terrace Saint-Exupéry occasionally camped out this summer. A distinguished-looking Russian émigré butler named Boris lorded over the home, on which the Saint-Exupérys did a great deal of work. Mirrors went up. Carpets went down. Walls were moved, cabinets hung, bookcases installed. The apartment was entirely painted. All of this appears to have been done under the supervision of an architect-decorator, hired in May. The furniture, however, was spare and, charitably speaking, eclectic; much of it had been donated by friends. The living room was furnished with green lawn chairs; a wooden plank laid over two horses served as a desk; the bookshelves were finished but their shelves never installed, leaving the writer's library in a jumble. The place Vauban represented Saint-Exupéry's only affair with bourgeois living, a half-successful arrangement that lasted just over two years. It was to be one of the great ironies of his life that—a native of the most stubbornly bourgeois of France's cities—he never quite mastered this art.

His immediate project in the spring of 1936—when amid much excitement the Front Populaire came to power—was the adaptation of *Courrier Sud* for the screen. Françoise Giroud, today one of France's better-known journalists and writers, worked with him daily on the project, typing out a number of versions of the screenplay in his room at the Lutétia. At the end of the afternoon the two would head off to the Deux-Magots or to the Café de Flore for a drink, often moving on to a neighborhood bistro for dinner. Saint-Exupéry was clearly at ease with Giroud, whose sex and age recommended her to him (she was eighteen at the time); he wrote her fantastic prose poems, made her drawings, shared the best of his musical repertoire, and generally unloaded his trunk of marvels. She remembered him as eternally broke, weighed down by debts but not belongings. He turned into her guardian angel when, in the fall, director Pierre Billon began to film *Courrier Sud* in southern Morocco. There was some question as to whether or not Giroud should be allowed to accompany thirty men into the desert for a shoot that was to last three weeks. She was on the verge of being replaced by a script boy when the writer gallantly saved the day: "Let her go," he declared. "She will be my ward." At the Hôtel Mogador he insisted that Giroud's room be adjacent to his, the better for him to defend her virtue.

Saint-Exupéry played the role of knight in shining armor better than that of beleaguered husband. Giroud knew him in 1936, as did many people, to be "crucified by his wife, whom he loved and who was unfaithful to him." While he had once written Consuelo letters when they were in the same room he now corresponded with her of necessity. In his early communications he sounded—stung by her caprices, by the missed engagements, the late nights out—like a disappointed parent. ("I like to be proud of you"; "Behave so that I can always, always trust you.") Now he wrote with the fury and anguish of a lover spurned. ("Oh, these sleepless nights spent waiting up for you. . . . Inside I am the same young man who loved you so—but you are the same Consuelo who deserts our home.") He was by no means blameless himself, but he knew how the game was played and was at least discreet about his diversions. After years that should have taught him better he continued to hope that some of this prudence would wear off on his wife, a woman whom he had married for her vivacity and unconventionality, who might appear swaddled in floor-length mink in July, who made a noisy entrance as the Countess de Saint-Exupéry. In a particularly patient mood he pleaded with her, after she had been less than circumspect in her remarks:

> I beg you one day to understand true dignity and true nobility, which is not to speak of such things. You are a little châtelaine now, you must forgo the language and reactions of a young girl. They must say of you, 'How dignified and proper that little Consuelo is. What admirable reserve. She had many faults but she has changed so much!' And not what they are bound to say when you flaunt our intimate problems. I want to protect you, but first you must help me protect you from yourself. Forgive me for having to say this once again, but I so much want you to become what you should be: a blushing, poetic young woman, adorable and discreet, and not a noisy muse for Surrealist brasseries.

Neither of the Saint-Exupérys could have been easy to live with, and Consuelo suffered equally at her husband's hands. She was as proud and jealous as she was inconstant, and was hurt that her husband's friends did not have much patience for her. She complained to one—who had been assigned to keep an eye on her—about the bad rhythms to which she and Saint-Exupéry were prey. Even as she pursued her own interests she felt humiliated by her husband's increasingly official liaison. She did not hesitate to attack Madame de B publicly, causing her enough embarrassment that family members wrote to ask that Madame de B do her best to tone things down. Consuelo may or may not have known her husband's sentimental life was messier still, at least on paper: he had not relinquished his fascination with Louise de Vilmorin, on whom he doted from afar. In the mid-1930s he continued to write his ex-fiancée tenderly of his devotion: "Whisper to yourself, very softly, as you fall asleep tonight, that someone loves you."

Late in 1936 Consuelo called a lawyer who had been recommended to her by a sculptor friend. He was on his way to Vichy for a cure; she told him her business could not wait and volunteered to meet him there. In the lobby of his hotel she went straight to the point: she wanted a divorce. "Do you have a lover?" asked the lawyer. "No," replied Consuelo. "Do you have money?" he asked. "No," answered Consuelo. "Do you intend to remarry?" Once again Consuelo answered in the negative. "Then why do you want a divorce?" asked the pragmatic lawyer. "May I make a telephone call?" responded Consuelo, excusing herself. Shortly she was overheard saying, "Don't worry, I'm not divorcing you." Saint-Exupéry, too, considered divorce but felt hampered by his background; he admitted as well—later, to another woman—that the idea of remarriage tore him apart. Preferring, it seemed, his ideals to the reality of his situation, unable to relinquish the sense that he was above all responsible for his wayward wife, he endured the marriage in much the same way as did she. The strategy suited him; he left town often.

In late May and early June Saint-Exupéry made a short trip to Germany and Romania, either as the pilot of a borrowed airplane or as a passenger. In July 1936, expecting to acquire a new Simoun with the insurance collected after the Libyan crash, he applied for permission to overfly Russia in a Paris–Tokyo *raid*. (The permission was, notwithstanding the Franco-Soviet pact of the previous year, denied.) On August 10, *L'Intransigeant* announced on its front page that he had left in the company plane for Barcelona. Two days later the first of his five articles, on Barcelona and the Lérida front, appeared. The Spanish pieces ring with Saint-Exupéry's usual themes—seen from either side the war seemed senseless to him; he was horrified by the loss of respect for the individual demonstrated by both Loyalists and Rebels; he abhorred the idea of a man being reduced to his political affiliation—but are generally uninspired. The exception was his account of having made the rounds with Pépin, a French Socialist and anti-Church worker who had for some reason taken it upon himself to negotiate with the revolutionaries for the release of French monks. When he succeeded in his mission he hurled insults at the ex-prisoners for whom he had just risked his life; in response the priests threw their arms around their savior, crying with joy. The whole seemed to Saint-Exupéry a perfect demonstration of the absurdity of the situation.

He must have been happy to be back in Paris, where a new red Simoun—identical to the first, save that it was more powerful and already outfitted for a *raid*, its two back seats having been torn out to make room for additional fuel—awaited him. He flew when he could at Le Bourget, usually in the late afternoons, often inviting a friend along for the ride. This was not often enough for his tastes, however; his writing assignments still claimed the bulk of his attention. The adaptation of *Courrier Sud* continued apace, which meant that at least provisionally the distractions of Paris were best left behind. The film's producer installed a group including Saint-Exupéry and Pierre Billon, in a small inn overlooking the Seine, a mile or so north of Fontainebleau. It seemed to him that a bit of calm would do the project good. Unfortunately for Pan Ciné the distractions of Paris sought out the film's writer. Billon remembered that one after another Saint-Exupéry's friends drove out to surprise him, guaranteeing long evenings of electrifying conversation and impossible-seeming card tricks. At the same time Saint-Exupéry's attention was diverted by the last of his Barcelona pieces. Predictably, he knocked on Billon's door one morning at 2:00 a.m. to read an article he had just finished. He proved no less hungry for approbation as his literary reputation grew than he had as a neophyte: Jeanson recalled a similar incident the following year, after a second Spain reportage, when Saint-Exupéry forced him away from the lunch table and thrust into his hands the proofs of a *Paris-Soir* article. A messenger was due to take them back to the paper in minutes; Saint-Exupéry insisted that Jeanson look them over immediately. "Do you think it's readable?" he badgered his friend. "Is it worth publishing?" (Jeanson hardly felt himself worthy of such questions and chose to evade them. *"Oui, Monsieur Molière,"* he answered, after a quick review. *"Merci, Monsieur Boileau,"* replied Saint-Exupéry.) Billon good-humoredly chauffeured Saint-Exupéry and his 1936 pieces to *L'Intransigeant*'s offices, trips that, naturally, did little to speed the work on *Courrier Sud.* The director finally admitted his concern on one such excursion, when the writer asked if they might pass by his tailor's on the rue des Pyramides while in town. "You'll see," he promised, "I'll be out in two minutes." Billon obliged. Saint-Exupéry raced into the shop, waved his jacket at the tailor, cried, "Hello! The same!" and was back at the director's side in seconds. "That took no time!" he exclaimed as they drove off.

Work on the dialogue and cutting of *Courrier Sud* continued in October in Paris, where nearly every day toward four Saint-Exupéry dragged Billon to Le Bourget for a spin in his Simoun. Meanwhile Jeanson had involved Saint-Exupéry in a project with his London-based friend Alexander Korda, who was planning the first in what was to be a series of films on the history of aviation. Saint-Exupéry was thrilled by the idea and probably that fall traveled to London with Jeanson to consult on the project. The two men happily settled into a luxurious suite at the Savoy but were discouraged when it turned out that filming had already begun and that the results were not much to their tastes. An English-speaking Blériot with a glued-on mustache was more than the two Frenchmen could stomach; while they were happy to live in the lap of luxury at Korda's expense, they found themselves quickly out of ideas. During this trip Jeanson introduced his friend to the actor Charles Laughton and to the artist Fernand Léger, both of whom were working for Korda at the time; the producer introduced them as well to H. G. Wells, who had written an early draft of the screenplay. Saint-Exupéry also ran into an old friend in London. The two dejected Frenchmen sat down for a late drink one night in a run-down club, where a barmaid could not take her eyes off the aviator. After a few minutes she came by. "Tonio—don't you remember me?" "Paulette!" cried a revived Saint-Exupéry, recognizing an old acquaintance from a Dakar nightclub. Side by side the two gossiped happily about the entire Aéropostale clan, a conversation that amused Jeanson more than Paulette's manager, who instructed her to move on to the bar's other customers. At this Saint-Exupéry rose—"*Saint-Exupéry le pacifique. Saint-Exupéry le doux*," as Jeanson put it—and pulled the man toward him by the tie. "You will apologize immediately to this lady," he exploded, shaking the surprised manager. "Don't you understand that this lady is a friend of my friends?" A few overturned tables later the Frenchman got his apology. Doubtless he was already seething with frustration, having found that England inspired him not at all and that Korda had no real need for his counsel. When the producer generously proposed that the two writers might be more comfortable at a country estate he had found for them than at the Savoy, Saint-Exupéry took advantage of the occasion to ask for a ticket home. He explained to Korda that—odd though it sounded—he had no ideas in England; Shakespeare had claimed them all. The next day he was back in France.[*]

In October, in one of two Latécoère 28's on loan from Air France, Saint-Exupéry flew to Mogador (today Essaouira), on the Moroccan coast, to supervise the filming of *Courrier Sud*. He proved an invaluable asset to the production which already benefited from full civic and military cooperation. It was not always easy, however, to maintain order on a set peopled by authentic Senegalese guards (provided by the army), Moorish blue men (ostensibly recruited by Saint-Exupéry), Arab cameleers, and Mogador prisoners, freed briefly to assist in towing the Latécoères through the dunes. Nor was it easy to impress upon the Moors what, exactly, cinema was: in the first simulated attack, they came hurtling over the dunes, roaring realistically, and overturned the camera. Its operator managed a narrow escape. Saint-Exupéry's primary concern, other than the verisimilitude of the set, was the direction of the Latécoères; he took the controls for most of the shots of the takeoffs and landings. Most memorably, he served as his own stuntman. For one scene a Latécoère needed to make a dramatic takeoff from between two 50-foot dunes, from a strip of sand about 200 yards long. The film's pilot, who had measured the distance, categorically refused to attempt the takeoff. Saint-Exupéry offered to take the airplane up alone. With four men holding it in place—the aircraft had no brakes—he throttled up. The airplane was then let go, and he taxied,

---

[*] Korda's aviation film ran into greater troubles than simply those caused by the defection of the two Frenchmen. Shelved repeatedly over the next years, *Conquest of the Air* was released finally in 1940, with a story credit to Antoine de Saint-Exupéry.

tail down, two-thirds of the way down the sand corridor. In the nick of time the Latécoère took to the air, having been catapulted off a rock hidden under the sand. Saint-Exupéry cleared the far dune by a matter of inches. He could not have known about the rock, and afterward admitted that he had been a little nervous. Still, he had wanted at all costs to prove the feat was possible. The film's official pilot was staggered, having estimated his chance of success at about one in ten.

~

On December 7, 1936, the Saint-Exupérys had guests to dinner at the place Vauban. The Swiss composer Arthur Honegger was there; so was Madame de B. Their host said little, and made trips to the telephone every five minutes. Finally he confided to Madame de B: "Mermoz transmitted a final message: 'Cutting off rear engine.' " His colleague had set out that morning with a four-member crew from Dakar to cross the South Atlantic in the flying boat *La Croix du Sud*. Three and a half hours into the flight he had transmitted the four-word message; it was not in itself cause for concern, but had been followed by a silence that had yet to be broken. When ten minutes had elapsed without any further communication every radio station from Paris to Buenos Aires snapped to attention, to listen and wait. "It would be ridiculous to worry over someone ten minutes late in our day-to-day existence, but in the airmail service ten minutes can be pregnant with meaning," wrote Saint-Exupéry, who was that evening in the middle of his vigil.

The two men had argued violently about politics but in the end had salvaged their friendship, largely by choosing to sidestep any ideological discussion. Saint-Exupéry was stricken by Mermoz's disappearance, which he only slowly came to admit was his complete loss. Naturally he became his friend's premier eulogist: in his first piece on France's most popular aviator he chose to draw up a catalogue of close calls. If Guillaumet had walked out of the Andes after five days, if Reine and Serre had disappeared into the Sahara and reemerged intact months later, if twenty aircraft searching the Libyan desert had failed to turn up two men walking directly below them, could Mermoz not still be alive, he asked on the thirteenth in *L'Intransigeant?* By the sixteenth he was a little more disposed to concede defeat, this time on the front page of *Marianne*. He was still not ready to ascribe to Mermoz all the virtues to which the dead are automatically entitled, however: "You are a friend, with all the marvelous failings that so endear you. And I am waiting to remind you of them. I don't want to respect you yet. I am keeping your place in all those little bistros where we used to meet. You will be late as always, oh, my insufferable friend . . . I am so afraid of never again getting on your nerves."

It was a threnody consistent with the nature of many of Saint-Exupéry's closest friendships—that with Ségogne, for example—which proceeded as much by endearing complaint and accusation as anything else. "When we lose a friend it is probably his faults that we mourn," Saint-Exupéry had written earlier, in a revealing statement. Soon enough he had grown accustomed to the idea that the thinning Aéropostale ranks had thinned again. A year after Mermoz's disappearance he spoke eloquently about the slow admission of loss, about the irreplaceability of old friends. "Old friends aren't made overnight. . . . It is useless, having planted an acorn in the morning, to expect to sit in the shade of an oak that afternoon." He began to grasp what was so unnerving about this kind of loss: "Mermoz has disappeared, and he was so much a part of us that many of us ache now with a melancholy that is unfamiliar, that is new to us: the secret regret of growing old."

There was every reason for Saint-Exupéry to feel an artifact. Not only had Aéropostale and its glories ceased to exist, not only did the desultory, directionless France of 1936 look shorn of any such grandeur, but the men responsible for the pioneering mails were fast disappearing. Mermoz's death left, of the early Aéropostale pilots, only Guillaumet, Reine, Serre, and Saint-Exupéry. He must have been thrilled when, a few days before Christmas, Pierre Cot, then the Air Minister, gave his consent to an African propaganda tour proposed by Saint-Exupéry and underwritten as well by *L'Intransigeant*, to whom he promised a write-up of the flight. Cot granted the author-aviator a 40,000-franc subsidy and agreed to see that the government pay for his insurance. Air France also backed the flight to Timbuktu, for which they offered to provide the fuel. (Their interest was presumably in an alternate France–Dakar route, passing inland via Oran instead of along the coast to Casablanca, a route that would once and for all have obviated the need to overfly Spanish territory.) Saint-Exupéry submitted to a medical exam at Le Bourget on January 29 and took off with Prévot, via Marseilles and Casablanca, a few days later. The *raid* took the two men over utterly virgin territory—"over blindingly white sand, tiring to the eyes and devoid of any trace of life," as the pilot described it—but this desert excursion of 5,500 miles went off without a hitch. (The two men were once again flying without a radio; having presumably learned his lesson, Saint-Exupéry had applied for one in January, but his request had been denied by the implacable French bureaucracy on the grounds that Prévot was not qualified to operate one.) Along the way Saint-Exupéry acquired a lion cub, which he attempted to bring back to France with him. The cub did not take well to flight, and the pilot was forced to fly north in a series of dives and climbs in an effort to keep the animal subdued by knocking it against the ceiling of the cabin. He found this good fun, especially in retrospect. Prévot must have been less amused by the cub's confused pawing, of which he wore the evidence all over his hands and arms. He had as well contracted malaria; his fidelity to Saint-Exupéry seemed destined to be compensated in medical bills.

Otherwise the pioneering trip went off splendidly, doing much to restore the pilot's faith in himself as what Noëlle Guillaumet described as "a man of the air and of the desert." From Algeria in mid-February he mailed several letters that shimmer with his satisfaction. To Madame de B he wrote from Oran that he was delighted with the trip, which he had made entirely outside of the existing trails, even when he could have followed them. "I felt confident and undertook everything lightly, sure of my eyes and of my calculations. . . . I return pleased with the trip and with myself . . . mountains, storms, sands, those are my household gods." A few days later, from Algiers, he boasted to Guillaumet of the flawless navigation he had performed with his top-of-the-line instruments. It was true that he had been graced by good weather, but he had all the same flown with impressive accuracy over thousands of miles of uncharted territory. He sounded, in his note to Guillaumet, like his lighthearted self. It was easy enough to see why: "I have just relived a few hours of the best years of my life," he signed off.

"I have an account to settle with the desert," Saint-Exupéry had said before setting off for Timbuktu. He had settled it; his feelings about writing for a living proved more difficult to resolve. The promised *L'Intransigeant* articles were never written. He may have negotiated a substitution: in the first week of April the newspaper carried a front-page account of Guillaumet's ordeal in the Andes, a near-final draft of what was to appear later in *Wind, Sand and Stars*. Evidently Saint-Exupéry preferred still the distant to the recent past. He sold a piece on a Saharan emergency landing to the Surrealist journal *Minotaure*, which appeared under the title "*Un Mirage*." He put the finishing touches on a screenplay—never filmed, and never unearthed—called "Radium," completed at the end of April, and he solicited assignments from *Marianne*. Any illusions he may have had about the integrity of the press were shattered on his return to Paris in late March, however, when he discovered that a sensationalist journal had published a story claiming he had concocted the Libyan accident. In January *Voltaire* alleged that he had landed quietly in a Cairo suburb, covered the wings of his Simoun with sand so as to disguise it, then stumbled into the city with his invented tale. Raccaud's desertion of the two airmen on the Continental steps had evidently fueled this accusation—against which Saint-Exupéry loyalists have had to defend the pilot as recently as 1987—although *Voltaire* was, as everyone knew, an inventive publication under the best of circumstances. Saint-Exupéry instituted a libel suit against the journal, which he won handily. The court found he had been defamed, awarding him 15,000 francs (today about $9,000) in damages. He was, however, cut to the quick by the entire incident. Once again this spring the man who claimed mountains, storms, and sands as his household gods found himself not on the offensive, fighting for his life in the Libyan desert, but on the defensive, battling men, whose stature was sometimes smaller even than it appeared from the air.

XIII

~

Civil Evening Twilight
1937–1939

> One must pay dearly for immortality: one has to
> die several times while still alive.
>
> NIETZSCHE, Ecce Homo

France, in 1937, was a country befuddled. When she looked around she seemed to be one of the last great hopes for liberal democracy in Europe, but she did not often dare to look around. There was constant talk of Franco, of Mussolini, of Hitler; the Spanish Civil War dominated the newspapers during the second half of 1936 and into 1937. But all the talk of the threat to the legitimate Spanish government, of the invasion of Ethiopia, of Germany's repeated aggressions, amounted to precisely that: talk. It was the chatter of a confused, divided people reeling with their own problems, obsessed with their own intrigues, bruised still by a war they could not conceive of fighting again. Across the Channel the British governments of Baldwin and Chamberlain followed the affairs of Europe with apathy and disinterest, convinced that Churchill's warnings were idle exaggerations; understandably, France had no burning interest in taking a lonely stand as the defender of European democracy. As early as 1935 the writing had been on the wall, however. Sometimes it was even eloquent. That year Jean Giraudoux published *Tiger at the Gates*, a play that trumpeted—in its keen-witted, agreeable manner—the news that war was inevitable.

France chose to look the other way when Hitler remilitarized the Rhineland in 1936, the first opportunity she had to stop him and arguably the last occasion on which she was still militarily strong enough to do so. When civil war broke out in Spain she again backed away, worried that intervention would plunge her directly into a confrontation with Italy and

Germany. That conflict, which France worked so hard to avoid, made itself felt all the same: it went a great way toward destabilizing the tentative alliance on which the Front Populaire government of Léon Blum, forged in the fury of 1934 and voted in with much enthusiasm two years later, had been based. When it was revealed that Blum had been approached by the Spanish Loyalists for arms and had not automatically refused, things began to go awry, enough so that the new premier, acting against his principles, was shamed into maintaining strict neutrality. He lost support on the Left—where cries of "Airplanes for Spain!" went up regularly—for treating Franco too gingerly. The Right—desperate for ground on which to break up the government—accused him of being anything but conciliatory. Its extreme elements painted Blum as a warmonger. France was at the time a country so much racked by infighting, so skittish, so bleary-eyed, that Blum's instinctive reaction was seen not as a heroic vote cast on a dark day in favor of liberty, fraternity, and equality but as a subversive act of a guileful politician bent on engaging France in a conflict with Germany because he was a Jew and had a personal account to settle with Hitler.

Between March 1936, when Hitler remilitarized the Rhineland, and March 1938, when he continued on into Austria, one could practically hear the heavy footfalls in the distance. In Paris this registered to many only as ripples in the café glasses. Those in power were intent on pursuing their own political agendas; *le Tout-Paris* merrily decanted its best vintages and threw balls at which to discuss these baroque goings-on; the man in the street focused on the country's pressing domestic problems. France still not having succeeded in pulling out of the Depression, these were years when bad economic news was the order of the day. Unemployment ran wild. The already-weak franc was devalued in 1936 (by the summer of 1939 it was not worth three pennies); the stock market crashed in early June 1937. The supposed villains, in the guise of the Banque de France—controlling "200 families," were denounced daily. High hopes for the Front Populaire fizzled quickly, replaced by a kind of last-resort despair. Despite the strikes and riots and unemployment, business went on as usual, however, 1937 amounting to a kind of squall before the storm. Not much actually happened in Europe that year: Germany continued on its course to rearm. The Spanish government did its best to hold out against Franco's forces. Italy defied the League of Nations in Abyssinia. And France muddled along. By now entirely pessimistic about the economy, no one was much surprised when the Front Populaire's ambitious and expensive reforms were put on hold in February. By now accustomed to the instability of the body politic, no one was much surprised when Blum's government fell in mid-June, after one year in office.

Paris itself—for all of the unrest—remained a garden of earthly delights. There were signs, however, that the city was beginning to look more like a fool's paradise. One thing that did happen in 1937 was the Paris World's Fair, officially known as the "Exposition Internationale des Arts et Techniques." By the end of the summer the city looked more splendid than ever, fitted with an ingeniously designed series of fountains and lights that together worked to produce "geysers of liquid electric color." If she could do little else France could still throw a fine party: a record-setting two hundred million tickets were sold to the Exposition of 1937, the largest such celebration of its time. Saint-Exupéry bought a ticket, late in August; he was even obliging enough to try the parachute jump off a 100-foot tower installed on the Esplanade des Invalides, a feat he claimed the single most terrifying moment of his life. (He suffered from vertigo.) For this demonstration of courage he was awarded a certificate, which he kept.

The fair hardly began as the success it became, however. Scheduled to open on May 1 along several acres of the Seine, from the Invalides to the Eiffel Tower, "l'Expo '37" was held up by a number of well-coordinated labor strikes. (By the end of the year the Left-leaning government would be forced to do its share of strikebreaking, an irony not lost on Henri Jeanson, who relished absurdity of any kind and reported on this one with gusto.) On May 1 the Esplanade des Invalides remained a muddy wasteland; only four countries' pavilions were finished. In a poor advertisement for democracy, three of them belonged to what Pierre Lazareff called "the three dictatorships," Germany, Italy, and Russia. The exhibition opened officially on May 24, although even then it was far from ready. Skeletons of buildings dotted the fairgrounds; the exhibition's vast array of lights did not fully function until August. Albert Speer's ambitious German pavilion, one of the first structures to be completed, stood grandly at the foot of the Pont d'Iéna on the Right Bank. Over it, perched atop a 170-foot tower, hovered an immense golden eagle, a swastika in his claws. Bathed in tones of topaz and emerald, Paris had never looked so beautiful. But from everywhere in the city—and most distinctly from the terrace of a sixth-floor apartment on the place Vauban—one could, if one looked, see the future.

René Delange noticed that, on the place Vauban, Saint-Exupéry began to show a little more patience for talking with the country's politicians. General Davet's impression was that he was somewhat embarrassed not to have taken the political scene more seriously; evidently their mutual friend Mermoz had interviewed everyone from the then-Communist Jacques Doriot to the Comte de Paris before settling on his Croix-de-Feu affiliation. It seems more likely that Saint-Exupéry feigned embarrassment out of deference to his friend, there being no record of his ever having regretted an active involvement in politics and plenty to the contrary. In any event this spring he began his crash course in political awareness which—if it failed to inculcate in him any particular ideology—did confirm him in his belief that war was no solution to anyone's problems.

This spring *Paris-Soir* offered Saint-Exupéry an astronomical 80,000 francs, roughly $32,000 today, to return to Spain. He was to deliver ten pieces to the newspaper. He accepted the offer, arriving at the Spanish border in the paper's plane on April 11. He spent the following day in Valencia, straightening out his papers and applying for letters of introduction that would enable him, in Madrid, to visit the Republican front. "I'm not interested in visiting a city, even one under bombardment, dining at a hotel and sleeping at night in my bed. I am absolutely not interested in interviewing generals," he wrote a friend. He did stay, either on the way to or from the front and during a heavy bombardment, at Madrid's Hotel Florida, but he does not appear to have spent time with Hemingway, Dos Passos, or any of the other foreign journalists assembled there. And he did meet Jeanson, in Madrid at the time as a correspondent for the satirical weekly *Le Canard Enchaîné*. Jeanson saw to it that Saint-Exupéry got out of town: He knew the leader of the Fédération Anarchiste Ibérique (FAI), who arranged for the transportation of the two journalists to the front. Buenaventura Durruti outfitted the Frenchmen with a chauffeured Rolls-Royce and affably sent them off, wishing them a pleasant stay in Spain. The driver conformed to what one might expect of an anarchist's chauffeur: he flew over the rutty, uneven roads that led to the city's southwestern edge at high speed, singing love songs and gaily engaging in a game the drivers had invented. When another of the party's cars approached, the two accelerated; by way of salute they attempted, at ninety miles per hour, to relieve the other of his fender. Jeanson disapproved of this manner of greeting and counseled the driver to be a little more considerate of his spanking-new Rolls. Saint-Exupéry was of little help: he wickedly informed the driver that his friend was prepared to give him a bonus of 500 pesetas for every fender removed. At this the chauffeur changed his tune to the "Internationale" and stepped on the gas.

On the front the writer proved no less intrepid, playing a version of Russian roulette that the anarchists had invented, performed with a lighted stick of dynamite. Equally courageous were his absentminded moments, on which he himself unabashedly reported. In the front-line trenches of the Guadalajara front a little over a week later he started one night to light up a cigarette. Two powerful hands put an end to his stupidity, which was met with the whistle of bullets. "One does not light a cigarette in the face of the enemy," Saint-Exupéry concluded. On another occasion, toward 3:00 a.m., he slipped into a prohibited area to observe the anarchists loading a shipment of matériel into a cargo train. Somehow he had convinced himself that he would be invisible in the dark; the barrel of a gun against his stomach proved him wrong. Hands in the air, he waited for the anarchist to fire ("It was a time of precipitous judgments," he noted), a moment that never came. Instead he was led, at gunpoint, to a dingy underground guard station. He was searched and his fate was discussed in Catalan, yet another language he did not speak. His camera, seemingly a piece of incriminating evidence, was seized and passed around. He tried to impress upon his captors that he was a journalist, but when asked for his papers had to admit he had left them at the hotel.

Saint-Exupéry proved as reluctant as ever to use the word "courage" but at the same time remained preoccupied by an old question, the one he had put to Henri Delaunay years earlier at Cape Juby. One night on the Carabanchel front he watched as an attack was prepared, then called off. The sergeant who was to have led it was awakened—by a group of soldiers and the Frenchman, all seated on his bed—with the news that he was not to race out to meet his death that morning. As Saint-Exupéry saw it, the sergeant had gone to sleep with a death sentence and risen with a pardon. "How does man receive the gift of life? I can answer that. A man sits still, pulls a bit of tobacco out of his pocket, nods his head slowly, looks up at the ceiling, and says, 'Suits me,' " he wrote. In his mind he had only one question for the officer: "Sergeant, what is it that makes you willing to die?" He had, of course, some experience with this mystery, which helped him to formulate his answer. Under Daurat's command he had fought a kind of battle and he understood its attractions; the camaraderie, the discipline, the higher calling of *la Ligne* had all been carried over from the Great War. He had loved that displaced war as much as he was now repulsed by the real thing, but was quick to see that all men thirsted for communion, for a cause. All ideology was simply a means to an end, an attempt to quench a deep-seated thirst. In satisfying that need man fulfilled himself, he argued, falling back on every one of his favorite images: it delivered man from his cocoon, it awakened in him the sleeping prince, it was as much a part of the natural order of things as eels flocking to the sea, wild gazelles returning from captivity to the desert. He had been as susceptible to this "brotherhood in the face of danger" as anyone; he had written odes to its liberating power for years. "Pilots meet if they are fighting to deliver the same mail; the Brown Shirts, if they are offering their lives to the same Hitler; the mountain climbers, if they are aiming for the same peak. Men do not unite by moving toward each other directly but only by losing themselves in the same god," he noted, unable to condemn any man for seeing to a need as basic as that for water.

In both of his absentminded moments Saint-Exupéry discovered another kind of communion. After enemy fire had deprived him of his cigarette he witnessed an amazing scene, which he recast slightly with a wink to Léon Werth. "Looks as if the lads across the way were awake," one of the Loyalists commented after the shots that had greeted the visitor's lighted match. "Do you think they'll talk tonight? We'd like to talk to them." From behind their stone wall one of the Loyalist sentinels called across to the enemy, "Antonio! Are you asleep? Antonio! It's me! Leo!" His call was not met by gunfire but, after a long silence, by "Quiet! Go to bed! Time to sleep!" Delighted by this bit of motherly advice from the enemy a Loyalist flew a second volley out into the night. It sounded as if he had been coached by the visiting Frenchman: "Antonio, what are you fighting for?" he called. "Spain!" came back the answer. "You?" "The bread of our brothers," responded the Loyalist, and the two wished each other a good night. "Their words were not the same, but their truths were identical," wrote Saint-Exupéry in *Wind, Sand and Stars*, displaying the same impatience for partisanship that had made him such a disarming moderator that night years before on the rue de Chanaleilles. In the guardhouse to which he had been taken by the train-loading anarchists he was held under surveillance by a team of very bored guards. He suffered mostly from their nerve-racking indifference, which offered no clue as to his fate. Again a cigarette saved the day. One of his jailers was smoking; with a vague smile Saint-Exupéry gestured that he would like very much to do the same. To his stupefaction the guard stretched, studied his prisoner for a moment, and smiled back. "It was like the break of day," wrote Saint-Exupéry, delivered by this simple exchange. The cigarette was offered, "and, the ice broken, the other guards, too, became men again; I entered into their smiles as into a new and free country. . . . We met in a smile above language, castes, parties."

Writing of such moments he was more than ever a man distinctly out of step with his time, searching for the common bond while those around him were busily clarifying their differences. In part a basic humility saved him from becoming a political creature. He who had written so vividly of his need for tenderness knew how vulnerable a man could be: "We men put on grand airs, but in our heart of hearts we know hesitation, doubt, distress." In part he was an innocent, applying to the body politic the lessons he had learned on the airline. His aristocratic birth helped to save him, too, hoisting him above the fray; he loved the species, he would say, but not the masses. He had never been a believer in systems—his was an overweening faith that life lay in the contradictions, not in the formulae, in the doubting, not the certainties, the needs rather than the riches—and political parties seemed to him little more than artificial structures designed to save man from his loneliness. He was as much opposed to war as reminded in Madrid of why men were attracted to it. While he had no respect for Franco—Jeanson said he sputtered when he so much as heard the name—he came back from Spain as agnostic as ever. Davet saw that in his respect for the Loyalists' courage he had somewhat identified with their cause. Difficult though it was, however—Saint-Exupéry left the country the day after German aircraft supporting Franco's Nationalists bombed the Basque town of Guernica—he continued to take only one side: that of the individual against whatever threatened his sovereignty. "Franco's soldier is noble; his opponent as well. I condemn any school of thought which—for coherency's sake—is forced to reduce the enemy army to a pack of pillaging, imbecilic peons," he wrote, as direct a political statement as he would make during these years, no heyday of ecumenicalism, in his notebook.

~

Saint-Exupéry returned to Paris at the end of April well-versed, as he had not been before, in the difference between an anarchist and a Communist, but without a scrap of paper to show *Paris-Soir*. When May began to slip by and no text appeared forthcoming Henri Mille and Jean Provoust began to worry: would the war end before *Paris-Soir* was able to publish its special correspondent's report? Fleury, then also employed by the paper, was this time dispatched to look after Saint-Exupéry. Every day he badgered him by telephone, and every day the truant supplied him with a fine excuse for delaying the delivery of his text. At last he was licensed to resort to more drastic measures: Fleury invited Saint-Exupéry to dinner at the paper's expense. "Terrific," responded the reporter, "we'll have foie gras!" Several days later Fleury carried Saint-Exupéry's first pages to the newspaper himself. Mille knew his writer well enough to proceed with caution, however, and did not run the piece immediately for fear that it might have no immediate successor. Sure enough Saint-Exupéry stalled again; only by the end of June did Mille have three articles in hand. These he began to run on the twenty-seventh of the month. A fourth installment was promised for early July but did not appear on schedule; Mille had spent two days biting his fingernails when his writer finally called to say it was ready. It was scheduled for the following day's paper, and a cyclist was sent to pick it up. Mille had just finished reading the article when its author strode into the *Paris-Soir* offices, toward five in the afternoon. He needed the piece back, he explained, as he had forgotten to add something. Mille handed him his pages and watched helplessly as Saint-Exupéry proceeded to tear them up, stuffing the scraps of paper in his pocket.

In the end Mille got only three of his ten pieces—for which Saint-Exupéry had been paid in advance—in 1937. The rest of his Spain reporting, the bulk of which appears, slightly reworked, in *Wind, Sand and Stars*, he kept to himself until the following year, partly because he procrastinated and had not yet had a chance to cast it as he liked. (Three additional pieces, for which he was presumably not paid a second time, appeared in *Paris-Soir* just after the Munich Pact on October 2, 3, and 4, 1938.) Many of the stories of Saint-Exupéry the perfectionist date from this time: Jeanson was not the only friend who was collared for an urgent, unbiased opinion (although Saint-Exupéry seemed to revise according to his own instincts and not according to the suggestions of those friends bold enough to offer advice), and Mille was not the only editor to see his text disappear before his eyes. Gallimard, too, watched as Saint-Exupéry began to cut ten unnecessary lines from a *Marianne* piece and—marking up the page proofs with his pen—proceeded to revise his entire text at the printer's. He was obsessed with the need to be perfectly understood or, as he put it, "*reçu*." He procrastinated and procrastinated, hurriedly cobbled together a draft at the last minute, then revised over and over, beyond the point where he could comfortably do so. He played, in short, as fast and loose with the rules of journalism as with those of aviation.

There were times and places in 1937 where it was better to play by the rules, as the writer discovered this July. In midmonth he set out for a trip of several days with Madame de B in the Simoun. The two went first to Amsterdam, then on to Berlin, where Saint-Exupéry was surprised to find the French air attaché waiting for him at the airfield. Already much of the German sky had been declared restricted, a fact he either did not know or chose to ignore. He had not filed a flight plan; as soon as the Simoun had been spotted a call had been made to the French embassy. Nor did his trespasses end here. From Berlin Saint-Exupéry and his companion flew to Frankfurt, with the intention of visiting friends in Rüdesheim, outside the city. Over central Germany, about 6,000 feet above Kassel, the Simoun filled with a foul odor. It seemed as if paint was burning; distressed, Saint-Exupéry turned circles over the city, where he knew he could safely make an emergency landing. He left Madame de B at the controls while he checked behind the seats but found nothing amiss. While the smell persisted the Simoun gave no sign of trouble, and after circling five or six times the pilot continued on toward Frankfurt. His friends had informed him that the airfield at nearby Wiesbaden was prettier than that of Frankfurt; it was here that the Simoun now headed. Saint-Exupéry was prepared for a lovely airstrip but surprised all the same by the surreal sight of a beautifully manicured but unmarked and deserted field. It was a hot day; a lone windsock fluttered in the light breeze.

Saint-Exupéry landed to find he was far from alone on the Wiesbaden airfield. Instantly a swarm of Hitler Youth, bare-chested and in black shorts, materialized out of nowhere. Chattering away excitedly they surrounded the Simoun, in which pilot and passenger were held captive. An officer soon arrived on the scene and made a half-successful attempt at interrogating the foreign pilot. Saint-Exupéry answered in all the languages he knew, none of which was German. After a laborious exchange he was, however, made to understand that he had landed on a highly restricted military airfield. Resorting to mime—which seemed to work better than Arabic or Provençal—he offered to take off and land properly at Frankfurt. Nothing doing, replied the officer, repeating something about Kassel, spies, and Berlin. It turned out that an important chemical plant was located in Kassel, accounting for the odor over the city and—thought the Germans—for the Frenchman's suspicious behavior. Changing tacks, Saint-Exupéry entered into a negotiation for permission to get out of the airplane. It was, after all, a blisteringly hot day, not the only reason he was drenched in sweat. Without mentioning that she spent it at her pilot's side, Madame de B provided the only account we have of the afternoon in her biography of Saint-Exupéry:

> After a thousand tergiversations, it was agreed that the airplane would be "pushed to the edge of the airfield" and that the suspects would be permitted to sit under its wings while awaiting a verdict. It was noon. A lovely summer afternoon went by in this manner: Saint-Exupéry, stretched out on the grass, sometimes laughing, sometimes fretting, smoked and downed the beers delivered to him by the future Luftwaffe pilots. Toward six in the afternoon an old officer drove up and walked toward the airplane. In fractured French he explained that Saint-Ex was accused of espionage, that he had circled Kassel to take photos and then had come to reconnoiter the military airfield at Wiesbaden.

Through Madame de B's excellent connections the two were finally allowed to continue on to Frankfurt. Although the French ambassador in Berlin vouched for their innocence, they were accompanied on their flight by a German officer; he took the only passenger seat in the Simoun. Madame de B squeezed in between the two men. On leaving the ground Saint-Exupéry saw that the Hitler Youth had assembled to see him off. He could not resist turning once around the field, initiating a dive, and flying over their heads. Directly below the wheels of the airplane fifty young arms went up in a Nazi salute. The German officer held on to his seat, unhappily.

Several hours later Saint-Exupéry was seated at a table overlooking the Rhine, drinking a beer and smoking a cigarette, discussing National Socialism with a young German woman. It was not yet too late for a theoretical conversation; it was still possible for a Frenchman to sit in a German restaurant and discuss the problems with that country's ruling ethos the way Frenchmen had sat in cafés at home and discussed what was wrong with their own for most of the 1930s. A fair number of Frenchmen had already begun to wonder aloud what it was the Germans were doing right: their country was in a shambles, and in leaps and bounds Germany was taking her place as the leader of Europe. As late as March

1938 Janet Flanner would report in *The New Yorker* that so long as war had not happened the French were willing to conclude that nothing at all had happened. They remained stubbornly preoccupied with their own problems—in particular with the state of the franc—as if those of the rest of Europe would go away if no Frenchman were around to hear the noise. There was all the same a sort of schizophrenia to the summer and fall, which began with a bang with the Semaine Artistique Allemande, an official Nazi propaganda week on the Champs-Élysées. German families traveled en masse across the border to the exposition, while at the same time, east of Strasbourg, at the French end of the Kehl bridge over the Rhine, a strange turret went up. "If it contains anything," wrote Janet Flanner, "[it] contains something that, if popped out, would aim straight toward the German sentries at the bridge's other end."

In what felt like the comfortable shade of the Maginot fortifications, France's were of course the feeblest of preparations. Nowhere was this more true than in the field of aeronautics. If the man in the street was tempted to think that Hitler was doing something right, any Frenchman vaguely associated with aviation had legitimate reason to agree. In 1935 France had had the largest military air force in Europe. In two years her production had fallen—despite a vastly increased budget—to thirty-seven aircraft a month. At the same time Germany was turning out 800 to 1,000 first-line warplanes a month. Many French aeronautics experts left for England; crippled by nationalization—at one point, with over 150,000 workers on strike, the entire industry skidded to a halt—France sought to purchase airplanes from the United States while she revamped her own program. The instability of the country as a whole took its toll on aviation: In the previous eight years France had had nine different air ministers and eight different air force chiefs-of-staff. By 1937 she held few of the new air records and was responsible for little that was new from an engineering point of view. Her presence in the air consisted less now of progress than of symbol: the world's largest flying boat, a Latécoère 521 christened the *Lieutenant-de-Vaisseau-Paris*, was her pride and joy.

Originally conceived as a luxury aircraft, the Latécoère's main salon had been exquisitely decorated with red-lacquered walls; its sixteen deluxe cabins—each of which bore the name of a constellation—included beds and bathrooms; its silver came from Puyforçat. Having sunk off the coast of Florida in 1936 the seaplane was now a less sumptuous vessel, but at the end of 1937 it nevertheless set five world records with Guillaumet at the controls. The fact remained, however, that the *Lieutenant-de-Vaisseau-Paris*, which dated from 1935, had been three years in the building at a cost exceeding $1.5 million. On the eve of World War II France had—for a whole array of social and political reasons, some of which had accounted for her earlier successes—still not managed to turn out either a cheap, mass-produced airplane or car. (Many "doodlebug-sized" vehicles were displayed at the thirty-first Salon d'Automobile in Paris in the fall of 1937, but these amounted literally to a case of too little too late.) The leading producer of aircraft matériel in World War I, the country found herself outpaced and outproduced by late 1939, when it mattered. As for the *Lieutenant-de-Vaisseau-Paris*, the aircraft fared slightly better than her first cousin, the *Normandie*. The seaplane, which was used briefly for maritime surveillance before the fall of France, was destroyed by the retreating Germans in 1944.

What was Saint-Exupéry, a man who could be counted on for nothing if not perspective, thinking as 1937 wore on? He had witnessed the bloodshed of Spain; he had met his Hitler Youth. He had seen France lose her lead in the air and he had listened to Mermoz and Guillaumet and Daurat and a host of friends and air ministry officials of different political persuasions expound on the tragedy. He continued to deal with these issues—and the others of the day—on a higher plane. In his notebooks he grappled with economic theory and its social implications, with the absurdity of any kind of patriotism founded on a forced conformity, with the invidiousness of politics. These ideas he set down more by way of meditation than by argument; dense with contradiction, these pages were never meant for anyone's eyes but his own. Taken as a whole, however, they are valuable in that they tell us where Saint-Exupéry was when he was not participating in the dinner conversation, not castigating the French government of the moment, not involving himself in the unfolding dramas of the air ministry. Trying to make sense of a minister's new policy with Werth one night, Saint-Exupéry stopped his friend in midthought: "Careful, I think we are anthropomorphizing." From Freud to Marx to Einstein he was entirely taken with the intellectual issues of his time, but the pages of his notebooks of the late 1930s so seldom address current events that they can prove near-impossible to date. At the heart of their ramblings lay several insistent concerns: how to reconcile an individual's thirst for profit with some social good; how to allow for a maximum of liberty in a world prone to tyranny; how to apply the happy lessons of Aéropostale to a social structure; how to nourish and motivate man in a machine age. Ségogne remembered that Saint-Exupéry returned from Moscow fascinated by the differences in speed with which a philosopher and a technician worked. Nothing in the world could make the former think more quickly while everything in the world—and profit first and foremost—conspired to make the latter produce more quickly. The result, Saint-Exupéry argued, is that we live in a technological age for which we are not yet spiritually prepared.

He conjured at the same time with a number of inventions. In 1937 he filed patents for two radio-navigation systems and a device for measuring fuel consumption. His reading had grown more and more technical; he read only science when writing himself. Madame de B reported that the pile on his bedside table included works by the mathematician James Jeans, the British astronomer Arthur Eddington, and the physicists Max Planck and Louis de Broglie, most of them pioneers in quantum theory. He was particularly fascinated by research into the nature of the atom and with the concept of entropy, investigations that yielded up a metaphysical side. He enjoyed lively discussions with Fernand Holweck, the French physicist and inventor. At the same time he also began the work he referred to as his "poem," a book that bore no resemblance at all to anything he had written before and had more in common with the florid, aphoristic style and near-biblical presentation of Gide's *Nourritures terrestres* or Nietzsche's *Thus Spake Zarathustra*. He remained on the Air France payroll. Though he seems rarely to have lectured this year, Renault was still, at the end of 1937, supplying him with the latest facts and figures regarding its aviation program for his publicity work. In June he was promoted to captain in the reserve. It is unlikely that he thought much about the honor, which amounted to a formality; nothing about his comportment over the next year suggested that Saint-Exupéry expected to see himself in an air force uniform, though by the summer of 1939 he was saying, half in jest, that in the event of an outbreak of hostilities his captain's cap was ready. Like the rest of France he had his own business to attend to: at the end of the year he stepped up his preparations for a third long-distance flight.

Madame de B asserted early on what has generally been accepted as fact: that Saint-Exupéry set out for what seemed at the time a gratuitous *raid* and would in retrospect appear to be a matter of pure folly because his life with Consuelo had become untenable. This was doubtless true, if conclusions can be drawn from the fact that by late 1938 the couple were living separately. As early as the summer of 1936 Saint-Exupéry had, however, been planning an American trip. It had initially been suggested to him by Conty; if I were you, Conty had told him in 1935, I would do something no Frenchman has yet done—fly the length of North and South America—especially as you already know the southern route. Saint-Exupéry seems to have been seduced by the fact that a straight line can be drawn longitudinally from Montreal to Punta Arenas. Evidently without consulting his friend, he sent his curriculum vitae to a New York–based journalist in June 1936 to ask for help in setting up a speaking tour. He proposed a month-long stay in America in April and May, during which he would lecture, in French, on "Aviation and Civilization." Conty, he proposed, would speak on the operations of the European and trans-Atlantic airlines.

The American network of Alliances Françaises evidently committed themselves to the venture, which over the next year evolved into a flight covering both American continents but involving no lecture work. Saint-Exupéry began to ready his papers in March 1937, by which time he must have known he had the support of the air ministry, if not of Air France as well. (Sending a prominent aviator abroad in a familiar airplane to herald the glories of a country's industry while at home that industry moldered amounted either to loose management of funds or an exercise in self-delusion, but the French faith in appearances was—in lieu of more substantive balms—by now stronger than ever.) By the fall of 1937 the Americas trip had become a reality; the ministry—billing the flight as a publicity trip to be undertaken by Saint-Exupéry in conjunction with the aviatrix Maryse Bastié, heading south from Montreal—wrote and cabled for the many necessary permissions. Saint-Exupéry's own correspondence this winter included a series of long letters to Renault and its insurers regarding Raccaud's expenses, for which the Wadi Natroun engineer was reimbursed only in November, twenty-two months after the Libyan crash.

~

Saint-Exupéry, André Prévot, and the crated-up Simoun F-ANXR sailed for New York on the *Île-de-France* during the first week of January 1938. The trip had continued to evolve, both in terms of schedule and itinerary. The French consular staff who had obtained landing rights for the pilot had been under the impression that he was to take off from Montreal on October 14, 1937; in November Prévot was still writing Saint-Exupéry notes about work that was being done on the Simoun's propeller and on its new radio. In December the air ministry thought the departure imminent; neither pilot nor mechanic obtained his American visa until after the New Year, by which time the Simoun's test flights had finally been completed (and when Maryse Bastié was already in Uruguay, as part of her goodwill tour of South America). Gaston Lavoisier, who test-flew the Simoun at Le Bourget, remembered Saint-Exupéry only in foul moods. The pilot was displeased with the flight results, expecting more of the aircraft than it could reliably deliver, and unappreciative of Lavoisier's cautions as to its limitations. Perhaps with his counsel in mind the pilot repeatedly made a curious claim in the weeks preceding his departure for South America. On the *Île-de-France* he told an acquaintance that he was setting off despite the fact that he was going to have a serious accident, which he would survive. In New York he told one friend he was doing "what he had to do," another that he knew the trip to be a vain conceit, but thought it probably his last shot at a long-distance flight. To others he confided, "This trip is risky." Then he would touch wood and add, "Fortunately I'm lucky. Nothing will happen to me." The record does not show if Prévot was on hand or not for these pronouncements; he was in any event to find out about his boss's clairvoyance soon enough.

In New York Saint-Exupéry checked into a twenty-fifth-floor room at the Barbizon Plaza Hotel on January 11. He saw friends, and he met with Eugene Reynal and Curtice Hitchcock. The vice president of the Century Company, which had brought out *Night Flight*, Hitchcock had known Saint-Exupéry since 1932, when the two men had met for dinner in Paris. (Consuelo had served memorably as interpreter, and Fargue as program director, until the wee hours of the morning.) He and Reynal, who had met Saint-Exupéry separately in Paris in 1932 and shared his colleague's admiration for his work, were now doing business as Reynal & Hitchcock. For some time they had been eager to make the Frenchman their author. (In an exchange fitting to the life, Hitchcock had asked a representative to speak to the author about the American rights to his books at the end of 1933. The representative had written back that December: "St.-Exupéry spent two minutes under the water in an airplane accident near Nice a few days ago. When he returns to Paris I shall get in touch with him.") Probably at this time the pilot agreed to let an impish man of courtly demeanor and quiet humor serve as his literary agent in America. A Cairo-born, Sorbonne-educated thirty-six-year-old of Austrian and French descent, Maximilian Becker had come to New York as a concert pianist, having seranaded the king of Siam. Shortly after his arrival he fractured both wrists while ice-skating; he never again touched a piano (or an ice skate), opening a literary agency instead. Among his early clients he counted Simenon and several other French writers; Jean Prévost introduced him to Saint-Exupéry.

With Becker's help the writer prevailed now on a fresh set of editors with a fresh set of results. (Parisian publishers and newspapermen had grown a little tired of his tin-cup routine. Gallimard remembered that on one occasion, when Saint-Exupéry had pushed his charity to the limit, the writer headed off to see Jean Provoust at *Paris-Soir*. Provoust had left strict instructions that he was not to be let in, but Saint-Exupéry managed to charm his way into the newspaper owner's office anyway, only to be told he could not have a loan. "Who do you take me for? God himself?" exploded Provoust. Taken aback, Saint-Exupéry replied, "Yes," and left with a check.) In New York he submitted a few disparate pieces of journalism to Eugene Reynal, billing them as the first three or four chapters of a new book. Reynal did not read French easily but was able to see that the pages—most likely the *Marianne* series of 1932 and an assortment of *Paris-Soir* articles—were rough and rather disconnected. They were beautiful, however, and Saint-Exupéry claimed to need some special equipment for the South American flight, and with Becker's help a very favorable contract was drawn up for a new book, separate from the author's standing agreement with Gallimard. All of this happened quickly; the contract—granting Saint-Exupéry the largest advance he had yet commanded—was signed a week after his arrival.

Saint-Exupéry was less impressed by the frenetic pace of New York life than by various aspects of American aviation, which he found to be superbly organized. He was especially taken with continual radio broadcasts, by which a pilot could navigate along aerial highways, an advance that had not yet come to France. He claimed it had taken him only two hours to familiarize himself with a system that was most of all superior in its very simplicity: "With the American navigation system, any tourist, even one unfamiliar with radios, can fly through the night in perfect safety," he marveled, probably lamenting a little his original Simoun. American broadcasts came in very handy in his case. As a test run for the new Simoun he offered to take Richard de Roussy de Sales, then a *Paris-Soir* correspondent in New York, to Washington, where Roussy de Sales had business. First he asked if Roussy de Sales had ever flown to Washington before; he had, often. Once in the air Saint-Exupéry turned to his passenger and asked, "Now, which way?" He could not believe that—having gone by air to Washington many times before—the journalist did not know the route, and he had brought no map. (Nor could the air traffic controller in the Washington tower believe that the pilot landed without contacting him, an oversight for which Roussy de Sales was forced to expiate through embassy channels.) The Simoun had been uncrated and reassembled at Newark airport, while Saint-Exupéry conferred on his routing with officials of Pan American Airways. The airline was then flying three times weekly from Brownsville, Texas, to Guatemala City and on to Panama; their representatives counseled the Frenchman to use this southbound corridor, after which he could continue down the west coast of South America to Punta Arenas. A sustained flight over the Caribbean—Saint-Exupéry's original intention had been to hop from Florida to Cuba to Panama and on to Ecuador—in a single-engine aircraft seemed inadvisable, although the pilot balked a little at the reasonable suggestion. "I prefer to be over water than lost among a bunch of stones with which I'm unfamiliar," he commented. He was, however, officially in America on a goodwill mission and not on a record-setting flight—his insurance covered him only for the former—and, deciding in favor of caution, he borrows Pan Am's slightly longer route to South America.

The Simoun was test-flown at least four times at Newark without incident, but Saint-Exupéry and Prévot's first two attempts at departures for their 9,000-mile flight were thwarted by heavy rains. On the morning of Tuesday, February 15, unwilling to wait any longer, Saint-Exupéry made a third start, although the weather had not entirely cleared and he was forced by fog and head winds to land in Atlanta and in Houston.

(Later he boasted that—the radio-navigation system being as good as it was—he had not once consulted his map between New York and Atlanta. He certainly had not pored over it at the last minute: Curtice Hitchcock attested that he could think of nothing on the eve of his departure but the highly elaborate wristwatch he had just acquired.) South of Houston the weather presented no problems, and Saint-Exupéry made only brief, scheduled stops in Mexico City and Veracruz. Madame de B called him in the coastal town as he had asked her to, having supplied the telephone numbers of all the airfields in advance. He was ecstatic to hear her voice; she could hear the noises from the airstrip in the background as they spoke. The Simoun continued on to Guatemala City, where the pilot must have made a last-minute decision to stop. His original intention—one to which the French minister to Central America had been alerted, though later than he liked to know such things—had been to fly from Veracruz over Guatemala and directly on to Nicaragua. Saint-Exupéry landed at the La Aurora airfield in Guatemala City at about 12:30 p.m. on the sixteenth and in his brief ground time again revised his itinerary. He now proposed to continue nonstop on to the Panama Canal Zone but changed his mind after conferring with Pan Am officials at La Aurora, who warned him he would have trouble taking off with enough fuel to make it through to Panama; the altitude of the La Aurora field favored a lighter aircraft. He revised his flight plan accordingly (the embassy officials had had the good sense to obtain visas for him for every country in which he might conceivably land), cabling the news to the *Paris-Soir* correspondents in New York who were following the trip: "IMPOSSIBLE TO TAKE ON SUFFICIENT FUEL BECAUSE ALTITUDE AND VERY UNEVEN STRIP. WILL STOP-OVER MANAGUA."

Several minutes later the two men climbed into the Simoun. Saint-Exupéry performed his run-up and at about 1:30 taxied down the mile-long runway. It was a windless, hot afternoon. At the north end of the field, beyond a low fence, lay an abandoned gravel pit, on the far side of which stood an aqueduct. These now began to approach although the Simoun had not yet picked up the speed necessary for takeoff. As the end of the field loomed Saint-Exupéry attempted to pull the airplane up anyway—he could have done little else—but it settled down again. He maneuvered to the left to avoid the oncoming fence and attempted to bounce the Simoun into the air, but the aircraft only shuddered back to earth a second time from a height of about seven feet, losing part of its left wing and the left aileron to a fence post, crashing nose first into the gravel pit, bouncing about forty feet farther along the ground, twisting around 180 degrees as it did so, and depositing Prévot in its wake, pinned down by the engine.

This time Saint-Exupéry did not leap from the wreckage. He was found still in his seat in the demolished cockpit. According to the head of the

American Legation in Guatemala, who was on the scene within fifteen minutes of the accident, the instrument panel, firewall, and engine had all been shorn from their places, leaving the front of the cockpit entirely open. None of this is obvious in photographs of the crash, in which the Simoun looks like a mangled lump of scrap metal and from no angle bears a resemblance to anything that flies. Saint-Exupéry was not much better off himself. As he commented later, "When they pulled me from the plane, I was the biggest piece of wreckage." He later ascribed his survival to the very fragility of the aircraft, which had crumbled on impact. In a more solid aircraft he imagined that he would have roasted to death.

An ambulance pulled up instantly to transport the two men to a military hospital. By all rights the Simoun should have burst into flames, taking the flyers with it, especially as the area around the crash was drenched in fuel. Saint-Exupéry and Prévot, who were still conscious as they were carried off the field, did not look particularly lucky, however, and the first reports had it that neither man would live. Both were bloody messes; Saint-Exupéry had clearly suffered extreme head injuries, and Prévot's right leg was mutilated, broken in several places. For a variety of reasons they had now flown together for the last time. The French minister to Central America, Monsieur Lavondes, sent word to the Quai d'Orsay a few hours after the crash that both men wanted to reassure their families that they were alive. Prévot supplied his father's name and address; Saint-Exupéry asked that Madame de B be contacted. Shortly after having done so he lost consciousness.

Saint-Exupéry's goodwill mission of 9,000 miles had generated few headlines outside the pages of *Paris-Soir*. His crash 3,400 miles into the trip made news in many countries, although French reporters generally shied away from the cause of it: the Simoun's gas tanks had, despite the Pan Am warning, been overfilled. Probably Prévot operated on the assumption that a Guatemalan gallon and an American gallon are the same, whereas in fact an Imperial gallon is closer to five liters and a U.S. gallon to about four. In any event it was Saint-Exupéry's responsibility as the Simoun's pilot to verify the state of the gas tanks. French journalists exonerated him by focusing on the inadequacies of the Guatemalan airfield, the result of which was a certain resentment in the Central American city against French aviation in general and French airplanes in particular, not exactly the intended fallout from an air ministry–sponsored goodwill mission. In some respects history had just repeated itself as farce, which may have explained why Saint-Exupéry—with an abundant sense of humor but a low tolerance for foolishness—did not anywhere write about this crash, which was to mark him more profoundly than any of the others. He could not have helped feeling a little embarrassed.

He did make occasional mention of his convalescence, which was long,

and which kept him in the Guatemala City hospital for over a month. He
was to claim that he lay for many days in a coma but no official report on
his condition corroborates this, and the fact that he managed to communicate daily with Madame de B would seem ample evidence to the
contrary. He did arrive at the hospital unconscious and displayed all the
signs of serious concussion, which goes in French by the impeccable name
of "*commotion cérébrale*," waking in a state of confusion no doubt exacerbated by the language barrier, a high fever, and a host of other injuries.
Listed by Dr. Echeverría Ávila, the colonel who headed the hospital, these
consisted of nasty bruises on his right wrist, elbow, and left forearm, and
damage to his left eye (Saint-Exupéry was particularly concerned about
his vision), the left side of his forehead, his bottom lip, his left shoulder,
and his chest. His heart was racing. Overlooked were several actual
fractures—Saint-Exupéry would maintain always that there had been
eight and doubtless now felt there were at least twice that many—including
one in his left shoulder, which as a consequence healed badly, preventing
the pilot from ever again lifting his left arm above his head.

Later he wrote in *Harper's Bazaar* of how he had floated back to the
real world in the Guatemalan hospital "through a thick syrupy atmosphere." One night he awoke, freezing cold, and begged his nurse for the
sheet "that heals wounds." The nurse protested that such a thing did not
exist. He tried to picture himself making his army bed, saw that there had
been a top and a bottom but no third sheet, and decided she must be
right. Nonetheless sometime after the crash he found himself back in
Lyons, at the little station at the top of the funicular that runs up to the
Fourvière basilica. There at the exit were the same advertisements he had
known as a child, among them a poster for "Girardot's Linen Sheets—a
sovereign soother of aches, pains, and wounds." The image, wrote Saint-
Exupéry, had been "tucked away in a dim corner of my mind for nearly
thirty years." In fact it had not been bundled away so neatly and never
would be. In signal acts of tenderness sheets get smoothed—or do their
soothing act—in every one of his works, from the short story "Manon
Danseuse" on.

Saint-Exupéry's friend Pierre de Lanux, an American-based professor
and lecturer, read about the accident in *The New York Times* of February
17. Within days he had decided to cancel his appointments for the week
and make the arduous trip from Cleveland—he had been on a lecture
tour when he got the news—to Guatemala City. He knew Saint-Exupéry's
life was not in danger but thought he must be lonely and in terrible pain.
(It was almost too perfect that he should have been reading La Boétie,
Montaigne's great friend, in the train from Louisville south.) A Guatemalan colonel accompanied him to the hospital on the twenty-second,

ushering him to a ground-floor room off a lushly planted courtyard. There was continual commotion in the court, but Saint-Exupéry's quarters were quiet, even without the luxury of a door. He must have been overjoyed to see Lanux, who in addition to being a stalwart and erudite friend spoke twice as much Spanish as did he, conjuring together Latin, French, and his abundant charm. Lanux found the patient lying on his back, his hands bandaged, on the mend but in poor shape. Most impressive was the wound to the face, which ran from Saint-Exupéry's eyebrow to his eyelid and pointed to an inflamed and bloodshot left eye. The patient complained of internal pains and moved his upper torso with great difficulty; he had an appetite only for milk and meat and suffered a burning sensation in his stomach. Moreover, as a result of the tetanus shots he had received, he was covered in hives.

His lodgings, however, were adequate and the personnel kind, which made sense since the race to pick up his hospital bill had been won by the Guatemalan government itself. The orderlies indulgently rolled his bed to a telephone so that he might call his Parisian friend. A French doctor had been sent from Mexico; having made a tour of Guatemala City's medical clinics, he decided that Saint-Exupéry was best off where he was. His patient was miserable and groaned a good deal; Lanux indulged him by slipping him aspirin, forbidden by the doctors, the only gifts, Lanux lamented later, he had ever been able to offer the friend who so often bestowed on him the middle-of-the-night pleasure of his half-minted prose.

Within forty-eight hours Lanux was off, leaving Saint-Exupéry to fend for himself. By nature he was of course the worst of patients: Guatemala left him with a number of persistent problems, some of them exacerbated by his imagination. Pélissier, himself a doctor, recalled having taken his friend to see an eminent colleague in Paris in 1939 for back pain which he suffered whenever he was upright. The doctor made his diagnosis and wrote Saint-Exupéry a prescription, which he felt would alleviate the worst of the problem. In the car leaving the appointment, the writer disputed the diagnosis point by point and proceeded to tear up the prescription, tossing its pieces to the winds. His immediate challenge in Guatemala was to keep his left arm, which became badly infected, and which the military doctors planned to amputate. He may have had some assistance in his campaign to hold on to it from Consuelo, who arrived in Guatemala aboard the *Wyoming* on March 5. She claimed later to have saved the arm but was not the only woman to say as much. After a few days at her husband's side she headed off to see her family in El Salvador, where Saint-Exupéry followed her for a ten-day stay after his release on the eighteenth, presumably now meeting his in-laws for the first time. As

Consuelo remembered the encounter, her father greeted her husband
warmly: "Come settle here. We will give you more plantations than
you can cross in an entire day in a powerful car." Respectfully Saint-
Exupéry responded: "My dear father-in-law, my dear mother-in-law,
it is too late for me to cultivate coffee beans. My job is to till the
clouds."

He was afterward flown back to New York on a Pan Am DC-3, an
airplane fitted with sleeping compartments, which he found roomy and
sensationally comfortable. He could not get over how far America had
taken night flying: the weather between Dallas and New York had been
dreadful, and the DC-3's pilots had flown the entire route on instruments.
Saint-Exupéry was shocked to find the aircraft's other passengers wholly
indifferent to this arrangement. He arrived in New York on March 28 and
fell into the arms of Guillaumet, in the United States on Air France
business at the time. Madame de B met him in New York as well and
arranged for him to borrow the Beekman Place apartment of a very close
friend, Colonel William J. Donovan, head of the OSS in World War II.
As Donovan's daughter's room had the best view, giving on to the East
River, Saint-Exupéry settled into her bright yellow quarters for the remainder of his convalescence. His friend stayed on with him for about a
month to see to his medical care, taking him to an osteopath daily. During
this time X-rays revealed a number of fractures that had been overlooked
in Guatemala, and the pilot discovered that, among other things, he had
lost his ability to hold his liquor.

He was, however, soon very much up and about, whipping up small
storms of static electricity by rubbing the soles of his shoes on Donovan's
carpet, then touching the key to the darkened apartment's door, and ac-
quainting himself with what seemed to him America's infinite variety of
gadgets, well-represented in the Beekman Place apartment. He enlisted
his host's law firm, Donovan & Leisure, to arrange for a sale of his patent
for a low-visibility landing device, something he had been eager to do for
some time. He ventured out to make his first real American purchases,
discovering to his joy that the language barrier afforded him the opportunity to assemble small harems of attractive salesgirls. He lost weight, as
he had after Libya, for the best. And he lunched now with Lewis Galantière, to whom both the Roussy de Sales brothers and Reynal and Hitchcock had introduced him before the crash. A Federal Reserve banker who
could claim the distinction of having found Hemingway his first Paris
apartment (slight and myopic, Galantière had not fared as well in the
ring as had Jean Prévost), Galantière had been educated in Paris and had
translated Sherwood Anderson into French. He continued to dabble in
criticism and fiction. He was now charged with the task of translating
Saint-Exupéry and of helping him to find a narrative device with which

to fit together his farrago of pieces. On Beekman Place the pilot began to sort through the journalism that had been his thirties, in search of a book.

~

Still looking haggard, Saint-Exupéry sailed back to France aboard the *Normandie* early in May. What little remained of the Simoun had already been arranged to be sold and returned separately; Saint-Exupéry had a merry time in July explaining to a Paris customs inspector, the kind of man who was his downfall, why he should not pay duty on the compass he was bringing back to France with him. Clearly this device had been part of the original Simoun, explained Saint-Exupéry through gritted teeth, "as it is impossible for an airplane to leave the factory, and navigate, without this instrument." A few items of sentimental interest—including a strip of red metal that Lanux had admired the previous year at Le Bourget—had been salvaged and carried by Lanux back to New York, wrapped in newspaper. These may or may not have included the pilot's maps and documents, which were sent back to France via the embassy and some time later returned to him. When they arrived he called Pélissier to join him in a package-opening ceremony. Together they tore at the paper; out of a fake leather briefcase in which Saint-Exupéry had filed his maps fell a quantity of Guatemalan earth and dried blood. Both men were silenced. Generally speaking it was a quiet return, not the kind of which headlines are made, and it was to be a quiet couple of months before Saint-Exupéry was—both spiritually and physically—recovered.

He moved about restlessly this summer. He was in Paris briefly in July when Eugene Reynal and his new wife came through town; the three enjoyed a long and festive lunch at the Ritz, ably translated by the lovely Elizabeth Reynal, who was as much at home in French as in English. Saint-Exupéry appeared in fine form, which must have been a relief to a publisher who had signed him on only to watch him check into a Guatemala City hospital. He kept the Reynals long at the table. The honeymooners were to head off for a trip around France; their new author insisted on providing them with a complete gastronomical itinerary, beginning with a four-star establishment outside Lyons, where the next day the Reynals found themselves sampling pâtés at 11:00 a.m. Having mentioned Saint-Exupéry's name they were not allowed from their table until well into the afternoon.

The writer was almost certainly in Agay when King George VI and Queen Elizabeth came to visit Paris in midmonth, a visit billed as the most extravagant public event since the Armistice. Planned as a gesture toward preserving European peace, the celebration—on which the French government spent over 24 million francs—turned into a four-day party, during which only those in Paris who were in uniform did anything resembling work. In Agay Saint-Exupéry got to know his sister Gabrielle's children, entertaining them with the magnificent new car he had managed to acquire, the most memorable feature of which from his niece Mireille's point of view was the electric razor on the dashboard. Her uncle explained that it was extremely practical for the man who was late, gleefully demonstrating his ability to shave and drive simultaneously. He tried to encourage Mireille to draw, producing for her a quick sketch of her future husband. The drawing of a handsome young man was captioned "A husband for Mireille, by her venerable and revered uncle, Antoine de Saint-Exupéry." Mireille was counseled to hang it over her bed and study it before sleep every night, so that she would recognize her intended when she met him.

Saint-Exupéry went on to Geneva and revisited his childhood haunts, in Fribourg and in Saint-Maurice-de-Rémens. He spent part of August with Yvonne de Lestrange at Chitré, where his conversation continued to dazzle André Gide and where his card tricks left his mentor convinced he was clairvoyant. He made a stop in a tiny town in southeastern France to call on Marguerite Chapeys, the former Saint-Maurice housekeeper, about to be made famous as the mistress of the linens in *Wind, Sand and Stars*. And most likely that summer he and Madame de B paid a visit to the Benedictine monastery at Solesmes, which Saint-Exupéry remembered from his childhood, and where he was overwhelmed by the beauty of the chants at vespers.

Everywhere he went he carried with him his bundle of journalism. By the time he arrived in Vichy for a cure in September—it was during this stay that he ran into his Strasbourg aviation instructor and recalled for the Aébys his first solo flight—the bundle had grown. He was still enough troubled by his injuries to consider surgery for some lingering problems but continued to work in his sporadic fashion, fixated on the book. Lewis Galantière spent the summer at Sherwood Anderson's estate in Trout Dale, Virginia, under a constant rain of letters from the author, whom he was translating furiously, although each missive—which instructed him to cut large portions of the adventure writing and proposed a multitude of tiny, stylistic revisions—did considerable damage to his schedule. (When he complained of this to Lazareff, the *Paris-Soir* editor could only regale him with stories of all the others who had suffered at the hands of Saint-Exupéry's perfectionism.) Galantière had made a number of editorial suggestions, chief among them that Saint-Exupéry concoct better transitions between various sections (the Spanish sections proved especially problematic), that he write an expanded chapter on the machine, that he give some thought to unifying his remarks on aviation and its place in the modern world, that he add new material to the manuscript. More action, less philosophy, counseled Galantière, who had from the start a clear vision of the book. As their translator could communicate with their author better than either of Saint-Exupéry's publishers Reynal and Hitchcock deferred to him editorially; it is unclear when Gallimard learned of the project, but it is certain that Galantière had no counterpart in France.

A great number of people were credited in a great number of dedications with the birth of *Wind, Sand and Stars*. (In Jean Prévost's copy Saint-Exupéry thanked the writer for having forced him to work and added that he hoped Prévost liked the book, as he had suggested he write it.) In France few were as instrumental as Hervé Mille, to whom Saint-Exupéry went in October because he once again found himself short of funds. (As interminable as his pecuniary difficulties seemed, they were to end with the publication of *Wind, Sand and Stars*, which Becker that month sold as well to a British publisher.) A percentage of the monies the writer had been advanced for the Guatemala trip had gone to the government as payment of back taxes, and the authorities were still after him. It seemed Saint-Exupéry had not felt it necessary to declare various subsidies he had received for the trip, as he had never seen this money himself; the French tax collectors felt differently. His accounts had been further depleted by the month's stay in New York, which had somehow, despite Donovan's hospitality, cost him more than 30,000 francs. He complained as well that he was running up substantial medical bills as a result of the crash. When the writer went to Mille looking for help the editor did not balk, despite the fact that Saint-Exupéry was already famously in debt to *Paris-Soir*. Instead Mille suggested that he might already have—among his *Air France* pieces, among the miscellaneous articles he had contributed to specialized aviation publications, among his rough drafts and false starts—something that he could sell the paper. He instructed him to collect all of his writings and to meet him the following evening near the Gare Montparnasse, at a comfortable restaurant. Saint-Exupéry arrived at Chez Jarraud with two bulging briefcases. After an excellent dinner author and editor cobbled together a series of three pieces, consisting as much of the writer's reflections as of his adventures.

Saint-Exupéry had been out of touch with his American publishers for large parts of the summer, much to their despair. By early fall Hitchcock had taken to telephoning Becker daily for news of his author, of which there was none. By October, however, Saint-Exupéry was ready to send on these 10,000 words, strung together at Chez Jarraud. "I think that this last chapter gives the book all its breadth," he wrote Becker on October 7, having cabled that the pages were traveling to New York on the *Normandie*. "I published it in three installments in *Paris-Soir* this week, to test the waters, and it was very well received." The articles in fact consisted of his delayed impressions of the Spanish Civil War; in October 1938 they were more timely than ever, less concerned with Spain than with man and war. Three days before they had begun to appear, France and Britain had agreed in Munich to the dismemberment of Czechoslovakia, an act about which few in France harbored illusions. When he returned to Paris after the signing of the pact, French premier Édouard Daladier was met by crowds at the airport; his initial reaction was that they were there to lynch him. Daladier knew very well that he had paid an enormous price for a brief delay of the inevitable. When it turned out that the airport crowds were admiring ones, he said under his breath, "The idiots, they don't know what they're applauding!" France was not, however, going to go to war over Czechoslovakia—57 percent of the population favored the Munich agreement, as did both *L'Intransigeant* and *Paris-Soir*, Paris's two most popular evening papers—even though troops had been in place along the Maginot Line since March.

Saint-Exupéry was as disturbed by the course of events as anyone— "When we thought peace was threatened, we discovered the abomination of war. When we thought war had been averted, we tasted the shame of peace," he wrote—and suggested to Becker that his agent try to cash in on the topicality of his pieces by selling them to an American magazine. They might run, he suggested, with a revised opening, with a few lines about the anxiety with which the French were following events in Central Europe. At Chez Jarraud Saint-Exupéry and Mille carved out six additional articles on the desert adventures, most of them reworked versions of the *Marianne* series of 1932 and the Air France pieces. These ran in *Paris-Soir* in November to extraordinary acclaim and were later folded, nearly word for word, into *Wind, Sand and Stars*.

Saint-Exupéry's had been a profitable housecleaning, though it drove Galantière to despair. He had been working as quickly as he could, shaping the book as he went. He had his hands full, given Saint-Exupéry's many convictions, great and small, and the writer's supple prose, cleaner now but no easier to translate than it had been years earlier for Stuart Gilbert. Translating from French into English is always a reductive act: it takes more words to say almost anything in French, and a translator working in that direction finds that whole seas of nuance evaporate when an attempt is made to channel them into English, a more specific language, that of business, not diplomacy. Raoul de Roussy de Sales put it best, speaking of literature of a different kind: "The difference between an American cookbook and a French one is that the former is very accurate and the second exceedingly vague. A French recipe seldom tells you how many ounces of butter to use to make *crêpes Suzette*, or how many spoonfuls of oil should go into a salad dressing. . . . American recipes look like doctors' prescriptions." Nowhere was this more true than with Saint-Exupéry's lyrical, image-heavy prose: what sounds lush in French—from Chateaubriand to Proust—will in a poor translation turn purple in English. From these kinds of embarrassments Galantière saved Saint-Exupéry, making no secret of his hard work, "because translating you is a little like translating Rimbaud." Privately, a little tug of war went on, as it will between editor and author, this one aggravated by the distance, by the author's constant emendations—he tried to cut nearly a quarter of his pages, though Galantière insisted on salvaging them for the American edition—and by the sheer size of the task. Early on Galantière told Saint-Exupéry that he was a miserable judge of his own prose. After a second collaboration he would allege that the author was virtually incapable of putting a book together on his own.

Ultimately Saint-Exupéry complied with Galantière's request for an additional chapter. Late in the year, at the suggestion of Hitchcock, who had presumably heard him tell the story, he wrote up his oft-told tale of the Patagonian cyclone. Titled "The Elements," the chapter makes for one of the most marked differences between two very different books, the English-language edition of *Wind, Sand and Stars*, in which it figures, and the French-language edition of *Terre des hommes*, in which it does not. This chapter was by no means written in the neat little hurricane in which it is said to have been: Saint-Exupéry worked and reworked these fourteen pages long after the rest of the book had fallen into place. Later he explained that the difficulty had come in casting the struggle in the simplest possible terms; he had needed to pare down his language so as to accentuate the enormity of the battle. He was still finishing the account when he asked Galantière to read through the American text from start to finish, probably in November, to see if it flowed well and seemed less a recycled series of articles, and if the last section, of which he was so proud, did not indeed seem a "crowning achievement." He wanted desperately for the whole to add up not to an adventure book but to a sort of moral call to arms, and to this end moved the section "The Men" to the front, so that the reader might be inspired by the examples of Guillaumet and Mermoz. This was not what Galantière had in mind—the philosophizing overlay is certainly what dates the book most—but it was what his author wanted. Moreover, it was, wrote Saint-Exupéry, applying a little pressure, also the right decision in the opinion of Gide, to whom he had shown the text. (At some point before or during the preparation of *Wind, Sand and Stars*, Gide is said to have pressed a copy of Conrad's 1906 *Mirror of the Sea* into Saint-Exupéry's hands, proof that it was perfectly legitimate to forge a book out of a loose collection of sketches.)

Saint-Exupéry was sufficiently obsessed with the project to talk of coming to New York at the end of the year to work with Galantière on the last chapters. He imagined a few days at sea to be just the kind of rest he needed, and thought he might continue on toward the heartland of America, where he hoped to begin a novel. (Becker encouraged him in this direction, promising that he could sell serial rights alone in the novel for $35,000 after the success *Wind, Sand and Stars* was bound to have.) The author did neither in 1938, when he appears more than anything else to have been casting about for a place to go. He found it at the Hôtel Lutétia, to which he returned in late September. The place Vauban was abandoned; Consuelo settled a few blocks away in a smallish apartment on the rue Barbet-de-Jouy, a hundred yards or so from the old rue de Chanaleilles apartment. Henceforth, save for a brief period in America, the Saint-Exupérys were to maintain separate addresses.

The writer was, all the same, often enough reduced to scouring the town—or the country—for his wandering wife. Toward the end of the year he moved as well to an apartment of his own, a small studio that he and Madame de B found together, at 52, rue Michel-Ange, in the 16th arrondissement. As he traveled to Algiers to see Pélissier just after Christmas 1938 and corrected the French proofs of the new book in Agay in January, the rue Michel-Ange initially provided him with little more than a mailing address. He did finally manage a two-week stay in America early in February 1939, by which time Reynal and Hitchcock had already bitten off their nails, as they had announced an early spring publication date for *Wind, Sand and Stars*. Their author arrived with revised text in hand but was spared his publishers' rage for two reasons: the pages were good, better than anyone had dared hope, and the book had been sold to the Book-of-the-Month Club, making it necessary—and profitable; Saint-Exupéry received nearly $5,000—to delay publication until summer. The writer spent his time looking over Galantière's shoulder and helping to coordinate the two editions, which for all his perfectionism he did not object to adapting to their different audiences. Probably it helped a little that for all his discussions with Galantière, he was unable to vet the English-language edition closely.

Nowhere is the difference between *Terre des hommes* and *Wind, Sand and Stars* more obvious than in the book's titles. Reynal and Hitchcock settled quickly on theirs, four words borrowed from the description of the enchanted desert evening Saint-Exupéry, Riguelle, Bourgat, et al. had spent outside Cape Barbas with their uncooperative Breguet 14's. The Americans were eager to publish a concrete text, not a philosophical treatise; the very name *Terre des hommes* made them tremble with fear before the book-buying public. Probably this emphasis on story accounts for the omission in the English-language edition of the four paragraphs that preface the French and read as a sort of personal manifesto. Borrowed from a 1937 eulogy to Mermoz, they establish Saint-Exupéry as a kind of anti-intellectual and a humanist of the first order, more Pascal than Conrad: "The earth teaches us more about ourselves than do all the books. Because it resists us. Man discovers himself when he measures himself against the obstacle. But to do so he needs a tool, a saw, or a plow. The farmer, in his labor, slowly coaxes out a few of nature's secrets, and the truths he unearths are universal. In the same way the airplane, tool of the airlines, involves man in all the old problems." There is more room in France for *moralisme* and at the time there was certainly more reason to indulge in it; Europe in 1939 was far more message-hungry than America. Room was found in the English edition for mysticism—at Galantière's suggestion Saint-Exupéry added a kind of apologia for the machine, called "The Tool," of which only a skeletal version appears in the French edition— but generally an attempt was made to rein in his meditations, to see that *Wind, Sand and Stars* remained first and foremost a book about flying. Saint-Exupéry thought of it as much more, as is obvious from his long search for a French title. This culminated in an offer he made his cousin André de Fonscolombe: 100 francs for a perfect title. Fonscolombe drew up a list of thirty possibilities, from which, one evening, on the rue Michel-Ange, *Terre des humains* emerged as the front-runner. On the proofs of the French edition, printed in mid-December 1938, the title *Étoiles par grand vent* has been crossed out and *Terre des hommes* substituted in Saint-Exupéry's hand. The proofs are dotted with additional minute corrections, and the author continued even at this point to add new pages of text, which were further revised. When he cabled from New York in 1939 to ask that his new chapter on the cyclone be included as well the book was already on press, and he received from Gallimard an answer he was not used to hearing.

This was pure Saint-Exupéry. The Prix Fémina laureate of 1931 had had eight years to produce his next book, and yet the manuscript had very nearly to be physically torn from him as deadlines came and went. In the end *Wind, Sand and Stars* came into being rather suddenly; it was not a book written over the course of eight years, but a book into which eight years of writing were hurriedly stitched. Much though it represents the wide range of his thinking it is not a volume he mulled over for years, the way, for example, Twain composed his account of piloting on the Mississippi. Richer in passion than in ambition, Saint-Exupéry's was not— either on the page or in the air—a life by design. He had never actually courted adventure; his post-1931 flying amounted less to adventure than to restlessness. In French aviation circles before the war one tended to smile in speaking of him as a great pilot, a distinction for which he did not seem to possess the requisite attention. When he earned accolades they were less often for his expertise or audacity than for his finesse, a double-edged word, implying as it does a special sort of adroitness. In his most famous act of valor he had staggered for four days through the Libyan desert, but he had done so in unlucky pursuit of 150,000 francs of prize money. The book that would earn him the reputation as the Conrad of the skies, *Wind, Sand and Stars* came about not because Saint-Exupéry had planned the volume for years, or even because he was one day struck by the idea for it. It was a work of expedience, to which his convalescence had contributed.

A sort of Saint-Exupéry omnibus conceived and shaped by publisher and translator (and possibly by Gide, depending on when he mentioned *Mirror of the Sea* to its author), everything went into *Wind, Sand and Stars*: the Saharan flights and crashes; the South American flights and near-crashes; the Libyan adventure; Guillaumet in the Andes; the enchanted evenings with the Fuchs family, with the Nouakchott sergeant, with Néri, with the Aéropostale crew in mid-desert; the story of Bark the Senegalese slave; the *Paris-Soir* reportages, even the eulogies to Mermoz. Combined—with a dash of mysticism and a generous sprinkling of hymns to fraternity—those writings make for some of the most glorious descriptions of flight ever published. Proof that a writer and his books may go their separate ways, nothing about these very personal pages hints at the circumstances behind them however. *Wind, Sand and Stars* reads as a hugely intimate work—women fell for its author over and over after reading it —but a very good deal of Saint-Exupéry gets left out of a volume we would classify today as a memoir or personal essay. Nothing about this humane book so bursting with heroism and innocence suggests that it was written out of dire financial necessity by a man with an exhausting sentimental life, who had not flown a mail route in eight years and was never again to pilot an airplane in peacetime.

XIV

~

Where Is France?
1939–1940

So foul a sky clears not without a storm:
Pour down thy weather: how goes all in France?

SHAKESPEARE, *King John*

Gallimard published *Terre des hommes* on March 3, 1939. Newly returned from New York, Saint-Exupéry submitted to his first related interview on the rue Michel-Ange at the end of February. Fortified by whiskey
and nicotine, doodling as he spoke, he expounded on a number of themes;
his visitor, from *Les Nouvelles Littéraires*, was not the first person to remark,
respectfully, that he felt as if he were in a lecture hall at Sciences Po.
Others as well were eager to engage in such conversation with the author,
who that month traveled to Germany, where plans to bring out a translation
of the book were under way. As skeptical of anti-Nazi propaganda as he
was of any propaganda, he drove to Berlin with Madame de B in her
Chrysler during the second week of March; he wanted to see for himself
what was happening with France's neighbor. The first reviews of *Terre
des hommes* appeared in his absence.

It was at once apparent that there was, in Germany, cause for concern.
Saint-Exupéry was awakened in a small Bavarian town by a middle-of-
the-night military convoy clanking its way through the streets; from a table
in a Nuremberg beer hall he watched as a group of Hitler Youth marched
by, hailed on all sides. In Berlin he met with Otto Abetz, who was then
in the business of courting well-placed Frenchmen with Nazi doctrine,
and who took the writer on a tour of the capital. Saint-Exupéry asked to
see an art exhibition and found he had company for this visit as well.
"Curious," he remarked, "how totalitarian countries always prefer guided
tours!" Abetz proposed an excursion into Pomerania, where one of the

country's three elite Führerschulen was located. Madame de B stayed in
Berlin, but another visiting French writer, Henry Bordeaux, joined Saint-
Exupéry for the trip. It was unsettling; later he was to tell Raoul de Roussy
de Sales that he had expected to find in the Führerschule a nursery for
the elite but had instead toured a school for sergeants. In a library bursting
with volumes the Frenchmen asked the school's director if the leaders-
in-training were permitted to read, say, Marx and Comte. They were
indeed, reported the director, so long as they did not find in those volumes
any objections to National Socialism, in which event they were expelled.
With a smile the German assured his visitors there was no cause for
concern; this never happened. Saint-Exupéry was indignant, as he was at
another point during the week when he asked a group of German physicists
the obvious question—were they allowed to read Einstein?—and got the
obvious answer. Back in the car he was direct with Abetz: "The kind of
man you are creating does not interest me." It was one thing for Hitler
to pose as the new Mohammed, another for him to outlaw a free exchange
of ideas. Abetz spent the long ride to Berlin summoning argument after
argument in a vain attempt to sway his opinion, a conversation that may
indeed have resembled one from the hallways of Sciences Po.

On March 15, in direct violation of the guarantee given at Munich the
previous fall, Hitler marched into Czechoslovakia. Fearing that the borders
might be closed at any moment, Saint-Exupéry and Bordeaux packed
earlier than they had intended. On the morning of the eighteenth Saint-
Exupéry drove back into France, stopping along the road at regular intervals to call Pélissier, who was staying in his apartment, to ask him to
wait for him for lunch, a meal he successfully delayed until four in the
afternoon. They have so many airplanes, he told his friend on arriving,
that they have no hangars for them, and this can only mean one thing.
Raoul de Roussy de Sales was later to say that Saint-Exupéry's was "a
philosophical analysis of Nazism"; he returned to France convinced of the
impossibility of reaching an understanding of any kind with Germany's
leaders, whose agendas went far beyond the political. He had not seen all
he had wanted to see, and he had not met with any high-ranking officers,
but he was certain that there was to be no such thing as a lasting peace
with a Nazi regime. (Clearly he was not alone in this thinking: on
April 1 the French army was partly mobilized; as of that date the French
press was censored.) Saint-Exupéry's discomfort with fascism could be
mutual. The first review of Terre des hommes appeared in L'Action Française, the formerly Royalist newspaper cited that month as Germany's best
friend among the French press. The notice was unflattering. Robert Bras-
illach thought Saint-Exupéry's cult of the individual smacked of anarchism
and felt the volume overwritten, fair charges both, but neither of them

enough to derail a master storyteller, or even enough to cost him a great number of right-wing admirers.

Generally *Terre des hommes* either made poets of its reviewers or drove them to hyperbole. "This volume is put together with rigor, with an evenness and a dignity that evoke fierce admiration. This universe in which danger, anguish, fear, and death must constantly be surmounted is described with a total lack of theatrics, without affect. No word seems to me better to characterize this work than modesty, which is, as we know, both a virtue in the world of heroics and a secret of literary effectiveness," wrote Sartre's great friend Paul Nizan in *Ce Soir*. "Saint-Exupéry, aviator and moralist, is blessed with a sumptuous and refined talent. The most striking images and passages of the most exquisite style abound in his work. Since the Vicomte de Chateaubriand, I do not know if anyone has so skillfully coaxed poetry out of prose," declared André Thérive in *Le Temps*. Edmond Jaloux placed Saint-Exupéry squarely in two traditions, evoking the names of Plutarch and Emerson on the one hand and Columbus and Magellan on the other.

In America, *Wind, Sand and Stars* was hailed on the front page of *The New York Times Book Review* as "a beautiful book, and a brave book. and a book that should be read against the confusion of this world, if only that we may retain our pride in humanity and our excitement in this modern age." Launched with fanfare by Reynal & Hitchcock, it was reviewed as well on the June covers of *The Saturday Review* and the New York *Herald Tribune Books* section, and quickly became a best-seller. "To read it is to forget we are earthbound," raved the *Atlantic* reviewer, who like several American critics knew little of Saint-Exupéry but made of him a quick study, describing the book's "contrasting moods of loneliness and human warmth, of exhilaration and the merciless exposure of nerves and sanity." (Many of Saint-Exupéry's friends would have howled with laughter had they read the *Herald Tribune* review, in which Ben Ray Redman, noting the author's quibble that most men are half-asleep in their lives, wrote, "Antoine de Saint-Exupéry is awake and would awaken others.") In October, a month after war had been declared, *Wind, Sand and Stars* read just as well in London, where *The Spectator*'s reviewer was struck by Saint-Exupéry's "God-like tolerance for the pettiness and folly of mankind." "He touches nothing which he does not illuminate," wrote the *Times Literary Supplement*'s critic of this book of "visions and dreams," rarely described in any country as anything less than a "hymn," a "poem," an "adventure in prose," or a "rhapsody." The fan mail poured in, from such disparate admirers as Le Corbusier and King Leopold of Belgium.

Otto Abetz perhaps did the most for the book. The German propagandist had put Saint-Exupéry and Bordeaux together for the visit to

Pomerania, during which the sixty-nine-year-old Bordeaux could not have helped but succumb to the force of the younger writer's personality. Probably on his return he read *Terre des hommes*, an experience he compared to a first hearing of *Le Cid* or a first reading of Descartes. He was overwhelmed by the freshness of Saint-Exupéry's vision; the author of a life of Guynemer and a veteran of World War I, Bordeaux was as close to a natural fan as Saint-Exupéry could have hoped for. He, too, had a *particule*; a member of the elite of France's elites, his name appeared in print always followed by "*de l'Académie Française.*" Without notifying its author, Bordeaux presented *Terre des hommes* to the Académie as a candidate for the Grand Prix du Roman, the first literary prize awarded each year. He had his work cut out for him; such decisions are as hotly contested in France as anywhere on earth, and *Terre* was not a novel. Fortunately for Saint-Exupéry there were few obvious choices among the books of fiction published in 1939 (the Goncourt went to another Gallimard author, Philippe Hériat), and Bordeaux was a talented debater. He challenged the Académie members to name a fiction writer who could match Saint-Exupéry's style. But there is no plot in the book, protested several of the other thirty-nine Immortals, to which argument Bordeaux countered, Does the human condition have a plot? The characters put in only fleeting appearances, noted someone else. It was true that the characters did little more than appear and disappear from the stage, Bordeaux conceded, but what magnificent entrances and exits they made! The debate, which Bordeaux had thought settled, flared up again unexpectedly just before the Académie cast its votes, but Bordeaux prevailed, and on Thursday, May 25, *Terre des hommes* was awarded the 1939 Grand Prix du Roman de l'Académie Française.

Saint-Exupéry could not have been more surprised by the news. In this he was not alone. The candidates for France's literary awards are generally well-known in advance, but the first reporter sent off to interview the Académie's new laureate—he arrived on the rue Michel-Ange at six that evening and was let in by Boris, formerly of the place Vauban—had not read the book. Understandably, he was under the impression that *Terre des hommes* was a novel. He found an apartment in which no one appeared to live and discovered that his subject was a difficult one. "His timidity intimidated," recalled Luc Estang. The *Figaro Littéraire* reporter had the same experience the following day: "Interviewing Monsieur Antoine de Saint-Exupéry is no easy feat. His modesty, his distaste for talking about himself, the near timidity of this big man, put an end to questions. They all seem pointless in the presence of someone whom one knows and senses to be accustomed to long meditations, who is at home with the dramas of the heavens and yet who stands so solidly on the earth." He made some headway with his subject, however, eliciting answers delivered with the aplomb one would expect from an author who claimed to want to throw out lifelines among men. Your books give us faith in humanity, the reporter told Saint-Exupéry. "I have much faith in man," responded the writer, "because I have only ever met agreeable men. There is an agreeable man in everyone, it goes along with the disagreeable. The mistake made by many is to address themselves stubbornly to the latter." From Saint-Exupéry's magnanimity his interviewer concluded that he had founded his ideas about humanity on the men he met through aviation and not through literature.

Everyone drew the same picture of an awkward, balding giant with a round face and a dreamy gaze, a *retroussé* nose that quivered when he talked excitedly, heavily lidded eyes that sparkled, then went flat. Saint-Exupéry conformed to their idea, as the *Revue des Deux Mondes* put it, of someone "on whom depend many fates," an impression to which his height and name surely added. No one mentioned the visible scars, one of which yanked his left eyebrow up, leaving a permanently quizzical expression on his face, the other of which pulled at his smile; he gave an impression of robust good health. He bore up well under the spotlight, never allowing his delight to melt into pride. The good news was celebrated with a couscous dinner at Consuelo's apartment on the rue Barbet-de-Jouy, attended by a dozen or so friends, including Madeleine Goisot, the Werths, the Fernandezes, Jean Lucas, and Léon-Paul Fargue. Saint-Exupéry was exultant, singing and recounting for a long portion of the evening. No one in Paris was more feted this May than he, who made for such good copy, especially at a time when France was not herself feeling particularly rich in glory or chivalry. "The name 'Saint-Exupéry' is one of the few that duchesses and café waiters pronounce with equal admiration," reported *Les Nouvelles Littéraires*. About the only discordant note sounded regarding *Terre des hommes* that spring came in the form of a telegram from Saigon. Simone de Saint-Exupéry cabled her brother that she had found a grammatical error in his text, a comment over which he was inconsolable.

By June the French reviews had dwindled to a few but the American raves had begun to come in. The book remained on the best-seller lists for nine months; by August more than 150,000 copies had been sold, swelling Saint-Exupéry's royalty account. In New York that summer he was thrilled to find his photograph in bookstore displays all over town, more delighted even with this very American tribute than he had been with the dignified honor bestowed upon him by the Académie Française. The book continued to seduce, as its elegiac accounts of the most harrowing of feats still do. Simone de Beauvoir picked up a copy in November and passed it on to Sartre; the two thought Saint-Exupéry talked drivel when he ventured into philosophy but fell under his curious spell all the

same. De Beauvoir wrote Sartre that *Terre* had been the first book in a
long time that had made her dream. Sartre agreed that it had left him
homesick for a world he did not know, nostalgic for a life he had not lived.
He talked of being "under the influence" of *Terre des hommes* as it is easy
to be, drunk on its author's images and idealism, urged on by his example
to overreach oneself. In its high-mindedness everyone saw what he wanted.
A volume that arguably did claim that work set one free, *Terre* was as
much admired in Germany as in France in 1939. Saint-Exupéry was later
co-opted by the *maquis* and the Vichyites, by existentialists and Catholics
and Marxists and humanists, the way Péguy was to be celebrated both by
the Résistance and by Vichy. It was entirely appropriate that *Wind, Sand
and Stars*, winner of the Académie Française's prize for the best novel of
the year, should be voted by the American Booksellers Association to be
the best work of nonfiction published in 1939.

~

France enjoyed a last gasp of frivolity that spring and summer, when the
stage and screen hits were Giraudoux's *Ondine* and Disney's *Snow White*.
Janet Flanner commented that it had "taken the threat of war to make
the French loosen up and have a really swell and civilized good time."
For Saint-Exupéry as well these were lighthearted months, spent among
the best friends he would know. On March 1 he attended the baptism of
Anne de Ségogne, his goddaughter. He was not known to have been a
father himself and expressed no more regret about this than about not
having a house full of fine furniture, but his feelings as far as others were
concerned had not changed in the ten years since Ségogne's first child
was born. Saint-Exupéry had written him: "You are going to be proud
and insufferable. Which is only natural: I don't think much creation in
life measures up to that of a little living being." The Easter holidays found
him in the south of France, first at the Werths' country house in Saint-
Amour, not far from Saint-Maurice.
    From here he set out late one morning with Suzanne and Léon Werth
and their fifteen-year-old son, Claude, in the family's Bugatti. In a leisurely
fashion—Saint-Exupéry was not at the wheel—they made their way north
to a small inn, in the village of Fleurville, overlooking the Saône. On the
terrace of the Café de la Marine, in the warm, spring sun, the two writers
ordered Pernods; they watched as a German bargeman, his wife, and a
French mechanic worked on the river. Saint-Exupéry hailed the trio and
invited them for a drink; they talked of war, which the foreigners assured
him the German people were unwilling to fight. The French mechanic
recognized Saint-Exupéry and asked him to autograph a postcard of the
Saône, which he did. Lunch was a straightforward affair, consisting of a

fine *saucisson* served with *pain de campagne, a friture de poissons,* and a *poulet à la crème*; for Saint-Exupéry the clear light of nostalgia transformed this simple repast and these few hours of perfect communion into the kind of totemic moment he had known under the stars in Nouakchott. As clean, well-pressed linens seemed to him always the very expression of civilization, he would later consider peace as that afternoon by the Saône. In *Lettre à un otage (Letter to a Hostage),* written in New York in 1942, he described the lunch—leaving out the autograph-seeker, and sacrificing the *friture* to the *saucisson*—as a true miracle, the kind that makes little noise. We know little of what was said at the lunch table but the afternoon was clearly not without its magic. More than a year afterward Werth wrote in his journal of the "shrines of memory" created by friendship: "At Fleurville, the Saône, the pale trees, the chicken, the *friture* will always have for me the taste of friendship." He was still thinking about the outing four years later, when, unbeknownst to him, Saint-Exupéry had written about it as well.

From Fleurville Werth drove to Lyons, depositing his wife and son at the train station. Saint-Exupéry had insisted that Werth accompany him on a visit to Sallès's, a scant 150 miles away at Tarascon; there was an added attraction in that Ségogne was vacationing with friends nearby, in Arles. By overriding Werth's objections that arriving at what was bound to be a rather advanced hour with a stranger in tow did not constitute proper behavior, Saint-Exupéry managed to assemble his two oldest friends and one of his two best friends. As they sat down to a late dinner, suddenly and visibly moved, he flung out his long arms and announced: "Tonight, three of my best friends are together. I have never been so happy in my life." It is unlikely that anyone got much sleep that evening. From Tarascon Saint-Exupéry moved on, with Ségogne and an architect friend, for a short tour of the region. In the Camargue delta Ségogne and Pierre Dalloz paused to admire the church of Saint-Gilles. A baptism had just released a group of screaming children into the square; Saint-Exupéry disappeared along with them. He turned up later, radiant, in the village *pâtisserie*, surrounded by twenty admirers busily licking sugar off their sticky fingers. At Aigues-Mortes he again proved, as Dalloz put it, that "he preferred human beings to old stones." While Dalloz and Ségogne visited the Tour de Constance, the Académie Française laureate-to-be inserted himself with the greatest of ease into a game of *boules* being played in the shadow of the town's fortifications.

At the end of May Saint-Exupéry and Madame de B rejoined what remained of the Aéropostale family outside of Biscarrosse, where Guillaumet had been working with the *Lieutenant-de-Vaisseau-Paris*. The occasion was Guillaumet's thirty-seventh birthday, as well as the awarding of Saint-Exupéry's rosette of the Légion d'Honneur; with Guillaumet as his sponsor, he had been named an *officier* in January. Lucas and Néri, who was also a member of the *Lieutenant-de-Vaisseau-Paris* team, joined them, as did the Guillaumets' terrier. There was singing and a cake with thirty-seven candles and some old-time boisterousness but there were no speeches, as both guests of honor were too moved to attempt one. Saint-Exupéry owed Guillaumet more than simply his decoration. The most quoted line in *Terre des hommes*, Guillaumet's "I swear that what I went through, no animal would have gone through," resounds even today: Gérard d'Aboville, the closest thing modern France has had to an adventurer, practically paraphrased the aviator when explaining what had possessed him to row alone across the Pacific in 1991. On reading Guillaumet's official report after the Andes crash Saint-Exupéry had written him that he deserved a chair at the Académie Française; it now appeared as if Guillaumet was winning one for his friend. Guillaumet even figured in the public announcement of the award in December, when the director of the Académie mentioned that what the Immortals had most of all admired about *Terre des hommes* was its author's "virile affection for his companions . . . his marvelous account of the martyrdom of Guillaumet." In inscribing *Vol de nuit* to his friend Saint-Exupéry had promised that his next book would be titled *Guillaumet*. It was not, although *Terre des hommes*—a specially printed copy of which Saint-Exupéry hand-delivered at 2:00 a.m.—is dedicated to him. During this Biscarrosse visit Guillaumet invited Saint-Exupéry to join him on the *Lieutenant-de-Vaisseau-Paris*'s crossing to New York, scheduled for early July, an idea that entailed a certain rewriting of Air France regulations. In his notebook Saint-Exupéry defined liberty as "the ability to defy probability"; he flexed this well-developed muscle again now, by no means for the last time that year.

After several conversations, Louis Couhé, the head of Air France Transatlantique, took the brunt of Saint-Exupéry's conviction. No passengers were allowed on test flights, and there was little reason for an exception to be made for someone who had no official relation with the company. At the end of what appears to have been a full day of discussions Saint-Exupéry succeeded in convincing Couhé to designate him "*pilote complémentaire.*" "Didn't he after all possess," reasoned the indulgent director, "all the necessary licenses?" So it was that Saint-Exupéry was officially listed as a second pilot of the forty-two-ton flying boat when in fact he spent the July 7 crossing from Biscarrosse to Long Island Sound mostly looking over Guillaumet's shoulder. During the four-day layover in New York he had his first glimpse of his likeness in bookstores and met with his happy publisher and with his agent, who took him on a late-night tour of the Harlem jazz clubs. At dawn on Bastille Day the flying boat—which all aboard knew to be a dinosaur in its time, when the Pan Am Clipper was zipping regularly across the ocean—took off from Long

Island in what unexpectedly turned into the first nonstop flight of a commercial airliner from the United States to France. Saint-Exupéry earned his keep during these twenty-eight and a half hours, regaling the crew with stories, reading Guillaumet passages from the French-language proofs of Anne Morrow Lindbergh's *Listen! The Wind*, to which he had agreed to write a preface. The diversions provided by this *"passager mascotte"* must have been particularly welcome at lunchtime, when it was discovered that the crew's meals had inadvertently been frozen with dry ice and would require hours to thaw.

On landing he left Biscarrosse immediately for Yvonne de Lestrange's, where the Guillaumets were to join him. (Guillaumet was longer than expected in Biscarrosse, and when he and his wife finally drove up to Chitré that evening they found a miserable Saint-Exupéry perched by the side of the road. He had spent two hours running between the road and his cousin's telephone, convinced that, having braved the North Atlantic, Guillaumet had been lost to western France.) The two glowed with triumph, a feeling the writer this time immediately conveyed to paper: *Paris-Soir* carried an account of the transatlantic flight on July 22. In it Saint-Exupéry expressed his usual regrets about commercial aviation having grown a little paunchy, a little *"embourgeoisé,"* but himself claimed to feel ten years younger after his trip, which had been like a childhood revisited. He sounded similar notes in two other pieces that appeared this summer, the first of which prefaced a special issue of a magazine on test-piloting edited by Conty. In it he made the case for intuition over mathematical equation, wisdom over science, a case entirely in keeping both with his approach to mathematics and his approach to piloting but heresy, had anyone noticed, in a country run by engineers. In July he tinkered with the preface to the Lindbergh book, the translated manuscript of which had been given him in mid-June. Henri Delgove, Lindbergh's translator, happened to be a native of Le Mans, and he had received a warm welcome on the rue Michel-Ange, where Saint-Exupéry had agreed to write the piece. Delgove may have rued the day. The author began his reading of the manuscript shortly before the *Lieutenant-de-Vaisseau-Paris* took off, cabling that he was so impressed with the work that he wanted to write a longer preface, provided that Delgove could wait until mid-July for its delivery. Mid-July came and went. The third week of the month Delgove and Jean Lucas locked Saint-Exupéry in his room for an evening and went off to Montparnasse to see a movie. After midnight they returned to the rue Michel-Ange to look in on their prisoner; they found him haggard, disheveled, and in a cold sweat, but they also found several sheets of microscopic text. They put the author to bed on the couch.

Delgove's battle was not yet over. The next weeks brought communications from Saint-Exupéry from Cannes and from the *Normandie*, on which he set sail again for New York on the twenty-sixth, less than two weeks after his return on the *Lieutenant-de-Vaisseau-Paris.* "Tell Delgove to replace page 3 line 10 '*rapports*' with '*relations*,' " he cabled. Robert de Saint-Jean, a *Paris-Soir* contributor, ran into the writer on the boat and heard all about Anne Morrow Lindbergh, the second time, appropriately, that Saint-Exupéry had sung her praises in mid-Atlantic. Their conversation was interrupted by a radiogram from Lindbergh's French publisher, the response to Saint-Exupéry's asking how much longer he might be allowed to make revisions in his nine pages of text. While he fiddled with his pages Saint-Jean inventoried the wonders of the *Normandie*, from the clay-pigeon range to the canine life vests to the prison. Among the ocean liner's marvels he listed Saint-Exupéry's card tricks. What most impresses you on board? he asked the prestidigitator. "The Camembert is always perfectly ripe," volunteered Saint-Exupéry, who spent a great deal of his time with the ship's captain discussing transatlantic travel and whether its future belonged to the sea or the air. His case was assisted once more by Guillaumet, who was crossing the North Atlantic again that week and who had promised to overfly the *Normandie*. During Saint-Exupéry's third night at sea he did so, flying as low as he could and circling the illuminated ocean liner twice in his Latécoère 522. All of the *Normandie*'s passengers turned out on deck for the superb sight. Néri hastily transmitted a message to the boat's captain; according to Saint-Jean, who had no reason to be privy to such information, it read: "HAVE CELEBRATED FIRST OVERFLIGHT NORMANDIE BY FRENCH FLYING BOAT WITH CHAMPAGNE. REGARDS TO SAINT-EX. GUILLAUMET." The Latécoère 522 arrived in New York the following day, followed, forty-eight hours later, by the *Normandie.*

The Saint-Exupérys evidently worked out a truce this summer after a miserable winter of abuse and crises and "*sacrifices acrobatiques*," the first two on Consuelo's part and the third, claimed the writer, on his. He was by now far more often with Madame de B than with his wife, who given the opportunity did her best to slander her rival. Nonetheless Saint-Exupéry continued to see and write Consuelo regularly, not only to keep her on the straight and narrow, a job he entrusted, in his absences, to the patient Suzanne Werth or, when geography allowed, to his mother. This summer he spent about as much time with her as he did attempting to track her down. On June 16, for example, the couple had dinner with the Werths, but by the twenty-first Consuelo had disappeared again. Together they had found a charming three-story country home with a large garden, a pond, a greenhouse, a tennis court, an aviary, and a rabbit hutch in La Varennes-Jarcy, twenty miles southeast of Paris; Consuelo thought that her husband's health called for some time in the country. In the course of the two hectic weeks between trips to America Saint-Exupéry signed a lease for the property, to be rented at 15,000 francs a year. An option to buy the house—known as "La Feuilleraie"—was included in the lease, though it may have been suggested by the lessor. Consuelo installed herself here this summer, although she was less often at La Feuilleraie than her husband might have liked, and he was less often a visitor than he could have been.

He had been in New York for only three days when he received a Saturday morning phone call from Anne Morrow Lindbergh, who had just read his preface. She was flattered and thrilled (enough so to start in on her copy of *Wind, Sand and Stars*); would he like to come for dinner and the evening, she asked him in French, noting that he spoke "*pas un mot*" of English. The Lindberghs were newly installed in Lloyd Neck on the north shore of Long Island; it was agreed that Charles would call for their guest that afternoon. As things worked out Anne headed into town for him, a little nervous, more so after being told at the Ritz-Carlton that Monsieur de Saint-Exupéry was waiting in the bar. "One of those drunken aviators," she was thinking as she headed in to meet the enormous Frenchman, a full foot taller than she and in all ways overpowering, but somehow familiar and as charming as ever, maybe even a little more so. A block from the Ritz, the conversation already flying fast and furious, Anne's car stalled; Saint-Exupéry chose the moment to pull a copy of the preface from his pocket. Mrs. Lindbergh found herself in the arduous position of having to "talk back in French, always an effort, talk to the taxi driver who was pushing us, and explain what was wrong with the car in French and then in English, all at the same time."

By the time the two had made their way to Pennsylvania Station, where they sat on high stools drinking orangeade at the counter—like children, thought Anne, herself once described as Lindbergh's "child-wife"—they had got to the subject of rhythm in writing, than which Saint-Exupéry claimed nothing was as important. Between Manhattan and Lloyd Neck they had covered America, aviation, art, the desert, exile, poetry, and Alfred North Whitehead; read through the preface together; lost all track of their surroundings; and begun to finish each other's sentences. In her diary afterward Anne described all the symptoms of having been on an idyllic first date: she had suddenly found that she had had an enormous amount to say; she had gone ahead and said it; because her companion understood her so well she was moved to say more; she worried she had bored him. For his part Saint-Exupéry was a little flirtatious. When Anne quoted D. H. Lawrence as having said of marriage that men and women should be like two poles that held a world between them, he laughed: "Oh—not so far apart as all that!" He offered his own definition: they should be like bees, gathering honey and bringing it home to the hive.

In the Lindbergh kitchen there was no sign of Charles. His wife and Saint-Exupéry had dinner alone after a few card tricks, which Anne saw as her guest's bashful way of putting himself at ease. Legends in their own time, Antoine de Saint-Exupéry and Charles Lindbergh did not meet until almost ten that evening. Anne felt relieved to observe the conversation—which she translated—move immediately to a "higher" plane, one which could also be described as a less personal one. The two pioneers compared notes on the thrills of the early days in the air: "But I never know," confessed the Frenchman, "whether it is not my own youth I am regretting." He steered Lindbergh around to his favorite subject— man and the machine, and man's spiritual needs in a technological age —making known his distaste for fascism, evidently rather gently. Lindbergh, whose friendship with Germany was already well-enough established that his name was hissed in newsreels, took no offense, although he also admitted to having had trouble following the brilliant tumult of Saint-Exupéry's conversation.

Sunday morning Saint-Exupéry came down to breakfast to report good-humoredly that he had got lost upstairs in search of his bathroom. (It adjoined his room.) He met two-year-old Land Lindbergh; it seemed to Anne that their guest was overwhelmed by the beauty of her golden-haired son. He played happily on the beach with Land and with Land's elder brother, Jon, who must have shared his mother's enthusiasm for the Frenchman; the following year he asked if he were one of the saints of France. After a swim the Lindberghs drove Saint-Exupéry the few miles to Huntington, where Raoul de Roussy de Sales, seriously ill with cancer, had taken a summer home. Saint-Exupéry spent the twenty minutes in the car relating the story of his near-drowning. The Lindberghs retrieved their guest late in the afternoon, finding him and his deck of cards on Roussy de Sales's porch; the ride home was devoted to the desert, and to the importance of danger and solitude. The talk went on and on—"There are the people one can talk to and there are the people one cannot talk to," explained the indefatigable Frenchman, "there is no middle ground"—through dinner, during a walk on the beach, over a nightcap of milk and ginger ale. It continued the next morning, when the Lindberghs drove Saint-Exupéry back into New York. By now he had explicated the story of Jacob and Esau, addressed the subject of faith, and launched into a fabulous parable about sheep farming in Patagonia, which to his mind proved that nature always exacted a price for man's progress. So distracted was the ordinarily meticulous Lindbergh by the conversation that his wife was feverishly translating that he ran out of gas on the ramp to the Fifty-ninth Street bridge. "For the second time in two days," wrote Anne, "Saint-Ex stands bent over the hood of an engine of a Lindbergh."

She had plenty of other reasons to remember the weekend guest, who left her feeling as if her "mind had been quickened" and whom she was never to see again. She perhaps best described what had taken place as "summer lightning," which was as it should have been for the petite, French-speaking diplomat's daughter who had caught so much of her husband's aviation fever and the courteous, subtle-minded Frenchman who between them wrote nearly all of the most lyrical accounts we have of flight. Anne Lindbergh continued to think and worry, often, about Saint-Exupéry, who "became for me the lens through which I saw the war." Her novel *The Steep Ascent* went out "like a letter to him," the one person she felt sure would understand it. Five years after the visit she felt the need to remind herself that she could not have asked for a better marriage. If Charles was the earth to her Saint-Exupéry was, she wrote, like a sun or a moon or a star. She was surprised by the depth of her grief when she heard of his death, a loss she felt as she had that of her sister and over which she was still mulling months later. "Are you going to look back all your life to an hour's conversation on a train with a stranger who could not even speak your language, and you only haltingly, his? But obviously he spoke 'my language' better than anyone I have ever met, before or since," she chastised herself. Her husband was a little surprised to hear of her attachment to Saint-Exupéry, owning up to some jealousy. He had his own, more prosaic reason to remember the Frenchman. Two months after his visit, Lindbergh went to Abercrombie & Fitch for a new pair of tennis shoes; he had lent his previous pair to Saint-Exupéry. "I think he probably left them on the beach; he could not possibly have packed them in his suitcase wet," noted Lindbergh, who would focus on the events of the next few years through a different lens altogether.

Saint-Exupéry spent the following weekend in Vermont at the Middlebury College summer school, at the invitation of André Morize, its director. He gave no formal lecture but in a series of casual talks proved to be charm incarnate; when he was not regaling his admirers (two-thirds of the summer-session students were women) with his account of having piloted over Africa with a lion cub breathing down his neck he delighted with sleight-of-hand. On both counts he drew crowds. In one of his more memorable stunts he asked a member of his audience to pick a card from his deck and return it to him; he then reversed it, producing a different card. So adept was he that he left the French faculty—many of them old friends—convinced that he operated with a trick deck. A luncheon held in his honor at the Dog Team Tavern on the twelfth proved equally convivial. Dorothy Thompson was in the vicinity and dropped by, evidently having heard that the French writer was in town. Pierre de Lanux, himself a brilliant conversationalist, sat between the two dignitaries, ostensibly to translate. In photos of the afternoon Saint-Exupéry appears relaxed and in his element, at times ebullient. That evening he set out for a drive with Yvonne Michel, a Parisian friend who was on staff for the summer, and a young consular official; he spent the excursion recounting the progress that had been made on the atomic front, describing nuclear fission in vivid detail. In the middle of his lecture, rather eerily, the aurora borealis flickered across the sky.

He was back in New York by August 20, 1939, when he spent a long evening talking with Roussy de Sales. It seemed to both men now that war was inevitable. Saint-Exupéry confided his fears of the kind of conflict aviation could make possible, a war in which a front is no longer a front. Three days later German foreign minister von Ribbentrop was in Moscow to sign the nonagression pact, to which the French reaction was the classic "*Nous sommes cocus*" ("We are cuckolded"). Holed up at the Ritz-Carlton Saint-Exupéry spent his day calling France. On the twenty-fourth—or, as he put it later, "when the headlines got too big"—he sailed home on the *Île de France*, as did Yvonne Michel and several other friends. He spent most of the trip in the captain's cabin, where he familiarized himself with all the details of the crossing, an especially agreeable one as there were vast provisions and few passengers. The travelers lived on caviar until August 30, when the *Île de France* docked in Le Havre. Hitler having invaded Poland, France declared war on Germany four days later, and Saint-Exupéry returned to Paris to find his mobilization letter waiting for him. On September 9 he reported to the Toulouse-Francazal airfield, in uniform.

~

Captain de Saint-Exupéry was thirty-nine years old and the military doctors were not much impressed with him. The best use of him seemed to be as a navigation instructor, and so he spent the early days of the war—which most of the French pretended for some time had not yet begun—in the rear; it may have been the only time in his life he was not happy to be in Toulouse. He began flying a Simoun as often as four times a day and, at least at the outset, performing mathematical feats on a blackboard more for his own contagious amusement than in connection with any course of study. Naturally this was not sufficient; the greatest regulation-busting campaign of his life was now launched, from the site of his first triumphs in the air. He appealed to his friends for help in being assigned a more active role in the war but chose among them wisely; some were intent on keeping him as far from any battle as possible. No one was better connected or more likely to accede to his wishes than Madame de B, to whom he wrote passionately late in October. He was suffocating, he was disgusted with the idea of being kept from danger, he begged her with all his might to get him transferred to an active unit. She must save him, by which he meant get him to the front.

It should be said that at least some of Saint-Exupéry's frustration was shared by the majority of mobilized men, bored and exasperated by a war that was not yet a war. They had headed off with near-relief that the long, post-Munich suspense was behind them; over the course of the winter what Winston Churchill termed an air of "calm aloofness" gave way to a frustration that was to leave the French military unprepared and hugely demoralized when the *drôle de guerre* turned, in the spring, into the Battle of France. Early in November though, having visited a military field and briefly retasted the joys of plain, ordered squadron life, Saint-Exupéry was more desperate than ever. "I am not embarrassed to ask this of you. It's not about a job or a grant; it's for an assignment to the front, in a fighter squadron. This is vital to me. And even if it's difficult, even if it's complicated, I have no scruples about my request, because it's the first time I have a total favor to ask of you," he pleaded with Madame de B. He got as far as a medical examination but was declared unfit to fly. Among the obvious impairments were a frozen left shoulder, a body stiff with old fractures, and a history of headaches.

Undeterred, he called on his old friend General Davet, then commander of the bomber school in Pau. Davet felt strongly that if a man's heart was in the job he should be allowed to take on that job, even if his was a thirty-nine-year-old heart; he personally walked Saint-Exupéry through a maze of bureaucracy that led ultimately to Guy La Chambre, the Ministre de l'Air. Saint-Exupéry no longer had the reflexes to pilot a fighter plane; he was unwilling to fly a bomber. In a happy compromise he was assigned on November 26 to a reconnaissance group, the 2/33, then based 120 miles east of Paris in the Champagne village of Orconte. As if testimony were needed to his powers of persuasion (or those of his connections) Guillaumet, who had also requested to be assigned to a fighter squadron, was refused on the grounds of his age and called up instead as a transport pilot. He was two years younger than his great friend. Saint-Exupéry celebrated his transfer twice, once in Paris at the Deux-Magots, in what must have seemed a very different celebration than that following the Libyan crash. In Toulouse he assembled his comrades for a drink, before his departure. The small gathering was marred by one remark, reflecting a belief widely enough held that someone had to voice it. Asserted a young lieutenant: "In order to fly in the military the airline pilot has everything to learn." "Except modesty," parried the irritated captain.

No one in Orconte was particularly happy to see Saint-Exupéry. He was legendary—as were his distractions—and a young, eager military pilot would have been far preferable to a legend. "All the same he isn't coming to fly?" asked Lieutenant René Gavoille, who served double-duty as the group's mechanic. "Is he going to make a movie or what?" wondered Lieutenant Jean Israël. "Isn't he forty?" moaned Lieutenant-observer Jean

Dutertre. None of them yet suspected that they were to become the characters in his next book. He was the object of much fascination as he emerged from the staff car in a less-than-natty uniform and stepped onto the muddy terrain on the afternoon of December 3. Once over the threshold of the barracks he seemed more timid than pretentious but did not flinch under the curious stares. François Laux stepped forward: "Lieutenant Laux, squadron commander." "Saint-Exupéry, pilot," replied the newcomer, who outranked him. The rest of the introductions made, Saint-Exupéry declared—as only a man who has romanticized a desolate strip of sand has the authority to do of a rustic, freezing barracks—"It's very nice here. If you will accept me, I should be happy to stay." He had worked his magic; within a day or two, remembered Israël, "he had tamed us." The extroverted Gavoille was charged with Saint-Exupéry's initiation into his new métier; aware of his reputation, he approached the novice with some apprehension. In the eyes of the French air force Saint-Exupéry had always been a fine pilot, however, and with Gavoille's help he adapted quickly to the first modern aircraft he was to fly, the Potez 63. (Unfortunately the Potez—a brand-new, 700-horsepower machine—was an airplane obsolescent from the start, outpaced by nearly 100 miles an hour by a Messerschmitt.) As the squadron's caution melted into respect, Gavoille's attentions became doting; he would later be said to be the aging aviator's equerry.

Saint-Exupéry remained true to form in most respects. He suited up in his sixty-five pounds of equipment for a first high-altitude flight, which took him to 30,000 feet, where the temperature drops to $-55°F$. You must not have been very warm, observed his colleagues afterward. The newcomer demurred, cataloguing only slight discomforts; he was interrupted by the news that he had forgotten to plug in his pressure suit. He daydreamed in the corner of the mess, where no one disturbed him; his room was littered with American-made gadgets, the pride of which was his electric razor. And counter to all regulations Saint-Exupéry was allowed to bring the second-hand De Soto he had bought that fall—a rare compromise in his life; he had wanted a Bugatti, and thought the De Soto hopelessly bourgeois—to Orconte, where it quickly became the entire squadron's car. In it he would pilot his friends at forty to ninety miles an hour, depending on the intensity of the conversation. This amounted to a hair-raising experience for his passengers. Hurtling along the icy roads the reconnaissance pilot generally missed the turnoff for Orconte, an oversight no one dared mention to him until he had decelerated. Israël remembered a trip back to Orconte from a dinner with a neighboring squadron as the most terrifying of all his war missions: at high speed Saint-Exupéry skated over the ice, headlights out due to the blackout, bent on proving to his passenger that he had not had too much to drink.

In Orconte he was billeted with a farming family and their three children, in the largest room of the house. He had not initially been welcome here either. When the captain appeared at her home, stooping so as to clear the doorway of the bedroom in question (something he would not always remember to do), Madame Scherschell informed him he would be more comfortable in the nearby château. Saint-Exupéry took one look around the room, of which the street offered a full view, and declared, "I like it here. I'll stay." To the Scherschells, whose home would be immortalized in *Flight to Arras*, he was a strange man indeed. He was often in the house in the afternoon, and one day came upon Madame Scherschell making butter in the kitchen. He installed himself at her side. "You know, Captain, butter takes a long time to make and it can't be very interesting to a man like yourself," she objected. Her house guest was not so easily dismissed. In his room he wrote furiously every evening, rapidly turning out what were to Madame Scherschell long sheets of yellow paper and what were in fact his ideas for a screenplay of *Wind, Sand and Stars*, as well as those for a screenplay of the still-unfinished "Igor"; his thoughts on the war, in the form of a long essay; contributions to his ongoing book, the "poem" to which his attachment was growing; a fair number of letters. Madame Scherschell resisted neither the temptation to read these nor that to discourage her guest's eccentricities by turning off his electricity when his light burned too late. Saint-Exupéry wrote tributes to his bed at the Scherschells, which could not have surprised anyone who tried to wake him to report to the field for a 7:00 a.m. breakfast. "A freezing bed is wonderful because if you keep still you luxuriate in a warm river, but if you move a foot you tumble into a polar current; the bed is full of mystery, with its Gulf Stream and its ice berghs (is that the correct spelling?)," he wrote Léon Werth when he had moved on to less primitive accommodations, with which he was less enthralled. "In temperate climates I wilt with boredom," he concluded, having come to know himself a little.

Orconte in 1939 was mild compared to Orconte in 1940, when Saint-Exupéry wrote Becker that it was a far cry from the Ritz-Carlton. France's mood changed generally that winter, the coldest in fifty years; the public that had feasted its eyes on *Snow White* now made *Nostradamus* a best-seller. Only one mission was flown by the 2/33 Reconnaissance Group in December, and it ended badly. The snow fell and fell, which made missions—vexing enough given the vast zone to be covered, the very precise German fighter planes, and a complete absence of radio navigation —impracticable. All was white as far as the eye could see; the unsheltered Potezes looked like a mutant breed of polar hedgehogs. There was little to do but wait, a particularly nerve-racking exercise for those in the air force who had discovered that their equipment was as flawed as it was scarce. The Potez's guns and controls froze at the high altitudes for which the aircraft was designed; nine months after the war was declared the sight of a French airplane in the sky was so rare that the antiaircraft batteries fired at anything they saw on the generally correct assumption it was German. "It's understandable but it's not funny," commented Saint-Exupéry, his aircraft grazed by friendly fire. The population of Germany was half as much again as that of France, but in the air there were ten to twenty German aircraft for every French one. A. J. Liebling, who had taken over Janet Flanner's *New Yorker* beat, was told by one French flyer stationed near Orconte: "Some of the German pilots are good, but most not so good. Nearly all the planes are good, though, and since the man in the plane you're after may by chance be one of the good pilots, you cannot afford to take anything for granted." Saint-Exupéry was given a brief summary of the pleasures of reconnaissance flying shortly after his arrival: "You'll be flying over Germany without guns or controls. But don't take it too hard, for it really doesn't matter. The German fighters always down you before you know they are there."

He trained for high altitude before Christmas, spent with the Scherschells, and in the New Year, but was to fly no war missions until late March, when the Potezes were replaced by the new Bloch 174's. He had plenty of time to write, to prove his prowess at chess, to reflect, and to draw; in 1939 he began scribbling a little man over and over, often with wings, or standing on a cloud, in one case menaced by a tiny devil representing a Messerschmitt. A member of the squadron asked why he often drew the figure chasing butterflies; Saint-Exupéry answered that he had endeared himself to him for his pursuit of "a realistic ideal." Increasingly demoralized as the winter wore on, he began to speak and write of "this odd planet on which I live." "The next time around," he vowed, "I'm going to change planets."

Frustrated by what he perceived as the sheer ineffectuality of the French war effort, he applied himself to solving some of the more acute problems that plagued the 2/33. He met with Fernand Holweck several times; the two devised and applied—apparently without the sanction of the High Command—an elegant solution to the problem of the freezing guns, to which methylglyoxol was added. Later he met with the scientist to discuss his idea for "luminous camouflage." Remembering from his Argentine year that a night pilot is blinded more effectively by sudden, bright light than by the dark, he suggested that a carpet of lights be set out to hide strategic sights from the enemy. Also this winter he invented a range finder; experimentation with both devices ended with the fall of France. Holweck summed up the talents of the irrepressible inventor: not being a trained man of science, Saint-Exupéry managed to see the forest for the trees. He was granted leave to make the trip to Paris whenever he liked, which was regularly, often in the company of a fellow officer. And, as ever, he provided the entertainment at Orconte. Almost immediately after his arrival Saint-Exupéry's exploits begin to show up in the squadron's logbook. On December 10 General Vuillemin, the commander of the French air force, came to make an inspection; he left overwhelmed by Saint-Exupéry's virtuoso card tricks. The writer attracted a series of visitors to Orconte, in addition to the planned entertainment: Ramon Fernandez, Joseph Kessel, and Pierre Mac Orlan dropped in, as did Werth and Holweck and, on several occasions, Madame de B.

As he had been at Juby, he was in his element among his fellow officers at Orconte, even allowing for the fact that he was now the elder statesman. "In the kind of adolescent atmosphere in which live men who are entirely willing to die, Antoine de Saint-Exupéry, more than anyone else, became again the marvelous child he was," remembered one comrade. He saw to the spirits of the group, entertaining with his mathematical conundrums, his word games, among the few consolations that spring, when the 2/33 at last began flying on a regular basis and their numbers quickly began to dwindle. He asked Becker to send him the best portable phonograph available in New York and a selection of French music of the fourteenth, fifteenth, and sixteenth centuries, as well as some Bach and Handel, which Becker did, via the diplomatic pouch. At one point the prized phonograph went on the blink; terrified of electric shocks, Saint-Exupéry invited his colleagues to see to its repair. In part he seems to have ordered up the music in an attempt to coax barrack standards up to his own. As much as he claimed to be delighted to be "an entirely anonymous soldier," to share with his comrades the cold, the rain, the rheumatism, the fear and the long, empty evenings, he now admitted that he had all his life preferred those who admired Bach to those who liked the tango. Like all squadrons the 2/33 sang a good deal: Werth observed during his visit to the squadron's mess that this gaiety was probably the only means of keeping the terror of war at bay. When Saint-Exupéry arrived the 2/33's repertoire was typically earthy; he introduced a number of frivolous but somewhat more refined airs.

In plenty of earthbound ways Captain de Saint-Exupéry proved his mettle this winter. In 1939 Henri Jeanson had been arrested and charged, because of an irreverent article he had published, with inciting military disobedience. His friend turned up unexpectedly at the Palais de Justice to testify in his defense, making what sounds from Jeanson's description to have been an entrance worthy of Cyrano. Looking like "a sort of aerial deep-sea diver, from a[n H. G.] Wells screenplay, directed by Fritz Lang," Saint-Exupéry introduced himself to a military judge who asked him to spell his name. In Jeanson's eyes it was as if the two men hailed not from different planets but from different solar systems. Without a hint of condescension or impatience Saint-Exupéry made his argument, though he could see it falling on deaf ears. Later in the winter, in a scene worthy more of Louis Malle than of Fritz Lang, he issued what may have been the only order of his military career. Having returned from a mission, he sat down for dinner with a friend in a restaurant outside of Laon. A group of noncommissioned officers occupied a second of the restaurant's tables; at a third sat a woman in mourning and her two young daughters, who appeared to be waiting for a car to come for them. The soldiers had had a good deal to drink, and they began to sing, raucously. When they worked their way up to a particularly bawdy tune Saint-Exupéry turned to them and motioned toward the two young girls. The soldiers paid him no heed and continued on with their concert, moving to a yet more tasteless song, of which the rendition was made as obscene as possible. In three steps Saint-Exupéry was upon the ringleader. "I order you to be quiet," he said evenly. Slowly, after a few objections, the table fell silent. The captain returned to his place, accompanied only by the sound of rattling dishes. The woman who had been at the center of the incident acknowledged him with some embarrassment: "Ah, Monsieur, thank heavens there are still men like you!"

His demeanor did not alone undermine his claim to be a "*soldat anonyme*"; his very presence at the front did. He had pulled strings to sit out the winter at Orconte and he continued to pull them so as to stay. Giraudoux, who had been appointed Ministre de l'Information during the summer, before France was even at war, had elicited from him a text that he read over the airwaves in mid-October, titled "Pan-Germanism and Its Propaganda." (Saint-Exupéry's mother graded it severely—"Diction excellent though a little hurried"—but was proud of her son and thought his address an effective weapon against the pernicious broadcasts of Radio Stuttgart.) Giraudoux felt Saint-Exupéry could be put to better use in this line of work and made a formal request in December that he be assigned to the propaganda service. The pilot refused. He had, he said, no Bible to offer Frenchmen, and he felt a Bible of some sort—as opposed to neat clichés about patriotism and the glories of France—was what they now needed.

By the day he was becoming a more valuable spokesman, however. In January, *Le Figaro* recommended that all young men heading off to the front pack a copy of *Terre des hommes* in their bags. In February, the American Booksellers Association named Saint-Exupéry the winner of the National Book Award. In May the Ministère de l'Information argued its case more vehemently; by all reports, Saint-Exupéry was the Frenchman whose word carried the most weight in America. The ministry hoped it could enlist him for a mission to America, where Lindbergh was doing his best to keep his country out of the conflict, and pleaded with Henri Alias, then Saint-Exupéry's commanding officer, to talk him into it. "We urgently request that you explore with Saint-Exupéry the conditions under which he might be able to reconcile his officer's duties with his responsibilities as a man of letters," wrote the general secretary of the information ministry, appealing to the luminary on his own terms. Major Alias claimed the letter never arrived.

In January 1940, the National Center of Scientific Research (CNRS), France's prestigious government-run research bureau, attempted to recruit him as well. Again he dug in his heels. This required some doing: for the second time, he was forced to plead his case with the Ministre de l'Air. Alias accompanied him on this visit; while Saint-Exupéry met with Guy La Chambre, the minister's chief-of-staff confided in Alias that the assignment had been concocted by friends of Saint-Exupéry's, eager to see he did not kill himself. To the same end Didier Daurat asked his former pilot to meet him in Paris for lunch that winter. Saint-Exupéry knew full well what Daurat wanted and this time prevailed upon Captain Max Gelée to accompany him. Explaining that he had never been able to say no to Daurat and would not be able to do so now, he begged Gelée to steer the conversation away from any discussion of a reassignment. Gelée succeeded until the end of the meal, when Daurat was forced to tackle the matter head-on. The captain managed to reason with the World War I hero all the same: Saint-Exupéry had not yet flown a single war mission; how could he be asked to leave the squadron now? Infuriated by his friend's stubbornness, Werth reminded him over the winter that he was worth more alive than dead and begged him to reconsider his assignment. To this Saint-Exupéry replied, "That would be discourteous toward my comrades." Dorothy Thompson told him the same thing in May; she was in Paris and asked Madame de B to arrange for her to see the writer again. It was outrageous, she told him, that he should be flying reconnaissance missions, which were claiming such high casualties. "You are absolutely wrong. . . . If I did not resist with my life, I should be unable to write. . . . One must write with one's body," the pilot informed Thompson, heading off on a long, mystical riff about making the word flesh. (On the other side of the world Anne Lindbergh read Thompson's account of her talk with Saint-Exupéry with a lump in her throat and tears in her eyes. She spent the next few days attempting to apply his philosophy to her own life, sorry that—in light of her husband's public opposition to America entering the war—she seemed to stand on the other side of his heroism.) Paradoxically, Saint-Exupéry had to make himself the exception to the rule in order to keep from being treated preferentially.

Why was he so much invested in flying missions he knew to be entirely futile? He was old enough to have outgrown any childish confidence in his own invulnerability, scarred enough to have relinquished the notion that he led a charmed life, acquainted enough with what he termed his "*absences de moi-même*" that he could brag to his commanding officer that he had reported his car stolen when he had in fact forgotten where he had parked it. Furthermore, he admitted that he knew he could be of far greater use to his country in another capacity. He had no logical argument with which to defend himself against those who sought his transfer. At the same time he could not shake his instinctive sense that he should be at the front, where he knew the odds were absurd. He was the first to admit that France's war effort amounted to a game of "cops and robbers," a "grim charade"; there was nothing vaguely rational about the reconnaissance missions flown by the 2/33, the hard-won information from which would be useless if it made its way to the General Staff, which it generally did not. (On one occasion when it did—in mid-May an observer on a low-altitude mission reported German tanks in the Ardennes, which the French staff continued to think of as impermeable—it was roundly disbelieved. The observer was told he had been hallucinating.) But the alternative to what seemed certain death did not interest Saint-Exupéry. "We face the prospect of a return to our native sordidness—the greasy food of avaricious relatives, the cantankerousness of family squabbles, the bad conscience born of money cares, the disappointed hopes, the degrading flight before the rent-collector, the arrogance of the landlord; squalor, and the stinking death in hospital. Up here at any rate death is clean," he wrote, having known some of these ills.

Because he should not have been at the front, his reasons for flying were necessarily more complex than those of his comrades, as expressed by Jean Dutertre: "We knew that the Germans were stronger, but we had a job to do, and we did it. We didn't pay attention to whether it served a purpose or not." Among other things, a certain *noblesse oblige* colored the issue for Saint-Exupéry. Even his mother, mobilized as a nurse in September 1939, wrote that she was delighted to be of use; she could not bear the idea of inaction. Her son admitted to "a desire to take charge of everything," and more and more thought of himself as a kind of shepherd. He realized a truth vital to his existence: "When you are in danger, you are responsible for everyone." Moreover, he had always mistrusted intellectuals; he had no stomach now for the formulae they concocted with which to assuage the pain of a miserable country. Over and over he insisted that true passion could be measured only in acts. He was unable to admit, with Sartre, that "words are deeds," still believing—as he had told Renée de Saussine years before—that he had to live in order to write, which naturally meant to risk not living.

He was much pained in January when accused in the press of making literature of his failed flights. A jealous writer led the charge, but managed to hit a nerve. Saint-Exupéry knew he was in large part fighting this battle for himself: He was the first to admit that he loved and needed that which forced him out of himself, that he found a certain serenity when under siege. He knew well the purifying power of sacrifice. In December he had written to Madame de B that he had loved his crash landing in Libya, the necessity which had forced him to walk and to keep walking. He told the Lindberghs that in his twenties he had sometimes found the desert flat and uninteresting—until he was fired at, when it became beautiful again. The philosopher Maurice Merleau-Ponty saw this clearly on reading *Flight to Arras*: he recognized Saint-Exupéry as a man who found himself "to the extent to which he runs into danger." While he had no taste for blood, or for high altitude, he needed to fight this war, which for all its futility and absurdity, for all it reminded him of his age, was the closest thing he had known to Aéropostale and its life of action, a front from which he had for nearly ten years now been exiled. He stayed on with the 2/33 when, as he well knew, he could have been of greater service to his country elsewhere, for the most noble and selfish of reasons.

~

On February 27 Saint-Exupéry left for Marseilles for two weeks to train on a Bloch 174, the new pride of the French air force, an aircraft that could, at an altitude of 30,000 feet, rival the Messerschmitt. At the end of March the first Blochs arrived in Orconte; the 2/33—one of the three reconnaissance groups that reported directly to the High Command—received them before any other squadron. There was a tussle over who would claim the honor of the first mission in the new aircraft, which Laux, Gelée, and Saint-Exupéry were all qualified to fly. Each had his own good reason for making the trip over eastern France and Belgium; Saint-Exupéry based his claim on the fact that he was the only one of the three who had experience as a test pilot. Laux won the day, but had a problem with his oxygen mask and was forced to abort his mission. With his gunner and observer Saint-Exupéry took off on Laux's return, gloating a little. "I knew that the first sortie was mine *ex officio*," he informed Laux before heading off on what was as well his own first mission. He turned back when at 27,000 feet his controls froze.

Three days later, on April 1, having flown two missions, Saint-Exupéry was scheduled to go up again as Gelée's observer. Like a child insisting he must ride in the front seat, he protested that he got sick in bad weather if he was not at the controls. He so much pressed the case that his commanding officer wound up as observer and Saint-Exupéry as pilot, over-flying western Germany together at 30,000 feet. On the return to Orconte, Gelée could not help but remind him over the intercom of the mnemonic he had taught him for preparing his landing gear. Threatening to fine Gelée if he distracted him again, Saint-Exupéry executed a perfect landing. He remained as gluttonous, and as stubborn, as he had been years before when polishing off Escot's plate. "If you had your way," Alias exploded one day, "you would fly all the missions." With the campaign of 1940 in mind, Alias coined the formula that fairly summed up his illustrious colleague's flying career: "When the flight is normal Saint-Exupéry is dangerous; given complications he's brilliant." On April 16 the 2/33's confidence in the Bloch was shattered when Laux was shot down over Belgium. His gunner and observer were killed, and Laux was badly burned. Everyone wanted to know how it had happened—the 1,140-horsepower Bloch had been thought invulnerable to attack—but only one person made the trip to Laux's bedside, posing as a *Paris-Soir* reporter, to find out. In his Neufchâteau hospital room on the twentieth Laux was surprised to see through the gauze of his bandages what looked like Saint-Exupéry. He stayed for a few hours, leaving Laux with a check for 1,000 francs, which the captain never cashed. With him Saint-Exupéry took back to France the unhappy news that a new model Messerschmitt was in the air.

The 2/33 had moved on April 11 to Athies-sous-Laon, eighty miles northwest of Orconte. Saint-Exupéry had by this time begun to suffer from a high fever that attacked without warning, sometimes even when he was on the runway. He got little satisfaction from the doctors he consulted, who seemed to want to blame his gallbladder, a theory with which he disagreed. With the help of sulfa drugs he managed to get along, barely; he carried a supply of the medicine in his pocket at all times, in the event he was taken prisoner. He told no one of the problem. "If anyone in the group had suspected these attacks they would have seen to it that I was sent back to my desk and not entrusted with the responsibility of an airplane and a crew. Since I couldn't complain without being forcibly cashiered, I flew high-altitude missions with a raging fever," he explained later. It does not appear to have crossed his mind that his gunner and observer may have had a vested interest in his health. Trouble came in the form of an unannounced medical examination, for which he had to invent an absurd story about an attack of malaria, an illness from which he had never suffered. It seems likely that a military doctor—who would almost certainly have known that Saint-Exupéry had been deemed unfit to fly in the first place—simply chose to look the other way; he probably would not have believed that anyone would attempt a war mission with a 104-degree fever. On May 10, when the Battle of France actually began, Saint-Exupéry was in Paris for medical reasons that—so far as his squadron knew—had to do with trouble he was having with some old fractures, which can be painful at 30,000 feet, at which altitude the body's tissues swell.

At 4:00 a.m. that day he was awakened in Paris by a phone call from

René Delange, the newspaper editor. The Germans had invaded Holland, Belgium, and Luxembourg. The *drôle de guerre* was over; on Saint-Exupéry's return to Laon he found—as did most of the 2/33's pilots, nearly all of whom were on leave when the Blitzkrieg began—that the terrain had been bombed. The aircraft had been camouflaged and had all survived the incident. By the fifteenth, however, when Holland surrendered, the enemy was within sixteen miles of the base. The 2/33 again moved west, in what was to be the first step in a pell-mell race across France. Saint-Exupéry was back in Paris on the sixteenth, partly to vent his outrage. Why had no one made it clear to the French people that the situation was dire, that the front was not holding? Did the leaders of France know where the Germans were? He did; he had seen them along the road outside Laon, a little over an hour's drive from Paris. He found the capital's calm extraordinary, as indeed it was. It was as inconceivable that the Germans would march into Paris as it had been that tanks would roll through the Ardennes, and the Luxembourg Punch-and-Judy show, the Drouot auctions, went on for weeks after this visit.

Saint-Exupéry is said to have met with Premier Paul Reynaud at 6:00 p.m. on the sixteenth, which he could not have done, as Reynaud had welcomed Churchill to an emergency meeting at the Quai d'Orsay thirty minutes earlier. (There Churchill learned that the Sedan front had been broken and that eight or ten German divisions, having cut the French forces in half, were now speeding toward Amiens and Arras. He was told in the next moment that the French had no strategic reserve, an announcement he remembered as one of the greatest surprises of his life. He must have been equally dumbfounded by the bonfires then burning in the Quai d'Orsay garden, into which foreign ministry officials were busily dumping years of French diplomatic archives.) Saint-Exupéry did at some point request to be sent to the United States to plead for aircraft, France having in a matter of weeks lost three-fourths of her fighter planes, and to ask Roosevelt to intervene in what was otherwise clearly a losing battle. His offer was turned down; about two weeks later the same mission was entrusted to René de Chambrun, a young lawyer who, like Saint-Exupéry, was both a captain and a count, but who made for a more natural envoy because—in no particular order—he spoke perfect English, was a direct descendant of Lafayette, and happened to be Pierre Laval's son-in-law.

Disgusted by the seeming indifference he felt in Paris, where the policemen were now equipped with rifles, Saint-Exupéry returned to his squadron on the twenty-first, the day they moved west again, to Orly. On the twenty-second two of the group's Potezes failed to return from missions over eastern France. In one of them Jean Israël was shot down; he was to spend the next five years in prison camps, where—in 1943—he would read Saint-Exupéry's account of what was to transpire the next day. On the twenty-third Saint-Exupéry set off from Orly with Jean Dutertre as his observer, on one of the two missions he was to conflate into the long, hair-raising meditation that is *Flight to Arras*, the supreme description of aerial warfare. The mission had been ordered by the High Command to determine whether Arras was holding its own; it was the first that had fallen to Saint-Exupéry in more than six weeks, which made it his first since the fighting had really begun. He flew north to Meaux that morning to join up with his fighter escort; when the pilots of the 1/33—whose group commander had initially refused to cooperate with the mission—learned that the reconnaissance pilot was the Académie Française laureate they scrambled for the honor of defending him.

Saint-Exupéry took off from an overcast Meaux just before 2:00 p.m. with an escort of nine Dewoitine 520's; from a height of 1,000 feet Dutertre was to establish the enemy position between Arras and Douai. Saint-Exupéry turned the machine-gun fire into poetry; Dutertre—one of the only men in the world to whom *Flight to Arras* is a novel—tersely described the apocalyptic sight that lay below. Hundreds of tanks were gathered less than two miles southwest of the city, waiting to attack. Arras was smoking like a volcano; the sky was alternately thick with dark smoke and brilliantly lit by fire. Suddenly Dutertre saw that the Bloch was about to overfly a tank formation; he cried to the pilot to turn, but was late in doing so. The Germans opened fire and the Bloch lurched violently. The observer waited a few seconds before asking, "Is something broken?" An oil tank was punctured, Saint-Exupéry reported; Dutertre directed him to return to the base. Minutes later they were flying through the sunny skies of Normandy, gasping with relief. At 3:30, without further incident, they landed at Orly. The two men laughed together as they jumped out of the aircraft, the observer more nimbly than the pilot. Saint-Exupéry offered Dutertre a cigarette, although he was unable to find a match, as he is unable to do throughout *Flight to Arras*. Later they learned that two of the escort pilots had been shot down; one pilot had been taken prisoner, and another had been hurt when he parachuted onto a chimney. Captain de Saint-Exupéry expressed his gratitude to the 1/33 with his customary wit. Without their help, he wrote in their visitors' book, "I would now be playing poker in heaven with Helen of Troy, Vercingétorix, and company—and I continue to prefer to live on this planet, despite its drawbacks."

That evening he sat down to dinner at a Porte Maillot bistro called Chez Georges with Madame de B and a doctor friend, who heard the first account of the hour and forty minutes that would become the better part of *Flight to Arras*. (In theory Saint-Exupéry spared Alias, to whom he made his official report, the observations he made now.) The pilot looked dejected and tired, mumbling a little as he described what appeared from the air to be an "interminable syrup" of refugees flowing south. He was used to frequent displacements but not entirely to the contrast between a war mission and a cozy dinner with friends, and felt it a little perverse to be holding forth in a good Parisian restaurant after having so narrowly escaped death. One minute, he told a reporter later, he could be eating his breakfast in a café, flirting with the waitress; two hours later he was back for lunch, having in the meantime gone off to survey the Rhine. "I felt like a fish being walked on the beach," he said of the schizophrenic existence that allowed him to wax poetic about German fireworks while devouring a well-prepared *Châteaubriand aux pommes*. For his front-row seat at those pyrotechnic displays he was awarded a Croix de Guerre avec Palme early in June.

Saint-Exupéry flew three additional high-altitude missions between May 31 and June 9, by which time Dunkirk had fallen and German tanks were swarming all over eastern France, their officers waving amiably to the population. On Monday the tenth and Tuesday the eleventh everyone who could left Paris, including the government, which retired provisionally to Tours. Said Werth, himself part of the mass exodus, "We amount to nothing but links in a chain, drawn slowly along the road, at speeds of six, of three miles an hour." He blamed Saint-Exupéry for having further slowed his trip south; he was weighted down by an inscribed copy of *Terre des hommes*, his most valuable possession. It is not known exactly when Consuelo left Paris, where she had been early in May; evidently on one of his trips to Paris her husband saw to it that she was evacuated, initially to Lyons.

What remained of the 2/33—now about two-thirds of its original size—began its withdrawal that Monday as well, a retreat that was not without its moments. In La Chapelle-Vendômoise, eighty-five miles southwest of Orly, Saint-Exupéry and Guy Bougerol, a lieutenant observer who happened to be a Franciscan father, were billeted in the local château, the owners of which were unhappy about the arrangement. Fearing German reprisals, they issued their guests strict instructions to observe the blackout and to keep as quiet as possible, easy conditions to meet as their rooms adjoined and the two men spent the night talking. Before going to sleep Saint-Exupéry had to leave the room; he turned the handle of his door to find that it came off in his hand. The same was true of Bougerol's, the two officers having been imprisoned by their nervous hosts. Outside the window ledge hung a bell cord; the not-very-spry flyer edged toward it and began, at about 2:00 a.m., ringing the château bell with all his might. As soon as his hostess appeared in the courtyard with a faintly lit gas lamp he launched into a vehement speech, inciting the populace to rebellion, from the ledge above her. When the châtelaine grasped the physiological urge behind this call-to-arms she released him immediately from his room, falling all over herself with apologies. "Monsieur de Saint-Exupéry, allow me to kiss you!" she cried. "Never!" responded Saint-Exupéry superbly, heading past her to the toilet.

The 2/33 was still in La Chapelle-Vendômoise when the Germans entered a deserted Paris on Friday, June 14, and swastikas began to fly from the Arc de Triomphe, the Quai d'Orsay, and the Eiffel Tower. The squadron was moving on to Bordeaux—"driven by the enemy from field to field like poor devils pursued by a relentless bailiff," as Saint-Exupéry put it—as Reynaud handed in his resignation, unwilling to break with the British and make a separate peace with the Germans, and Marchal Pétain, the eighty-four-year-old embodiment of French military glory, came to power with the aim of seeking an immediate peace. "The news from France is very bad," Churchill conceded on the seventeenth. In New York Raoul de Roussy de Sales went further: "France has fallen from the height of ten centuries of history in thirty-eight days. This is the inescapable fact, but it is so tremendous no one is capable of grasping it." One Frenchman who did was in London; the following day Charles de Gaulle broadcast his call-to-arms over the BBC, a speech that lasted four minutes and did more at the time to make him a persona non grata in France than to establish him as his country's savior. Another Frenchman continued south: "We're off to Algeria. . . . Don't expect mail as it will be impossible, but know of my affection," Saint-Exupéry hurriedly wrote his mother.

On the Bordeaux-Mérignac tarmac stood a fabulous array of aircraft, packed wing to wing. Saint-Exupéry piled a number of spare parts and some forty passengers—including a woman, a cage of birds, and a dog, because of which he would refer to the aircraft later as "Noah's Ark"—into a four-motor Farman 220. It was not the airplane he was meant to take—he should have salvaged a Bloch—and the hulking machine resembled nothing he had ever flown. But as the Farman could carry ground personnel and parts to North Africa, where the 2/33 was to continue its operations, Saint-Exupéry took it upon himself to appropriate the passenger plane. It was an unfinished prototype, however, and its bolts began to give over the Mediterranean, a fact the pilot took great pleasure in announcing to the exhausted Red Cross nurse on board. He woke Suzanne Massu repeatedly with terrifying bulletins and—misconstruing fatigue for sangfroid—was impressed to find her unflappable. Saint-Exupéry piloted the Farman through a heavy fog pierced on all sides by other aircraft; it was as if he and his passengers took advantage of a flock of wild birds for their escape, as would one of his later heroes. On the afternoon of the twenty-first he landed in Oran, where he expected to find his squadron; the signals had been crossed, however, and they were waiting for him in Algiers. The following morning he was over the Maison-Blanche field, again pestering Suzanne Massu. Most of the French air force had retreated to Algiers, and he saw no room to land. After circling the field several times Saint-Exupéry maneuvered the Farman to the ground in what was deemed an acrobatic feat. The armistice having been signed the previous day, the pilots and parts he had transported were now useless. He was, as he put it, out of work. That day Hitler treated himself to a tour of Paris, sullen and silent, but still beautiful.

In Algiers the French officers checked into the Hôtel Aletti, the center of French political intrigue for the four years to come. Saint-Exupéry called Pélissier, who crept through a pitch-black night to join him in his room. Pélissier found his friend exhausted and horrified, increasingly resigned, as the days wore on, to the impossibility of continuing the fight. In the Aletti bar a group of flyers gathered every evening to discuss the ardent battle they hoped to wage; they had airplanes—some 800 in fact, and in the 2/33's case more than they had had at the beginning of the war—but were hopelessly short on fuel, parts, and ground crews. Saint-Exupéry was rarely in attendance, entirely silent when he was. With a sad smile the author of *Terre des hommes* explained his discretion to Suzanne Massu: "Pointless to extinguish their faith."

XV

~

Resistance on Fifth Avenue
1940–1942

*Set down three Frenchmen in the deserts of Libya:
before a month is out they will be wrangling and
scratching at one another.*

MONTAIGNE, *Essays*

As a reserve officer, Saint-Exupéry was demobilized on July 31, five
weeks after his arrival in Algiers. With regrets of all kinds he left his group,
effusively inscribing a copy of *Terre des hommes* to Gavoille before doing
so. On the dedication page he sketched a dazed-looking version of his
little *bonhomme:* "This is me, demobilized and uncertain of the future,"
he scrawled underneath. On August 4 Alias and a few other members of
the squadron saw him off on board the *Lamoricière,* on which he was to
sail for Marseilles. In a few poignant moments in the ship's bar Saint-
Exupéry confessed that he had been nervous about making a late debut
as a military pilot, that he had been in over his head in Orconte at first,
and that he was extremely grateful to the 2/33—the spirit of which had
so reminded him of Aéropostale—for having welcomed him as warmly as
it had. For its part, the 2/33 reported that with the pilot's departure the
group had "lost its soul."

He arrived in Marseilles the following day with three francs and fifty
centimes to his name, doubtless in large part because, ever the *grand
seigneur,* he had treated the group to a lavish banquet before leaving
Algiers. Fortunately Madame de B was waiting for him in Marseilles. She
accompanied him to Agay, where he buried himself in his writing; she
settled in at a nearby villa with her son and her family. She had no trouble
understanding his disillusionment, about which she was more than articulate: under the name Hélène Froment she published a novel with Gal-

limard a year later about the impossible love affair between a military doctor and a married nurse who has loved him since childhood, a novel that bears certain echoes of *Southern Mail* and much louder ones of Saint-Exupéry. Writes the hero of *On ne revient pas* (*No Way Back*) from the front in 1940, "My companions are all fine men, and I am happy to share their lives, their rain, their mud, their melancholy days," paraphrasing Saint-Exupéry, whose vocabulary he shares, and who had written that letter in December 1939. Captain Bernard Fontaine thirsts for the absolute, is cut to the quick by the dissensions among men, and prefers the higher calling of his profession to a life of domestic calm. Overwhelmed by the cataclysm around him, he proves wed to his métier, impossible to tame.

Mireille d'Agay, Saint-Exupéry's niece, remembered the summer of 1940 as one of preoccupied, whispering adults, of the same kind of late-night sobriety that Saint-Exupéry had sensed in the corridors of Saint-Maurice in 1914. Her uncle worked nearly all the time—he himself compared the occupation to being in a monastery, an appropriate analogy, given the tone of the pages at hand—and his nieces and nephew got used to tiptoeing past his door. In Mireille's eleven-year-old eyes the highlight of the stay, the writer's longest at Agay and his last, were the late-night readings. She and her sister would slide out of bed and down the hallway to the living room, where their mother, a finger to her lips, would signal for them to install themselves on the carpet. Bewitched, the adults sat perfectly still as Saint-Exupéry read from his long "poem," a book of parables set in the desert into which he was busily inserting the sum of his experience, an ambitious undertaking that—at the age of forty—he began to refer to as "my posthumous work." Drunk on its images, a little dizzy from the haze of cigarette smoke that accumulated around a declaiming Saint-Exupéry, the children stumbled off to bed late in the evening without a word. Their uncle went back to his room and back to work. By the end of the summer he had a good-sized chunk of manuscript, which he rarely let out of his sight.

He was not, however, one to spend the war writing on the Riviera. No obvious alternative presented itself: there were few places where a Frenchman could hold his head high in the autumn of 1940. Over the course of several August weeks Madame de B's brother tried to convince him to join de Gaulle in London, but Saint-Exupéry—who had been put off by de Gaulle's bitter BBC attack on Pétain just after the armistice—had already heard as much as he cared to about the renegade general and his aspirations, which in 1940 seemed far-fetched at best. Nor did he have any taste for Vichy, particularly as the autumn wore on and the regime's anti-Jewish measures were promulgated. Hardly a proponent of compromise under the best of circumstances, he was unwilling to enter into the

double game many played with the occupying power; any argument to
sauver les meubles ("salvage the furniture") was lost on a man who had
none. Gallimard had burned its files and retreated to the Riviera, leaving
a number of worried writers tugging at Gaston's purse strings; it looked
as if the influential *NRF* would be salvaged by the Nazis for their own
aims. Saint-Exupéry could not have been entirely certain that he would
be able to publish in his own country, at least without being conscripted
by forces with which he did not wish to associate. To complicate matters
his health continued to deteriorate, taking a toll on his nerves. The south
of France was packed with refugees, creating shortages of food and gasoline; he had no reserves of cash. He also had a wife to support: La
Feuilleraie being in the occupied zone, Consuelo had now settled—against
her husband's wishes—in a sort of artists' colony in the abandoned old
city of the tiny Vaucluse town of Oppède, an experience she was to write
about later. On the subject of her husband at this time her description
was entirely accurate: "He turned in circles like a caged bear."

Saint-Exupéry considered himself "half-separated" from Consuelo,
on whom he had come to learn he could not rely, and with whom honesty
was not always the best policy. When he had sent instructions to Becker
from the front as to how he would want his estate divided in the event of
his death he left a third of it to his mother, an installment he begged
Becker not to mention to Consuelo. All the same he felt as responsible as
ever for his wife, and since he was not particularly versed in domestic
responsibility and she was particularly adept at acting irresponsibly, he
often had reason to feel guilty on her account (as, doubtless, did she on
his). Madame de Saint-Exupéry assured her son that he had done all he
could for Consuelo, given a set of imperfect circumstances. He spoke of
her rarely, except to the Werths, who before the debacle so often passed
on messages from one spouse to the other. That summer Suzanne Werth
finally confided her utter mystification about their friend's love life to
Madame de B, who explained—rather lucidly, for someone in the thick
of it—that while Antoine felt like a parent with Consuelo he was with her
like a child. He came to her for refuge, as Fontaine does Beatrice, the
heroine of *On ne revient pas*. Like Beatrice she "wanted to protect him,
care for him, sustain him," to dress him and reassure him and send him
back out to the battle with a word of encouragement. She loved him enough
to provide these services, although he was not her only child—her son
was quite young —and she was therefore not able to be with him as much
as she might like. Their periods of separation would only increase in the
years of muddled geography that followed, as three-fifths of France was
occupied by the Germans and residents of the capital headed their letters
"Paris, Germany."

Saint-Exupéry flew around from the Werths to the Gallimards to Sallès early that fall, soliciting advice. Sooner or later the idea of America came up, as it was bound to. "Out of a thousand Frenchmen of whom you ask the question 'What country would you like to see?' 999 will answer 'the United States,' and the last one will reply 'New York,' " wrote a resident of occupied France the following year. Reynal & Hitchcock represented an end to Saint-Exupéry's financial embarrassments; America stood clearly as the answer to France's humiliation. He ran the idea past Werth, the friend he claimed was his conscience, who applauded it, and past Sallès, who put him up in Tarascon while he waited for his papers to be processed in Vichy, the makeshift capital, where he collected them in mid-October.

In Vichy Saint-Exupéry ran into a number of old friends. One was Robert Boname, an Air France Transatlantique engineer and executive to whom he described his plans in the words he was to use repeatedly over the next few weeks: "My friend, there is nothing left to be done here. I'm off." As the expression on his face indicated that Boname should do the same, the engineer replied, "See you soon, then, on the other side." Saint-Exupéry explained his thinking to Ségogne with the same shrug of resignation and informed Joseph Kessel that he was going to New York for a month. With Roger Beaucaire, an old Aéropostale colleague who would wind up in America as well, he had dinner at the Hôtel du Parc, Pétain's headquarters in Vichy, a resort town in which each ministry claimed its own hotel. A private table had been set up in the middle of the dining room for Pierre Laval. According to Beaucaire, when the vice premier (there was no premier and there was no legislature, France now having—not counting the Germans—a government of two, Pétain and Laval) made his entrance Saint-Exupéry said loudly, "There goes the man who's giving France away." When informed that every word of his seditious conversation had been overheard by a compatriot who would go on to become Vichy ambassador to Berlin, Saint-Exupéry commented, "Oh, well, now that we've said enough to be shot at dawn let's go for a walk." If his actual performance was slightly less cinematic the conviction was no less intense.

There were a great number of helpful people in Vichy. Chief among them from Saint-Exupéry's vantage point was Pierre Drieu La Rochelle, a Gallimard writer who in 1940 was a fascist in all but name. He was in Vichy on *NRF* business, having been charged by his old friend Otto Abetz, now German ambassador to France, with producing a literary journal of which the occupying power could be proud. With hindsight Saint-Exupéry would doubtless have picked a different travel agent, but Drieu (whom he knew through the Gallimards) managed to see that his papers were readied promptly: The American visa was issued on the twenty-first, and a *laissez-passer* was provided for Paris, where he wanted to collect his papers. Drieu agreed to drive him to the capital the following day, saving Saint-Exupéry the long wait for a crowded refugee train. On reaching the demarcation line and seeing how easily Drieu glided past the German sentinels at the border of occupied France Saint-Exupéry realized with whom he had accepted a ride. Neither man left any mention of what was discussed during this trip but the subject of NRF must have come up: earlier in the week Gallimard had called on Gide to suggest that the publication could be kept in business with an editorial board composed of Drieu, Paul Éluard, Jean Giono, Malraux, Saint-Exupéry, and Gide, a proposition to which Gide did not lend his support. (He proffered a contribution from his journals instead.) As late as December, in his first issue of the NRF, Drieu promised to publish work by Saint-Exupéry. The latter's political convictions remained just vague enough for a Nazi sympathizer to make this claim—as for Vichy officials to consider him for a ministry post.

In Paris Saint-Exupéry was asked to submit to an interview with a German officer, a meeting arranged by Drieu. Leaving it at 9:45 p.m. he discovered—with fifteen minutes to curfew—that the Métro had already closed. This time in the manner of "a nimble bear" he ran from the Rond-Point of the Champs-Élysées across the Seine to the 7th arrondissement, terrified that he would be apprehended and his notebooks seized. After the marathon he concluded, disheveled, "I'm not made to live under the Occupation." Forty-eight hours later he was back in the unoccupied zone, where he set about saying his good-byes. In the course of these weeks, before and after the trip to Vichy, he saw nearly everyone he knew, for the simple reason that nearly everyone still in France who could afford to be—and many who could not—were huddled in the south. He had dinner with his old Saurer boss, from his days as a truck salesman. He saw Guillaumet, more discouraged even than he, largely because he had not witnessed the war firsthand and understood less well why it could not continue. He lunched in Cannes with André Beucler, who did not entirely approve of his hurrying off. "I think it imperative to commit to the home-land, even trampled, even profaned," said Beucler. "I think it is time to step back, to gain perspective, and I am going to try to get to New York," countered Saint-Exupéry.

In Lyons he dined with Jean Prévost and a group of friends, among them Françoise Giroud. He finished off the dinner with his usual display of card tricks, offering to let Giroud in on one of his secrets. "You will show me when France is free," she said, as tears welled in their eyes. He spent three days before the Vichy trip with Werth in Saint-Amour, a visit that left his friend to meditate anew on the marvels of friendship. During his stay Saint-Exupéry expounded on his belief that the obstacles presented to man were but "opportunities for his deliverance," perhaps an encour-aging thing to mention to someone named Werth living in Vichy France less than two weeks after the Jewish Statute had come into effect. Saint-Exupéry had his own way with obstacles, of course: in front of his old Aéropostale colleague Jean Lucas he pulled out a pack of Cravens, almost impossible to find that summer. Lucas expressed surprise. "When I want something," explained the writer, "I always get it." He scoured Cannes for Pierre Billon, whom he had heard was in town; dismissing Billon's fiancée, he told the *Courrier Sud* director over lunch of his opportunity to leave for America and entrusted him with his sole copy of the treatment for "Igor." "If I come back," he promised Billon, "we'll work on it together." In Cannes he ran into the director Raymond Bernard, who had brought his parents to the unoccupied zone, and whom he told as well of his imminent departure. Saint-Exupéry was on his way to see his mother in Cabris and suddenly thought it imperative that he introduce Bernard to her, which he was unable to do. He left his mother with a portable radio, which she accepted with tears.

No one forgot these meetings with Saint-Exupéry, which were to be their last; at a time like this one remembered one's impressions. At the end of October, during his final days in France, he spoke with a reporter from a Lyons newspaper. He rehearsed the story of the Arras flight in his hotel lobby. The reporter accompanied him to the station; as the Académie Française laureate boarded his train, he fired a last question. What did Monsieur de Saint-Exupéry like to read? Elsewhere he was to say that his constant companions at the front were Rilke, Pascal, and Baudelaire; from the running board of the train he summed up this literature quickly: "I like books which give the impression that civilization still exists."

Saint-Exupéry made his way west via North Africa, for which he sailed on November 5. Naturally he called on the 2/33, who were then stationed, rather idly, near Tunis. He was thrilled to discover in Algiers that René Chambe, an air force officer and writer whom he had known for some time, was also a guest at the Aletti; he rang the colonel's room at 1:00 a.m. to say he was waiting for him with a bottle of cold champagne, to which the two did justice some time before they parted at four. (Another reunion that week came to an abrupt end when an Italian from the Armistice Commission complained to the hotel about his lively neighbor.) They were in agreement that there was nothing to be done in France; Saint-Exupéry outlined for Chambe his plans for New York, which he now described as embarking on a public relations campaign so as to persuade America to intervene in the war. Chambe was in North Africa on what was meant to be a journalistic assignment but was a trip for which he had a larger agenda: he had been asked to take the temperature of public opinion, but personally wondered about the loyalty of the 115,000 troops the armistice allowed France to keep in the colonies. With pleasure he took his friend with him on a high-level tour of Morocco, during which it was established that the native population was generally indifferent to the fate of France. More worrisome was the attitude of the military, who reacted coolly to the idea of Americans setting foot in North Africa. The two officers said their good-byes in Marrakech, on the balcony of Chambe's room at the Hôtel Mamounia. "So, Saint-Ex, when will we see each other again?" asked Chambe over a sustained handshake. "Right here, damn it all, in Africa! When the Americans land I swear to you I will be with them," the captain assured him.

He arrived in December in Lisbon, a city overflowing with refugees of every kind but in no other way touched by war. He was lucky to find a hotel room in Estoril, a resort town just outside the city, and began the wait for a boat, a debilitating, bureaucratic ordeal for most people. Clearly he still had misgivings about his decision; leaving his country in her hour of need tallied with none of his ideals. An acquaintance from the 1930s who met him again now commented: "Rarely have I seen a person in such an indecisive frame of mind." He was sickened by the sight of many of those headed in his direction, whom he observed in the Estoril casino: "I felt neither indignation nor disrespect but a vague anguish, the kind you experience at a zoo before the last of an extinct species. . . . They were gambling fortunes that were—perhaps at the moment they were staked —worthless. They were playing with currencies that may at that moment have been taken out of circulation. Their wealth consisted of factories that might already have been confiscated. . . . It was unreal, a kind of puppet show." On the twenty-seventh he received what must under the circumstances have felt an especially cruel blow. Guillaumet was dead, having been shot down over the Mediterranean while flying the new French High Commissioner to Syria. His last words had the same syncopated feel as Mermoz's—"Under attack. Fire on board. SOS. SO"—and echoed as loudly in Lisbon as anywhere. Saint-Exupéry, who had just lost one world, now found that another had evaporated out from under him. He wrote an especially distraught letter to Madame de B:

> Guillaumet is dead. It seems to me tonight as if I have no more friends. I don't feel sorry for him; I have never been able to pity the dead. But it will take me so long to come to terms with his disappearance, and I'm already burdened by such miserable tasks. It will be months and months; I will need him so often. Does age really claim us so quickly? I'm the last survivor of the old Casa/Dakar team. . . . All the others are dead, and I have no one left on earth with whom to reminisce. I'm like an old toothless man, ruminating over all this by myself.

Poised on the far edge of the continent he teetered a bit. He cabled and telephoned France incessantly, a luxury he could ill afford. He had little desire to emigrate: "I've learned so many things at home that will be useless elsewhere," he was to write later. If Madame de B thought he should return to France, he informed her, he would.

On the day he received the news of Guillaumet's death Saint-Exupéry was scheduled to give a talk at Lisbon's École Française. Soberly he sang the praises of the simple man who had always seemed to him the incarnation of courage, dwelling on his misadventure in the Andes, segueing into the message of *Terre des hommes.* He cried openly in the course of the talk; he did not neglect to mention that he was the last survivor of the airline's early days. He pulled himself together afterward at a reception held in his honor and for the filmmaker Jean Renoir, who had also lectured, sampling a vintage port and mesmerizing with his sleight-of-hand. On December 4 he was scheduled to speak again on the subject of Aéropostale at a highly regarded engineering school. In a statement Giraudoux might have appreciated, he began by saying that he would prefer to brave a cyclone than to deliver his lecture. He went on to say that he wanted to change his subject, so as to speak about a topic with which he was preoccupied of late. "I would like to talk to you about fear," Saint-Exupéry announced, sending an excited murmur through the audience. In an even tone the pilot went on to analyze the spectrum of his emotions under fire in a reconnaissance plane, underwater in the bay of Saint-Raphaël, under the heat of the Libyan sun. In the middle of the first ordeal he had forged what he claimed was a new definition of life: "To live is to be conscious that you are not dead, second by second, as bombs burst around you, which amounts to an extraordinary anguish."

On December 21 he and the gray-paper parcel from which he had refused to be separated during his stay in Lisbon boarded the *Siboney,* a tiny boat of the American Export Lines. His neighbor turned out to be Jean Renoir, whom Saint-Exupéry had known only peripherally. Before embarking he cabled Becker, asking that he inform only Hitchcock of his imminent arrival. He wanted very much to avoid interviews.

∼

Saint-Exupéry got on the *Siboney* as a refugee and off as a celebrity; there was no avoiding reporters, some of whom had turned up to meet Jean Renoir and settled for the other outsized Frenchman, an even better catch. Among them was a young news service correspondent who worshiped Saint-Exupéry and spoke a little French; the writer good-naturedly engaged him as a translator for an impromptu press conference at the pier. In a tweed topcoat, his hairline having crept high up on his forehead, his face creased with lines and scars, he looked particularly monumental. He gave away no secrets in ascribing France's fall to a group of leaders who had little concept of modern war but veered away from making any po-

litical statements, refusing to offer an opinion of Pétain. He expressed his
confidence that France would rise again but when pressed as to how
squinted at the Manhattan skyline and answered a little bitterly, "I am
not a crystal gazer." He was more at ease describing the *Siboney*'s stormy
crossing, which had taken two days longer than expected and proved soggy:
sea water had risen through the wash basins and invaded the cabins. On
board the vessel, which bore little resemblance to the *Normandie*, Saint-
Exupéry had said he sympathized with Columbus. The ship's captain was
relieved to see Jersey City: it was now New Year's Eve, and because of
the delay the *Siboney*'s bars had run dry. Saint-Exupéry was no less relieved, although he spared reporters an account of the seasickness that
had kept him loyal to a weeklong diet of tea and beef bouillon. For the
former he had imposed on Renoir's wife to place his order. "All you have
to say is 'tea,'" Didi Renoir informed him. "I don't want to. I should
rather go without," pouted the writer, who told reporters—and doubtless
believed—that his stay in the English-speaking world was to last three to
four weeks. At the conclusion of the interview the young reporter impul-
sively asked Saint-Exupéry to autograph his interview notes. The more
seasoned journalists followed suit, admitting later that they had never
before done such a thing.

New York looked dazzling and wild with animation after the ashen
skies and curfews of Europe. Saint-Exupéry had spent New Year's Eve
in some unusual places, but accustomed as he was to blackouts Times
Square proved nearly as exotic as the Libyan desert. The city's high spirits
left him—as a party in full swing will a man in mourning—with a deep
sense of malaise. He checked into the Ritz-Carlton and quickly made his
first calls. With Renoir in tow he turned up on the doorstep of his old
Beaux-Arts companion Bernard Lamotte, now painting in a studio on East
Fifty-second Street, today La Grenouille's upstairs dining room. Here and
on his rooftop terrace Lamotte was to entertain the major and minor
celebrities of the extended artistic community over the next years. Better
supplied with charm than with money, he did so in bohemian splendor;
Saint-Exupéry was to visit regularly, and in the odes he wrote to the refuge
at Lamotte's he generally evoked spinning heads and rotating sidewalks.
Lamotte welcomed "the two mastodons" with open arms, rustling up a
Sunday lunch of sardines and veal Marengo from the restaurant below,
washed down over the course of the afternoon with a fair number of bottles
of Byrrh. Also this first weekend Saint-Exupéry called on Raoul de Roussy
de Sales, who found him less merry. The former *Paris-Soir* correspondent
reported that his friend seemed "more like a bird than ever, a bird with
a tendency to hide its head under its wing. He is, so to speak, weather-
beaten by the war." Saint-Exupéry was not only unhappy and at a loss
for what to do; he was painfully aware that the British—up against the

same miserable odds as the French had been—were still fighting a war his own country had surrendered.

What he most wanted was a minute to think, a respite, a time-out, and this America was not prepared to offer him. Two weeks after his arrival—a year late, but with one fine excuse—he collected his 1939 National Book Award at a Hotel Astor luncheon attended by 1,500 people. The press could not help but descend upon him in the days following the ceremony; perhaps because Reynal & Hitchcock laid the groundwork for him, perhaps because he was now, despite himself, on a sort of propaganda mission, Saint-Exupéry handled them with aplomb, far more at ease than he had been when the Académie Française had thrust him into the spotlight two years earlier. He made for good copy, not only on account of his derring-do: a six-foot two-inch Frenchman will stand out in any crowd. Legends of all kinds attached themselves to him, more so after his publishers volunteered that the only way to get the globe-trotting author to write was to lock him in a room; when his agent expounded on his sartorial quirks; when in the middle of an interview with Stephen Vincent Benét the pilot had to summon a Ritz waiter to turn off the electric fireplace in his room so that the two men did not roast to death. He could not himself make head or tails of the contraption. He was charming, always able in relating his adventures to make himself half hero, half clown. "He has a nice perception of the fact that conversation is not a book or a lecture; that it should be interesting," noted an admiring Otis Ferguson, who found the Frenchman a master of timing: "You never have to wonder what his point is: it explodes." And he was forthcoming on any subject outside of politics, volunteering that he was planning to put his other manuscript aside so as to concentrate on a book about his war experiences.

To this end he received nothing but encouragement from Eugene Reynal and Curtice Hitchcock, who—along with their wives—did everything in their power to make the foreign author feel at home. It was not their understanding that Saint-Exupéry was in town for a short stay, and Elizabeth Reynal and Peggy Hitchcock scoured the city for an apartment that would be to his liking. They found one with magnificent views on the twenty-third floor of 240 Central Park South; visitors often described it as a cockpit of a place. They equipped the kitchen and stocked the bar and refrigerator and filled the closet with hangers. Only when a fire was burning in the fireplace and a few friends were assembled for an afternoon cocktail was their author allowed to see his new home. He was touched and delighted, close to tears. He needed looking after, and Reynal, Hitchcock, and Becker were happy to oblige.

His immediate problem was, of course, one of money. *Wind, Sand and Stars* had already earned him over $17,500 in royalties—roughly $200,000 today—but Saint-Exupéry's bank account was blocked because of the war.

Reynal and Hitchcock helped their author to draft an application for permission to draw on his account. Outlining a rather unusual budget, he explained to the authorities that he would require an additional $1,500 a month over and above the nominal sum he was allowed. He would need not only to rent an apartment and hire a secretary and a translator, but was also to require immediate medical and dental attention for lingering troubles from the Guatemala crash. (He spoke only of his jawbone, which he claimed had been broken in three places and never properly treated, but was suffering more from the still-unexplained fevers.) Given the circumstances under which he had left France he did not have so much as a change of clothes; he anticipated that he would run up a fair number of travel and entertainment charges. The Reynals vouched for the accuracy of his statements and generally opened their door to Saint-Exupéry, who became a frequent and unannounced caller at their East Sixty-sixth Street apartment. Elizabeth saw to it that he was well entertained and, as importantly, well translated; she, Galantière, and Becker ran the bulk of his linguistic interference. (Of Curtice and Peggy Hitchcock their daughter has said that his French was more fluent and hers more grammatical.) Few services were more valuable.

Saint-Exupéry came to New York for four weeks and stayed for over two years but was no more willing to learn English—or able to speak it —in 1943 than he had been in 1941. He could read signs, and he could count. He could coax sense out of a text, probably more than he let on. He had no idea what people said when they talked. He was as accomplished a mime as he had proved to be in the Río de Oro and got along admirably with a smattering of French, Spanish, and German—he held whole tables of English-speakers breathless with his tales—but his refusal to so much as attempt a sentence in English was to color his exile greatly. He was not the first expatriate to fail to take to the language of his new country—F. Scott Fitzgerald proved equally impervious to French—but Saint-Exupéry did so in wartime, after having justified his exile by saying he had hoped to present France's case to the American people and her government.

He made light of his handicap, which was all unwillingness and not inability: when at last, under unusual circumstances, he submitted to English lessons in 1942, he proved to have an acute ear and an uncanny gift for imitation. "When I want a cup of coffee, I head toward the prettiest waitress and make her understand, through a series of gestures, that I need a cup, a saucer, a spoon, coffee, cream, and sugar. My act makes her laugh. Why in the world should I learn English when it would deprive me of that smile?" he told friends, in some company substituting an "*oeuf à la coque*" for the cup of coffee. In a more serious mood he would growl

"I haven't finished learning French yet" when asked why he made no effort with English, which his publishers, among others, were eager for him to master. This response hinted at the truth about his tenaciously held unilingualism: in any language he had a horror of miscommunication. Particularly during the hair-splitting arguments of the war years he valued little as much as lucidity. In interviews he insisted on a translator so as not to traffic in possible misstatements or stumble into awkwardness. At the same time, like all those who hesitate to speak the language of the realm for fear of embarrassing themselves, he was indulgent, encouraging even, of those who spoke a modicum of French. He preferred that they mangle the language of Molière than that he flounder around with words that might distort his meaning.

His intransigence on this matter had its comic and tragic sides. Saint-Exupéry folded himself into New York taxis and—as if it were the most natural thing in the world—rattled off his destination in French. He played out extraordinary bits of theater with his cleaning woman, whom he called—pushing the limits of the French language—his *"arrache-poussière"* (roughly, his "dust-puller-upper"). He became expert at corraling friends into running errands with him. Robert Boname, the Air France Transatlantique engineer, accompanied him to the drugstore. Becker took him shopping for a new wardrobe. Lamotte translated while he priced Dictaphones, of which the writer went through several; he watched as Saint-Exupéry handed over nearly $700—for which he could equally well have had a car, and which sent Reynal and Hitchcock back to pleading with the bank on his behalf—for a sophisticated recording device. Doubtless he would not have done any of these errands alone had he been able to. He needed an audience, and this arrangement suited him. Madame de B spent nearly two months in New York this winter and did her share of communicating on her friend's behalf. Yvonne Michel went with him to movies, despite the fact that he spent his time in the theater asking, "What's going on? What's happening?" Elizabeth Reynal found him French-speaking doctors; a long search for a bilingual secretary who could work a French typewriter, decipher Saint-Exupéry's handwriting, and tolerate his eccentric hours turned up a Lyons native, Marie Bouchu McBride, who spent two years in the writer's service. In situations that he was forced to tackle alone he turned to his other great friend, the telephone. From Saks he called a friend to ask him to explain to the sales clerk at his side that he would like the tie in the window with the red background. In a doctor's office he and his physician went for several rounds like this, handing the phone back and forth. On one occasion he found himself alone with the doctor in a consulting room, which had no telephone. *"Sprechen Sie Deutsch, Herr Doktor?"* asked Saint-Exupéry, at which the two men tripped their way through an involved matter in a language of which each had only an elementary grasp. Under the circumstances it seemed the appropriate one to mangle.

The language barrier proved more of an obstacle than Saint-Exupéry liked to admit, however. Generally it increased his sense of isolation: he arrived in New York a defeated man, and as the months wore on felt more and more a disenfranchised one. He had little love of America—it seemed to him that a country capable of designing a state-of-the-art washing machine might also apply itself to saving France—and he could hardly get to know her better when he could not speak her language, read her newspapers, glimpse what lay behind a culture that seemed to consist primarily of baseball, Coca-Cola, and chewing gum. As America had, in his mind, turned a cold shoulder to France, he felt personally rebuffed by her now. Raoul Aglion, an emissary of de Gaulle's who arrived in Manhattan a day after Saint-Exupéry, reminded him that New York represented only a part of America. "Yes," agreed the aviator, "but the heart of the country is here, and the heart is hard." He cut a lonely figure, as the author of *Mary Poppins*, P. L. Travers, who met him through their mutual publisher, was quick to observe. More than ever he appeared to hail from a different planet. In part because he spoke a different language and was not of his world, in part because his concerns soared higher than ever above the practical or the immediate, he began to seem a kind of religious figure. Galantière saw him in retrospect as a "kind of preaching friar." Others—responding more to his manner and his balding crown than to his lifestyle—took him for a monk. Some of his best friends in America were children, with whom language is optional. An adolescent girl on whom he lavished hilarious lessons in deportment saw the halo as clearly as anyone. It was not that of a saint, Natacha Stewart Ullmann remembered later, "It was more like the ring around the moon."

He made contact with the War Department soon after his arrival, though not exactly for the reasons he had implied. In March he met with a representative from the army's military intelligence division to whom he spoke about two inventions, probably the navigation devices he had been perfecting in Orconte. He came on strong. Reported Colonel Ralph Busbee to his superiors:

> The point is—this man—a genius almost to the point of being nuts— claims to have two inventions with respect to airplanes, which *may* prove of value. He is reluctant to ask for patents on them or proceed with further development for fear that the ideas are already under patent secretly by the U.S. Army. While not pro-Vichy, he has a wife and children [sic] in France, and naturally cannot sever connections. He wants to offer his inventions to the U.S. Army, of course hoping to make money, but is leery

of telling anyone of them unless he is fully protected. He speaks French only but has an agent who speaks English [probably Galantière].

Another officer followed up on this visit but nothing came of Saint-Exupéry's proposition.

In May, still insisting he would be returning to France in a month or so, he met a State Department official at a dinner at the Lazareffs, to whom he expounded on the taking of North Africa. "If at the time of France's collapse anyone had offered the troops in North Africa a thousand planes with replacement parts, lubricating oil, gasoline, and all the necessary adjuncts, North Africa would be fighting today. If anyone turned up there now with the offer of a lot of planes and armored units, it would turn the tide . . . the seizure of North Africa would mean the seizure of unoccupied France," he predicted. It was suggested that the War Department be in touch with the Frenchman, who seemed exceptionally well-acquainted with the geography of North Africa, a part of the world of which an accurate map was hard to come by in America at the time. In June the War Department made contact with him. It reported back to State a little dismissively: "For the record, this Division evaluates M. de Saint-Exupéry's knowledge of French African territories as 'good' in some respects but does not consider it to be 'exceptional' by any means." They did not feel he contributed anything to the War Department's expertise. In part he seems to have been rebuffed because he was not a military man. Just as clearly, it did not seem as if anyone in the U.S. War Department was willing to put much weight in unsolicited advice offered them by a foreign reserve captain unable to speak a word of English.

No one refused to speak Saint-Exupéry's language more adamantly than the French colony in New York. After the fall of France some 20,000 Frenchmen had joined the existing American community, about ten times that size. A great number of these new arrivals were diplomats, artists, scientists, industrialists, financiers; most of them settled temporarily in and around New York and Los Angeles. Immediately they divided, less than neatly, into sects and subsects; in the same issue of *The New York Times* that carried the story of Saint-Exupéry's arrival in New York, Pétain was quoted as asking the French people to put aside their rancors, prejudices, and mistrusts in the New Year. The Vichy faction—into which category most Frenchmen fell in 1941—were pro-Pétain, pro-Laval, or outright collaborationists; the *résistants* divided between Gaullist supporters and detractors. So institutionalized were the factions that when Raoul Aglion arrived in New York he was obliged to present his credentials at three Free French addresses. The resulting tour of Manhattan made for a kind of riddle; each representative claimed to be the only true friend of de Gaulle's, an intimate since their St. Cyr days, and proceeded to discredit his rivals. Nor did the divisiveness confine itself to Fifth Avenue. Léon Werth, who spent the war unobtrusively in Saint-Amour, provided the following political profile of his son's eleventh-grade class in Lyons: "20 Anglophiles, be it Pétainist or Gaullist; 14 fervent Vichyites, of which 2 Nazis; 3 Action Françaises; 3 advocates of collaboration; 6 indifferent." At the Lycée Français in New York half the students refused to speak to the other half. A community humiliated is one eager to blame, and a community in exile is by definitioń one of gossip and betrayal. The behavior of America's French refugees—as fine an example of collective bad behavior as exists—seemed to Washington in and of itself ample explanation for the defeat of France.

Into this hornets' nest walked Antoine de Saint-Exupéry, a man determined to remain above politics. His prestige was incomparable; each political faction was determined to recruit him to its cause. He got his first taste of the level of discourse at the end of January, when word arrived —ostensibly from Vichy, but more likely from the mouth of an ill-wisher—that he had been appointed by Vichy to a council of notables. Saint-Exupéry was forced to call a press conference to repudiate the report. He wrote up a statement that Roussy de Sales translated, Galantière revised, Reynal and Hitchcock approved, and Becker's secretary typed, and which he presented to the press in his suite at the Ritz-Carlton. The January 31 Times headline announced "Saint-Exupéry Dislikes Vichy Appointment/Writer-Aviator Says He Would Have Refused If Asked" and quoted him as saying he had no political agenda whatsoever. He indignantly denied all accounts to the contrary, as he would still be doing eighteen months later regarding the same charge. In one particularly bitter letter from a series of bitter letters addressed to André Breton he explained that he had done his best with the Vichy appointment: he had found it awkward to resign from a position to which he had never been formally appointed. It was true that he believed Pétain to be not the lesser of two evils but the least of three—he could be replaced at any time by a number of rabidly pro-Nazi French officials—and true as well that he had believed the armistice had been necessary. (It was also true that Vichy was capable of handing down appointments to individuals who were not only unwilling to associate with the spa-based government but whom—as was the case of the filmmaker René Clair—that government had declared persona non grata moments before.) Saint-Exupéry was reduced to an uncharacteristically shrill contention that he had amply proved his principles: Look at it this way, he told Breton: Half of my friends are dead, and all of yours are living.

Allying himself with no camp, he was calumniated by all. He engaged in a number of heated conversations with de Gaulle's representatives, instructed to convert the influential writer to the cause at all cost. In Saint-

Exupéry's eyes, however—as in those of the U.S. government—de Gaulle was a potential dictator. The writer instinctively mistrusted him and failed to understand what gave the headstrong general the right to say he spoke for a nation. Obstinately he continued to believe that Pétain had saved France from total destruction—he refused to listen when Aglion pointed out that no other country Hitler had invaded had signed an armistice with the Germans—and begrudged the general his ambition. ("How can you expect him to be otherwise? Ambition is the source of leadership," Aglion vainly protested.) Like several of his Gaullist friends, Aglion was chastised for socializing with Saint-Exupéry. Yvonne Michel, who went to work for the French desk of the Office of War Information (OWI), was told to steer clear of him. Fanned by both sides, the rumors flew fast and furious. As the Gaullists had more to lose they did a particularly virulent job: the writer was seen lunching in Washington with Vichy officials (when he had never left town); he was known to be purchasing airplanes for Vichy (even while most of his friends leaned toward de Gaulle). When he was invited to speak at the Lycée Français in December the school received a series of menacing phone calls protesting that it was about to subject its students to "a Nazi." To this day there are those who believe Saint-Exupéry to have been an anti-Semite, which he was not, for the same reason that got him blackballed in 1941: he refused to see men in terms of labels. De Gaulle, perceived as an interloper by the U.S. government, paid dearly for being unable to rally the celebrated writer—Aglion holds that of all those who refused to weigh in for the general, Saint-Exupéry did him the most harm—and de Gaulle, not the forgiving type, saw to it that he paid many times over for his lack of cooperation. Backs turned, doors closed, tongues wagged, even while Saint-Exupéry remained to American eyes the most famous of Frenchmen, a high-minded proponent of brotherhood.

While he was unrealistic to think he could steer clear of partisanship, he persisted in believing this the only conscionable tack to take. Publicly he refused to criticize Pétain's government—privately he referred to it as "that great jellyfish which is Vichy"—in which he thought, as late as mid-1942, the hopes of a majority of Frenchmen still to be invested. Unity seemed to him to be the order of the day and not at all a priority of de Gaulle's. "They are not waging war against the Nazis," said Saint-Exupéry of the general's followers, "but against the French chef or elevator man at the Ritz who refuses to join them and whom they therefore consider a traitor." One other person—who was for reasons of her own cut off from the world this year—shared his naïveté. Anne Morrow Lindbergh kept up with Saint-Exupéry through the press but did not dare call on him: having published *The Wave of the Future* in the winter of 1941, she felt she was now "the bubonic plague among writers." She did not know

enough about the French community to realize that Saint-Exupéry was
already infected. Instead she prayed that the Frenchman could "stay *free*,
pure and untouched, in an age when everyone is being smeared black or
white, forced to take sides." Her husband's terse comment on the subject
was that Saint-Exupéry represented the saint's point of view, but that saints
have a well-known habit of shirking their earthly responsibilities.

Saint-Exupéry remained more intent on seeing America enter the war
than on throwing his weight behind either Pétain or de Gaulle, a conviction
shared by Renoir, whose profile was lower and whose opinion therefore
more his own. "I detest the French in America," Renoir wrote his friend
in 1942, listing only a few exceptions. "I am happy to renounce the politics
of my ex-country altogether. I like Monsieur Roosevelt, and I like neither
Vichy, which permits a few too many executions, nor de Gaulle, who strikes
me as a bit too opportunistic." By this time Saint-Exupéry was finding
the American climate one of outright hostility. "I have been more courageous in not deviating from the road set by my conscience, in spite of
two years of insults and defamation, than when photographing Mainz or
Essen," he wrote a friend toward the end of his American stay. He reported
to Renoir that he could barely breathe, that he was in dire need of an
archangel who might guide him past his ill-wishers and show him the
way. Once a citizen of the world he was now profoundly French, down,
as they say, to the marrow; his patriotism, however, was of a different
stripe from de Gaulle's, ironic given Saint-Exupéry's famous faith in strong
leaders and what should have been a certain tolerance for reinventing the
rules. He might have been consoled by the fact that half the French in
occupied France were now in the business of informing on the other half,
a practice that left the Germans as perplexed by the Gallic character as
was Washington. He would not have been any happier had he stayed
home; he thought he would be happier anywhere else in the world, save
London. The defamatory bordered finally on the hilarious: to the list of
accusations leveled against Saint-Exupéry was added, with the publication
of *The Little Prince*, the assertion that he was a Royalist. No one in the
French community had more reason to complain of the intolerance, the
pettiness of his countrymen than he, whose publications over the next
years were to leave a trail of acrimonious political debate—and an exhausted author laboring futilely to clarify his unforgivably neutral stand
—in their wake.

~

Reynal and Hitchcock, to a great extent oblivious to the nuances of this
drama in 1941—from their vantage point it seemed simply as if all the
French in New York were having nervous breakdowns—were well aware

that they had on their hands a best-selling author with no immediate project. Saint-Exupéry was allowed a few weeks to settle in at 240 Central Park South and then reminded that he should be writing. "When tact failed, a little pressure was applied," remembered Galantière, who told him, "It is your duty to explain France, to explain the defeat to people who believe that the French did not put up a fight." Saint-Exupéry bristled at the idea of having to defend his country and, as always, at the idea of writing for a fee. He was made to see the virtues of the idea: some twenty volumes on the fall of France had already been published, many by people who had been in America since 1939 (an exception was René de Chambrun, whose *I Saw France Fall* came out in 1940); the embassy Vichy supporters in Washington and the Gaullist factions in New York spent so much time denouncing each other that France was lost in the shuffle. Protesting that he had nothing to say, Saint-Exupéry wrote a few chapters, but the book went nowhere.

His heart was not in the project. As late as May 1941 he was still hoping to get back to North Africa, if not to fight for France then to devote himself to the pages he had been honing since 1938, to be published as *The Wisdom of the Sands*. (Of this idea Galantière and Elizabeth Reynal, to whom fell the task of dragging the war book out of him, remained unaware.) His telephone rang incessantly, with invitations or with news of the lastest piece of gossip making its way around town on his account. Madame de B went back to France at the end of March, leaving him to fend for himself. His crippling fevers continued, cutting him down in the middle of a dinner, making it impossible for him to remain on his feet, waking him—teeth chattering and freezing cold—in the middle of the night. (The language barrier caused him pain on this count, too: Saint-Exupéry found that no one felt sorry for him when he reported he was running a 41° [105°F] fever.) The sulfa drugs allowed him to function by afternoon, when he suffered only mild fever and a bit of nausea. His teeth continued to bother him; he found that as a result of his 1923 accident his left eye was prone to infection. He wore dark glasses and complained to various friends of his pains. Even with the help of sedatives he was unable to sleep, although this particular affliction may have had more to do with the pots of black tea he consumed while he worked at night than with anything else.

He was further distracted by a number of projects that came of the new friendship with Jean Renoir. In Hollywood in March Renoir read the copy of *Wind, Sand and Stars* that Saint-Exupéry had given him days after the *Siboney* had docked in January. He was overwhelmed, and spent the next two months trying to get Darryl F. Zanuck, to whom he was under contract at Fox, to read the book. He felt he could make of it a great film, "without a doubt the most beautiful film of my life." Saint-Exupéry admired Renoir's work tremendously and was thrilled by the idea. In all modesty he concurred that Renoir could extract from *Wind, Sand and Stars* "something truly monumental." The filmmaker knocked himself out looking for someone in Hollywood who felt similarly; while the book's synopsis made its way around town he energetically plotted his next steps, providing Saint-Exupéry with a crash course on the baroque workings of the studios, careful always to make sure that his enthusiasm for the project could be heard above the producers' rejections. At the same time Saint-Exupéry joined the battle closest to Renoir's heart: to extricate his twenty-one-year-old son from North Africa. That spring he wrote a diplomat friend in Rabat on Alain Renoir's behalf: "I wouldn't bother you for a favor for just anyone. I detest recommendations and have always refused to pass manuscripts along to Gallimard. This leaves me with a certain available credit, for those I truly love. It is on this credit that I now draw."

In early April he flew to California for a brief stay. By then it had been agreed that the unifying drama of the *Wind, Sand and Stars* film would be the Libyan adventure and that the book's other episodes would be folded in as the trek across the desert progressed. A love interest was added, and the hero—rechristened Bernis—was supplied with a confidante in the form of a mischievous twelve-year-old sister. Renoir set up an appointment for the two men with an influential agent, whom he hoped would handle the project. The agent held court in a plush neo-Georgian office lined with beautifully bound books; so offended was Saint-Exupéry to discover that nothing lay inside their bindings but a concealed bar that he refused to charm during the interview. Afterward he was capable only of sputtering "He's a pig! He's a pig!" about one of the most powerful men in Hollywood. Over the weeks that followed he bombarded Renoir from New York with his ideas for the project, recorded on twelve-inch acetate lacquer disks. These late-night monologues were peppered with his usual treasures. He might interrupt himself to address Dido Renoir, whom he assumed was listening. In a typical aside he would say, "Dido, I know you're there, and I know you think I'm a fool," continuing on to defend himself. Often the recordings closed with a card trick. He admitted to being stumped by the ending of the film but outlined a number of comic and picturesque touches, some more convincing than others.

He experienced his usual share of technical difficulties with the recording device, which had a habit of whistling. At other times he complained about its efficacy, more constant than that of the human mind: "It's problematic because the disk turns quickly and that prevents me from thinking," he complained to Renoir after one long pause, admitting he had not done his homework. When there was nothing to say he discoursed on the nature of silence. On one occasion he had to concede that he had nothing further to add but could not stop talking because he could not very well send Renoir a blank disk. He lamented that a long, friendly silence could not be conveyed from one coast to the other and begged Renoir to understand that this was not his fault, simply a mystery of nature.

> So it [the machine] forces me to speak without having anything to say. . . . So you are going to find me a bit of a cretin. I'm forced to cast about for ideas, but with ideas, when you go looking for them a priori like that, without knowing for what or about what or why, you find nothing. Nothing at all. You don't find any ideas. It's as with fishing—you know, when you go in search of a fish and you have a piece of line and a net and a float— myself I've noticed that you never catch anything. Fishing for ideas is like that, it yields the same result.

One thing that did stimulate the manufacture of ideas was difficulty. "Did you notice that, during the war," Saint-Exupéry continued, ice cubes rattling in the background, "the French General Staffs, since they didn't know they had any difficulties, didn't have any ideas? Since they knew nothing, they had no problems."

The arrival of his recordings in Hollywood was as much cause for apprehension as celebration. The monologuist expected an immediate response. He sent the disks to California by overnight mail and signed out, "I think that I will have a cable tomorrow night if you are kind." If he heard nothing he telephoned immediately. Renoir was hard at work on a film; it was impossible for him to keep up with his New York–based friend, and the records came to represent a kind of torture. Relief came in the form of the author himself, who took the train to California in mid-August. He had a long-standing invitation from the Renoirs, who were aware that he was homesick and depressed. In no way inspired by the New York heat, he was making little headway with the book; he may have thought he could salvage the film of *Wind, Sand and Stars*, which had by now fallen by the wayside.* The events of 1940—and a crossing like that on the *Siboney*—could be in themselves sufficient to draw two Frenchmen of the same generation together, but with the genial Renoir Saint-Exupéry already had a good deal in common. Six years his senior, Renoir had learned to fly in Ambérieu; he had flown reconnaissance missions in World War I. (Jean Gabin wears his pilot's tunic in *Grand Illusion*.) He, too, had an abundant sense of humor and a hearty appetite for life. He had no

---

* Ultimately a discouraged Renoir conceded that the studios had a taste only for a "certain familiar treacle." In retrospect he mellowed a little, allowing that the book's exoticism had worked against it: in 1941 no one yet filmed on location, and it would have been difficult to make any studio look like the Libyan desert. For his part Saint-Exupéry appears to have begrudged Renoir the disappointment. He chastised his friend for having lowered himself to Hollywood's standards and could not resist informing him that—blessed with the talent of a Michelangelo—he was spending his time embroidering pillows.

taste for polemic and a clear enough view of the foibles of his countrymen that his mordant 1939 masterpiece, *The Rules of the Game*, had been reviled. More temperate than Saint-Exupéry, Renoir adapted quickly to America, settling in easily to a shingled house on Hollywood Boulevard. Here he installed Saint-Exupéry in an upper-floor suite, where every effort was now made—on the Renoirs' part, and on that of the California-based Lazareffs'—to reduce the number of obstacles that stood between the writer and his work. Someone turned up an electric typewriter, though this proved more a novelty than a help with the book. A number of secretaries volunteered their services, working off Dictaphone recordings the author left when he retired for the day, at breakfast time.

Saint-Exupéry and Renoir's rapport did not extend to their hours. As the author continued to work at night and the director by day the two rarely saw one another. Saint-Exupéry's presence made itself felt, however; he took up a lot of room in a house. He had acquired the habit of making a meal of toast spread with congealed olive oil, said by a doctor to be beneficial to the liver, and promptly emptied the Renoirs' refrigerator to make room for his collection of oil-filled saucers. He shuffled around loudly while he worked at night. He tacked papers to the walls of his room, scribbling on or near them; he kept Renoir—who was terrified of fire—on the verge of emotional collapse by throwing lighted cigarettes into his wastepaper basket. Few complaints were filed, however, at least in part because Saint-Exupéry was not up to being chastised. He was dispirited and ill, by now far beyond the point where he could make a secret of his fevers. In the middle of an afternoon he would be sick to the point of delirium. Pale and dripping with sweat, he seemed—especially to those shorter than he, which was nearly everyone—as if he might at any moment keel over. Hélène Lazareff looked after him, helping him to a couch when she could, putting him in touch with Jean-Louis Lapeyre, the foremost French physician in Los Angeles. In eight days he suffered three such attacks, each with a fever of 104° or higher. One afternoon he fainted; a few days later he agreed to an operation proposed to him by a specialist, who diagnosed the problem as urological in origin. Saint-Exupéry heard out Dr. Elmer Belt with a little more patience than he had accorded most physicians—at least in part because Belt had no designs on his gallbladder—but put his own gloss on the diagnosis. He claimed the ailment resulted from his 1923 crash, in which a splinter from the aircraft's wooden seat had sliced through his perineum, leaving him with a lump of scar tissue just outside the neck of the bladder. Belt theorized that a pocket of urine collected here from time to time, playing host to infections.

It was generally not a pretty subject, though Saint-Exupéry described

the surgery in great detail—and with several modest illustrations—to Galantière. He felt he owed his translator an explanation for his irregular
behavior and for a litany of complaints that he feared Galantière might
have heard as ravings of "a neurasthenic little girl."* In this respect he
was happy to report that he was—and had been for three years—seriously
ill. (He may have written for a second reason: he sounds positively enchanted with Belt's clever diagnosis.) Otherwise he was exceedingly eager
to see to it that the nature of the surgery remain confidential. Most of his
acquaintances in California were told he had malaria. In New York word
went around simply that he had been treated for an old fracture. The
patient and his physician ultimately fell out because Lapeyre divulged
Saint-Exupéry's condition to a New York surgeon who looked after the
writer as well and who called Lapeyre for details of the operation. "Everyone in New York is going to know why I'm here, which is none of their
business," cursed the writer, before deciding to treat his physician to the
cold shoulder.

The convalescence was as indecorous as the truth. The operation having been performed in what the writer described as a "not very sterile
zone" he suffered afterward from a long series of infections. There was
some postoperative hemorrhaging, accompanied by a number of excru-
ciating spasms. Saint-Exupéry's eye flared up as a result, and the whole
ordeal took a toll on his nerves. He was several weeks in the hospital. It
was, he said, Guatemala all over again, a little less painfully. It was nearly
as long this time until he was up and around, but he did not so much
want for company: among others, the Renoirs, the Lazareffs, and René
Clair came to see him. Annabella, the star of *Anne-Marie* and now the
wife of Tyrone Power, paid him a visit when she heard where he was. She
found him in a darkened room with no flowers, demi-moribund, a huge
man in a tiny bed that looked as if it were about to collapse under his
weight. He told her she was kind to come, that it was sad to die. The two
made awkward attempts at conversation until Annabella spotted a book
on the writer's bedside table. It turned out to be a collection of Andersen's
fairy tales, which she opened to "The Little Mermaid." She began to read

---

* Saint-Exupéry took two different tacks with his health concerns, which mounted in his
forties. With women and with several intimates he discoursed upon his pains in great detail.
More often he tried to rise above them. Declares the desert chieftain in *The Wisdom of the
Sands*, whose teeth are rotting and whose kidneys give him trouble as well: "I have found
my consolation, which is not to let myself be cast down by these portents of a failing body,
nor worn down by infirmities which are base and personal, locked up within me, and to
which the historians of my empire will not accord three lines in their chronicles. It matters
little that my teeth are loosening and that they will be pulled, it would be unseemly on my
part to expect the least sympathy."

the story but finished it by heart; she was rewarded by a magnificent smile as the patient returned to life and to an hour-long conversation about his favorite characters. His petulance, too, revived him. He called Dido Renoir to ask that she arrange for the hospital staff not to put carrots on his dinner plate. "But he doesn't have to eat them," the nursing staff informed Madame Renoir, who passed the message on to Saint-Exupéry. "Of course I don't eat them. It's the sight of them I can't stand; they make me sad!" he exploded, as he did again the next day when a fresh helping of carrots appeared before him. His convalescence continued in a rented two-room apartment, where he spent his day prone on a couch, receiving few visitors other than Annabella, who brought him picnic lunches and listened appreciatively as he spun his tales.

In October Renoir finally prevailed upon him to move back to Hollywood Boulevard. Gradually he returned to work, abashed that the book Reynal & Hitchcock hoped to publish this fall had barely progressed. He apologized to Galantière for his tardiness, promising that he was more despairing of it than his translator could possibly be. He got out a little, meeting various Caltech scientists, including Theodore von Kármán, with whom he shared descriptions of his inventions. He attended a dinner at the home of Dr. Belt and his wife, at which he was asked what America could do for the war effort. He was ready with his answer: "As things stand your country devotes 90 percent of its industrial potential to making consumer goods Americans want—in other words cars and chewing gum—and 10 percent to stopping Hitler. Only when those figures are reversed—10 percent to cars and chewing gum and 90 percent to stopping Hitler—will there be any hope," he responded, cramming all of his feelings about America into a single statement.

By November, when he took the train back to New York, Saint-Exupéry had written a portion of *Flight to Arras*. He was feeling better—he had gone a full month without a relapse—but could still not say he was entirely cured, and would be rehospitalized in New York. He traveled east in the same train as Dr. Belt and his wife, whom he joined for the three-hour stopover in Chicago. On leaving the station he refused to check one of his bags, evidently a cumbersome one. Dr. Belt explained that they would hardly be able to maneuver around the city with the suitcase in tow but was long in convincing his patient, who protested that it contained his "brain child," by which he could have meant *Flight to Arras*, *The Wisdom of the Sands*, or some combination of the two. With some misgiving he handed over the valise, but its absence soon began to torment him. He checked his watch so often that the Belts decided to return to the depot early; at the station doors the Frenchman raced ahead through the crowd. The Belts arrived at the baggage check as the case was being handed over.

Saint-Exupéry hugged it to this chest and—rolling his eyes to the heavens—proclaimed in the language that may have seemed to him appropriate to a moment of invented drama, "*Gracias a Dios! Mi niño está salvado!*"

In New York, shamed by Galantière and Elizabeth Reynal, he returned single-mindedly to *Flight to Arras*. He buried Galantière in an avalanche of revisions; to the person most familiar with the extent of his perfectionism, Marie Bouchu McBride, he later dedicated a copy of the book with thanks for her having typed it ten times. For all of his delays—from his barrel of excuses he now offered up the one about the interfering guardian angel—he had never written a book more quickly. This one took eight months from start to finish, and much of that time Saint-Exupéry was out of commission or procrastinating. On the one hand, shaken by Guillaumet's death and by his own ill health, he was suddenly aware of his mortality and inclined to hurry; he wrote Madame de B that he thought *The Wisdom of the Sands* probably required another ten years' work, more than he had in him. On the other hand he railed against Reynal & Hitchcock's deadlines, which he naturally did his best to mow down. Patiently Galantière explained to him that he could not wait ten years to write the book just because he felt he would think more clearly in ten years. Less patiently Saint-Exupéry responded that ideas, like fruit and children, had to mature. Later he was to say—groundlessly—that he had been too hurried to work his alchemy with *Flight to Arras*.

The timing was more crucial than he realized initially. Scheduled for a November 1941 publication, *Flight to Arras* read differently when it appeared in February 1942, two months after the Japanese attack on Pearl Harbor. Topicality carried little weight with Saint-Exupéry at this point in his life, however. He was more determined than ever to express himself with the utmost of lucidity, claiming that he preferred to starve than to put his name on a book with which he was not happy. "I prefer the sale of 100 copies of a book I don't have to blush for to the sale of 6 million copies of a bad book," he wrote during the tug-of-war with Galantière that consumed November and December, pointing out that Descartes had changed the world but that *Paris-Soir*, with its millions of readers, was unlikely to. He spent long hours railing at his translator, in letters usually written as the sun was rising, when he might have been finishing the volume; it was imperative to him, however, that Galantière understand his perspective. He was not writing for February 22, the publication date Reynal & Hitchcock proposed when December came and went, but for the next decade. Accordingly he was most interested in extracting some kind of lasting truths from the events he was to describe. When shortly after Pearl Harbor he lectured to a group of students, an appearance into

which he was bullied by Dorothy Thompson, he dwelt not on the conflict
at hand but on how his audience might enrich their lives. He knew of
only one method: sacrifice to a higher cause. Similarly *Flight to Arras*—
a book conceived as an apologia for France and touted by Reynal &
Hitchcock before its publication as the story of a day in the life of a
reconnaissance pilot—was for its author a work about responsibility, about
charity. He was enraged by his publishers' emphasis on the journalistic
when he wanted to produce a volume rich in philosophy. The former, he
wrote Galantière one January morning before the sun was up, he could
have tossed off at the age of five. "What is the use of overcoming a host
of diseases, accidents, exams, ill-fated love affairs, tax audits, and other
assorted nuisances if it all leads to my repeating—without progressing
one iota—what my nanny already told me? I see no need to propagate in
1942 what she knew perfectly well in 1900. That can wait until the year
2000. It might then even be thought original, as it will then have been
forgotten."

His health did not finally delay the book but did leave its mark. It was
appropriate that Saint-Exupéry should now write about danger: if anything
he felt more vulnerable physically in America in 1941 than he had when
flying through enemy fire in 1940. (When his health gave him no cause
for concern he succumbed to hypochondria, not a common disease for a
man who had repeatedly bluffed his way past medical examiners. Born
years before of his fear of syphilis, that anxiety was to plague him increasingly in his forties.) At the top of a sheet on which he sketched a new
invention he set down a list of friends and relatives he had lost, beginning
with his brother. He claimed that his sudden sense of his mortality released
him from certain concerns, among them his irritation with the chatter in
New York; it also inclined him, and *Arras*, in a more spiritual direction,
where he was headed anyway. Galantière would have liked to have stopped
him—especially after Pearl Harbor, he felt Americans wanted a demonstration of democracy and not a hymn to charity—but Saint-Exupéry
mostly got his way. His quasi-mystical musings (he was incapable of sys-
temic philosophical analysis) color the book. So does his divorce from his
body, which he appears to have wished he had left in California. He seems
to conclude somewhere over Arras that his body is "a kind of flunkey"
that he has taken an inordinate amount of time to dress, bathe, groom,
and feed over the years. It was in 1941, however, that he was inclined to
slough it off: "I don't care a button what becomes of you. . . . One way
and another, I have dragged you through life to this point; and here I
discover that you are of no importance." Not everyone recognized in this
a cry of faith. Anne and Charles Lindbergh read and discussed the excerpt
of *Flight to Arras* that appeared, the second in a series of three, in the
February issue of the *Atlantic*. Declared Charles: "I think it was awful the

way he talked about his body. . . . If *I'd* been his body I'd have gotten
chicken pox just to get even with him!"

~

Nearly everyone who mattered to Saint-Exupéry heard portions of the
book before it was published. The telephone is a dangerous weapon in
the hands of a dejected man who needs constant reassurance and keeps
odd hours; Saint-Exupéry did not shy from using his, to the tune of about
seventy-five dollars a month, half of what he paid his secretary. At his
dining room table or at an all-night deli he scribbled until dawn, dictating
his illegible pages for Marie McBride, who did not see him before noon.
At any point during this time his friends' sleep was in jeopardy. Like most
writers, Saint-Exupéry was incapable of keeping to himself a passage with
which he was happy. Unlike most writers, he retained from his Aéropostale
days the conviction that nothing was more thrilling than a middle-of-the-
night call from a friend in need. Galantière, who was translating chapter
by chapter, took the brunt of his generosity. When the telephone rang at
2:00 or 3:00 a.m. he knew immediately who was calling; he got used to
hearing himself dole out half-asleep praise. "I don't think that it ever
occurred to him that of the two of us, only he was awake," he said later.
Yvonne Michel, Lamotte, Lanux, Lazareff, Becker found they could not
stay angry at Saint-Exupéry for costing them their rest, although not everyone was honestly able to tell the difference between the text they heard
in the middle of one night and the previous version of the same text, which
they had heard in the middle of the previous night. Only Lamotte grumbled a little. "Listen, Bernard, I've just written four pages, do you want
to hear them?" Saint-Exupéry woke the painter to ask one evening. Lamotte wondered if the reading could wait until the next day. "Why tomorrow?" Saint-Exupéry persisted. "Because it is two in the morning and
in theory people sleep at this hour, even if you don't," Lamotte informed
him, though he was still on the phone twenty minutes later. Saint-Exupéry
had better luck with his West Coast friends, less easy to disturb. When
he called Annabella and Tyrone Power late in the year to read them
chapters of *The Little Prince* they thought him only hopelessly extravagant.

One person who had been spared these impositions was Consuelo,
who arrived in New York toward the beginning of 1942, as Galantière
was wresting the last pages of the book from her husband. The writer had
agonized for some time over whether or not to bring his wife to America;
his friends seemed to think she would cause him less trouble in New York,
where he could keep an eye on her, than in France, where—with predictable results—he was unable to. (He got her news from Madame de
B, who encouraged him to send for her, and relied on his mother to run

interference.) Probably in the end the decision to come to America was Consuelo's: it would have been a difficult trip for anyone to make against her will. (She would claim that she had shamed her husband into bringing her over, threatening to make a scandal if he did not take her back, and this may have been true.) Back in New York, Lazareff, the former *Paris-Soir* editor, helped collect a number of affidavits in support of Consuelo's visa application. Saint-Exupéry—who had not found female companionship to be in short supply in New York—by no means broadcast the news of his wife's arrival. One night he called Jean-Gérard Fleury, himself recently arrived, to requisition him and his car for the next morning. He did not mention a destination; Fleury found himself at the Hoboken pier before he was told why he was there. Dutifully he loaded Consuelo's bags into his Pontiac and chauffeured her—as she regaled the men with stories of Oppède—to Central Park South. That afternoon Saint-Exupéry telephoned the Reynals, frantic. Consuelo had arrived and he had to be decent to her; were they possibly free for dinner? The Reynals joined the Saint-Exupérys on a circular banquette at the restaurant at 240 Central Park South that evening. On one side of the table the author, under his breath, told Elizabeth how relieved he was that his wife was in town only for a few nights. Across the table Consuelo gaily informed Eugene Reynal of her delight to be in New York on a six-month visa. Without her husband's knowledge she then arranged to move into a twenty-second-floor apartment in the building. Saint-Exupéry made the best of the situation; some of his greatest trials now began.

According to Fleury, it was Consuelo who—in a late-night brainstorming session—put forward the French-language title for the book, *Pilote de guerre*. (New York had by now become a center of French-language publishing—an edition of André Maurois or Saint-Exupéry could sell 15,000 copies—and *Pilote de guerre* was brought out simultaneously with *Flight to Arras* by the Éditions de la Maison Française.) Reynal & Hitchcock, after much casting about, had already settled on *Flight to Arras*. Saint-Exupéry was bad with titles, and there is no record of how he felt about these. He was not—despite his protests—altogether displeased with his text. He had laced the account of the reconnaissance flight with memories and musings, stitching exactly the kind of personal credo he had been lobbying for to the end. It was not a perfect match. His riffs about the primacy of Man over the individual and the duty of charity date the book more than the events it describes, though they won him comparisons to the Bible in 1941. While he agonized over these statements the volume engages more successfully on another level: it provides a very true portrait of a man, no run-of-the-mill hero. German antiaircraft fire brings out a Saint-Exupéry the Libyan desert did not; *Arras* is a deeply personal book. Renoir, with whom Saint-Exupéry had fallen out of touch this year, wrote

Becker that he missed their mutual friend but that when he wanted to spend fifteen minutes with him he leafed through *Pilote*. In the first line we catch Saint-Exupéry the reconnaissance pilot, a man for whom attention is all, daydreaming. He performs his card tricks, confides his late-night anxieties, fumbles for a match, loses his gloves, grouses, daydreams some more. He is proud, impatient, in pain. He hums into his oxygen mask ("Hum like that, Captain, and you'll pass out," Dutertre warns him), he admits he has good days and bad, has lost a brother at a young age (which he gets wrong). He is stubborn, he is bitter, he is cocky about his chess game, he is not immune to the effects of alcohol. He confides his feelings on being asked to autograph one of his books. All of this he does—eighteen months after the events in question—mostly in the present tense, which lends the account of the man and the mission a fierce immediacy. He does not mention, in a volume awash in humility, tenderness, fraternity, that his life as he writes is devoid of all such things, though he may have intended to. The original first line of the manuscript—dotted with cigarette burns and coffee stains, scribbled so much in haste as to be in parts wholly illegible, the margins decorated with a series of little figures—read, "It is becoming so difficult to live."

Conceived as a volume on the fall of France, *Flight to Arras* was a war book by the time it was published. It won raves on both counts. It was universally thought to dwarf all other accounts of the French defeat; writing in the *Atlantic* Edward Weeks declared, "This narrative and Churchill's speeches stand as the best answer the democracies have yet found to *Mein Kampf.*" Published on February 20 the book sold out its first printing before any reviews had appeared. Lamotte had contributed a series of illustrations to the volume, enlargements of which hung in bookstore displays all over New York. Copies of *Arras* were piled high in Bloomingdale's windows. Reviewed on the front pages of *The New York Times Book Review* and the New York *Herald Tribune Books* section, the best-selling volume turned into one of the ten biggest books of 1942; Reynal & Hitchcock made every effort to keep it in stock despite a tightening paper situation. Not all of the critics fell for Saint-Exupéry's brand of mystical rambling, but everyone agreed that he wrote "like a soliloquizing angel." He was allowed more latitude than most essayists not because he was a stylist but because he was a soldier. It seemed doubly noble that a man who had risked his life for his country in near-suicidal reconnaissance missions should be so much obsessed with making some larger sense of the whole war experience.

Wail though Saint-Exupéry did about the project, *Flight to Arras* proved the best use of his American time, more or less what he claimed he had left France to accomplish. The prestige of France was low in 1942, and *Arras* was judged by many to be the single most redeeming piece of propaganda on her behalf. As the first indication many Americans had had that the French had made an effort to resist the Germans, the volume greatly influenced public opinion. (Saint-Exupéry saw to it that a copy found its way to the White House via Supreme Court Justice Felix Frankfurter, whom he knew socially. He inscribed the book: "For President Franklin Roosevelt, whose country is assuming the immense task of saving the world.") Having defended his country once with his person and once on the page, he was in some eyes twice a hero. The language barrier spared him readings and an author tour, but he became a most sought-after lecturer and guest, the jewel in every hostess's crown. These engagements he accepted reluctantly. Anne Morgan, head of the Coordinating Council of the French Relief Societies, invited him to lecture in her living room to a group of fifty socially prominent women, for whom Saint-Exupéry was to sign copies of *Arras*. He snapped his way nervously through a box of wooden matches as he spoke. After his remarks he was rushed by the crowd, in which he recognized a familiar face: that of "Ping" Lawrence, the wife of Laudy Lawrence, who represented MGM in Europe. "I want to talk to you," he said, leading her by the hand into the next room, where he engaged her in conversation behind an oversized armchair, entirely out of view. After he was introduced to a crowded meeting of the American Association of Teachers of French in a New York University hall he whispered something to the chairman, who brought forward a chair that he placed sideways on the stage. Saint-Exupéry addressed his muffled remarks to the far wall of the auditorium. An hour before he was to lecture at the French Institute Pierre Bédard, its director, decided to check in on him. He found the writer in his bathrobe, oblivious to the commitment. He managed to get him dressed, fed, and bundled off— nearly on time—to the Institute, where 450 people were waiting to hear him speak.

Saint-Exupéry did not think he had written a controversial book but braced himself, if only out of habit, for "the calumnies and resentments." He was well-advised to do so. In March the French consul-general in New York reported respectfully on the success of *Arras* to the Vichy ambassador in Washington, a fervent Pétainist, describing the book as the first account of the war to rise above politics. Soon enough politics rose up to meet it. The last lines of the book, which are enigmatic, created great consternation. Read by Vichy as a call-to-arms, they were seen by the Gaullists as defeatist. For once the two sides had something in common: they joined in denouncing the text. Saint-Exupéry racked his brains to try to make sense of the objections; he could not defend himself on one count without opening himself to attack on three others. (Ironically, he had meant to damn no one but the Americans, for not having come to France's rescue.) He looked long and hard for evidence of his solidarity with Vichy but could find only one line of text regarding the government, which he thought a rather subtle condemnation. Flabbergasted, he interrogated every Gaullist he knew. He had defended Vichy, they told him, in defending the armistice. "But I didn't write about the armistice," objected Saint-Exupéry. "Yes, but you made it look to the Americans as if the French army had been beaten," came the reply. Why had he written about only one mission, they moaned. The word on the street—in this case Park and Fifth Avenues—was that Saint-Exupéry had made the war effort look skimpy.

The controversy heated up after the French publication of the book at the end of the year. By moving to America Saint-Exupéry had neatly sidestepped the to-appear-or-not-to-appear question with which writers who were living under the Occupation—and France was at the end of 1942 fully occupied—had to wrestle. To submit a book for publication at this time was to do business with a group of men committed to collaboration. There were many reasons to do so, of course, not the least of them that writers have to eat. Jean Guéhenno cited another: "The man of letters is not the noblest of human species. Incapable of living very long in obscurity, he will sell his soul to see his name *appear*. A few months of silence, of disappearance, drive him to his wits' ends. He can take it no longer." Saint-Exupéry was more fortunate than most writers in that his publishing fortunes were as good if not better outside France, but it was imperative to him that *Pilote de guerre* appear in his own country; he had not written the book expressly for Americans. He saw to it that a copy of the manuscript made its way to Ségogne, who was instructed to have it published in France at all cost. Nothing appeared in France without the approval of the censors, to whom Gallimard submitted the text in the fall. Saint-Exupéry's was an account of doing battle with Germany but mostly it was an elegiac description of war; his work had already been held up by the Germans as an example of the best kind of French literature. Gerhard Heller, the young, literature-loving German at the head of the review section of the Propagandastaffel, was closest to Gaston Gallimard, of all the French publishers. He passed the book for a December 1942 publication, although one line was censored and its print run limited to 2,000 copies.*

The Gallimard edition sold out in a week, whipping up a storm of admiring reviews, then was recalled, though not because of the Germans. It had not escaped the notice of several Frenchmen that in singing the praises of the men of his squadron Saint-Exupéry had cited the heroics

---

* The line—in which Saint-Exupéry declared they were all fools, the orderly who had misplaced his gloves no less than Hitler who had unleashed the war—has never been restored in the French edition of the book.

of a certain "Jean Israël." This was more than they could stomach. In all fairness Saint-Exupéry had trumpeted Israël's identity for all it was worth, making fourteen references to his Jewish nose in two pages of text. He must have been aware of what he was doing: he used Israël's loaded name again later, deliberately, and when a careful writer uses a word fourteen times in quick succession it can safely be assumed he has done so for effect. Pierre-Antoine Cousteau led a virulent crusade against the book, "another demented Judeo-bellicose act." "M. de Saint-Exupéry chooses his associates badly," he snorted, reminding readers that the author of *Pilote de guerre* was also a great friend of Léon Werth. Surely a French writer had better things to do than to vaunt the courage of a Jew? He denounced the book as an act of treason, an appraisal with which other Nazi sympathizers agreed. As for the reviewers, asked another Frenchman, had they forgotten how to read? In mid-January the Vichy Commissioner of Jewish Affairs wondered what the censors had been thinking when they passed such a book, so insulting to the occupying power. The Gaullists remained deaf to these accusations of philo-Semitism, preferring those of their own.

Like many banned books, *Pilote de guerre* soon became as popular—at least in reputation; copies were not easy to come by—as *Gone With the Wind*. (Saint-Exupéry was in good company: French collaborators objected as well to the Germans having passed Camus's *L'Étranger*, and the *Larousse Élémentaire* was banned.) Two clandestine editions of *Pilote* appeared, one in December 1943 and one in 1944, but Gallimard was not allowed to reprint Saint-Exupéry's earlier titles and his work fell out of print in France. Once the darling of the right-wing Académie Française, he was now off the shelves. In Casablanca a request for one of his books in 1943 raised booksellers' eyebrows. Heller was severely reprimanded for his oversight and placed under house arrest for several days. For Gallimard, eager during the war years to direct attention away from the firm and unhappy about this tussle, the trouble caused by *Pilote de guerre* proved well worth it. He was later able to cite his publication of the volume as proof of his proper allegiances during the Occupation. (The blame for collaboration was directed entirely to Drieu La Rochelle and the *NRF*.)

In the prison camp where he had been since the day before that described in *Arras*, Jean Israël read in the collaborationist press of the uproar his friend had caused. A month or so later a copy of *Pilote de guerre* was smuggled into the camp and passed around covertly. Israël read it with pride. In reality it is his name which betrays his heritage—his nose is entirely unremarkable—but he was happy to serve by whatever means he could. No other French writer in 1942 would have gone out, or went out, on a limb for a lieutenant named Israël. Few other French writers would have failed to admit that doing so was provocative. Only Saint-Exupéry —who spoke too eloquently to be ignored but too softly to suit anyone's political agenda—could get himself banned for singing the praises of Jean Israël and condemned as a Vichyite, all at once.

XVI

~

Anywhere Out of This World
1942–1943

*"Women are an inspiration. It's because of
them we put on a clean shirt and wash our socks.
Because of women we want to excel. Because
of a woman, Christopher Columbus discovered
America."*
"Queen Isabella," Mary [Cheever] murmured.
*"I was thinking," John said, "of Mrs. Colum-
bus."*

SCOTT DONALDSON, *John Cheever*

A solitary, awkward Frenchman trailing behind him a colorful past and
floating in an aura of celebrity, Saint-Exupéry attracted a certain following
in America. Fay Wray, who met him briefly through Ping and Laudy
Lawrence, was smitten: "Oh, he was wonderful to look at! Big, tall, great
black eyes that themselves looked like radiant stars." In the New York
Post, Elsa Maxwell described the man she considered the greatest living
French writer as "a virile male, with great charm, a sort of power and
enchantment, for women." Kitty Carlisle Hart, who was introduced to
Saint-Exupéry at Bernard Lamotte's, thought him enormously sexy; like
many who met him, she did not know he had a wife. (Those who did, like
Anne Lindbergh, believed it common knowledge that the two were separated.) A member of his 1941 Lycée Français audience remarked fifty
years later, "I don't know if a nine-year-old can sense sex appeal or not,
but he had it."

He did little to solicit attention. He did not need to; the "*mignonnes*"
or "*mignonettes*," as he called them, flocked to him, the swashbuckling
celebrity who could vanquish anything but day-to-day life. For all of his
shyness Saint-Exupéry was not unaware of the effect he had on women.

He detested coarseness of any kind and did not speak of his conquests, but, now quite bald, did take to calling himself *"le beau blond."* He rarely mentioned Consuelo, save to the other women in his life. Becker knew of his client's variegated love life because he often performed commissions for his author (in an attempt to lure him to the United States in 1940 he promised he would meet him at the dock with six blondes, each more ravishing than the next); Galantière knew of the women because the two men were in constant touch. He volunteered more of an opinion on this subject than most of the writer's friends. "Like all virile men," noted Galantière, "he preferred the company of one woman to the company of several women, and the company of several men to that of one man alone." He observed that while Saint-Exupéry's taste ran to the frail, the ship-wrecked, "he found himself now and then involved with women who were 'not his type'—handsome viragoes, so to say, who attached themselves to him, listened with calculated attention to his reflections, tried to arrange his existence for him, and whom he had a hard time getting rid of because he simply did not know how to be brutal."

With one of the latter the writer and his translator dined in Chinatown late in November 1941. Galantière had known the woman in question from childhood and was disappointed that Saint-Exupéry had taken up with her. At thirty-eight she was stunning; her appeal extended to women as well as men, although Galantière thought Saint-Exupéry knew nothing of this history. At dinner she began to talk about *Night Flight*, which she had just read. As she spoke it became clear that she was an anti-Semite and a fascist; her interpretation of the novel provoked an explosion from Galantière, who held that she had entirely misconstrued the word "leader." With his outburst the conversation turned to one about democracy, a subject on which the two men violently disagreed. To Saint-Exupéry democracy was the creation of a corrupt, bourgeois government, the Third Republic; he had a certain nostalgia for authority figures, to which France is known to deliver herself when in trouble. (Said Pétain in 1940, "They only call me in a crisis.") The debate continued in the car uptown, in which Galantière lost his temper. "Let's stop right here; you've spent the evening defending the most loathsome ideas. You are clearly a fascist," he fumed. As he got out of the car Saint-Exupéry put a hand on his translator's shoulder. "You know that I love you dearly," he said quietly. "Only please don't call me a fascist, I'm not one." For all of her tenacity Saint-Exupéry's escort could not have seen very much of him in the hours that followed; Galantière woke to find a seventeen-page letter of explanation under his door. In it Saint-Exupéry quickly dispensed with the cornerstones of French democracy as practiced in America. There was more liberty to be found in a monastery than in the choice among three of Zanuck's films; equality, he argued, like Tocqueville, reduced man to the lowest common denominator; fraternity hardly existed in a nonhierarchical society. There was more of it in the French army, insisted the man who had never been able to tolerate communal quarters, than in all of America.

On the other kind of woman, who more resembled his wife, Saint-Exupéry lavished—by necessity—more attention. In 1942 he took up with the stunning wife of a Brazilian prince who fit what a friend described as the writer's three criteria: she was tall, blond, and titled. He was often seen about town with Nada de Bragance, who looked disarmingly familiar; many of those to whom Saint-Exupéry introduced her thought at first that Madame de B was back in New York. (She was not, and for much of this period was on the outs with Saint-Exupéry, distance having taken its toll. To make a telephone conversation that she suspected was being tapped more palatable she threw in a few tributes to de Gaulle. Saint-Exupéry flew into a rage, convinced she had converted to the cause he so disdained.* He forgave her only later, in Algiers. After one particularly tempestuous conversation he hung up in a fury. The operator, still on the line, heard Madame de B crying at her end. "Don't work yourself up about it," she said, having come to recognize Saint-Exupéry's voice. "You know he'll call you back in five minutes.") The writer admitted straight out that he was attracted to Nada because she was unhappy, not that any man would have been pressed to justify this particular attraction. "Her face, which is that of someone who is drowning, is so beautiful when she smiles," he told a friend, who happened to be Madame de B. Displaying the kind of ingenuousness that was to drive the women in his life to despair he once asked her to check up on Nada, as both women were then in London. Madame de B complained that Nada was unbalanced. "Don't speak like that of my women," Saint-Exupéry chided her, "they are all crazy." (Nada committed suicide after the war, jumping from a London hotel window.)

The affairs were not necessarily sequential. Women were one of the few consolations New York had to offer a lonely man in poor health and at the mercy of a hostile climate; these were to be the most female-heavy years since Saint-Exupéry's all-female childhood. As his anguish increased his need for refuge did as well: he bounced from woman to woman, although not all of these relationships were sexual and some were more notable for re-creating the intimacy he had known with his sisters. Hedda Sterne was a twenty-five-year-old painter, a Romanian refugee who had

---

* During this time the U.S. government also expressed concern about Madame de B's political leanings. As she was well acquainted with high-ranking ambassadors of all stripes, she traveled with seeming ease throughout wartorn Europe. This gave rise to speculation—based on evidence that was flimsy at best—that she was engaging in secret service work, under a variety of aliases, for Pétain.

studied in Vienna and Paris, when an acquaintance introduced her to Saint-Exupéry in October 1941. Her family, which was Jewish, was in Europe; she was alone in New York and riddled with guilt. The two became instant friends. In long monologues the Frenchman poured out his heart to her, a tiny, striking young woman who made for a rather brilliant fairy princess. Hedda Sterne was to say that Saint-Exupéry nearly saved her life at a desperate and friendless time but she clearly saved his a little as well: she knew how to hold up her end of a relationship that was anything but conventional, which she describes as having been "entirely private, out of the ordinary world, soul-to-soul." She felt privileged to open her door to an anguished writer who, once or twice a week, climbed five flights of stairs, late at night, to talk. In her vulnerability and with her discerning eye she may have provided Saint-Exupéry with a sort of substitute for Léon Werth. She helped the writer with an essay on his French friend and encouraged him mightily with *The Wisdom of the Sands*, which she adored. He wrote her that she had provided more "spiritual assistance" with that project than she could imagine.

At least some and possibly all of the physical relationships were not consummated. Naturally this brought sex—which according to Pélissier Saint-Exupéry had generally regarded as "an episodic necessity"—to the fore. A deeply sensual man, his New York socializing amounted in part to attempts to feel like a cosseted boy, in part to desperate attempts to feel like a man. In this very private quest he was not helped by Consuelo, who had never been above making public statements about her husband's superb legs, and who ran around New York announcing—much to ballast her own image as a *femme fatale*—alternately that her husband had just ravished her and that, having flown at high altitude, he was no longer able to satisfy her. In this and numerous other ways she made it clear to other men that she was accessible. Other women did all they could for Saint-Exupéry; one went so far as to drug him with Seconal to see if this might relax him a little and help him to perform. With Natalie Paley—an actress with whom Cocteau had also been enamored, a Romanov princess by birth—Saint-Exupéry found for some months the comfort he was looking for: "I desperately need to be pitied and consoled. . . . I am entitled to absent myself temporarily from the demands of life. I am entitled to have a heavy heart, and to entrust it to you to lighten." Natalie soothed his nerves, diverting him with "that light of milk and honey which you radiate and which makes opening your dress as magical as daybreak." In the course of a deeply erotic letter he admitted he had been fleetingly unfaithful; in another he admitted that he knew they would hurt each other in the end, "but such is the nature of existence. To experience springtime is to risk living through winter; to be present is to risk one day being absent." Still, he assured her, despite his numerous affairs he had used the word "love" perhaps three times in his life. He did not think he would use it again, after her.

Even while he was explaining to Natalie his feelings about divorce and remarriage—a statement to which he appears to have been moved by her elusiveness—he was cultivating a new friendship. In March 1942 he was speaking with Galantière at a Sunday cocktail at a friend's house when twenty-eight-year-old Silvia Reinhardt, an acquaintance of Galantière's, sidled up to the two men. She had recently read *Wind, Sand and Stars* and asked to be introduced to the book's author. "Tell him I love him," she instructed Galantière who, able translator that he was, got the message wrong. Silvia insisted; Galantière failed a second time to rise to the occasion. "Would you like my phone number?" she asked Saint-Exupéry directly, facing him square in the chest. "*Oui, oui,*" answered the man who claimed not to understand a word of English. The two began to see each other daily, inventing a private language that consisted of an approximation of several known ones and a fair amount of gesticulating. Silvia must have proved a master at this, as Saint-Exupéry bestowed on her one of his finest compliments: you know so well how to tell a story, he wrote her later. Evidence of their easy compatibility can be found in Lillian Ross's *Picture*, in and out of which Silvia, as Mrs. Gottfried Reinhardt, flits eccentrically with her black poodle. Ross catches her at John Huston's birthday party in 1950, "a slender, attractive, sardonic-looking lady with large skeptical brown eyes and a vaguely Continental manner, [who] moved with a sort of weary impishness among the guests." When told by her husband to mingle with the wives Silvia responds, "I won't mingle. I have an odd interior climate," and wanders off. When the men adjourn to the next room for a game of poker she throws up her hands in despair: "Gottfried, nobody ever listens to anybody else! It's a condition of the world."

No one else communicated like Saint-Exupéry and Silvia, who—in a series of evenings that stretched over the course of a year and often began with a late dinner at Silvia's Park Avenue apartment or at the restaurant Ruby Foo's—saw no one else. As the telephone proved useless Saint-Exupéry rarely called. He appeared unannounced with a knock on the door, usually hours after Silvia—who never left the house for fear of missing him—had given up hope of his materializing. When Saint-Exupéry needed to communicate a point too fine to be trusted to their private Babel, Silvia asked him to write it down; she then passed on his note to the woman she had hired to tutor her in French. With pursed lips the Browning School teacher—clearly scandalized by the American woman's involvement with a man who was to her a minor deity—translated these missives, as she did Silvia's English-language responses. If Saint-Exupéry knew of this system he never let on. What mattered to him was that Silvia grasped the essential: she welcomed him with open arms (if with tears over his tardiness); she made him laugh; she never questioned him about the limits of their sex life, for which the writer offered no explanation; she fed and bathed and sheltered him; she encouraged him in his work, even in his singing, which she thought abominable. In fact the language barrier screened out most of what Saint-Exupéry liked to avoid. Silvia had no sense whatever of the French community's vilification of her lover. Nor did she have any inkling of Saint-Exupéry's shame over the French defeat, or his attempts, which multiplied late in 1942, to return to the front. She knew only that he was, by his own account, broken, sick of this world, tormented, drinking heavily. And that he was a most entertaining—and frustrating—companion. *"Je suis usé,"* Saint-Exupéry repeatedly told her, a statement she took to be an explanation of his impotence. At the end of an evening he would install himself on a chaise longue in her bedroom and read to her from his unfinished work, tears rolling down his face as he did so. Half-asleep on the floor, Silvia understood not a word.

Afterward, with no explanation, Saint-Exupéry would disappear. Two other obligations called—his wife, whom he liked to check up on late at night, and his work—though he told Silvia little of either of these. (When, sometime after the two had begun seeing each other, he admitted he was married, Saint-Exupéry left Silvia with the impression that his wife was mentally frail, a malingerer who had moved into Central Park South without giving him any choice in the matter.) These late-night exits drove Silvia to despair. She assumed her rivals were women and did not know that her lover returned to a hell of his own; as late as he returned to Central Park South, Consuelo got home later. He struck up a different sort of correspondence with his wife, composed of an acrid series of "Where were you?" 's and "Weren't you going to stop by before you went out?" 's and "I thought we had a date at midnight" 's and "I waited for you in vain" 's and "Why are you so cruel?" 's. One evening he kept up an irate vigil, marking the time across the top of a page at ten-minute intervals, which he spent pacing. He had imagined the worst and was particularly incensed that Consuelo had so taken advantage of what he called his tenderness. With a bitter reminder to his wife that he had never come home after she did, he conceded defeat at 3:00 a.m. In an unsent letter that had plenty of counterparts but which Saint-Exupéry tore to pieces and relegated to his wastebasket (from which his secretary retrieved and reassembled it) he wrote after a missed midnight rendezvous: "You are low to hurt me like this. I don't deserve it. Of course I am full of rancor against life. You never give me what I need. . . . I give everything and get nothing in exchange but hateful words." By the end of these months of near-cohabitation he was neither bitter nor accusatory but perfectly hys-

terical: "When I'm dead you will know what you've lost." Consuelo told
people, including those she barely knew, that her husband would do anything to be rid of her, even go off and get himself killed in the war.

Those who saw the Saint-Exupérys together were not spared the sight
of this strife. A housekeeper invited a guest to inspect a closet of broken
furniture, victims, she claimed, of Consuelo's rages. Bita Dobo, an assistant
of Pierre Lazareff's who had met Saint-Exupéry in California, watched a
number of objects fly through the air between them. Another friend reported, optimistically, that the couple had worked out a nonaggression
pact. Becker checked in on his author nearly every day and remembered
the Saint-Exupérys arguing bitterly, although he also noticed that the
writer suffered when apart from his wife. Indeed the tone of his letters
changes instantly when the couple is separated for any length of time,
complying with La Rochefoucauld's dictum that absence will make a
strong passion stronger and a weak one weaker. Robert Tenger, who was
to publish Saint-Exupéry's work in French the following year, remembered the author telling his wife, "If you're not here I can't think, and if
you talk I can't write." Saint-Exupéry wore a wedding ring and invitations
came addressed to Monsieur and Madame, but the writer rarely appeared
in New York with Consuelo, who found comfort—but not an antidote to
her jealousy—elsewhere. When the Saint-Exupérys entertained together
she was late, or prone to vanish at the end of the meal. She stepped out
for dinner one night in a dark blue ski suit and leopard-skin boots, a
brilliant wool scarf thrown over her shoulder. Her husband asked if she
might care to change; Consuelo declined. "Do you think you will look
presentable?" he patiently inquired. "Oh yes," she assured him, as they
headed to a midtown bistro with a guest.

Consuelo confounded even the Americans. Her jealousy knew no
bounds; she managed to go so far as to corner Saint-Exupéry's prim
English tutor in the fall, drilling her for the secret of her success with her
husband (it was in fact entirely marginal), Saint-Exupéry having remarked
offhandedly that he wrote better after a lesson. (The tutor did not have
the courage to tell the truth, which was that she concentrated on calm
before entering the couple's turbulent household.) Galantière, who did
not like Consuelo, perhaps best described her as "Surrealism made flesh";
he could not forgive her her lack of curiosity about the world, her lack of
conversation. The general consensus was that she was out of her depth
with her husband and to be pitied; some were better at this than others,
generally depending on how entertaining they found Consuelo, who could
be vastly entertaining. She told Helen Wolff, the New York publisher, of
having as a child smeared her naked body with honey and run into the
tropical forest in Central America, attracting butterflies, who soon dressed

her in a scintillating coat. She spent a cocktail party to which she was invited by the Wolffs under a large writing desk, from which a pale arm occasionally emerged, an empty martini glass affixed to its end. Asked that winter how she had managed the priest at confession she laughed and answered quickly, "Well, I was honest. I said, '*Mon Père*, I am a daughter of Eve. What can you expect?'" She was on the one hand "incurably infantile," on the other enough like her husband to complain, world-weary and sick in the 1950s, "All I ask for is someone with whom to play to distract me from all the serious, mean, and mighty people."

All of the writer's American tribulations came together to conspire against him in May 1942. Precipitously he flew to Montreal at the invitation of his Canadian publisher, who had reissued *Wind, Sand and Stars* and who had been after him for some time to visit. Saint-Exupéry asked Consuelo to join him for what he thought was to be a trip of forty-eight hours but was alone when he checked into the Hotel Windsor on April 29. He held a press conference the following day. Asked about his political views he provided a series of sincere but noncommittal answers, much to the frustration of the reporters. The press badgered him, for all the usual reasons and then some. An *Amérique Française* reporter made the mistake of promising the celebrity that he could vet the text of their interview. One interview turned into a series as Saint-Exupéry repeatedly asked Pierre Baillergeon to come back for the piece, with which he had not finished. In the meantime he expounded on his theory of what made a writer great: his syntax. Writing was a business of the same precision as flying, explained Saint-Exupéry, demonstrating how language, too, "amounted to a sophisticated machine, very scientific, where one word too many—like a grain of sand or the slightest clumsiness, like an incorrect maneuver—could result in a crash." He had plenty of time to expand on these themes, to share with Baillergeon his draft of a preface to *Les Fleurs du Mal* that had been commissioned but that never saw the light of day. On his arrival in Montreal he discovered that his visa was not, as he had been promised it would be, in proper order, and that he was barred from reentry into the United States. He was advised to reconcile himself to a six-month stay.

The Reynals were the first to hear of the writer's plight. Well acquainted with his gift for the practical, their reaction was a weary "Oh, my God, he's done it again." Saint-Exupéry concluded—based on evidence that, if it existed, is lost today—that he was the victim of a Gaullist plot. He had been assured that his papers would be arranged for him by a Canadian embassy official in Washington who had even insisted a little on the trip, which Saint-Exupéry had repeatedly put off. His Montreal publisher felt—either for his own reasons or because he was encouraged to do so by Saint-Exupéry—that the Washington Gaullists had denounced him to

keep him trapped in Canada. This was possible but unlikely, as the writer's
visa trouble was with the Americans, and de Gaulle's word carried little
weight in Washington in mid-1942. What seems most likely is that he
was allowed into Canada without the requisite papers—he left in a hurry
and before his U.S. exit permit was officially registered, on the embassy
official's assurance that all could be arranged in Montreal—and that the
wheels of bureaucracy had to grind a bit to catch up with him. This
explanation was too pedestrian for Saint-Exupéry, who, in letter after
letter, phone call after phone call, sputtered that his Canadian stay
amounted to a Chinese water torture. He had plenty of time to vent his
spleen, which he directed at his American publishers, whom he essentially
ordered to get him out of Canada. The day after the author's arrival in
Montreal Curtice Hitchcock wrote the U.S. State Department to vouch
for him: a best-selling writer with a monthly income of well in excess of
$1,000, he was "in no danger whatsoever of becoming a public charge."

As the forty-eight hours melted into five weeks Saint-Exupéry grew
increasingly petulant. Once again he waged a battle—this time across a
friendly border that suddenly loomed grotesquely high—to make himself
understood. He knew he was behaving badly but could not help himself,
given the stupidity of the situation. In a ten-page letter he explained to
Hitchcock that his calls to Elizabeth Reynal had been trying; she had
persisted in treating him like a five-year-old. It was important to him
that his publisher know he was neither ungrateful nor an idiot. Over
and over he rehashed the history of the trip: "If I insist on the details
it's because I cannot bear for you to think that the grave concerns and
the trouble I have caused you might in any way be due to my thought-
lessness." It is easy to take a measure of his insistence; it drove the equa-
nimous Elizabeth to lose her patience. She was furious with the writer
for passing off the blame on everyone else. Regardless of the promises
made him by the embassy he had been irresponsible in leaving without papers. As for the State Department, she reminded Saint-Exupéry,
"It has other things to do than to worry about you. It's waging a war.
You're best off going to bed." By the end of May she had nothing but
reproaches for him when all he wanted—aside from an American visa—
was sympathy.

He had long since given the lectures he had been asked to deliver, of
which he acquitted himself with his usual relish. Speaking on his war
experiences and on France's need for unity, he won over his Montreal
audience on May 2 not with eloquence but with shyness and sincerity. He
was ill at ease on the dais, correcting his first sentence three times before
launching into the rest of his talk; he was now more l than ever careful
with his words. On May 4, by which time it was clear to him he was going
nowhere soon, he spoke in Quebec City, at the Institut Canadien, to a

packed auditorium. Over the next weeks he saw a good deal of his Canadian publisher, whom he held responsible for his predicament, but spent most of his time in his room at the Windsor, much of it brooding over his visa trouble. Several times he visited with Philippe Roy, an army officer who was the son of the former Canadian minister to France, as well as with Roy's friends and family, who found their guest so charming they were doubtless little tempted to help him return to America. In a stylish Montreal restaurant one night with Roy and his future wife, Katherine Ethier, Saint-Exupéry proceeded to pull the tablecloth out from under four place settings without disturbing a single piece of silver or stemware. The Café Martin's waiters were astonished. So were the children to whom Saint-Exupéry was introduced in Montreal, for whom he performed the better part of his repertoire. He let a deck of cards fly all over Katherine Ethier's living room then excused himself, inviting her family to choose a card and replace it. On his return he correctly identified each of their choices.

On Hotel Windsor letterhead he wrote tenderly to both Natalie and Silvia, promising his newer friend that he would come to see her as soon as he returned to "the promised land." She thought he had left for two days and when he was not back dispatched a private detective to track him down. Nor was she the only woman combing the eastern seaboard for the hulking aviator. One sizzling hot afternoon in early June Katherine Ethier's maid came to find her to announce a visitor. Ethier was in the final stages of moving house; she went downstairs to find Consuelo in a floor-length mink in the empty living room. Had anyone seen her husband? She claimed she was to have met him for a cocktail party at this address, which she had probably misunderstood. She and the coat left in a taxi, to general consternation. To make matters worse Saint-Exupéry suffered toward the middle of his stay from a series of painful spasms that he attributed to an inflamed gallbladder, an infection for which he had been hospitalized in New York.* He was forced to consult a Montreal doctor, who took one look at him and diagnosed the problem, confirming the patient's belief that science was as often a detriment to medicine as to aviation. The man who had walked out of the Libyan desert spent two sleepless weeks in bed with an icepack on his stomach, subsisting entirely on a diet of belladonna. "It makes you a bit stupid," he wrote, twice exiled, to Hitchcock. "Odd planet, odd problems, odd language. Maybe there is

---

* These may have indicated that the 1941 California surgery had not addressed the problem. (Some four months after Dr. Belt's ingenious diagnosis, Saint-Exupéry had written the surgeon that his condition had improved but that he was not yet ready to declare the operation a perfect success.) Equally well, the cholecystitis that plagued him in Montreal and throughout 1942 may have been unrelated.

a star where life is simple," he wrote Natalie at about this time, Consuelo having opened a telegram from his lover.

~

Out of these labors came *The Little Prince*. The book was proposed as a sort of therapy; Saint-Exupéry returned to New York in June 1942 with no immediate project. Once again Elizabeth Reynal came to the rescue. In the margins of the manuscript pages of *Flight to Arras* danced the little figure Saint-Exupéry had been drawing—on letters, dedication pages, in the midst of mathematical equations, over restaurant tablecloths—since the mid-1930s. Well attuned to the author's despair Elizabeth asked if he might not be distracted by writing a children's story about his *"petit bonhomme."* She may have put forth the idea vaguely at dinner one night, when Saint-Exupéry's only response to it was a long look, or she may have mentioned it to her husband, who relayed it to the author over lunch. (Reynal & Hitchcock enjoyed a phenomenal success at the time with P. L. Travers's *Mary Poppins* books.) A great many people remember having offered Saint-Exupéry paint sets in 1941 or 1942 and may well have done so, but he began the book, very much on whim, with a set of children's watercolors he bought himself in an Eighth Avenue drugstore.

Saint-Exupéry wrote and drew *The Little Prince* that summer and fall in his usual distracted manner, in long, late-night bursts of energy fueled by coffee, Coca-Cola, and cigarettes, generous traces of which show up on the manuscript. He wrote with a different series of pens and pencils and edited and crumpled and scribbled in margins. He painted on the wrong side of the onionskin. Galantière was to say that he tore up one hundred pages for every one he sent to the printer, and he was if anything more exacting of this slim text. Saint-Exupéry had told a reporter that the most difficult thing about writing was beginning but did not seem to have had this difficulty with *The Little Prince*, the plot of which emerged full-blown. The illustrations were more problematic. The author had particular trouble with the Little Prince's baobab trees, arriving finally at a satisfactory result only by turning his drawing 120 degrees and beginning again. He was proud enough of the result to boast of it a little in the text. The Little Prince's wardrobe went through a number of transformations, as it does in the finished book. Certain decisions were easy: "Kings *always* wear ermine," the author explained to a visitor in the fall with a knowing smile. He did not settle immediately on the boa digesting the elephant which opens the tale. Originally he offered as proof of his lack of artistic abilities a drawing of a boat, which he claimed a friend took for a potato.

Silvia Reinhardt lent the fox—really a fennec, from Cape Juby—his most memorable speech after she complained to Saint-Exupéry of the pain his tardiness caused her. What difference can it make, protested the author, who evidently for some incidental purpose wore a watch. "My heart begins to dance when I know you are coming," explained Silvia. He settled down to write in her living room; she nursed him through the project with gin-and-Cokes, and with fried eggs and English muffins served by candlelight. A doll in her apartment posed as the Little Prince, giving him a mop of golden curls. (In previous incarnations, the Little Prince's hair was, like the writer's, thinning.) Mocha the poodle modeled for the sheep; a boxer Silvia bought for Saint-Exupéry in August—she thought he needed a pet, and he christened this one "Hannibal"—became the tiger. She listened to Saint-Exupéry chuckle and chortle his way through the manuscript, which it did not seem to her that he took altogether seriously but which clearly represented one of the few solaces he would know in America, a judgment echoed by his secretary. At all times Silvia encouraged him with the project; later he wrote her that she had understood him better than those who had had the benefit of language. "Words," counsels the Little Prince's fox, "are the source of misunderstandings." It is altogether appropriate that the book's most quoted line —"What is essential is invisible to the eye," a line that caused Saint-Exupéry a great deal of trouble although he had been turning out versions of it for five years—should be spoken by the fox.

Silvia Reinhardt and Elizabeth Reynal were not the only women who left their marks on the book, a tenderhearted one in which no women appear. It was hotter in Manhattan in July than Saint-Exupéry could bear, and—after a few weekends as a house guest on Long Island with the Reynals and the Roussy de Saleses—he dispatched Consuelo to locate a summer home. He turned out the remainder of the book's pages in a twenty-two-room mansard-roofed mansion in Asharoken, overlooking Long Island Sound, a house about which he groused, "I wanted a hut and it's the Palace of Versailles." The Bevin House was, nonetheless, the best place he had had to work since Agay, which it resembled, to the extent that the north shore of Long Island can resemble the Riviera. The Saint-Exupérys' was not a quiet household, and to its chaos was added a steady stream of celebrity visitors. André Maurois spent a weekend at the Bevin House in the fall and did not find his stay restful. Saint-Exupéry kept to his usual schedule and thought nothing of summoning his guests at any time to show off a drawing of which he was particularly proud. He did not hesitate to awaken Consuelo—and with her the entire household— at two in the morning to announce he was hungry and in dire need of a plate of scrambled eggs. In another two hours everyone might be aroused again when, from the foot of the stairs, he demanded that his wife come down and indulge him in a game of chess. When the writer was not exhausting the house guests his wife was, with enchanting tales of Oppède;

Maurois felt afterward as if he had been in the clutches of two sorcerers. The Swiss writer Denis de Rougemont made the two-hour trip to the Long Island home regularly, less at the invitation of Saint-Exupéry than of Consuelo. Posing on his stomach, feet in the air, for the Little Prince, he watched Saint-Exupéry manipulate his tiny paintbrushes with fierce concentration, his tongue glued to his upper lip. After a late-night reading from *The Wisdom of the Sands* de Rougemont would stumble to his room, only to find that his host had followed him, eager to talk and smoke some more. He took away from these weekends the impression of a mind that could not be switched off. He became a neighbor of the Saint-Exupérys when both men moved to Beekman Place in New York in December. De Rougemont claimed he never afterward got a full night's sleep. "You are less a couple than a full-time conspiracy against your friends' sleep," he informed them.

Having thus far resisted all of Reynal and Hitchcock's efforts to see that he learn English, Saint-Exupéry submitted in Asharoken to a series of tutorials with a well-intentioned young Northport French teacher named Adèle Breaux. She had originally approached Consuelo about English lessons; Consuelo fobbed her off on her husband. He did not have the courage to send her away but proved a difficult conquest. "Mademoiselle, I am a very busy man. . . . I have very little time to give to English. I don't care whether I ever speak it easily. As a matter of fact, I don't wish to know it too well; I want no other language to impinge on my own. . . . Furthermore, don't count on me to study!" he informed her at the outset of their first session in September. He warmed up only a few lessons later, when the generally circumspect Breaux—initiating her student into the mysteries of the negative in the English language—produced the statement "All children do not love their parents." For the first time she saw the writer's face light up. "Ah, Mademoiselle, do you realize that you have just enunciated an immoral statement?" he boomed, collapsing in laughter over her discomfort. Inadvertently she had allied herself with the irreverence of the Little Prince; from this day on Breaux was a welcome visitor in the house. She found this honor carried with it certain obligations: Saint-Exupéry was as ever on the lookout for people to tend to his wife, and twice prevailed upon Breaux to dine with her in his absence. He used the same words—and no one was quite as scrupulous in setting down Saint-Exupéry's as Adèle Breaux, who kept a flashlight in her car and furiously recorded everything the great man had said by the side of Bevin Road upon leaving him—on both occasions: "She does not like to be left alone."

The Oregon-born Breaux, in whom substance triumphed over style, did not find these the most cordial dinners of her life. Although she took no offense, she was treated with prickly condescension. She heard a good deal about Consuelo's travails in getting her husband's attention, about what Saint-Exupéry admired in a woman. She learned about Consuelo's idea for a book, based on her experiences at Oppède, a project that was clearly earning little support from the author of *Flight to Arras*, who had forbidden his wife to publish under her married name. (Consuelo de Saint-Exupéry's *Kingdom of the Rocks* was brought out by Random House two years after her husband's death. Its reviews as much described the woman Breaux met that summer as they did the work in question: "It is irritating only because it is so constantly on the verge of being good," noted Albert Guérard, the *Times* reviewer. "There are times when she seems a little fey, a little over-poetic and romantic but she is never dull," wrote another. She reminded Guérard of Rostand, not at his best, of Bernhardt, in her decline.) Breaux was treated to an intimate view of the marriage but—she had not yet read *The Little Prince*—did not recognize the rose. While Consuelo was not, as has been claimed, responsible for the volume's drawing, she was in part responsible for the story's whimsical atmosphere. She did not provide her husband with a healthy climate but always assured a fertile one; nothing, in her hands, was or remained prosaic. Her asthma bothered her in New York; she was as sensitive to the air around her as the Prince's globe-protected flower. Like the rose she hid her half-truths with a troubling cough. Few people familiar with the text of *The Little Prince* would have boasted of being the inspiration for the rose, a distinction on a par with having served as the model for Charles Bovary. Consuelo did not hesitate to do so.

She tried unsuccessfully that fall to claim and hold her husband's attention, confiding in Breaux that she felt lonely and abandoned. (In Breaux's opinion the writer was not himself much better off; he appeared, she said later, "never to really seem anchored, in spite of the many friends. What a lonely individual, and how greatly his marriage added to that.") Saint-Exupéry, however, had eyes mostly for France. As the year wore on he stepped up his assaults on Washington. Early in April Jean Monnet, who had come to the United States as a representative of the French government but whom Churchill had appointed to the British Supply Council after the *débâcle*, had arranged for Saint-Exupéry to meet with the American General Staff. On the eighth he attended a meeting in the Munitions Building, probably to discuss the inventions he had mentioned to the government earlier. A week later Henri Giraud, the French general who had commanded the principal sector of the Maginot Line, made a miraculous escape from a German prison. Overjoyed, Saint-Exupéry devised an intricate scheme to unite Giraud and the Americans, themselves delighted to be presented with an alternative to de Gaulle. The writer outlined his scheme to Galantière: the United States would transport him to North Africa, from which he could make his way to France. There he would secure an airplane and fly Giraud to an American ship, which would convey the general to Washington. Giraud and the Combined Chiefs of Staff could work out the details for a North African invasion, Giraud being the only French officer behind whom the troops in North Africa were likely to rally. Galantière was enough taken with this immodest proposal to present it, in July, to two Washington friends, one from the OSS and the other from the Combined Chiefs. It was dismissed as "a grotesque pipe dream," and Galantière was severely rebuffed. "My friend Saint-Exupéry might perhaps be a genius, but he was certainly a complete idiot," Galantière remembered having been informed. Furthermore, if either he or his friend should breathe a word of their hair-brained idea to anyone they could look forward to twelve years in a federal penitentiary.

It was in this way that Saint-Exupéry and Galantière learned, earlier than most, of Operation Torch. "So that's how it is! They're cleverer than I had imagined," was the writer's reaction to the uproar his translator had caused in Washington. (Before the landings Giraud was smuggled out of France to meet with General Eisenhower in Gibraltar. His code name during Operation Torch was "Kingpin.") Saint-Exupéry told a few friends, discreetly, that he made regular trips to Washington, at which he offered up his knowledge of the geography of North Africa, its airports and installations, but there is no evidence that he actually did so, at least in a formal capacity. Even if he was not in touch with the U.S. government the government kept in touch with him: the State Department regularly monitored his sympathies, listening in on his telephone calls and soliciting reports on his dinner table conversations, a task that was presumably facilitated by his friendship with William J. Donovan, with whom Saint-Exupéry remained in touch at least periodically. Through the fall and the early winter he did commute between Silvia's apartment in New York and the house on Long Island, making precipitous departures and unannounced arrivals at both ends, where he was greeted and waved off with torrents of tears.

He responded to these crises with a correspondence suffused with the imagery of *The Little Prince*. Generally as 1942 wore on his letters to Silvia devolved into a litany of explanations and his letters to Consuelo into those of recriminations. On both fronts he pleaded for understanding. To Silvia he wrote:

> I am more devoted to you than you think. This is not obvious because of the difficulties I have with love; this is my mystery, and a very tiring one. Love doesn't give me a voice; it silences me. It does not free me; it locks me up. And yet I cannot live without it. . . . I get terribly confused in love. I disappoint and am contradictory. But tenderness and friendship, once instilled in me, never perish. Little Sylvia [sic], I am a poor sailor. I cannot offer you a smooth trip; I don't know where I am headed. All your re-

proaches, without exception, are merited. And yet my tenderness for you is extreme. When I rest my hand on your forehead I would like to fill you with stars. . . .

To Consuelo he wrote: "I am so alone, so lost, so bitter." His wife was "an odd kind of desert." When not attempting to explain away his erratic behavior he extolled Silvia's unaffected charms. This he did in perfect Little Prince–like metaphors, comparing her to an expanse of unremarkable countryside, one where the grass is green and the water fresh, where the exotic blossoms do not clamor for attention, do not demand to be admired as if in an exhibition.

He had the complicated man's love of the simple; he seemed to have realized he had married an orchid when he wanted a daisy. Even his letters to friends smacked of the themes of *The Little Prince.* Evidently to thank Lamotte for the drawings he had contributed to *Arras* he scribbled an eloquent two-page tribute to the artist. A scraggly willow that Lamotte had potted on his rooftop terrace allowed him the opportunity to expound on one of his favorite themes. Lamotte doted on the spindly tree, which was neither lush nor sturdy, and which did not last long in midtown Manhattan. "We never know if the owner of a $1,000 greyhound likes dogs, but of the man who invites in a mongrel we can be more sure," wrote Saint-Exupéry, noting the care Lamotte took to chase birds from the tiny willow, for fear they would damage its branches.

~

The Little Prince's adventures seem exotic: he is a cosmic urchin who leaves his asteroid because of a misunderstanding with a troublesome rose; he makes a speedy survey of adult logic in six visits to neighboring asteroids, each populated by a man more ridiculous than the last; he lands in the Sahara, where he meets the aviator who serves as the book's narrator; and he learns a few crucial lessons from a fox before disappearing into thin air. The book hardly represented a departure for Saint-Exupéry, however, whose first novel had consisted of equal parts flight and failed love and who had been writing of secret gardens and roses and fairy princes ever since. *The Wisdom of the Sands*, meant to be a philosophical meditation, part Old Testament and part Pascal, shares all the preoccupations of the children's book. An airplane Bernis flies in *Southern Mail* bears the same number as does the Little Prince's asteroid, B-612.* The worst insult the Little Prince can hurl at a man is the same with which the author berated the complacent when in his twenties: such men are "mushrooms."

* It was originally A-612.

In Moscow the author had—in a context about as sensible as that in which the Little Prince poses the same question—asked a diplomat friend to draw him a sheep on the corner of a table. He confessed to Adèle Breaux that the boa swallowing the elephant resembled a sketch he had made as a child. He had himself fallen to earth countless times; he had written from the start of interplanetary space. A man of broad horizons, he had spoken about planets—of changing planets, of his luck in having landed on the same one as the Werths, given the size of the solar system—for several years. He had dreamed of escape for even longer.

The landscape of Saint-Exupéry's travels became his hero's: the volcanoes come from Patagonia, the baobabs from Dakar. Of all the places he lived, only New York is absent from the book, having been excised in an early draft in a reference Saint-Exupéry appears to have thought too parochial. (It was replaced by "a small Pacific islet.") He had a Frenchman's attachment to the earth, of which he never owned a piece; gardening remained for him an emblem of integrity in an increasingly complicated world. (The Little Prince originally presided over a full-scale vegetable garden.) Pastoral metaphors proliferate in his work, as does the image born in Nouakchott of his twin obsessions—with the earth, and with the human duty to cultivate—of a man tending a frail and isolated plant in an inhospitable place. In addition to the tribute to Lamotte, he had worked the image into three books, three articles, countless letters, and a screenplay. The supporting cast of *The Little Prince* also traveled around with him for years: the relatives, administrators, and bureaucrats who had resisted his winning and unorthodox ways, who had made it difficult for an aristocrat to become a pilot, for a pilot to become a writer, for a distracted pilot to remain in the air, for a prominent pilot to abstain from taking a political stance. It took the war, and a mountain of personal problems, to bring them all together in a book.

In early incarnations the Little Prince resembles a Kewpie doll, a baby puffin, or R. Crumb's rumpled Keep-On-Truckin' figure. One early Little Prince, not yet shorn of his eyebrows, looks like the French actor Jean-Louis Barrault. Occasionally in 1940 these ancestors sported wings which—like Saint-Exupéry—they lost with the fall of France. When the writer was asked later how the child-hero had entered his life, he said he had looked down on what he had thought was a blank sheet of paper to find a tiny figure. "I asked him who he was," he explained. "I'm the Little Prince," came the reply. How much did Saint-Exupéry resemble his hero? "You are an extraterrestrial," Aglion informed him one day, before he had yet read the book. "Yes, yes, it is true, I sometimes go for walks among the stars," admitted Saint-Exupéry, who made several sketches of the aviator-narrator but chose not to include any of them in the text. (He is as much that narrator—who has "lived his life alone, without anyone that

I could really talk to"—as the Prince, who cries, "Be my friends, I am all alone" from a desolate mountaintop, to hear only his own echo.) His gestures, Hedda Sterne remembers, were entirely those of the Prince. Others said the same of his speech patterns. He was as inquisitive as his hero but better at answering questions. In an early draft of the manuscript, poking fun at his fame, he wrote that his opinion has been solicited on a great number of subjects; while he did not in fact have strong feelings on such weighty matters as neckties, he had never dared admit as much to a journalist. The tone of the Little Prince's voice was very much that of the man who had informed a woman who shuddered at the thought of boarding an airplane, "It is without precedent, Madame, that an airplane has gone up and not come down"; Saint-Exupéry's charm consisted too of equal parts awkwardness and intimidation. When he grew unhappier still he used the figure to illustrate his despair. For Silvia he sketched a captioned series of Little Princes, wedged in crevices, marooned in bleak landscapes, perched atop craggy cliffs. To Hedda Sterne—for whom he had waited in vain through a despondent afternoon—he sent a Little Prince wading in text: "If I knew how to write letters I would write you a long one, but four or five years ago I turned into an idiot and I no longer know how to communicate very well. I detest myself." In Algiers in 1943 he drew the figure for Madame de B—in prison, in the company of a spider he has tamed. He offered up the book there proudly, boyishly, the autobiography of an innocent abroad, handing it over as if he were offering up his photograph.

Saint-Exupéry's was the brand of purity possessed by two sorts of people: children and monks. He had plenty of faith but little investment in religion; between the dismal days in which he wrote *The Little Prince* and the more dismal days that followed he was to regret this. He said repeatedly that if only he had religion he would retire to a monastery, usually harking back to Solesmes, where he had been so taken by the Gregorian chants. In his habits he seemed ill-suited for such an existence, but in his last years especially he appeared a man with a stubborn faith in search of a place in which to invest it. Publicly he clung always, on all levels, to a dignified idealism. In 1939 Joseph Kessel asked him derisively why he contributed to second-rate publications like *Paris-Soir*. Saint-Exupéry responded without any trace of irritation that if other talented writers were to do the same *Paris-Soir* would no longer be a second-rate publication. (Faced some time earlier with a variation on the same question, Theodore Dreiser shrugged, "One must live," which was of course the operative answer as well for Saint-Exupéry, who admitted elsewhere that he could not so much as bring himself to read *Paris-Soir*.) Through the trials of the early 1940s he remained, for all his despair, indomitable, unwaveringly faithful in the manner a psychologist might identify as that of the *puer aeternus*, what a layman might term unrealistic. He assured a woman friend that while Consuelo tormented him she did not do so maliciously or even intentionally. He never relinquished hope that he might one day reform her, that he might save her from herself. He described his wife to one lover as his cross to bear; his last communications to her are the most adoring of love letters.

No one who met Saint-Exupéry the adult ever forgot him, but the children of his friends and colleagues—with whom, outside of language, politics, and the emotional, he was entirely at ease—preserve the most vivid memories of him. They remember him at the height of his powers, experimenting with a sort of thick green soup in his Central Park South bathtub, filling the sky outside of his apartment with fleets of paper airplanes, tossing water bombs out over Gramercy Park, blowing pumpkin-sized glycerine bubbles with a rolled-up newspaper, setting Hannibal and a tube of toothpaste loose on the luscious carpets of Beekman Place, offering teenage girls lessons in deportment, fabricating helicopters out of maple seeds and hairpins. He rarely hesitated to draw cousins of the Little Prince for the children he met and went so far as to promise René Gavoille's daughter a work on the Little Princess. As children will, he understood what he was to describe in *The Wisdom of the Sands* as the difference between the urgent and the important. While writing *The Little Prince* he called Hélène Lazareff, then the assistant women's editor at *The New York Times*, to ask how many stars were in the sky. (His businessman is engrossed in counting them when the Prince arrives.) Hélène passed the question on to her assistant, Dorothy Barclay, who called the Hayden Planetarium on the author's behalf. She did not succeed in her mission, but her effort was well-rewarded. Her copy of *The Little Prince* bears an extra prince. "You would have to be crazy to choose this planet. It is agreeable only at night, when its inhabitants are asleep," announces the little figure on the half-title page. Underneath him Saint-Exupéry scrawled: "The Little Prince was wrong. There are on earth those whose integrity, kindness, and generosity make up for the greed and the selfishness of others. For example, Dorothy Barclay." For days after the book was sent to Barclay its author hounded Lazareff. What had her assistant thought? Had she liked his drawing?

His playmates were often older children as well. When Annabella Power came to New York for an acting job, Saint-Exupéry coaxed her out of her room at the Hotel Pierre to feed the squirrels in Central Park. She was eager to perfect her accent for her performance and excused herself to race off to an English lesson. He was indignant she could think of abandoning his squirrels. "We were twelve years old when together," reported Annabella, echoing many of Saint-Exupéry's escorts. At Silvia's he devised a game he called "*des oranges sur le piano.*" By rolling one orange up and down the black keys and a second over the white he was able to produce what sounded to most ears like honest Debussy. He got a great deal of mileage out of his Dictaphone, on which he recorded a series of animal noises, or a Mozart symphony, overlaid with several friends' recitations of French classical verse, scanned to accord with the tempi. One visitor arrived to find him amusing himself by "recording his voice on top of itself: singing first one part of a sailor song into the mike, then, in the same track, another, and listening rapturously to the strange results." He played the recordings—to which his guests had no choice but to contribute—forward and backward; he replayed the solos he bullied them into performing at the most compromising times. He interviewed his visitors. Gleefully he directed his friends in a hilarious rendition of a group of French provincials getting their first glimpse of New York from the top of a Fifth Avenue bus.

The diversions were not always as puerile as they seemed. Many friends and acquaintances visited with Saint-Exupéry while he played in his Central Park South bathtub but few who did—apart from those he designated his "wave-maker"—were aware that they were visiting with him in his laboratory. The Reynals found their author hunched over the bathtub one morning when he was to have met them for an important lunch with the head of research for Bell Laboratories. He had proved oblivious to repeated knocks on the door, which the building's superintendent had had to open; in his bathtub he was toying with methods with which to launch a silent invasion of France. He experimented with wave motion, convinced that the difference between the velocity of the waves at the surface and below the surface of the Atlantic could power a tiny submarine. Robert Boname, the engineer who was often Saint-Exupéry's consultant in these matters, built him a wood-and-plastic model with which he continued his tubside experiments—barefoot, his pant legs rolled to his knees, paddling a hand vigorously in the water—in a Northport inlet. The paper helicopters with which he littered Central Park South—a basket of which he once unloaded from the top of the Empire State Building—were designed to the same end: he thought the enemy could be surprised by a motorless autogiro. (Boname was skeptical about the invention, which he did not feel could function without an impossibly long rotor, but the writer ignored his counsel.) Several of his ideas Saint-Exupéry conveyed to von Kármán, then an adviser to the air force. Galantière's favorite was a fleet of large underwater barges on which dismounted airplanes could be hauled, by submarine, across the Atlantic. Equally intriguing was the underwater vessel in which the inventor proposed to make his way back to France, said to have consisted of a sort of fish-shaped coffin outfitted with a rudder and mobile scales. Of course he was not the only one experimenting in such realms; the U.S. War Department received some fantastic mail during

these years. Saint-Exupéry's irrepressible inventing and high-level international contacts appear to have caused some concern among government
agencies, however. A curious May 1942 intelligence report had him organizing an aircraft construction enterprise in Brazil with Fleury, not what
the United States wanted a resident alien who was believed to be "if not
pro-Vichy, at least pro-Pétain" to be doing.

The starry-eyed innocence and the deep-seated sense of responsibility
caused Saint-Exupéry more trouble than they did the Little Prince, who
traveled better, who had the good fortune to meet a wise fox, and of whom
less was expected. The latter half of the writer's American stay turned into
a struggle between two conflicting sets of needs: those of a small boy in
search of comfort and a grown man who either was or felt he was shirking
his duty. He dreamed of liberating France but was done in by all lesser
obligations. Having failed to appear for a dinner at the Reynals he wrote
Elizabeth with his excuses. He was dead tired, he was unhappy and anxious. "So I'm a bit scatter-brained, and I forget dinners and appointments.
Know that I am horribly distracted but don't think that I am negligent,"
he begged her. He remained, with mixed results, childishly addicted to
honesty. When Consuelo was mugged in 1942—the thief hit her over the
head before making away with her bag—he chose to confide his anguish
to Silvia. This was patently not a subject on which she cared to hear him
expound. He had not moved from Consuelo's bedside for forty-eight hours,
he could neither eat nor sleep, he had suddenly realized that if anything
were to happen to her he would not be able to go on living. She had her
flaws but she was his wife, and he felt responsible for her "like a captain
for his ship." He realized he had abandoned his post, a painful admission
for a man who acknowledged that he had little aptitude for affairs of the
heart but who prided himself on being a loyal friend, an excellent shepherd. The remorse was the same he suffered for living far from his besieged
country. There was ample reason why—in the only line of *The Little Prince*
in which Saint-Exupéry reaches out and collars his reader—he offers up
a version of "*Mais il faut cultiver notre jardin.*" His regret that he could
not do so ate away at him. And yet, writing from the next room, to the
sound of Consuelo's labored breathing, he could not help but tell Silvia
how alone he felt, how exhausted he was, how much he needed to see
her.

Idealistic, or fussy, he remained too much the individualist to submit
to behavior that might have simplified his life. As Maurois said of him,
"Either he dominated the conversation or he dreamed of another planet."
Renoir put it more bluntly: "I think it is fair to say that, throughout his
entire stay with us, and no doubt in America until the day he left, Saint-
Exupéry was not in the United States." He was unable to make himself
heard—clearly—in Washington or in the French community in exile, and

by his taste for grandeur and his obsession with lucidity was condemned to the margins. In 1942 the rest of his countrymen took sides, although they often enough had to struggle with their consciences to do so, and although they often disagreed violently with their fellow partisans. Not having to search very far for his inspiration, Saint-Exupéry wrote a satire of the adult world.

~

The bulk of the manuscript was completed by mid-October. Reynal and Hitchcock—who had heard little about the project in the preceding months—were very happy with it; Hitchcock wrote of the title that would turn into the best-seller among Saint-Exupéry's works, "I am perfectly delighted with the little book, and have high hopes for its success." A contract was drawn up in November, when Saint-Exupéry was again short on funds and when the text was ready to be typeset. Reynal & Hitchcock began advancing their author his monies immediately, although nothing was finalized until the last week of January 1943. By that time it was clear that *The Little Prince* would not, as its publishers had hoped, appear in February, and the contract had grown to a two-book agreement. Saint-Exupéry was granted a $3,000 advance for the children's book and for a short volume he was to deliver on the position of France and the French in the modern world, a work that doubtless would have corresponded little to that description but that he was not in any event to write. (An amendment to his Canadian contract signed in March turned that project into a novel, due in the fall.) He continued, through the early part of the winter, to fiddle with his illustrations for *The Little Prince* and to agonize over their proper placement in the text.

On November 8, 1942, in one of the most complex maneuvers in military history, American troops landed in North Africa. The news reached New York that evening. Among the many prophecies of Saint-Exupéry proved true by Operation Torch was one that he had made to a French restaurateur who had despaired of the objectionable table manners of an American couple in his New York establishment. "They are barbarians," the Frenchman had sniffed. "Yes, barbarians who will help us to win the war," Saint-Exupéry had agreed. Reactions to the momentous news varied. The French army, under the orders of Pétain, fired on their once and future allies. De Gaulle, who had not been informed of the military operation, partly because of his unpopularity among the Vichy troops in North Africa, partly because he had behaved badly toward Roosevelt, partly because Roosevelt did not like him in the first place, was incensed. Roused from bed and told of the American move the six-foot five-inch pajamaed monument sputtered: "Well, I hope that Vichy will throw them back into the sea. One doesn't make one's way into France by breaking and entering." Saint-Exupéry, of course, was jubilant.

In response to the landings the Germans occupied all of France. Vichy was no longer, which again dramatically changed the political landscape, notably in America and in North Africa. Those members of the French embassy and consulate in the United States who refused to reconsider their loyalty to Pétain were escorted with their families by the FBI to a luxury hotel in Hershey, Pennsylvania, where they were sequestered until they changed their minds or—as was the case of neary twenty diehards —were later exchanged for American diplomatic personnel held by the Germans. Along with several other groups (one attempted to recruit Saint-Exupéry, asking him to put in a word on their behalf with Donovan), de Gaulle's representatives lobbied to be recognized as the French authority in America. This left Washington to wonder once again who, and where, was France. Was an opportunistic renegade general based in London any worse than an illegitimate puppet government that had just cost the United States 1,500 casualties? Aglion remembered that wartime France represented a situation so far afield of American State Department experience that the United States fell back on policies forged in Latin America, where illegitimate governments were often recognized for want of a better alternative, and armies could be counted on to rise up against their leaders.

Not having forgotten the bitterness of his experience with *Flight to Arras* (which was only now published in France) but evidently feeling as if he could this time adequately brace himself, Saint-Exupéry dipped a toe into the polemical surf. On November 29 *The New York Times Magazine* carried his "An Open Letter to Frenchmen Everywhere," a version of which the author also read over the air in French. Once again he pleaded with his countrymen to set aside their differences, to focus not on representing France but on serving her; the American action in North Africa should have put an end to all discussion of Vichy's real and alleged sins. Leave those, he argued, to the historians and the war tribunals. As for any discussion of who should command: "Our real chief," he wrote, "is France, now condemned to silence." And as for the provisional organization of France, this could be entrusted to Britain and the United States. With Vichy out of the picture there was no longer any excuse for sects, clans, divisions. Frenchmen should be asking only how they could free their country. Saint-Exupéry suggested that all those who had thus far been silent—by which he meant the non-Gaullists—should write Cordell Hull, the U.S. Secretary of State, of their desire to serve in whatever way the American government saw fit, stipulating that in the interests of French unity the organization remain outside of politics. "The State Department will be astonished at the number of Frenchmen who will take their stand for unity. For, despite our reputation, most of us at heart know only love of our civilization and our country," he wrote.

His sincerity left him open to ridicule, which was what he earned from most of his American-based compatriots. A fair number saw in his text a direct attack on de Gaulle. One former French air force officer wrote in a letter to the *Times* that Saint-Exupéry was himself furthering divisions among the French by implying that de Gaulle was the leader of a sect. He got endless flak—and still does today—for having suggested that any political organization of France could be entrusted to the Allies, an idea that was anathema to de Gaulle, who went so far as to appoint the full cast of a shadow government, down to the *préfets* and the *sous-préfets*, before setting foot back in France. Henry Bernstein, the outspoken playwright who had written so vitriolically of Vichy as to have been stripped in absentia of his French citizenship, took Saint-Exupéry to task for having gone easy on Pétain. "We cannot, however touching the appeal, by however brilliant a writer, by however courageous an aviator, by however nice a man, say mildly, 'We'll let bygones be bygones,' " he wrote, patronizingly, in a long letter to the *Times*. A few praised the author's noble sentiments, but generally the piece only incited to riot. Why, fumed Bernstein, are the Americans and British entitled to their differences of opinion, whereas the French are labeled—the words were Saint-Exupéry's—"little baskets of crabs" when they quarrel? American readers were moved by the writer's eloquence but did not see how his appeal would amount to much, given what they had seen of those same "little baskets of crabs." For them the piece fell squarely in the realm of literature.

Once again, too, Saint-Exupéry proved a master of poor timing. The Americans had backed the wrong man in North Africa—loyal to Pétain, the army had no interest in accepting Giraud as Supreme French Commander, proving that the Latin American analogy only went so far—and had to engage in some nimble, behind-the-scenes negotiating to bring around Admiral Darlan to the Allied cause. As the American press was quick to point out, this was an expedient but distasteful solution; Darlan was known to be antipathetic to the British and thought by many to be a Nazi. Named High Commissioner in North Africa, the admiral shared control of the French armed forces in North Africa with Giraud as of mid-November. The American landings entailed all kinds of treacheries, but nothing compared to the Alice-in-Wonderland logic of the Darlan solution: the admiral's power stemmed from the fact that he gave orders in Pétain's hallowed name. Arguing that Pétain was now a prisoner of Germany and no longer responsible for his own decisions, he continued to do so, and was obeyed, despite the fact that he was now issuing anti-Axis orders. In Vichy one of Pétain's staff members remarked, "We live in sad times when we cannot trust our traitors anymore."

The American press objected fiercely to Roosevelt's installation of Darlan, who for all of his usefulness caused the president an enormous amount of embarrassment. (Roosevelt and many people were put out of their misery when Darlan was assassinated on Christmas Eve.) Darlan's unexpected entrance on the scene—only because of an odd twist of events was he in North Africa at the time of the landings in the first place—muddied the waters for Saint-Exupéry as well. In one of the most painful attacks upon him after the *Times* piece appeared, Jacques Maritain, the esteemed Catholic philosopher, published a long article entitled *"Il faut parfois juger"* ("Sometimes One Must Judge") on the front page of the anti-Vichy weekly, *Pour la Victoire*. Maritain was more cool-headed than most of Saint-Exupéry's detractors but made the unassailable point that the writer could not publish such a piece and claim to be above the fray, could not publish, in fact, without himself ceding to language, which he claimed he distrusted. In a most dignified manner he accused his compatriot of being vague and unrealistic. Saint-Exupéry was shown Maritain's article by its author before it appeared and allowed to contribute a statement to the newspaper; essentially he blamed his troubles on the *Times* translation and asked *Pour la Victoire* to carry his piece in the original French, which it did. (Galantière could not be blamed on this count, having left for London in October, but the writer would have been hard-pressed to find fault with the *Times*, which had evidently paid four different translators to render him into English, at least one of whom did a perfectly serviceable job.) He wrote Maritain directly on December 19; he had been profoundly hurt by his criticism, especially as it came from someone who did not generally stoop to polemic and whom he greatly esteemed.* He had written his piece for the non-Gaullists, in French, before the Darlan problem; he wished Maritain would read it in that light. He engaged in a certain amount of hair-splitting and pleaded a little: say what you will, he entreated, but please do not misconstrue my intentions. He showed less restraint when arguing about the piece with Raoul de Roussy de Sales, who had been on the Gaullist payroll since the previous fall, though with mixed feelings. The two men nearly came to blows over "An Open Letter" in December. They never patched up their differences; two days after this bitter argument Roussy de Sales died of cancer.

Saint-Exupéry's *litiges* were not confined to the political. Over the winter he continued the feud with André Breton that had simmered—a little bit tended by Consuelo—through the summer. In June he had been raked over the coals in *VVV*, the Surrealist magazine, which again made hay of the 1941 Vichy nomination. The argument took a more personal turn later in the year. Breton had evidently visited the Saint-Exupérys and

* Maritain advised the Gaullists but never considered himself a Gaullist.

had not been charmed by his host's habit of reading to his guests. (Consuelo had let her husband know Breton was bored, and Saint-Exupéry had immediately desisted.) Saint-Exupéry was clearly very bothered by Breton's criticisms; claiming he had never been difficult with any of his friends, he repeatedly invited Breton to Northport for a conciliatory afternoon. We probably do disagree about a hundred thousand things, he conceded, but we doubtless agree about another hundred thousand. There was no reason for the two men to avoid each other; Saint-Exupéry had nothing but respect for those whose opinions differed from his own, and no time for disagreements. Surely Breton could turn a deaf ear to the lies that were being spread about him. He had risked his life to be here today to argue with Breton; they would not change each other, but why not come to lunch anyway? His saintly approach had a predictable effect on the heretic, who responded by throwing more mud in his face.

On the home front, more than ever, he found himself harassed at the end of 1942. Consuelo vacated her Central Park South apartment during the last week of November and the couple—having left the Bevin House, the multiple fireplaces of which had to be stoked daily to keep the house livable in winter, as Saint-Exupéry did not like furnace heat—moved in December to a town house at 35 Beekman Place. Consuelo had found the duplex apartment, which probably did not represent any more strain on the family's finances than did two Central Park South apartments and the Long Island home; New York City rents were particularly modest at the time. She may have sold her husband on the idea because the house, separated from the East River by a private garden, represented the most tranquil accommodations Manhattan had to offer. From her point of view it meant that the couple could continue to live together, as they had on Long Island. Much impressed by the cream-colored carpets, the huge walls of mirror, the cozy, upper-floor library, Denis de Rougemont said he knew of no more charming residence in New York. Adèle Breaux found the spacious living room, with its brown velvet upholstery and its dark wood wainscoting, a definition of perfect taste.

Most of these charms were lost on Saint-Exupéry, whose own tastes continued to run to the ascetic and who gave Hannibal free rein of the place. He was wholly inconvenienced by the move, which allowed Consuelo an excuse to buy him a $600 antique Spanish writing table. ("I consider that a useless waste of money. Our stay here is temporary and besides, you know that I don't care what kind of table I write on as long as it is stable," he reprimanded her in front of Breaux, with whom he shared the page proofs of *The Little Prince* one Sunday just after the move.) Between the return from Northport and the departure from Central Park South he wrote Silvia of the uproar, which had caused him in turn to mislead her about a rendezvous:

I understand why you are upset with me. I understand fully, I understand too well. I am terribly upset with myself. I am in despair over the missed trains, the bungled appointments, the lost addresses, the bills, the unreturned phone calls, the reproaches, the difficult reconciliations, the hurt friends, the headaches when it is time to talk, the vacuum of ideas when it is time to write, the three dinners accepted for the same evening.

She had to forgive him; he had been cooped up for forty-eight hours in two rooms along with the movers, Consuelo and her friends, Marie McBride and her typewriter, a cook gone mad who persisted in making scenes, a telephone that had not stopped ringing, and a constant stream of visitors. It had been like working in Grand Central Terminal. His head was bursting; the last thing he needed on top of it all were Silvia's reproaches. In a matter of weeks he would learn that *Flight to Arras* had been banned in France.

On the thirty-first the Saint-Exupérys hosted a late-night dinner for the Bonames and four or five other couples at Beekman Place. The Bonames came into town from the suburbs and so arrived before their host and hostess, who had gone to mass at St. Patrick's Cathedral. Saint-Exupéry showed up with a red nose but all the same barely made it through the introductions before exploding: "For goodness' sake! If you don't catch pneumonia in the church you can't possibly feel as if you've attended midnight mass!" (He raged in a similar fashion against American progress as manifested in precisely the kind of gadgetry he so admired: "If they continue to mechanize everything," he told Fleury as he accompanied him through the sliding doors of Pennsylvania Station, "in a few years no one in America will know how to open a door.") After hors d'oeuvres the group sat down to a New Year's Eve dinner, with Saint-Exupéry and Consuelo at far ends of a vast table. A flutist—a friend of Consuelo's on whom her husband claimed he had never before set eyes—installed himself behind the writer and periodically entertained the guests with airs. Saint-Exupéry was in an entertaining mode as well; he plunged into the story of a breakdown in dissident Africa. He held his guests spellbound with the account, leading up to the repair of the aircraft just as the Moors appeared, rifles in hand, on the horizon. At this critical moment a volley of saucers flew toward his head from the opposite end of the table, where they had been dexterously launched by Consuelo. Her husband bore up under this siege with more facility than most of the others of 1942 (there is no record of how he fared with the *oeufs en gelée* that Consuelo boasted of having bombarded him on an earlier occasion): according to Madame Boname, who was seated, *en garde*, to his immediate left, Saint-Exupéry reflexively caught each missile in midair, extending his right arm, then his left, each time without blinking, and all without missing a beat of his

story. The assaults—that of the Moors, and that of the flying saucers—
let up simultaneously, claiming no casualties.

~

Since his arrival in New York, Saint-Exupéry had said he wanted only to
fly again. For two years there had been no front on which he might do
so, although as early as Pearl Harbor he had drafted a proposal for a
squadron of French volunteers who might fight under the Americans. In
1942 he talked incessantly about getting back in uniform, if not always
when expected to: Elizabeth Reynal introduced him to Helen Gahagan
Douglas in the hope that the congresswoman would be able to help him
with what Elizabeth described as his obsession, but the writer, for whatever
reason, did not broach the topic of his reenlistment. In "An Open Letter"
he as much as announced he would leave as soon as he could for the
front, the landing in North Africa having created one. According to Maurois, he and Saint-Exupéry offered up their services immediately. The two
officers were told at the end of 1942 that an emissary of Giraud, General
Antoine Béthouart, would be making his way to America and were advised
to take up their case with him. Béthouart arrived with the new year. The
first item on his agenda was to ask the Americans for weapons for the
French army in North Africa. The second—on which Béthouart had probably not counted—was to dispel the American impression of two rival
French armies, one behind Giraud and the other behind de Gaulle.* Saint-
Exupéry did all he could to see that he never amounted to anything less
than the general's third priority.

Most of the readers of "An Open Letter" saw in it Saint-Exupéry's
announcement of a return to the front. Anne Lindbergh read in it something stronger, "the pull to sacrifice, to death." She thought her friend
felt a need to pay his debt to what he referred to as the saints of France,
the 40 million people living under the German boot. He had in fact nearly
said as much in an essay completed in 1942, originally meant to have
prefaced a book on the exodus from Paris by Werth and originally entitled
"Lettre à Léon Werth." In it he initially sang the praises of his great
friend—"If I write a page, and then I imagine Werth critiquing it, I discover in that page imperfections that I would not otherwise have detected"
—although the specific references to Werth and the long passages in which
his friend paid him tribute were later cut. Brentano's planned to publish
Werth's *33 jours* with Saint-Exupéry's preface—by then titled "Lettre à
un ami"—in the spring of 1943 but did not do so (*33 jours* appeared forty-

* General Béthouart was only too well-qualified for the job: he had been jailed in Morocco
for not having resisted the Allied invasion.

nine years later, in Paris); ultimately they did issue Saint-Exupéry's *Lettre à un otage*, on its own, in June 1943. The text was still directed at Werth, whom his friend addressed in the second person, although his name does not figure in the essay. As he stood in for all of France Saint-Exupéry took a little artistic license: he added that the friend over whose fate he anguished was in danger not only because he was French and a Jew but because he was sick, which Werth was not.

Lettre à un otage (Letter to a Hostage) is a haunting essay, shot through with the "pull to sacrifice" Anne Lindbergh noted in "An Open Letter." It arguably stands as the most crystalline expression of Saint-Exupéry's thinking. In its fifteen pages he compresses all of the ideas that, bloated by parable, bulk out the pages of *The Wisdom of the Sands*; he urgently recapitulates those to which he slyly gave voice in *The Little Prince*, a book dedicated to Werth. On the crowded boat to America he looks back to Juby and realizes that in its desolation it was the home he most loved; he makes the only mention he will make in a published work of the loss of Guillaumet; he pays tribute to the Fleurville lunch; he pours out his anguish. He expresses suddenly a need for his past—not his childhood, but his past, for the "lovely shipload of experiences" that is his hard-won maturity. He had always written odes to friendship but nowhere else on the page—save in *The Little Prince*—is he so alone, having lost the ties, the relationships that for him constitute France. These friendships are his only riches: especially in the early drafts of the much-worked-over manuscript he pleaded with his friends to survive the war, to make sure the storm passed them by. If they no longer existed, neither did he. They could age later. Above all he was haunted by the image of Werth, a man he loved and who loved him beyond reason, the friend who had taught him, as he had tried to teach Breton, that "If I differ from you, far from undermining you, I enhance you." It was for Werth, for that brand of friendship, for a lunch on the banks of the Saône that he wanted to fight again. That was the best he could do: he might be a soldier, but the 40 million hostages in France were nothing less than saints.

Comfortably installed on Beekman Place, he clearly envied them their sacrifice. He shared his misery with Hedda Sterne, stopping by her East Fiftieth Street apartment in the evenings when he was out walking Hannibal. Repeatedly he grumbled that he had no truths to offer men, that he had no desire or ambition but to save his country, that he must have been put on earth for some reason but did not know how to make himself useful. His work of the last year had convinced him, if he needed convincing, of one thing: "Words," he told Yvonne Michel, "are noises emanating from the mouth. You must judge people on who they are and what they do." He had long said that he preferred to waste his sweat to his saliva; the written word now seemed to him entirely insufficient. (In better spirits he was to quip that language was like sex among turtles: not terribly well-designed.) In 1943 he began to talk about signing only with his blood. Consuelo heard the most fervent articulations of this despair: After General Béthouart had seen to his reenlistment, early in 1943, her husband informed her that she would be better off without him and that he would be better off dead. There are all kinds of torture, and Saint-Exupéry had his preferences. He went into a rage when—having realized he did not have an article of clothing he could pack for North Africa and that he was running low on funds—Consuelo came home with an armload of new dresses. He asked her how much she had spent; she jumped down his throat. Yet just before he sailed or during the crossing he wrote her: "I'm off to the war. I cannot bear to be far from those who are hungry, and know only one way to make peace with my conscience, which is to suffer as much as possible. To search out the greatest possible suffering. . . . I am not leaving *in order* to die. I am leaving in order to suffer and thereby be united with those who are dear to me."

He learned in February that he would be mobilized and he expected to leave on or around March 1. He was thus making his preparations when, on February 15, the French battleship *Richelieu* docked in New York for repairs, setting off what was to become a nightmare of public relations for the Gaullists in America. Lured by various forms of propaganda, 350 members of the ship's crew deserted to join the Free French while in New York harbor. (By that time two rival French recruiting offices had been set up only a few doors from each other on Fifth Avenue; more than a few confused sailors enlisted with Giraud when they meant to enlist with de Gaulle.) Fascinated by life on board the battleship, Saint-Exupéry evidently visited the *Richelieu* with Consuelo, Maurois, and several other friends. On the last Saturday of the month he ran into a *Richelieu* sailor in a midtown jewelry store and plied him with a series of questions. The twenty-year-old sailor, Georges Perrin, had no idea who Saint-Exupéry was but submitted all the same to the interrogation. With great enthusiasm the older man then mentioned that he, too, was to be reenlisted. "In what branch?" Perrin asked, in perfect innocence. "In the air force," replied Saint-Exupéry, who remained entirely composed when asked his rank. He was in no way put off by the sailor's questions and may even have been relieved to be traveling incognito. He spent some two hours discussing the war with Perrin, making on him an indelible impression, mostly of humility.

"Saint-Exupéry changed people—at least while they were with him," Galantière was to write. "His presence put heart into the timid, abashed the impudent, closed the liar's mouth. . . . He had a glance that stopped witless smut in mid-telling." Like all idealists he brought people up to his level. This was the quality the writer so admired in Werth, whom he wrote could "ennoble" the mechanic looking after his Bugatti with a simple handshake. He claimed that Werth had taught him that grandeur and civility were contagious, and he lived as if they were. In an early draft of *Lettre à un otage* he wrote that a smile was no less binding than a pact between empires. He got to know the late-night Red Arrow messenger who carried his missives all over Manhattan well enough to accompany him home to Brooklyn for a bachelors' dinner. When he called on the Hitchcocks at Gramercy Park one Saturday afternoon he rang at the wrong apartment; he spent an hour charming their Irish neighbors and left without seeing his publisher. De Gaulle spoke always of France and of the grandeur of France; Saint-Exupéry, for all his lofty perspective, for all his weighty pronouncements, planted himself at the other end of the telescope. For him, the individual was the empire.

Throughout February he saw to—or delegated—the necessary arrangements. He submitted to Hélène Lazareff a shopping list that she and Dorothy Thompson filled for him, Hélène seeing to the Alka-Seltzer, the toothpaste, the aspirin, the shaving cream, the socks, and the cigarettes, Dorothy to the equally specific list of art supplies, including ink for Saint-Exupéry's Parker pen, with which he was enamored. Not only had he no respectable clothes, he had no uniform. On February 26 he wrote a check for $100 to the Brooks Uniform Company, having located the closest approximation of a French air force uniform New York had to offer. His travel orders did not come through in early March, however, which left him with plenty of time to put his affairs in order. On the twenty-ninth he signed two agreements with Reynal & Hitchcock. He granted Becker power-of-attorney to make all decisions concerning *Wind, Sand and Stars, Flight to Arras*, and *The Little Prince*. Everyone who saw him during these weeks reported him to be in effusively high spirits. De Rougemont—with whom Saint-Exupéry spent nearly an entire night demonstrating that only two economic systems, Stalinism and feudalism, were viable (de Rougemont did not think he would be able to repeat the argument)—described the condition as one of "intellectual euphoria." Beaming, he received Ping Lawrence and a few other guests for what he billed as a farewell dinner. Late in the night he assembled them in the upstairs study, where he read *The Little Prince* from beginning to end, in the middle of a blackout test, by candlelight, as the snow fell outside. Midway through, Consuelo arrived for dinner.

Generally Consuelo behaved badly throughout the month of March, crying and screaming in the hope of preventing her husband from leaving New York; she told visitors he was going off to be free of her. Saint-Exupéry had taken leave of his wife often enough to have predicted the results: the Little Prince's rose at first refuses to say good-bye to him, then, in a miserable attempt to send him off graciously, overcomes her vanity long enough to lash out, "Don't linger like this. You have decided to go away. Now go!" Consuelo carried on as she had before the Libyan misadventure, though a little closer to home. "Hers is the worst case of self-induced hysteria that I have ever witnessed. Whoever heard of a wife carrying on like that when her husband is about to set off for war! The screaming has been unbearable. It is absolutely shameless," announced the nurse who opened the door to Adèle Breaux early in March. She was on her way to administer sedatives. The strain showed on Saint-Exupéry, whom Breaux found jumpy and fatigued.

He appears to have said his good-byes several times. On what he thought was to be his last night in America, or said was his last night, or what others chose to remember as his last night, he did some or all of the following things: visited with the Hitchcocks, and joined their children in a water-bomb attack on the pedestrians of Gramercy Park; put in an appearance as the guest of honor at a small farewell dinner given by Jean Mercier, a prominent engineer and inventor, and his wife, Simone, who asked Saint-Exupéry what he would like her to serve and obliged with a platter of *cuisses de grenouille à l'aïoli*; dropped off the drafts, typescript, and proofs of *Lettre à un otage*—as well as a disk on which he had recorded "The Prayer of Loneliness" from what would become *The Wisdom of the Sands**—with Hedda Sterne; signed a great number of copies of *The Little Prince*. The next morning at seven he woke Silvia Reinhardt. In an old flannel nightgown she opened her door to find her friend standing before her, looking ridiculous in a uniform of which he was clearly very proud. The sleeves billowed out over his hands; the skin-tight jacket pulled over the chest; the gold-embroidered emblem on the breast pocket looked "like an amoeba run amok." He told her he had come to say good-bye. "I wish I had something splendid for you to remember me by, but this is all I have," he said, handing over his Zeiss Ikon camera and tossing a rumpled brown paper bag onto her entryway table. In it was the preliminary manuscript of *The Little Prince*.

A little after noon on April 13, 1943, Saint-Exupéry boarded the S.S. *Stirling Castle*, which in an apt metaphor was accomplished by walking over the hull of the *Normandie*, lying on its side in a bed of mud more than a year after having gone up in a blaze in New York harbor. Within an hour he turned up in the *Stirling Castle*'s sickbay, accompanied by a young naval officer. A small cinder had lodged in his eye, and was removed. Also while the ship was docked in New York Saint-Exupéry read *The Little Prince* to a French-speaking officer on board, a Jungian psychoanalyst

---

* He filled the remainder of the twelve-inch disk with music, singing several deeply felt refrains of "*V'là le bon vent*," an old French air he said he had rediscovered in Canada and found exquisite, which in his rendition it is.

named Henry Elkin. The book had officially been published on the sixth; its first major reviews had appeared that week. The critics were as befuddled as impressed. A winsome fairy tale was not exactly what America was expecting from the virile author of *Flight to Arras*. (In their advertisements to the trade his publishers had taken the coy way out: "Reviewers and critics will have a field day explaining to you just what kind of story it is. As far as we are concerned it is the new book by Saint-Exupéry.") Few reviewers saw *The Little Prince* as a children's book and not everyone recommended it for adults; when they did, the book earned its author comparisons with writers as different as Montesquieu and Hans Christian Andersen.

Among *The Little Prince*'s more astute readers were Anne Lindbergh and P. L. Travers. Both women immediately recognized the book as a bitter tale of lost childhood. Anne Lindbergh found it far sadder than *Arras* and was quick to see that Saint-Exupéry "must have been miserable and sick and lonely when he wrote it." She thought he would "throw himself into self-sacrifice—war and death. Thinking that is the answer—and it is not." Travers—who has said the book seemed to her a distillation of suffering—saw the crux of it in the line, "So I lived my whole life without anyone I could really talk to." She greeted *The Little Prince* warmly in a front-page review in the New York *Herald Tribune* and, curiously, reminded readers that "all fairy tales are portents." The book spent one week on the *New York Times* best-seller list in June and two months on the *Herald Tribune* list, not a hugely impressive performance for its author. By the fall it had sold only 30,000 copies in English and 7,000 in French. Some good things nearly happened for it: Orson Welles, who had adapted material from *Night Flight* and *Wind, Sand and Stars* for radio propaganda programs in November, discovered the work in May. He summoned his business partner to his home for a 4:00 a.m. reading, which the partner —yet another person to lose a night's sleep to the Little Prince—attended in his bathrobe. He got no rest until he had secured a two-month film option for Welles, who wanted to bring the book to the screen with a combination of live action and animation. The project came to naught when Welles was unable to enlist the help of Walt Disney.*

The *Stirling Castle* sailed, part of a thirty-ship convoy, at nightfall. Saint-Exupéry spent the next three weeks playing excellent chess and revising his pages of *The Wisdom of the Sands*, the manuscript of which he had had microfilmed and now carried, along with his papers, in a beautiful pigskin Mark Cross bag Silvia had given him. (She had also

---

* Acting like a character from the book, Disney failed to appreciate the attention Welles commanded when he outlined his plans for *The Little Prince* in a Disney boardroom. He walked out of the meeting and away from the project.

given him a gold identification bracelet inscribed with his name and blood group, although she claims she never knew, at least on a conscious level, that he really meant to leave.) Later he remembered this crossing as having elicited in him "the joy of a crusade." In the course of it he told Henry Elkin that as soon as the war was over he planned to enter the monastery at Solesmes. As if to press the point, he closed each of their conversations with a liturgical chant.

XVII

~

Into Thin Air
1943–1944

I shall see to it, if I can, that my death makes no
statement that my life has not made already.

MONTAIGNE, *Essays*

Saint-Exupéry was not to set foot in mainland France in the last year
of his life. North Africa and Corsica were as close as he was to come; he
reported to Algiers, the only major French city not subjected to the Occupation, at the end of April 1943. It made for a curious kind of promised
land. One young American diplomat posted to North Africa at the time
found himself reminded, at various moments, of a Hollywood melodrama,
of *Alice's Adventures in Wonderland*, and of *The Pirates of Penzance*. More
often the Borgias were evoked. Nowhere was the political atmosphere
thicker, or more sticky, than in Algiers, a city overrun by adventurers,
diplomatic personnel, secret agents of all nationalities, the remnants of
café society and its demimondaines, black marketeers, wealthy natives.
Nothing went unnoticed; no rumor went unrepeated. Bitter enemies sat
elbow to elbow on the terrace of the Hôtel Aletti or in the old Moorish
palace that was now the Club Interallié; intelligence officers made over-
tures to the wrong people. The plots and counterplots hatched overnight.
It was as if the political passions of France played themselves out all the
more fiercely for being forced to do so in a hothouse climate on a small
piece of atypical turf. A. J. Liebling tried to make sense of North Africa
for his *New Yorker* readers by saying that the situation was a little like
what would result if the United States were to extend statehood to Puerto
Rico, then—finding itself occupied by a foreign power—were to allow the
island, acting under the thumb of the powerful sugar companies, to carry

on as the United States. Saint-Exupéry offered a few memorable descriptions of Algiers as well, but these were to come later.

It was not a city in which one had to announce oneself, but he lost no time in making his presence felt. For the most part his timing was good. Having dropped his bags at Pélissier's he began flying a Simoun almost immediately, outside of Algiers. On May 1 he was officially reassigned to his old reconnaissance squadron. A few days later the 2/33 came through Algiers; they were on their way to Tunisia, where they were to join the American 3rd Photo Group under Elliott Roosevelt, the president's son, then head of the Mediterranean Allied Photo Reconnaissance Wing (MAPRW). Gavoille, now in command of the 2/33, dropped in on Pélissier and to his amazement found Saint-Exupéry in the doctor's living room. The two men fell into each other's arms with much emotion. The same day Gelée, Saint-Exupéry's commanding officer in Orconte, was named the head of General Giraud's cabinet, an office of which Saint-Exupéry was happy to avail himself. He waited a few weeks before asking his friend if he did not think it high time he was promoted to major. When Gelée agreed that it was, the captain instructed him, "Well, see to it!" (Gelée did, though not without effort.)

Probably on May 5 Saint-Exupéry called on René Chambe, now a general and—more fortuitously yet—now Giraud's minister of information. Chambe found the new arrival thinner but otherwise unchanged; he made no comment on the writer's attire, which was without equal in North Africa. "Here, per our agreement," announced Saint-Exupéry, not having forgotten his Mamounia promise, "but six months late, for which apologies." He wrote off his tardiness to the Gaullists, whom he said had done everything in their power to detain him. Chambe more than made up for any inconvenience, arranging for his friend to rejoin the 2/33 immediately in Laghouat, Algeria. This return conformed eerily to what Anne Lindbergh imagined when she had read of the writer's departure and predicted that his greatest happiness would come in rejoining his squadron: "He will go back to them. He will walk in shyly, stooping a little. They will shout, 'Saint-Ex!' That will be his reward." The following day he went up for a training flight in a Bloch 174; that evening he treated his colleagues to a lavish barbecue, at which he paraded out all of his card tricks. The neighboring squadron was beside itself with envy. For the first time in two and a half years he was back in the French-speaking world, aloft and among friends.

On two other counts his timing was exceptional as well. Saint-Exupéry's return to the 2/33 coincided with the arrival of the squadron's first Lockheed P-38's (Lightnings), the remarkable twin-boomed fighters that had been adapted for reconnaissance missions and were among the fastest airplanes in existence in 1943. Capable of speeds nearly twice that

of a Bloch 174, the rugged P-38 so much represented a new generation
of aircraft that, in the words of one American officer charged with retrain-
ing the French, they made the Potez that Saint-Exupéry had flown in
1940 look like Wilbur Wright's plane. The P-38 was not a temperamental
machine—one pilot claimed he could practically fill out his paperwork as
he came in for a landing—but it was a sophisticated one. Saint-Exupéry,
who had learned to fly in an airplane with virtually no controls,. was
impressed by the 103 controls of a Bloch 174. A Lightning had 148.
Strapped into his gear its pilot monitored two engines, eight fuel tanks,
innumerable electric circuits, four cameras, and his oxygen supply while
he piloted, navigated, photographed, and kept an eye out for enemy aircraft. As Saint-Exupéry was not authorized to fly a P-38 he was fortunate
as well that in June Giraud's star was still ascendant; no sooner had the
pilot rejoined his squadron than he was off to Algiers. Possibly for this
trip he made the departure that Jules Roy, then an aspiring writer assigned
to a neighboring squadron, was to remember vividly. Saint-Exupéry having
been fitted into a Bloch, the members of the 2/33 formed a sort of honor
guard along the palm-lined Laghouat airstrip to see him off. He was to
make his way west via Bou-Saada; as Roy was to lunch in the Algerian
town that day he followed a few minutes behind him in a Simoun. On
landing on the Bou-Saada airfield Roy noticed a Bloch lying on its side
at the end of the airstrip, its landing gear crumbled. Its pilot had already
continued on to Algiers in another aircraft.

In the capital Saint-Exupéry called on Chambe at the Palais d'Été,
where Giraud and his staff had their offices. The 2/33 was to begin its
P-38 training; Chambe had to see he was added to the list. "How old are
you, Saint-Ex? I can't remember," asked the information minister. "Forty-
two," answered the pilot, who would not have bothered Chambe in the
first place had he been unaware that the age limit for P-38 pilots was ten
years less than that. Chambe informed his friend that his quest was noble
but futile; the Americans were intractable on this point. Saint-Exupéry
insisted that Giraud intervene. Good-naturedly Chambe set up a meeting
for him: the French commander-in-chief customarily received, in the company of his aides, at breakfast, and Chambe saw to it that Saint-Exupéry
was accorded an 8:30 appointment. The captain, however, did not endear
himself to the general, a man better known for his military mettle than
for his political acumen, of which he had none. At the time Giraud was
considering inviting de Gaulle to Algiers to share in the government. Saint-
Exupéry thought the idea preposterous—was Giraud so naïve as not to
know what de Gaulle's men were saying about him in New York?—and
lost no time in telling him so. Were de Gaulle to come to North Africa,
he swore, Giraud would be finished. Giraud had some advice for the
aviator, too. He had decided that Saint-Exupéry would be better off in his

cabinet than in a cockpit, and let drop another word guaranteed to send the writer into a tirade: propaganda. Less than graciously, Saint-Exupéry declined the offer. The meeting ended badly. Rising abruptly to dismiss his guest, Giraud declared, "It seems you think me a complete idiot," which was true.

Neither man was much impressed by the other but Chambe saved the day, arranging for Giraud to be able to announce to Saint-Exupéry over a second breakfast that he had seen to his request. (Chambe had convinced Giraud to telephone Eisenhower directly to obtain the favor.) Under the circumstances the pilot could hardly refuse to undertake a short propaganda mission throughout North Africa, in the course of which he was meant to raise the spirits of the French officers and NCOs moldering in training camps, waiting for the battle of liberation to begin. "Here I am, a traveling salesman in propaganda, and it's your fault!" he grumbled to Chambe as he installed himself behind the controls of a Simoun. He was not encouraged by a tour he had undertaken half-heartedly in the first place and which confirmed that in North Africa, as in New York, Gaullist propaganda had made for what were effectively two French armies. What was more, his admiration for Giraud—the only ranking French leader likely to view him in a sympathetic light in 1943—had not survived this initial encounter. "A scarecrow who as such is not threatened by noise but who fears the wind" was how he later dismissed the man he wrote off now—while on a Giraud-sponsored propaganda mission—as *"le mur élastique"* ("the rubber wall"). Before the month was out de Gaulle was in Algiers, and in a matter of days the French Committee of National Liberation (CFLN), a provisional government headed jointly by the two generals and hustled into being by the Allies, was formed. Within a week of his arrival de Gaulle had managed to rearrange that body so that his representatives outnumbered Giraud's, two to one. So handily outdone was Giraud by his co-president's machinations that he essentially voted against himself on the matter.

Feelings about this conflict ran as strong in Algiers that summer as those about the greater one. The Americans insisted that Giraud retain control of the French army under any circumstances. De Gaulle proved equally adamant that all French troops swear allegiance to him. The situation was not improved by the fact that the United States refused to recognize the CFLN as the reigning authority in metropolitan France, nor by the fact that most of the French barely respected it. Kenneth Pendar, the American diplomat who had been quick to see traces of Gilbert and Sullivan in North Africa, overheard a particularly bitter conversation between General Béthouart and Saint-Exupéry at the Interallié; the two men were heartsick about the divided state of the army. In a letter to Curtice Hitchcock Saint-Exupéry wrote of his continued distaste for de Gaulle,

whose politics hardly represented a salvation for France; in a stern, un-
mailed letter to Jules Roy, who had recently endorsed de Gaulle, he
summed up his arguments with the line, "Sectarianism always leads one
astray." He was more vocal still with American diplomatic personnel. To
them he compared Gaullism to National Socialism.

The skirmish on this front could not help but distract him from what
should have been the greater battle. He officially rejoined the 2/33 as a
P-38 reconnaissance pilot on June 4, taking up a Lightning four days later
at the La Marsa airfield, outside of Tunis. Gavoille kept a close eye on
him. Both the pilot's age and his physical condition were handicaps at
high altitude in a nonpressurized cabin, and he was hardly familiar with
the P-38. The cold at 30,000 feet is formidable, as was the sheer weight
of a reconnaissance pilot's gear. Saint-Exupéry was not only ten years too
old but nearly too large as well; the cutoff point for P-38 pilots was six
feet four inches, and stiff as he was he practically had to be fitted into the
cockpit with a shoehorn. Nor did his resistance to the English language
facilitate his work; the control towers were now staffed by Americans, and
the sky over Oujda was crowded. He came down from his first training
flight less than impressed with the new aircraft; soon enough it was discovered that his discomfort had had to do with the fact that—having been
instructed to go up to 2,000 meters (6,500 feet), and having misread his
altimeter—he had gone up to 20,000 feet without an oxygen mask. On
another training flight he evidently marveled over how clearly he could
examine Tunisia from 10,000 meters. He had been flying, this time with
an oxygen mask, at 10,000 feet.

Gavoille kept an eye on Saint-Exupéry for all the reasons that had led
him to be termed his equerry (and his nanny) in 1940 and then one: the
Americans were watching over his shoulder. Not all of them thought highly
of their allies, and some officers were openly hostile. One American major
took delight in assembling the 2/33 to inform them that the French had
lost the war and now that the Americans had come to bail them out they
had best comport themselves as in the presence of a superior people.
Fortunately the designated translator did not speak French; Gavoille
gracefully thanked the visitor for his allocution. Matériel was not initially
in great supply, and relations were impaired both by the French impression
that they were getting the Americans' castoffs and by the related American
impression that the French were not properly maintaining their aircraft.*
It was easier for the Americans to say that the French—who were in fact
generally more seasoned pilots, and who knew the territory far better than
their Allies—were incompetent, and it was easier for the French—who

* There was a glimmer of truth in the former accusation and none at all in the latter. Generally
the best aircraft were reserved for combat missions and the most worn for training flights.

carried with them a certain sense of shame and frustration—to assume that the Americans were not treating them evenhandedly. Rearming the French had been as much a political gesture as a military necessity, a fact that created resentment on both sides. Sometimes the hostility was reflexive. When Gavoille was asked what call sign he would like for his squadron he asked for one without an "r" so that his men might be able to signal clearly to the control tower. He was given six choices, each with an "r." (He settled on "Dress down," the least difficult for a French speaker to pronounce.) More often the run-ins centered on questions of discipline, of which the Americans thought the French incapable. Leon Gray, who as MAPRW Operations Officer reported directly to Elliott Roosevelt, said he could make the French do everything except take off on schedule. Others held that the French were slow to adapt to P-38's, aircraft with which the average American pilot had at least fifty hours' experience before being sent overseas. They could not understand why the French were not applying themselves to the task, choosing to overlook the fact that they were being instructed in a foreign language and that a P-38 differed in many crucial respects from the aircraft to which the French were accustomed. Frustrated by his attempts to train the French to fly the equally new B-26's, one officer was overheard to remark, "The quicker the SOBs kill themselves, the quicker we'll get to France."

At first Saint-Exupéry sailed easily through these troubled waters. Most of the Americans were unaware of his stature—Leon Gray asserted that "he didn't know him from a bale of hay"—and those who were stood more in awe of the aviation pioneer than of the Académie Française laureate. He reinvigorated the 2/33, entertained the American ground personnel, and—away from the base—engaged in a little propaganda on his own and the 2/33's behalfs. Mid-June found him back in Algiers, begging Robert Murphy, President Roosevelt's brilliant right-hand man in North Africa, to set up a meeting for him with Elliott Roosevelt. The writer had already called once on Roosevelt shortly after his arrival; he now hoped to lobby for the 2/33 to be entirely outfitted with P-38's and immediately assigned a full slate of missions. Characteristically he did not feel he had made himself clear at the meeting with Murphy on the sixteenth and sent a lengthy follow-up letter the next day. For the first time since his 1933 correspondence with Air France he resorted to selling himself to get what he wanted: it was a different approach altogether from the one he had used seventeen years earlier with Latécoère's Beppo de Massimi, before whom his ardor to fly had made him mute on the subject of his first published story. For Murphy he listed the titles of his books and the honors that had accrued to them (he had some difficulty remembering what the National Book Award was called) and made the case that he could write a new *Flight to Arras* only if he were to fly regular missions again. At the same time, he thought it best he dispense with "an absurd myth," the one about the effects of high altitude on the older pilot. Nothing could be further from the truth, explained Saint-Exupéry, who knew full well that an older pilot is a less resilient pilot, one far more susceptible to the effects of G-forces. To Murphy he must have sounded like a child insisting that swimming after a meal will not bring on cramps. While he was at it, without naming names, he expressed his deep disaffection for de Gaulle.

A matter of weeks before he stoically argued his case before the American Saint-Exupéry had painted a very different picture for his wife, to whom he had reported essentially that he was a walking wreck. His liver gave him trouble two days out of three; when it did not he suffered from nausea. As a result of the Guatemala crash one of his ears hummed continuously. Only with great pain could he carry a five-pound package, or get out of bed, or bend to the floor. He had already taken enough sulfa drugs to kill a horse; without them, he claimed, he would be dead. In 1942 Consuelo had observed—rather astutely, as it turned out—that no country other than France would allow her husband to fly again at his age and in his condition. Nine days after the visit to Murphy his promotion came through. Four days later, on his forty-third birthday, Major de Saint-Exupéry was cleared by the French air force medical examiner in Algiers for high-altitude missions.

He alternately gloated and grumbled about this dubious triumph. He was quick to inform Hitchcock—who had remained skeptical that his author would see active service in the air—that he had proved him wrong, that he had resisted all the usual efforts to be turned into a propagandist, that he was flying the fastest airplane in existence. (The word "petulance" exists in French but means "exuberance.") He had, a little late, or so it must have seemed to Hitchcock, rather fallen in love with America. He was in awe before its war effort. (A kind man, Hitchcock wrote back that he was not going to attempt to dissuade Saint-Exupéry from flying, as he knew his efforts would be futile. A canny publisher, Hitchcock took the liberty of sharing his author's kind words for America with *The New York Times*. In a press release he announced to the world that the writer was once again in the neighborhood in which he had met the Little Prince.) To Chambe and Pélissier Saint-Exupéry wrote—even as he continued to prove the life of the squadron—of his despair, of his disgust with camp life. He hated standing in line for his food and devouring it, standing up, in ten minutes; nothing was a greater torment to him than sharing a room with two other men. (His roommates in turn fell asleep to the sound of his pen scratching its way across the page.) He confided in Pélissier that the simplest of physical tasks was to him as great a challenge as scaling the Himalayas. He inveighed even against the coveted P-38: the marvel of American technology amounted to "a sort of flying torpedo that has nothing whatever to do with flying and, with all its screens and buttons, makes of its pilot a sort of chief accountant."

Gavoille and the members of the 2/33 were more conscious of the pilot's resistance to the P-38 than of his despair, which was for the most part confined to his letters. A parachutist from a nearby training camp commented that the Lightning's speed seemed both to intoxicate and to frighten Saint-Exupéry, who could not get over the fact that Algiers and Tunis were now eighty-five minutes apart. A new recruit to the 2/33 who translated his voluminous American fan mail thought its recipient allergic to the aircraft's sophisticated instrument panel. On the one hand he had no interest in wasting his time learning to master the machine; on the other while in the air he did everything in his power to exceed the call of duty, which in the military is known as defying orders. With a little over ten hours' training under his belt he flew his first mission, over the Riviera, on July 21. It was his first view of the homeland since the summer of 1940; he was in the air for nearly six hours and was—by all but one report— perfectly successful. A few days later in a little basement restaurant in Algiers where he dined with Pélissier, the French actor Jean Gabin, and a few others, he talked of how moved he had been to see France again. Initially he had been put off by the sterility below him; from 30,000 feet he could detect no signs of life. France is dead, he had thought, growing melancholic. Then little gray puffs of smoke began to appear around his aircraft. "They were firing at me! France was alive! I was so happy," he reported. "My dear friend," countered Gabin, "myself I prefer melancholy."

In July the Americans began to catalogue Saint-Exupéry's eccentricities with a different concern from the French. They kept a close eye on their P-38's: it was a little bit a case of one national treasure versus another. According to Colonel Frank Dunn, Roosevelt's second-in-command, Saint-Exupéry had on an early training mission cranked down the window of his Lightning at 30,000 feet, losing his oxygen mask in the process; he had descended so quickly the wings of the aircraft had been damaged. Gavoille, who got on well with the Americans, had dutifully but awkwardly reported the mishap to Dunn. On August 1 he appeared again at the commanding officer's side. "This is very, very difficult," he began. Saint-Exupéry had gone up for his second mission, from which he had been forced by engine trouble to return after forty minutes. He had not pumped his hydraulic brakes and had, after touching down at about 100 miles per hour, run off the end of the airstrip, crashing into an olive grove. As the pilot described the damages later, the undercarriage had collapsed, after which the left wing and engine had hit the ground; the aircraft had then tipped and the right wing and engine had taken a hit. The result was a

Lightning that would never fly again. The 6,000-foot runway was more than long enough and all the pilots had been briefed about the braking system; as hydraulics were new to the French, the Americans "jabbered and hollered and screamed about them constantly." Dunn's and Gray's memories diverge a little at this point. As Gray remembered things, he discovered on consulting the record that Saint-Exupéry had had an earlier mishap with his brakes. He recalled having told Gavoille that he was to take his pilot off flying status until he was properly trained. Dunn was certain that he had himself initiated this disciplinary action (Gray reported to Dunn, but either man had the authority to make the decision on his own, and the two did confer either just before or just after it was made). Dunn maintained that he had grounded the pilot as much for the August incident as for a set of photographs Saint-Exupéry had taken of a French château—probably Agay—while he was meant to be surveying military installations on his earlier mission. He remembered having grounded the pilot immediately, as Gavoille looked on. One thing was certain: it was not the case, as the pilot would repeatedly claim in the diatribes of the next months, that he was taken off flying status on account of his age.

The accident came as no great surprise to anyone but the severity of the punishment did. To the French it seemed as if American chauvinism was at work. To the Americans the incident proved yet again that the French were hopelessly irresponsible.* Saint-Exupéry naturally railed against what seemed to him an injustice, pure and simple. "Yes, the Lightning would never fly again, but all the same, to ground a man for that!" he sputtered, to some ears a cavalier statement to make about an $80,000 airplane in the middle of a war. He could not fathom the Americans' severity; neither could he accept the decision as final. (He probably did not know that some of his friends grudgingly approved of the Americans' action. Even Gavoille felt that medically and technically Dunn and Gray had been in the right.) A few days after the incident he threw a lavish banquet for the entire French squadron and a handful of American officers, nearly 100 men in all; Dunn and Gray were seated to the immediate right and left of their host. Invitations from the French were rare at the time, and neither officer had any doubt about why he was there. "If he was taken off flying status on Monday and he had a big couscous dinner on Thursday, why, there was a reason for it," recalled Gray.

---

* Dunn argued that an American pilot would, at the very least, have been stripped of his rank for Saint-Exupéry's accumulated record. Richard Rumbold, an RAF flyer and Saint-Exupéry biographer, has written that an RAF pilot would have been fined, while an equally careless French flyer would have been asked to stand the mess to a round of drinks.

The candlelit banquet took place in a magnificent villa overlooking the bay of Tunis. Saint-Exupéry's guests were seated on the floor, where they were waited on by a small army of local girls. The wine flowed freely through nine or ten courses, and the "Marseillaise" was sung. Saint-Exupéry swore at the outset of the meal that he would be able to empty all the water carafes during the course of the evening without anyone noticing and succeeded in doing so. He appears to have had the same conversation with each of the two guests of honor, both of them twenty-eight, the age he had been at Cape Juby. Toward the end of the evening the veteran leaned in toward Dunn. Slowly knocking his fist against his chest he declared, "I want to die for France." (The actual emotion may have been more complex than his English allowed.) Dunn shook his head. "I want to talk with you for three minutes," Saint-Exupéry persisted. "The answer is no, no, and no," replied Dunn. On Gray—who had earlier been pressured strenuously by Gavoille to reconsider the order—he used the same line. A more moderate man than Dunn and one who was not haunted by the alleged château photographs, Gray had come more slowly to the conviction that the Frenchman be grounded. Nonetheless he felt, like Dunn, that orders were orders, and when the pilot turned to him to repeat, "Sir, I want to die for France," he was ready with his answer. "I don't give a damn if you die for France or not," he informed Saint-Exupéry, many bottles of superb wine into the evening, "but you're not going to do so in one of our airplanes."

~

In Dunn's opinion, René Gavoille had in Saint-Exupéry the most difficult command in all of North Africa. He could not have been said to have been proved wrong by the few days that followed. In a joint show of patriotism and impertinence, the pilot flew about frantically in search of someone who might put him back on flying status, a little like Jacob wrestling with the angel. He could not help himself: he was used to military regulations crumbling under his weight as all regulations tended to. The morning after the banquet he evidently left Algiers at dawn to seek out OSS Chief Donovan. Within the week he was back on Chambe's doorstep, pleading that Giraud, who was still to be in power for a few more months, take up his case with Eisenhower. He was lucky; the object of his scorn had just read *Flight to Arras*, with which he had been pleased (if only, suggested Chambe, because he knew the volume had distinctly displeased de Gaulle). While Saint-Exupéry paced in Algiers Giraud badgered the Americans; according to Chambe, the French commander-in-chief ultimately won a concession of a sort from the Allied commander. After a number of entreaties Eisenhower is reported to have exploded: "This Frenchman is driving us crazy! Reenlist him! With luck he'll bother us less in the air than on the ground!" In the end Saint-Exupéry was not authorized to rejoin his squadron, however. On August 8 he made a brief visit to La Marsa; the squadron's logbook reports that he was on the verge of leaving for a mission to the United States. The same day de Gaulle made a triumphant entrance into Casablanca, where he felt his presence "served as a symbol and a center of French authority."

Saint-Exupéry wound up not in America but at Pélissier's, his headquarters for the next eight months, the bleakest of his life. The doctor installed his guest in a narrow, half-furnished room, originally a linen closet, in his second-floor apartment. Overnight the space disappeared under a sea of paper, on which floated Saint-Exupéry's rumpled shreds of American khaki. Pélissier's was a bustling household. His medical offices were in the apartment and his living room served during the day as a waiting room; as lodging in Algiers was scarce, he often took in other boarders. His housekeeper did her best to look after the esteemed house guest (and to contain his damages) but he was, despite her attentions, far from comfortable. Most of those who visited him here—and a constant stream of American, British, and French visitors rang for Saint-Exupéry at 17, rue Denfert-Rochereau—were struck by the fact that the writer seemed perpetually on the point of leaving. He indeed was, at the outset; he had been more settled at Cape Juby. He had moved in only provisionally and soon enough discovered that his lodgings allowed him neither to write nor to receive as he liked. When Pélissier heard that his guest intended to decamp he flew into a rage, however; not wanting to appear ungrateful, Saint-Exupéry changed his mind. He remained deaf to the advice of friends who counseled him to move on. And so the world's worst house guest—it was Pélissier who noted that Saint-Exupéry automatically lost your keys and managed to burn everything in sight with his cigarettes—refused to budge from the half-furnished, underheated linen closet, out of politeness.

It was not long before he began to refer to the room as his cell. Nor was it long before he came to realize that the walls he was butting up against were not the gray ones at Pélissier's but the more rigid ones of another man's intransigence. Despite his claims to want to remain above the fray he had been vocal and direct in his first months in Algiers; if he had been ostracized in New York for his silence he now found that every word he had uttered against de Gaulle in North Africa was to come back to haunt him. He was hardly installed at Pélissier's when he wrote Madame de B, then in Lisbon, that he had proof that the Gaullists were intercepting his mail: "It's as if I were in prison. Letters sent to me end up in a dark closet, God only knows where, from which they never emerge."* Few punishments could have been more cruel to a cloistered man who had so often risked his life for a bag of mail, but the worse was yet to come. De Gaulle's stock had at last begun to rise—by November Giraud was no longer even a member of the CFLN—and his ascent was prepared by what Kenneth Pendar saw as his "warriors of propaganda," men ready to direct their pens of vitriol at anyone who dared stand in the general's way. The future French leader's behavior on Saint-Exupéry's account did nothing to betray the impression formed of him by the American, who for his own reasons thought de Gaulle "revengeful, unforgiving, treacherous, disloyal, and filled with hate." (The ex-premier Paul Reynaud perhaps said it as well but more delicately: "De Gaulle has the character of a stubborn pig, but he *has* character.") On good authority Saint-Exupéry was advised to watch his back and to tread lightly, which he was not often able to do. One ill-wisher hailed him publicly with "Hello, my dear member of Pétain's council." (All Saint-Exupéry could muster by way of response was a near-gentlemanly "Of course you know that at this moment you are behaving like a bastard.") Some time that winter he asked for, and was denied, an audience with de Gaulle. Early in 1944 he made friends with the commander of the *Curie*, a Free French warship, and with his men; the crew applied for permission for the writer to join them on their next patrol. The Admiralty was succinct in its refusal: "Saint-Ex is not a Gaullist!" When Pierre Dalloz, Ségogne's friend who had met Saint-Exupéry in 1939 and who was now active in the Resistance, returned to Algiers at the end of November, he found the writer living in a state of total disgrace.

There was a more effective way still of humbling Saint-Exupéry. In late October de Gaulle delivered a speech in Algiers in which he named those French writers who were to be applauded for having chosen exile over collaboration. Saint-Exupéry's name—like that of Maurois, who was Jewish, who had fled to New York, who was at the time a French army captain in North Africa, but who was not a Gaullist—was conspicuously absent from the list, which included a number of lesser writers. (Had Saint-Exupéry behaved properly he would have done what Joseph Kessel did: Kessel met with the general in London at the beginning of 1943, was instantly won over, and happily lent his pen to the cause.) When *L'Arche*, an Algiers literary review, proposed including *Lettre à un otage* in its premier issue that winter other writers protested that if Saint-Exupéry's work appeared in the publication theirs would not.† In what was surely

---

* He was probably right.

† The February 1, 1944, issue of *L'Arche* included *Lettre à un otage* along with work by, among others, Gide, Maritain, Kessel, and Robert Aron.

the heaviest blow, his works were banned in North Africa. He watched, indignantly, as crates of French-language titles arrived from New York but his own did not. For the second time *Flight to Arras* had effectively been censured by his own countrymen. (By a supreme irony the book was actually less available in Free France than in occupied France, where an underground edition was now circulating.) Under the circumstances it was not surprising that when the author lent out *Arras*, *The Little Prince*, or *Lettre à un otage*—he traveled always with a few copies of each—he did so only for intervals of twenty-four or forty-eight hours. For different reasons he lent *The Little Prince* to Gelée on the condition that it be returned with a written report and he read over the shoulder of Dalloz, circling his old friend and checking regularly on his progress, when he sat him down in Pélissier's living room with pages of *Citadelle*. Tell me what you think, he implored Dalloz, only don't say anything that might hinder my work. With Pélissier he was more forceful yet. "Admit it," he prodded after a long reading to which the doctor did not immediately respond, "It's without a doubt the best writing I've done."

Insofar as he was to do any writing this desperate fall and winter he devoted himself to that manuscript, a work that exalts the unfulfilled, obstacle-rich, sacrifice-prone life and reads like a hymn to all that cannot be bought, held, or even attained. André Beucler was well justified in saying later that *Citadelle*—*The Wisdom of the Sands* to English-language readers—would better have been titled "Memoirs of a tortured soul or meditations of a disillusioned hero." Saint-Exupéry was far too miserable and far too uncomfortable at Pélissier's to work in any sustained fashion; he managed to add to the existing work but not to perfect it. Still, he continued to bill the manuscript as "*l'oeuvre de ma vie.*" On August 7 one of its greatest admirers arrived in Algiers: Madame de B flew in from Gibraltar on an American airplane, raising a number of eyebrows. André Gide, who was not overly fond of her, went out of his way to attend a reception purely for the malicious pleasure of seeing the couple in action. The U.S. State Department continued to be amazed by her ability to travel freely around Europe and suspected her still of collaboration; they followed her and her sentimental life closely. In the end they concluded that she had made the trip to North Africa primarily to see Saint-Exupéry, whom they had been told (erroneously) she was to marry. She, too, eventually settled in at Pélissier's. Two nights after her arrival she dined with Gaston Palewski, the chief of de Gaulle's personal staff. "You must convince Saint-Exupéry that he is altogether wrong not to join de Gaulle," he told her. She conveyed the message to her friend, who had not been in Algiers when she arrived, and whom she found balder, heavier, graying at the temples, but somehow more imposing than ever. He shrugged.

Saint-Exupéry greeted Madame de B with 500 pages of *Citadelle*, which he expected her to read immediately. Naturally he shuffled around her nervously in Pélissier's living room as she did so. Also as she read the sirocco began to pick up; before long the heat in the room grew unbearable. At about page 100 she proposed a trip to the beach. Saint-Exupéry was indignant. "If you put my book down now, it's because it bores you!" "But I find it magnificent," she objected. "Impossible, because you are tired of it!" pouted the author. "I am not tired of the book. I am tired from the trip, and exhausted from the heat. When I have stretched my legs a little I will be able to read more carefully," Madame de B explained evenly. Amused by the familiar display of tyranny, she agreed to read two more pages. Saint-Exupéry disappeared while she did so, returning to thrust two tablets into her mouth. She was now free to go to the beach, he conceded. She would be able to review the manuscript that evening, when she was not sleeping; she had just swallowed a sizable dose of Benzedrine. Awake for forty-eight hours she had in fact nothing better to do than to read and reread his pages, after which she offered her written comments, with which the author was delighted. Madame de B had an appreciation of *Citadelle* which many of its author's friends did not share and the two discussed the work at length, tossing out the names of translators who might render its ornate, highly stylized prose into English. "You are a little like Christ when you write your *Citadelle*," Madame de B had observed, a statement with which the author had quietly agreed, eyes to the ground. In her opinion the manuscript was the only thing for which he continued to live. She remained in Algiers until early November, when she returned to London. Saint-Exupéry continued to write her that he had forgotten all of their little misunderstandings, that she was of capital importance in his life, that her advice was invaluable, and that he loved her, but the two were never to see each other again.

In September 1943 the author paid a month-long visit to Henri Comte, the genial surgeon who had been a mainstay of his Casablanca days and who lived in a lovely villa in Anfa, overlooking the Moroccan capital. Comte's hospitality did not in itself prompt the trip: Madame de B has suggested that Saint-Exupéry left Algiers so that Consuelo's friends would not report back to her that her husband and his lover were staying together at Pélissier's. In Anfa Saint-Exupéry continued his work on *Citadelle*, slipping his most recent pages under his host's door as he wrote and interviewing him over breakfast. (Comte was not particularly forthcoming, having spent the night sleeping.) At the same time he vainly pursued the possibility of being parachuted into France to join the Resistance. The two made a pilgrimage to Marrakech, to the landscapes that had inspired *Citadelle*, but very little actually cheered Saint-Exupéry, who had begun most of all to fear the bloodletting the liberation was bound to unleash. "A lot of people are going to be shot next year," he warned friends.* Sedgwick Mead, an American army doctor stationed in Casablanca, dined with the writer at Comte's on two occasions and found him—despite his volubility and a virtuoso performance of his *faux*-Debussy, executed this time with eggs—visibly brokenhearted. He bristled at the mention of de Gaulle and snapped at Mead when the American mentioned a book that painted a rather unflattering portrait of the French military command. Mead also was offered a loan of *The Little Prince* in exchange for his comments. "He seemed generally preoccupied, as if it were a constant effort to recall his whereabouts," he noted, an assessment with which the friends who visited with Saint-Exupéry in Algiers concurred. More and more he retreated to his bathtub, or immersed himself in math problems and word games. He was now more interested in diversion than in creation; he wrote few pages in Algiers, and his tubside experiments yielded up no new inventions. The result was that he forgot appointments, of which he made many. One morning an acquaintance stopped off to see him on his way to the Maison Blanche airfield. He found Saint-Exupéry shaving, and volunteered to check for mail for him at the field. An hour and a half later the writer opened the door to him with some consternation: "Have you forgotten something? You were just here three minutes ago," he said. He had indeed lost track of time; he was still shaving.

So much in need of diversion himself, he proved a sought-after guest in weary, worried Algiers. He was as ever capable of his highly original displays of humor—one acquaintance drew an unforgettable portrait of Saint-Exupéry dancing a kind of samba in a restaurant with a friend's kepi, on which he joyously bounced a gargantuan soap bubble—though few friends took them at face value. Even those who knew him slightly remarked that he occasionally seemed on the verge of tears. For the most part, however, he remained so mesmerizing a raconteur, so accomplished a magician, that his presence was in constant demand. Jean Macaigne, with whom he had flown in South America, came to his former colleague's rescue on one awkward occasion. Two hostesses had prevailed upon the writer for the same evening, and he had been unable to decline either invitation. On the night of reckoning he installed Macaigne at his window to assist in his decision. Macaigne deemed the company that arrived in the first car more than acceptable-looking and—having sent off his friend—genially stepped out to advise the latecomers that their guest regretted to have been suddenly called away.

* In a particularly black mood he imagined a conversation about himself: "A very nice man, very nice indeed, but he will have to be shot." "Why?" "He's the reason that the United States hasn't recognized de Gaulle."

Saint-Exupéry wrote Silvia Reinhardt that he had played his *oranges sur le piano* all over North Africa and from the memories left behind he indeed seems to have left no keyboard untouched. He kept up a busy calendar—aside from his regular chess dates with Gide and with the writer Emmanuel Bove, his datebook shows that he had at least a lunch or dinner engagement every day—although he had never thrived on the social whirl and did not now. It was in this way that he made the acquaintance of Pierre Sonneville, the Free French captain who had invited him aboard the *Curie*. Sonneville and his whiskey had found refuge from a reception in the entry of a cloakroom, where a clearly bored gentleman sized them up warily. Suspecting that, despite Sonneville's Croix de Lorraine, he was in the company of a kindred spirit, Saint-Exupéry motioned toward the crowd. "Does this interest you?" he asked. "I have a Jeep outside at my disposal; shall I give you a lift?" He then introduced himself.

He stayed out late. Max-Pol Fouchet, an editor who briefly roomed next to him at Pélissier's, noted that he inevitably knocked something over when he came in, generally long after Fouchet had gone to sleep. "Saint-Exupéry needed a propeller," he concluded, as apt a statement as anyone made about the wretched months in Algiers. He could not rise above the situation, could not extricate himself from the pettiness. There was nothing lofty about his existence this winter, anathema to this reverse Antaeus who late in the year was to state in a bitter letter explaining his politics, "Everything is ugly, seen close up." As if in perfect dramatization of his floundering, his distraction and clumsiness combined with painful results early in November. On the fifth, in the middle of a blackout, he fell down the stairs in Pélissier's entryway. "I failed to make out six marble steps, designed to be elegant under lights, back in the happy days when there were lights. Suddenly I found myself suspended in midair—but not for long. I heard a tremendous crash. It was me," was how he described the incident to Comte, to whom he sent an X-ray of his back nine days later. Rattled, he had sat for five minutes in the stairwell. He had then proceeded, painfully, to the dinner to which he had been headed, at which the news that he had just broken a vertebra was greeted with general laughter. After consulting with Pélissier he kept his engagements the next day, proceeding on the seventh to a lavish reception thrown by the Soviets in a palace garden. He was in agony. In the middle of a lawn he found himself suddenly immobile; he prayed that people would continue to come over to talk to him, as otherwise he was sure to look idiotic. In a series of tiny steps he ultimately managed a more or less dignified escape.

The mishap was one of several that poisoned the atmosphere on the rue Denfert-Rochereau. Saint-Exupéry was convinced he had fractured his spine. Pélissier, who had examined him, knew he had not. The patient countered by pressuring an X-ray technician to confirm his diagnosis. He

then declared war on his host: November and December passed in a
blizzard of notes and interminable letters, testimony to his pain (as to the
time on his hands) and, as he saw it, to Pélissier's inability to understand
him. Mostly he begrudged the doctor his lack of sympathy. What he
wanted—clearly on more than one level—was for someone to order him
to take to his bed; he was in search of the license for the respite he had
wanted since the fall of 1940. This Pélissier did not and stubbornly would
not issue; Saint-Exupéry concluded that the doctor was heartless. Only
after five weeks was he—still very much crippled by the accident—prepared to sound apologetic:

> I am well aware that you are neither the inventor of staircases, nor the
> inventor of the blackout, nor the cause of my distraction. And I know well
> that your science cannot restore my hair, or my teeth, or my youth, even
> if it might indeed save me on numerous occasions. I no longer reproach
> you for not being God. You are a friend, which is already a great deal.
> And you are "certainly" right, which is also a great deal, though extremely
> annoying.

To Madame de B, to whom he had written a series of rambling letters
over the course of his nonconvalescence, he at one point confided that the
shock of the fall had actually helped clear his head.

It did not, however, raise his spirits. He had been drinking heavily and
did so more now, to dull the pain. The attacks of cholecystitis continued.
Christmas left him meditating once again on his childhood, this time from
a different angle: he spoke of it not as a refuge but as a resting place.
Although he never said as much, he may have been aware that he was
now three years older than his father had been at the time of his death.
He wrote Consuelo as well as Madame de B of his despair, appealing to
one for her sympathy and the other for her understanding. If there were
distractions in Algiers there were no great loves. Silvia had stopped writing
him and the mail to France was a difficult matter. A note scribbled to his
family just after the New Year was delivered by parachute, but nothing
came in the opposite direction. (To Madame de Saint-Exupéry her son
wrote that he wished only that he could again sit by her side, in front of
the fire, for a long talk. He would contradict her as little as possible, as
she was in the end right about all things in life.) From Consuelo he had
infrequent news and what he did have could be disturbing. During the
summer he had cabled that he thought her idea to share an apartment
with Denis de Rougemont unwise; that autumn Becker wrote to inform
his client that his wife was receiving the regular sum they had agreed
upon but had also presented him with a hefty clutch of bills. (His royalty
account, from which Becker could wire money to North Africa, was not
empty, and in Algiers Saint-Exupéry received his army salary through

October.) He wrote Consuelo of his misery, of the senselessness of his existence, of his continued love. He desperately needed her; he asked her to row him gently toward old age. "Take care of yourself, watch out for yourself, guard yourself, never go out at night, never catch cold, never forget me, pray for me," he closed one particularly poignant letter. He was incapable of taking care of himself and found the cold, for which he was unprepared, oppressive. The days of the tributes to freezing beds were over: he complained that he slept in his underwear, two pairs of pajamas, and a bathrobe. Not only was there no one to look after him but the man who had left America hoping to suffer as much as possible for those dear to him could not pretend to have anyone in his charge. He caved in to despair.

At the end of the year several attempts were made to rescue him. In December General René Bouscat, the commander of the French air force, suggested that Saint-Exupéry be assigned to the air force section of the French military mission in America. (The pilot had ideas of his own: while this proposal was pending he wrote Consuelo to say he hoped to return to the United States to appeal Dunn and Gray's August verdict.) De Gaulle judged the idea "inopportune." At about the same time General François d'Astier de la Vigerie, long a close associate of de Gaulle's, mentioned that he would like to put the pilot to work in England; Saint-Exupéry did all he could behind the scenes to influence the matter. When Bouscat inquired into the affair he was informed by the chief of de Gaulle's cabinet that in the end d'Astier had not taken up Saint-Exupéry's case with the general, who in any event saw no reason to take the captain off reserve status. "It would not appear opportune for this officer, whose military service does not now seem necessary, to be sent to England," reported the aide. (Quickly enough de Gaulle's veto was quoted on North African café terraces as "Leave him in Algiers, he's only good for card tricks," a comment that made its way back to Saint-Exupéry.) He received the news on January 10 from a friend who was almost too abashed to deliver it. It sent him into a rage. Now more than ever he heaped abuse on de Gaulle, sometimes alienating friends—among them Gide and Kessel, who tired of his tirades—in the process. He was going nowhere and reserved some of his anger for Algiers: the city was "a trash heap," "a basket of crabs," "a dump for the dregs of humanity," "a tomb," "a human desert," "a moldy, provincial police station."

Jean Genet's prescription for saintliness was pain put to good use; Saint-Exupéry had nothing to do, no cause in which to enlist his suffering. He wanted to cry, he did cry, he shivered with cold, he chain-smoked, he cursed his room at Pélissier's, he ranted and raved—to the tune of a note dispatched every fifteen minutes—when his host had the ill sense to borrow his sole remaining copy of *The Little Prince* on the January afternoon when a representative of Alexander Korda's was meant to carry it off to the London-based producer. He could not produce a decent sketch of the Little Prince. He wanted to burn *Citadelle*. He wrote in the most desultory of fashions. He decided to be flattered to be single-handedly credited with de Gaulle's failure in the United States; at least then he could pride himself on being—as Anne Lindbergh saw her husband to be in 1941—a sort of Antichrist. In the New Year he suffered a brief, imagined bout with stomach cancer, from which he won a reprieve only late in February, when tests incontrovertibly showed that he was free of the disease and Pélissier managed to convince him that his gastrointestinal distress was the result not of cancer but of too many sulfa drugs and too much spicy food. The hypochondria served a purpose: Saint-Exupéry's imaginary ills provided a viable reason for him to be sidelined, in defiance of all his principles. He wanted to enter a monastery; he wanted to turn the clock back a few centuries; he wanted to become a gardener. He weighed the advantages of prison over death. (They were few.) He thought back repeatedly, with near-longing, to the last night and last morning in Libya, to the last seconds under the bay of Saint-Raphaël. At the end of January 1944 he attended a small dinner thrown in honor of the newly arrived British representative to the CFLN (the position amounted to the closest thing that existed at the time to ambassador to Paris), Duff Cooper, and his wife, Lady Diana. The evening ended gaily with a glass of cognac at the Coopers' home. Saint-Exupéry held forth with a deck of cards, entirely enchanting the diplomat's wife. Suddenly he paused in midshuffle. "This morning I consulted a fortune-teller," he announced to the assembled guests. "Clearly she didn't recognize the insignia on my uniform and took me for a sailor, because she predicted my imminent death in the waves of the sea." The room fell silent.

~

Toward the end of February 1944 John Phillips, a young *Life* magazine photographer and journalist, arrived in Algiers. Phillips was an unusual American in that he had been born in Algeria and spoke perfect French; he had long admired Saint-Exupéry, whom he telephoned directly. "Colonel," he began. "Major," Saint-Exupéry corrected him. Otherwise the older writer was entirely welcoming, preparing drinks for his visitor in Pélissier's kitchen. Into a frying pan he poured muscatel and a harsh, distilled wine; he then lit the concoction with a match, producing delectable results. Much of the available liquor in North Africa was undrinkable; Phillips thought his host ingenious. Saint-Exupéry lost no time in telling the war correspondent that he was the sole survivor of a bygone era: "I'm the last one, and I can assure you that it's a very strange feeling," he said, glancing moodily out the window. In the living room he described the grave injustice the Americans had committed on his account. When his visitor asked if he was writing he replied that he did not have the right to, as he had no role in the war. He went on to make Phillips a casual proposal: "I want to write, and I'll donate what I do to you, for your publication, if you get me reinstated into my squadron." The American, who had every reason in the world to sympathize with the balding legend before him, promised to do his best. A few weeks later he returned to Naples, where he kept an apartment, and where he met with Colonel John Reagan ("Tex") McCrary, then in charge of the photo press in England and all air force press in Italy. McCrary reported to General Ira Eaker, the commander of the Mediterranean air force, with whom he in turn pursued the subject of Saint-Exupéry. Eaker, who was the head of the world's largest air command and who had just lost a society-page American flyer, handed down no immediate decision, however, and when Phillips returned to Algiers he did so empty-handed.

He found Saint-Exupéry in a state of high dudgeon. In Phillips's absence the pilot's old Brest instructor, Lionel-Max Chassin—a colonel who had been powerless to help his former student although that winter he was personnel director at the air ministry (he had played a great deal of chess with Saint-Exupéry instead)—had taken command of a bomber squadron in Villacidro, Sardinia. Chassin had seen to it that Saint-Exupéry was assigned to the 1/22, where he was meant to co-pilot a medium-sized bomber, the B-26. In the weeks since Phillips had seen him the writer had stopped grousing about the "imbecilic Americans" and begun to grumble instead about his new assignment. He could not possibly serve as a co-pilot, he explained, as he suffered from air sickness. (The truth doubtless had more to do with the fact that—feted though he was by the 1/22—he wanted to return to his own squadron, whose reconnaissance work he considered a more noble pursuit than bombing work.) Convinced that he could himself persuade Eaker, probably tempted, too, by the fact that the 2/33 had been based in Pomigliano, outside of Naples, since January, Saint-Exupéry flew back to Italy with Phillips late in April. He crammed a mass of papers and his treasured Parker pens into his Mark Cross bag for the trip. To ensure that it would not be lost he entrusted his inkwell to Phillips. (To ensure that he and his manuscript would not both be lost he generally saw to it over the next months that he and his bag flew separately.) So far as Phillips could tell, the pilot, who was now officially a member of the 1/22—he had begun to collect his army pay again as of April 1—made the trip AWOL.

In Naples Phillips took Saint-Exupéry to his apartment, where the two ran into the assistant managing editor of *Life*. Phillips made the introductions. "*The* Saint-Exupéry?" asked the editor, who was startled to learn from Phillips that the Frenchman was to contribute something to the magazine. "We've tried for two years to get him to write a piece for us and he never has," he explained; the publication had clearly never offered the proper form of payment. At the bar of a Naples officers' club a few days later the writer met McCrary. Phillips handled the translating, speaking as if he were Saint-Exupéry. His new friend was relentless on this point, admonishing his broker throughout the meeting to do his job well. "Look, Saint-Ex, I've done a beautiful job, an eloquent job," Phillips finally objected. He clearly had—McCrary felt that the Frenchman had been "hugely selling"—and Saint-Exupéry underestimated the simple power of his presence. He made a deep impression on the American colonel, who had done his homework for the meeting but had not previously been in the writer's thrall. With Phillips as his spokesman Saint-Exupéry voiced all of his habitual arguments, mentioning his shame at not being able to serve his country, citing his Book-of-the-Month Club honors. As Phillips knew, the two were preaching to the converted; McCrary was already of the opinion that any man who wanted to fight in the war should be allowed to do so. "I was charmed and respectful and quite frankly I, too, was jealous of the young men who flew not out of a sense of guilt or out of a sense of adventure but because they had to," remembered McCrary. He had his own pound of flesh to exact, however: Saint-Exupéry was to write a chapter about the Allied air forces for the book McCrary was putting together. The Frenchman agreed—there was no escaping the propagandists—and McCrary called Eaker to report on the meeting. "It's a hell of a deal for the air force," he advised the general, who did not immediately concur, but who was generally making it his business to reequip and retrain the French pilots. They would, he had noted in an admiring March memo, "cut a German throat probably with more relish than anybody."

On April 23 in Pomigliano, Saint-Exupéry visited with the 2/33, which was at the time applying its aerial talents to photographic forays over an erupting Vesuvius. A Swiss geologist was visiting as well; at the officers' table he and Saint-Exupéry enjoyed a wide-ranging discussion. The Frenchman spoke at length about molecular physics, the philosophical implications of which most interested him; he stunned his colleagues with the news that an atomic bomb was in the making and with the prediction that it would be deployed before the end of the war. According to Phillips, with whom he lodged, he spent the rest of his time in Italy "watching Vesuvius erupt, reading Kafka, and being a good winner at chess and a poor loser at word games." A game of chess with the writer required particular grace on his opponent's part: no one forgot the sadistic pleasure he took in winning. Phillips was repeatedly disarmed by Saint-Exupéry sweetly chanting, "I'm going to checkmate you, I'm going to checkmate you," as he played.

At the end of the month he was back in Algiers, tending to another front of his campaign. Henri Frenay, a Resistance hero who now held a CFLN post, arranged a lunch at which he might introduce the writer to Fernand Grenier, a former Communist deputy who had recently become head of the provisional government's air commission. (De Gaulle was now supreme military commander as well as the French civilian authority, having finally succeeded in stripping Giraud of all power; the cabinet was again reshuffled in the process.) On one of the last afternoons of the month, Grenier, Saint-Exupéry, and two of Frenay's Resistance friends gathered at Frenay's apartment outside Algiers. They fell instantly into a discussion of the underground movement's activities, its arrests and its tortures, the fraternity that it instilled in its members, a war experience utterly foreign to Saint-Exupéry's of the previous three years. He listened to these tales with a wide-eyed fascination, one which must have bordered on jealousy. Before long the atmosphere was thick with emotion; by Frenay's account the tears began first to roll down Saint-Exupéry's cheeks. The five men soon joined hands around the table, from which they discreetly disappeared by turns to collect themselves. " 'Ah, France,' we sighed," one of them recalled, "and she was there among us, wounded and shorn, bloodied and miserable."

The afternoon worked its magic in more ways than one. Shortly afterward Frenay wrote to Grenier to remind him of the lunch and to report more fully on Saint-Exupéry's plight. The pilot was naturally dissatisfied with his present assignment, and would be *"follement heureux"* to rejoin his own squadron, with which he had so brilliantly served in the campaign of 1940. Eaker, who was to meet with Bouscat that week, had let it be known that he would reconsider the posting as long as the French air force voiced no objection. (McCrary had heard the news earlier: "You win, I'm going to do it," Eaker had informed him by telephone.) Frenay felt compelled to add two small disclaimers to the end of his May 2 letter. He knew that Saint-Exupéry's past actions had won him much criticism but reported—a long limb on which to venture out—that he could personally vouch for the writer's present sympathies. Moreover, he added, he was by no means seeking preferential treatment for a friend. He wanted only for a man determined and qualified to fight to be granted permission to do so. Once again, Saint-Exupéry's career advanced not through favoritism but through exception. On the twelfth Grenier okayed the request.

Four days later corks popped in Alghero, on the northwest coast of Sardinia, to which Saint-Exupéry and Phillips were flown in a B-26. In the months since the pilot had left his squadron most of the kinks in the

Franco-American enterprise had been ironed out, at least on the military level. (The CFLN would not be recognized as the legitimate French government until October, and the Americans—both in Washington and in the field—continued to wring their hands over their allies' constant squabbling over politics.) Dunn and Gray had moved on; Colonel Karl Polifka had replaced Elliott Roosevelt and had seen to it that the 2/33 was equipped with spanking-new Lightnings. Spirits had improved overnight and, in Polifka's words, "the arrival of Saint-Exupéry put the 2/33 in the clouds." The squadron had taken over a villa on the rocky Sardinian coast eight miles from the airfield; the newcomer was moved into the best room in the house. The signs of his arrival were unmistakable. The following day the 2/33's logbook reported that its wayward member had "inoculated all the officers with the dangerous word-game virus, a formidable disease that immediately decimated the villa." He was soon discoursing brilliantly on spiritualism. On May 24 he took up a P-38 for an hour-long training flight. He had not been at the controls of a Lightning for nearly nine months; one flyer who had not seen him in the interim noted that he moved more slowly and with infinitely more trouble than he had in 1943. Nonetheless the man who had written his wife at Christmas that he had aged 100 years while in Algiers now reported that he felt twenty years younger, that follicle by follicle his hair was growing back, that his flowing white beard had fallen off overnight. He made no further mention of cancer, Eaker's intervention having miraculously cured him of all his ills.

Phillips, who had by now come to know well the Algiers entertainer who could keep friends locked in heated conversation on a street corner until 3:00 a.m., stayed on with the 2/33 for two weeks; he was thus able to observe and to photograph the reconnaissance pilot in action. Though few of Saint-Exupéry's colleagues admitted as much it was a poignant sight. He grimaced and growled as he was dressed for his flights; his boots were laced for him, as he could not bend over. He had to be fitted into and extracted from the cockpit. Wedged into a P-38 he was a heavy consumer of oxygen; some colleagues estimated that he used as much as twice the norm, partly because of his size, partly because he had a habit of turning on his oxygen before takeoff. It was difficult work, a fact the veteran acknowledged in his own way: "I have enough to worry about with my flying, my navigation, my radio work, and my photography," he told Jean Leleu, the 2/33's new operations officer. "I'm not going to waste my time watching out for the Krauts [les Boches]." Six hours at high altitude in a nonpressurized cabin left a twenty-three-year-old feeling limp the next day. Saint-Exupéry could only have felt worse, but did not dare mention this distress to his colleagues. He was doted on anyway. He was the pride of the 2/33, a squadron to which new pilots had been added but which was still recognizably the group immortalized in *Flight to Arras.*

There was no civilian life at Alghero—as one pilot put it the men lived "in the middle of nowhere"—but Saint-Exupéry in his baggy American fatigues and faded French air force cap more than compensated for the posting. He hauled out his intoxicating stories, of the Spanish Civil War; he offered a minute-by-minute re-creation of the Libyan adventure (he never talked about the Guatemalan crash, from which less poetry could be extracted); he overwhelmed the squadron's American colleagues with his sleight-of-hand. From his seat at the head of the table in the mess he delivered captivating talks on his favorite topics. Two that obsessed him at this time were brothels, which he vehemently argued should be closed, and the penal system, for which he proposed a dramatic reform. Gleefully he shared his recipe for a lion hunt: "You go to the desert with a sieve. You sift the sand. On the sieve, you will find the lions." With relish he shared in one of the squadron's favorite pastimes—fishing with dynamite—although he was reportedly never trusted with the explosives, only with the net with which to collect the victims. Once again he was, as he had been to his Aéropostale colleagues in the 1920s, a little bit the group's Queen of England.

The missions the 2/33 flew from Alghero were undertaken to map southern France for an eventual Allied landing. They were highly dangerous but not all-consuming; the pace of life in Sardinia was leisurely. Either for a liaison or a training flight Saint-Exupéry was in the cockpit of a P-38 nearly every day between May 24 and June 6, when he attempted his first mission, but these flights rarely lasted more than two hours. This allowed him ample time to torment Phillips with the word game he had invented the previous year, his infamous "game of the six-letter words." Each player wrote down a word consisting of six letters; the winner was the first to guess his opponent's choice. This was accomplished by systematically proposing other six-letter words and noting how many letters of the suggested word fell in the same places as in the word in question. For hours, often with an audience, Saint-Exupéry kept Phillips at this pursuit, at which he was expert. One day the room fell uncomfortably silent when it became clear that the American was about to win. He had chosen "zigzag." "In the name of God, Phillips," Saint-Exupéry exploded when the inevitable came to pass, " 'zigzag' is not a French word!" Evidently he had been able to do little more than sputter when on another occasion a young lieutenant bettered him with "St-Cyr"; he was very nearly driven to homicide by an opponent who wrote down six random letters.

"I seem happy when performing card tricks," Saint-Exupéry had written Madame de B from Pélissier's, "but I can't amuse myself with card tricks, only others." In the privacy of his room he remained as alone and as despairing as ever. He was disgusted by "this civil war between civilized peoples." In his letters he protested again and again that he was indifferent to calumny. Where he was once elegiac he was now bitter; where he was once nostalgic he was now desperately homesick, longing for a time, a place, and an ethos that were more remote than Cape Juby or Patagonia had ever been. Much though he felt isolated and alone among his squadron not all of his colleagues were fooled by his merrymaking. "Saint-Ex was done for and he knew it, but he never mentioned it to anyone," observed one pilot. Nonetheless he specialized in good cheer, which he spread around generously. To Anne Heurgon-Desjardins, Gide's hostess in Algiers, he cabled: "Prepare mayonnaise and court-bouillon. Am arriving from Sardinia with seven lobsters and will be with you in one hour." (This at a time when Heurgon-Desjardins was reduced to bartering her illustrious's house guest's presence for several grams of butter or a bottle of oil.) He dropped in on the 1/22, of which he was still officially a member; he flew regularly to Tunis. His high spirits were much in evidence on the night of May 28, when he arranged for a huge barbecue in Phillips's honor. A group of Sardinian shepherds roasted ten lambs for the squadron and their American colleagues; for a group of Frenchmen whose stomachs had begun to rebel against a steady diet of Sardinian lobsters and doctored Spam the meal was heaven-sent. Having arranged for the 230-liter belly tank of a P-38 to be filled with wine in Algiers, Phillips spent the evening scampering over the villa's rooftop, photographing the results of his largesse.

The next night was Phillips's last in Sardinia, and Saint-Exupéry returned to his room with the American in tow. He was finally to produce the promised article. Phillips watched as he fitted himself into a wicker chair, lit a cigarette, and—with loud sighs—proceeded to fill several pages of a writing pad that he balanced on his knees.* Evoking the same images on which he had relied since the 1930s, Saint-Exupéry essentially added his new concern to the message he had sounded in *Wind, Sand and Stars*, a book he now claimed he had written "in order to tell men passionately that they were all inhabitants of the same planet, passengers on the same ship." Technological progress had shrunk the globe to a point where humankind now constituted one vast organism, yet as he saw it that living entity so far lacked a soul. The world's greatest Luddite aviator at the same time gloried in some of the engineering advances of which he so despaired: he offered his American readers a thrilling sense of what it was like to overfly one's country as the enemy at 35,000 feet, though he had yet to fly a mission in 1944. After two drafts of the piece he stepped out on the villa's terrace for a breath of air; Phillips imagined that he gazed

* Overtaken by events, "Lettre à un Américain" did not appear in *Life*, which never did publish a Saint-Exupéry piece. The short text was read over the air in the United States by the actor Charles Boyer in April 1945.

through the cool darkness with longing, trying to make out the contours of France. At dawn the American was greeted by Gavoille, with whom he was sharing a room. "Well, did he write, or did you play chess all night?" asked the squadron leader. Phillips offered him Saint-Exupéry's six half-legible pages. "Damned Saint-Ex," declared the energetic captain, who had risen through the ranks, "five spelling mistakes."

Phillips left on the thirtieth, though not without first having witnessed some of his friend's other old tricks. The pilot remained as indifferent as ever to the English language, the exclusive language of the Allied airwaves.* On an early flight the control tower was so much confused by the indecipherable messages coming in over the intercom that the antiaircraft batteries were put on alert. They were called off only when a perfectly clear "*Merde!*" came through and the controllers—equally clumsy when it came to pronouncing the pilot's name—were able to announce that the approaching aircraft was only that of "Major X." (For his part Saint-Exupéry complained that his headphones served no purpose other than to give him a migraine. He barely understood a word of what was said to him.) At this point in his career it was difficult to maintain that he was not absentminded, or out of his depth, in the cockpit. The gentlest way of framing this truth was perhaps Gavoille's, who in a weak moment later admitted to Pélissier that Saint-Exupéry was not distracted in the air— where he was in fact meticulous—but that he was distracted on the ground, when receiving his instructions. He maintained his tendency of lowering his landing gear only at the very last minute; an ambulance rushed to the field to meet him on one occasion, when it looked as if he was not going to do so at all. On June 24 he took off for a test flight which he inadvertently performed with only one engine. Fooled by the fact that his right propeller continued to turn in the wind he did not notice until he landed that he had been flying a single-engined aircraft.

Nor were the peccadilloes confined to the air. Ten days after Phillips's departure the thirteen pilots of the 2/33 paid a visit to the frantically busy control room for their sector. The highlight of the visit made its way into the squadron's logbook: "Major Saint-Ex, stepping into a tangle of wires, pulls down a half-dozen telephones in a frightening crash, throwing the entire system out of commission." He continued his lifelong habit of writing in the air; the 2/33's mechanics routinely removed rumpled balls of paper in his cockpits. In Algiers he had been known to read while he shaved and now he read while he flew. On July 6 he appeared immersed in a detective novel when he was meant to take a P-38 to Tunis. He read in the operations rooms as his aircraft was readied and continued to do

---

* According to one member of the 2/33, he signed off simply with "Out" because he was unable—or unwilling—to pronounce "Over."

so when he was called to the field. Ultimately a Jeep arrived to carry him off; he read all the way to the airstrip. "He reads on the field while everyone waits for him to deign to get into his aircraft; he reads in the Lightning while someone goes back to fetch his bags, which naturally he has forgotten; he refuses to let go of the book before departure on the pretext that only a few pages remain; and he takes off with the book on his knee," reported the logbook. On this or another occasion he circled the Tunis airfield for nearly an hour before landing. He said afterward he could not have approached the runway with a clear head had he done so without having learned the identity of the novel's culprit.

Under the circumstances the 2/33 experienced a kind of collective worry every time their celebrated colleague flew. "We always admired him; he was our big brother and we loved him greatly and he could be incredibly foolish [il faisait les grosses bêtises]," explained Lieutenant Raymond Duriez, the assistant operations officer. The major attempted a first mission on June 6 over Marseilles despite reports of bad weather but was forced to turn back when a fire broke out in his left engine. (The logbook noted that a gaping hole had opened in the engine cowling but had fortunately escaped the pilot's notice, sparing him further worry.) He returned to the base to learn that the Allies had landed in Normandy, news which left some in the squadron to wonder if they might not be home for Christmas but which Saint-Exupéry greeted with no particular joy, at least on paper. He remained preoccupied not with the outcome of the war but with the ugliness that was certain to accompany the peace. He no longer boasted, as he had in May, of being "the dean of all war pilots," but succumbed more and more to a deep pessimism about the future and his place in it. He summed up his concern with a simple formula: We are preparing a world capable of producing 5,000 perfect assembly-line pianos a day but incapable of cultivating a worthy pianist, he sighed, a twist on the "condemned Mozart" of Wind, Sand and Stars. As ever he expressed his disdain for the modern world by writing it off as "an anthill." Phillips was not surprised to come across the writer lying on his stomach on the airfield one day, moving ants from one colony to another with a piece of straw so as to study their confusion.

On June 14 he flew his first successful mission from Alghero, over the Riviera. He took off again the next morning but was forced to turn back after he had trouble with his oxygen mask and nearly passed out in flight. His missions over the course of the next month were generally to follow this pattern. Saint-Exupéry had prevailed upon Jean Leleu for those sorties that would take him over the southeast of France, a demand to which Leleu acceded, not without noting, however, that by some quirk of fate the pilot experienced a brush with danger every time he overflew the territory so dear to his heart. To Dalloz he summed up the record himself at the end of July. Since his return to the 2/33 he had known every kind of near-disaster: he had experienced engine trouble, he had nearly fainted in flight, he had been pursued by enemy aircraft, he had had a fire on board. On his forty-fourth birthday he took off for France for the fifth time, for a mission that was again to take him over Annecy and Chambéry. Over France his left engine gave him trouble and had to be switched off; handicapped by its loss he headed south through the Alps, where he was less likely to meet a German fighter. On radioing in from the Mediterranean he was directed not to Alghero but to Borgo, on Corsica's eastern coast, where he spent the night. The mocha birthday cake and the mounds of ice cream that had been prepared for him by the 2/33's gifted chef and ace pilot, Lieutenant André Henry, were consumed in his absence.

On his return to the squadron Saint-Exupéry was able to offer Gavoille what was at best "a rather fanciful account" of his flight. The photo developer was able to shed some light on his whimsy: the pilot had made his way back to the Mediterranean via the Po Valley, then dotted with enemy bases. Probably he owed his life to the fact that no German would have assumed a slow-moving aircraft flying 8,000 feet overhead to have been that of the enemy. He had neglected to turn off his cameras during this casual stroll from Turin to Genoa; inadvertently, he had produced a stunning series of photographs of the German installations below. (One photograph revealed an enemy aircraft, to which Saint-Exupéry claimed he had been oblivious.) Over these Gavoille made a fuss; he said nothing at the time of another group of photographs the pilot brought back from this mission. He had overflown and photographed the coast around Agay, another area that did not figure in his assigned itinerary, probably because he had learned that his sister's home had been destroyed that spring by the Germans. A virtue was made in the end of Saint-Exupéry's inexactitude which, transformed into audacity, earned him a posthumous Croix de Guerre avec Palme.

He knew well that he was trafficking in miracles. On the morning of his forty-fourth birthday his mind had not been on the present danger, however. While he had been casually gliding through the Po Valley with a feathered propeller Saint-Exupéry had been cursing a different enemy: the "superpatriots" in North Africa who had banned his books. "I love France, on my own, more than all of them put together. They love only themselves," he had written that winter. He did not know any more than he had in 1940 what he was fighting for but this time he did know what would be said of him if he were to stop. He flew, as ever, out of duty, but also a little out of self-defense. In 1944 Saint-Exupéry had something to prove; he had been shaped, as he wrote in *Citadelle*, by the enemy. He was a writer who had never believed the pen to be mightier than the sword, yet in 1944 he felt as much defeated by internecine bickering and slander as by international conflict. His war missions were no longer his only peace, as he had claimed them to be the previous year. They did not offer the same taste of purity. Before one flight he asked André Henry for a seemingly unnecessary bit of advice. "Why," asked Henry, "are you scared?" "No," replied Saint-Exupéry, "but if only you knew, there are so many out there who would love to see me fail in my mission." Even in the cockpit he gritted his teeth now with anger.

For all of the obvious reasons Leleu did not accede to the pilot's second demand, the same one with which he had tormented Alias in 1940. "For the rest of you," the major argued, "one mission more or less makes no difference. For me, who started late, you must understand, it is vital." The month of July—he returned after his Italian escapade on Sunday the second and spent much of the next week in Algiers—passed in one drawn-out attempt to ground the pilot and, on Saint-Exupéry's end, in one sustained plot to thwart the intentions of his friends and superiors. On the eleventh he took off for a mission over Lyons, although he was told in no uncertain terms that the weather was unfavorable and returned after less than three hours with no photographs. Two days later he was scheduled to fly again but was forced to cede the mission to Duriez. He was told there was not enough oxygen for him to go up, which may have been a ruse; Gavoille had begun to do all he could to keep him out of the air. Polifka later claimed that he, too, had decided that Saint-Exupéry had had enough flying and that he attempted that month to ground the pilot, twice, although no official documents support the claim. The invasion of France was growing nearer, and as Polifka remembered, "I wanted Saint-Ex there when we hit the beach." His decision, if indeed it was made, was overruled from above. All of the arguments that had been used on the pilot during the campaign of 1940 failed again; Chassin tried to talk some sense into his ex-student, who calmly replied: "I'll follow through now. The end is no longer very far off, I think." Several members of the squadron were surprised that Saint-Exupéry continued to fly as they had heard a rumor that Eaker had granted him exactly five missions, which was Phillips's understanding as well. If Eaker had issued such an edict word of a limitation never made its way either to Gavoille or to Leleu, who could have enforced it. Saint-Exupéry could not have been relied upon to have done so himself; on this count it seems safe to say his honor would have failed him.

On July 14 President Roosevelt sent de Gaulle a telegram wishing the General a happy Bastille Day and acknowledging that the complete liberation of France seemed in sight. At about the same time the 2/33 moved physically closer to the homeland, to Corsica. They were billeted in a villa in Erbalunga, six miles north of Bastia. Here Gavoille decided to make a direct appeal to his pilot; he had long been haunted by a line he had uttered half-seriously in 1940, which had made its way into *Arras*: "Surely you don't mean, Captain, that you expect to come out of the war alive?" On the eighteenth he paid Saint-Exupéry a late-night visit in his room. He found the 2/33's record-holder of close calls reclining in his bed, fully dressed, his hands behind his head, thinking. Gavoille began rather awkwardly by teasing him about his birthday mission; Saint-Exupéry could see where the conversation was headed and quietly at first, then with great intensity, cut his commanding officer off at the pass. He would not survive being grounded again; it was clear to him he was going to disappear in one fashion or another, and he told Gavoille he would greatly prefer to do so on a war mission. This favor, at least, his old colleague could surely accord him. He had another service to ask as well: that evening he entrusted his pigskin bag and its papers to Gavoille, to whom he issued detailed instructions in the event of his death. The two men left each other in tears.

The following week Gavoille's three-week-old son was baptized in La Marsa. Saint-Exupéry was named godfather, as he had asked to be. After the ceremony on the twenty-fourth he told Marie-Madeleine Mast, the wife of the governor-general of Tunisia and the child's godmother, that flying was becoming more and more difficult, that it was likely he would not return. General Mast and Gavoille meanwhile engaged in a little plotting. They agreed that the easiest way to be sure Saint-Exupéry survived the war would be to see that he was told the details of the imminent landing, after which he would be unable, for security reasons, to fly. Henry and Leleu had already been grounded for this reason; Saint-Exupéry had taken to gliding past Henry with a curt "Henry, say hello to me, and then don't utter another word." (According to the squadron's logbook the two pilots used their knowledge to extract whatever they wanted from their colleagues, "by threatening to reveal the information and thereby condemn them to the same fate.") During the week that followed it was decided that Henry would inadvertently let the information slip, in the middle of a meal, or over a game of cards. It seemed a foolproof tactic; Saint-Exupéry would not be able to claim he had been grounded for the wrong reasons.

In Algiers that week he bequeathed his chess set to a diplomat friend. "Keep it," he advised Raoul Bertrand. "We'll play again on another planet." The next day both Gavoille and an American pilot took off for missions over France; the American, Lieutenant Eugene Meredith, was shot down on his return sixty miles from the base, minutes after waving to Gavoille in midair. Saint-Exupéry probably heard the news when he returned from Bastia, where he had been visiting with the American squadron and in particular with Colonel Paul Rockwell, whom he invited to dinner the next evening at the French mess. A flyer was most vulnerable

as he made his descent toward Corsica, and—out of relief and fatigue—
reconnaissance pilots often made this descent prematurely, exposing
themselves to additional danger. Perhaps through Gavoille's intervention,
perhaps because of his frequent absences, each of which relegated a pilot
to the bottom of the ladder, Saint-Exupéry had not flown a mission since
the eighteenth, despite the fact that two of the 2/33's pilots were out of
commission, but he appears to have assumed he was to fly the following
day. He may have managed to profit from Gavoille's exhaustion on the
thirtieth to see that he was assigned a mission; there was to be as much
confusion about his departure on July 31 as about the subsequent mission
itself. Gavoille claimed that he had not been scheduled to go anywhere;
Leleu—who distributed the missions—felt certain he had; several American officers were under the impression that he had been grounded and
that when he took off that Monday he did so against orders. Duriez, who
saw him off, could not remember if Saint-Exupéry's name figured at the
top of the roster of pilots. He well enough remembered that if it had not
he would have been incapable of denying Major de Saint-Exupéry a mission had the major imposed on him for one, however.

That afternoon or evening the pilot wrote two letters, one to Dalloz
and one to Madame de B, in which he again expressed his loneliness, his
distaste for the Gaullists, and his "breathtaking indifference" to life. To
Consuelo a week or so earlier he had written that his only regret were he
to be shot down would be to make her cry. He spent part of the evening
of the thirtieth entertaining a group of young women with a deck of cards
in a seaside restaurant in Miomo, from which he disappeared just before
midnight, alone. If he went back to his room that evening he did not sleep
there. He reappeared for a 7:30 breakfast, joining Duriez in the mess for
a *pain beurré* and a *café crème*. The two men spoke little. The assistant
operations officer drove the pilot to the field and checked the weather for
him. It was glorious. He then helped Saint-Exupéry into his gear and into
a P-38, which a mechanic had already warmed; he waited while the pilot
completed his eleven engine checks. Several minutes later Saint-Exupéry
motioned that he was ready to taxi. Two squadron mechanics pulled away
the blocks from the Lightning's wheels. Duriez waved him off. In English
the pilot radioed to the control tower for permission to depart and at 8:30,
according to Duriez, or at 8:45, according to the logbook, he took off for
what was intended to be a mapping mission east of Lyons. Nothing about
the previous twenty-four hours—not even the desperate letters in his room,
which were to have been given to Colonel Rockwell that evening—was
unusual, save for the unexplained absence, and for the fact that Gavoille
was not on hand for the departure, which seems to support the notion that
the pilot had traded or bargained for a mission. "In the name of God,"
Gavoille bawled out Duriez later that afternoon, "what got into you that

you didn't find a way to prevent him from flying?" The radar at Cape Corse tracked Saint-Exupéry crossing into southern France. "When your gods die, you die. For you live by them," he had written in *Citadelle*. He was due back at 12:30, but was not heard from again.

Two weeks later the remaining twelve pilots of the 2/33 participated in the Allied landing they had helped to prepare in the south of France. On August 25 Paris was liberated. The following day Charles de Gaulle led a triumphant procession down the Champs-Élysées.

Epilogue: Saint Antoine d'Exupéry

~

It's worth it, it's worth the final smash-up.

MERMOZ, as quoted in *Wind, Sand and Stars*

What happened between the time Saint-Exupéry took off from Bastia on July 31, 1944, and the time he would have run out of fuel six hours later remains a mystery. Toward 1:00 o'clock Gavoille summoned Vernon Robison, the American liaison officer assigned to the 2/33, to sector control. Saint-Exupéry was late returning, Gavoille explained, his mouth twitching; would the lieutenant please call for him? Robison did, repeatedly. (There had been a dress rehearsal for this afternoon: Saint-Exupéry had been overdue returning from a previous mission, when Gavoille had also handed Robison a microphone. The pilot was thought to be over the Mediterranean; he radioed from the skies of France that he had not yet completed his mission and asked for permission to do so, which his commanding officer reluctantly granted.) This time no response was forthcoming. The two men hoped against hope; it all came down to the kind of pregnant wait, heavier by the minute, which the lost pilot had himself so indelibly described in *Wind, Sand and Stars*. At 3:30 Robison filed the interrogation report for Saint-Exupéry's eighth and final mission: PILOT DID NOT RETURN AND IS PRESUMED LOST. Not everyone understood the enormity of the loss as Gavoille felt it: one American who was in the operations room that day remembered having been told that "a Frenchie" had failed to return and that he was a writer but did not recognize his name. ("I was twenty-three and illiterate," he explained years later.) That evening, Rockwell and a fellow American officer showed up at the French mess, to which the pilot had invited them the previous day. They, too, were shattered by the news, although, as Gavoille put it, "the traditions of aviation were maintained." The evening passed in song. Most of the 2/33 clung to the hope that their illustrious colleague had landed in Switzerland or been taken prisoner. When the 1/22—of which squadron Saint-Exupéry was officially still a member, having only been detached to the

2/33—called around to see if they might pry additional information out of the Allied command they got nowhere. They were unable to impress upon the security-conscious Wing that the rules applied to everyone but not to Saint-Exupéry.

The day after his disappearance the Algiers newspapers began to speak of him, then fell silent. The gossip-mongers were happy to step in where the news left off. It would not be surprising, tittered one camp, if Saint-Exupéry had delivered his airplane to Vichy. Was it really true, asked another, that Saint-Exupéry had been assassinated by the Gaullists? Pélissier received word on August 2 from the High Command; he had been listed as the party to alert in case of accident. In part obscured by happy events, the news that the writer was lost filtered out gradually. The acceptance of his death was yet slower in coming. It was as if all of the eulogies he had written over the years now came back to attach themselves to him; his friends and family were as reluctant to grant him the respect and perfection due the dead as he had been reluctant to grant them to Mermoz in 1936. Late in the evening of August 9 Léon Werth was half-listening to the radio when he heard that his great friend was reported missing. He thought back to the wide-ranging discussions and the mind-boggling card tricks—to the years of tardiness—and concluded that his Tonio was lost but alive. A week later he had not abandoned this hope. Jean Israël heard the news over the radio as well; he was entering his fifth and last year of captivity in an officers' prison camp. His response to the announcement was that of Daurat, who reported that the news threw him into total shock.

Anne Lindbergh read of Saint-Exupéry's disappearance on August 9 and put her finger on one of the reasons for the ache it caused. There was, wrote a woman supremely qualified to know, a vast, terrible difference between "lost" and "dead." She imagined "the man who spoke 'my language' better than anyone I have ever met, before or since" to be like a soul in Dante, drifting between heaven and hell. On August 10, when American troops were within eighty-seven miles of Paris, *The New York Times* reported the writer missing. Not all the indications of a forthcoming Allied victory were positive ones: Jean Guehénno, who had remained in France throughout the war but had not published, heard about Saint-Exupéry just before reading that Drieu La Rochelle had attempted suicide. (Drieu, who had kept the *NRF* afloat for the Germans, would succeed the following year.) Seven days later *Pour la Victoire* announced the aviator's news to French-speaking New Yorkers. The paper's editor imagined Saint-Exupéry to be hidden away in France and wagered he would resurface.

That same week, acting on Saint-Exupéry's instructions, Gavoille asked one of his pilots to deliver the writer's manuscripts to Pélissier. He did so in direct defiance of military regulation (his affairs should have gone to the ministry) "but for Saint-Ex," the officer wrote Pélissier, "it's the least I can do." It was an appropriate gesture: from the grave Saint-Exupéry continued to corrupt the rule-bound. Colonel Rockwell had seen to it that the letters to Dalloz and to Madame de B were delivered; Dalloz took his to Gide, who read the dispiriting document aloud, sentence by sentence, emitting a pained "Ah!" as he put down the paper. De Gaulle's acting foreign minister, René de Massigli, carried the second letter to London, where Madame de B had already received the news of its author. At the end of the month Curtice Hitchcock sent on the article Saint-Exupéry had drafted for Phillips to the editor of *Life*. In his covering letter he wrote: "I can't somehow believe Saint-Ex won't show up somewhere back of the *maquis* lines before this thing is over." He was sure enough that his daredevil author would again reappear to treat the matter of payment for the piece lightly. He wrote that if the author was still alive he was certain to need the money, and that if for some reason he was not, his wife would.

Reluctant though his friends were to accept his death, few were surprised to hear of Saint-Exupéry's disappearance. He had been saying his good-byes since 1942—when he saw Fleury off in New York late that year he did so with a handshake and with the comment, "And if I disappear, you can be sure, it will be without regrets"—and letters to his intimates over the year that followed amount to variations on "I don't give a damn if I die." Hedda Sterne and Silvia Reinhardt knew when he left New York they would never see him again (Silvia met her future husband the night after Saint-Exupéry's departure, when, still in tears, she cut a particularly fetching and tragic figure); Madame de B very strongly suspected when she saw him in Algiers that he would be shot down. Anne Lindbergh— who over the course of the next two and a half months was to pass through every stage of grief on the Frenchman's account, which loss she compared to that of her sister or her baby—conceded that she had expected the news for some time. "He wanted to make the supreme sacrifice," she wrote, feeling as if she had been stabbed through the heart; "he went back for that." Like others of his friends she breathed a sigh of relief for him. "It's for the best. He's free now," commented an officer who had seen him regularly in Algiers. We do not know how or when Consuelo—who had so many times before lost her husband—received the news of this final separation. Although her behavior often belied her attachment, she, too, was long in believing him to be actually gone.

Max Becker felt his client had been courting death for some time. Those who did not think he was flirting with an early end nonetheless had to admit that he had fallen prey to a deep despair. "Let's be honest," said Anne Heurgon-Desjardins, who visited with the writer every time he called on Gide and for the last time on July 26. "Saint-Exupéry no longer wanted to live." He had clearly prepared his death—he had said his good-byes, had issued the equivalent of a last testament to Gavoille, had made known his plans for his manuscripts, had harped on his indifference to life—and the fact that he did so has been construed by some as his having arranged for it. This seems unlikely. All reconnaissance pilots flew alone, unarmed, into enemy territory with only their speed, their altitude, and their wits to protect them, and all reconnaissance pilots flew with fear. While Saint-Exupéry may not have expected to have survived the war it is not at all clear that he had truly lost his desire to do so. More and more he fell into expressions of despair and explosions of disdain—he was by 1944 no longer either the open-minded dialectician of the 1930s or the high-minded mystic of *Wind, Sand and Stars*—but his life's correspondence can be read as one long roar of discontent. Nor did he entirely shy from embracing the future. Bill Donovan reported that the pilot had come to see him in mid-1944 to ask if he might serve in the OSS; the second week of July he had written Pélissier that he hoped the war would end soon, before he was entirely exhausted ("*avant que j'aie fondu tout entier*"), as he had work to see to later.

All the same, dying for France was consistent with Saint-Exupéry's principles and, for once, entirely within the realm of what was expected of a man of his background. Raoul Bertrand, to whom the writer's chess set had gone, did see a sort of implied death wish in his friend's last days. He termed this a sister of charity, the noble response to small-mindedness. Denis de Rougemont, who like almost everyone who had known Saint-Exupéry became his eulogizer, put this best: "As for honor, it is easier to die for than to live by." Saint-Exupéry had never been a man of his time; the hour of history in which he had felt at home lasted only so long as pilots flew without the benefit of instruments. Many men outlive their time but Saint-Exupéry, stooped and stiff, had grown rigid, unrealistic to the point of gracelessness. Since he was a young man he had bemoaned the end of an era; had he survived the war he would as well have had to admit that his days of active duty were over. This—more than the *épuration*, more than de Gaulle's ascension, more than what he accurately predicted would be an age of bowling alleys and assembly lines—he would have abhorred. John Phillips has pointed out that in the twenty years since his friend had learned to fly aviation had grown stronger while he had grown weaker; the men with whom he lived in Corsica could fly circles around him and knew as much. Probably they were less aware that for pilots of his generation a certain nearly senseless risk-taking was an integral part of the sport, the foolishness that lent duty its flavor. Pilots of his era knew only one end. They did not aspire to breathing their last at home in their beds.

Dying for France was not a prerequisite of the second of Saint-

Exupéry's chosen professions. Four hundred and fifty French writers per-
ished in World War I, but when *Publishers Weekly* called the roll of prominent French writers in October 1944 it went something like this: Benjamin
Crémieux dead in a Nazi concentration camp; Gide in refuge in Rome;
Jules Romains in refuge in New York; Roger Martin du Gard in Nice.
Malraux, Eluard, Aragon, and Sartre were all well, several of them veterans of the Resistance or of prison camps. Jean Prévost also fought with
the Resistance; he had died the day after Saint-Exupéry had disappeared,
when he walked into a German ambush in the south of France. Céline
was in exile (and ultimately in prison) in Denmark. Saint-Exupéry was
missing. He was to go down in history as the most celebrated French man
of letters to die in the war for the simple reason that most French men of
letters did not see active combat after the fall of France in 1940. In a
country which an American intelligence agent reported "had been made
almost psychopathically sensitive to defeat," this was to prove, as the pilot
himself might have guessed, a thankless distinction. In 1945 he was the
most prestigious French author in the eyes of the Americans, but by the
time his generation had come to take over French letters he was gone.

     Saint-Exupéry did not reappear; a mass was finally said for him in the
east of France a year after his last mission. In April 1948 he was officially
deemed to have died for his country, for which sacrifice a French writer's
copyrights are extended by thirty years. Speculation continues to this day,
however, as to the circumstances surrounding the last flight, the mystery
of which is conclusively solved every few years, or with about the same
regularity as Amelia Earhart's final moments are reconstructed. We know
that the Cape Corse radar tracked Saint-Exupéry into but not out of France
on the thirty-first. It is possible that he went down over France, probably
in the Alps; it is slightly less possible that he overflew the Riviera at a very
low altitude, too low for the radar to pick up any sign of his aircraft, and
disappeared into the Mediterranean. (If he was flying "on the deck," as
it is called, he presumably was doing so either because he had had trouble
with his aircraft or was paying a visit to Agay, not part of the scheduled
mission.) No one can be sure exactly why he fell from the sky. The spectrum
of possibilities is evenly represented by his previous missions, plagued by
mishaps, any one of which could equally well have proved his last. Over
the years a number of eyewitnesses have stepped forth to testify that they
saw a P-38 go down off the coast of France between Cannes and Saint-
Tropez on the thirty-first; they may actually have seen Meredith go down
on the thirtieth, however. The sky over Corsica in late July was thick with
Allied bombers and fighters preparing the invasion. None of those
airmen—or any of the air-sea rescue units in the area—noticed a P-38
shot down that afternoon, as they would have been likely to.

     In 1981 an unofficial report from a Luftwaffe flyer named Robert

Hiechele came to light in which the young German claimed he had shot down a Lightning on the thirty-first although he was on a routine surveillance mission and had not been authorized to do so; there seems no viable explanation for why an official report was not filed by the Focke-Wulf pilot, who under any circumstances should and would have been proud of his victory, especially one over a mighty P-38. (Heichele, who had just turned twenty-one, died a few weeks later and was buried about fifteen miles from Saint-Maurice-de-Rémens.) His account, energetically denied by the Germans, cannot be substantiated. Searches of the Mediterranean have been inconclusive, although at this writing an American-made screw found in the sea near Toulon was thought to yield some clue to Saint-Exupéry's death. No one has yet undertaken a wide-scale search of the Alps, which would be exceedingly difficult.

Whether he went down because of an inhaler problem (probably the most humane alternative as oxygen deprivation goes undetected by the pilot, who blacks out first) or because of an enemy fighter, Saint-Exupéry's was a noble death, what is called in French *"une mort glorieuse."* Instinctively right about so many things, Consuelo said in 1946 that her husband's had been a perfectly appropriate death, nearly a custom-designed one; at the end of a star-chasing life, his had been a meteoric fall. We may hope he got exactly the brand of death he wanted, a subject on which, like most, he had an opinion. In the 1930s a *Marianne* editor asked him if—after all of his close calls—he had come to prefer one end to another. He knew Saint-Exupéry would not be offended by the unusual question, the kind he liked. Stipulating that his answer was not for publication, at least not until he was "truly dead," the pilot readily catalogued the options. He had concluded that water was best: "You don't feel yourself dying. You feel simply as if you're falling asleep and beginning to dream."

~

His untimely and enigmatic death—or as some saw it, his martyrdom—would assure Saint-Exupéry's legend. It did not, however, bring out the best in everyone. Pélissier held on tightly to the manuscripts that Gavoille had gallantly passed on to him; the ministry of air was forced to sue for their return and retrieved them finally—at some cost—late in January 1945. Gavoille remained a loyal friend on all counts. That month the ministry asked how to contact the flyer's family. His commanding officer provided the name and address of Madame de B, who maintained that Pélissier had not released all of the documents in question. During these proceedings an inventory was drawn up of the writer's Corsican belongings, which makes for a poignant comment on a life. In the end his possessions amounted to little more than his 915 typed pages of *Citadelle* and a host of other notebooks and papers (one typescript of Teilhard de Chardin, another spiritual man with deep ties to the natural world, was initially credited to Saint-Exupéry), a stapler, a broken pipe, a regulation GI wardrobe, seven pairs of shoes, four pairs of pajamas, a bathing suit, fourteen handkerchiefs, a set of watercolors, a deck of cards, a bag of toiletries, two electric razors, a small sum of money in various currencies, a silk bathrobe. In July Consuelo took legal action to reclaim the remainder of her husband's possessions, the last of which finally made their way, via the air ministry, back to his family three years after his death. The distribution of the estate proved equally messy. A man with a professed taste for the simple, Saint-Exupéry left two women—his wife and his mother —to profit equally from his work,* and a third—Madame de B—as his literary executor. This sensible if awkward arrangement left Madame de B in the position of having to remind Saint-Exupéry's American agent that while Consuelo was to receive half the royalties on her husband's work she was not to be in any way involved in the publishing plans for those volumes.

It was not with Consuelo but with Gallimard that Reynal & Hitchcock had their troubles. Saint-Exupéry's French publisher charged in 1945 that all of the American editions of the writer's work were illegal, as they had never consented to them. Gallimard claimed they had had no prior knowledge of the U.S. editions, an astonishing allegation given that Reynal & Hitchcock had had a contract with the best-selling writer since 1938, had corresponded with Gallimard about the copyright for *Arras*, and had heard no objections from the French publisher in their mutual author's lifetime, during a year of which the author received his Gallimard mail in care of his New York editors. Gaston Gallimard approached what probably resembled the truth when he wrote Hitchcock that many French publishers found themselves in embarrassing positions in 1945, having been deprived of relations with the world for many years, during which time the works of their authors had appeared—and turned a profit—elsewhere. Reynal & Hitchcock had nothing to gain financially from circumventing Gallimard, whose proceeds came out of the writer's earnings; having always been generous in their dealings with their profligate author and circumspect in their contractual negotiations (the French rights in *The Little Prince*, for example, were automatically to revert to Saint-Exupéry upon the liberation of France) they were flabbergasted. In part they wrote off the misunderstanding to their author's clumsiness in his business dealings, imagining him telling Gallimard of the arrangements he had made independently with a shrug of his wide shoulders and a "Gaston, I have done a terrible thing." (Even such nonchalance on Saint-Exupéry's part

* His mother's share was to be divided among his mother and his two sisters.

does not explain how Gallimard could have been oblivious to the best-selling American editions of his titles; the world was smaller than that.) Litigation between the two firms—Reynal repeatedly referred to it as their "impasse"—continued until 1948. An envoy from the French side, Albert Camus, ultimately served as intermediary. The suit was resolved exactly four years after Saint-Exupéry's death with a court order that allowed both of his publishers to claim victory.

Each of the women in Saint-Exupéry's life offered memorials to him. Madame de Saint-Exupéry wrote a book of poems, published by Gallimard. Consuelo—who in 1946 became the second Saint-Exupéry to publish in America with *Kingdom of the Rocks**—sculpted effigies of her husband and of the Little Prince. Madame de B published a biography of her friend under the name Pierre Chevrier in 1949. Three very different women, their grief took them in separate directions. Madame de Saint-Exupéry put in sober and discreet appearances at commemorative events for her son, as she had at the Hôtel Pont-Royal in 1936. She was on hand when a plaque was added to the Panthéon in 1965 but died three years before one was affixed to the apartment building on the place Vauban in 1975. She was ninety-seven years old, and had survived all but two of her children.

Madame de B masterfully managed her friend's literary legacy, evidently not without emotion at the outset. In October 1946 the British writer Richard Aldington reported to the poet H. D. that Madame de B had asked him to contribute a piece on Saint-Exupéry to a sort of *Festschrift* she was putting together.† "She is a rather tragical figure, doping herself with 'Scotch' to try to forget him—they were to have been married the day after he was killed, so how can I refuse?" he wrote, stretching the truth a little. In her correspondence with Saint-Exupéry's American publishers, Madame de B acknowledged her grief but did not allow it to interfere with the business at hand. She discreetly arranged for all publishing decisions and all manuscript copies to bypass Consuelo and remained on good terms with all parties while Gallimard and Reynal & Hitchcock ironed out their differences. She has proved one of the most stalwart defenders of the faith: to this day a biographer's query sent to the Association des Amis de Saint-Exupéry in Paris—an organization in which she holds no official position—is answered by Madame de B. The Saint-Exupéry family controls the rights in their uncle and great-uncle's works; Madame de B remains in possession of the greatest cache of papers, those entrusted to her by Saint-Exupéry when he left France in 1940, the notebooks, the datebooks, his correspondence, and the original typescript of *Citadelle*.

---

* The manuscript was originally titled *Harvest of the Stones*.
† The 1947 issue of *Confluences* is dedicated to Saint-Exupéry.

Consuelo—whose tantrums and crises Madame de B felt it her obligation to attempt to minimize—continued on her independent way. She was seen around New York shortly after her husband's disappearance on the arm of Denis de Rougemont, for some time her official escort, best known in America as the author of *Love in the Western World*. In November 1945 Anaïs Nin caught a glimpse of her at a party for André Breton; in her diary she noted that Madame de Saint-Exupéry had about her "the consumed look of a woman who has lived, loved, taken drugs, lost her husband to his passion for air and space" and that she was living with de Rougemont. For a brief time after the war she operated a restaurant-barge on the Seine called Le Petit Prince, endearing herself to no one by appearing in a sailor's cap bearing the name "Saint-Ex" in gilt lettering. She made spectacular entrances and exits for the next years as the Countess de Saint-Exupéry. In the 1950s she continued to be described as exceedingly beautiful; her voice raspy from alcohol and cigarettes, she remained fully capable of throwing herself into the arms of choice, unsuspecting strangers with tremendous effect, of lording girlishly over an entire room, of beguiling with the story of the earthquake that had turned the house around. She remained troubled by her asthma and burdened by financial woes. In the 1960s she pleaded with French government officials to forgive several years of back taxes; she had no savings and had been threatened with seizure of her property. She spent most of her last days in Grasse, where she died after a prolonged illness in 1979. She was buried in Père-Lachaise next to her second husband, Gómez Carrillo. At the time of their marriage Saint-Exupéry probably thought he would be happy with her and probably also thought he would not; he had been right on both counts. One other woman, a first-rate seductress to the end, paid her own kind of tribute to the author-aviator. Louise de Vilmorin, the writer's ex-fiancée, is said to have quipped that she would have been better off as Saint-Exupéry's widow than she had been as Malraux's mistress.

Five years after Consuelo's death her papers were sold at auction, much to the displeasure of the family, who formally registered their objection to a sale they could not prevent. Generally traffic in the relics fueled misunderstandings, sometimes escalating into religious wars. Honoring Saint-Exupéry's sense of discretion while at the same time ensuring his place in the public eye (and, occasionally, paying one's bills) proved a difficult balancing act. Ségogne fell out with Dalloz when Dalloz sold his 1944 letter; everyone fell out when Pélissier published a fine biography of his house guest in 1951; Ségogne and Renée de Saussine fell out when she published her early letters; many of Saint-Exupéry's friends were furious when Madame de B allowed Gallimard to publish *Citadelle*. Although the writer had never expected the work to appear in his lifetime it was not necessarily in any shape to appear. Pélissier claimed that its author had prohibited the publication of the book in 1942. Werth thought *Citadelle* had been brought out prematurely. Galantière, who had done more to order the work of Saint-Exupéry than anyone else, found it "an unorganized, repetitive bulk" even in the English-language edition, which is two-thirds the length of the French. The mild Becker was on this count severe: "If Saint-Ex knew they had published it," he groaned, "he would die all over again."

Citadelle was the third of Saint-Exupéry's works to be published posthumously in France, after *Lettre à un otage* and *Le Petit Prince*. All of the earlier titles found their way back into print after the war, when Gallimard, no longer the embarrassed publisher of *Pilote de guerre*, was resurrected as the anti-German publisher of Saint-Exupéry. *Lettre à un otage* was published at the end of 1944; the appearance of the elegiac text—hailed by one critic as "*le plus beau texte depuis la Libération*"—was in the wake of its author's disappearance cause for hagiography.* *Le Petit Prince* followed in 1946: the tale of the imperious innocent who falls to earth, makes a quick study of the men behind its curtains, and ultimately disappears without a trace read differently in France than it had in New York in 1943. As it had been true to its author's life it was now seen as having eerily predicted his death. The reaction of Adrienne Monnier—the rue de l'Odéon bookseller who, at Jean Prévost's suggestion, had been the first to publish Saint-Exupéry—was representative. Initially *Le Petit Prince* struck her as puerile, but she found herself drenched in tears by the end. She realized she was crying not over the book but, belatedly, for Saint-Exupéry, who had poured so much of himself into it. The critics were less moved. In a country that maintains a near-religious faith in appearances it is somewhat blasphemous to claim that the essential is invisible to the eye, sacrilege on a par with the advice Saint-Exupéry had offered years earlier, when he had counseled that a fault of grammar was preferable to one of rhythm. Thirty years would pass before reviewers on either side of the ocean saw in *The Little Prince* "a thoroughly Gallic and slightly sophisticated version of J. M. Barrie's *Peter Pan*." By the time they might have been ready to concede as much the book had become so popular that it was more tempting to go at it with a hatchet.

In 1948 Gallimard brought out *Citadelle*, a work better read as a gauge of its author's mood than as a work of philosophy and one that constituted a first strike against his posthumous glory. The book of meditations, delivered in the guise of a desert chieftain handing down his wisdoms to his son, appears a far cry from *Night Flight* or *Wind, Sand and Stars*. It was a little bit the Bible Saint-Exupéry wished he could offer men; its language

---

* Léon Werth did not see the text for which he was so much responsible until five months after his friend's death, when Gallimard sent him a special edition.

is high-flown, a victim of the timelessness for which he was striving when—intent on rising above his age—he was constantly ambushed by it. ("I have found the necessary style for an English version of *Citadelle*," Stuart Gilbert wrote Reynal triumphantly in 1948, having settled on a language rich in "whithers" and "wherefores," "but it's rather like walking on a tightrope all the time!") For all its religious veneer *Citadelle* departs little from the rest of its author's oeuvre. The omnipotent, Solomonic chieftain is but an extension of the steely, Old Testament Daurat, both of them creations of a man who had neither a father nor a son. The volume's insistent harping on the need to barter oneself for a greater good is the message of *Night Flight* revisited; rich in sand foxes and rose trees, the Berber Arcadia of *Citadelle* is half real, half the land of the Little Prince. The aging chieftain and the impertinent prince are in fact blood relations, detached, tyrannical, well-traveled in their own ways, both of them disdainful of everyday realities. From the Patagonian leper to the transposed squabbles of wartime New York, the arc of Saint-Exupéry's life can be traced in the text; it represents a piece of spiritual ground marked out by a weary man with a vestigial sense of Catholicism and an innate sense of responsibility who has lived a life thirsting for the values but free of the bounds of both. What is surprising about *Citadelle* is ultimately not that the author of *Night Flight* could or would have written such a book but that his themes could remain constant throughout a novel of aviation, a book of personal essays, a children's allegory, and a succession of philosophical dialogues spoken at the desert court of an imaginary ruler.

France is a country of *moralistes*; one attempts philosophy there at one's own risk. Gallimard considered then rejected the idea of bringing out *Citadelle* in an abridged form, which may have been a disservice to its author. In any event by 1948 the moment was ripe for backlash, and an inaccessible, repetitive tome of didactic suras from an aviator who already seemed on shaky intellectual ground did nothing to enhance Saint-Exupéry's reputation. He had well enough mastered the cadence of holy writing but his thinking had never been systematic and was not now. Critics took him to task on all counts, even while some of those close to the man continued to think of *Citadelle*, as had its author, as his masterpiece. (Madame de B has remained a particularly staunch defender.) The work may well represent the fullest expression of his personal convictions but it is his least lucid: only the most energetic admirer can claim *Citadelle* is not sleep-inducing. V. S. Pritchett railed against the volume's "tiresomely archaic language" when it was published in England as *The Wisdom of the Sands* in 1952; French critics found the book "muddled and failed." It is easy enough to target the inconsistencies in a work that makes a simultaneous case for self-fulfillment and enlightened oligarchy; *Le Monde*'s reviewer contented himself with pointing up the naïveté of *Ci-*

tadelle by noting that Saint-Exupéry's was an Arabian utopia altogether lacking in oil.

By the time a collection of Saint-Exupéry's journalistic pieces appeared in the 1950s the most indulgent reviewers were asking that for his own sake the author not be treated as an intellectual, which he was not. Nonetheless there were those who chose to attack him as an imposter, a dabbler, as a doler-out of "prop-driven platitudes." His heroic message has been more and more heard as unfashionably aristocratic or fascistic; the insistent popularity of *The Little Prince* has opened him up to regular charges of mawkishness and *"boy-scoutism."* "Saint-Exupéry's image has aged badly," conceded Françoise Giroud. "He has been made into a Boy Scout, a kind of simpleton." Once again he has not been redeemed by success. His popularity enrages the critics, who have made a punching bag of the awkward, oversized author. It is easy to argue that Saint-Exupéry was a great writer who—with the possible exception of *Night Flight*—never wrote a great book, and it is altogether tempting to do so when speaking of the most translated author in the French language. *The Little Prince* can be read in nearly eighty languages; it continues to sell some 125,000 copies annually in America alone and another 300,000 a year in France. It has assembled a motley fan club and evoked a host of tributes. James Dean had an obsession with the book, which he had hoped to film. Anaïs Nin, experimenting with LSD in the 1950s, could not get the image of the Little Prince out of her mind; the little man teetering on the edge of his planet had become for her the very image of loneliness. The 1/33 has adopted the figure as part of its insignia; Little Princes appear on the tails of the squadron's Mirages. Paris's chief gardener has bred a blue rose that bears Saint-Exupéry's name; in 1987 Soviet astronomers named an asteroid—one large enough to accommodate more than a few sheep—in his honor.* Saint-Exupéry, the Little Prince, and the boa digesting the elephant now appear on the fifty-franc note. The work has been adapted several times for both the screen and television; stage productions proliferate; songs have been written in its honor; *The Little Prince* even had its moment as a Broadway musical. The book has proved Saint-Exupéry's most popular and enduring work, even if—as a classic of flight—it survives on a shelf alongside *Mary Poppins*, *Peter Pan*, and *The Wizard of Oz*.

Saint-Exupéry himself has been less well-served, not only by those who point to his sales figures in France—he is among Gallimard's best-selling authors—and argue that his largest audience is among those studying at vocational schools. Particularly in light of his death his myth has been cultivated at the expense of the man; survived by nearly everyone he

---

* The asteroid Saint-Exupéry, twelve miles in diameter, orbits between Mars and Jupiter, about 280 million miles from the sun.

knew, he has been buried under decades of eulogies. Some like him there, where they consider him safe; he is not often allowed to go out with a biographer unchaperoned. His admirers, like his critics, are left to attend not to the man but to the legend. He was a visionary but he was no saint, as he had himself reminded Pélissier in 1943 after the mishap on the stairs, when he felt he had reached the limits of his endurance. His fall from literary grace has been a particularly painful one because he occupied such an uncomfortable seat in the first place. One of his French apologists has explained his maddening offenses along these lines: "He manages to eschew Cartesian thinking, to sidestep the subtlety of our rhetoricians, to rise above our Talmudic taste for criticism—in short, to escape all of our national vices." The independence of mind that cost him so dearly in his lifetime was to continue to undermine him afterward. In the end popular because he speaks to all men, he remains suspect precisely because he is too broad for any category.

Perhaps because he lived so much tangled up in paradox Saint-Exupéry was fated to be misconstrued. He slips through nets, embraces inconsistencies. As a pioneer, he lived in the past; as a man of science, he believed above all in instinct; as a writer, he mistrusted language—and intellectuals. He shied from the trappings and obligations of the aristocratic life while retaining a worldview that was entirely seigneurial. He staked his reputation on the fraternity of men and yet was in his heart an elitist and in his life unclubbable, drafting hymns to discipline and duty while routinely pushing the limits of both. Co-opted by every school in turn—even the existentialists found a use for him—he was at the end of the day claimed by no one. Down to the smallest detail we have fumbled in our attempts to pin him down. The plaque to his memory at Saint-Maurice (plans to convert the château into a Saint-Exupéry museum are only now underway) gives the wrong date for his birth; the plaque on the place Vauban wildly exaggerates his tenure there. His name is spelled incorrectly on the original issue of the fifty-franc note. Doubtless Saint-Exupéry would have forgiven these peccadilloes, almost appropriate given his own clumsiness with a calendar. Others mellowed, too, on his account. In 1959 his name came up at a luncheon when de Gaulle was reminded of a visit he had made to New York during the early years of the war. Sadly the president of the Republic recalled the writer and his stubbornness: "Several years later, we both wound up in Algiers. He tried to make an appointment with me. I thought about it; I said to myself: 'I think after all I'll make him wait a bit.' And, *hélas,* I never saw him. This has caused me tremendous sorrow. The fact is, there are two men in me: the man and the general. Sometimes the man is willing to do something that the general cannot do, not yet, not right away."

Saint-Exupéry would have appreciated the predicament. On the page he could sound every ounce the adventurer but he remained as much the vulnerable, anguished child with the insatiable appetite for understanding as the daring *Übermensch* of legend, as much the cosmic urchin as the desert chieftain. Rarely realistic, never practical, he was as overly human as he was larger than life. He knew well that—as he phrased it in an early draft of *Lettre à un otage*—man blushes, hesitates, doubts, stutters. He romanced his time more than it courted him; especially in the last years of his life he was the last to know the kind of grandeur of which he wrote, the open minds and open spaces conjured by his name. He had a greater experience of failure, of chance, than most who shared his taste for the heroic. On paper he turned this—along with the loose grasp of reality that in his lifetime was known as distraction—to his advantage. He made a virtue of the obstacle; he knew, or discovered, that grandeur lurks in unexpected places. From a decidedly earthbound life he culled the loftier moments and the best of these, with much effort, he committed to the page. The work adds up only to an armful, some of it dated, much of it flawed. But it is all of it rich in spirit: it makes us want to overreach ourselves. It makes us dream.

Afterword

~

On September 7, 1998, a fisherman trawling off the coast of Marseilles plucked a silver identity bracelet from his net. It was pitted and blackened, but a swipe of the thumb revealed the words "Antoine" and "Saint Exupéry." With further scrubbing the New York address of Reynal and Hitchcock emerged, along with Consuelo's name. "The ocean is so vast, and a bracelet so small," exulted the fisherman. "It's a miracle." He had a point. The hulking carcass of an airplane had eluded searchers for years, and yet here a simple piece of jewelry — seemingly too modest even to enclose a male wrist — had risen from the depths. Quietly (and illegally) the fisher man turned his discovery over to a local specialist in underwater explorations. The two agreed that the bracelet would remain their secret. Six weeks of discreet and intensive searching followed. Dives over a vast swath of the Mediterranean located seven shipwrecks — including the remains of a Roman vessel — but turned up no aircraft.

Meanwhile, news of the fisherman's unexpected catch found its way into the newspapers. Vigorously Saint-Exupéry's heirs, the grandchildren of his sister Gabrielle, challenged the authenticity of the bracelet, which was not sent their way. The discovery had hardly been treated in a legitimate fash ion. And the d'Agay family had long opposed any search, which they considered undignified, the more so as Saint-Exupéry's wreck, wherever it was, constituted his burial ground. The best way to ensure that the writer's sun never set was to keep him from being exposed to the light of day. The disap pearance guaranteed the legend; it elevated the author to Earhart/Atlantis status. Some might argue that the mystery was worth its weight in royalties.

While discussions dragged on as to whether or not the bracelet was a counterfeit, a professional diver named Luc Vanrell set to work. He knew the ocean floor off Marseilles well; he had photographed a wreck near the Ile de Riou more than fifteen years earlier, under the impression that he had been surveying the remains of a French or German aircraft. Over the next months he made a diligent study of the Lockheed Lightning. By May 2000 he was able to ascertain that the landing gear bay, hunk of fuselage, and tur bocompressor parts strewn over nearly a half mile of ocean floor, 250 feet below the surface, could belong only to a P-38. Four such aircraft had crashed in the Mediterranean, of which three had already been identified. Vanrell notified the authorities.

Saint-Exupéry had always been a master of poor timing, and he remained one after his death. He had missed the liberation of Paris by a matter of weeks. He had made his way on to the fifty-franc note shortly before the franc was replaced by the euro. He should have known better than to attempt to turn up in 2000; having performed one of the most celebrated vanishing acts in memory, he was unwise to materialize in his centennial year. Death was prosaic, disappearing into thin air anything but. And his myth was at its apogee in 2000. Translated into nearly one hundred languages, *The Little Prince* continued to outsell every book on the planet except the Bible. Little Prince dolls—pillowcases, pens, watches, and notebooks—had landed in giftshops all over the world. The Lyons airport was renamed in the author's honor, as was the street on which he was born.

Everyone who could claim a piece of the legacy did. A plaque went up on the façade of La Grenouille, the successor to a New York restaurant that Saint-Exupéry had frequented. It was now asserted that he had written *The Little Prince* at that East 52nd Street address. (The house in Northport and 240 Central Park South, where he indeed wrote the tale, remain plaqueless.) Consuelo's memoirs were suddenly discovered and published, reworked by a critic. They made for a bestseller. *The Tale of the Rose* offers a wrought account of an impossible life with an impossible man, one who— despite the best intentions in the world—tortured those around him. A portrait of marital bliss was hardly to be expected from the party Saint-Exupéry had informed, "If you're not here I can't think, and if you talk I can't write."

"His inner world was too rich," Conseulo observed of her husband, altogether accurately. The same could have been said of his love life, although in her pages Consuelo desisted from exacting revenge on Madame de B, her chief rival. Madame de B was Nelly de Vogüé, married at the time she had been involved with Saint-Exupéry, and reluctant to be named in print even a half-century later. She had had her say years earlier as Pierre Chevrier, although her letters from Saint-Exupéry have yet to appear, and may well one day reveal more of the man. ("They will not be published until after *you* are dead," she assured this biographer, with relish.) Those pages are currently in the collection of the Bibliothèque Nationale, sealed to readers for the next half century.

Dissimilar through they were, Saint-Exupéry's wife and mistress painted consistent pictures of their subject. Pierre Chevrier tells of Saint-Exupéry forcing Benzedrine down her throat so that she might read his new pages with unflagging attention. What did he do on his first evening with Consuelo? Saint-Exupéry treated his wife-to-be to passages of his first novel, then plied her with sedatives. Small wonder he was not allowed to go out with a biographer unchaperoned. The clumsiness— with both the practical and the emotional worlds—remained constant, if more vivid in Conseulo's description. Her husband could manage to find something over which to trip in the middle of the North African desert. Having already resuscitated him from one near death experience in the Mediterranean, she was by no means pleased when Saint Exupéry had proposed a flight to Saigon. In 1936 she pleaded with him: "Promise me, Tonio, that you won't fly over water or even anything that looks like water. It's silly of me to bother you with my superstitions, but I don't believe water likes you."

~

Three years would elapse before the French government granted permission to dredge up the disintegrating remains that Vanrell had located. In September 2003 they were lifted by crane to the surface, disassembled, and subjected to an acid bath. Quickly enough a stainless steel panel of turbo compressor casing yielded the numbers 2734 - the Lockheed serial number for the aircraft in which Saint Exupéry had taken off from Corsica on July 31, 1944. There was no longer any doubt. The relics reside today in the Musée de l'Air at Le Bourget, along with the identity bracelet, of which the Saint Exupéry family have reluctantly accepted the authenticity. Sixty years after the fact, one mystery about Saint Exupéry's end was resolved at last. He was where he was supposed to be, by no means a given.

What impact does the corroded metal have on the myth? The relics actually resolve little; if you fall from the sky, sooner or later you wind up on earth. The law of gravity was never on trial. The evidence indicates only that Saint Exupéry's P-38 dove vertically, at extremely high speed, and presumably during the return to Corsica, into the ocean. Why he wound up there is and will remain a matter of speculation. There is no reason to believe he was shot down; the wreckage bears no sign of bullet holes. Nor is there any reason to believe he did himself in. While nothing about the discovery of the aircraft will discourage those who read a death wish into *The Little Prince*, there is no evidence either to further their cause. All that can be said is that that crash hardly qualifies as unexpected, following as it did Saint-Exupéry's catalogue of close calls. Any one of his 1944 missions could have been his last.

The myth does yield a little to the martyr; human error, or inattention, or sheer bad luck plainly played a role. Can the legend survive if Saint-Exupéry's fate and the Little Prince's no longer coincide? That book reads differently today, at last restored to what it was in its author's lifetime: a work of fiction. It has too long been asked to carry a heavy load. We do not expect P. L. Travers to have been swept off by the west wind, or C. S. Lewis to have dissolved into the arms of Aslan. The debris on the ocean floor reminds us that Saint-Exupéry did not vanish into his pages. While its discovery strips away a level of mystery, it also enhances the text. Once again *The Little Prince* is a slim volume that conjures not with the riddle of the author's death, but with the hefty ones that so befuddled him in his lifetime.

August 2005

Acknowledgments

~

A great number of people contributed in a great number of ways to this project. No one has been more helpful than the National Air and Space Museum's R. E. G. Davies, whom I initially sought out for his expertise in airline history and who turned out to be a polymath and a grammarian of the first rank, in short the best friend a writer could have. His additions to the manuscript have been invaluable, as have his deletions from it. I doubt I have taught him anything but dearly hope I amused him a little. I stand as well in debt to the prodigious research conducted by Jean Lasserre and Colonel Edmond Petit of the French aviation journal *Icare*, whose twenty years of documentation often proved difficult to better.

Those interviewed for this volume are too numerous to thank individually but I am indebted to each of them and hope they will accept this collective mention of my gratitude. Many of them are thanked in the notes for their contributions. I should also like to offer collective thanks to the members of the American 23rd Photo Reconnaissance Squadron, who were forced to endure my endless queries. They may all blame Captain Sylvester Bernstein and Colonel John S. Masterson, who passed on their names. For memories, insights, documents of all kinds, and suggestions for further research I am particularly grateful to: Raoul Aglion, Max Alder, Sergeant Richard L. Andrews, Annabella, Paul Barthe-Dejean, Maximilian Becker, Royce Becker, Jean Bénech, Robert and Mary Evans Boname, Pierre and Dorothy Brodin, Anthony Cave Brown, Guillemette de Bure, Pierre Chevrier, Jean-Marie Conty, Aleta Daley, Elizabeth Reynal Darbee, Colonel Frank Dunn, Colonel Raymond Duriez, Colonel Jean Dutertre, Marius Fabre, Stephen Freeman, Norman T. Gates, General René Gavoille, Françoise Giroud, Madeleine Goisot, Colonel Leon Gray, Colonel André Henry, Henry Hyde, Colonel Jean Israël, Colonel Alain Jourdan, Ormonde de Kay, Nikos and Laurie Kefalidis, Mary S. Lovell, Fernand Marty, Anne Morrow Lindbergh, Tex McCrary, Yvonne Michel, Colonel Edmond Petit, John Phillips, Silvia Reinhardt, Alain Renoir, Colonel Vernon V. Robison, Selden Rodman, Anne Roque, Richard de Roussy de Sales, Ysatis de Saint-Simon, Henri-Jean de Saussine, Howard Scherry, Arnaud de Ségogne, Dr. Sheldon Sommers, Hedda Sterne, Bikou de Lanux Strong, Joseph Tandet, Robert Tenger, Dorothy Barclay Thompson, Jacques Tiné, P. L. Travers, Claude Werth, and Helen Wolff.

Saint-Exupéry was a gypsy, which puts his biographer at a considerable disadvantage. As he had no fixed address he had no top desk drawer; the clue-rich clutter of a life barely existed for him. That which did has been dispersed throughout the world. He was in the habit of entrusting his papers to the women in his life: many of these pages have survived, though not all of them can be located and the largest portion of those that can are not available to a biographer. For documents of all kinds I am therefore especially grateful to the following individuals, institutions, libraries, and their staffs: The Académie Nationale de l'Air et de l'Espace in Toulouse, where Martine Ségur could not have been more welcoming; the Air Force Historical Research Agency, Maxwell Air Force Base; the Smithsonian Institution's Archives of American Art; the Archives Nationales, with a special thanks to Michel Guillot; Françoise Grimmer and the archives of the Association des Amis de Saint-Exupéry in Paris; the Bibliothèque Nationale and its superbly helpful staff at the Versailles annex; the Rare Book and Manuscript Library, Columbia University; the Bibliothèque Litéraire Jacques Doucet; the French Cultural Services in New York; the French Institute in New York; Lilly Library at Indiana University and its assistant curator of manuscripts, Rebecca Campbell Cape; the McGill University Library; the Bibliothèque Municipale de Montréal; the Musée Air France; the Musée de la Poste; the Archives Division of the National Air and Space Museum in Washington; the National Archives, where I leaned heavily on John Taylor and Ken Schlessinger; the New York Public Library; the Pierpont Morgan Library, where I owe special debts to Robert E. Parks and to Dr. Ruth Kraemer, who kindly allowed me an early look at her transcription of the manuscript of *The Little Prince*; the Harry Ransom Humanities Research Center at the University of Texas, Austin; the Service Historique de l'Armée de l'Air in Vincennes and its director, General Lucien Robineau; the University of Alberta Library; Brigitte J. Kueppers at the Arts Library Special Collections, University of California, Los Angeles; Ned Comstock at the Cinema and Television Library, University of Southern California; and the Westmount Public Library in Montreal, which quietly houses what may well be the best collection of Franco-American books in North America.

Special thanks must go to Frédéric d'Agay, Saint-Exupéry's great-nephew, for permission to quote from Saint-Exupéry's unpublished work. I badgered him shamelessly with queries throughout the long course of this project. I should like to express my appreciation to Harcourt Brace as well for having shared with me documents from the Reynal & Hitchcock archives and for allowing me permission to quote from them in the text.

Karen Weller-Watson at Harcourt was also unfailingly generous with her time when she had no reason to be.

I have leaned very heavily on my friends and family in writing this book and owe a variety of huge personal debts, chief among them to Nancy Barr, Susan Bergholz, Emmanuel Breguet, Walter Bode, David Colbert, François Cornu, Mary Deschamps, Harry Frankfurt, Mitchell Katz, Elinor Lipman, Maclab Enterprises, Dona Munker, Clarita Puyaoan, Mort and Ellen Schiff, Geri Thoma, Andrea Versenyi, and Meg Wolitzer. The New York University Biography Seminar provided spiritual and intellectual sustenance. I cannot help but thank Apple Computers, over whose wizardry I marveled every day.

For the early enthusiasm of Ashbel Green, my Knopf editor, I am very grateful, as I am to Carmen Callil and Jonathan Burnham. Also at Knopf, Jenny McPhee and Jennifer Bernstein adroitly shepherded this book through the production process. Marc de La Bruyère has proved a model of several rare qualities, none of which was more appreciated in the long course of this project than his unfailing savoir-faire. He read these pages with fierce attention while his home life collapsed around him. Without the constant ministrations of the most extraordinary of literary agents, Lois Wallace, the pieces of that life would have been impossible to fit back together again. Pétain complained that he was called only in a crisis; Lois did not, and kindly refrained from pointing out that the situation at hand rarely ever constituted one.

Notes

~

Notes for primary sources follow, keyed to the first few words of each quotation. (A selected list of secondary sources can be found in the Bibliography, page 511.) There is no central repository of Saint-Exupéry's texts. Several typescripts have made their way into the collection of the Bibliothèque Nationale; an early manuscript of *The Little Prince* remains in New York, at the Pierpont Morgan Library; the drafts and proofs of *Lettre à un otage* can be found at the Smithsonian's Archives of American Art. Saint-Exupéry's letters to his family, published and unpublished, are conserved at the Archives Nationales in Paris. Madame de B has retained her correspondence, which no researcher has yet consulted. Most of the rest of Saint-Exupéry's correspondence remains either in the hands of the families of his correspondents or has found its way—via auction houses—into private collections around the world.

Saint-Exupéry appears throughout the notes as SE. His texts, and the collections in which his papers or essential documents concerning him can be found, have been abbreviated as follows:

LSM	*Lettres à sa mère* (Paris: Gallimard, 1984)
LJ	*Lettres de jeunesse* (Paris: Gallimard, 1953)
SM	*Southern Mail* (New York: Harcourt Brace Jovanovich, 1971)
NF	*Night Flight* (from *Airman's Odyssey*, New York: Harcourt Brace Jovanovich, 1984)
WSS	*Wind, Sand and Stars* (from *Airman's Odyssey*, New York: Harcourt Brace Jovanovich, 1984)
FA	*Flight to Arras* (from *Airman's Odyssey*, New York: Harcourt Brace Jovanovich, 1984)
LP	*The Little Prince* (New York: Harcourt Brace Jovanovich, 1971)
OTAGE	*Lettre à un otage* (Paris: Gallimard Pléiade, 1959)
CITAD	*The Wisdom of the Sands* (Chicago: University of Chicago, 1979)
CARNETS	*Carnets* (Paris: Gallimard, 1975)
EG	*Écrits de guerre, 1939–1944* (Paris: Gallimard, 1982)
SLV	*Un sens à la vie* (Paris: Gallimard, 1956)
AAA	Archives of American Art, Smithsonian Institution, Washington, D.C.
ANAT	Archives Nationales, Paris
BL	Rare Book and Manuscript Library (Butler), Columbia University, New York
BN	Bibliothèque Nationale, Paris
ML	Pierpont Morgan Library, New York
NA	National Archives, Washington, D.C.

QO   Archives of the Ministère des Affaires Étrangères. Quai d'Orsay, Paris
SHAA   French air force files, Service Historique de l'Armée de l'Air, Vincennes

All of Saint-Exupéry's books appear in their published translations unless noted. Translations of *Lettre à un otage*, Saint-Exupéry's letters, and the journalistic pieces are the
author's, except where noted.

INTRODUCTION

i x   forty-four sunsets: Inexplicably, forty-three sunsets in the French edition.
  x   his wedding date: He got it wrong on a 1937 Air France information sheet, now in
      the archives of the Musée Air France.
x i   "*un beau nom*": Quoted in Jean Escot. *Icare* 69. Summer 1974 (hereafter *Icare* I). 111.
      "Is he one of the saints": See Anne Morrow Lindbergh. *War Within and Without* (New
      York: Harcourt Brace Javanovich, 1980). 122.

I A KING OF INFINITE SPACE

3   "I have never": OTAGE, 392.
    his worldly possessions: LSM, 125.
4   "the most desolate": Jean-Gérard Fleury, "Antoine de Saint-Exupéry," *Pour la victoire*,
    August 4, 1945. Generally Fleury's rank among the supreme descriptions of the glory
    days of the airline. See especially *La Ligne* (Rio de Janeiro: Atlantica Editora, 1942).
    "tragic solitude," "strange silhouettes," and "Did you really": Joseph Kessel, *Vent de
    sable*, Les Éditions de France, Paris, 1959, 149–50.
    "had so much an impression": Jean Mermoz's 1927 letter to his grandparents is
    reproduced in Jean Mermoz, *Mes vols*, Flammarion, Paris, 1957, 49–50.
    "1,000 kilometers": SE's letter to Lucie-Marie Decour was published, along with
    several others, as "Lettres intimes d'Antoine de Saint-Exupéry à une jeune fille," *Le
    Figaro Littéraire*, July 8, 1950, 1. The pioneering description of the Río de Oro appears
    in G. Louis, "Casa-Dakar à bord d'un avion postal," *Les Reportages de "La Vigie
    Marocaine*," May 1923, 1–24. I am grateful to Marie-Vincente Latécoère for having
    provided additional archival accounts of the early days of the airline. A fine, detailed
    history of the Río de Oro is to be found in John Mercer, *The Spanish Sahara* (London:
    Allen & Unwin, 1976). I have relied as well on John Gretton, *The Western Sahara*
    (London: Anti-Slavery Society, 1976).
5   "secret language" and "read the anger": WSS, 84.
6   "We had created": Quoted in Jean-Gérard Fleury, *La Ligne*, 170.
    "The ability to come crashing": Louis Blériot, in Claude Grahame-White and Harry
    Harper, *The Aeroplane: Past, Present, and Future* (London: T. Werner Laurie, 1911),
    205.
    Lindbergh commented on fog and sleet in *We* (New York: G. P. Putnam's Sons, 1928),
    176.
    SE to his brother-in-law, LSM, 180.
    SE on the Moors' poor aim, cited in Jean-Gérard Fleury, *Chemins du ciel* (Paris:
    Nouvelles Éditions Latines, 1955), 41.
7   "to set off to the rescue": Didier Daurat, "Saint-Exupéry Pionnier de la Ligne," *Le
    Figaro Littéraire*, July 31, 1954.

8 ··The bearers of water": From SE's preface to José Le Boucher, *Le destin de Joseph-Marie Le Brix* (Paris: Nouvelle Librairie Française, 1932).

"Don't put 'Count' ": Reproduced in *Icare* 37, Spring 1966, 10.

··a little bit our Queen": Jean-René Lefèbvre, cited in Claude Mossé, *Mécano de Saint-Ex*, Éditions Ramsay, Paris, 1984, 119.

9 ··I have turned out": LSM, 164.

··a constant need": Unpublished letter to Charles Brun, evidently a former professor of SE's, from the SE family archives. The postmark is blurred but the letter appears to have been mailed on March 31, 1927.

··a superficial, chattering": LSM, 164.

··a marriageable man": LSM, 171.

"*un beau gigolo*" and "I wish I were": LJ, 94.

"Mickey-Mouse nose": General L.-M. Chassin, "Souvenirs sur Saint-Ex," *Forces Aériennes Françaises*, April 1959, 537. Chassin described SE's looks many times but never strayed far from this description.

10 "I am delighted": From SE's correspondence with Lucie-Marie Decour, *Le Figaro Littéraire*, July 8, 1950.

"When my engine coughs": SE family archives, from the Charles Brun letter, op. cit., presumably March 31, 1927.

··a heavy-footed explorer": SM, 22.

··barriers of breeding": Lindbergh, *War Within and Without*, 442.

··when in France": to Decour, *Le Figaro Littéraire*, July 8, 1950.

"You're engaged": SE's letter to Charles Sallès is included in *Cahiers Saint-Exupéry I*, Association des Amis de Saint-Exupéry, ed., Gallimard, Paris, 1980, 25–27.

··It is my role": LSM, 187.

11 ··Frankly it's sweet": LJ, 121.

··tasted of the forbidden": Sallès letter in *Cahiers Saint-Exupéry I*, op. cit., 26.

··goodness, his rectitude": Didier Daurat, *Miroir de l'histoire*, June 1962.

··great white dervish": Didier Daurat, *Saint-Exupéry tel que je l'ai connu*, Dynamo, Liège, 1954, 7.

12 "Captain of the Birds": LSM, 191.

··strangely dressed": Marcel Migeo, *Henri Guillaumet* (Paris: B. Arthaud, 1949), 99.

··Say hello": Jean-Gérard Fleury goes on at length about Toto in *La Ligne*, 100–101. See also Migeo's *Guillaumet*, op. cit. For additional details regarding Toto and about Juby in general I am indebted to Marius Fabre, whose letters of February 6, April 9, and October 4, 1992, dispense with whole chapters of legend.

··locks and bolts": Migeo, *Guillaumet*, op. cit., 63.

Henri Delaunay's account of the Juby evening is from *L'Araignée du soir* (Paris: Éditions France-Empire, 1968), 68ff., and is reprinted in *Icare* I, 150–53.

13 "Our nearest neighbors": SM, 4.

··We are as much strangers": To Decour, *Le Figaro Littéraire*, July 8, 1950.

14 ··Let me describe": ibid.

··There is a silence": OTAGE, 394.

··it was impossible": Henri Delaunay, from *L'Araignée du soir*, reprinted in *Cahiers* I, 35.

"By virtue of what": ibid., 31–32.

··The mail is sacred": SE quoted in Richard Rumbold and Lady Margaret Stewart, *The Winged Life* (London: Weidenfeld & Nicolson, 1953), 33.

··Anyone who has": OTAGE, 394.

15 "like opera lights": LSM, 187. SE described the canned foods and the early evening to Decour, op. cit.

15 "That's a lot": In LSM, 189, the line is quoted as *"Enfin c'est toujours ça."* The original, ANAT, looks more like *"Enfin c'est long ça."*
"chicks" and "I ready myself ": Decour, op. cit.
Only SE's account of the February trip to Casablanca survives, ANAT.
On SE's reading habits, Léon Werth, from his catalogue preface to the Bibliothèque Nationale's Saint-Exupéry exhibition, Paris, 1954, and Suzanne de Verneilh, unidentified clipping of July 31, 1950, Association des Amis de Saint-Exupéry archives. On his reading list, LSM, 193.
"He did not actually": Suzanne de Verneilh, ibid.
16 On Gide and Fernandez, LSM, 191.
"interior world": Edmond Jaloux, *Les Nouvelles Littéraires*, July 6, 1929.
better left unpublished: In the 1940s it was not unusual for SE to cross *Southern Mail* out in the front matter of the copies of the books he dedicated. In 1941 he told a reporter he had written a novel before *Night Flight* and "wished he hadn't": Otis Ferguson, *Common Sense*, May 1941, 131.
Joseph Kessel's (possibly imaginative) re-creation of the readings is from *Mermoz* (Paris: Gallimard, 1938), 119–21.
Conty's recollection of the reading: Interview with author, January 5, 1991.
"But you've already": *France-Amérique*, March 9, 1952, 10.
17 Lola's appetite for CS: Fleury, *La Ligne*, 104.
"Is it good?" and the conversation with Guillaumet, Migeo, *Guillaumet*, 87.
"You eat greens": WSS, 93.
"The children play" and the rest of the account of Bark to "golden slippers" is drawn from WSS, 99–107. Additional details come from Didier Daurat's confidential note of August 18, 1928, to the Paris Latécoère office (Musée Air France, D39), in which Daurat makes much of the Spanish mismanagement of their territory, as well as from Kessel, op. cit., 140.
19 "We were sending": SM, 80.
20 "a salad" and the mechanic's-eye view of the mishap to "happy as a child" are René Lefèbvre's, from Mossé, 192–200. SE's version, WSS, 26–27.
21 "We unloaded": WSS, 27. The original *Paris-Soir* account appeared on November 10, 1938.
22 "Covering himself" and "The North Star": Mossé, 198–99.
"a little nothing": LSM, 194.
23 "At times like these": LSM, 194.
"I have never": LSM, 196.
SE's caravan rescue became the stuff of lore; among others, Fleury (*La Ligne*) and Kessel (*Vent de sable*) reported on it. His official report, on which I have relied heavily, is dated August 1, 1928, and reproduced in *Icare* I, 175ff.
25 "I folded this paper," "technically perfect," and "Don't reproach me": SE's private report to Tête, July 26, 1928, quoted by Raymond Vanier in *Icare* I, 175.
"Saint-Exupéry was never": Lefèbvre, from Mossé, 121.
26 The best account of SE's rogue rescue attempt is that of Paul Nubalde, *Icare* I, 184.
27 "irregular conduct": Quoted in Pierre Chevrier, *Antoine de Saint-Exupéry* (Paris: Gallimard, 1949), 62.
"who had been carried away": Archives of the Musée Air France, D39.
"where one politely": LSM, 196.
28 "It may be": LSM, 196.
"Two Spanish planes": Albert Tête's official report, quoted in *Icare* I, op. cit., 181.
"One does not pacify": SE's report on the Río de Oro is reproduced in its entirety in René Delange, *La vie de Saint-Exupéry* (Paris: Éditions du Seuil, 1949), 189–99.

"with a lifting motion": Otis Ferguson, *Common Sense*, May 1941, 132. Ferguson's little-known piece provides one of the supreme portraits of SE the awkward, unwilling celebrity.

29   "I am decidedly": LSM, 198.
       "where 200 men": LSM, 192.
30   "is more mysterious": LSM, 208.
       "Somewhere there was a park": WSS, 65. SE first published this account under the title "Un Mirage" in the Surrealist journal *Minotaure*, Winter 1935, 19.

II THE MOTHER COUNTRY

32   For the histories of the Saint-Exupéry and Boyer de Fonscolombe families I am tremendously grateful to Frédéric d'Agay.
       In one of the rare lines: EG, 584.
       "marvelous gaiety": From an interview conducted by Helen Elizabeth Crane with Amici de Saint-Exupéry Churchill, included in Crane, *L'Humanisme dans l'oeuvre de Saint-Exupéry* (Evanston, Ill.: Principia Press, 1957), 245.
33   For SE's birth certificate I am again indebted to Frédéric d'Agay, who also provided information on the birth dates of Saint-Exupéry's siblings and on the château of Saint-Maurice and the Château de La Mole. I am grateful as well to Maggy Herzog, from the Caisse des Écoles de la ville de Lyons, for having graciously shown me around Saint-Maurice-de-Rémens. Simone de Saint-Exupéry wrote more on the Saint-Maurice years than did any of her siblings, including her better-known brother; Frédéric d'Agay kindly shared her unpublished manuscript, *Cinq enfants dans un parc*. I have relied heavily on her descriptions of her brother's antics. On Madame de Saint-Exupéry, see also Olga Baget, "Marie de Saint-Exupéry," *Les cahiers bourbonnais*, 2ème trimestre, 1978.
       The family was no sooner complete: *La Croix du Littoral*, March 20, 1904.
34   a very private anxiety: In 1923 SE wrote his mother (ANAT) that—in light of heredity—he felt he had best submit to a Wassermann test before what he thought were to be his imminent nuptials. A close friend who has asked not to be identified confided in an interview on December 4, 1991, that SE submitted to these tests regularly and repeatedly insisted on SE's obsession with the subject. SE also told that friend that he should like to have a child with a desert woman, whom he would not worry about infecting with the syphilis of which he feared he was a carrier; he knew that venereal syphilis (actually bejel) was prevalent in North Africa.
35   "He followed me": Cited in Françoise de Quercize, "Saint-Exupéry raconté par les témoins de sa vie," *Marie-France*, May 1965, 129. SE makes mention of the little green chair himself in LSM, 128.
       from the age of six: SE, "Books I Remember," *Harper's Bazaar*, April 1941, 82.
       accomplished *metteurs en scène*: From Crane's interview with Charlotte Churchill, *L'Humanisme dans l'oeuvre de Saint-Exupéry*, 250.
       "When you are awakened": Cited in Quercize, *Marie-France*, May 1965, 129.
       "Enough, Tonio": Simone de Saint-Exupéry, "Antoine, Mon Frère," *Lettres Françaises*, December 12, 1963, 3.
36   "Antoine is extraordinarily": From Simone de Saint-Exupéry's unpublished *Cinq enfants dans un parc*.
       "The bizarre object": Simone de Saint-Exupéry, *Icare* I, 59.
       to take to the air: Odette de Sinéty, "Quand Saint-Exupéry jouait au Petit-Prince dans la Sarthe," *Le Maine Libre*, July 29, 1982.

36 "You would say": WSS, 66. For Simone's version, in which her brother more accurately
    tortures the housekeeper with his tales, see *Cinq enfants dans un parc.*
    A village child: Annette Flamand described her childhood memories of SE to Howard
    Scherry, who kindly lent me a tape of their conversation of July 18, 1989.

37 On the succession of SE family pets, see Simone de Saint-Exupéry, *Lettres Françaises*,
    December 12, 1963, and Simone de Saint-Exupéry, *Les Nouvelles Littéraires*, July 29,
    1954.
    "He often asked me": *Cahiers Saint-Exupéry II*, Association des Amis de Saint-
    Exupéry, Gallimard, 1981, 37.
    His appetite seemed: Chevrier, 2.

38 The story of the offending green beans comes from a conversation with Madame de
    B, January 22, 1991.
    refused the job: Simone de Saint-Exupéry's "Antoine mon frère" in *Saint-Exupéry*
    (Paris: Hachette, 1963), 59.
    "an infinite gentleness" and "He was a first-rate devil": From Crane's interview with
    Amici de Saint-Exupéry Churchill, Crane, 243.
    "Mother, you leaned": LSM, 209.
    "Antoine was talented": Mme. de Saint-Exupéry noted that Simone in fact appeared
    the most intellectual of her children in her interview with Crane, op. cit., 240.

39 "profound musical ambiance" and "The house resonated": From André de Fonsco-
    lombe's recollections of his cousin's childhood home in *Cahiers de l'Aéro-Club de
    France*, June 1991, 20–21; also in an interview with the author, January 21, 1991.
    "What a family": LSM, 201.
    "What? This man": Marie de Saint-Exupéry, *J'écoute chanter mon arbre*, Gallimard,
    Paris, 1967, 39.
    "She sent delightful": From Crane's interview with Alix Churchill, Crane, 246.
    The visit with the Countess du Mesnil du Buisson was written up by her son, R. du
    Mesnil du Buisson: "Antoine de Saint-Exupéry au pays d'Argentan," *Le Pays d'Ar-
    gentan*, September 1955, 75–77.

40 "a respect for the real" and "As in truth": Chevrier, 16.
    "noisy, vulgar": Simone de Saint-Exupéry, *Cinq enfants dans un parc.*
    "My two brothers": Simone de Saint-Exupéry, *Lettres Françaises*, December 12,
    1965, 3.
    SE's recollections of his uncle Hubert can be found in FA, 344–45.

41 "Both, being from the South": Crane interview with Charlotte Churchill, Crane, 250.
    "was like the reign": Mme. de Saint-Exupéry, cited in Chevrier, 25.
    "I have lived": LP, 5 (translation mine). As an adult SE was to remark, "*J'ai une
    famille qui est tout à fait végétative*" (interview with a friend who has asked not to be
    identified, December 17, 1991), although it should be said that any family—in fact
    the very concept of family—would have seemed "vegetative" to SE.
    "The life of Antoine": Simone de SE, *Lettres Françaises*, December 12, 1963, 1.
    "house without secrets": WSS, 70–71.

42 "When we were ten": CS, 94.
    "It is of you I think": ANAT.
    "What taught me": LSM, 209.
    "Once you are a man": FA, 380.
    "like the tides": FA, 345.

43 "the little stove": LSM, 208.
    "You must be like": SE to Consuelo, 1939–40, ANAT.
    "This world of childhood" and "I am not sure": LSM, 208–209.

"There is one thing": I am grateful to Jean Bénech for having shared with me the writings of his father, Captain Pierre Bénech, who remembered this incident.

III THINGS IN HEAVEN AND EARTH

44 A vestige of Le Mans: I am inestimably grateful to Frédéric d'Agay for this observation (disputed by some) and for much of the background regarding SE's paternal grandfather.
Mont Saint-Barthélmy: Mme. de Saint-Exupéry told her son's first biographer, Pierre Chevrier, of this early education, of which no record exists.
"Tatane": For this nickname and a sense of Notre-Dame-de-Sainte-Croix I have relied heavily on the recollections of Jean-Marie Lelièvre, *Icare* I, 73–77. SE's academic record comes from the school.
45 "in no way": Simone de Saint-Exupéry, in *Saint-Exupéry* (Hachette), op. cit., 58.
"incapable of sitting": Chevrier, 22.
"dreamy and meditative": Letter from the Abbé Vérité to Crane, published in Crane, op. cit., 255.
"off in space": Again, the descriptions are from Lelièvre, *Icare* I, 73–77.
On Solesmes, LSM, 37.
46 "he made us read": Lelièvre never forgot the reception that greeted "Odyssey of a Hat." See *Icare* I, op. cit., 74.
"lived in peace and quiet" and all other quotations from "Odyssey of a Hat": SE's early masterpiece has been reproduced frequently. It can most easily be found in Crane, op. cit., 257–58 (translation mine).
47 "Far too many spelling": 1984 Archives Nationales exhibit catalogue, 5.
"for his escape": LP, 38.
"wrote poems, tragedies" to "more or less like a bear": Odette de Sinéty's recollections of the courtship are from *Le Maine Libre*, op. cit., July 29, 1982. I am grateful to Roland de Belabre for having shared SE's poetic tributes to his aunt.
48 "hands as dirty" and the general report on SE's clumsiness: Lelièvre in *Icare* I, op. cit., 73–77.
"He flies!": Curtis Prendergast, *The First Aviators* (New York: Time-Life Books, 1980), 34.
"acrobat" and "four-flusher": Reports of the French press's skepticism about Wright are cited in Fred Howard, *Wilbur and Orville Wright* (New York: Knopf, 1987). Reports of their about-face are cited in Charles H. Gibbs-Smith, *The Aeroplane* (London: Her Majesty's Stationery Office, 1960), 62–63. See also Orville Wright, *How We Invented the Airplane* (New York: David McKay Company, 1953).
"A new era": Blériot is quoted in Howard, 258
"We are beaten": ibid., 262.
49 "You never saw anything": Wilbur Wright to Orville, cited in Howard, 263.
Wilbur Wright's letter to his brother regarding Chanute's Aéro-Club de France speech dates from June 28, 1908 and appears in Marvin W. McFarland, ed., *The Papers of Wilbur and Orville Wright*, II (New York: Arno Press, 1972).
For a sense of the early days of the Aéro-Club de France, and for a general sense of early aviation in France, see Edmond Petit, *La vie quotidienne dans l'aviation de 1900 à 1935* (Paris: Librairie Hachette, 1977).
50 I owe the observation regarding high-quality, small-scale production and the aviation industry to Herrick Chapman, *State Capitalism and Working Class Radicalism in the French Aircraft Industry* (Berkeley: University of California Press, 1991).

50 Both Fred Howard and Tom D. Crouch (*The Bishop's Boys*, Norton, 1989) provide ample accounts of the Wright brothers' difficulty in selling the Flyer. So does Orville Wright in *How We Invented the Airplane*, op. cit.
On Léon Bollée, his generosity, and Wright's need for it in Le Mans, see Howard, op. cit., and *The Papers of Wilbur and Orville Wright*, op. cit. In the latter (page 906) Wilbur confided his difficulties to Chanute, noting that the Le Mans mechanics' grasp of English was "rather more limited than I had hoped to find it." I am grateful as well to Léon Bollée's family for their help with several details.
"almost as much": *The Papers of Wilbur and Orville Wright*, op. cit., 906.
51 On the tourist trade at Auvours, see Howard, op cit.
He wrote Orville: Wilbur's letter of October 4, 1908, is included in *The Papers of Wilbur and Orville Wright*, op. cit.
For more on Blériot, his crashes and his triumphs, see Eric Hodgins and F. Alexander Magoun, *Sky High* (Boston: Little, Brown & Company, 1929), 216–20.
On the Reims air meet: ibid., 219–21.
52 The observation that all airplanes flying today descended from the generation represented in Reims in 1909 is Charles H. Gibbs-Smith's, from *Flight Through the Ages* (New York: Thomas Y. Crowell, 1974), 98.
I am grateful to R. E. G. Davies at the Smithsonian for having provided the Igor Sikorsky information.
On the prize money in 1914: *Sky High*, 235.
53 For all of the information concerning the Wroblewski brothers I am grateful to René Wroblewski.
"Sir, Maman has now": Alfred Thénoz in *Icare* I, 78.
For having gone to extraordinary lengths to straighten out the record regarding SE's first flight every biographer stands indebted to Colonel Edmond Petit and Jean Lasserre, who published their research in *Icare* I, 78–79. I am grateful as well to Howard Scherry for having shared with me his tape of a July 17, 1989, interview with Georges Thibaut, the "younger schoolboy" who introduced SE to the fliers.
"he jumped for joy": From Scherry's interview with Thibaut, op. cit.
"The wings quivered": Quoted in Chevrier, 25.
54 "*mon petit Antoine*": René Wroblewski kindly shared these letters of condolence.
For the information on Guy de Saint-Exupéry, I am again grateful to Frédéric d'Agay.
On SE at Mongré: Crane interviewed Louis Barjon in 1951; see Crane, 262–63.
"Our man was": R. P. Ract, quoted in Crane, 261. P. Solly at Notre-Dame-de-Mongré kindly shared SE's grades with me.
"Of course I was convinced": SE, "Books I Remember," *Harper's Bazaar*, April 1941, 123.
"bad Racine": Maurice Métral, "Saint-Exupéry a été champion d'escrime à Fribourg," *La Femme d'aujourd'hui et patrie Suisse actualités*, Geneva, March 2, 1963.
55 "At school I wrote": I am grateful to Seldon Rodman for having shared with me his record of a lunch with SE in early April 1941, during the course of which the Frenchman—surprised to learn that Leonardo da Vinci's notebooks read from right to left—greeted the news with a demonstration of this early talent.
"Guess what?": Charles Sallès's recollections appear in *Icare* I, 81.

IV LOST HORIZONS

56 "With melancholy": SM, 13.
57 A fine description of the Villa Saint-Jean and its curriculum appears in the catalogue

from the 1984 Saint-Exupéry exhibit at the Archives Nationales in Paris, 6. "Not to be less" to "its worst drawbacks": The school's prospectus is partially reproduced in that catalogue, 6. Also for background on the school: "Le Père de Miscault égrène des souvenirs," *La Liberté* (Fribourg), March 13, 1973, 11.

"I like it here": ANAT.

"It's a helpful subject": LP, 10 (translation mine).

"dutifully with compass" and "From an industrious": FA, 283.

58 "You stiffened": FA, 394.

"flunk like a schoolboy": FA, 395.

"erstwhile sloth": CS, 14.

"Is being a man": CARNETS, 44 (translation mine).

"I felt at once" and "I worshiped Baudelaire": SE, "Books I Remember," *Harper's Bazaar*, op. cit., April 1941, 123.

"Already a great concern": Letter from Abbé Fritsch, reprinted in Crane, op. cit., 266. On SE's athletic prowess, see Métral, *La Femme d'aujourd'hui et patrie Suisse actualités*, op. cit., March 2, 1963.

"tipped over the table": Chevrier, 28.

"Very agile": Cited in Michel Prévost, *Les Nouvelles Littéraires*, August 1, 1946, 1.

59 "left permanent wounds": Léon-Paul Fargue, *Revue de Paris*, September, 1945. Both Bonnevie and Sabran are mentioned frequently in SE's correspondence with his mother and by Simone de Saint-Exupéry in her *Saint-Exupéry* (Hachette) essay, 60–65. For more on Bonnevie, see André Chagny, *Le Lieutenant Louis de Bonnevie* (Lyons: Librairie Pierre Masson, 1930).

"lost his faith": Interview with Madame de B, January 13, 1992. SE said as much in a letter to his mother of 1931, ANAT.

60 On SE and confession, ANAT.

"offering himself up": CS, 66.

"*Maman*, you cannot know," "And I was congratulating," and "And each time": ANAT.

61 SE's suggestion that his mother take a holiday, ANAT.

The statistics regarding the *baccalauréat* are from J.-B. Piobetta, *Le Baccalauréat* (Paris: J.-B. Baillière et fils, 1937), 250–52, and from Theodore Zeldin, *France 1848–1945*, II (London: Oxford University Press, 1977), 269ff. and 841ff.

"I this minute left," as well as SE's description of the stay in Paris for his *bac* are included in his letters to his mother, ANAT.

62 "The body is an old crock" and the remainder of the account of François's death, FA, 388–89.

"remained motionless": LP, 108.

"He reckoned that he had": Unpublished text of a March 17, 1974, interview with Henry de Ségogne, conserved in Edmond Petit's archives at the Association des Amis de Saint-Exupéry, Paris.

"I will do my best": Chevrier, 29.

Simone de Saint-Exupéry wrote of her mother's attempts to distract her brother after François's death in *Cinq enfants dans un parc*. The itinerary can be mapped through his unpublished letters, ANAT, in which figure his impressions of the summer visits. Simone revealed her brother's summer infatuation with Jeanne de Menthon.

63 SE's opinions on the *flottards*, *cyrards*, et. al. can be gleaned from his letters to his mother. ANAT.

"a big guy, very strong," "Saint-Exu," and "A cloud would pass": From Henry de Ségogne's recollections in *Icare* I, 91. Ségogne's observations regarding SE's work habits come from the same text.

64 "I am well": LSM, 48.
65 "an appalling mess": Generally the best descriptions of the drama leading to the writing of the ballad come from Ségogne's published text (*Icare* I, 91–92) or his unpublished interview (archives of the Association des Amis de Saint-Exupéry). The ballad has been reprinted frequently and can be found in its entirety in the catalogue from the 1984 Saint-Exupéry exhibition at the Archives Nationales, 9.
66 "the album, not the binder": LSM, 39. "I don't like rissoles" and *"Antoine propose"*: LSM, 41. The remainder of his requests figure either in his published letters from Paris (LSM, 41ff.) or in the unpublished texts, ANAT. "Shoes—rubbers": LSM, 84.
67 "hugely tender-hearted": Ségogne, unpublished text. "He had a fierce": Ségogne, *Icare* I, 91.
"I will rent": LSM, 46.
The morality report and "oddly enough": LSM, 43.
"I believe I will always": LSM, 52.
68 SE's report on Madame Jordan's brochures, LSM, 56.
"Yvonne is a marvel": ANAT.
69 The "irreproachable" wardrobe and "It was with her": LSM, 53.
On Parisian life during World War I and especially on its gastronomic habits, no book is as delightfully informative as Gabriel Perreux's *La vie quotidienne des civils en France pendant la grande guerre* (Paris: Hachette, 1966). See also William Wiser, *The Crazy Years* (London: Thames & Hudson, 1983).
"Aunt Rose is as ever": LSM, 62.
"All of Paris is painted": ANAT.
70 "witnessed a bit of war," "It was just after," and the plea for chocolate truffles: "Lettre d'un adolescent" published in *Cahiers Saint-Exupéry* I, 15.
On SE's reenactment of the bombing, Simone de Saint-Exupéry in *Cinq enfants dans un parc*, as in most of her other pieces.
71 "very well-seated": ANAT.
On the censors, and "That will put an end alive": LSM, 57.
"What a bunch": LSM, 58.
"The Gothas are back" and "N.B. I am": LSM, 60.
"It's a beautiful evening," "I wish you were," and "Useless to take": LSM, 63.
72 SE's letter to Simone regarding his Besançon schedule belongs to the family archives and was shown to me by Frédéric d'Agay.
SE wrote his mother of his enlistment plans, LSM, 71.
On the hijinks at the Lycée Saint-Louis, see Ségogne, *Icare* I, 92, and unpublished text, Association des Amis de Saint-Exupéry archives.
73 The irony of his having: LSM, 78.
"Grown-ups never question": LP, 16 (translation mine).
"When I'm an engineer": LSM, 86.
On his newfound love of theater, LSM, 82.
74 SE's citation for drawing at Saint-Louis figures in the Archives Nationales 1984 exhibition catalogue, 9.
The École des Beaux-Arts has no record of SE having attended the school. Bernard Lamotte remembered him there, or at least in the neighborhood, *Icare* I, 96.

V   SILVER LININGS

75 For a vivid and lively description of postwar literary Paris, see Noel Riley Fitch, *Sylvia Beach and the Lost Generation* (New York: W. W. Norton, 1983). I have drawn as well

on Marcelle Auclair and Françoise Prévost's *Mémoires à deux voix* (Paris: Editions du Sevil, 1978) and Pierre Assouline's *Gaston Gallimard* (New York: Harcourt Brace Jovanovich, 1988).

76 "He himself must have" to "always a bit awkward": Bernard Lamotte, *Icare* I, 96.

"But . . . what the devil": ANAT.

Theodore Zeldin has suggested that the *bac* failure rate has taken its toll on the French population, in *France 1848–1945*, II, 293.

77 "feed my nascent": ANAT.

"everywhere I come across": LSM, 79–80.

Renée de Saussine recalled SE's toga recitations in "Les miroirs de l'Hôtel Créqui," *Miroir de l'Histoire*, January 1958, 82.

78 "What a magnificent" and on SE's silence: Renée de Saussine in her preface to LJ, 10.

On the Hôtel La Louisiane, Chevrier, 32. Carlos Baker gives a fine idea of Saint-Germain and its prices at this time in *Ernest Hemingway: A Life Story* (New York: Charles Scribner's Sons, 1969).

"well-liked friends": LSM, 80.

79 "the sound of Niagara Falls" and "Why are you being": Yvonne de Lestrange, *Icare* I, 95.

"What I shall be": Jean Escot, "Un grand ami: Saint-Exupéry," undated, unidentified clipping, Association des Amis de Saint-Exupéry archives, 20.

80 SE described his Strasbourg lodgings to his mother, LSM, 94. "An exquisite city" comes from the same letter.

"there is categorically": LSM, 95. In the same letter he lobbied for a motorcycle and wrote of his boredom.

81 For the best account of the training of civilian and military pilots in the 1920s, see Petit, *La vie quotidienne dans l'aviation*, 177. Additional details of these years came from Edmond Petit during a conversation with the author, December 9, 1992.

"I will have a classroom": ANAT. The arrival of the texts—and the requests for money—figure in this correspondence as well.

Asking his mother to take up his case with Captain de Billy, LSM, 97. Asking Gabrielle to do same, LSM, 99.

Robert Aéby wrote up his account of the odd goings-on at the Neuhof field a number of times. The account in *Icare* ("Le complot de Strasbourg," *Icare* I, 98–101) is the most complete, but additional details can be gleaned from his article in *DNA*, April 14, 1973, and that in *La France de l'Est*, January 21, 1936.

82 "rather a pleasant thing": *Icare* I, 99.

"memorable acrobatics sessions": André Huguenet, *Icare* I, 102.

"My senses of space" and "the spins, the loops": LSM, 102.

SE on the friends who took him up and "It holds the air": LSM, 102–103. On the idea of volunteering for Morocco, LSM, 101.

83 "*Maman*, if you only knew": LSM, 104. "It seems to me": ANAT. "I've *thought*": LSM, 106. "I swear to you" and "You told me": LSM, 107.

"I need an occupation": LSM, 107.

On Commander Garde's conditions, see Aéby, who refers to him as Commandant Moser in his *DNA* article but as Garde in his other accounts. "A veritable conspiracy": Aéby, *Icare* I, 98.

"I beg you, Mother": LSM, 107.

The air time figures come from Aéby's records, as SE—piloting clandestinely—had no logbook. Aéby's logbook was in fact confiscated by the Germans in 1940, but he had previously copied out passages from it.

84 On the required hours of training, see Petit, *La vie quotidienne dans l'aviation*, 190. "conservative flying": LSM, 115. In the same letter SE voiced his frustration with the Farman.

85 Aéby recalled the conversation leading up to SE's first solo in *Icare* I, 100. "If you only knew, Madame:" Aéby, *Icare* I, 101.
    SE reported on the ministry's decision, LSM, 114–15.

86 SE's complaints about the heat and "To go *as a pilot*": LSM, 115–16.
    "Where are the banana": ANAT, and cited in the 1984 Archives Nationales exhibition catalogue.
    "When I come across": LSM, 123.
    "You cannot commune": From the original typescript of *Terre des hommes*, BN, microfilm no. 2343.
    "The open-air barrack": LSM, 120.

87 "Still this anguish": LSM, 131. On SE's newfound love of drawing, LSM, 121.
    "Verse, drawing, all that": LSM, 131.
    "Tonight, by the peaceful": LSM, 127–28.
    "I spread out my maps": WSS, 6–7.

88 "You've done everything": LSM, 124.
    "Send me photos": LSM, 125.
    For SE's air time and his itinerary, I am grateful to General Lucien Robineau at SHAA.
    "of the Crusaders": LSM, 134.
    "If you could see me": LSM, 131. On the cold: LSM, 134.
    There is some confusion about Marc Sabran, who is always assumed to be the friend SE lost in 1926. French air force files do reveal the existence of two Sabrans (Marie Charles Emmanuel, born in 1897, and Marie Paul Émile, born in 1890), but neither died in Morocco in 1926. No other branch of the military has any record of a Marc Sabran. SE's letters home allude to a death that seems to have been that of Sabran, of whom he never speaks after 1926; Simone de Saint-Exupéry as well reported in *Saint-Exupéry* (Hachette), 64, that Sabran had died in Morocco at that time.

89 "an appalling school," on the planned resignation, and "mechanical and insipid": LSM, 126.
    "One feels as if": LSM, 127. The descriptions of the stays with Priou: LSM, 126–30.
    "I write you from": LSM, 129.
    "greatness comes first": CARNETS, 66.

90 "I can't complain" and the anticipated return: LSM, 136–37.
    SE told Escot he had done all he could to fail the exam: Escot, *Icare* I, 107. The results of the qualifying exam are reproduced in *Icare* I, 106.
    "Pants too large": Escot in *Icare* I, 105. Louis Noirot remembered choosing his kepi with SE. *Icare* I, 120. SE bragged to Noirot about his Beaux-Arts background. "I didn't like the looks": Noirot, *Icare* I, 117. Emmanuel Breguet at SHAA very patiently fielded my questions about the early days of French military aviation.

91 "a surprising density of occupation": The phrase is Jean Leleu's, from his portrait of SE in *Icare* no. 30bis, Summer 1964 (hereafter *Icare*), 54.
    "I am writing": LSM, 140.

92 "Then I will marry," "hard and bitter man," and the request for money: LSM, 140. if his mother's telegram": Louis Noirot reported on SE's habit of borrowing funds, *Icare* I, 117. Maximilian Becker gave him high marks for repaying his loans in a conversation with the author, November 8, 1991.

94 it is important to all that came: In all air force appraisals of his talent, SE was deemed a gifted and intelligent pilot. "*Excellent pilote, ayant le feu sacré*," reads one report of

1924; "*très consciencieux, excellente tenue et bon esprit militaire,*" reads another. "*Très bon pilote fin et précis ayant beaucoup de cran. . . . Apte à rendre les meilleurs services. Bel espoir, beau service,*" read a report filed after an April 1926 training period. Dossier IP 6678, SHAA.

VI WALKING ON AIR

95 "I wonder what there is": From Curtis Cate's splendidly researched *Antoine de Saint-Exupéry* (New York: Paragon House, 1990), 68.
96 "At the very top": Ségogne, unpublished interview, op. cit.
SE on the three Americans and "I don't need her": LSM, 142–43.
97 "to foster among," "frugal bursar," "Grand Poète": Henri-Jean de Saussine very kindly provided me with a copy of the GB Club's hilarious charter.
the magic of her childhood: Jean Chalon, *Florence et Louise les magnifiques* (Paris: Éditions du Rocher, 1987), 131.
98 "You spend your days": ibid., 140.
"The queen of Italy" and "There was once": ibid., 138.
"The magician of our adolescence": Louise de Vilmorin, "Antoine de Saint-Exupéry, *Carrefour*, August 26, 1944, 4.
"a tamed sprite": Chalon, 116.
"They wanted to marry me": Quoted in Jean Bothorel, *Louise, ou la vie de Louise de Vilmorin* (Paris: Grasset, 1993), 64.
an heirloom string of pearls: The story of Louise and the ill-fated necklace can be reconstructed from SE's unpublished letters at ANAT.
99 "If Louise loved him": André de Vilmorin, *Essai sur Louise de Vilmorin* (Paris: Pierre Seghers, 1962), 35–36.
The report of SE's accident appeared in *Le Figaro*, May 2, 1923, 3. Additional details concerning the accident are drawn from Lt. Col. Delafond's reports of May 1, 1923, and May 11, 1923, Air Force files, SHAA.
"I beg your forgiveness": ANAT.
"lieutenant Saint-Escupéry": Charles Sallès in *Icare* I, 82.
100 "his too-lively interest" and "Made to be a fighter": Air Force files, SHAA.
"There is nothing": ANAT.
"general staff ": Cocteau, cited in Vilmorin, *Essai*, 47.
101 "vague pachyderm": Cited in Eric Deschodt, *Saint-Exupéry* (Paris: Lattès, 1980), 62.
in light of his upcoming nuptials: ANAT. He thought only of Louise: SE to his mother, ANAT ("*Je ne pense qu'à Loulou,*" he reported). "I've been trying": ANAT. The jointly written letters are conserved at ANAT as well.
"He describes for me" and the rest of Louise's description of the Reconvilier trip—including "Secretly, we manage" and "Like all the youth"—come from "Fièvre Promenade," *Marie-Claire*, October 1955, 107–11.
102 "My wife's opinion": ANAT. SE was explaining to his mother why he was staying in Paris with Louise, at her suggestion, and not coming to Saint-Maurice.
"diplomatic calls": ANAT.
"The practical side" and "Your impoverished son": ANAT.
103 "Nothing satisfies Antoine": Louise de Vilmorin, "Antoine de Saint-Exupéry," *Carrefour*, August 26, 1944, 4. Renée de Saussine nearly repeated the same words, to Quercize, *Marie-France*, op. cit., May 1965, 251.
brother-of-the-bride: An especially fine photograph of the October wedding is reproduced in *Icare* 1, 67.

103   He was aware: SE's apology is articulated most fully in the correspondence at ANAT. It figures in part in LSM, 144–45.
104   "clear things up" and SE begging for silence on the matter of the broken engagement: ANAT. The taxi incident is here as well. Marcelle Auclair saw SE just after this near-encounter with Louise and found him pale and shaken, *Mémoires à deux voix*, 179.
      "I shall love you": Cited in Chalon, 136.
      "I have no faith": Louise de Vilmorin, *Carnets* (Paris: Gallimard, 1970), 12.
      "Oh, Loulou": Quoted in Vilmorin, *Essai*, 37.
      "What I need": Cited in Bothorel, 65.
105   "*Ne m'oubliez pas trop*": Ibid., 47.
      "I should so much like": Vilmorin, *Essai*, 39.
      her father-in-law's home: Frank Wright of the Nevada State Museum and Historical Society provided invaluable details on the Hunts and on Las Vegas in the 1920s.
      "She knew the sesame": SM, 36.
      "She was a woman": Chalon, 129. "Marilyn Malraux": Chalon, 131. "Her union": Chalon, 156. Louise confided the names of her great loves to Chalon, 142.
106   "frail child": SM, 27. "underwater fairy": SM, 30.
      golden-haired sister: It was Simone who speculated as much, in *Cinq enfants dans un parc*.
      "heavy-footed explorer": SM, 22. "light-footed as the moon": SM, 30.
      "a habit of fortune" and "the 1,000 objects": SM, 50.
107   "It was as if I had": SM, 103.
      "The day dawns": WSS, 74; translation mine.
      "the smile of superiority": Anaïs Nin, *Paris Revisited* (Santa Barbara, Calif.: Capra Press. 1972), 7.
      "Love me": Cited in Chalon, 162.
      "in which no action": Cited in Vilmorin, *Essai*, 36.
108   "retain the light imprint": SM, 117.
      "I wasn't made": LSM, 153.
      "I've tried every trick" and "It is precisely": Letter to Charles Sallès, reprinted in *Icare* I, 88.
      "like an evening gown": Cited in LJ, 15.
109   "You would laugh to see me": LSM, 149.
      "*douce intimité*": LSM, 150.
      "Like a broken heart": Sallès letter, *Icare* I, 88.
      "When I am rich": LSM, 160.
      On Saint-Maurice, its sale, and SE's financial burdens: ANAT.
110   "I will probably get to be": ANAT.
      "I am the most discouraged": Sallès, *Icare* I, 89.
      On the Titania: Mme. Sautour kindly showed me around the hotel and verified the dates of SE's stay. The writer occupied what is today room no. 75.
      "Let me go first" and "Leave me the bigger": Escot, *Icare* 1, 114.
      shirt collars from his socks: LSM, 155.
      "It will be my first joy": LSM, 152.
      no two joys resemble each other: LJ, 37.
111   "*Je me porte*": ANAT.
      "*refaire son trousseau*": LSM, 156.
112   "special rates": SM, 60.
      "*une cure de silence*": LJ, 53. Also in a letter to Ségogne reproduced in the 1984 Archives Nationales exhibition catalogue, 67.
      "The I-haven't-the-foggiest," "Midnight sharp," "The twentieth century," "because

it was nighttime," "the day after yesterday," "I don't give," and "The annual client": A fine selection of Escot's letters is reproduced in *Icare* I, 112–14.

113   "What a responsibility" and "full of little": Sallès, *Icare* I, 88.

"*sous-préfet*'s ball": LJ, 43. Also, LSM, 166.

"I set my hat down": LJ, 45.

"My life is empty": From a 1925 letter to Marie-Madeleine de Saint-Exupéry, reproduced in the Archives Nationales exhibition catalogue, 17.

114   an aristocrat-salesman: The point is made by Jesse R. Pitts, *In Search of France* (Cambridge: Harvard University Press, 1963), 244–49.

"Customers are selfish," "Don't even bother," and "Here lies the last": Escot letters in *Icare* 1, 112–14.

The average Saurer salesman: Or so reported Louise Regner in an interview with the author, November 18, 1991. It was Mlle. Regner who was to remember SE—with some consternation—as a different breed of salesman.

115   "After so long": SM, 21.

"like an explorer": LSM, 168.

"I don't like people": ANAT.

"You must forgive me": LSM, 165.

"The more intimate the feeling": ANAT.

116   "One needs to learn": LJ, 35.

"One needs to live:" LJ, 22.

"*Métaphysique de concierge:*" Renée de Saussine recalled the line and the incident in a radio interview broadcast on France-Culture, July 30, 1974.

"concerned themselves overly": LSM, 157.

"I have never loved anything": ANAT.

"Café society" and "I like people:" LJ, 69–70.

117   "the obstacle": SE, *Oeuvres* (Paris: Gallimard Pléiade, 1959), 139. Hereafter cited as *Pléiade*.

"*Mozart assassiné*": *Pléiade*, 261.

"I cannot live": ANAT.

VII   FRIENDS IN HIGH PLACES

119   Hemingway on shortchanging Prévost: Fitch, 145. After 45 seconds, Baker, 145.

"Go sit in back": Michel Prévost, *Les Nouvelles Littéraires*, August 1, 1946, 1.

120   "I met him through friends": Prévost's editorial note appears at the end of "L'Aviateur," *Le Navire d'Argent*, April 1926, 287.

121   "Dear Sir: I regret": Auclair and Prévost, *Mémoires à deux voix*, 177.

"an aviation and mechanical expert": *Le Navire d'Argent*, April 1926, 287.

"who flies like a pig": ibid., 284. "Shut down": ibid., 285. "*Ils font un métier*": ibid., 282.

123   "is wholly contained": Guéhenno cited in Herbert R. Lottman, *The Left Bank* (Boston: Houghton Mifflin, 1982), 9.

"*l'esprit NRF*": Pierre Assouline, *Gaston Gallimard* (New York: Harcourt Brace Jovanovich, 1988), 24.

124   General Édouard Barès: For many details concerning the general's position and responsibilities I am grateful to his son, José Barès. Barès's inscribed copy of *Wind, Sand and Stars* belongs today to the Musée Air France.

like a dance card: The CAF flights appear in SE's early logbook, a copy of which is conserved in the archives of the Association des Amis de Saint-Exupéry.

124 "Madame, let me": Quoted in Deschodt, 75.
125 SE complained to Escot: Escot, "Un grand ami: Saint-Exupéry," op. cit., 20.
"with sadness and humiliation": Cited in Richard McDougall, *The Very Rich Hours of Adrienne Monnier* (New York: Charles Scribner's Sons, 1976), 196. See also Adrienne Monnier, *Les Gazettes d'Adrienne Monnier, 1925–45* (Paris: Julliard, 1953), 49.
"this perpetually temporary life" and "*beaucoup de petits*": LSM, 16. Only ever met one woman: LSM, 161.
"That's what one needs": LSM, 168.
126 "unreal little existence": This letter—which SE had written to Diomède Catroux in early 1944—was published for the first time in *Le Monde*, July 29, 1950. The line in full reads: "*J'éprouve un vague malaise à vivre ces nuits hors du temps, parmi cette végétation parasite; ces gens me font l'effet de champignons qui, greffés sur un arbre qu'ils ignorent, poursuivent avec candeur leur cruelle petite existence.*"
"All my friends get married": Decour, *Le Figaro Littéraire*, July 8, 1950.
The qualifications: LSM, 162.
"You are not the first": Anne Roque and Arnaud de Ségogne kindly shared this letter to their father.
Lucie-Marie Decour: Jean-Marie Scapini described to me the history of his mother's relationship with SE.
127 "*trop aventuré mon coeur*": From a letter to Ségogne, reproduced in part in the 1984 Archives Nationales exhibition catalogue, 67.
"Drearily I court" and "waiting rooms": LSM, 162.
The publication touted: Cited in Theodore Zeldin, *France 1848–1945*, I (London: Oxford University Press, 1973), 99.
128 "this tall young man": Beppo de Massimi, *Vent debout* (Paris: Plon, 1949), 296. Massimi's memoirs are invaluable in reconstructing the circumstances of SE's arrival at Latécoère.
"And then?" and the conversation that follows. Massimi, 296–98.
"I'm not a very nice": LJ, 75.
129 On October 11: Latécoère's letter is reproduced in part in Chevrier, 46.
130 "People write every day": Cited in Deschodt, 108.
Daurat noted in his memoirs: Didier Daurat, *Dans le vent des hélices* (Paris: Seuil, 1956). Daurat's accounts of these events are legion but offer up little to no variation.
"possessed a clear moral": Didier Daurat, *Saint-Exupéry tel que je l'ai connu* (Liège: Éditions Dynamo, 1954), 7. See also Daurat, "Saint-Exupéry, pionnier de La Ligne," *Le Figaro Littéraire*, July 31, 1954, 1.
131 "You should take the boat!": From the text of a lecture given by Daurat at the Cercle des Transports, Paris, April 18, 1958, 18.
"Massimi referred him": Mossé, 117. Lefèbvre was remembering a conversation he had had with Daurat in 1967, more than forty years after the events in question.
132 "I learned that any delay": *Marianne*, October 26, 1932, 2. (The translation is from *Living Age*, January 1933, 425.)
"armor of pride": Didier Daurat, "Souvenirs sur Saint-Exupéry," *Historia*, July 1964, 52.
"without brio": ibid., 53.
133 a book floating, and "Are you sick?": Léon Antoine, *Icare* I, 147.
"like skeptics lost": Fleury, *La Ligne*, 44.
"When I joined": *Marianne*, October 26, 1932, 2.
Along with two additional restaurants: Marius Fabre, Jean Macaigne, and Jean-Marie Conty generously supplemented the written accounts of the early days in Toulouse with their recollections.

134 "But, on the other hand": Fabre letter to author, October 4, 1992.
"manifested the imperious": LJ, 92.
135 "One is who one is": LSM, 165.
"*Mermoz défriche*": Quoted in Marcel Moré, *J'ai vécu l'épopée de l'Aéropostale* (Paris: Éditions de l'Aéropole, 1980), 69.
136 He said: "You leave": WSS, 4–5. "It's easier" and "Guillaumet did not teach": WSS, 6–7.
137 reprimand the countryside: LJ, 133–34.
"Little by little": WSS, 7.
"*à l'oeil et à la fesse*": The apt comment is mechanic Marius Fabre's, from a conversation with the author, January 23, 1991.
138 "Late in the night": Daurat, *Icare* 1, 136.
In an interview: Daurat confided as much in Edmond-Marie Dupuis during a recorded interview in Dupuis's Paris apartment, December 6, 1978.
"I am immensely fond": LJ, 102.
"I alone was in the confidence": WSS, 8. "wrapped in the aura," "smelled of the dust," and "their dreary diurnal": WSS, 9. "the birth within him": WSS, 10. "Old bureaucrat": WSS, 12.
140 Daurat's copy: A copy of SE's inscription can be found in the archives of the Association des Amis de Saint-Exupéry, Paris.
"a knight of the Holy Grail": Jules Roy, *Saint-Exupéry* (Paris: La Manufacture, 1990), 43.
"Don't forget that imagination": Petit, *La vie quotidienne dans l'aviation*, 194.
"The proprietor and the waiter": To Decour, op. cit., 1.
141 "little provincial path": LJ, 110.
fear of habit: LJ, 114.
"Would you call" and "It doesn't mean": WSS, 11.
"where dates ripen": LJ, 119.
"Monsieur . . . the plane": Raymond Vanier, *Tout pour la Ligne* (Paris: Éditions France-Empire, 1960), 135.

VIII THE SWIFT COMPLETION OF THEIR APPOINTED ROUNDS

142 an ambitious young industrialist: The best source of information on Pierre-Georges Latécoère is Emmanuel Chadeau's *Latécoère* (Paris: Olivier Orban, 1990).
143 "I've reworked": Chadeau, 99. Beppo de Massimi's memoirs make for invaluable reading here: *Vent debout*, op. cit.
144 "It's a handkerchief": Fleury, *La Ligne*, 10.
"That didn't go": ibid., 10.
Less than a month later: For the most scientific overview of the airline's early days see Raymond Danel's two-volume history: *Les Lignes Latécoère 1918–1927* (Toulouse: Éditions Privat, 1986) and *L'Aéropostale 1927–1933* (Toulouse: Éditions Privat, 1989). Fleury's, Massimi's, and Daurat's accounts are equally invaluable but anecdotal.
145 "We have a fair amount": Afrique 1918–1940, file no. 361, report from the French ambassador in Spain to the minister of foreign affairs, Madrid, May 26, 1928, QO.
SE's trip to Timbuktu: London *Times*, January 23, 1937, 14.
"a series of forays": Chadeau, 182.
146 the company's annual report: I am grateful to R. E. G. Davies at the Smithsonian Institution for having opened his extraordinary archives, which include a copy of the Latécoère 1927 annual report.

146   "It's hardly worth": LJ, 142.
147   crowded history of early aviation: For overviews of these years I have consulted a great number of texts. Generally the voices of Gibbs-Smith and R. E. G. Davies ring loudest.
148   "You apply for the right": LJ, 134.
      "took the opportunity": Decour, op. cit.
      On another occasion: LJ, 118.
      fear, he was to say later: From an unpublished interview with Gaston and Raymond Gallimard, conducted for *Icare*, archives of the Association des Amis de Saint-Exupéry, n.d.
149   Just before he left: LSM, 171.
      "I was startled": WSS, 76–77. Supplementary details are drawn from SE's original account of the incident, *Marianne*, November 2, 1932.
      "a handsome crash": 1984 Archives National exhibit catalogue, 68.
150   *"baptême de solitude"*: *Marianne*, November 2, 1932.
      "Sitting on the dune," "You weren't frightened?" and "I said no": WSS, 78–79.
      "The trip went well": LSM, 172.
      gauge its accuracy: Fleury sums up the evening in only one line, *La Ligne*, 99.
151   In one account: The sergeant weeps in SE's description of the evening in *Paris-Soir*, November 14, 1938. The first published account of the Nouakchott evening is that in *Marianne*, November 2, 1932.
      "all present": WSS, 80.
      "We went to sleep": Reproduced in Archives Nationales exhibit catalogue, 68.
      the incident found its way: The account of the Nouakchott visit differs greatly—more so than any of the rest of the text—in the excerpt from SM that appeared in the *NRF* (May 1, 1929) and in the final text of the novel. The WSS account comes directly from the November 1932 *Marianne* article. SE made an additional reference to the evening in a piece of Russian journalism for *Paris-Soir*, May 14, 1935.
      "Are you the Sergeant" and the remainder of Bernis's story: CS, 110–12.
152   "Our hostess shows us": BN, manuscript microfilm no. 2543.
153   "It is a little lonely" and "It is also lonely": LPP, 72.
      SE complained: ANAT, and very eloquently in the letter to Sallès reproduced in *Cahiers* I, 21–22, as in the letter to Brun in the d'Agay family archives.
      Noëlle Guillaumet never forgot: See "L'album de Noëlle Henri Guillaumet," in *Icare* 37, Spring 1966, unpaginated. On reading Plato: Werth (who did not know him at the time), *Icare* (Summer 1964), 92.
      "those little village": Sallès letter, *Cahiers* I, 22.
      "Everything is here": To Brun, op. cit.
154   "I have a little parcel": Cited in Chevrier, 49. Similarly, LJ, 128.
      in a letter to Sallès: *Cahiers* I, op. cit.
      "I know that I am": To Brun, op. cit.
      "Sometimes I think" and "I wonder what": To Decour, op. cit., 5.
155   he wrote his brother-in-law: LSM, 183.
      He dreamed: To Decour, op. cit. Similarly LJ, 133.
      "The world would not lose": LJ, 127.
      "It's hogwash": To Decour, op. cit., 5.
      "I don't even know": ibid.
      "a touch of anger": SE supplied his description of courage in a letter to Yvonne de Lestrange, from which Gide quoted in his preface to NF, 6.
156   "Good aircraft" and "Look here, Lefèbvre": Lefèbvre recalled the incident in Mossé, op. cit., 120–22.
      "Flying an airplane": ibid., 123.

"Once you have learned": William T. Piper, "Plain Facts About Private Planes," *The Pocket Atlantic*, 1946. 19.

157 One went so far: See Léon Antoine, *Icare* I, 147–48. Fabre corroborated the statement in a conversation with the author, January 23, 1991.

"How is it possible": Anne Morrow Lindbergh reviewing WSS in the *Saturday Review*, October 14, 1939, 8–9. "the frozen glitter": SE, WSS, 117.

158 "there is no fraternity": *Journal de Moscou*, May 23, 1935, 15.

excerpt from *Vent de sable*: The excerpt appeared in *Le Figaro Littéraire* on November 30, 1929. For a sense of the legend that had begun to flourish around SE, see Yves Courrière, *Joseph Kessel* (Paris: Plon, 1985).

Cendrars admitted: *Confluences*, Vols. 12–14, Paris, 1947, 54.

two distinct individuals: Joseph Kessel, "Portrait de Saint-Exupéry, *Gringoire*, January 10, 1936.

160 "this big, rough-hewn devil," "on behalf of the civilian," and "clumsiness and his lively": From General Lionel-Max Chassin's account in *Icare* I, 188–90.

as Daurat had also observed: Daurat in *Le Figaro Littéraire*, July 31, 1954.

161 "not much fun": ANAT.

In a melancholic mood: My thanks to Anne Roque and Arnaud de Ségogne for having shared this letter to their father of May 1929.

was quick to note: Ch.-Yves Peslin, "Antoine de Saint-Exupéry à Brest," *Les Cahiers de l'Iroise*, no. 1, 1975, 25–26.

162 His Parisian cousin: Honoré d'Estienne d'Orves fought in the Resistance and did not survive the war. Entries from his journal were reprinted in *Biblio*, March 1955. See also Rose and Philippe Honoré d'Estienne d'Orves, *Honoré d'Estienne d'Orves* (Paris: Éditions France-Empire, 1990).

"My publisher, who is also": André Beucler, *Les instants de Giraudoux* (Geneva: Éditions du Milieu du Monde, 1948), 14.

Gaston Gallimard's roommate: Beucler, *De Saint-Pétersbourg à Saint-Germain* (Paris: NRF, 1980), 102–105.

"Saint-Exupéry is not a writer": From Beucler's preface to the original edition of CS (the preface was omitted in subsequent editions), i.

"He seemed to hold": From an unpublished interview with Beucler, conducted by Madame Castillon du Perron, 2.

163 "Give me the name": Chassin, *Icare* I, 190.

"superb blonde": Verneilh, op. cit.

the eminent Edmond: *Les Nouvelles Littéraires*, July 6, 1929.

164 "the music-lover," and "*pour avoir à exprimer*": Henri Delaunay, *Araignée du soir*, op. cit. These pages are reprinted in *Cahiers Saint-Exupéry* III (Paris: Gallimard, 1989), 30–31.

165 "bad businessmen": Noëlle Guillaumet in *Icare*, Spring 1966, unpaginated.

IX TOWARD THE COUNTRY WHERE THE STONES FLY

166 "No one was around": Decour, 5.

167 He reported that: ibid.

"You'll be more comfortable": Cited in Fleury, *La Ligne*, op. cit., 218.

168 the Great Pyramid: LJ, 139.

Buenos Aires in 1929: For facts and figures pertaining to the development of Buenos Aires I have relied especially on Charles S. Sargent, *The Spatial Evolution of Greater Buenos Aires* (Tempe: Arizona State University, Center for Latin American Studies,

1974), J. A. Hammerton, *The Real Argentine* (New York: Dodd, Mead & Company, 1916), and R.M. Albérès, *Argentina* (Paris: Hachette, 1957).

168   "a giant slab": Cited in Chevrier, 75.

"the world's most prodigious": Hammerton, 37.

So disenchanted was Le Corbusier: The architect is quoted in Sargent, 91.

169   like a set for Charlie Chaplin's: "Escales de Patagonie," *Marianne*, November 30, 1932. dented, he wrote later: WSS, 45.

"gratifying revenge": ANAT.

"succeeded not so badly": Cited in Chevrier, 76.

170   The photograph of the October 29, 1929, banquet figures in the collection of the Archivo General de la Nación Argentina.

171   The speed limit: Fleury, *La Ligne*, 218–19.

172   landing was another ordeal: The best description of this odd exercise figures in Paul Vachet's *Avant les jets* (Paris: Hachette, 1964), 185–90. Jean-Marie Conty recalled SE's description in an interview with the author, January 15, 1991.

173   SE and the cyclone: *Marianne*, August 16, 1939, and WSS, 44–57. "I was a man who": WSS, 48. "I had been spat": WSS, 50.

Later, too, he was to say: Conty interview of January 15, 1991.

174   "I climbed out": WSS, 56.

"Yet, in passing over": Charles Darwin, quoted in W. H. Hudson, *Idle Days in Patagonia* (London: J.M. Dent & Sons, 1924), 205.

"in which one traded": "Escales de Patagonie," *Marianne*, November 30, 1932, 7.

"Imagine," he wrote: "Princesses d'Argentine," *Marianne*, December 14, 1932, 2.

175   "We will come to fetch": ibid.

"Nowhere have I encountered" and "Arrived to build": *Marianne*, November 30, 1932, 7.

"Ambition, jealousy, honor": ibid. The leper made a huge impression on SE, who was still writing of him ten years later, in *Citadelle*.

"a town born of": WSS, 60.

176   "these men who, accustomed": LSM, 210.

"as if from a cracked": "Une Planète," *NRF*, April 1, 1933, 584.

Madame Guillaumet's tales: See *Icare*, 29, and *Icare* II, 34.

In a piece he wrote later: "La Fin de l'Émeraude," *Marianne*, January 24, 1934, 1.

177   "the delta of the Nile": Albérès, 90.

He reported having covered, LSM, 210. On writing in midair: Jean Macaigne recalled this habit of his colleague's in an interview, January 4, 1991.

178   "But you're sick" and "We would have got": Raoul Roubes, *Icare* I, 215.

179   "to play the fool": ibid.

"second by second": LJ, 139.

"one of the most remarkably": Hammerton, 131.

Now that he had bought himself: SE complained to Renée de Saussine of the weight of his possessions, LJ, 138.

Later SE was to write: Introduction to *Terre des hommes*, Pléiade, 139. The four-paragraph introduction does not figure in the English-language edition of the text.

180   Rosamond Lehmann and "tribe": LSM, 208.

"a friend of time" and the description of the Fuchses: *Marianne*, December 14, 1932, and repolished for WSS, 70–71.

"I would be so incapable": LSM, 211.

"You vaguely hold": Decour, 5.

181   "an engagement with an elsewhere": Breyten Breytenbach, "The Long March from Hearth to Heart," *Harper's*, May 1991, 12.

One gets ambushed by it and "And it gets no better": LSM, 212. The unabridged version of this revealing letter is at ANAT, as are SE's enraged missives to his mother. "Listen to this": Paul Dony, "Saint-Exupéry: Jeux littéraires et souvenirs," *Vie et langage*, November, 1958, 563. All of the descriptions of SE's South American word games are taken from this fine article.

182   *"Je recommence la littérature"*: Dony, 565.

"I began out of a love": Joseph Kessel, "Saint-Ex," *Paris-Soir*, May 27, 1939, 6.

"The Argentines are crazy": Fleury, *La Ligne*, 259.

"demonstrated a remarkable": The citation is reproduced in the Archives Nationales exhibition catalogue, 46.

183   SE flew the Laté 28: Danel reported on the incident in *L'Aéropostale*, 57; Dony remembered its fallout with a chuckle, 568. For Bouilloux-Lafont's version of the events I am grateful to Guillemette de Bure, who dove into her archives to produce her grandfather's handwritten notes from the Río Gallegos trip.

184   AIRCRAFT ACCIDENT: Jean Brijon, "Avec ceux de la ligne historique France-Amérique du Sud," *Philatélie*, February 1972, 47.

The French ambassadorial staff: The background on Lindbergh's promotion to Commander of the Légion d'Honneur can be gleaned from *Amérique 1918–1940*, file no. 124 (aviation), QO. The suggestion that Lindbergh be elevated so as to reinforce *"les bonnes relations"* was put forth on October 13, 1930, and okayed a week later.

185   The plane was immediately: Fleury, *La Ligne*, 239–49; also Daurat, *Dans le vent des hélices*, 134–35. Daurat includes Guillaumet's official report of June 26, 135–38, which appeared in expanded form in *Le Figaro Littéraire*, June 11, 1949, 1–4. "I leave to my readers": ibid. SE's account: WSS, 28–38, by way of *L'Intransigeant* ("L'aventure pathétique de Guillaumet"), April 3, 1937, 1–3.

"My last thought": The complete text of Guillaumet's message is preserved in photos of the overturned airplane, *Icare* II, 48.

186   "My wife, if she": WSS, 33 (translation mine).

"What saves a man": WSS, 35.

"Guillaumet is saved!" Lefèbvre, *Icare* II, 48 (though in no other of his accounts).

187   "without a doubt": Lefèbvre in Mossé, 221.

"was splotched and swollen": WSS, 32.

"They're from joy": Fleury, *La Ligne*, 247.

"I swear that what": WSS, 36. Lefèbvre in Mossé, 221.

"Yo soy l'aviador": Guillaumet, *Le Figaro Littéraire*, June 11, 1949, 4.

"I'm Mrs. Markham": Mary S. Lovell, *Straight on Till Morning: The Biography of Beryl Markham* (London: Hutchinson, 1987), 175.

"Which way is Ireland?": Charles Lindbergh, *We*, 222.

188   "It's obscenely late": Noëlle Guillaumet, *Icare* II, 35.

189   "I shall never": André Gide, *The Journals of André Gide*, III (New York: Alfred A. Knopf, 1949), 158. The entry is dated March 31, 1931.

190   There is no reason to think: It has been suggested that Crémieux and Consuelo were intimate at this time although no evidence supports this claim. For more on Crémieux, see A. Eustis, *Trois Critiques de la NRF* (Paris: Nouvelles Éditions Debresse, 1961). A native of Guatemala City: For more on Gómez Carrillo see Charles A. Solé, ed., *Latin American Writers* (New York: Charles Scribner's Sons, 1989), vol. II, 465–69; Julio Cesar Anzueto, *Enrique Gómez Carrillo* (Guatemala City: Universidad de San Carlos de Guatemala, 1968); Amilcar Echeverría, *La Obra de Enrique Gómez Carrillo y su Protección en la Literatura Hispanoamerica* (Guatemala City: Guatemalan Cultural Services, 1974); and Gómez Carrillo's own *Treinta Años de Mi Vida*, vol. II (Buenos Aires: La Casa Vaccaro, 1919), in which Maeterlinck's homage can be found.

191 On hearing this story: Robert Tenger in an interview with the author, January 19, 1991.
"I know why" to "You're not ugly": Consuelo's variations are as legion as her reports of the courtship, but these details—from *Icare* II, 25—generally remain constant. See also Rumbold and Stewart, who were able to interview Consuelo, 112–13.

192 "Your husband, if you consent": Interview with Madeleine Goisot, January 2, 1992. Sometimes the line read *"Votre fiancé, si vous . . ."*, as in *Icare* II, 26.
ceremoniously worded reprimand: The note is reproduced in Chevrier, 81.
From July to September: For a sense of Renée de Saussine's whereabouts I am indebted to Henri-Jean de Saussine and to Howard Scherry, who passed on press clippings from her concerts abroad.
He tended to sidle up: The description is from Lewis Galantière. "Antoine de Saint-Exupéry," *The Atlantic*, April 1947, 133–46. Galantière's ranks among the premier descriptions of SE.

193 "The Count de Saint-Exupéry": cited in Deschodt, 202.
"frail, young, gentle persons": Galantière, *The Atlantic*, April 1947, 138.
"who scorned both": Werth, "Tel Quel," in René Delange, *La Vie de Saint-Exupéry* (Paris: Seuil, 1948), 159.
"little eternity": Cited in Bothorel, 47. The passage, which SE would have written in 1929, reads: *"Je suis toujours un peu un étranger sans patrie. C'est sans doute pourquoi je parais timide. J'aimerais qu'une femme me dise: 'tu vas entrer dans cette petite éternité qui est enfermée dans mon village ou dans mon parc. C'est ça une patrie. Et vivre là où les choses ont un sens durable.' Mais je me sens fugitif et je n'ai su aimer qu'une femme. . . ."*

194 Her son had seemed: SE blew hot and cold about the visit, ANAT.
SE had the time: Dony, 568–69. The account of the trip to Asunción is also Dony's, 569.

195 The abandoned French hangars: Eve Curie, *Journey Among Warriors* (Garden City, N.Y.: Doubleday Doran & Company, 1943), 9–10.

X BRIGHTNESS FALLS

196 Evidently she thought it: I owe this portrait of Consuelo to her niece, Ysatis de Saint-Simon, interview of December 2, 1990.

197 At the same time he: Yvonne de Lestrange, *Icare* I, 95.
"Greatly enjoyed seeing": Gide, *The Journals of André Gide*, III, 158–59.
"When will you finally marry?: Consuelo in *Icare* II, 29.

198 "done in by political": Mermoz cited in Danel, *L'Aéropostale*, 178.
"belle aventure" and *"l'ère de l'administration"*: Gaston Vedel, *Le pilote oublié* (Paris: Gallimard, 1976), 166.

199 never forgot the reception: Fleury, "Saint-Exupéry, l'aviateur du désert," *Candide*, January 9, 1936.

200 SE painted a particularly vivid picture of Port-Étienne in an early draft of WSS, BN, microfilm no. 2343.
Once, having been advised: Jacques Mortane, *L'Air*, Smithsonian Institution file on Saint-Exupéry, n.d.

201 The preserved Néri-SE correspondence: *Icare* II, Winter 1974, 71, 57–59. "I told you to write" to "In my opinion": ibid.
"slipped beyond the confines": WSS, 15.

SE dreams of the breakfast: He dreams in these words in his *Paris-Soir* account, November 9, 1938, and in slightly less elaborate form in WSS, 16.

"would not, incorruptible": WSS, 16. "The old flirt": *Marianne*, October 26, 1932, 2.

"All's well": WSS, 17 (translation mine).

202 "I find," he sighed: Mortane, *L'Air*, n.d. See also SE's wistful report from the 1934 airshow, "Le 14ème salon de l'aviation," *Marianne*, November 21, 1934.

"You're going to set" to "Acknowledge, what's going on?": The incident was related anonymously in *Présence des Retraités d'Air France*, April 1973.

203 he could be more nervous: Noëlle Guillaumet, *Icare* II, 38.

Evidently SE spent and "*ministrou*": Néri, *Icare* II, 52–53.

"Come live with me": Ader Picard Tajan auction catalogue, July 6, 1984, Drouot sale, item no. 1.

204 down to the last detail: Fleury, *Icare* II, 73.

their next bottle of Cinzano: Léon Antoine, *Icare* I, 48.

"I have come down": Henri Comte recalled the incident in *Icare*, 96, Spring 1991 (hereafter *Icare* III), 59.

205 "I have never forgotten": Henri Jeanson, *70 ans d'adolescence* (Paris: Stock, 1971), 225. Most of the pages concerning SE have been reprinted in *Icare* III, 74–83.

"will relegate all novels": André Thérive, *Le Matin*, December 11, 1931.

"It is not a novel": *Les Nouvelles Littéraires*, October 24, 1931, 3.

"the man of the century": Yvonne Sarcey, *Les Annales politiques et littéraires*, December 15, 1931, 520. Madame Sarcey shared with her readers the logic behind the Fémina jury's deliberations.

206 "the service of the mails" and "Those are the orders": NF, 25.

"If only you punish": NF, 24.

"Am I just or unjust?": NF, 41.

"a Jack London superman": Henry Miller, *Letters to Anaïs Nin* (New York: G. P. Putnam's Sons, 1965), 28. Miller's enthusiasm for SE did not wane; thirteen years later he wrote Nin to say he thought FA a magnificent achievement.

In Hollywood: I am grateful to Ned Comstock at the Cinema and Television Library at the University of Southern California for having supplied numerous documents from the MGM Collection, including the enthusiastic August 11, 1932, reader's report on the property.

"Not one of the peasants": NF, 65.

207 "By virtue of what emotion": Delaunay, *L'Araignée du soir*, 90.

"The mail." SE had concluded: Rumbold and Stewart, 33.

from his fictional counterpart: Daurat went so far as to title a chapter of *Dans le vent des hélices* "Je ne suis pas Rivière."

in search of a blessing: Interview with Madame de B. January 17, 1992.

"On what does our salvation": *Cahiers* II, 32–34.

208 "as a divine hand": NF, 46.

mechanic at San Antonio Oeste: Decendit recalled the incident in *Icare* I, 211–12.

"talismans to open doors": NF, 30.

"All his long life": NF, 31.

airing of his grievance: Georges Pélissier, *Les cinq visages de Saint-Exupéry* (Paris: Flammarion, 1951), 129.

209 "another theory of life": NF, 64.

210 "And before I was through": Cate, 237.

"Usually considered" and "the action takes place": *Harper's Bazaar*, April 1941, 123.

One critic counted: André-A. Devaux, "Un devoir plus grand que celui d'aimer," *Cahiers* I, 86.

210 "an enduring modern classic": *Commonweal*, November 30, 1932, 17.
"modern courage": André Maurois, *Saturday Review*, August 13, 1932.
"For the first time": Louis Kronenberger, *The New York Times Book Review*, August 14, 1932, 7.

211 in the running for the Prix Goncourt: *Les Annales politiques et littéraires*, December 1, 1931.
Mermoz sent: James Milhaud kindly provided a copy of this cable.
The 1931 Fémina laureate: The description is from André Dubourdieu, *Forces Aériennes Françaises*, 34, July 1949, 444.
"If a friend approached": Chevrier, 98.
While one newpaper: *L'Ami du Peuple*, December 5, 1931.
another noted that: Maurice Bourdet, "Notre Aviation," *Le Petit Parisien*, December 10, 1931.

212 he told Yvonne de Lestrange: Lestrange, *Icare* I, 95.
"I'll never be able to find" to "Must one then be": *Les Annales politiques et littéraires*, 97, December 15, 1931, 534. SE may have protested a little too fiercely. He wrote up the Néri episode four times in all, more and less ornately. In 1932 he spoke of being lost in interplanetary space, *"parmi cent étoiles en trompe-l'oeil, à la recherche de la seule planète véritable."* ("Among 100 stars painted in trompe-l'oeil, in search of the only real planet.") If the image was indeed born over the Río de Oro in 1931 SE evidently considered it too literary for future accounts, in which it does not appear. In most other respects the story—wholly mature in WSS—became more image-heavy as it aged.
"an afternoon stroll": *Marianne*, October 26, 1932, 2.

214 "fat green mosquito": Mireille d'Agay, *Icare* 75, Winter 1975 (hereafter *Icare* III), 20–21.
"You should see your name": Didier Daurat quoted in Petit, *La vie quotidienne dans l'aviation*, 194.
"For having written": Reproduced in Yvette Guy, *Saint-Exupéry* (Monaco: Éditions Les Flots Bleus, 1958), 99.

215 "You don't know": *Icare* II, 41.
In an interview on the twenty-seventh and "Infamies!": Papers of Raoul Dautry, 307 AP 92, ANAT.
SE said he spoke: From a letter of February 20, 1933, from SE to Daurat, reproduced in full in *Dans le vent des hélices*, 175–77.
"he has obvious failings": Mermoz, *Mes vols*, 108.

216 "The most insignificant": SE to Dautry, October 31, 1932, reproduced in part in the 1984 Archives Nationales exhibition catalogue, 60–61. The original resides at ANAT, 307 AP 92.
"like lost chicks": ANAT. In the same letter SE protested that the Château de La Mole by no means qualified as a family seat, as was clearly the opinion of his mother's brother, SE's Uncle Emmanuel.
According to a letter: Reproduced in Chevrier, 99.
He was short even with, and "*Maman*, the more I've": ANAT. The letter is one of the few in which SE entirely loses his patience with his mother.

217 the rental and ultimately the sale: My thanks to Mireille Massot for having scoured the archives of the city of Nice and thereby put to rest the misapprehension that the Cimiez home was sold in 1932.

218 "Although there is": The *Marianne* piece of October 26, 1932, was reprinted in *The Living Age*, January 1933, in a translation I have only slightly reworked here.

219 "This seemed to me," "in a brutal and painful," "But it seems to me," and "the petty grudges": SE to Dautry, October 31, 1932, ANAT, 307 AP 92.

220 "infinitely regrettable": Dautry's masterfully worded letter is at ANAT (307 AP 92) but is reproduced in part in the 1984 Archives Nationales catalogue, 61.

"a dangerous book": Clifton Fadiman in *The Nation*, September 7, 1932, 135.

"as terrible an exhibition": Pare Lorentz, *Lorentz on Film* (New York: Hopkinson & Blake, 1975), 127.

a hopelessly drunk John Barrymore: For more on the production see Margot Peters, *The House of Barrymore* (New York: Alfred A. Knopf, 1990).

By the time Aéropostale: Danel and R. E. G. Davies, "Marcel Bouilloux-Lafont: Where Is the Glory?," *Air Pictorial*, September 1981, provide the most evenhanded assessments of the demise of Aéropostale and the subsequent birth of Air France. Resurrected, Daurat got his issue of *Icare* (no. 140, 1er trimestre, 1992). A biography of Marcel Bouilloux-Lafont remains, not surprisingly, to be written.

221 "people's ineradicable love": Luigi Barzini, *The Europeans* (New York: Simon & Schuster, 1983), 132.

"*notre vieille propension*": Cited in Barzini, 137.

"the France of the Right": Fleury, *La Ligne*, 255.

"Our country does not": Mermoz quoted in Fleury, *La Ligne*, 269. See also *Mes vols*, 312.

222 "A ship's captain": Mermoz, *Mes vols*, 181.

"It is terribly difficult": SE to Dautry, October 31, 1932, ANAT, or partially reproduced in exhibition catalogue, 60–61.

XI BEYOND THE CALL OF DUTY

223 "Saint-Ex had not an ounce": Jeanson, *70 ans d'adolescence*, 220.

As one colleague observed: Dubourdieu, *Forces Aériennes Françaises*, July 1949, 445.

totaled 33,000 francs: Marie-Vincente Latécoère provided the firm's January 1934 summary of SE's income for the previous year.

224 Louis Marty, the chief: *Icare* II, 67.

"floating above the concerns": Jean Gonord, *Icare* II, 69.

"I know no one" to He wrote that he was most: Cited in Chevrier, 102.

225 On December 21: Gilbert Vergès, one of SE's passengers that day, provided the most reliable account of the mishap, *Icare* II, 70–73.

"In truth, death": Mortane, *L'Air*.

226 "Air and water": WSS, 43–44.

comb through his hair: Or so he told an audience at the Lisbon École Française in December 1940, according to an account published in Crane, op. cit., 281.

How much easier: Unpublished Gallimard interview, op. cit.

he wrote a long and urgent: SE's letter to Foa, dated February 2, 1934, is reproduced in its entirety in Daurat, *Dans le vent des hélices*, 241–44.

"After all I've done" to "*la Ligne* should be": *Dans le vent des hélices*, 242–43.

227 "As you slowly descend": From SE's preface to Maurice Bourdet's *Grandeur et servitude de l'aviation* (Paris: Corrêa, 1933), reproduced in SLV, 243–44. (SLV appeared in slightly different form and in uneven translation in English as *A Sense of Life* [New York: Funk & Wagnalls Company, 1965].)

"collection of parameters": From SE's preface to an anthology on test-piloting compiled by Jean-Marie Conty, reproduced in SLV, 259.

227   In 1934 he applied: Both passports are conserved at ANAT. I was unable to locate
      SE's last passport.
228   "bloody Tuesday": Alexander Werth's *The Twilight of France* (New York: Howard
      Fertig, 1966) and Janet Flanner's *New Yorker* columns of the time were of particular
      help here.
      "I have no taste": SE to Foa, February 2, 1934, in *Dans le vent des hélices*, 242.
229   "an immense difficulty": CARNETS, 25.
      "To sell a man": ibid., 92.
      "Finished *Le Rouge et le Noir*": Gide, *Journal 1939-1949* (Paris: Éditions Gallimard,
      1954), 151. The entry is dated December 11, 1942.
230   "Peace, without Tonio": Jean Lucas in *Icare* II, 104.
      He painted a picture: Fleury, *Icare* II, 81.
231   "When I read your letters": SE's poignant missive to Luro Cambaceres—who was to
      write his own account of the early days of the airline—is reproduced in *Icare* I, 197.
      "You're not up to anything" to "It's not much": Jean Chitry, *Icare* II, 85.
232   Generally he kept his distance: A fascinating statement to this effect is partially re-
      produced in Chevrier, 124: *"Je ne considère point une pellicule comme mon oeuvre. Elle
      est, en effet, toujours oeuvre collective, issue tant bien que mal de compromis qui ne
      contentent jamais un auteur, et j'évite au contraire avec le plus grand soin de trop y
      attacher mon nom. Je ne puis empêcher les producteurs de jouer sur une signature qu'ils
      ont payée, mais je ne joins pas mes efforts aux leurs."* The statement may explain why
      the story credit for "Anne-Marie" went to one "A. de Saint-Exupéry."
      "The Sahara seems": *Air France Revue*, Spring 1935, 5.
233   As the sun set: Gaudillère re-created the incident in *Icare* II, 113.
      "un artiste en souvenirs": Jean Prévost, *Les Caractères* (Paris: Éditions Albin Michel,
      1948), 109.
      SE reported a gross income: Frédéric d'Agay kindly shared his great-uncle's tax returns
      of 1935 and 1937 with me.
234   "How much do you have" and "Good. I'm leaving": Fleury, *Icare* II, 82–83.
      In the most dramatic: Fleury, *Icare* II, 83. Similarly, Chevrier, 119–121. The report
      on SE's cellmate was issued by Captain Pierre Bénech.
      "A night flight": "Mermoz, le pilote de ligne," *Marianne*, August 7, 1935, 1.
235   "Gaston Gallimard is": Crémieux cited in Assouline, 181.
      One friend was to say: Léon-Paul Fargue, "Souvenir de Saint-Exupéry," *La Revue
      de Paris*, September 1945, 53.
      "to sit on chairs": Jean-Paul Sartre, *The War Diaries of Jean-Paul Sartre* (New York:
      Pantheon, 1984), 248–49.
      "One couldn't write": Léon-Paul Fargue cited in Lottman, 36.
236   "I the undersigned": July 6, 1984, Drouot sale, item no. 29.
      "Straddling a chair": Cendrars in *Confluences*, Vols. 12–14, 59–60.
237   "A shooting star" and entire episode: André Beucler, "Quand Saint-Exupéry imaginait
      des contes de fées jusqu'au retour de l'aube . . . ," *Le Figaro Littéraire*, July 30, 1949,
      1. Also Beucler, *20 ans avec Léon-Paul Fargue* (Geneva: Éditions du Milieu du Monde,
      1952), 110–13. The two accounts differ slightly.
      "If it was cold": Jeanson, *70 ans*, 226.
      The party broke up: Jean Galtier-Boissière's account can be found in *Mémoires d'un
      Parisien II* (Paris: La Table Ronde, 1961), 297.
      On the lunches with Prévost, Giraudoux, Beucler: See Beucler, *Les instants de Girau-
      doux* (Geneva: Éditions du Milieu du Monde, 1948).
238   One night he attracted: Escot, *Icare* I, 114.
      "Ça, c'est Guillaumet": Werth, *Tel Quel*, 152.

borrowing a domestic's tie: Unpublished Gallimard interview, op. cit.

239   a Fernandez-moderated panel: The account of the evening—it was June 8—can be found in Van Rysselberghe, *Cahiers André Gide* V, 451–52.

"I'd very much like": Werth, *Tel Quel*, 157.

In the front seat: Pélissier, 128.

"That day, I understood": Lamotte, *Icare* 1, 97.

he loved to sing: Beucler, *Les Instants de Giraudoux*, 21.

"he liked honesty": Beucler in René Tavernier, *Saint-Exupéry en procès* (Paris: Belfond, 1967), 141.

"He appreciated disguises": Beucler, "Quand Saint-Exupéry imaginait des contes de fées jusqu'au retour de l'aube," *Le Figaro Littéraire*, July 30, 1949, 1.

a fairly constant thirst: Madame de B remembered her friend's having been hugely—and unappealingly—"puffed up" by whiskey in the late 1930s, conversation with the author, January 18, 1994. She claimed that he lost fifteen kilos nearly overnight when she informed him that she did not like heavy men, interviews of January 7, 1991, and January 18, 1994.

240   "Tonio, sing!" Interview with Madeleine Goisot, January 2, 1992.

"Have you noticed?" and "That reminds me": Gaudillère, *Icare* II, 113.

"lighter than air": Werth, *Tel Quel*, 166.

"You're a sorcerer": Interview with Madame de B, December 4, 1991.

"Dunno. Do you count": Dony, 568.

241   "He spent less time": Prévost, *Les caractères*, 109.

Beucler remembered: Beucler, *Le Figaro Littéraire*, July 30, 1949.

He devised psychological: Werth, *Tel Quel*, 164.

He liked to torment: Each of his friends retained a favorite Exupérien theory as well. Maximilian Becker never forgot an eloquent defense the writer offered of capitalism and the accumulation of great fortunes, without which the arts would languish; for Hedda Sterne SE explained the value of reactionary thinking. (It saved the world from evolving too quickly, which could be dangerous.) Another friend was struck by his intriguing argument that plants and creatures occurred in greater variation the higher one moved on the evolutionary scale.

"Only with difficulty": ANAT.

"slow to take off" and "He would leave us": Jeanson, *70 ans*, 226. André Maurois left a nearly identical description in *From Proust to Camus* (Garden City, N.Y.: Doubleday & Company, 1966), 210–1.

242   "He gestured with his left": Cendrars, *Confluences*, 60.

short aviation pieces to *Marianne*: January 25, 1933 ("Mermoz"), January 24, 1934 ("La fin de l'Émeraude"), and February 28, 1934 ("Servitude et grandeur de l'aviation").

243   "an outright surrender": *Paris-Soir*, May 14, 1935. The translation is from *A Sense of Life*, 33. The Russian pieces appeared on the front page of *Paris-Soir* on May 3, 14, 16, 19, 20, and 22, 1935.

"unified solid mass" and "like any Paris suburb": *Paris-Soir*, May 3, 1935; the translation is from *A Sense of Life*, 32.

244   years later he was patiently: Interview with John Phillips, December 4, 1990.

"cut an unswerving path" to "lumps of clay": *Paris-Soir*, May 14, 1935; translation from *A Sense of Life*, 38–40. SE ended WSS on this note, 204–206.

Hervé Mille impatiently: Mille interview with author, January 6, 1992.

"What's wrong" and "I can't continue": Interview and Mille, *Icare* III, 56.

245   "speak above the roar" to "My impression": *Paris-Soir*, May 20, 1935.

"This dedication to the métier": *Journal de Moscou*, May 23, 1935.

245 "as invisible as virtue" to "I'll be the first": *Paris-Soir*, May 22, 1935.
246 "Theirs is a hard and bitter": Frédéric d'Agay provided a copy of the *Anne-Marie* screenplay. I am grateful to Annabella for having lent me her tape of the film.
247 "quite amazingly silly": Graham Greene, *The Pleasure Dome: The Collected Film Criticism* (New York: Oxford University Press, 1972), 73.
248 to secure an airplane: Daurat says as much in *Dans le vent des hélices*. Madame de B and Jean-Marie Conty—who would have been more personally acquainted with SE's financial and personal affairs—continue to think it more likely that the airplane was bestowed on the pilot for publicity purposes; Madame de B did not, as has been claimed, purchase it for her friend. The Renault archives yield no clues on this count, or at least have not done so to date.
249 "I wanted to dazzle": Werth, *Tel Quel*, 158.
"Come and see me" and "I will come by air": Conty recalled the conversation and the subsequent tour in two interviews, January 5, 1991, and January 18, 1992. He wrote of it as well in *Icare* II, 93–97.
"Do you see" and "Yes, I see": Interview of January 18, 1992.
250 "As for Monsieur de SE": Archives Nationales catalogue, 54.
"Yes, gentlemen" and "But you must forgive": Conty, *Cahiers Saint-Exupéry* I, 73.
Consuelo's address: In tracking the nomadic Saint-Exupérys through the 1930s I have relied heavily on the recollections of Jean-Marie Conty and Madeleine Goisot. Edmond Petit published a guide to his cousin's addresses in *Icare* II, 33.
251 "kindly caretaker": Ernest Hemingway, *The Snows of Kilimanjaro and Other Stories* (New York: Charles Scribner's Sons, 1927), 11.
"Dear Lord, save": Archives Nationales catalogue, 54.
"Can you hear": Interview with Ysatis de Saint-Simon, December 2, 1990. Similarly Hervé Mille, interview of January 6, 1992. Mille remembered SE as having been amused and greatly touched by this communication.
to be a fine shepherd: To Silvia Reinhardt, in an exquisite love letter, a copy of which Silvia Reinhardt shared with me.
He could speak inexhaustibly: R.-L. Bruckberger, *Au diable le Père Bruck!* (Paris: Plon, 1986), 171.
252 "She's a tough little number": Simone de Saint-Exupéry writing as Simone de Rémens, *Météores* (Hanoi: Taupin & Company, 1943), 204.
"He has always been": ibid., 220.
"like two kids": Goisot interviews, January 2, 1992, and January 20, 1992.
"*métier d'homme*" and "From the moment": Michel Georges-Michel, *Le baiser à Consuelo* (Paris: Éditions Baudinière, 1935), 125–26.
253 "The first three, four": Pélissier, 131.
"Put your mind": FA, 319.
as his new acquaintance read: I have based this account in part on many conversations with Madame de B, especially that of January 22, 1991, and in part on the description of the meeting included by Richard Rumbold and Lady Margaret Stewart—who also interviewed Madame de B on the subject—in *The Winged Life*, op. cit.
254 "his sweet Egeria": Marcel Migeo, *Saint-Ex* (New York: McGraw-Hill, 1960), 142.
"who brought him both": Maja Destrem, *Saint-Exupéry* (Paris: Éditions Paris-Match, 1974), 28. "guardian angel": Nicole Marino, *Écoute*, January 1993, 28. "a charming and intelligent": Rumbold and Stewart, 87. "*la blonde*": Deschodt, 209.
"perhaps there was" to "was it": Rosalind Baker Wilson, *Near the Magician* (New York: Grove Weidenfeld, 1989), 206. I am grateful to Rosalind Wilson for having put me in touch with Eva Thoby-Marcelin.
"a crisis never arises": Gertrude Stein, *Paris, France* (New York: Liveright, 1970), 29.

like her Zorro: Bruckberger, op. cit., 173.
255 "sizzling letters": Interview with Maximilian Becker, December 13, 1990.
"L'une le déséquilibrait": Conversation with a relative requesting anonymity, January 13, 1991.

XII "TAYARA BOUM-BOUM, TAYARA BOUM-BOUM!"

256 "Aviation unites": Malraux cited in Selden Rodman, ed. *The Poetry of Flight* (Freeport, N.Y.: Books for Libraries Press, 1969), 11.
Under no circumstances: General René Davet contributed his recollections to *Icare* III, 87–95. His preface to Daniel Anet, *Antoine de Saint-Exupéry, poète, romancier, moraliste* (Paris: Corrêa, 1946) is also informative.
nothing was more boring: Maggie Guiral, "Saint-Ex," *Voilà*, n.d., Saint-Exupéry file (1P 6678) at SHAA.
257 Mermoz was to say: *Mes vols*, 13.
"a combination tea party": Marcel Migeo, *Saint-Ex*, 168. Jean-Marie Conty more than confirmed this report, interview of January 5, 1991, and reported that Mermoz had no faith at all that his former colleague would succeed with the raid.
258 *"l'aviation sportive"*: *Le Figaro*, December 30, 1935, 1.
he assumed he had already: SE's initial account of the crash—and of the reasoning that preceded it—was delivered to reporters in Marseilles on his return and reproduced in *La Nef*, February–March 1951, 114–16.
"I was sure": WSS, 125.
"Our situation was": Cited in Chevrier, 132.
"vague foreboding," "in a confused way," and all quotations regarding the crash except where noted: WSS, 129–57. SE's original account of the crash appeared on the front page of *Paris-Soir* between January 30 and February 4 under the general title "Prison de Sable." The six pieces bore an inspired series of subtitles: "Un avertissement du Destin," "Soudain, un formidable craquement," "La soif," "Le délire," "Le supplice du 3ème jour," and "Résurrection."
"Oh, because of that": Madame de B, writing as Hélène Froment, *Confluences*, 279.
"I ask my wife's": *Paris-Soir*, January 5, 1936, 1. "WE HAVE HEADED": *Paris-Soir*, January 8, 1936, 3.
A number of journalists: *Marianne*, January 8, 1936. Nearly everyone present either wrote up his memories of the vigil or shared them with a journalist or biographer who did.
260 He paid a call: Ségogne, *Icare* III, 67.
"Ah, Saint-Exupéry, he's gotten": Conty interview, January 5, 1991.
"Have no fear": Fleury, "Saint-Exupéry, l'aviateur du désert," *Candide*, January 9, 1936.
One of Saint-Exupéry's editors: Hervé Mille interview, January 6, 1992.
"reprendre le flambeau": Conty, January 5, 1991.
When she sat down: The interview appeared in *Le Figaro*, December 31, 1935, 1f.
where she claimed: Madeleine Goisot, letter to author, February 6, 1992.
Madame Vidi swore: The report of the visit with the clairvoyant appeared as "Votre mari est vivant," *L'Intransigeant*, January 11, 1936, 2.
261 "Held up by two": Marcellin Cazes, "Derrière Thorez, je vois entrer Léon Daudet," *Paris Presse L'Intransigeant*, October 29, 1965.
At the same time: Lucas, *Icare* II, 104.

261 ring forever in his ears: Suzanne Raccaud, *Cahiers* 1, 57. Madame Raccaud's recollections provide a magnificent counterpoint to SE's account of the crash. The other Madame de SE: *Paris-Soir*'s reporter published his account of the early-morning visit to the Pont-Royal on the third in the January 4 paper, 3. For Gide's reaction, see *Cahiers André Gide* V, 509–10.

262 entirely disoriented: *Marseille-Matin*, January 4, 1936, 1–4.
"canoeing in mid-ocean": WSS, 155.
"After three days of walking": Jacques Baratier, "Retour d'Amérique, Antoine de Saint-Exupéry nous dit . . . ," *Les Nouvelles Littéraires*, March 18, 1939, 1.
"that caravan swaying": WSS, 154.
"*Tayara boum-boum!*": Raccaud, *Cahiers* I, 56.
"like young calves": WSS, 155.
"Could you pay my guide": Raccaud, *Cahiers* I, 50.

263 "When you have nothing": *Paris-Soir*, January 6, 1936, 5.
"Yes, tea—and whiskey": Raccaud, *Cahiers* I, 51.
"Don't forget, sir": Cited in Deschodt, 225.
the Continental's porter: *L'Intransigeant*, January 4, 1936, 1.
Evidently at this moment to "Tell them for me": Gabriel Dardaud's account—which sounds a bit overexuberant in the original—is from *30 ans au bord du Nil* (Paris: Lieu Commun, 1987), 60–65. He offered a shorter but no less dramatic version of the activity on the Continental's steps in *Le Point*, January 27, 1986, 135–39.

264 "ARE SO HAPPY": WSS, 157 (translation mine).
"SAFE AND SOUND": ANAT.

265 "A few hours' sleep": *Le Figaro*, January 4, 1936, 1.
Breakfasts in the desert: *L'Intransigeant*, January 4, 1936, 5.
Marseille-Matin went so far: "Saint-Ex," *Marseille-Matin*, January 8, 1936, 1.
"I cried reading": LSM, 214–15.
The order Witasse had placed: Dardaud, 63.
doubtless remembering the words: SE quoted Le Brix in his preface to José Le Boucher, *Le Destin de Joseph-Marie Le Brix* (Paris: Nouvelle Librairie Française, 1932) years before his stay in the Libyan desert: " 'Buvez,' me répétait Le Brix, 'sans quoi vous le regretteriez un jour: j'ai vu défiler, dans mon délire, tous les bocks bien glacés que j'avais refusés dans ma vie.' Plus tard, il ajouta: 'Et ça—il me désignait le mirage où les dunes se reflétaient dans une eau pure—vous croyez que c'est drôle, ça, quand on crève de soif!' "
"I started a sentence": I am grateful to Paul Barthe-Dejean for sharing his dedication, and for his crystal-clear recollections of the Garden City luncheon and the days that followed, outlined in letters of February 8 and March 17, 1995.
Not having seen each other: The return to Wadi-Natroun was written up in *Paris-Soir*, January 8, 1936.

266 "tour de force": A portion of SE's December 23, 1936, letter to his insurers is reproduced in the auction catalogue from a Drouot sale, Paris, June 16 and 17, 1990, item 29.
taken off in haste: *Le Figaro*, January 5, 1936, 1.
"la véritable grandeur": The La Bruyère comparison is invoked in *Le Figaro*, January 4, 1936, 5.
implying that no pilot: *Les Ailes*, January 9, 1936.
"Finally you've come!": *Le Radical* (Marseilles), January 21, 1936, 1. See also *Marseille-Matin*, January 22, 1926, 3, for a fine account of SE's return to France.

267 The Lipp proprietor: Cazes, *Paris Presse L'Intransigeant*, October 29, 1965.
"I suffered such thirst": *Algérie-Soir*, August 13, 1944.
"She's going to throw" to "If I had appealed": Jeanson, *70 ans*, 236–37.

268 Consuelo burst instantly: Raymond Bernard, *Icare* III, 28.
proved equally impressed: René Davet, in his preface to Daniel Anet, *Antoine de Saint-Exupéry, poète, romancier, moraliste* (Paris: Editions Corrêa, 1946).
not all of the hotel bills: Madame de B, interview of January 8, 1992.

269 "refresh one's wardrobe": Quoted in Françoise Giroud, *Si je mens . . .* (Paris: Éditions Stock, 1972), 38.
"I am going to write": Pélissier, 157.
"I feel like a prisoner": The letter has been reproduced several times but is perhaps most available as "Métier et vocation d'écrivain," *Preuves*, October 1957, 20–21. Françoise Giroud remembered SE complaining of same, letter to author, April 1992.
Early in March Émile Raccaud: Reproduced in part in Drouot catalogue from sale of June 16 and 17, 1990, item no. 24.
"Furthermore, I already miss" and "Here the world": ibid., item no. 25.
"Money burned a hole": Taped Radio France interview with Consuelo, conducted by Jacques Chancel, n.d.

270 "a spousal holiday": Goisot letter of August 21, 1993.
All of this appears: I have based this account of the renovation of the place Vauban apartment on bills reproduced in the Drouot catalogue, June 1990 sale, items no. 38–53.
remembered him as: Françoise Giroud, *Si je mens . . .* , op. cit., and Giroud, *Leçons particulières* (Paris: Librairie Arthème Fayard, 1990). Also letter to author of April 1992. "Let her go" and "She will be": *Si je mens . . .* , 38. Similarly, *Icare* VII, 47.
"crucified by his wife": Giroud, 69. In the original the line reads: ". . . *il vivait perché comme un oiseau sur la branche, toujours fauché, crucifié par sa femme qu'il aimait et qui le trompait.*"

271 "I like to be proud": From the Arts Anciens auction catalogue, sale held in Geneva on November 22 and 23, 1986, item no. 13A.
"Behave so that": From the Ader Picard Tajan catalogue, sale held in Paris, July 6, 1984, item no. 3.
"Oh, these sleepless nights": ibid., no. 15.
"I beg you one day": ANAT.
She complained to one: Consuelo to Suzanne Werth, n.d. "*Je souffre toujours de ce mauvais rythme qui existe entre Tonio et moi. Bientôt sera la fin car je n'ai plus de courage. Je n'ai pas envie de continuer,*" wrote Consuelo on Lutétia stationery.
"Whisper to yourself": Cited in Bothorel, 96.

272 "Do you have" to "I'm not divorcing you": Interview with Robert Tenger, January 19, 1991.
tore him apart: A portion of an anguished, five-page letter to Natalie Paley appeared in the catalogue for the Laurin-Guilloux-Buffetaud-Tailleur sale, December 4, 1991, Drouot, item no. 30, letter 7.
applied for permission: NA, 2081–1422, 4 (July 1936).
The exception was his account: *L'Intransigeant*, August 19, 1936, 1. The balance of the front-page pieces appeared on August 12, 13, 14, and 16, 1936.

273 Billon remembered: *Icare* III, 30–32.
"Do you think" to "*Monsieur Boileau*": Jeanson, *70 ans*, 222.
"You'll see" to "That took no time!": Billon, *Icare* III, 31–32.

274 "Tonio—don't you" to "friend of my friends": Jeanson's is the only account we have of the London visit. He appears to have related the nightclub story for the first time in *L'Événement-Journal* (Quebec), May 30, 1939. For the full report of the trip see *70 ans d'adolescence*, 229–35. Alexander Korda's ill-fated *Conquest of the Air* exhausted a long series of directors and was released six years after its conception.

275 The film's official pilot: Quoted in the recollections of Charles Bultel, *Icare* III, 44.
"Mermoz transmitted": Chevrier, 142–43. Also interview with Madame de B of January 7, 1991.
"It would be ridiculous": WSS, 23.
in his first piece: *L'Intransigeant*, December 13, 1936, 1.
"You are a friend": "À Jean Mermoz," *Marianne*, December 16, 1936, 1.

276 "When we lose a friend": *Paris-Soir*, May 19, 1935, 1.
"Old friends aren't made": WSS, 25 (translation mine).
"Mermoz has disappeared": SE can be heard reading a piece entitled "Adieu à Mermoz" on a Festival recording (FLD 23) from the series "Leur oeuvre et leur voix." He is clearly moved; his voice cracks partway through the short address.
"over blindingly white sand": Drouot auction catalogue, June 16 and 17, 1990, item no. 67.
SE had applied for one: ibid., item no. 58.

277 "a man of the air": Noëlle Guillaumet, *Icare*, Spring 1966.
"I felt confident": Reproduced in Chevrier, 151.
he boasted to Guillaumet and "I have just relived": Reproduced in *Icare* III, 84. At the top SE scrawled in pencil that he thought he had mailed the letter a month earlier but was sending it on anyway, as *"Mieux vaut tard que jamais . . ."*
"I have an account": Chevrier, 149.
Surrealist journal: "Un Mirage" appeared in the Winter 1935 issue of *Minotaure*, 19.
solicited assignments: Jacques Paget, *Le Méridional*, October 28, 1962.
loyalists have had to defend: See "À propos de Saint-Exupéry," *Le Monde*, December 11, 1987, 16.

XIII CIVIL EVENING TWILIGHT

279 France, in 1937, was: The most colorful accounts I know of France in the 1930s are Olivier Bernier, *Fireworks at Dusk: Paris in the Thirties* (New York: Little, Brown & Company, 1993); Janet Flanner's (Genêt's) columns, both in *The New Yorker* through those years and as collected in *Paris Was Yesterday* (New York: Harcourt Brace Jovanovich, 1988); and Werth, *The Twilight of France*. I have drawn on them all.

281 "geysers of liquid electric color": The phrase is Flanner's, "Letter from Paris," *The New Yorker*, August 28, 1937, 36.
a feat he claimed: The "diploma" issued to SE for his jump of August 24, 1937, was sold in Paris at Drouot, June 16 and 17, 1990, catalogue item no. 15. SE told Pélissier that he would not have jumped if he had not been pushed, Pélissier, 28–29.
He suffered from vertigo: Or so he told Jacques Baratier, *Les Nouvelles Littéraires*, March 18, 1939. Wrote Prévost of him in *Les caractères* after a description of SE jubilantly piloting: *"Et il aurait le vertige à pied sur un toit."*
"the three dictatorships": Cited in Alexander Werth, 87.
René Delange noticed: Delange, 73.
General Davet's impression: Davet, *Icare* III, 91.

282 "I'm not interested": Cited in Chevrier, 152.
he did meet Jeanson: Jeanson, *70 ans*, 227–29. The account of the "Internationale"-singing chauffeur is here as well.
"One does not light": *Paris-Soir*, October 3, 1938. The translation is from *A Sense of Life*, 141. The first Spain pieces appeared on the front page of *Paris-Soir* on June 27 and 28, 1937. A third appeared on July 3, 1937, 4.

283 "It was a time": OTAGE, 399 (translation mine).

"How does a man receive" to "Sergeant, what is it": *Paris-Soir*, July 3, 1937. Translation from *A Sense of Life*, 119. See also WSS, 190–91.

"Pilots meet if they are fighting": *Paris-Soir*, October 4, 1938. Translation is from *A Sense of Life*, 156.

"Looks as if" to "Time to sleep!": *Paris-Soir*, October 3, 1938. "Antonio, what are" to "Their words were": The same account as revised for WSS, 184.

284   "It was like the break," "and, the ice broken," and "We men put on": OTAGE, 401. Jeanson said he sputtered: Jeanson, *70 ans*, 227.

285   "Franco's soldier is noble": CARNETS, 201.

as he had not been before: See Davet, *Icare* III, 94.

"Terrific," responded the reporter: Fleury, *Icare* II, 82.

Mille handed him his pages: The story is the stuff of legend but was confirmed by Mille, interview of January 6, 1992.

286   In midmonth to "After a thousand tergiversations": Chevrier, 157–58, supplemented by details provided by Madame de B, interview of January 22, 1991.

288   "If it contains anything": Flanner, "Letter from Munich," *The New Yorker*, September 11, 1937, 38.

still not managed to turn out: I owe this observation to Zeldin, *France 1848–1945*, II, 640. Zeldin is also the author of the word "doodlebug-sized."

289   "Careful, I think we are": Werth, "Tel Quel," 154.

Ségogne remembered that: Ségogne, *Icare* III, 69. The idea amounts to an obsession in CARNETS.

filed patents: For a full description of SE's various patents and addendum thereto, see Gérard Trocmé, *Icare* III, 116–21.

290   only science when writing: Chevrier, 163.

his captain's cap was ready: Néri, *Icare* II, 53.

initially been suggested to him: Conty, interview of January 18, 1992.

291   SE's own correspondence this winter: Many of these documents figure in the auction catalogue from the Drouot sale, June 16 and 17, 1990, 11–14.

The French consular staff: Amérique 1918–40, dossiers généraux, no. 136, QO. See also 811.7961/236, NA.

In December the air ministry: QO, Amérique 1918–40, no. 136, QO. SE and Prévot's visas were issued during the week ending January 8, memo from Robert D. Murphy to the U.S. Secretary of State, 811.111, 11347, NA. I have insisted somewhat on the disparate impressions of SE's departure date and itinerary as they seem to me to give a sense of the casualness with which the trip—gratuitous in the first place—was ultimately undertaken.

only in foul moods: Gaston Lavoisier, *Quartier Latin*, March 23, 1945, 3.

On the *Île de France*: Pierre Massin de Miraval, *Icare*, 96, Spring 1981 (hereafter *Icare* VI), 80.

"what he had to do": Bernard Lamotte, *Icare*, 84, Spring 1978 (hereafter *Icare* V), 83.

a vain conceit: From the notes of Lewis Galantière, BL. In his *Atlantic* piece (April 1947, 137) Galantière quotes SE as having said, "It's a silly thing to do, perhaps, but I want to do it."

"This trip is risky" and "Fortunately I'm lucky": Raoul de Roussy de Sales writing as Jacques Fransalès, *Paris-Soir*, February 18, 1938, 1. The headline of the piece—published after the accident—read: " 'Ce voyage est un casse-gueule mais je suis verni,' disait Saint-Exupéry."

292   Hitchcock had asked a representative: Letter from Walter Batsell to Hitchcock, December 27, 1933. Solange Herter unearthed the letter and kindly passed it on.

292 Gallimard remembered that, "Who do you take," and "Yes": Unpublished Gallimard interview.
They were beautiful, however: For the history of the publishing relationship between SE and Reynal & Hitchcock I am especially grateful to Harcourt Brace for opening their files (hereafter referred to as the HBJ archives).

293 "With the American navigation": Alexandra Pecker, "Antoine de Saint-Exupéry," *France-Amérique*, May 17, 1938.
"Now, which way?" and rest of incident: Richard de Roussy de Sales, in a February 18, 1991, letter to author.
"I prefer to be over": *Paris-Soir*, February 18, 1938.
Atlanta and in Houston: On the fifteenth the Associated Press reported that "a sizeable delegation"—it included a representative of the French Line who had evidently been a classmate of SE's—waited in vain for him for several hours at the New Orleans airport.

294 Later he boasted that: Pecker, *France-Amérique*, May 17, 1938.
Hitchcock attested: From Curtice Hitchcock's press information for FA, June 1939, HBJ archives.
He was ecstatic: Interview with Madame de B, January 21, 1992.
"IMPOSSIBLE TO TAKE ON": Jacques Fransalès (Raoul de Roussy de Sales), *Paris-Soir*, February 18, 1932, 1.
pinned down by the engine: In weeding through the many diplomatic and journalistic reports of the accident I have favored that of the head of the American legation to Guatemala, who arrived on the scene within fifteen minutes of the crash and had no particular stake in Franco-Guatemalan or Guatemalan-Franco relations. 814.7965/15 and 16. NA.

295 "When they pulled me": Quoted in Patrick Kessel, *La vie de Saint-Exupéry* (Paris: Gallimard, 1954), 65.
He later ascribed: I am grateful to Bikou de Lanux Strong for having offered up pages from her father's unpublished memoirs. Chapter 7—entitled "La route de Guatemala"—includes a report on the hospital conversation with SE, during which the pilot stated that in a more solid aircraft he would have been roasted alive.
the first reports: Lavondes's round-the-clock telegrams can be found in Amérique 1918-40, no. 136, QO. It was he who noted that the men were eager to reassure their families they were alive and that for his part SE had asked the Quai d'Orsay to alert Madame de B.
a certain resentment: Navy Intelligence Attaché's Report, April 12, 1938, 814.7965/16, NA.

296 Listed by Dr. Echeverría Ávila: A portion of Avila's report appeared in the catalogue for the Drouot June 1990 sale, no. 23.
"through a thick syrupy" to "tucked away in a dim": *Harper's Bazaar*, op. cit., 123.
Within days he had: In his account of the trip to SE's bedside Pierre de Lanux provided all of the details, down to the hives and the forbidden aspirin. Yvonne Michel remembered that Lanux "s'est précipité pour aller voir" SE, letter of April 23, 1992.

297 Lanux lamented later: Lanux, *Confluences*, 115.
In the car leaving: Pélissier, 136.

298 "Come settle here" and "My dear father-in-law": M. Laure, "Consuelo, la femme-oiseau," *Détective*, December 18, 1959, 6-7. The visit—recalled only by Madeleine Goisot, who was told of it by Consuelo—appears to tally with the exit and entrance visas in SE's passport. *The New York Times* reported that Consuelo had arrived in Guatemala to join her husband, March 6, 1938, 29.
which he found roomy: DC-3: Alexandra Pecker article, May 17, 1938.

and arranged for him to borrow: Interviews with Madame de B, January 7, 1991, and December 9, 1992.

299   "as it is impossible": Drouot auction catalogue, June 1990 sale, item no. 89.

enjoyed a long and festive: Interview with Elizabeth (Reynal) Darbee, July 12, 1993.

300   anything resembling work: Flanner is most eloquent on the visit in *Paris Was Yesterday*, 183–86. See also Bernier, 279–81.

"A husband for Mireille": Mireille d'Agay's memories of the summer visit are from *Icare* III, 21–23.

convinced he was clairvoyant: Maria van Rysselberghe, *Cahiers André Gide* VI, (Paris: Gallimard, 1975), 19. The entries are dated August 19 and October 9, 1938.

he was overwhelmed: Interview with Madame de B, January 30, 1992.

301   a clear vision of the book: Anyone doubting the long reach of Galantière's editorial arm has only to consult his papers, BL, or to compare the American and French editions of the text, all of which have greatly informed this discussion of the two volumes. SE writes repeatedly in his correspondence with Becker of the changes and additions requested by Hitchcock and, especially, by Galantière. He harped on the idea that he wanted the book to amount to more than simply a collection of memories and can be heard saying as much on the Festival recording, "Leur Oeuvre et Leur Voix," on which he prefaces his reading from the French-language preface. See also Curtice Hitchcock's chronology of the publishing relationship between Reynal & Hitchcock and SE (prepared for the Gallimard lawsuit), HBJ archives.

In Jean Prévost's copy: Auclair and Prévost, 181.

A percentage of the monies: SE's financial woes are revealed in his letter to the FISC of July 12, 1938, Drouot catalogue, June 1990 sale, item no. 98.

Chez Jarraud: Mille, *Icare* III, 59, and interview of January 6, 1992.

"I think that this last" and "I published it in three": SE to Becker, October 1938. I am indebted to Royce Becker for her assistance with her father's papers.

302   "The idiots, they don't know": The report is Pierre Lazareff's, cited in Bernier, 292. "When we thought peace": *Paris-Soir*, October 2, 1938.

"The difference between an American": Raoul de Roussy de Sales, "Love in America," *The Pocket Atlantic*, 1946, 8.

303   "because translating you": Galantière to SE, June 1939, quoted in 1984 Archives Nationales exhibition catalogue, 102.

After a second collaboration: I am grateful to Howard Scherry for having shared his correspondence with Galantière from the 1970s, in which Galantière reflected openly on his editorial relationship with SE.

at the suggestion of Hitchcock: SE to Becker, October 1938.

Later he explained: See Jacques de Dampierre's memories of SE in Lisbon in 1940, EG, 140. SE spoke freely with several acquaintances of the trouble he had had depicting the cyclone; in order to impress the enormity of it on the reader he had needed to minimize his terms. Imagine a man in a rowboat, he argued; would he be any more frightened before a hundred-meter-high wave than before a thirty-meter-high wave? Would the reader reading of his plight not have more trouble imagining, *sensing*, the former? See also Jean Macaigne. *Icare* VI, 44.

"crowning achievement": To Galantière, BL. Similarly to Max Becker, early fall, 1938.

He wanted desperately: A running theme in the Galantière papers, BL.

Gide is said to have pressed: Pélissier, 68. As Gide brought Conrad to the attention of Europe's literary circles in the first place it is highly likely that he spoke of him to SE. There is no proof, however, that he actually mentioned the 1906 *Mirror of the Sea* to SE, or that SE ever read the book.

He imagined a few days at sea: SE to Becker, October 1938. Becker actively discouraged

his client from making the trip if he was planning on doing so only in order to finish
the book, letter of October 1, 1938 and interviews.

304   promising that he could sell: Becker to SE, letter of June 6, 1939.
      for his wandering wife: Claude Werth made available a string of SE's telegrams, the
      gist of which is *"Inquiet, Consuelo introuvable"* ("Uneasy—Consuelo nowhere to be
      found"). Werth recalled Consuelo's relationship with his mother, interview of January
      24, 1991.
      a small studio: Interview with Madame de B, January 13, 1992.
      early in February 1939: See SE's passport, ANAT. There was no fall 1938 trip to
      America, as has been reported.
      the very name *Terre des hommes*: Conversation with Elizabeth Darbee, July 12, 1993.
305   "The earth teaches us": *Terre des hommes*, Pléiade, 139 (translation mine).
      This culminated: Interview with André de Fonscolombe, January 25, 1991.
      proofs of the French edition: The title page is reproduced in the 1984 Archives Na-
      tionales exhibition catalogue, 103, as is a long list of possible titles written in SE's
      hand.
      In French aviation circles: Letter from Robert Boname, December 12, 1992.

XIV WHERE IS FRANCE?

307   Fortified by whiskey: Jacques Baratier, *Les Nouvelles Littéraires*, March 18, 1939, 1.
      "Curious," he remarked: Chevrier, 176. Her published account of this visit is supple-
      mented by our conversations and by the writings of Henry Bordeaux.
308   later he was to tell: Raoul de Roussy de Sales, *The Making of Yesterday* (New York:
      Reynal & Hitchcock, 1947), 43–44. The journal entry is dated August 7, 1939. See
      also 48–49.
      Marx and Comte: Henry Bordeaux, "Antoine de Saint-Exupéry," *Écrits de Paris*, Sep-
      tember 1948, 89.
      to read Einstein: EG, 114.
      "The kind of man": Chevrier, 176.
      They have so many airplanes: Pélissier, 33–34.
      "a philosophical analysis": Raoul de Roussy de Sales, *The Making of Yesterday*, 44.
      The first review: Robert Brasillach, *L'Action Française*, March 16, 1939.
309   "This volume is put": Paul Nizan, *Ce Soir*, March 30, 1939.
      "SE, aviator and moralist": André Thérive, *Le Temps*, April 27, 1939.
      Edmond Jaloux placed: Jaloux, *Les Nouvelles Littéraires*, April 8, 1939.
      "a beautiful book": Clare Leighton, *The New York Times Book Review*, June 18,
      1939, 1.
      "To read it is to forget" and "contrasting moods": Edward Weeks, *The Atlantic*, August
      1939.
      "Antoine de SE is awake": Ben Ray Redman, New York *Herald Tribune*, June 18,
      1939, 1.
      "God-like tolerance": Cecil Lewis, *The Spectator*, October 6, 1939, 478–79.
      "He touches nothing" and "visions and dreams": *The Times Literary Supplement*,
      September 23, 1939.
310   an experience he compared and the account of the Académie Française's deliberations:
      Bordeaux, *Écrits de Paris*, September 1948, 89.
      "His timidity intimidated": Lucè Estang recalled this 1939 interview in his biography
      of SE, *Saint-Exupéry par lui-meme* (Paris: Éditions du Seuil, 1958), 16.
      "Interviewing Monsieur Antoine de SE" and "I have much faith": Luc Estang writing

as Boisgontier, "Cinq minutes avec Monsieur Antoine de Saint-Exupéry, lauréat du grand prix du roman." *Le Figaro Littéraire*, May 27, 1939, 1.

311 "on whom depend many": Fidus, *Revue des Deux-Mondes*, May 27, 1939, 854.

a couscous dinner: I am again especially grateful to Madeleine Goisot for her memories of this evening.

"The name 'SE' ": Jeanine Delpech, *Les Nouvelles Littéraires*, May 27, 1939, 1.

he was inconsolable: Pélissier, 81.

more delighted even: Madame de B, interview of January 30, 1992.

the two thought SE talked drivel: Simone de Beauvoir, *Letters to Sartre* (New York: Arcade Publishing, 1991), 175–76. See also Jean-Paul Sartre, *Witness to My Life: The Letters of Jean-Paul Sartre to Simone de Beauvoir, 1926–1939* (New York: Charles Scribner's Sons, 1992), 370–75.

312 "under the influence": Jean-Paul Sartre, ibid., 371.

"taken the threat of war": Flanner, *Paris Was Yesterday*, 220.

He was not known to have been: But he may have been surprised by several claims made after his death.

"You are going to be": SE to Ségogne, courtesy of Anne Roque and Arnaud de Ségogne.

Lunch was a straightforward: Based on Werth's descriptions of the afternoon, including those in several unpublished pages passed on by Claude Werth, who also remembered the lunch vividly.

313 "shrines of memory": Werth, *Déposition* (Paris: Viviane Hamy, 1992), 61. "At Fleurville, the Saône": ibid., 61.

"Tonight, three of my": Sallès, *Icare* I, 86.

"he preferred human beings": Pierre Dalloz, *Confluences*, 160.

314 "virile affection": A portion of the December 14, 1939, address of Louis Gillet, the director of the Académie Française, is reproduced in *Icare* III, 121.

"the ability to defy": CARNETS, 234.

"*pilote complémentaire*" and "Didn't he after all": Louis Couhé, *Icare* III, 106. Also Louis Castex, "Antoine de Saint-Exupéry tel que je l'ai connu," *Illustration*, August 1954.

315 "*passager mascotte*": Georges Bouchard, *Icare* III, 106.

"*embourgeoisé*": "Avec Guillaumet l'homme des miracles de New-York à Biscarrosse," *Paris-Soir*, July 22, 1939, 3.

316 "Tell Delgove to replace": Henri Delgove, *Icare*, 108, 1er trimestre, 1984 (hereafter *Icare* VII), 73.

heard all about Anne Morrow Lindbergh, "The Camembert is always," and "HAVE CELEBRATED": Robert de Saint-Jean, "Avec Saint-Ex en plein Atlantique j'ai recontré Guillaumet," *Paris-Soir*, August 11, 1939, 2.

"*sacrifices acrobatiques*": Ader Picard Tajan auction catalogue, Drouot sale of July 6, 1984, item no. 11, part 3.

317 "*pas un mot*" and "One of those drunken": Anne Morrow Lindbergh, *War Within and Without* (New York: Harcourt Brace Jovanovich, 1980), 21. The account of the Lindbergh weekend comes entirely from *War Within and Without*, Anne Lindbergh's preface to SE's *Wartime Writings*—an abridged version of *Écrits de guerre* (New York: Harcourt Brace Jovanovich, 1986)—and my interview with Anne Lindbergh, December 5, 1990.

"talk back in French": Lindbergh, *War Within and Without*, 22.

"child-wife": Nigel Nicolson cited in Dorothy Herrmann, *Anne Morrow Lindbergh* (New York: Ticknor & Fields, 1992), 194.

"Oh—not so far apart": *War Within and Without*, 26.

318   "But I never know": ibid., 27. "There are the people one can": 30. "For the second time": 35. "mind had been quickened": 35. "summer lightning": 23.

319   "became for me the lens": Lindbergh, *Wartime Writings*, xii. "like a letter to him": *War Within and Without*, 447. If Charles was the earth: ibid. "Are you going to look": ibid., 449.

"I think he probably": Charles Lindbergh, *The Wartime Journals of Charles A. Lindbergh* (New York, Harcourt Brace Jovanovich, 1970), 269.

Middlebury College summer school: For two very different perspectives on the August 11–13 visit, I am grateful to Alain Guilloton (who was eleven at the time) and to Stephen Freeman, then dean of the French School. Yvonne Michel was also able to offer invaluable help, interview of January 4, 1991. The photos are Professor Freeman's.

320   SE confided his fears: Raoul de Roussy de Sales, *The Making of Yesterday*, 48–49. "when the headlines": SE used the expression in his interview with Robert Van Gelder, published as "A Talk with Antoine de Saint-Exupéry," *The New York Times Book Review*, January 19, 1941, 2. to whom he wrote passionately: The letters are cited in part in Chevrier, 215–17, and in slightly larger part in EG, 54–56. "I am not embarrassed": EG, 55.

321   "In order to fly" and "Except modesty": Delange, 80–81. "All the same he isn't": Gavoille's response was recorded by Jean Dutertre, *Icare*, 78, Autumn 1976 (hereafter *Icare* IV), 69. "Is he going to make": Jean Israël, interview with author, January 22, 1991. "Isn't he forty?": Dutertre, interview of January 16, 1991, and *Icare* IV, 69.

322   "Lieutenant Laux" and "SE, pilot": Dutertre, *Icare* IV, 69. "It's very nice here": ibid., 69–70. Also *Icare*, 40. "he had tamed us": Israël, interview, January 22, 1991. You must not have been: The legendary incident was reported by SE himself, EG, 67. had wanted a Bugatti: Madame de B, interview of January 21, 1992. Israël remembered a trip: Interview of January 22, 1991, as in *Icare* IV, 59.

323   "I like it here" and "You know, Captain": An interview with Madame Scherschell appeared in *L'Est Républicain*, February 3, 1961, 4bis. "A freezing bed": EG, 97. Similarly, to Madame de B, EG, 69–70. "In temperate climates": EG, 97. polar hedgehogs: I have drawn on many accounts in this section but chief among them are Jean-Marie Chirol, *Groupes de Chasse et de Reconnaissance à Oronte et Saint-Dizier* (Paris: Langres, 1981), Guy Bougerol, *Ceux qu'on n'a jamais vus* (Grenoble: Arthaud, 1943), and the 2/33's *journal de marche* and *historique*, which can be found at SHAA.

324   "It's understandable but": EG, 108. "Some of the German pilots": A. J. Liebling, *The Road Back to Paris* (Garden City, N.Y.: Doubleday, Doran, 1944), 88. "a realistic ideal": Max Gelée, *Icare* VI, 82. "this odd planet": EG, 66. "The next time around": Gelée, *Icare* VI, 82. Also this winter: Jean Israël, an engineer by training, has been eloquent on the subject of SE's inventions of 1939–40. See "Saint-Exupéry inventeur," *Cahiers de l'Aéro-Club de France*, June 1991, 10–12

325   "In the kind of adolescent": André George, *La Nef*, September 1945, 23. "an entirely anonymous soldier": EG, 57. Werth observed: Werth, *Déposition*, 123. "a sort of aerial deep-sea diver": Jeanson, *70 ans*, 237.

326 the only order to "Ah, Monsieur, thank heavens": The account is entirely from Chevrier, who was there, 220.

"Diction excellent": Unpublished letter of October 1939 from Madame de SE to her son, Frédéric d'Agay archives.

pack a copy of *Terre*: *Le Figaro*, January 6, 1940.

"We urgently request": Frédéric d'Agay provided a copy of the Ministère de l'Information's May 24, 1940, letter. Copies of all of this correspondence can be found in the air force files, SHAA. These include a polite but firm letter dated March 25, 1940, from the French commander-in-chief to the Ministre de l'Air explaining why SE could not be separated from the 2/33, where he was said to be invaluable (true) as an instructor (false).

327 The captain managed to reason: Gelée, *Icare* IV, 66–67.

"That would be discourteous": Werth, *Tel Quel*, 184.

Dorothy Thompson told: Interview with Madame de B, January 8, 1992, and Dorothy Thompson, New York *Herald Tribune*, June 7, 1940, 21. "You are absolutely wrong": ibid.

On the other side of the world: Lindbergh, *War Within and Without*, 102–107.

328 *"absences de moi-même"*: "Lettres de guerre à un ami," *Le Figaro Littéraire*, July 27, 1957, 1. The letter, to Madame de B, is reprinted as well in EG.

brag to his commanding officer: Henri Alias, *Icare* IV, 94.

He had no logical: EG, 68–70, among other such admissions.

"cops and robbers" and "grim charade": FA, 311–12.

On one occasion when it did: Israël, *Icare* IV, 57.

"We face the prospect": FA, 348.

"We knew that the Germans": Dutertre interview, January 16, 1991.

"a desire to take charge": EG, 68.

"When you are in danger": EG, 72.

Over and over he insisted: See Ader Picard Tajan auction catalogue, July 6, 1984, Drouot sale, item no. 76.

329 serenity when under siege: EG, 63.

He told the Lindberghs: Lindbergh, *War Within and Without*, 27.

"to the extent to which": Maurice Merleau-Ponty, *Sense and Non-sense* (Evanston, Ill.: Northwestern University Press, 1964), 306.

"I knew that the first": Cited in Delange, 84.

He so much pressed: Max Gelée, *Icare* IV, 65.

330 "If you had your way": André George, *La Nef*, September 1945, 25.

"When the flight is normal": Alias, *Icare* IV, 94.

Laux was surprised: Laux, *Icare* V, 49.

He got little satisfaction and "If anyone in the group": SE went on at length about his medical condition to Galantière in 1941, BL. In FA he admits only that his old fractures were giving him trouble, 301.

331 Why had no one: Chevrier, 225. Chevrier has him meeting with Reynaud on the sixteenth.

an announcement he remembered: Winston Churchill, *Memoirs of the Second World War* (Boston: Houghton Mifflin, 1987), 252.

332 tersely described the apocalyptic: see Dutertre, *Icare* IV, 71–73.

"Is something broken": Dutertre, ibid., 72. I have based the account of the flight on my interview with Colonel Dutertre, on his 1940 contribution to the 2/33's *historique* (SHAA), on his published accounts over the last fifty years, on those of the 1/33's veterans (*Icare* IV, 78–83), and on the 2/33's *journal de marche* (SHAA).

"I would now be playing": Archives of the Association des Amis de Saint-Exupéry.

333 "interminable syrup": FA, 349.
     One minute, he told a reporter: *Le Devoir* (Montreal), April 26, 1942. The recollections
     of Michel Albeaux-Fernet, the third at dinner that night, can be found in EG, 106–108.
     "I felt like a fish": *Le Devoir* (Montreal), May 2, 1942.
     "We amount to nothing": Werth, *33 jours* (Paris: Viviane Hamy, 1992), 13. He blamed
     SE": ibid., 49.
334 "Monsieur de SE" and "Never": J.-G. Bougerol, *Icare*, Spring 1971.
     "driven by the enemy": FA, 286 (translation mine).
     "The news from France": Churchill, *Memoirs of the Second World War*, 254.
     "France has fallen": Raoul de Roussy de Sales, *The Making of Yesterday*, 133.
     "We're off to Algeria": LSM, 218.
     a fact the pilot took great pleasure: See Suzanne Massu, *Icare* IV, 96–99. an acrobatic
     feat: So Massu was told by "the connoisseurs," ibid., 99.
335 Pélissier found his friend: Pélissier, 36.
     "Pointless to extinguish": Suzanne Massu, *Icare* IV, 99. Also, Massu, *Quand j'étais
     Rochambelle* (Paris: Grasset, 1969). The two accounts differ slightly.

                          XV   RESISTANCE ON FIFTH AVENUE

336 "This is me": My thanks to the late René Gavoille for a copy of this dedication page,
     reproduced in *Icare* VI, 28–29.
     confessed that he had been nervous: Henri Alias, *Icare* IV, 93.
     "lost its soul": *"historique"* of the 2/33. SHAA.
337 "My companions are all": Hélène Froment, *On ne revient pas* (Paris: Gallimard, 1941),
     193. Fontaine, too, writes odes to his freezing bed.
     preoccupied, whispering adults: Mireille d'Agay, *Icare* III, 22–23.
     who had been put off: April 13, 1942, memorandum to Donovan from John C. Wiley,
     OSS files, INT 12FR21, NA. SE was put off as well by the anti–de Gaulle sentiments
     expressed by various friends in the military.
338 "He turned in circles": Gisèle d'Assailly, "En Parlant de Saint-Exupéry," *La Gazette
     des Arts et Lettres*, December 21, 1946.
     "half-separated": Interview with Maximilian Becker, September 21, 1990. SE uses
     the word himself in his 1939 correspondence with his agent when discussing the
     distribution of his assets in the event of his death.
     Suzanne Werth finally confided: Her query—and Madame de B's response—can be
     found in Claude Werth's archives.
     "wanted to protect him": Froment, 198.
     "Paris, Germany": The observation is Flanner's, *The New Yorker*, December 7, 1940.
339 "Out of a thousand": Eve Curie, Philippe Barrès, Raoul de Roussy de Sales, eds.,
     They Speak for a Nation (Garden City, N.Y.: Doubleday, Doran, 1941), 237.
     he claimed was his conscience: EG, 98.
     "My friend there is" and "See you soon, then": Robert Boname, *Icare* V, 107. Also,
     interview with Robert Boname, December 20, 1990. Joseph Kessel wrote his brother
     from Vichy: *"J'ai vu ici Saint-Ex, et ç'a été une joie rare. Tu le verras prochainement.
     Il va pour un mois à New York"* (Courrières, *Joseph Kessel*, 538).
     "There goes the man": Roger Beaucaire, EG, 128. The story exists in many variations;
     Beaucaire's account, among the plainest, seems closest to the truth.
340 Gallimard had called on Gide: van Rysselberghe, *Cahiers André Gide* VI, 199–200.
     For more on Drieu La Rochelle and the *NRF*, see Pierre Andreu and Frederic Grover,
     Drieu La Rochelle (Paris: Hachette, 1979), 451–60.

"I'm not made": Chevrier, 229.
"I think it imperative" and "I think it is time": Beucler, *Icare* IV, 113.
"You will show me": Giroud, *Leçons particulières*, 104. See also Odile Yelnik, *Jean Prévost* (Paris: Fayard, 1979), 150–51.
"opportunities for his deliverance": Werth, *Déposition*, 61.
341 "When I want something": Lucas, *Icare* II, 104.
"If I come back": Billon, *Icare* IV, 117. The film was never made, despite Billon's best attempts.
"I like books which give": Georges Altman, *Le Progrès* (Lyons), October 30, 1940, 1. See also Altman, *Volonté de ceux de la Résistance*, February 21, 1945.
Another reunion that week: Jean Macaigne, interview of January 4, 1991.
SE outlined for Chambe to "Right here, damn it all": Chambe, *Icare* IV, 121.
342 "Rarely have I seen": Prince Alexander Makinsky, cited in Cate, 427.
"I felt neither": OTAGE, 391 (translation mine).
"Under attack": Migeo, *Henri Guillaumet*, 187.
"Guillaumet is dead": Chevrier, 230.
"I've learned so many": OTAGE, 392.
343 "I would like to talk": Jacques de Dampierre, EG, 141.
"To live is to be": Mlle. Dutheil, of the École Française of Lisbon, cited in Crane, 280–81.
He wanted very much: SE cable to Becker, December 21, 1940. Becker papers.
the writer good-naturedly engaged: I am indebted to Joseph Laitin for his recollections, which greatly supplement the *New York Times* report of SE's arrival, January 1, 1941, 20.
344 "I am not a crystal": ibid. Cécile Busignies provided helpful details regarding the *Siboney* crossing, interviews of October 8, 1990, and August 24, 1993. She remembered SE's quip about Columbus.
"All you have to say" and "I don't want to": Jean Renoir, *Ma vie et mes films* (Paris: Flammarion, 1974), 183.
"the two mastodons": Lamotte, *Icare* V, 83. See Wendy Goodman, "The Man Upstairs," *New York*, June 19, 1989, for more on Lamotte in New York.
"more like a bird": Raoul de Roussy de Sales, *The Making of Yesterday*, 175.
345 Legends of all kinds: See Robert Van Gelder, *The New York Times Book Review*, January 19, 1941, 2, and Stephen Vincent and Rosemary Benét, "Saint-Exupéry, Flyer and Thinker," New York *Herald Tribune Books*, January 19, 1941, 5.
half hero, half clown: From the diaries of Selden Rodman, the young poet and editor of *Common Sense*, who visited with SE on several occasions in 1941.
"You never have to": Otis Ferguson, *Common Sense*, May 1941, 133.
It was not their understanding: Interview with Elizabeth (Reynal) Darbee, August 28, 1993. He was touched and delighted: ibid.
346 Outlining a rather unusual: From a deposition written by SE and prepared by Reynal and Hitchcock for the U.S. government, January 13, 1941, HBJ archives.
Of Curtice and Peggy Hitchcock: Interview with Joan Rich, August 7, 1991.
He had no idea: SE explained his grasp of English to Adèle Breaux; see Breaux, *Saint-Exupéry in America, 1942–1943* (Cranbury, N.J.: Associated University Presses, Inc., 1971), 38. It was she who deemed his ear for English acute.
"When I want a cup": SE used this excuse on everyone; this version comes from John Phillips, interview of November 28, 1990.
347 "I haven't finished learning": Interview with Maximilian Becker, September 21, 1990.
"arrache-poussière": Jacques Tiné, letter of January 1993.
"What's going on": Yvonne Michel, interview of January 4, 1991.

347 From Saks he called: André Maurois. "Saint-Exupéry." *Les Nouvelles Littéraires*, November 7. 1946, 1. Max Becker remembered having been at the receiving end of some of these calls.
"*Sprechen Sie Deutsch*": Ruth Belt, Cited in Crane. 287.

348 He had little love of America: SE was not shy on this front, confiding his disdain with nearly everyone he knew, always in the same terms. Madame de B, interview of January 7, 1991; Elizabeth Darbee, interview of July 22. 1991.
"Yes," agreed the aviator: Raoul Aglion, interview of October 4. 1990.
"kind of preaching friar": Galantière letter to Howard Scherry, April 8, 1972.
"It was more like": Natacha Stewart Ullmann. "Let's Play Portraits," *The New Yorker*, January 27, 1962. The piece stands as a shining example of a perfect match of subject and author.
"The point is—this man": Lieutenant Colonel Busbee to Colonel Ralph C. Smith, MID, March 22, 1941, MID 2307-C-109, NA.

349 "If at the time of": His opinions made their way to the State Department in a memo of May 8, 1941, written by R. Gordon Wasson, 740.0011/11539, NA.
"For the record, this Division": Memo of June 23, 1941, from War to State, G-2/2307-C-109, NA.
Pétain was quoted: *The New York Times*, January 1, 1941, 24.

350 "20 Anglophiles": Werth, *Déposition*, 126.
he had no political agenda: *The New York Times*, January 31, 1941, 7.
Look at it this way: SE's letters—biting, then conciliatory—to Breton are conserved in Paris at the Bibliothèque Jacques Doucet. I am grateful to Elisa Breton and Aube Gelleonët for having allowed me to consult them. The letters went through multiple drafts; a portion of one early draft—from which this thought was taken—was reproduced in the Ader Picard Tajan catalogue for the Drouot sale of July 6, 1984, item no. 26. A letter in which SE defends himself on the subject of the Vichy "appointment" is reproduced in *Cahiers Saint-Exupéry* 3, 9–21.

351 "How can you expect": Raoul Aglion, *Roosevelt and de Gaulle* (New York: The Free Press, 1988), 84. (A different version of the same book appeared in France as *De Gaulle et Roosevelt: la France libre aux États-Unis* [Paris: Plon, 1984].)
Fanned by both sides: The recollections of Raoul Aglion, Elizabeth Darbee, Lewis Galantière, and Yvonne Michel have all been of help here. Pierre Brodin's Lycée Français office received the indignant phone calls, interview with Pierre Brodin, December 17. 1990. See also Guy Fritsch-Estrangin's gossipy, invaluable *New York entre de Gaulle et Pétain* (Paris: La Table Ronde, 1969).
Aglion holds that of all: Aglion, interview of October 4, 1990. For one indication of de Gaulle's eagerness to bring SE into the fold, see his telegram of September 18, 1941, to René Pleven in de Gaulle. *The Call to Honor* (New York: The Viking Press, 1955), 365.
"They are not waging": Denis de Rougemont, *Journal des deux mondes* (Paris: Gallimard, 1968), 519. The entry is for July 10, 1942.
"the bubonic plague": Lindbergh, *War Within and Without*, 161. "stay *free*, pure and untouched": ibid., 166. The saint's point of view: ibid., 309.

352 "I detest the French" and "I am happy": Dido Renoir and Alexander Sesonske, eds., Jean Renoir. *Lettres d'Amérique* (Paris: Presses de la Renaissance, 1984), 103–104. The letter is dated June 2, 1942.
"I have been more courageous": EG, 272.
in dire need of an archangel: From a 1941 letter from SE to Renoir, Renoir papers, Arts Library, University of California, Los Angeles.
half the French in occupied France: Ted Morgan. *An Uncertain Hour* (New York:

William Morrow & Company, 1990), 110–11. See also Diomède Catroux, *Icare* VI, 72. from their vantage point: Elizabeth Darbee, interview of July 22, 1991.

353   "When tact failed": Galantière, *The Atlantic*, April 1947, 135.

he was still hoping: As he continued to tell many friends, among them the Rabat-based Pierre Charpentier, *Icare*, 108, première trimestre, 1984 (hereafter *Icare* VII), 57.

His crippling fevers: See Galantière's *Atlantic* piece (April 1947, 135) as well as his papers, BL. Forty-one-degree fever: ibid. Also Robert Boname, March 19, 1991; interview with Becker, September 21, 1990. He wore dark glasses: Rodman, interview of October 16, 1991.

"without a doubt the most": Renoir, *Lettres d'Amérique*, 37. The letter dates from April 29, 1941.

354   "something truly monumental": SE quoted in Renoir, *Lettres d'Amérique*, 27.

"I wouldn't bother you": To Charpentier, *Icare* VII, 57.

"He's a pig! He's a pig!": Renoir, *Icare* V, 28. See also Renoir, *Ma vie et mes films*.

"Dido, I know you're there": I am hugely grateful to Alain Renoir for having unearthed this recording, from which the information about the WSS screenplay is derived.

"It's problematic" to "I think that I will": ibid.

355   "certain familiar treacle": ibid., 78.

In retrospect he mellowed: See Jean Narboni, ed., *Cahiers du Cinéma: Jean Renoir, entretiens et propos* (Paris: Éditions de l'Étoile, 1979).

He chastised his friend: Renoir papers, Arts Library, University of California, Los Angeles.

356   he took up a lot of room: See Renoir, *Icare* V, 27–30. On the verge of emotional collapse: Alain Renoir, letter of October 18, 1991. Annabella also recalled SE's eccentricities, *Icare* V, 56–69.

sick to the point of delirium: Interviews with Bita Dobo, January 31, 1991, and August 29, 1993. Dobo was Pierre Lazareff's assistant at the time.

his own gloss: To Galantière, BL.

357   "a neurasthenic little girl": ibid.

"Everyone in New York": Recollections of Dr. J. L. Lapeyre, family papers.

"not very sterile zone" and Guatemala all over: To Galantière, BL.

She found him: Interview with Annabella, December 12, 1991. See also Annabella, *Icare* V, 56–69.

358   "But he doesn't" and "Of course I don't": Renoir, *Icare* V, 28–29.

"As things stand": Ruth Belt, cited in Crane, 288. I am grateful to Carolee Lapeyre for having granted me access to her father's papers.

"brain child" to "*Gracias a Dios!*": Ruth Belt, cited in Crane, 289.

359   he wrote Madame de B: See especially the New York letter reproduced in Paul Nayrac, *L'Angoisse de Saint-Exupéry*, Discours à la séance inaugurale du Congrès de Psychiatrie et de Neurologie de Langue Française, Strasbourg, July 21–26, 1958.

Patiently Galantière explained: Galantière papers, BL.

Later he was to say: Max Gelée, *Icare* IV, 65.

"I prefer the sale" and pointing out that Descartes: EG, 219. The original missives are at BL.

360   "What is the use": EG, 222.

At the top of a sheet: The page is now in the collection of Max Alder.

He claimed that his sudden: EG, 191. (From the second half of the letter cited in part in Nayrac, op. cit.)

"a kind of flunkey": FA, 387. "I don't care a button": FA, 388.

500 Notes

360 "I think it was awful": Charles Lindbergh cited in Anne Morrow Lindbergh, *War Within and Without*, 249–50.

half of what he paid: I am grateful to Howard Scherry for having provided a copy of the contract with Marie Bouchu McBride, as well as a copy of McBride's letter to Adèle Breaux of February 19, 1973.

361 "I don't think": Galantière, "The Most Unforgettable Character I've Met," *The Reader's Digest*, December 1957, 176.

"Listen, Bernard" to "Because it is two": Lamotte, *Icare* V, 85.

they thought him: Annabella, *Icare* V, 58.

The writer had agonized: Interview with Madame de B, January 17, 1992.

362 She would claim that: Breaux, 112.

the Hoboken pier: Fleury, *Icare* V, 36–37.

That afternoon SE telephoned: Interviews with Elizabeth Darbee, July 22, 1991, and September 6, 1991.

According to Fleury: Fleury, *Icare* V, 37.

363 missed their mutual friend: Renoir, *Lettres d'Amérique*, 120. The letter is dated August 21, 1942

"Hum like that": FA, 328.

"It is becoming": Original manuscript, microfilms 2336 and 2337, BN.

"This narrative and Churchill's": Edward Weeks, *The Atlantic*, April 1942.

"like a soliloquizing angel": E. Edman, New York *Herald Tribune Books*, February 22, 1942, 1.

364 "For President Franklin Roosevelt": My thanks to Raymond Teichman at the Franklin D. Roosevelt Library for supplying a copy of this inscription.

"I want to talk to you": Ping Lawrence provided the description of SE's appearance at Anne Morgan's, interview of April 1, 1991.

far wall of the auditorium: Breaux, 20–21.

An hour before: Pierre Bédard, letter of February 21, 1951, reproduced in Crane, 291.

"the calumnies and resentments": EG, 227. The note—probably to Nada de Bragance—was written in February 1942.

the French consul-general: Monsieur d'Aumale's letter, commending FA and its author for rising above politics, is dated March 27, 1942, and resides in the archives of the French Embassy in Washington. It was reprinted in part in the 1984 Archives Nationales exhibition catalogue, 120.

SE racked his brains to "Yes, but you made it look": EG, 284. SE grappled with these objections in a December letter to Jacques Maritain.

365 "The man of letters": Jean Guéhenno, cited in Assouline, 253.

366 "another demented Judeo-bellicose" and "M. de SE chooses": P.-A. Cousteau, "À propos d'une provocation," *Je suis partout*, January 15, 1943, 1. See also P.-A. Cousteau, "Antoine de Saint-Exupéry au secours d'Israël et de la guerre Juive," *Le Cahier jaune*, January 1943.

As for the reviewers: Pierre Masteau, "M. de Saint-Exupéry quarante-huitard attardé," *Au Pilori*, January 21, 1943.

Vichy commissioner of Jewish affairs: The astonishing document—the commissoner's response to an offended reader—is reproduced in Chevrier, 313–16.

In Casablanca a request: L. A. Triebel, *The Literature of Flying and Flyers* (Sydney: Les Éditions du Courrier Australien, 1955), 13.

Heller was severely: Heller, EG, 300.

He was later able: Assouline, 300, 312–15.

Israël read: Interview with Israël, January 22, 1991.

XVI ANYWHERE OUT OF THIS WORLD

368 "Oh, he was wonderful": Fay Wray, *On the Other Hand* (New York: St. Martin's Press, 1989), 226.

"a virile male": Elsa Maxwell, "Elsa Maxwell's Party Line," New York *Post*, July 20, 1943, 15.

enormously sexy: Interview with Kitty Carlisle Hart, September 28, 1990.

Those who did: Interview with Anne Morrow Lindbergh, December 5, 1990.

"I don't know": Interview with Nadine Bertin, November 6, 1991.

369 "*le beau blond*": Interview with John Phillips, December 4, 1990. Becker, Brodin, and Elizabeth Darbee all thought SE more than aware of his effect on women to whom, reported Mrs. Darbee, "he was catnip."

"he found himself": Galantière, *The Atlantic*, April 1947, 138–39.

"They only call me": Cited often, but early on by Janet Flanner in the second of her magnificent four-part profile of Pétain, "La France et le Vieux," *The New Yorker*, February 19, 1944, 32.

"Let's stop right here" to "Only please don't": Galantière papers, BL. A toned-down version of the same events appears in Galantière's *Reader's Digest* profile, December 1957.

the cornerstones of French democracy: Galantière papers, BL.

370 tall, blond, and titled: Elizabeth Darbee, interview of September 6, 1991.

Madame de B's political leanings: See OSS reports on Madame de B in RG 226, Entry 190, Box 380, Folder 514; Entry 108A, Box 133, BD 241–940; and NA76–785 London X2. With friends in all kinds of high places, she attracted her share of attention, although this did not guarantee that the OSS drew accurate conclusions regarding her activities.

"Don't work yourself" and "You know": Interview with Madame de B, December 4, 1991.

"Her face, which is that of ": Interview with Madame de B, January 13, 1992.

"Don't speak like that": Interview with Madame de B, December 4, 1991.

371 "entirely private, out of the ordinary": Interview with Hedda Sterne, October 25, 1993.

"spiritual assistance": SE to Hedda Sterne, Hedda Sterne collection, AAA.

"an episodic necessity": Pélissier, 125.

superb legs: Quoted in Renée de Saussine, *Icare* III, 63.

flown at high altitude: Radio France interview with Consuelo, conducted by Jacques Chancel. Also, interview with Pierre Brodin, December 17, 1990.

drug him with Seconal: The lover has requested anonymity; the attempt failed.

"I desperately need": From the bundle of letters sold at Drouot, December 4, 1991, item no. 30, letter 4.

"that light of milk": ibid.

"but such is the nature": Drouot, December 4, 1991, sale, item no. 30, letter 6.

372 "Tell him I love him" to "*Oui, oui*": Interviews with Silvia Reinhardt, March 23, 1992, and September 16, 1993.

"a slender, attractive": Lillian Ross, *Picture* (New York: Limelight Editions, 1984), 40–41. "I won't mingle": ibid, 42. "Gottfried, nobody ever": ibid., 44.

No one else communicated to "*Je suis usé*": I have drawn on a long series of conversations—especially those of September 26 and 27, 1991—with Silvia Reinhardt for these details concerning the relationship.

373 an irate vigil: Ader Picard Tajan catalogue, July 6, 1984, Drouot sale, item no. 15.
     The letter is wrenching; even SE's handwriting looks tortured.
     "You are low": The letter was generously supplied by Howard Scherry, who rescued
     it from Marie McBride's files under unusual circumstances years after Marie McBride
     had retrieved it—to the sound of SE's returning footsteps—from the author's waste-
     paper basket.
374 "When I'm dead": ibid.
     Consuelo told people: Breaux, 112.
     A housekeeper: ibid., 109.
     a number of objects fly: Interview with Bita Dobo, August 29, 1993.
     a nonaggression pact: Interview with Pierre Brodin, December 17, 1990.
     "If you're not here": Interview with Robert Tenger, January 19, 1991.
     prone to vanish: Pierre Brodin remembered as much, interview of December 17, 1990,
     as did many others.
     "Do you think" and "Oh, yes": Breaux, 130.
     "Surrealism made flesh": Galantière, letter to Howard Scherry, April 8, 1972.
375 She spent a cocktail party: Helen Wolff to the author, December 10, 1990.
     "Well, I was honest": Breaux, 136.
     "incurably infantile": Helen Wolff letter of December 10, 1990.
     "All I ask for": Consuelo de SE to Madeleine Goisot, May 2, 1955.
     Asked about his political: See Alfred Ayotte, "Entretien avec Antoine de Saint-
     Exupéry," *Le Devoir*, April 30, 1942, 2.
     "amounted to a sophisticated": Pierre Baillargeon's *Amérique Française* reporting can
     be found in the *Quartier Latin* tribute to SE, March 23, 1945.
     "Oh, my God": Interview with Elizabeth Darbee, September 6, 1991.
376 U.S. exit permit: State Department files do not indicate an exit permit for SE in May.
     A visa case was opened for SE on June 1 and a visa issued on the fourth, 811.111,
     NA.
     ordered to get him out: Elizabeth Darbee, August 28, 1993.
     "in no danger": From Curtice Hitchcock's Department of State affidavit in support of
     SE's re-entry into the U.S., April 30, 1942, HBJ archives.
     "If I insist" and "It has other things": SE to Hitchcock, ANAT. Elizabeth Darbee does
     not as much remember having lost her patience as she remembers SE's imperiousness.
     correcting his first sentence: Marcel Raymond, "Antoine de Saint-Exupéry," *Quartier
     Latin* (Montreal), March 23, 1945. For more on SE's lectures, see *L'Action Catholique*
     (Quebec), May 5, 1942, 13; *L'Action Universitaire*, January, 1944, 11; and *Le Devoir*,
     May 2, 1942, 1. In perhaps the least flattering description of SE on the dais, Jean
     Issalys noted the Frenchman had *"une tête de batracien rêveur."* (*Quartier Latin*, March
     23, 1945.)
377 Several times he visited: I owe these recollections to Katherine Ethier Roy, interviews
     of September 3, 1990, and September 25, 1993.
     He was forced to consult: Interviews with Bita Dobo, August 29, 1993, and with Hedda
     Sterne, October 25, 1993.
     "It makes you a bit": SE to Hitchcock, ANAT.
     "Odd planet": Drouot, December 4, 1991, sale, item no. 30, letter 3.
378 She may have put forth: Interview with Elizabeth Darbee, October 15, 1991.
     Galantière was to say: Galantière, *Reader's Digest*, December 1957, 178.
     most difficult thing about writing: Baillargeon, *Amérique Française*, op cit.
     "Kings *always* wear": Breaux, 75.
     Originally he offered: This text—along with its drawings—was part of an Arts Anciens
     sale, Geneva, November 22, 1986, item no. 22A.

379 "My heart begins": Interview with Silvia Reinhardt, February 10, 1992.
later he wrote: SE to Silvia Reinhardt, from Algiers, 1943. The letter has been sold, although Mrs. Reinhardt kindly shared a copy.
"Words," counsels the Little Prince's fox: LP, 84. "What is essential": LP, 87.
"I wanted a hut": de Rougemont, 521.
380 Maurois felt afterward: Maurois wrote of the visit in many places. See especially "Saint-Exupéry," *Les Nouvelles Littéraires*, November 7, 1946, and his article on Consuelo in *Pour la Victoire*, October 6, 1945, 7.
He took away: de Rougemont, 521. "You are less": ibid., 530.
"Mademoiselle, I am a very": Breaux, 36. Breaux's modest book—never published in France—provides an invaluable portrait of the celebrated English student in America. For more on Breaux see also Barbara Marhoefer, "Eatons Neck 1942: The Little Prince Is Born," *The New York Times*, November 28, 1971, 12.
"All children do not" and "Ah, Mademoiselle": Breaux, 48.
"She does not like": Breaux, 60, 105.
381 "It is irritating": Albert Guérard, *The New York Times Book Review*, December 15, 1946, 12. See also Consuelo de Saint-Exupéry, *Kingdom of the Rocks* (New York: Random House, 1946). The novel's translator, Katherine Woods, had been the translator of *The Little Prince*.
"There are times": Rose Feld, *Weekly Book Review*, December 29, 1946, 2.
She reminded Guérard: Albert Guérard, *The New York Times Book Review*, December 15, 1946, 12.
"never to really seem": From a November 17, 1972, letter from Adèle Breaux to Howard Scherry.
382 "a grotesque pipe dream" to "So that's how it is!" Galantière, *The Atlantic*, April 1947, 140–41.
listening in on: See for example RG226, M1642, Roll no. 105, NA, a report of a nine-minute telephone conversation taped and reported on by the OSS, November 13, 1942.
"I am more devoted": See Drouot catalogue of May 20, 1976.
383 "I am so alone": Ader Picard Tajan catalogue, Drouot sale, July 6, 1984, item no. 17, letter 2.
"an odd kind of desert": Ader Picard Tajan catalogue, Drouot sale, July 6, 1984, item no. 13.
"We never know": SE to Bernard Lamotte, n.d. I am indebted to Dorothy Barclay Thompson for having produced this sister text to *The Little Prince*.
384 asked a diplomat friend: Charpentier, *Icare* VII, 56.
He confessed to Adèle Breaux: Breaux, 81.
"a small Pacific islet": LP, 68.
"I asked him" and "I'm the Little Prince": John Phillips, from pages that appeared as an essay in his *Odd World* (New York: Simon & Schuster, 1959). The text is available in French in Phillips, *Les derniers jours de Saint-Exupéry* (Éditions Parkett/Der Alltag: Zurich, 1989).
"You are an extraterrestrial" and "Yes, yes, it is true": Raoul Aglion, letter to author, September 26, 1990.
"lived his life alone": LP, 5. "Be my friends": LP, 76.
385 His gestures: Interview with Hedda Sterne, October 25, 1993.
his speech patterns: Interview with André Henry, January 23, 1991.
"It is without precedent": Dony, 568.
"If I knew how": To Hedda Sterne, Hedda Sterne collection, AAA.
offering up his photograph: Pierre Guillain de Bénouville, EG, 492.
SE responded without: Israël, *Icare* IV, 59–60. On his disdain for *Paris-Soir*, EG, 391.

386 He assured a woman friend: Ader Picard Tajan catalogue, Drouot sale, July 6, 1984, item no. 21. SE felt compelled to attempt to explain his relationship with his wife to a lover named Suzanne.

He described his wife: Interview with Madame de B, December 4, 1991.

the Little Princess: Interview with René Gavoille, January 9, 1992.

he called Hélène Lazareff: Interview with Dorothy Barclay Thompson, February 5, 1993.

"You would have to be" and "The Little Prince was wrong": From Dorothy Barclay Thompson's inscribed copy of the book.

He was indignant and "We were twelve years old": Annabella, interview of December 12, 1991.

387 "recording his voice": I am grateful to Selden Rodman for having shared with me his journal entries of 1941 concerning SE. This one dates from April 4, 1941.

Gleefully he directed: Galantière, *The Atlantic*, April 1947, 135.

"wave-maker": Paul-Émile Victor, *Icare* V, 25.

The Reynals found their author: Interview with Elizabeth Darbee, September 7, 1993.

Boname was skeptical: Boname, *Icare* V, 108.

Galantière's favorite: Galantière, *The Atlantic*, April 1947, 140.

fish-shaped coffin: Chevrier, 238.

388 "if not pro-Vichy": T-5297, 0-15, May 27, 1942, Intelligence report from Thomas to Dostert, NA. Generally Fleury's behavior was thought to be suspect; the friendship concerned various State Department officials. See Dewitt Poole's memo to Donovan of March 13. 1942, OSS 57-75, Central File no. 759 (Entry 92, Box 8), NA.

"So I'm a bit scatter-brained": I am grateful to Elizabeth Darbee for having shared a copy of this undated note of apology from SE.

"like a captain": A portion of SE's letter to Silvia was reproduced in the auction catalogue from the sale of Silvia's papers, Drouot, May 20, 1976, no. 52.

"Either he dominated": Maurois, *From Proust to Camus*, 203.

"I think it is fair": Renoir, *Icare* V, 29.

389 "I am perfectly delighted": Hitchcock to Max Becker, October 16, 1942. I am indebted to Royce Becker and Aleta Daley for having provided a copy of the fully executed contract.

"They are barbarians" and "Yes, barbarians": Paul-Émile Victor, *Icare* V, 25.

"Well, I hope that Vichy": Jean Lacouture, *Charles de Gaulle*, vol. 1 (Paris: Éditions du Seuil, 1984), 607.

390 the United States fell back on policies: Interview with Raoul Aglion, September 27, 1991.

"Our real chief" and "The State Department": SE, "An Open Letter to Frenchmen Everywhere," *The New York Times Magazine*, November 29, 1942.

391 open to ridicule: Fritsch-Estrangin, 82.

One former French air force officer: *The New York Times*, December 7, 1942, 26. Pierre Benedictus—who claimed to have been on the Dunkerque airfield at about the time SE was overflying Arras—gently reprimanded his colleague for having remained "aloof, on neutral ground."

"We cannot, however touching": Henry Bernstein, *The New York Times*, December 6. 1942, 23.

"We live in sad times": Aglion, *Roosevelt and de Gaulle*, 146.

392 made the unassailable point: Jacques Maritain, "Il faut parfois juger," *Pour la Victoire*, December 19. 1942, 1.

say what you will: SE to Maritain, EG

393 We probably do disagree: SE's letters to Breton can be found at the Bibliothèque Jacques Doucet in Paris.
no more charming residence: de Rougemont, 526. I am grateful to Max Becker for having handed on a copy of the lease for Consuelo's apartment at 240 Central Park South. It was canceled as of November 30, 1942.
| a definition of perfect taste: Breaux, 129.
"I consider that": ibid., 134.

394 "I understand why you are upset": The bulk of this letter was published in the catalogue for the Drouot sale, May 20, 1976, item no. 47.
On the thirty-first the SEs: I owe the description of this evening to a magnificent letter from Mary Evans Boname, March 18, 1991. Consuelo bragged to Helen Wolff of the *oeufs-en-gelée* attack, letter to author, December 10, 1990.
"For goodness' sake!" Interview with Boname, March 19, 1991.
"If they continue to mechanize": Cited in Fleury, *Icare* V, 37.

395 he had drafted a proposal: Ader Picard Tajan catalogue, Drouot sale, July 6, 1984, item no. 43. SE toyed with the idea of a squadron of French volunteers fighting under the American flag, December 1941. Also OSS files (INT, 12FR21), NA. On April 15, 1942, John C. Wiley reported to Donovan that SE and Paul-Émile Victor had recently told their dinner companions they were "anxious to enter once more into active service. They would like to form a French foreign legion marching with them."
Helen Gahagan Douglas: Interview with Elizabeth Darbee, August 28, 1993.
According to Maurois: André Maurois, *Mémoires* (Paris: Flammarion, 1970), 353.
"the pull to sacrifice": Lindbergh, *War Within and Without*, 309.
"If I write a page": OTAGE, original manuscript. SE's pages and pages of draft manuscript—and the proofs of the very affecting original—can be found in Washington, D.C., AAA.

396 "lovely shipload of experiences": OTAGE, 400 (translation mine).
"If I differ from you": OTAGE, 404 (translation mine).
"Words," he told Yvonne Michel: Interview with Yvonne Michel, January 4, 1991.
In better spirits: EG, 465.

397 better off without him: Ader Picard Tajan catalogue, Drouot sale, July 6, 1984, item no. 5.
"I'm off to the war": SE to Consuelo, EG, 353.
visited the *Richelieu*: Cate, 482.
"In what branch?" and "In the air force": Interview with Georges Perrin, January 16, 1991.
"SE changed people": Galantière, *Reader's Digest*, December 1957, 175. Many of SE's friends and acquaintances echoed these words in interviews.

398 without seeing his publisher: Interview with Joan Rich, August 7, 1991.
a shopping list: Dorothy Barclay Thompson kindly shared the list, which she asked Hélène Lazareff if she might keep and which remains in her possession.
"intellectual euphoria": De Rougemont, 530.
Beaming, he received: Ping Lawrence re-created the evening, interview of April 1, 1991.

399 "Don't linger like this": LP, 40.
"Hers is the worst case": Breaux, 140.
"like an amoeba" and "I wish I had": Silvia Reinhardt, interviews of September 26, 1991, and November 6, 1991.
A little after noon: I am grateful to Dr. Sheldon Sommers for having shared his memories of the *Stirling Castle* and SE in sickbay, letters of January 8, 1991, July 16, 1991, and August 29, 1993.

400 "Reviewers and critics": Reynal & Hitchcock's two-page advertisement appeared in *Publishers Weekly*, February 20, 1943.
"must have been miserable" and "throw himself into self-sacrifice": Lindbergh, *War Within and Without*, 338.
distillation of suffering: P. L. Travers, letter to Adèle Breaux, May 30, 1970.
"So I lived my whole life": LP, 5.
"all fairy tales": P. L. Travers, New York *Herald Tribune Books*, April 11, 1943, 4–5.
summoned his business partner: On the ill-fated romance between Orson Welles and *The Little Prince*, see Barbara Leaming, *Orson Welles* (New York: Viking Penguin, 1985), 270–71. I am grateful to Barbara Leaming for having reminded me of this enthusiasm on Welles's part and to Rebecca Campbell Cape at the Lilly Library, Indiana University, Bloomington, Indiana, for having supplied the supporting documents. Welles's script is at the Lilly Library. Welles purchased broadcast rights in WSS and NF in November 1942 for three hundred dollars.
401 she claims she never knew: Silvia Reinhardt, interview of March 23, 1992.
"the joy of a crusade": SE, "Lettre à un Américain," EG, 495.
liturgical chant: See Henry Elkin, EG, 355–57.

XVII INTO THIN AIR

402 One young American diplomat: See Kenneth Pendar, *Adventure in Diplomacy* (London: Cassel & Company, 1966). Equally helpful as background for this chapter were *The War Memoirs of Charles de Gaulle* (New York: Simon & Schuster, 1959), Jean Monnet, *Memoirs* (Garden City, N.Y.: Doubleday & Company, 1978), Robert Murphy, *Diplomat Among Warriors* (Garden City, N.Y.: Doubleday & Company, 1964), and Pierre Sonneville, *Les Combattants de la Liberté* (Paris: Éditions de la Table Ronde, 1968).
A. J. Liebling tried: Liebling, 219.
403 to his amazement: Gavoille, interview of January 9, 1992. Also *Icare* VI, 30.
"Well, see to it!": Gelée, *Icare* VI, 82.
"Here, per our agreement": René Chambe, *Icare* VI, 38.
"He will go back": Lindbergh, *War Within and Without*, 341.
The neighboring squadron: See Jules Roy, *Saint-Exupéry* (Paris: La Manufacture, 1990), 45.
404 Wilbur Wright's plane: Interview with Leon Gray, July 16, 1991.
fill out his paperwork: Interview with John R. Hoover, August 9, 1991.
to remember vividly: Roy, 47–48. Roy has offered several variations on this tale. The only one that differs substantially was written nearly fifty years later and appears in *Mémoires barbares* (Paris: Albin Michel, 1989), 222–23.
"How old are you" to "It seems you think me": Chambe, *Icare* VI, 39.
405 "Here I am": ibid., 40.
"A scarecrow": He used the expression repeatedly; see for example EG, 462.
"*le mur élastique*": Comte, *Icare* VI, 60.
French barely respected it: Sonneville, 266.
at the Interallié: Pendar, 182–83.
406 "Sectarianism always": Cited without Roy's name in EG, 369.
He came down: François Laux, *Icare* VI, 42. See also Chassin's version, *Forces Aériennes Françaises*, April 1959.
On another training flight: Reynaud-Fourton provides the best account of this incident, which he retells in SE's words, *Icare* VII, 63.

One American major: Vernon V. Robison recounts the priceless story of the visit of the unilingual American major to the unilingual French squadron in *Icare* VI, 113.

407 He was given six choices: Interview with Vernon V. Robison, December 28, 1990.
except take off on schedule: Interviews with Leon Gray, July 16, 1991, and September 9, 1991.
"The quicker the SOBs": Letter from Dino A. Brugioni, January 1994.
"he didn't know him": Interview with Leon Gray, July 16, 1991.
begging Robert Murphy and "an absurd myth": The letter is reproduced in *Icare* VI, 43.

408 a very different picture: The letter to Consuelo appears in part in EG, 353.
enough sulfa drugs: Interview with Madame de B, January 17, 1992. In his biography, Pélissier attests that SE—moderate in few things—habitually abused medications.
Four days later: SHAA file. SE was cleared to fly by the medical examiner on his birthday, June 29, 1943. His 1943–44 *carnet de vol* is invaluable in charting his air- and ground time over these months, SHAA.
He was quick to inform: I am grateful to Royce Becker for supplying a copy of SE's June 8, 1943, letter to his publisher, who sent a copy on to Becker. An excerpt appears in EG, 371–73.
A canny publisher: Hitchcock's August 3, 1943, response to SE's letter—and the July 19 press release—are in the HBJ archives.
He hated: To Pélissier, EG, 373. Similarly, from an eloquent, unsent letter, EG, 376.
scaling the Himalayas: To Pélissier, EG, 373.

409 "a sort of flying torpedo": EG, 381.
A parachutist: Maurice Guernier, EG, 387.
could not get over: Diomède Catroux, *Icare* VI, 70.
allergic to the aircraft's: Henri Billard, EG, 396.
"They were firing" and "My dear friend": Quoted in Pélissier, 45–46.
cranked down the window and "This is very, very difficult": Interview with Dunn, March 1, 1991.
As the pilot described: See John Phillips's *Odd World* (New York: Simon & Schuster, 1959). I am hugely indebted to John Phillips, who is blessed with total recall, for a great number of details in this chapter.

410 "jabbered and hollered": Interview with Leon Gray, July 16, 1991.
Dunn maintained: Interview with Frank Dunn, July 16, 1991.
"Yes, the Lightning would never fly": SE to Phillips, Phillips interview of December 4, 1990.
"If he was taken": Interview with Gray, July 16, 1991.

411 "I want to die" to "The answer is no, no, and no": Dunn, interviews of March 1, 1991, and March 11, 1991. "Sir, I want to die" and "I don't give a damn": Gray, July 16, 1991.
with which he had been pleased and "This Frenchman": Chambe, *Icare* VI, 40. Dalloz felt that Giraud admired the book for the same reason.

412 "served as a symbol": *The War Memoirs of Charles de Gaulle (Unity)*, 143.
intended to decamp: See Chassin, *Icare* VI, 146. Madame de B provided the best description of the "underheated linen closet," interview of January 22, 1991. Chassin reported on the chaos therein, *Forces Aériennes Françaises*, April 1959.
"It's as if I were": EG, 407. The bulk of the dispirited correspondence reproduced in EG—the best barometer of SE's mood, which went from bad to worse—was addressed to Madame de B.

413 "warriors of propaganda": Pendar, 235.
"revengeful, unforgiving": ibid., 323.
"De Gaulle has the character": Cited in Liebling, 96.

413 "Hello, my dear member" and "Of course you know": EG, 455.
an audience with de Gaulle: See Roy, *Mémoires barbares*, 225. De Gaulle would admit as much later: see Marcel Achard's memories in *Icare* III, 65. Also Madame de B. January 18, 1994.
"Saint-Ex is not a Gaullist!": Sonneville, 270.
414 He watched, indignantly: EG, 477. Also Chassin, *Icare* VI, 147.
Tell me what you think: Dalloz, *Vérités sur le drame du Vercors* (Paris: Éditions Lanore, 1979), 13.
"Admit it": Pélissier, 101.
"Memoirs of a tortured soul": Beucler, in René Tavernier, *Saint-Exupéry en procès*, 148.
André Gide, who was not: Anne Heurgon-Desjardins, in a preface to *Entretiens sur André Gide* (Paris: Mouton and Co., 1967), 7.
The U.S. State Department: September 27, 1943, OSS report, See RG226, Entry 190, Box 380, Folder 514 and Entry 108A, Box 133, BD-241-940, as well as 77-785, London X2, Pts. 72, Folder 18, Doc. 28, NA.
"You must convince": Interview with Madame de B, January 30, 1992.
balder, heavier: Interview with Madame de B, January 18, 1994.
415 "If you put my book" to a sizable dose of Benzedrine: Chevrier, 264–65. Supplementary details from Madame de B, January 18, 1994.
"You are a little like Christ": Madame de B, January 8, 1992.
Comte's hospitality: Madame de B, January 18, 1994.
416 "A lot of people": From a letter to Comte, reproduced in *Icare* VI, 61.
In a particularly black mood: EG, 461.
"He seemed generally preoccupied": Sedgwick Mead, "My Dinner with Saint-Exupéry," *Harvard Medical Alumni Bulletin*, Autumn 1993, 68–69. Dr. Mead kindly supplied additional details regarding the visit, October 22, 1993.
"Have you forgotten something?" From an interview of May 19, 1987, with Pierre Reynaud-Fourton, SHAA. Emmanuel Breguet, who conducted the interview, kindly shared this tape with me. Delange tells a similar tale that I have not been able to substantiate: During the summer of 1943, SE landed soon after takeoff in a field several kilometers from the airstrip. He had not been wearing a watch and—suddenly convinced that he had been flying for several hours—thought he must be running low on fuel.
a kind of samba: Reynaud-Fourton, *Icare* VII, 66.
one awkward occasion: Interview with Jean Macaigne, January 4, 1991.
417 SE wrote Silvia: The letter has been published in *Icare* V, 111. Nearly everyone with whom I spoke from SE's Algiers days—including those who met the man on only one occasion—had been treated to recitals of the *faux*-Debussy.
regular chess dates: I am grateful to Madame de B for having shared portions of SE's Algiers date books.
"Does this interest you?" and "I have a Jeep": Sonneville, 267.
"SE needed a propeller": Max-Pol Fouchet, *Un jour je m'en souviens* (Paris: Mercure de France, 1968), 110.
"Everything is ugly": EG, 431.
"I failed to make out": EG, 435.
the news that he had just broken: SE to Madame de B, EG, 443.
The mishap: See Pélissier, pages 137–49, for the best account of the crisis on the rue Denfert-Rochereau and for portions of SE's voluminous correspondence on the subject, some of which is reprinted in EG.
418 "I am well aware": EG, 442.

The attacks of cholecystitis: SE reported as much to Consuelo. A portion of the letter in which he did so is included in the Arts Anciens auction catalogue for the November 20, 1986. sale in Geneva. item no. 13A.

he spoke of it: To Madame de B. EG. 442.

her son wrote: LSM. 220.

he had cabled: Arts Anciens auction catalogue, November 22. 1986. Geneva sale. item no. 16A.

Becker wrote to inform: Becker to SE. October 20. 1943.

419 "Take care of yourself": SE's winter letter to Consuelo is conserved at the ML, MA-4607.

slept in his underwear: To Madame de B. EG. 458–59. He wrote Consuelo as well of the cold. which he claimed prevented him from writing legibly.

judged the idea "inopportune": Included in a December 18, 1943. letter from Bouscat to the War Office. written on SE's behalf. Air Force file. SHAA.

"It would not appear opportune": January 8, 1944. letter from Colonel Billotte to the War Office. Air Force file. SHAA. SE wrote of his immense disappointment to Madame de B. EG. 475–76.

almost too abashed: EG. 476.

"a trash heap": SE's descriptions of Algiers pepper his letters and. evidently, peppered his conversations as well. All of these terms can be found in EG.

a note dispatched every fifteen minutes: See Pélissier. 152–55.

420 brief. imagined bout: ibid.. 149–50.

"This morning" and "Clearly she didn't": G. D. Morawski. EG. 481.

"Colonel." he began to "I want to write": Phillips. interviews of November 28, 1990, and December 4. 1990.

421 "*The* SE?" and "We've tried": Phillips, November 28, 1990.

422 "Look, SE, I've done": Phillips. December 4, 1990.

"hugely selling": Tex McCrary. to whom I am indebted for much background as well as for the details of this meeting, interview of November 27, 1990. "I was charmed" and "It's a hell of a deal." ibid.

"cut a German throat": Quoted in James Parton. *Air Force Spoken Here* (Bethesda: Adler & Adler, 1986). 419.

in Pomigliano: I have relied here on the 2/33's logbook as well as on Jean Leleu's piece in *Confluences*. 172–73.

"watching Vesuvius": Phillips. *Odd World* essay.

423 "I'm going to checkmate": Phillips, interview of November 28, 1990.

They fell instantly: The accounts of the lunch are from Pierre Guillain de Bénouville, *Confluences*. 144–49. and Henri Frenay. *La nuit finira* (Paris: Laffont. 1973), 425–26.

"Ah, France": Guillain de Bénouville. *Confluences*. 448–49.

"*follement heureux*": The invaluable letter is reproduced in *Icare* VI, 76.

"You win": McCrary. November 27. 1990.

424 "the arrival of SE": Karl L. Polifka's recollections of SE are cited in full in Crane, 309–12.

"inoculated all the officers": The 2/33's logbook. May 17. 1944.

more slowly and with infinitely more: Dino A. Brugioni. "Antoine de Saint-Exupéry Reconnaissance Pilot Par Excellence." *American Intelligence Journal*. Winter-Spring 1992. 77. Dino Brugioni's letters of June 5. 1993. December 10. 1993. and January 1994. much informed these pages as well.

now reported that he felt: Robert Aron. EG. 493.

"I have enough to worry about" and "I'm not going to": Leleu, *Confluences*. 179.

425 "in the middle of nowhere": Interview with Alain Jourdan. January 28. 1991. Fernand

Marty provided invaluable background for the Corsican days, interview of February 25, 1991. For more on the 23rd Photographic Reconnaissance Squadron, see their unit histories, microfilms B0746, B0747, and A0909, Department of the Air Force, Historical Research Agency, Maxwell Air Force Base.

425 "You go to the desert": The 2/33's logbook, July 11, 1944. Similarly, Pélissier, 137. "In the name of God, Phillips": *Odd World* essay, notes, p. 12. The best description in print of the "game of six letters" can be found in Beucler's *Figaro Littéraire* essay, July 30, 1949.
"I seem happy": From a letter to Madame de B. EG, 456.
"this civil war": From a letter to Chambe. EG, 513.

426 "SE was done for": Interview with Raymond Duriez, January 16, 1992.
"Prepare mayonnaise": Gide. "Saint-Exupéry," *Le Figaro*, February 1, 1945, 1.
"in order to tell men": From a letter to Chambe. EG, 391.

427 "Well, did he write" to "five spelling mistakes": Interviews with John Phillips and *Odd World* essay.
signed off simply: Interview with André Henry. January 23, 1991.
"*Merde!*": Phillips, interview of December 4, 1990. As Phillips remembers it, SE was attempting to call in with a Friday landing code on a Wednesday.
in a weak moment later: Pélissier quotes from his Gavoille letter, 31.
"Major SE, stepping into a tangle": The 2/33's logbook, July 10, 1944.
rumpled balls of paper: Duriez, interview of January 16, 1992.

428 "He reads on the field": The 2/33's logbook, July 6, 1944. Also interview with Alain Jourdan, January 28, 1991.
"We always admired him": Duriez, interview of January 16, 1992.
"the dean of all war pilots": To Galantière, EG, 499.
by some quirk of fate: Jean Leleu, *Confluences*, 178.
To Dalloz he summed up: EG, 515–16.

429 "a rather fanciful account": General Gavoille was kind enough to share his lecture notes, on which I have drawn often for this chapter. His accounts of SE are legion; they are consistent if sometimes overly indulgent.
he said nothing at the time: Interview with René Gavoille, January 9, 1992.
Croix de Guerre avec Palme: For the November 1944 citation, see the Archives Nationales exhibition catalogue, 131.
the "superpatriots": SE coined the word in a 1943 letter to Silvia Reinhardt, see *Icare* V, 110. He wrote of his anger to Madame de B just before his death, EG, 516.
"I love France": EG, 455.
"Why," asked Henry: Interview with André Henry, January 23, 1991.

430 "For the rest of you": Leleu, *Confluences*, 177.
"I wanted SE there": Polifka, Crane, 311.
"I'll follow through now": Chassin. *Visage de l'universel* (Liège: Éditions Dynamo, 1957), 15.
exactly five missions: Such was the rumor around the base, although Duriez (who had heard SE was to fly eight missions) remembered that while the idea floated about it never figured on any official document; André Henry wrote it off as the stuff of legend; and Gavoille always categorically denied that any limit had been imposed. Phillips remains equally convinced of the limitation and of Gavoille's knowledge of it.
On July 14 President Roosevelt: File no. 1633, Guerre 1939–1945. QO.

431 "Surely you don't mean": FA. 285 (translation mine).
The two men left each other: From Gavoille's lecture text. Also, letter to author of April 10. 1992.
likely he would not return: Marie-Madeleine Mast, *Icare* VI, 142.

"Henry, say hello": Interview with André Henry, January 23, 1991.
"by threatening to reveal": The 2/33's logbook, July 21, 1944.
Henry would inadvertently: Interview with André Henry, January 23, 1991.
"Keep it," he advised: Raoul Bertrand, "Les derniers jours de Saint-Exupéry," *Le Monde*, January 18, 1985.
A flyer was most vulnerable: Interview with Alain Jourdan, January 28, 1991.
432 several American officers: Among them was Harry Oakley, at the time a major with the 23rd Photo Reconnaissance Squadron. Letter to author, April 22, 1991.
"breathtaking indifference": EG, 516
To Consuelo a week or so: Ader Picard Tajan catalogue, Drouot sale, July 6, 1984, item no. 8.
a group of young women: Interview with Yvette Moiron, May 10, 1993.
joining Duriez in the mess to "In the name of God": Duriez, January 16, 1992, and letter of February 3, 1992.
433 The radar at Cape Corse. Some hold that the radar picked up SE on a portion of the return; Gavoille and Robison, in the control room that day, have disagreed. John Masterson, the intelligence officer at hand, recalled that the radar had worked particularly well on the thirty-first but that it followed SE into France on the outbound trip only. The official U.S. Air Force report indeed states that the radar control did not pick up SE crossing the French border on his return.
"When your gods die": CITAD, 292.

EPILOGUE: SAINT ANTOINE D'EXUPÉRY

435 Toward 1:00 o'clock: Interview with Robison, December 28, 1990, and *Icare* VI, 112ff.
"I was twenty-three": Letter from Whitman Bassow, March 13, 1991.
"the traditions of aviation": Gavoille, lecture notes.
When the 1/22: Georges Courtin, "Dernières images de Saint-Exupéry," *Le Figaro Littéraire*, July 31, 1948, 1.
436 was half-listening: Werth, *Déposition*, 703–704.
Jean Israël heard: Israël, interview of January 22, 1991.
total shock: Daurat's essay in *Saint-Exupéry* (Hachette), 82.
"the man who spoke 'my language' ": Lindbergh, *War Within and Without*, 449.
between heaven and hell: ibid., 448.
437 "but for SE," the officer wrote: Pélissier quotes from Gavoille's note in "Non, le mystère de la mort de Saint-Exupéry n'est pas encore éclairci," *Les Nouvelles Littéraires*, July 26, 1951.
emitting a pained "Ah!": EG, 530.
"I can't somehow": Hitchcock's letter is dated August 24, 1944, HBJ archives.
"And if I disappear": Fleury, *Icare* V, 37.
"He wanted to make": Lindbergh, *War Within and Without*, 447.
"It's for the best": Pierre Massin de Miraval *Icare* VI, 81.
was long in believing: Interview with Ysatis de Saint-Simon, September 26, 1991.
"Let's be honest": Anne Heurgon-Desjardins, EG, 500.
438 Bill Donovan reported: See his 1951 letter in Crane, 276. No official record of this visit exists, nor does any mention of Donovan appear in SE's date book at this time.
"avant que j'aie fondu": EG, 510.
"As for honor": de Rougemont, "Prototype T. E. L.," *La Table Ronde*, January 1952, 36. De Rougemont was himself quoting a biographer of T. E. Lawrence.
aviation had grown stronger: Phillips, *Odd World* essay.

439 called the roll: "What Has Happened to French Writers and Publishers?," *Publishers Weekly*, October 7, 1944, 1484.
"had been made almost psychopathically": From "The French Situation," an OSS report of February 5, 1944. RG 226, M1642, microfilm 50, NA.
a number of eyewitnesses: The historian Daniel Décot has painstakingly catalogued their testimonies; see *Icare* VI, 162.
The sky over Corsica: I owe this observation to photo reconnaissance and interpretation expert Dino A. Brugioni, letter of July 9, 1993.
an unofficial report from a Luftwaffe flyer: Agence France Presse announced that the mystery of SE's death was solved, May 20, 1981. For the response see Ulrich Scholz, "Wir haben Saint-Exupéry nicht abgeschossen!," *Bild am Sonntag*, June 21, 1981.

440 a custom-designed one: Gisèle d'Assailly, *Gazette des arts et lettres*, December 21, 1946.
He knew SE would not be to "You feel simply": Jacques Paget, "Saint-Exupéry cet inconnu," *Le Méridional*, October 28, 1962, 1.
an inventory: Can be found, along with a number of the documents from the lawsuits, in the Air Force file, SHAA.

441 "Gaston, I have done": Eugene Reynal was concurring with a description Madame de B had put forward about how the Gallimard imbroglio had come about, letter of November 27, 1946, HBJ archives. For a summary of the case see "Reynal & Hitchcock Makes Statement as to Gallimard Suit," *Publishers Weekly*, April 13, 1946, 2094.

442 "She is a rather tragical": Aldington's letter of October 26, 1946, to H.D. is included in Norman T. Gates, ed., *Richard Aldington: An Autobiography in Letters* (University Park: Pennsylvania State University Press, 1992), 216–18. The original is at Yale University.

443 for some time her official escort: Interview with Helen Wolff, December 19, 1990. Similarly Max Becker, interview of November 8, 1991.
"the consumed look": Anaïs Nin, *The Diary of Anaïs Nin*, Gunther Stuhlmann, ed. (New York: Harcourt Brace Jovanovich, 1971), 103.
choice, unsuspecting strangers: See Bruckberger, 171–77.
Louise de Vilmorin . . . is said: The remark was reported to the author by a member of SE's family, January 12, 1991.
formally registered their objection: A judgment was handed down in Paris on May 11, 1984, regarding the sale of papers that was to take place the following day at Drouot. The d'Agay family made it known that they in no way condoned the sale; at the same time they were allowed to ensure that several documents were not publicly displayed. One item was withheld from the sale, by order of the court.

444 "an unorganized, repetitive bulk": Galantière did so publicly, in his review of the book, New York *Herald Tribune Books*, October 15, 1950, 4.
"If SE knew": Interview with Becker, September 14, 1990.
the anti-German publisher: See Assouline, 312–13.
"le plus beau texte": Fouchet, "Le Plus Court Chemin," *Les Lettres Françaises*, January 13, 1945.
The reaction of Adrienne Monnier: See McDougall, 155–56.
"a thoroughly Gallic": Margaret O'Brien Steinfels, *Commonweal*, November 23, 1973, 211.

445 "I have found": Stuart Gilbert to Eugene Reynal, September 9, 1948, HBJ archives.
only the most energetic admirer: Even the otherwise admiring Luc Estang could not keep his eyes from glazing over: "*L'attention se dilue,*" he reported, "*l'ennui submerge l'admiration.*" Cited in Edmond Petit, "Le Cas Saint-Exupéry," *Forces Aériennes Françaises*, February 1963, nos. 244, 236.

"tiresomely archaic language": V. S. Pritchett, *New Statesman and Nation*, May 3, 1952, 52–53.

"muddled and failed": Émile Henriot, *Le Monde*, May 26, 1948.

446 altogether lacking in oil: ibid.

the most indulgent reviewers: André Rousseaux, *Le Figaro Littéraire*, April 24, 1956.

"SE's image": Giroud, *Si je mens . . .* , 41.

447 but he was no saint: EG, 440.

"He manages to eschew": Pierre de Boisdeffre, in Tavernier, *Saint-Exupéry en procès*, 177. Paget echoed his sentiments, *Le Méridional*, October 28, 1962.

"Several years later": See Achard, *Icare* III, 65.

Selected Bibliography

~

AGLION, RAOUL. *Roosevelt and de Gaulle.* New York: Free Press, 1988.

AMIRAULT, JEAN-MICHEL, ED. "Rencontre Saint-Exupéry." *Cahiers de l'Aéro-Club de France.* Paris, June 1990.

ANON. "The Little Prince." *The New Yorker,* March 21, 1983, 31–34.

Antoine de Saint-Exupéry. Direction des Archives de France, Archives Nationales exhibition catalogue. Paris, 1984.

ASSOULINE, PIERRE. *Gaston Gallimard.* New York: Harcourt Brace Jovanovich, 1988.

AUCLAIR, MARCELLE, and FRANÇOISE PRÉVOST, *Mémoires à deux voix.* Paris: Seuil, 1978.

BEAUVOIR, SIMONE DE. *Letters to Sartre.* Edited by Quintin Hoare. New York: Arcade Publishing, 1991.

———. *Witness to My Life: The Letters of Jean-Paul Sartre to Simone de Beauvoir, 1926– 1939.* New York: Charles Scribner's Sons, 1992.

BERNIER, OLIVIER. *Fireworks at Dusk: Paris in the Thirties.* Boston: Little, Brown & Company, 1993.

BEUCLER, ANDRÉ. *Les instants de Giraudoux.* Geneva: Éditions du Milieu du Monde, 1948.

BOTHOREL, JEAN. *Louise, ou la vie de Louise de Vilmorin.* Paris: Grasset, 1993.

BOUGEROL, GUY. *Ceux qu'on n'a jamais vus.* Grenoble: Arthaud, 1943.

BREAUX, ADÈLE. *Saint-Exupéry in America, 1942–1943.* Cranbury, N.J.: Associated University Presses, 1971.

BRUGIONI, DINO A. "Antoine de Saint-Exupéry: Reconnaissance Pilot par Excellence." *American Intelligence Journal,* Winter/Spring 1992, 75–79.

Cahiers Saint-Exupéry. Le Comité de l'Association des Amis d'Antoine de Saint-Exupéry, eds. Paris: Gallimard. no. 1, 1980; no. 2, 1981; no. 3, 1989.

CATE, CURTIS. *Antoine de Saint-Exupéry.* New York: 1970, rpt. Paragon House, 1990.

CHADEAU, EMMANUEL. *Latécoère.* Paris: Olivier Orban, 1990.

CHALON, JEAN. *Florence et Louise les magnifiques.* Paris: Editions du Rocher, 1987.

CHAMBRUN, RENÉ DE. *I Saw France Fall.* New York: William Morrow & Company, 1940.

CHEVRIER, PIERRE (pseudonym of Madame de B). *Antoine de Saint-Exupéry.* Paris: Gallimard, 1949.

CHIROL, JEAN-MARIE. *Groupes de chasse et de reconnaissance à Orconte et Saint-Dizier.* Paris: Langres, 1981.

CHURCHILL, WINSTON S. *Memoirs of the Second World War.* Boston: Houghton Mifflin, 1987.

Confluences. "Saint-Exupéry," no. 12–14. Paris, 1947.

COURRIÈRE, YVES. *Joseph Kessel, ou Sur la piste du lion.* Paris: Plon, 1986.

CRANE, HELEN ELIZABETH. *L'Humanisme dans l'oeuvre de Saint-Exupéry.* Evanston, Ill.: Principia Press, 1957.

CROSBY, CARESSE. *The Passionate Years.* New York: The Ecco Press, 1979.

DANEL, RAYMOND. *L'Aéropostale, 1927–1933.* Toulouse: Privat, 1989.

———. *Les Lignes Latécoère, 1918–1927.* Toulouse: Privat, 1986.

DARDAUD, GABRIEL. *30 ans au bord du Nil*. Paris: Lieu Commun. 1987.

DAURAT, DIDIER. *Dans le vent des hélices*. Paris: Seuil. 1956.

————. *Saint-Exupéry tel que je l'ai connu*. Liège: Dynamo. 1954.

DAVIES. R. E. G. "Marcel Bouilloux-Lafont—Where is the Glory?" *Air Pictorial*, August 1981, 308–12, and September 1981, 207–208. "Marcel Bouilloux-Lafont: The Shattered Dream." *Air Pictorial*, July 1983, 266–70 and August 1983, 306–10.

DE GAULLE, CHARLES. *The War Memoirs of Charles de Gaulle*. New York: Simon & Schuster. 1959.

DELANGE, RENÉ. *La vie de Saint-Exupéry* (includes *Tel que je l'ai connu* by Léon Werth). Paris: Seuil. 1948.

DELAUNAY, HENRI. *L'Araignée du soir*. Paris: Éditions France-Empire. 1968.

DESCHODT, ERIC. *Saint-Exupéry*. Paris: Lattès. 1980.

ESTANG, LUC. *Saint-Exupéry par lui-même*. Paris: Seuil, 1958.

FARGUE, LÉON-PAUL. *Souvenir de Saint-Exupéry*. Liège: Dynamo, 1945.

FITCH, NOEL RILEY. *Sylvia Beach and the Lost Generation*. New York: W. W. Norton & Company. 1983.

FLANNER, JANET. *Paris Was Yesterday 1925–1939*. New York: Viking Press, 1972.

FLEURY, JEAN-GÉRARD. *Chemins du ciel*. Paris: Nouvelles Éditions Latines, 1933.

————. *La Ligne*. Paris: Gallimard, 1942.

FOUCHET, MAX-POL. *Un jour je m'en souviens*. Paris: Mercure de France, 1968.

FRITSCH-ESTRANGIN, GUY. *New York entre de Gaulle et Pétain*. Paris: La Table Ronde, 1969.

FROMENT, HÉLÈNE (pseudonym of Madame de B). *On ne revient pas*. Paris: Gallimard, 1941.

GALANTIÈRE, LEWIS. "Antoine de Saint-Exupéry." *The Atlantic*, April 1947, 133–41.

————. "The Most Unforgettable Character I've Met." *Reader's Digest*, December 1957, 174–79.

GIBBS-SMITH, CHARLES H. *Flight Through the Ages*. New York: Thomas Y. Crowell, 1974.

————. *The Aeroplane*. London: Her Majesty's Stationery Office, 1960.

GIDE, ANDRÉ. *Antoine de Saint-Exupéry*. Liège: Dynamo, 1951.

————. *The Journals of André Gide*, III. New York: Alfred A. Knopf, 1949.

GIROUD, FRANÇOISE. *Leçons particulières*. Paris: Fayard, 1990.

————. *Si je mens* . . . Paris: Stock, 1972.

JEANSON, HENRI. *70 ans d'adolescence*. Paris: Stock, 1971.

KESSEL, JOSEPH. *Mermoz*. Paris: Gallimard, 1938.

————. *Vent de sable*. Paris: Éditions de France, 1929.

LACOUTURE, JEAN, *De Gaulle, The Rebel*. New York: W. W. Norton & Company, 1990.

LIEBLING. A. J. *The Road Back to Paris*. Garden City, N.Y.: Doubleday, Doran, 1944.

LINDBERGH, ANNE MORROW. *War Within and Without*. New York: Harcourt Brace Jovanovich, 1980.

LINDBERGH, CHARLES A. *The Wartime Journals of Charles A. Lindbergh*. New York: Harcourt Brace Jovanovich, 1970.

LOTTMAN, HERBERT R. *The Fall of Paris*. New York: HarperCollins, 1992.

————. *The Left Bank*. Boston: Houghton Mifflin Company, 1982.

LOVELL. MARY S. *Straight on Till Morning: The Biography of Beryl Markham*. London: Hutchinson. 1987.

MALRAUX, ANDRÉ. *Anti-Memoirs*. New York: Henry Holt & Company, 1968.

MARCK. BERNARD. *Il était une foi Mermoz*. Paris: Éditions Jean Picollec, 1986.

MASSIMI, BEPPO DE. *Vent debout*. Paris: Plon, 1949.

MAUROIS, ANDRÉ. *From Proust to Camus*. Garden City, N.Y.: Doubleday & Company, 1966.

————. *Memoirs*. New York: Harper & Row, 1970.

MERMOZ. JEAN. *Mes vols*. Paris: Flammarion, 1937; reprint 1986.

MIGEO, MARCEL. *Didier Daurat*. Paris: Flammarion, 1962.

————. *Henri Guillaumet.* Paris: B. Arthaud, 1949.

————. *Saint-Ex.* New York: McGraw-Hill, 1960.

MIGEO, MARCEL, ET AL. *Saint-Exupéry.* Paris: Hachette, 1963.

MONNIER, ADRIENNE. *Les Gazettes d'Adrienne Monnier, 1925–1945.* Paris: Julliard, 1953.

MORÉ, MARCEL. *J'ai vécu l'épopée de l'Aéropostale.* Paris: Éditions de l'Aéropole, 1980.

MORGAN, TED. *An Uncertain Hour: The French, the Germans, the Jews, the Barbie Trial, and the City of Lyon, 1940–1945.* New York: William Morrow & Company, 1990.

MOSSÉ, CLAUDE. *Mécano de Saint-Ex.* Paris: Éditions Ramsay, 1984.

PÉLISSIER, GEORGES. *Les cinq visages de Saint-Exupéry.* Paris: Flammarion, 1951.

PENDAR, KENNETH. *Adventure in Diplomacy: The Emergence of General de Gaulle in North Africa.* London: Cassell & Company, 1966.

PETIT, EDMOND. *La vie quotidienne dans l'aviation de 1900 à 1935.* Paris: Hachette, 1977.

————. *Nouvelle Histoire Mondiale de l'Aviation.* Paris: Albin Michel, 1989.

PHILLIPS, JOHN. *Les derniers jours de Saint-Exupéry.* Zurich: Editions Parkett/Der Alltag, 1989.

————. *Odd World.* New York: Simon & Schuster, 1959.

PRÉVOST, JEAN. *Les Caractères.* Paris: Albin Michel, 1948.

RÉMENS, SIMONE DE (pseudonym of Simone de Saint-Exupéry). *Météores.* Hanoi: Taupin & Cie., 1943.

RENOIR, JEAN. *Lettres d'Amérique.* Paris: Presses de la Renaissance, 1984.

————. *Ma vie et mes films.* Paris: Flammarion, 1974.

ROUGEMONT, DENIS DE. *Journal des deux mondes.* Paris: Gallimard, 1968.

ROUSSY DE SALES, RAOUL DE. *The Making of Yesterday.* New York: Reynal & Hitchcock, 1947.

ROY, JULES. *Mémoires barbares.* Paris: Albin Michel, 1989.

————. *Saint-Exupéry.* Paris: La Manufacture, 1990.

RUMBOLD, RICHARD, and LADY MARGARET STEWART. *The Winged Life.* London: Weidenfeld & Nicolson, 1953.

RYSSELBERGHE, MARIA VAN. *Cahiers André Gide,* V. Paris: Gallimard, 1974.

SAINT-EXUPÉRY, ANTOINE DE. *Airman's Odyssey (Wind, Sand and Stars, Night Flight, Flight to Arras).* New York: Harcourt Brace Jovanovich, 1984.

————. "Books I Remember." *Harper's Bazaar,* April 1941, 82.

————. *Carnets.* Paris: Gallimard, 1975.

————. *Lettres à sa mère.* Paris: Gallimard, 1984.

————. *Lettres de jeunesse.* Paris: Gallimard, 1953.

————. "Lettres intimes d'Antoine de Saint-Exupéry à une jeune fille." *Le Figaro Littéraire,* July 8, 1950, 1.

————. *The Little Prince.* New York: Harcourt Brace Jovanovich, 1971.

————. *A Sense of Life.* New York: Funk & Wagnalls Company, 1965.

————. *Southern Mail.* New York: Harcourt Brace Jovanovich, 1971.

————. *Wartime Writings, 1939–1944.* New York: Harcourt Brace Jovanovich, 1986.

————. *The Wisdom of the Sands.* Chicago: University of Chicago Press, 1979.

SAINT-EXUPÉRY, CONSUELO DE. *Kingdom of the Rocks: Memories of Oppède.* New York: Random House, 1946.

SAINT-EXUPÉRY, MARIE DE. *J'écoute chanter mon arbre.* Paris: Gallimard, 1967.

SARTRE, JEAN-PAUL. *The War Diaries of Jean-Paul Sartre.* New York: Pantheon, 1984.

SCHIFF, STACY. "A Grounded Soul: Saint-Exupéry in New York." *The New York Times Book Review,* May 30, 1993, 1.

SMITH, MAXWELL A. *Knight of the Air.* New York: Pageant Press, 1956.

SYNDICAT NATIONAL DES PILOTES DE LIGNE, EDS. *Icare: Revue de l'aviation française.* No. 30, "Saint-Exupéry, écrivain et pilote," Summer 1964. No. 69. "Saint-Exupéry 1900–1930," vol. I, Summer 1974. No. 71, "Saint-Exupéry 1930–1936," vol. II, Winter 1974. No. 75. "Saint-Exupéry 1936–1939," vol III, Winter 1975. No. 78, "Saint-

Exupéry 1939–1940," vol. IV, Fall 1976. No. 84. "Saint-Exupéry 1941–1943," vol. V, Spring 1978. No. 96, "Saint-Exupéry 1943–1944," vol VI, Spring 1981. No. 108, "Saint-Exupéry toujours vivant," vol. VII, first trimester, 1984. No. 140, "Didier Daurat," first trimester, 1992.

TAVERNIER, RENÉ, ED. *Saint-Exupéry en procès*. Paris: Belfond, 1967.

ULLMANN, NATACHA STEWART (unsigned). "Let's Play Portraits." *The New Yorker*, January 27, 1962, 31–33.

VACHET, PAUL. *Avant les jets*. Paris: Hachette, 1964.

VANIER, RAYMOND. *Tout pour la Ligne*. Paris: Éditions France-Empire, 1960.

VEDEL, GASTON. *Le pilote oublié*. Paris: Gallimard, 1976.

VERCIER, BRUNO, ED. *Les critiques de notre temps et Saint-Exupéry*. Paris: Garnier Frères, 1971.

VILMORIN, ANDRÉ DE. *Essai sur Louise de Vilmorin*. Paris: Pierre Seghers, 1962.

VILMORIN, LOUISE DE. *Carnets*. Paris: Gallimard, 1970.

WERTH, ALEXANDER. *The Twilight of France*. New York: Howard Fertig, 1966.

WERTH, LÉON. *Déposition, Journal 1940–1944*. Paris: Viviane Hamy, 1992.

———. *33 jours*. Paris: 1946, reprint. Viviane Hamy, 1992.

WILLEMETZ, G., and J. SUFFEL. *Exposition Saint-Exupéry*. Bibliothèque Nationale exhibition catalogue. with a preface by Léon Werth, Paris, 1954.

ZELDIN, THEODORE. *France 1848–1945*, two vols. London: Oxford University Press, 1973 and 1977.

Index

~

Permissions Acknowledgments

~

Photographic Credits

~